A-Z BIRMINGHAM
De Luxe Street Atlas

KU-618-809

CONTENTS

REFERENCE

Motorway	M6
A Road	A38
Under Construction	
Proposed	
B Road	B4284
Dual Carriageway	
One Way Street	→
Traffic flow on A Roads is also indicated by a heavy line on the driver's left	→
City Centre Ring Road & Junction Numbers	①
Restricted Access	
Pedestrianized Road	
Track / Footpath	------------
Cycleway (Selected)	🚲
Railway	Station / Heritage Station / Level Crossing / Tunnel
Midland Metro	
The boarding of Metro trams at stops may be limited to a single direction, indicated by the arrow.	Stop
Built Up Area	NEWTON PL.
Local Authority Boundary	— ·· — ·· —
Posttown Boundary	— · — · —
Postcode Boundary (within Posttown)	— — —
Map Continuation	20
Large Scale City Centre	4

Car Park (Selected)	P
Church or Chapel	†
Fire Station	■
Hospital	H
House Numbers A and B Roads only	20 ... 40
Information Centre	i
Junction Name (M6 Toll only)	BURNTWOOD JUNCTION
National Grid Reference	412
Park & Ride	Monkspath P+R
Police Station	▲
Post Office	★
Toilet:	
without facilities for the Disabled	▽
with facilities for the Disabled	▽
for exclusive use by the Disabled	▽
Viewpoint	☀ ☀
Educational Establishment	
Hospital or Hospice	
Industrial Building	
Leisure or Recreational Facility	
Place of Interest	
Public Building	
Shopping Centre or Market	
Other Selected Buildings	

SCALE

Map Pages 6-169
1:13,339 approx. 4¾ inches to 1 mile

0	¼	½ Mile

0	250	500	750 Metres

7.50cm to 1km 12.07cm to 1 mile

Map Pages 4-5, 170
1:6669 approx. 9½ inches to 1 mile

0	⅛	¼ Mile

0	100	200	300 Metres

14.99cm to 1km 24.13cm to 1 mile

Copyright of Geographers' A-Z Map Company Ltd.

Head Office:
Fairfield Road, Borough Green, Sevenoaks, Kent TN15 8PP
Telephone: 01732 781000 (Enquiries & Trade Sales)
01732 783422 (Retail Sales)
www.a-zmaps.co.uk
Copyright © Geographers' A-Z Map Co. Ltd.

 Ordnance Survey® This product includes mapping data licensed from Ordnance Survey® with the permission of the Controller of Her Majesty's Stationery Office.

© Crown Copyright 2005. All rights reserved. Licence number 100017302

EDITION 3 2005   EDITION 3A 2006 (Part Revision)

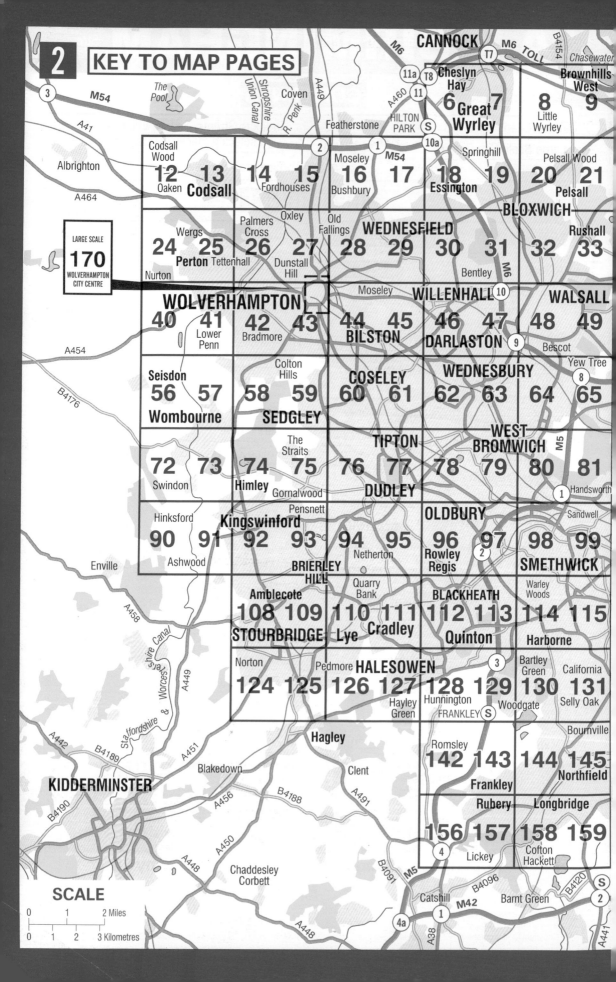

2 KEY TO MAP PAGES

LARGE SCALE

170

WOLVERHAMPTON CITY CENTRE

				6 Great Wyrley	7	8 9
12 13	14 15	16 17	18 19	20 21		
24 25	26 27	28 29	30 31	32 33		
40 41	42 43	44 45	46 47	48 49		
56 57	58 59	60 61	62 63	64 65		
72 73	74 75	76 77	78 79	80 81		
90 91	92 93	94 95	96 97	98 99		
108 109	110 111	112 113	114 115			
124 125	126 127	128 129	130 131			
		142 143	144 145			
		156 157	158 159			

Albrighton
The Pool
Coven
Codsall Wood
Oaken Codsall
Wergs
Perton Tettenhall
Nurton
Palmers Cross
Oxley
Dunstall Hill
Old Fallings
WEDNESFIELD
Featherstone
HILTON PARK
CANNOCK
Cheslyn Hay
Springhill
Pelsall Wood
Little Wyrley
Brownhills West
Essington
BLOXWICH
Rushall
Pelsall
WOLVERHAMPTON
Lower Penn
Bradmore
BILSTON
Moseley
WILLENHALL
Bentley
DARLASTON
WALSALL
Bescot
Yew Tree
Seisdon
Wombourne
Colton Hills
SEDGLEY
COSELEY
WEDNESBURY
Swindon
Himley
The Straits
Gornalwood
TIPTON
WEST BROMWICH
DUDLEY
Handsworth
Hinksford
Kingswinford
Pensnett
Netherton
OLDBURY
Rowley Regis
SMETHWICK
Sandwell
Enville
Ashwood
BRIERLEY HILL
Quarry Bank
BLACKHEATH
Warley Woods
Amblecote
STOURBRIDGE
Lye
Cradley
Quinton
Harborne
Bartley Green
California
Selly Oak
Norton
Pedmore
HALESOWEN
Hayley Green
Hunnington
FRANKLEY
Woodgate
Bournville
Hagley
Blakedown
Clent
Romsley
Frankley
Northfield
KIDDERMINSTER
Rubery
Longbridge
Chaddesley Corbett
Lickey
Cofton Hackett
Catshill
Barnt Green

SCALE

0   1   2 Miles

0   1   2   3 Kilometres

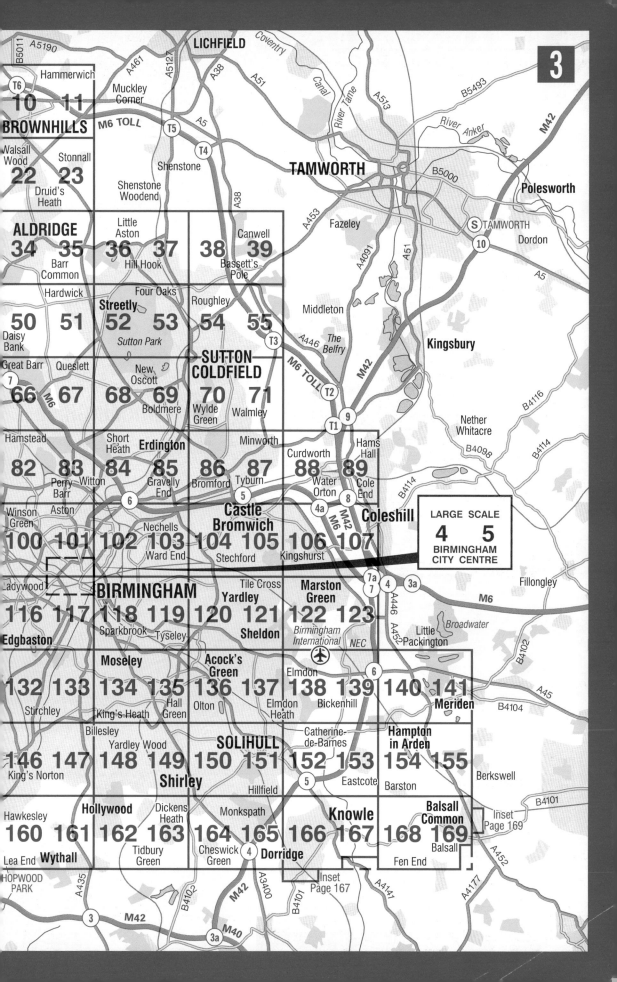

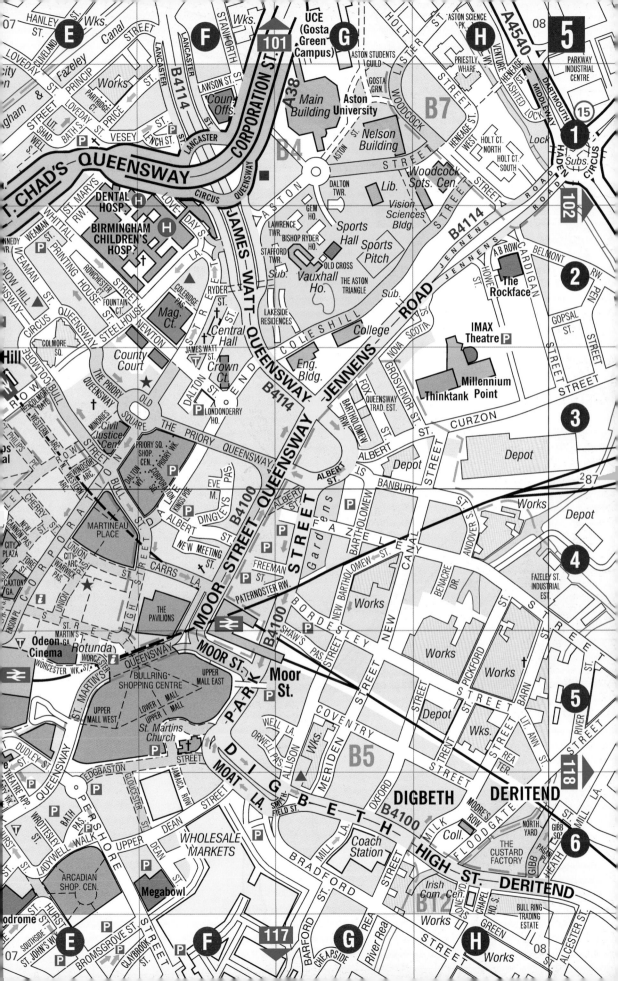

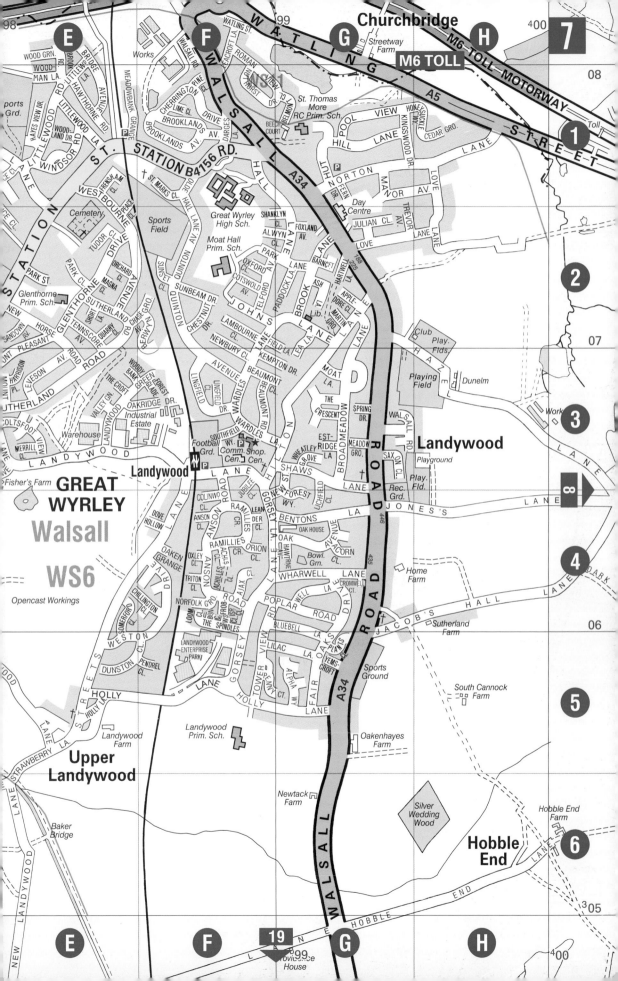

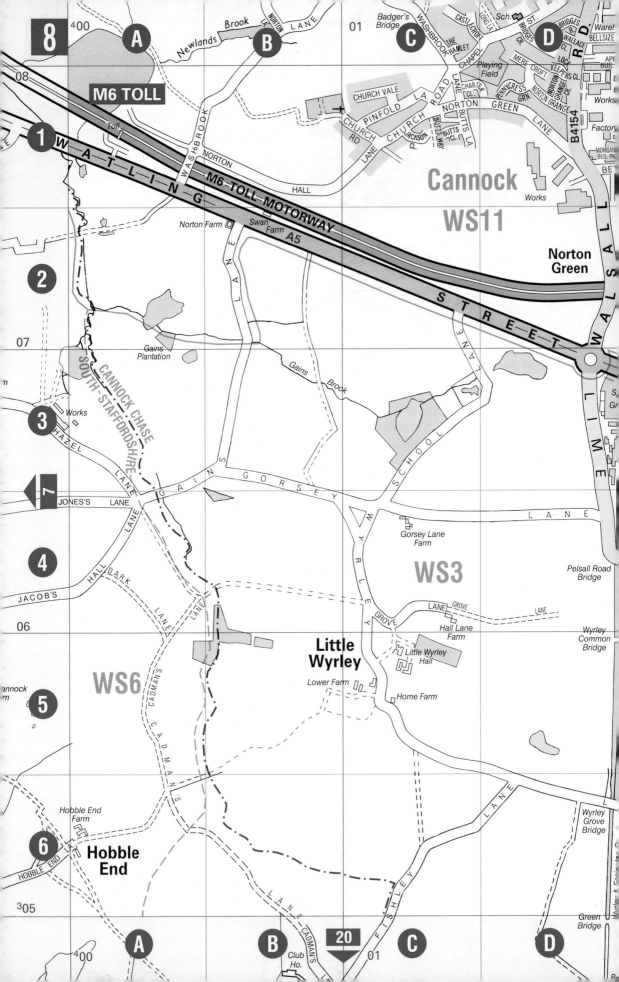

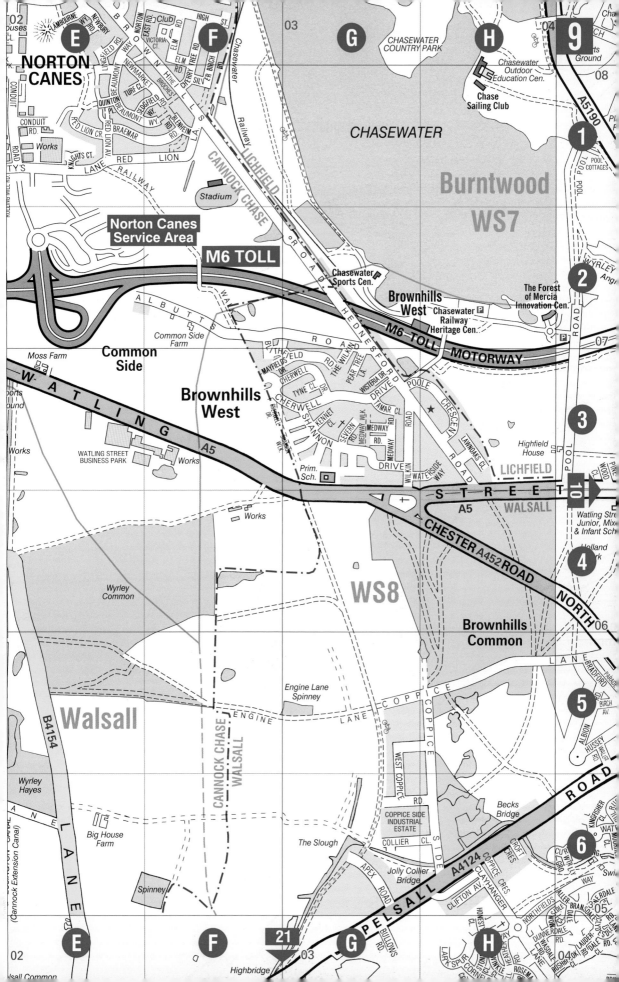

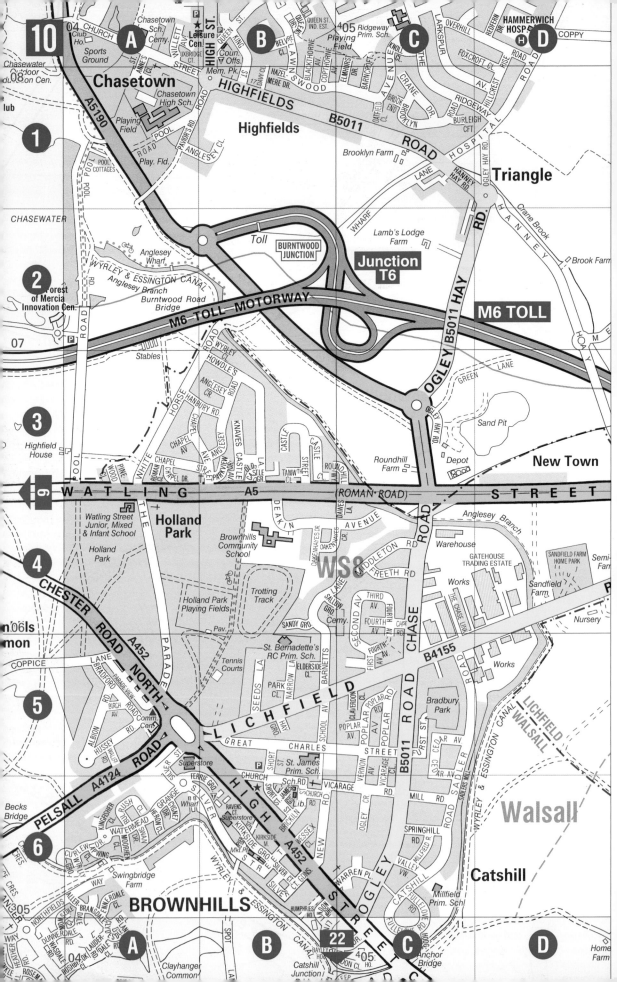

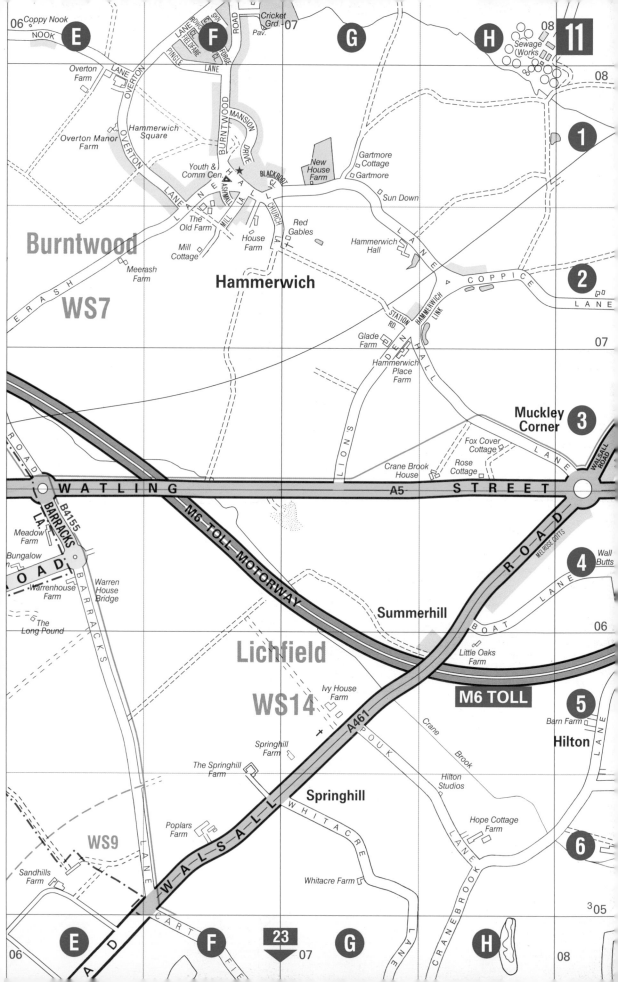

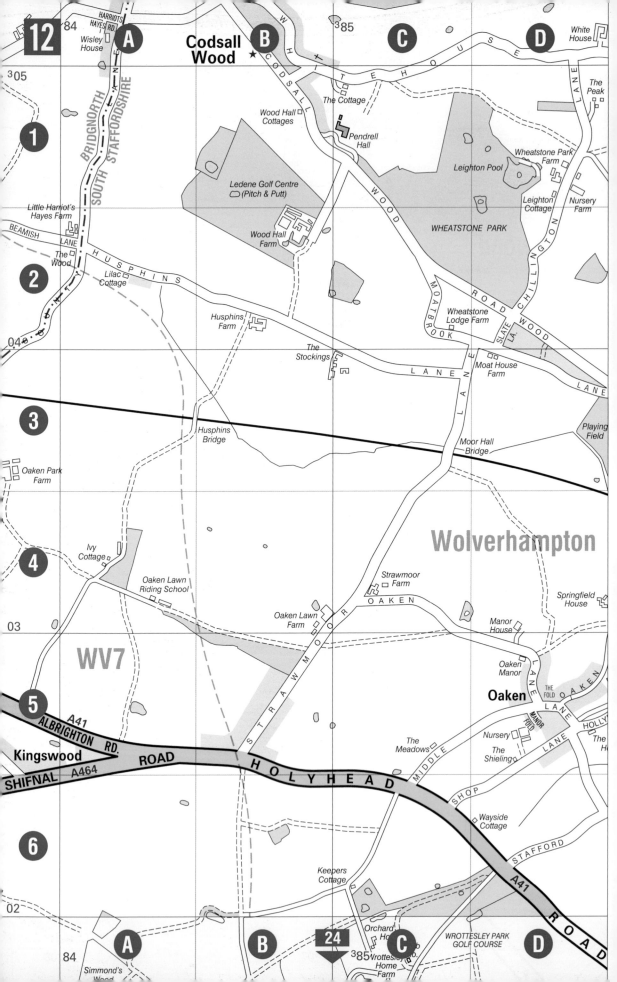

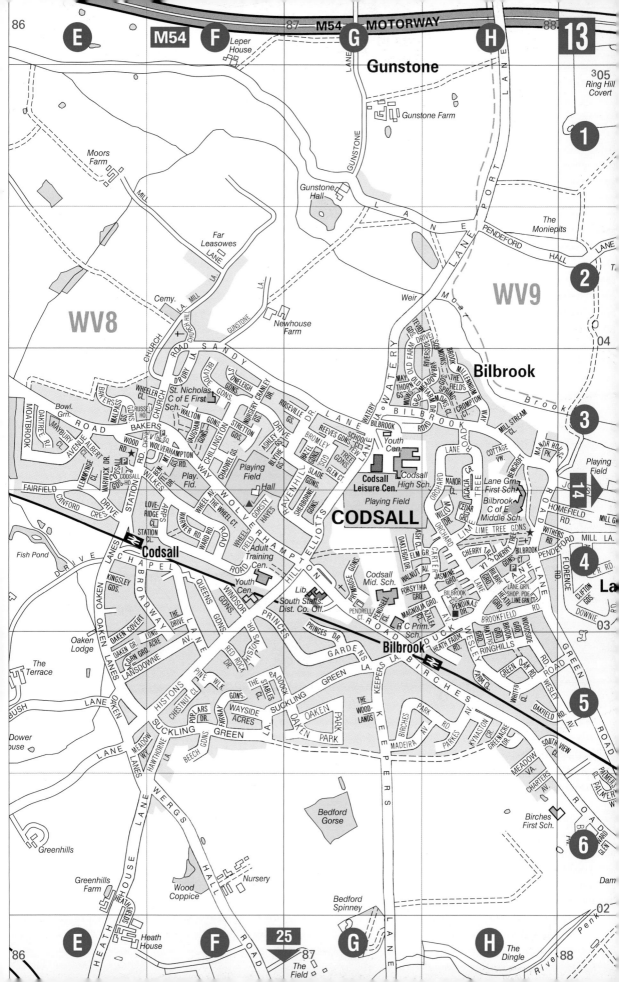

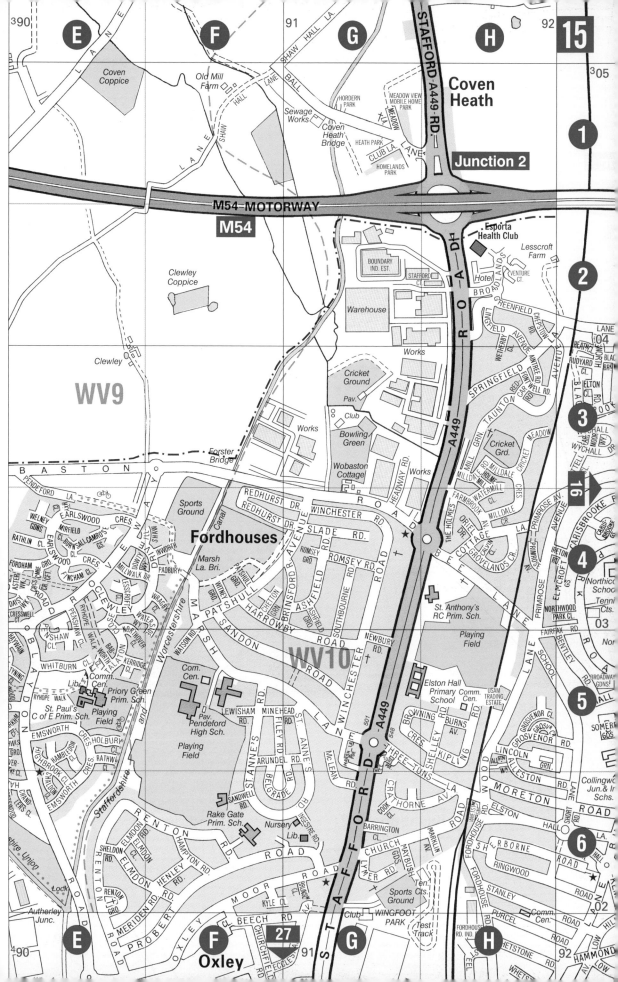

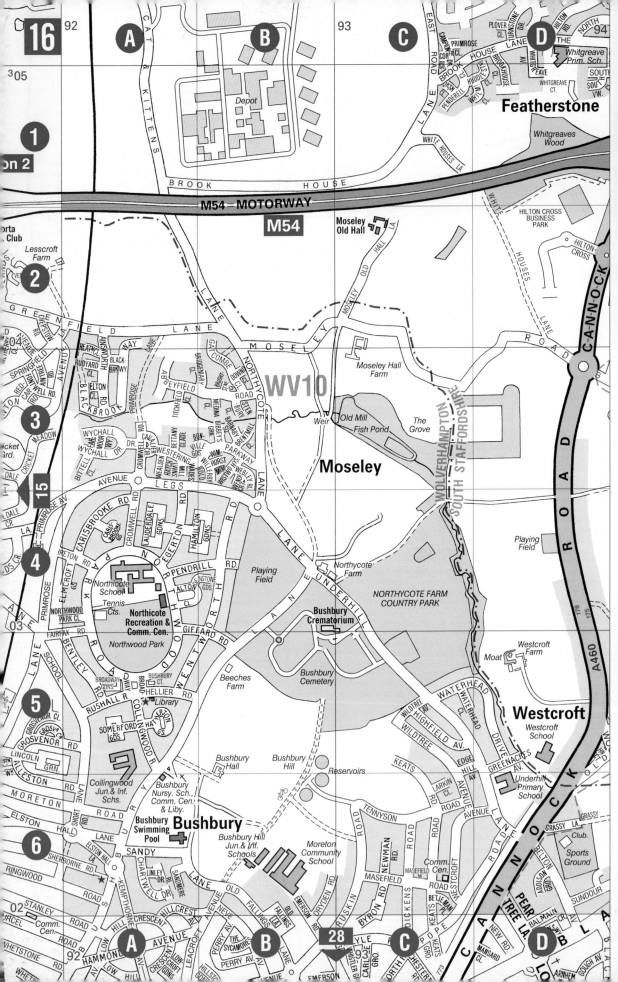

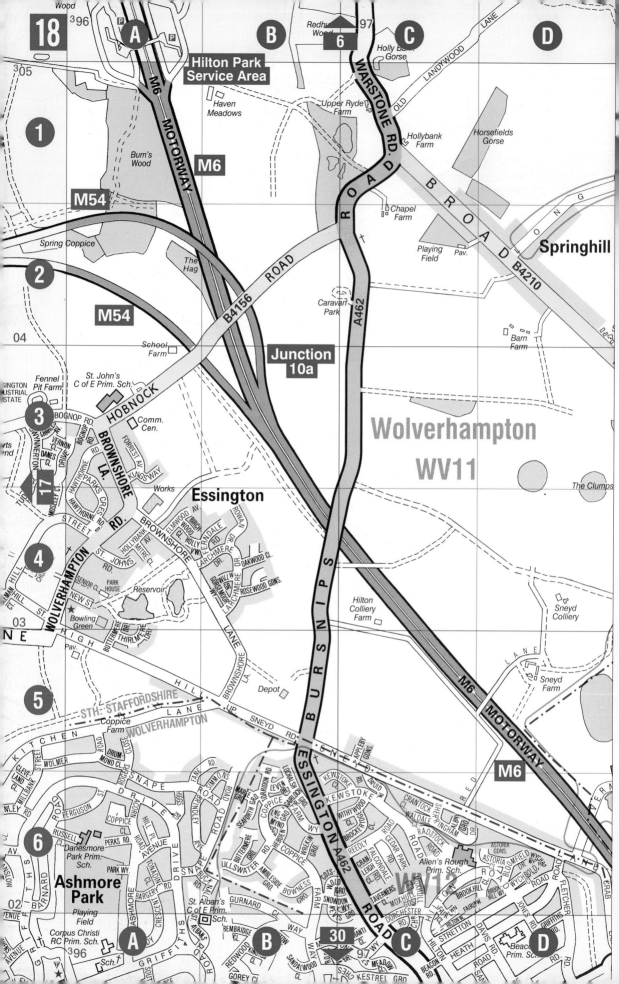

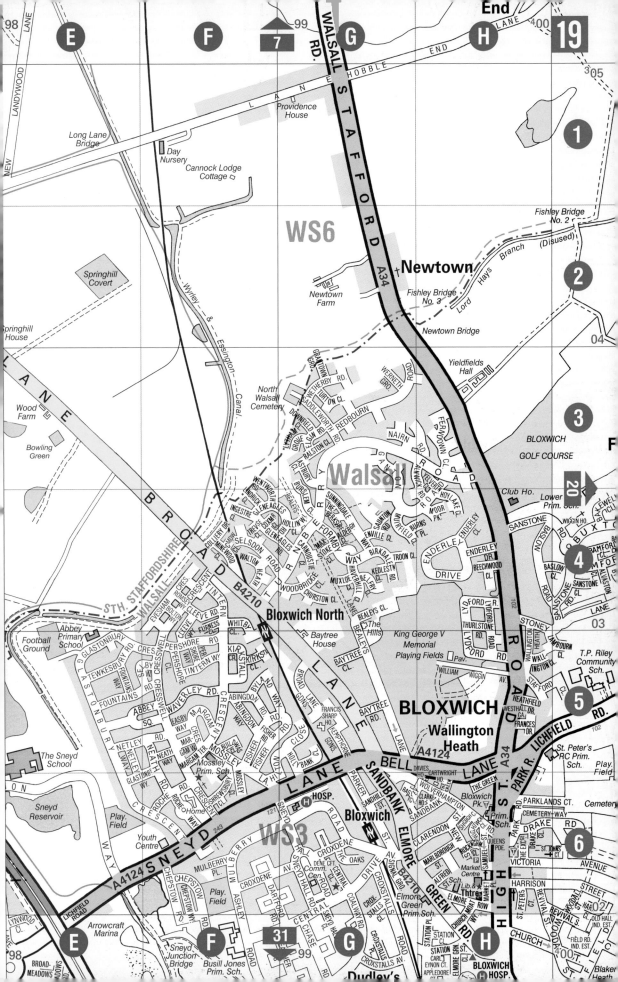

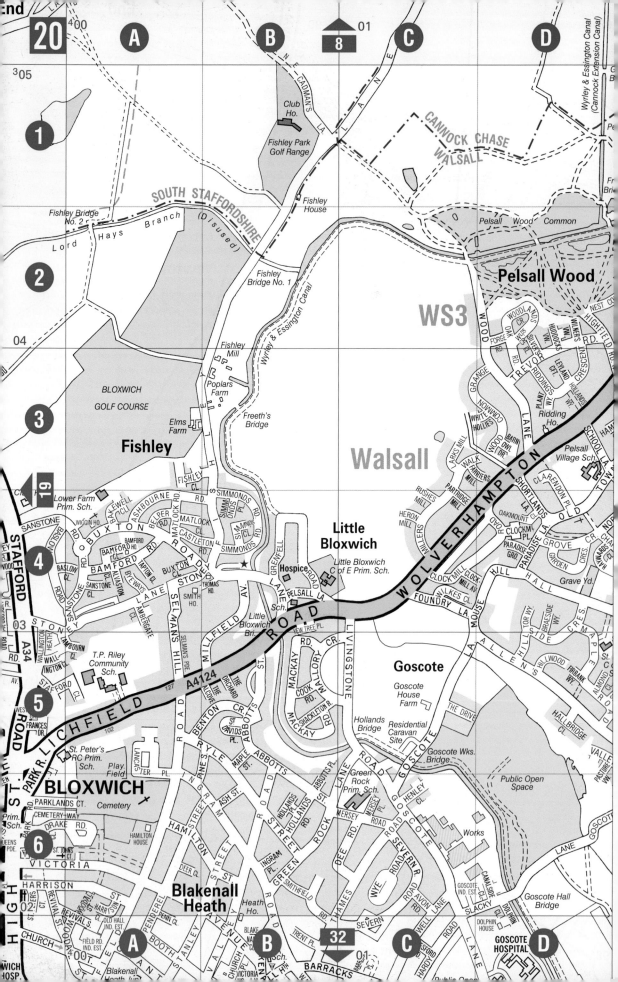

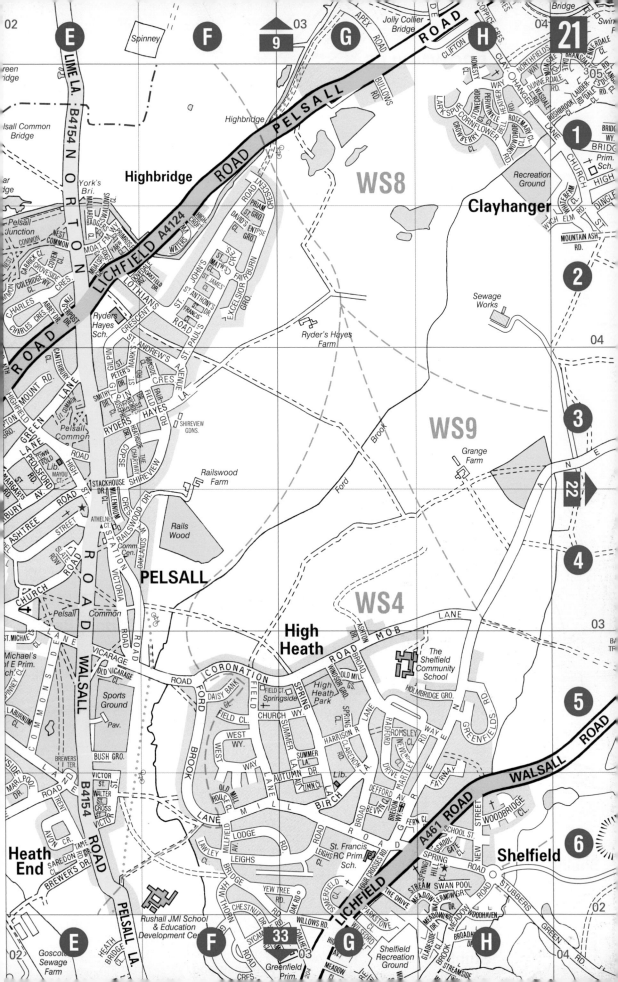

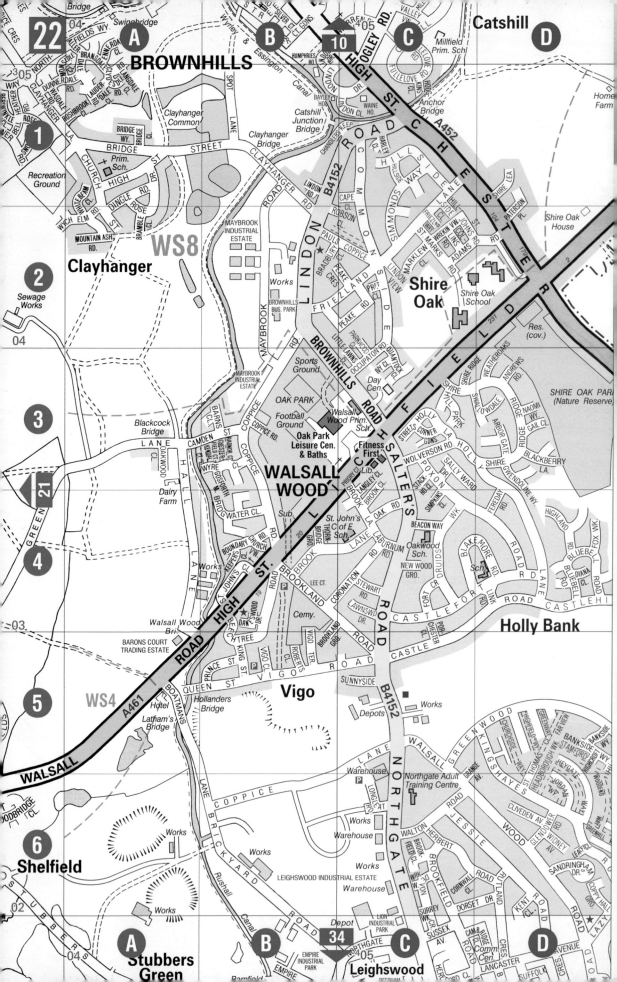

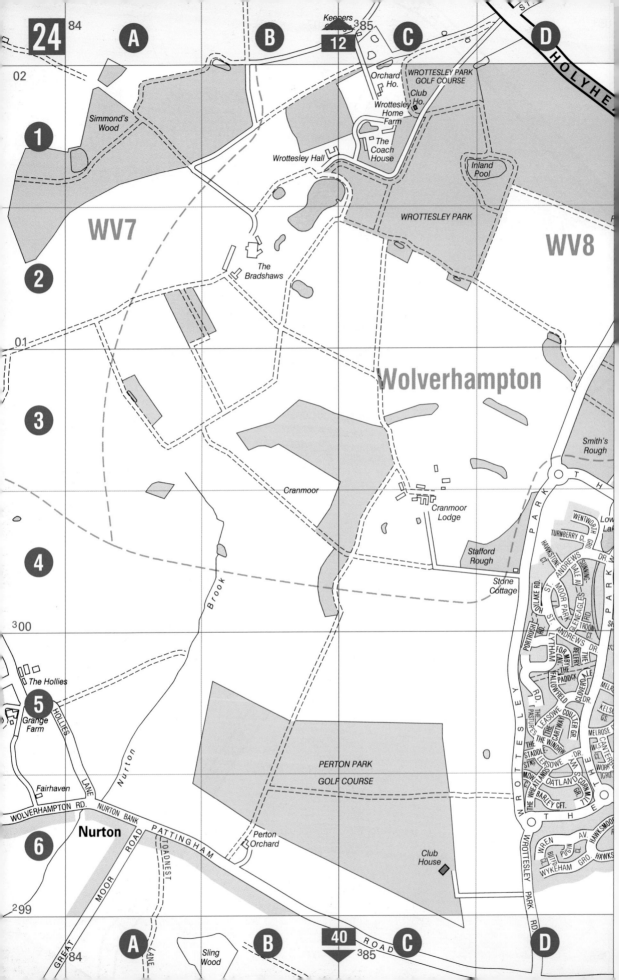

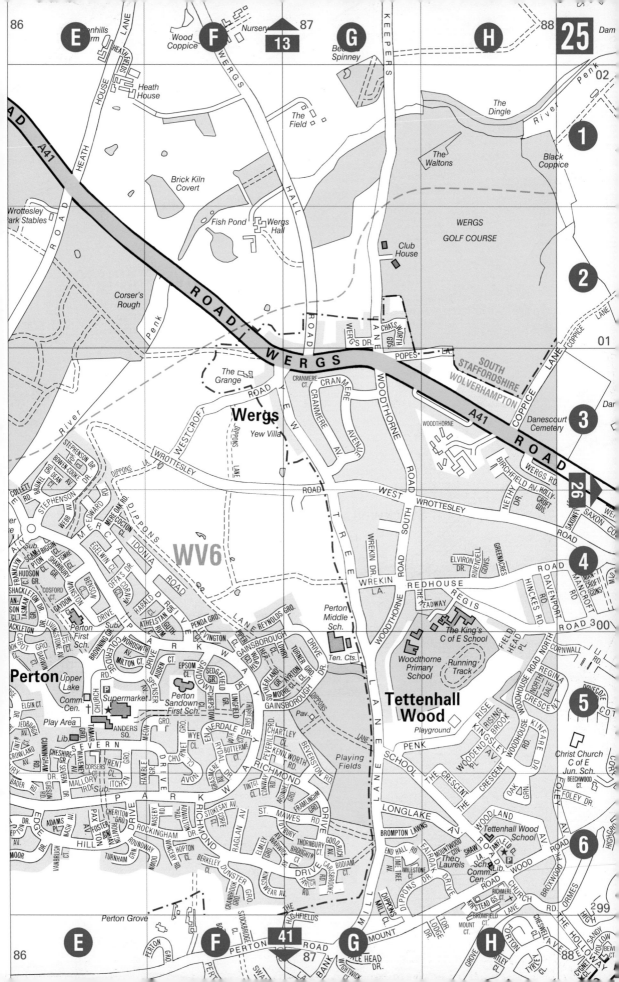

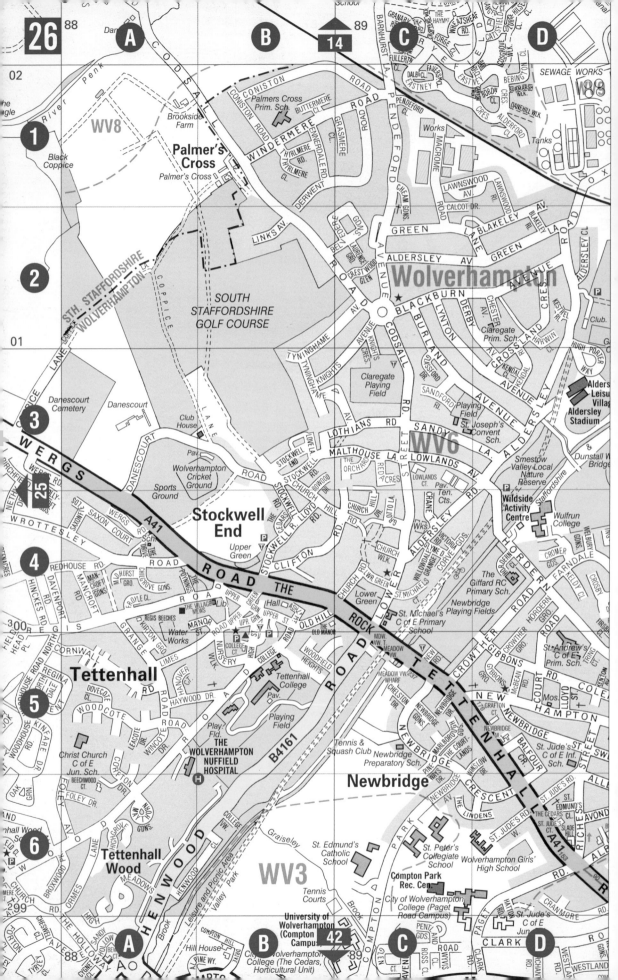

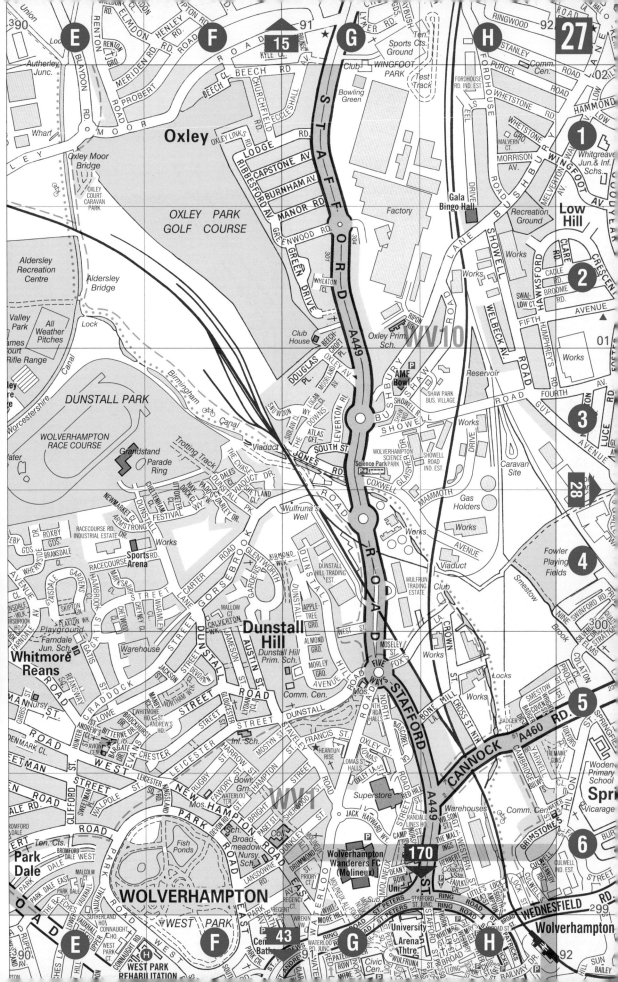

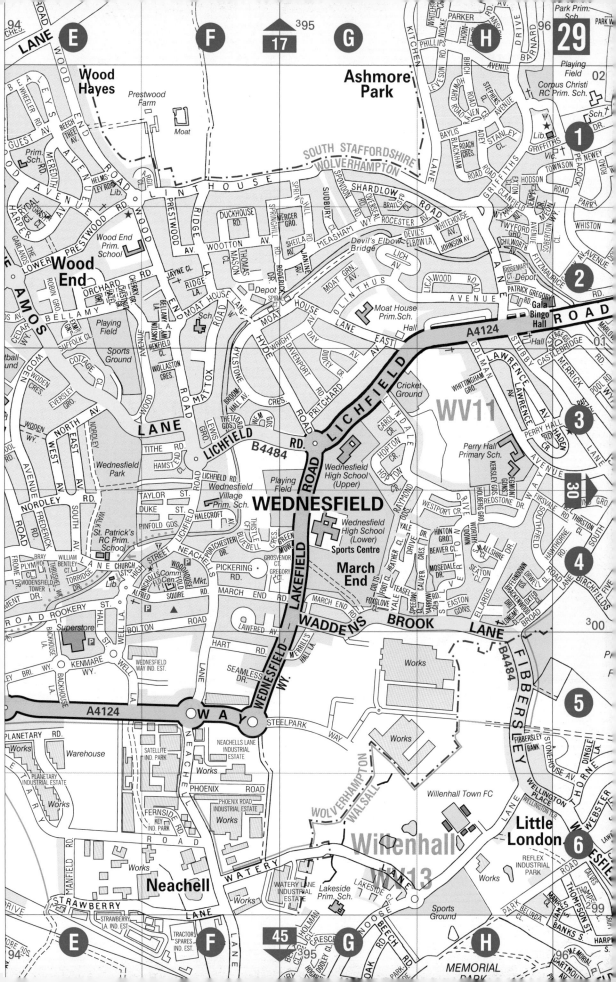

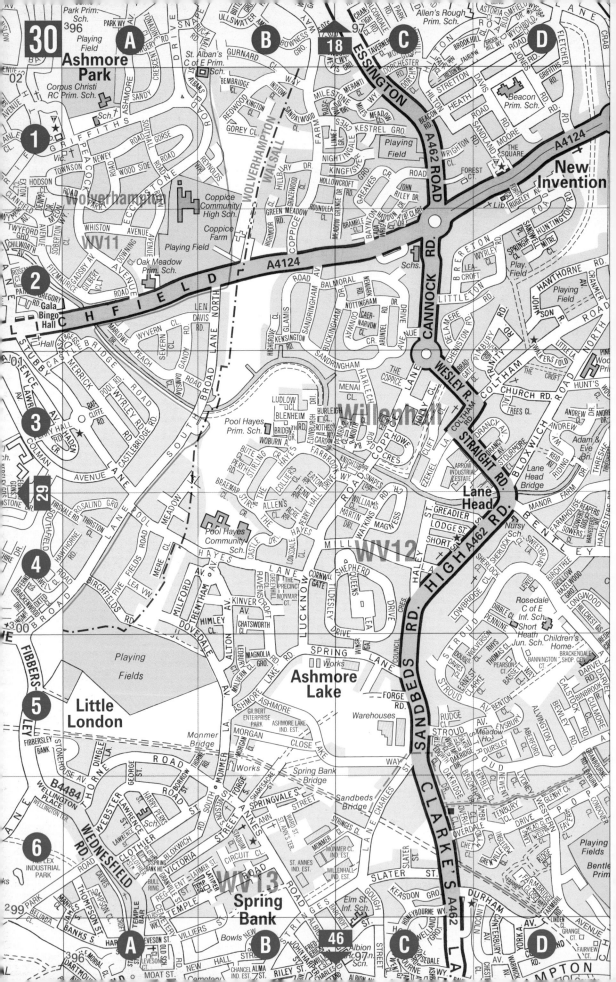

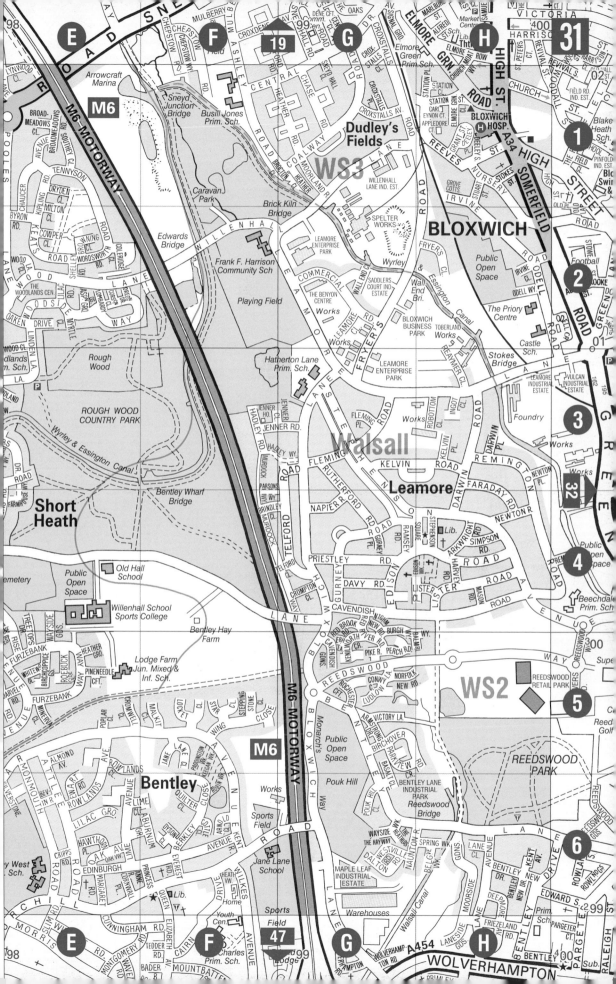

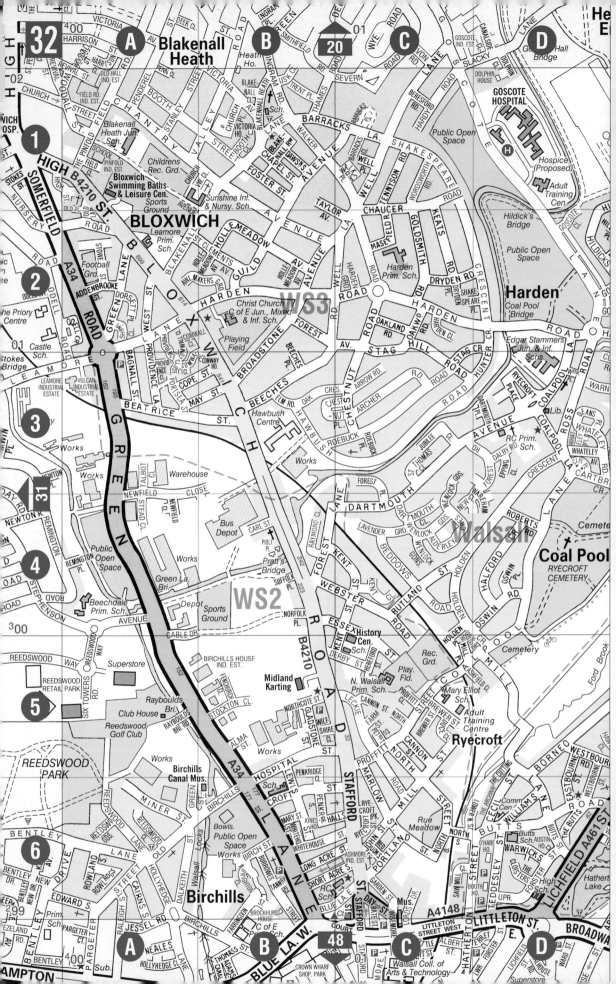

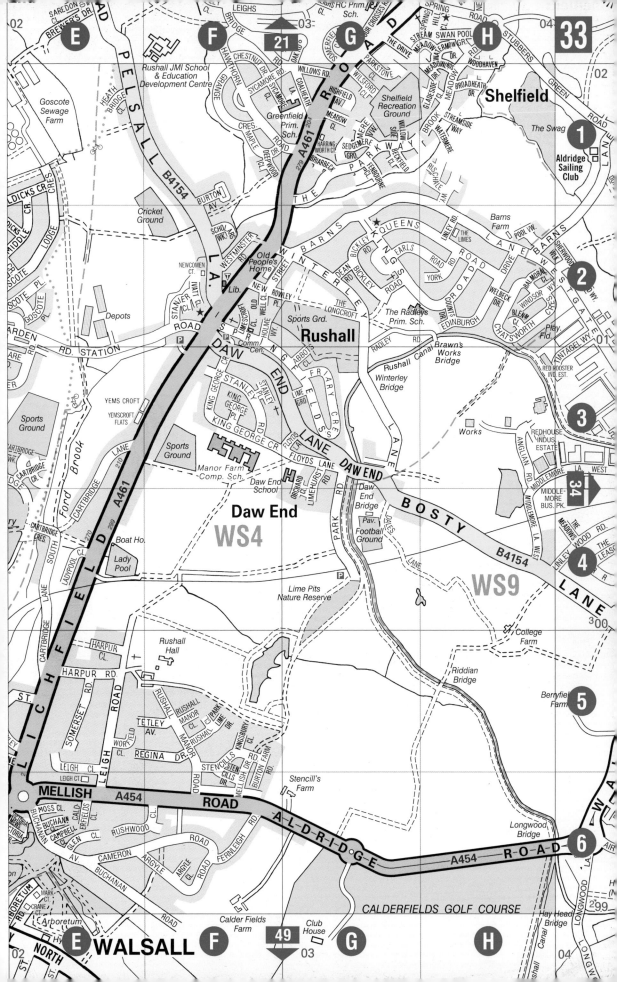

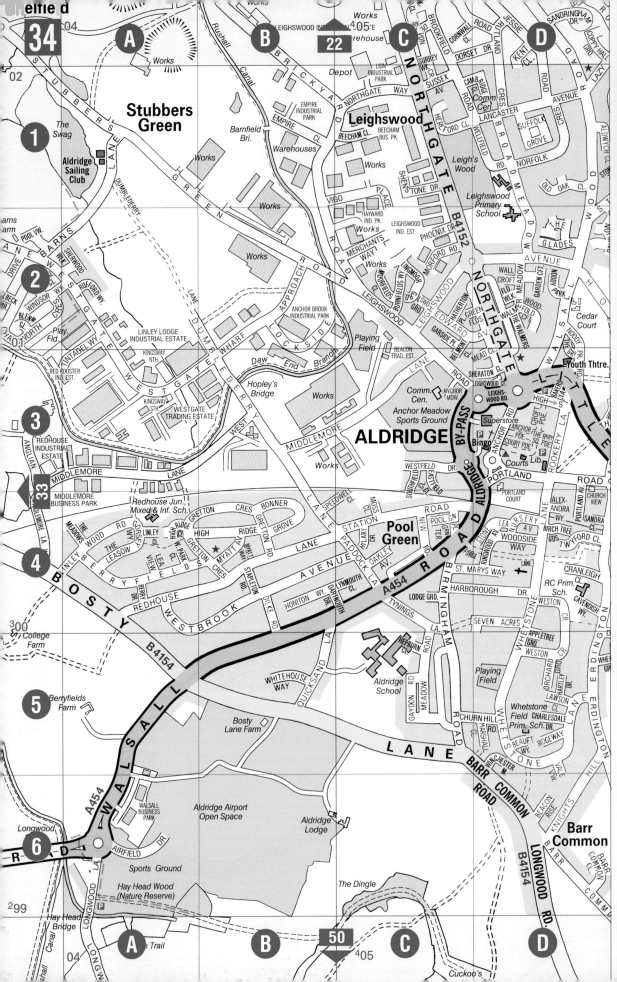

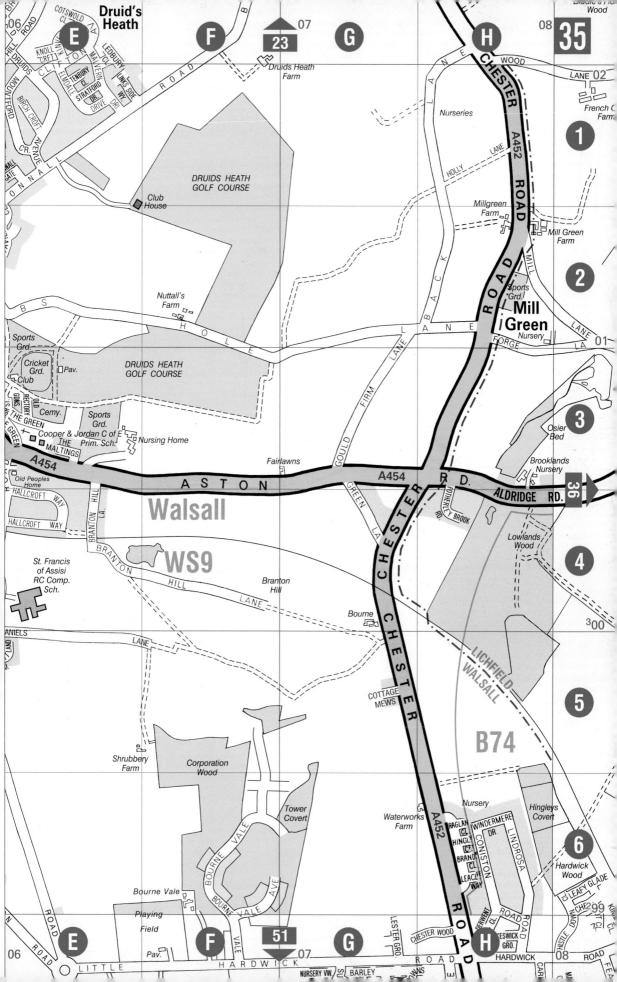

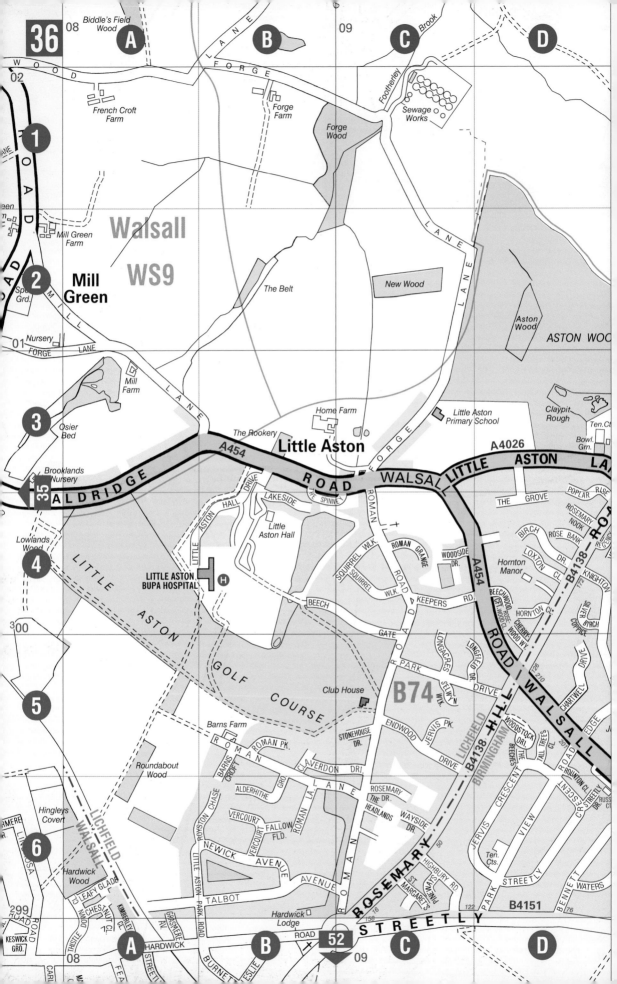

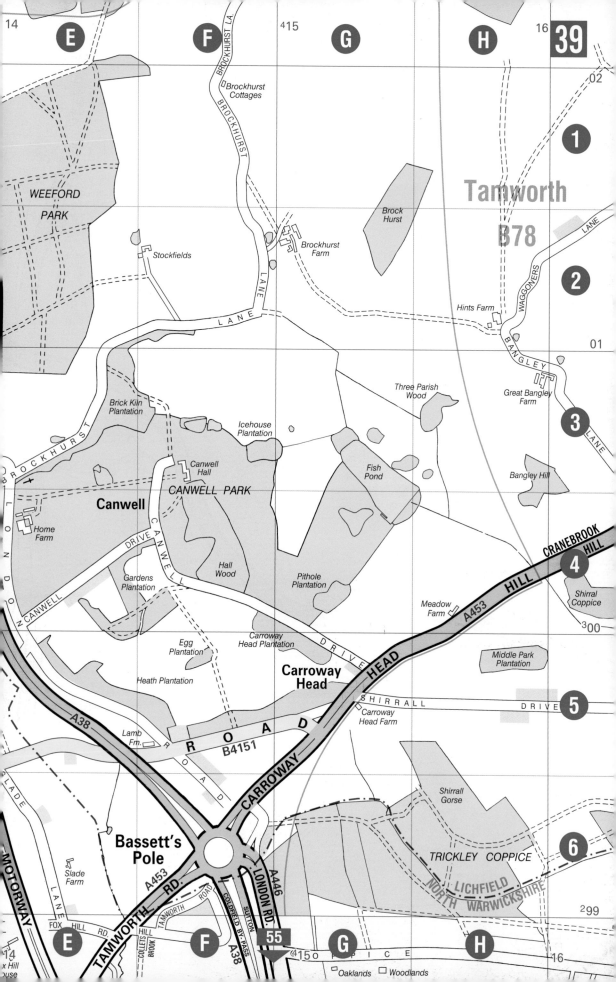

40 84

99

A

B | 385 | ▲ **24** ▼ | **C**

D

Club House

WV6

WV5

²96

84

A

B ▲ **56** ▼ 385

C

D

Ebstree

GREAT MOOR ROAD

TOADNEST

LANE

PATTINGHAM

WROTTESLEY PARK ROAD

WYKEHAM

GRO

HAWKS

Sling Wood

Middle Wood

Freehold Wood

South Perton Farm

Perton Court

WALKERS LANE

JENNY

ROAD

BRI

Sewage Works

Perton Mill Farm

BENNETT'S LA.

Ford

Pool Hall

STAFFORD

Trescott

East Trescott Farm

SHOP LA.

BRIDGNORTH A454

West Trescott Farm

Poolhall Cottages

The Pool

Trescott Grange

Brook

Furnace Grange

Smestow

Twin Oaks Farm

ROAD

EBSTREE

Wo

1

2

3

4

5

6

98

97

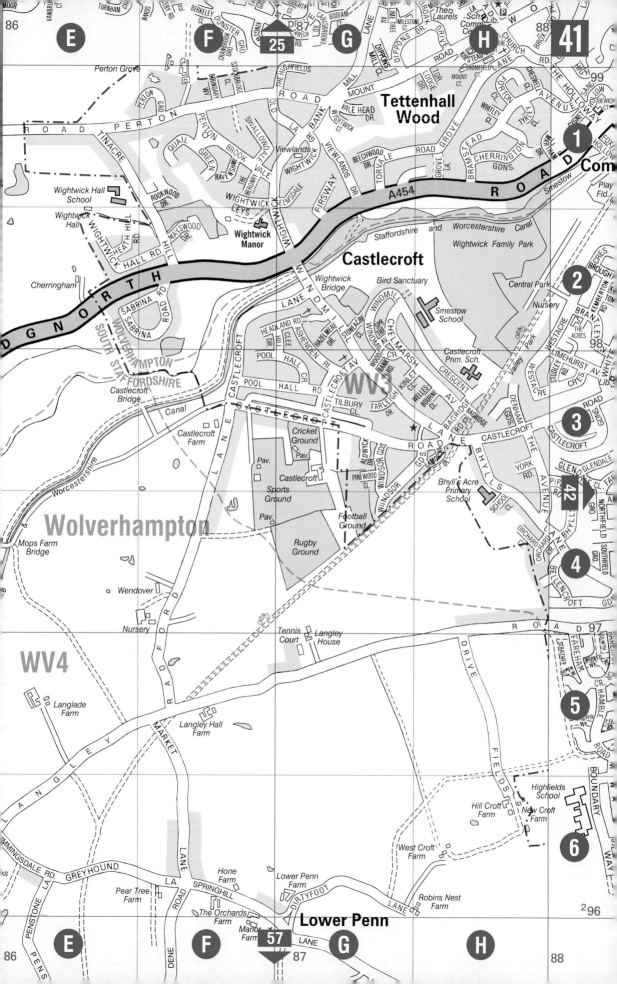

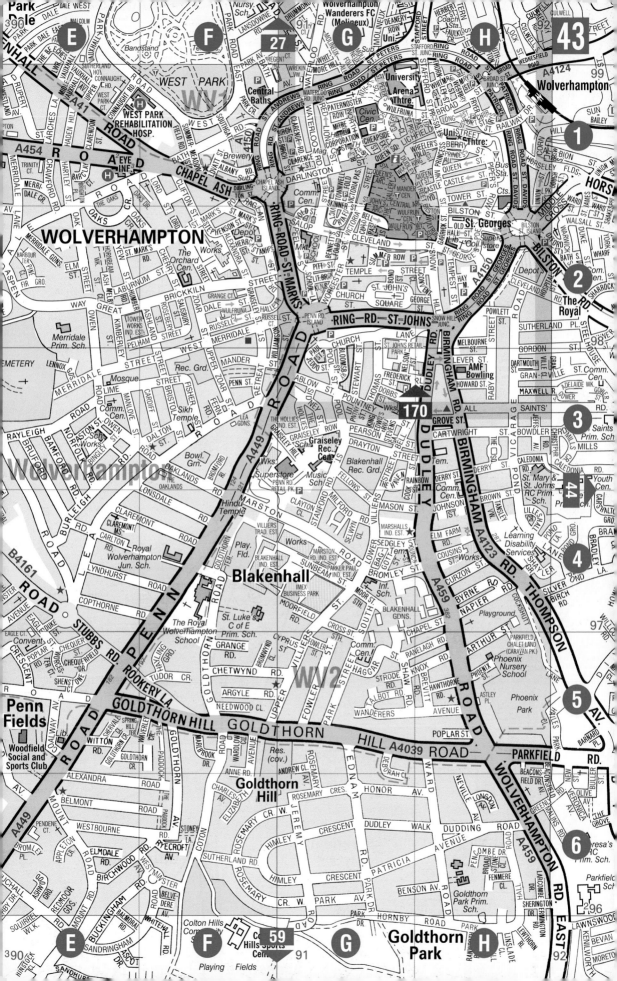

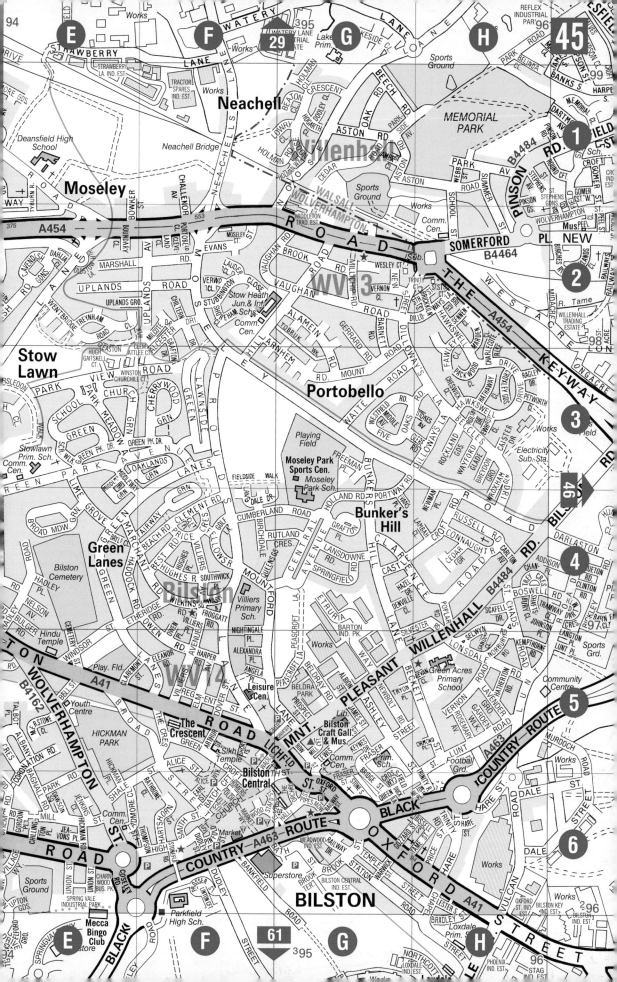

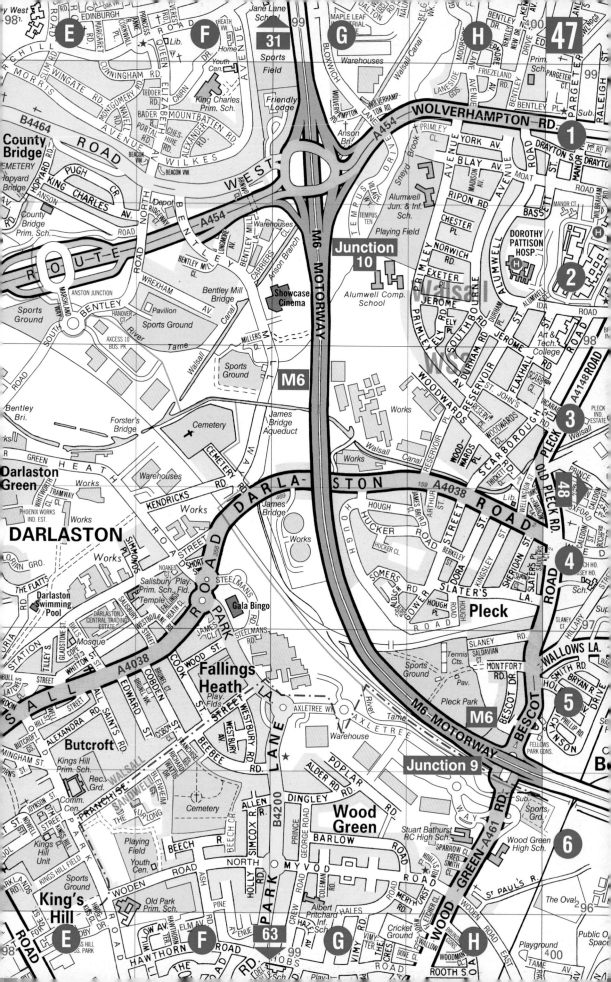

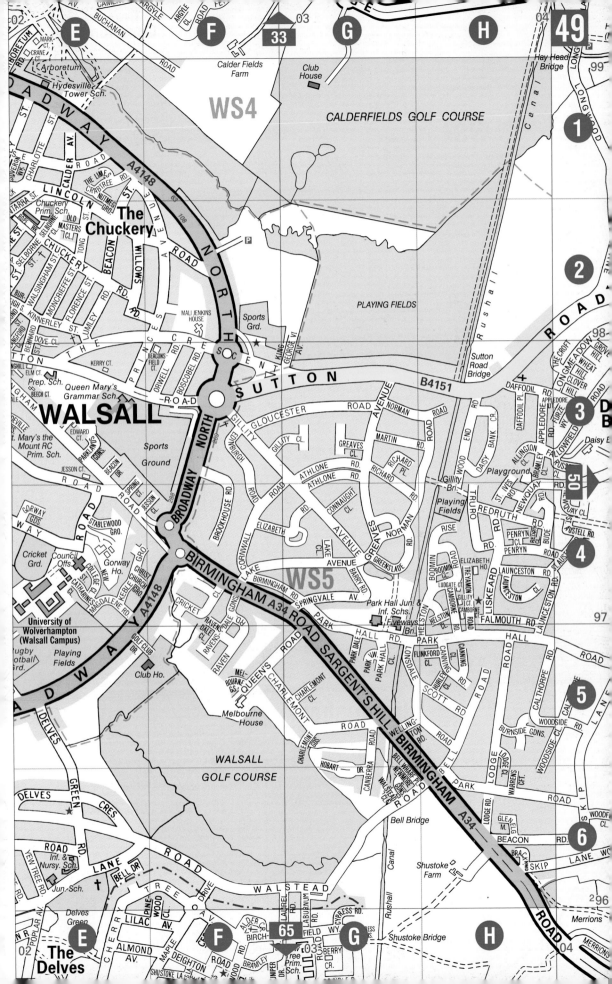

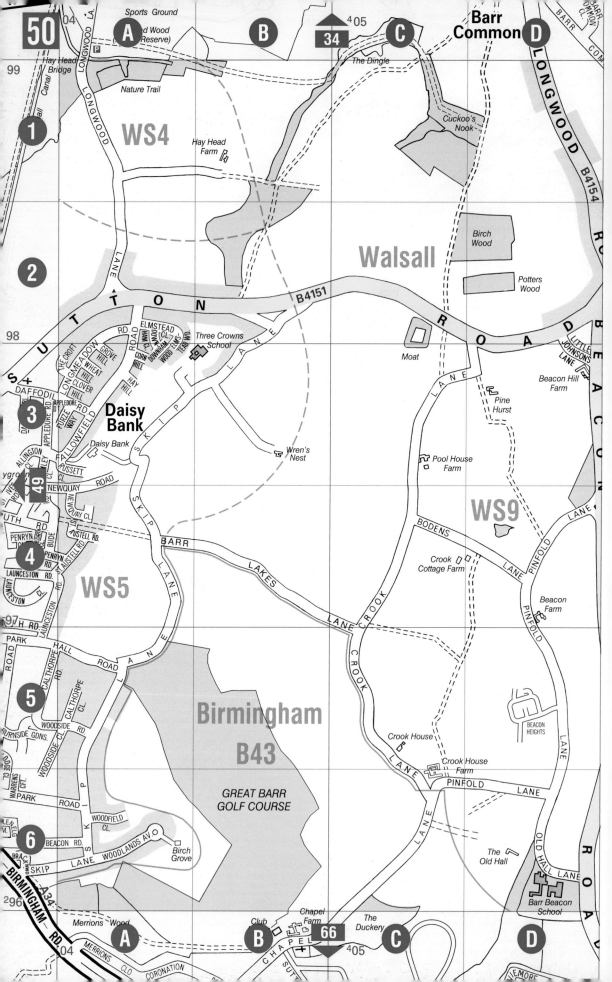

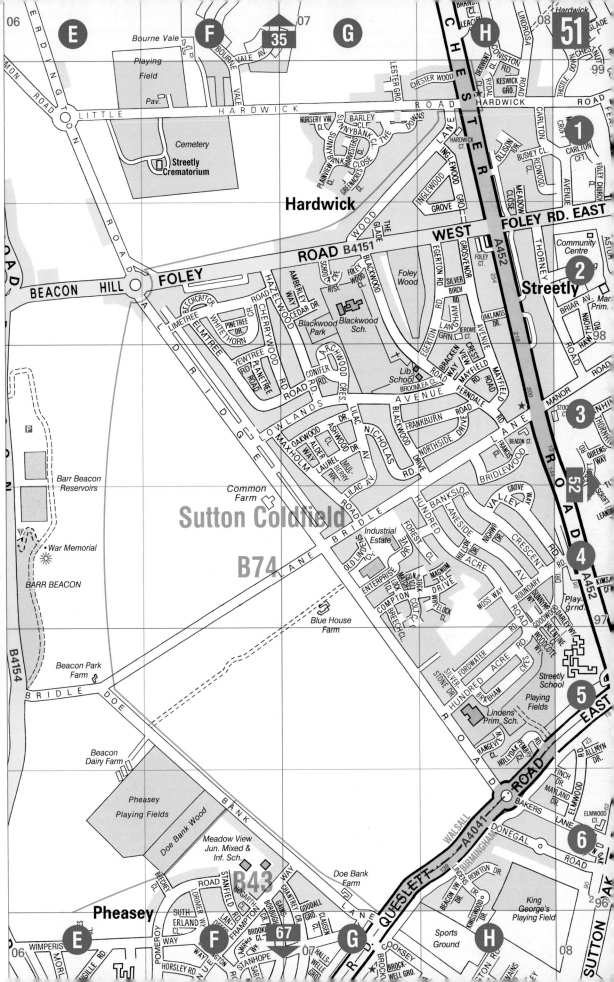

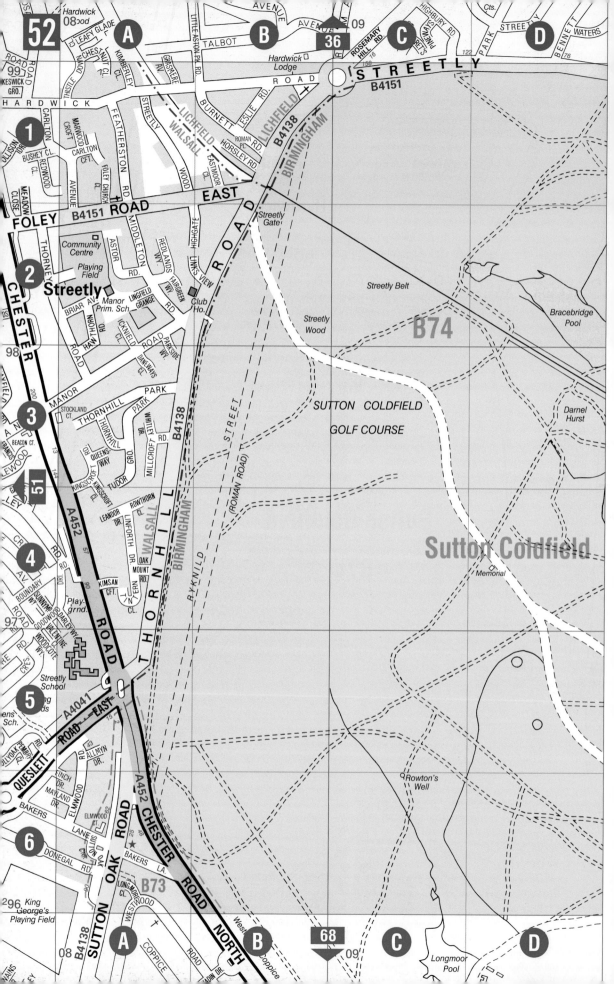

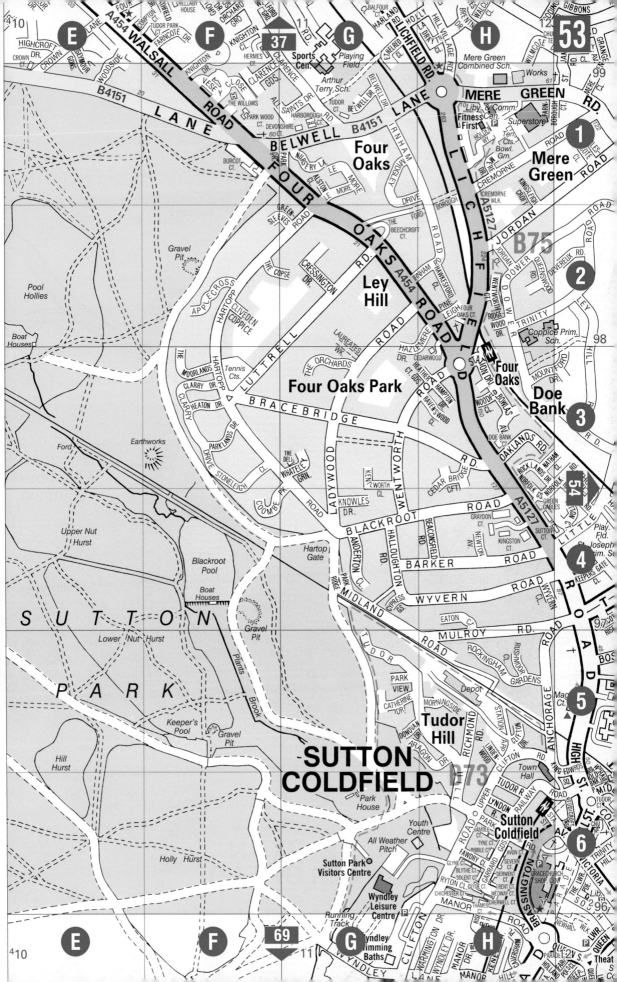

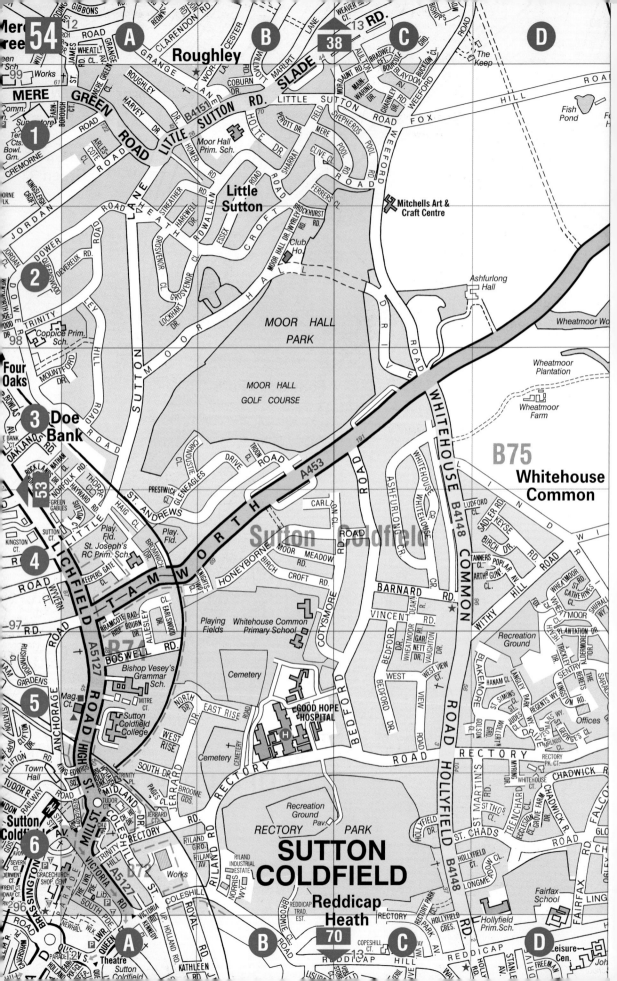

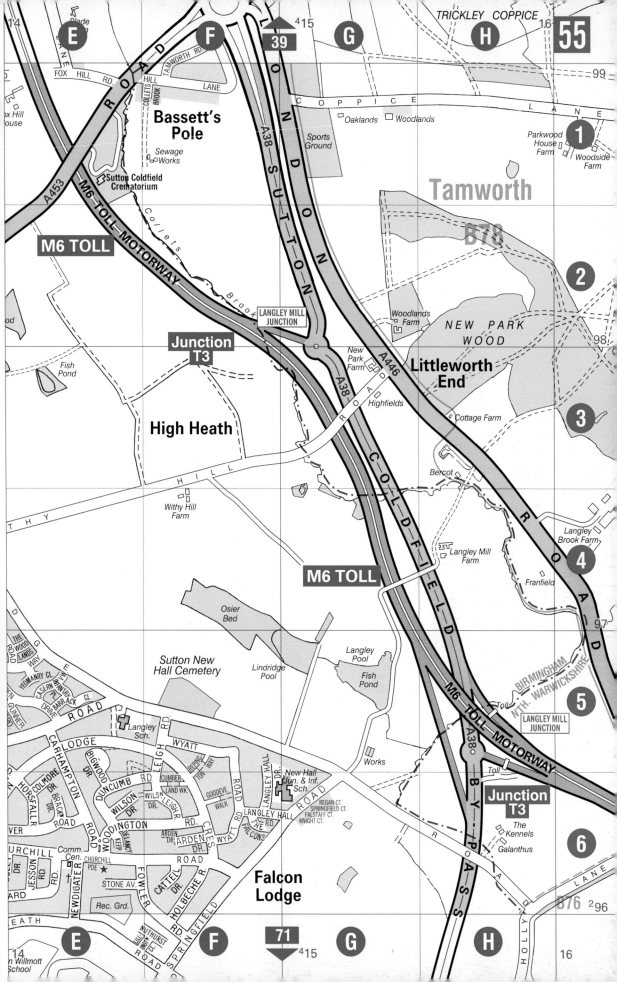

56

84

96

295

94

93

84

A   B   C   D

385
40

385
72

1
2
3
4
5
6

Ebstree

Old Smithy Farm

Greenacres

Ponderosa

Wolverhampton

Ebstree Bridge

The Elms

Ivy House Farm

Meadow Farm

Lanes Farm

SEISDON HOLLAWAY

Seisdon

Lea Farm

BEECH HURST GDNS.

Rock House

Roost Farm

Meadow Cottage

The Hall

Home Farm

Smestow

CROCKINGTON

SEISDON

CHURCH ST

EBSTREE MDW.

THE WILLOWS

OAK DR.

THE FOLD

ROAD

POST OFFICE

Sand Pit

TRYSULL

HOLLOWAY

Awbridge Farm

Warehouse

The Grotto

UNION

CHURCH LA.

Trysull

Trysull Farm

Monks Path

BELL

Manor Farm Cottages

Brook

LANE

ROAD

Manor House

WHITE ROW

The Croft

Ketley House

ROAD

WV5

LANE

BEECHHOUSE

The Beeches

All Saints C of E Prim. Sch.

SCHOOL

SCHOOL LANE

THE GREEN

WOODFORD

Playing Field

Woodford Grange

FEIASHILL

Feiashill

FEIAS-HILL CL.

Cherry Cottage

Loneacre

mestow Barn

The Farm

Works

Smestow Brook

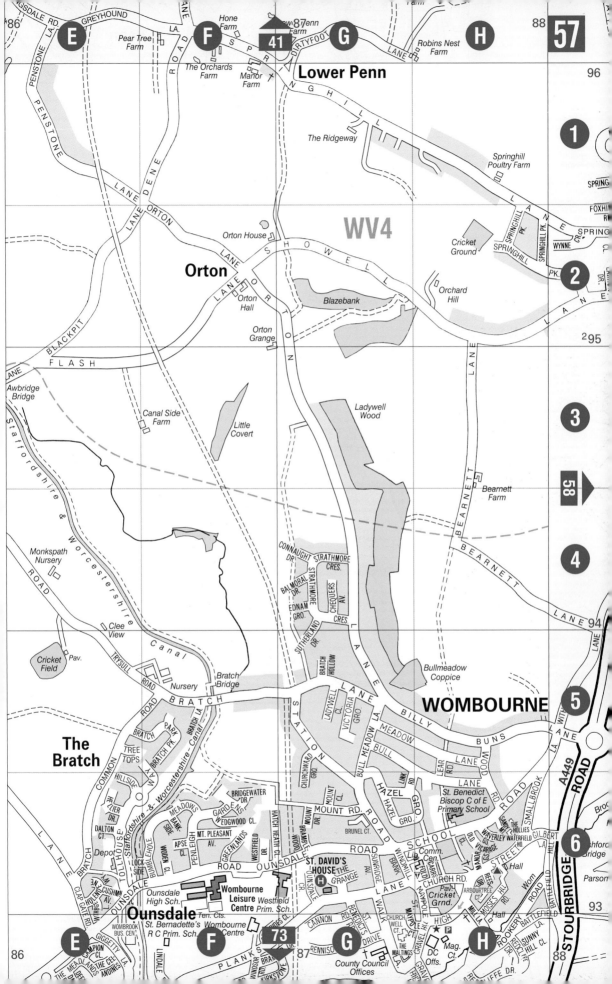

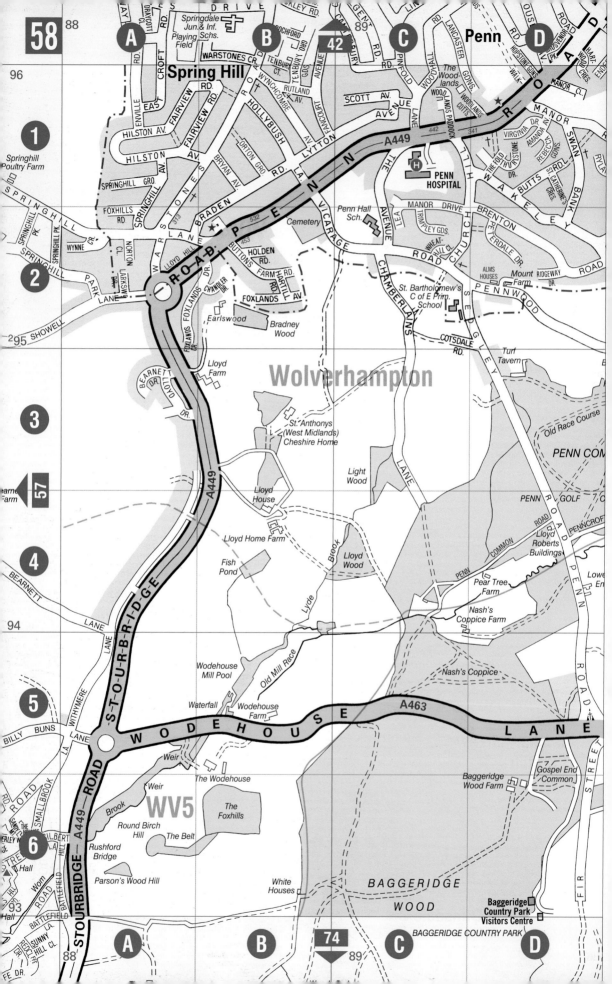

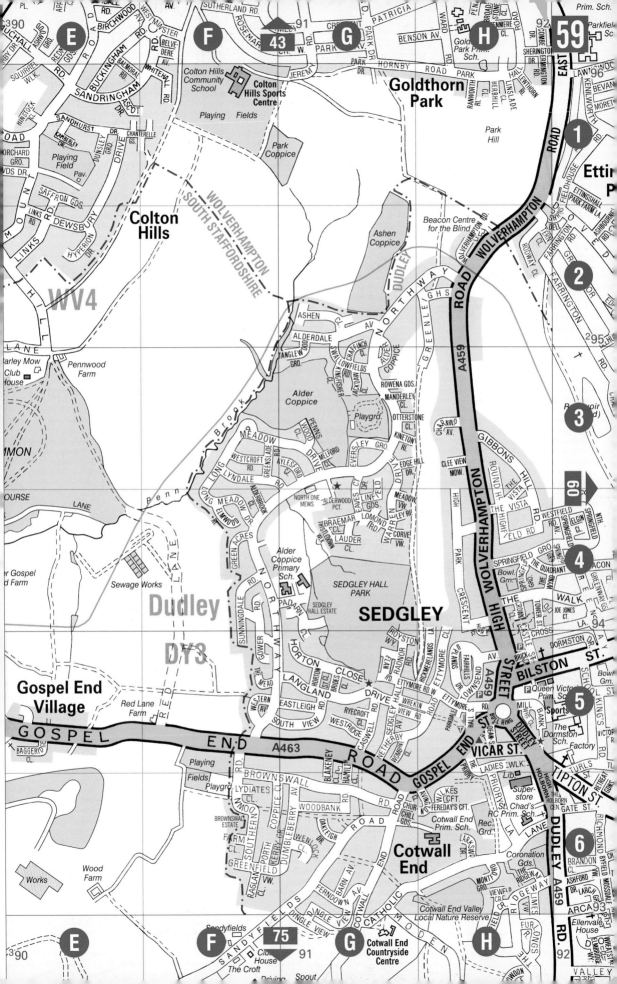

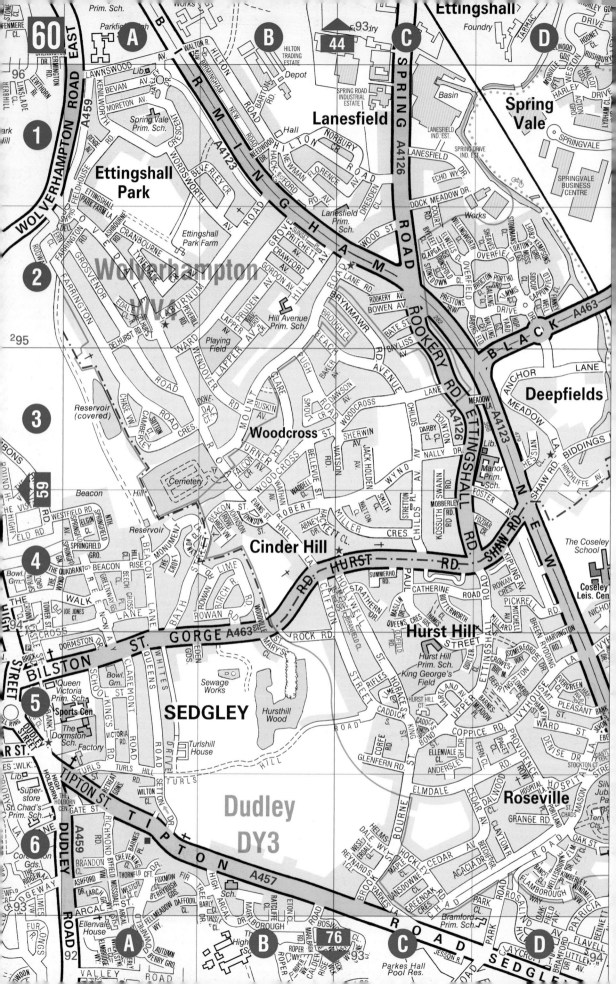

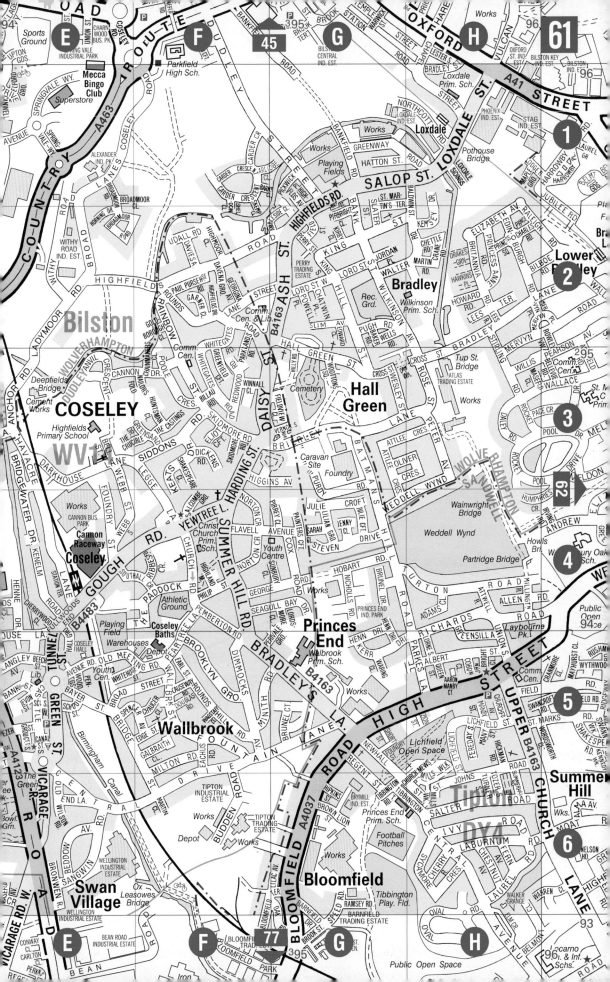

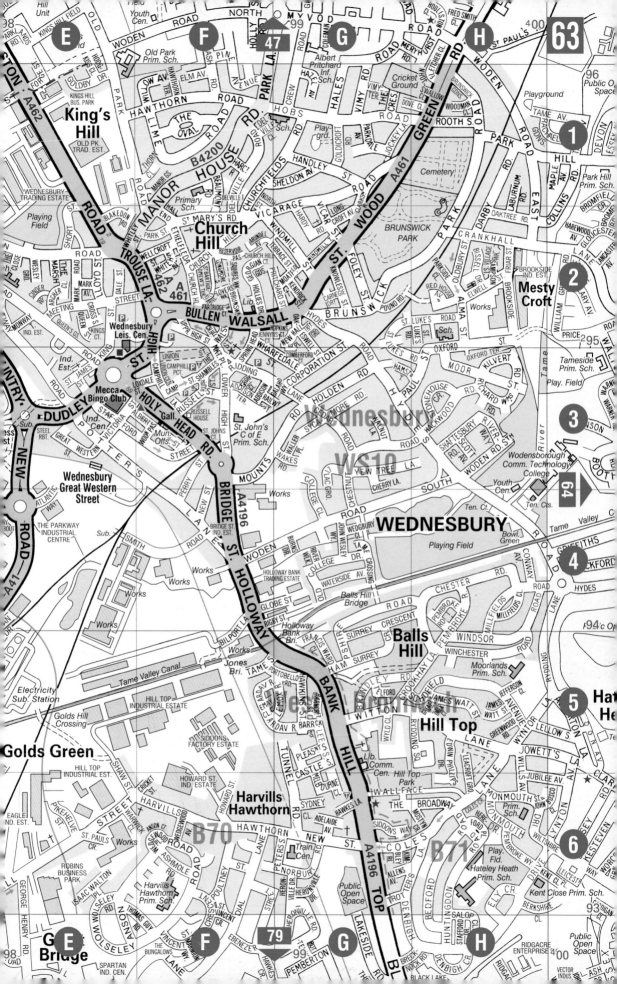

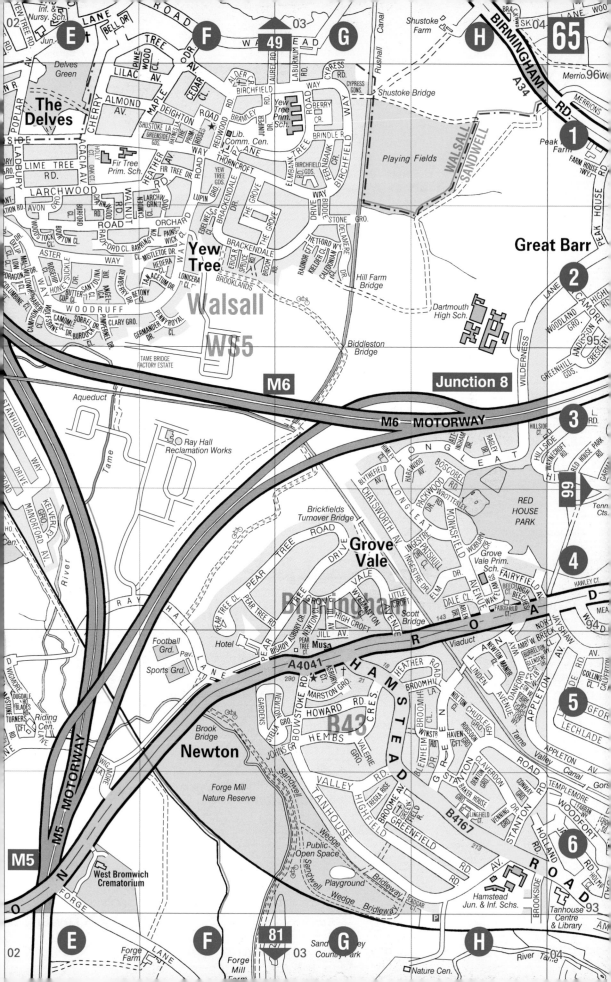

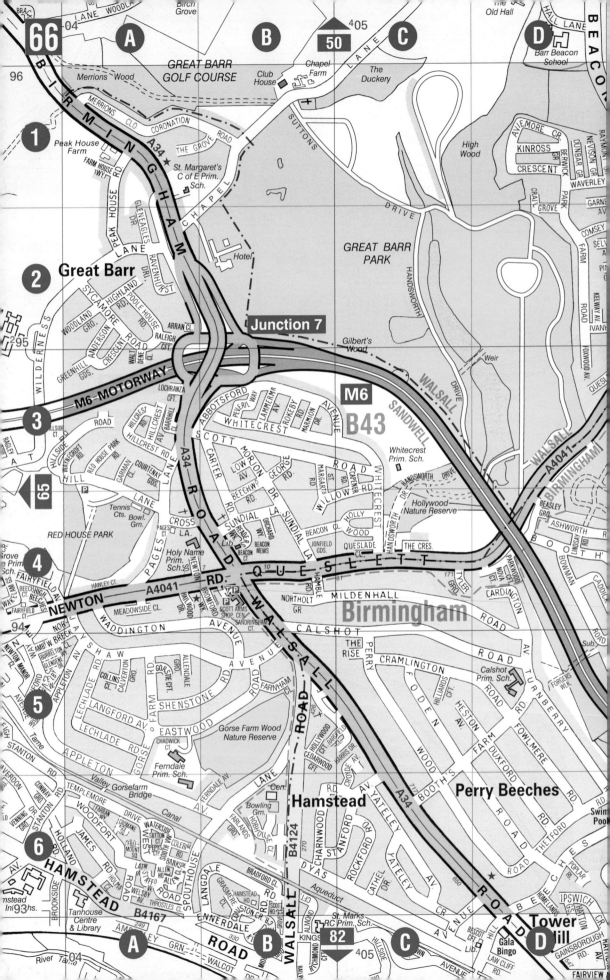

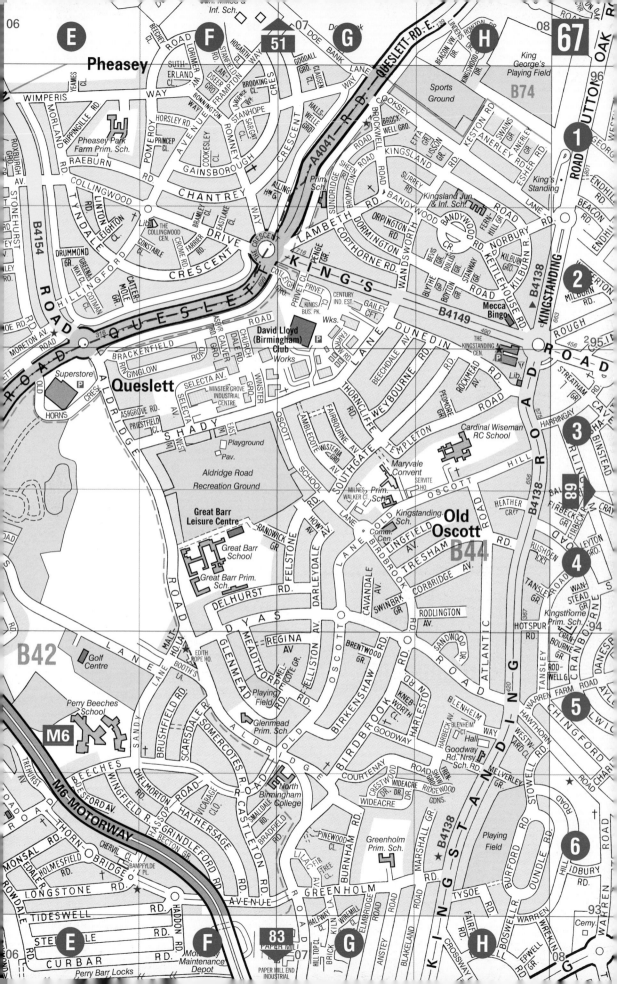

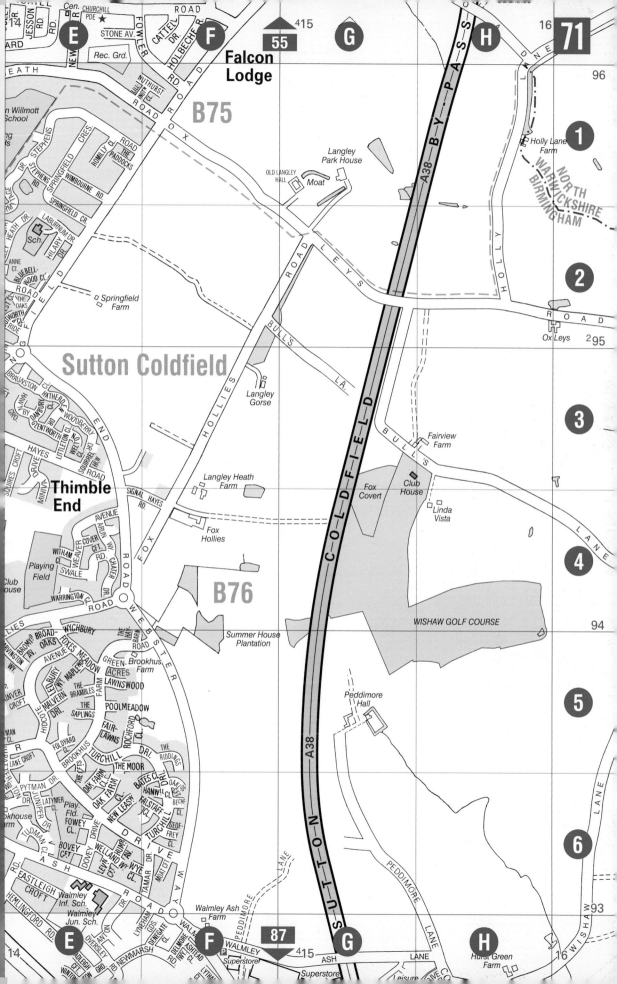

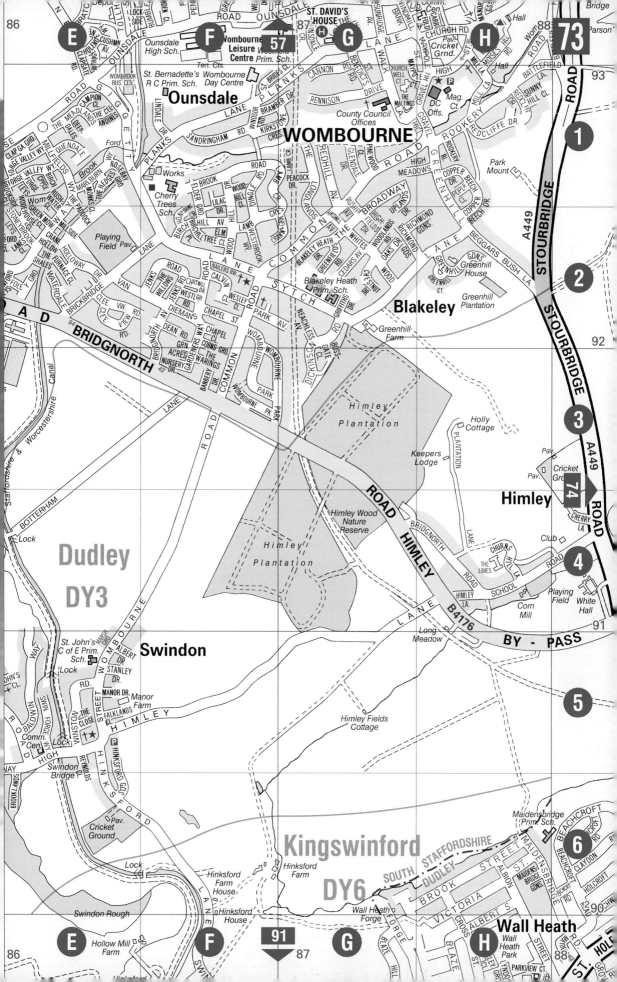

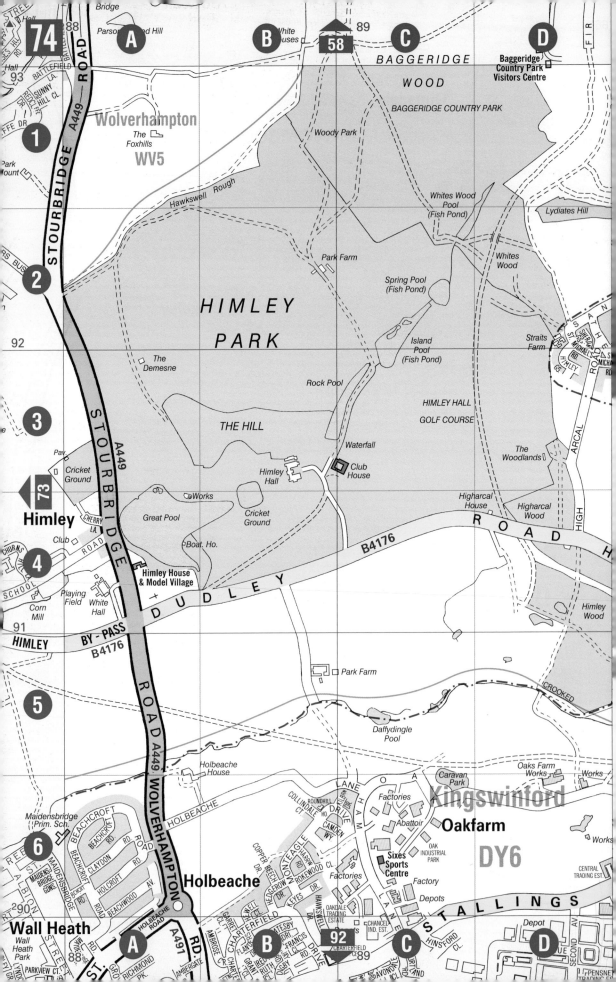

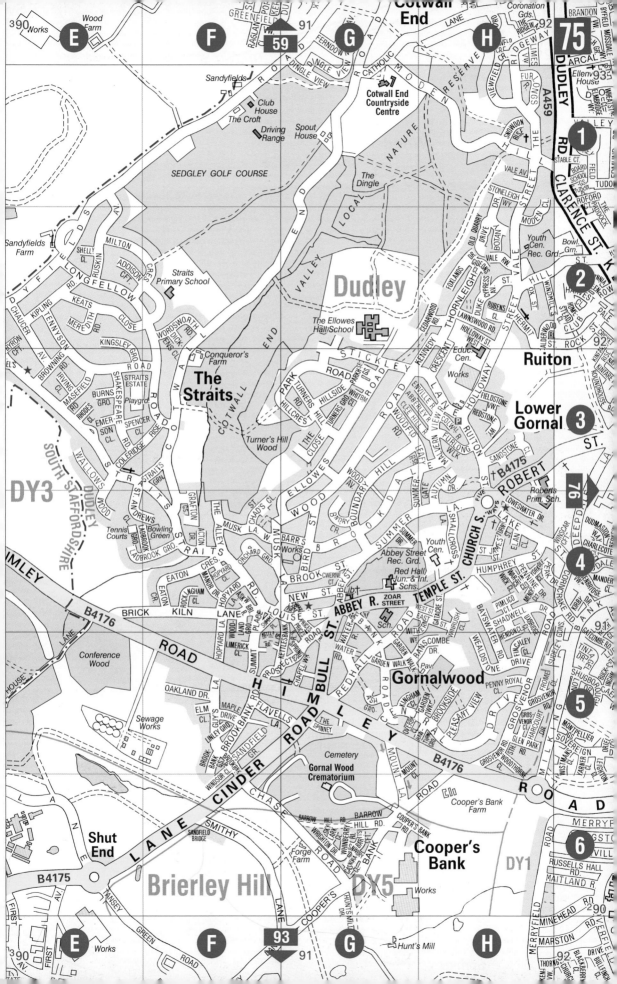

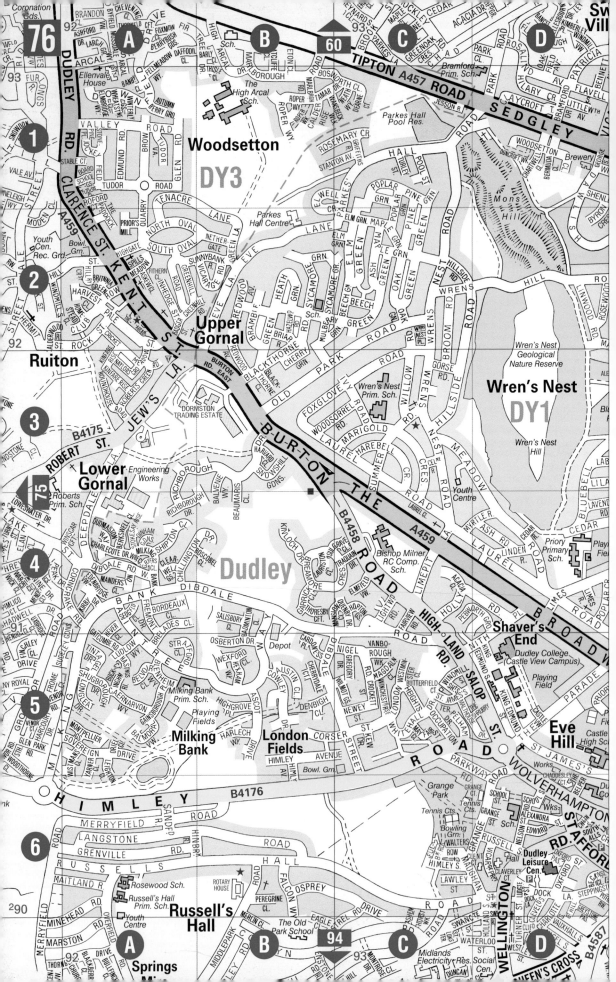

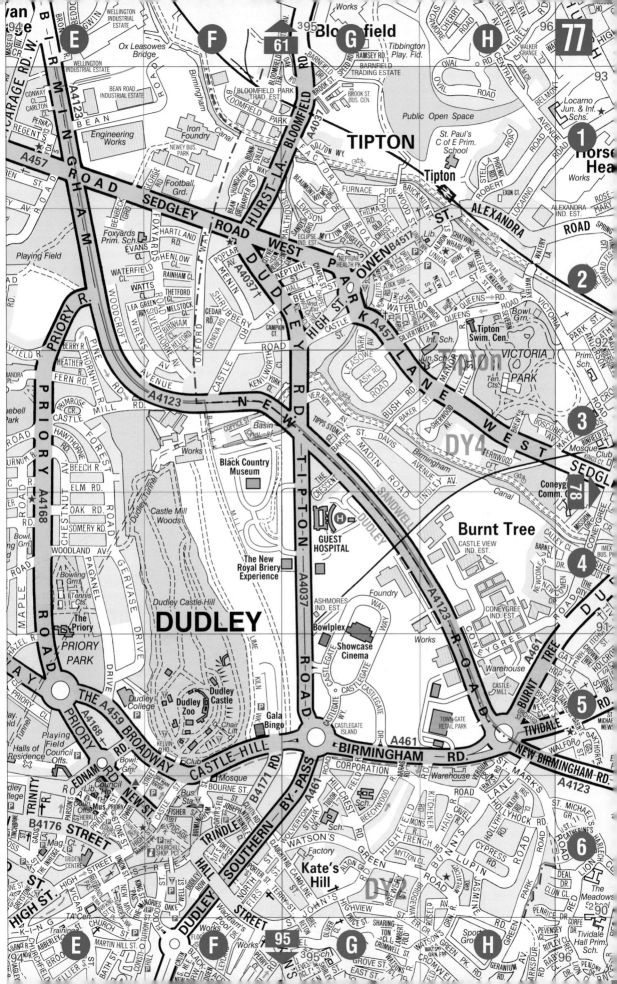

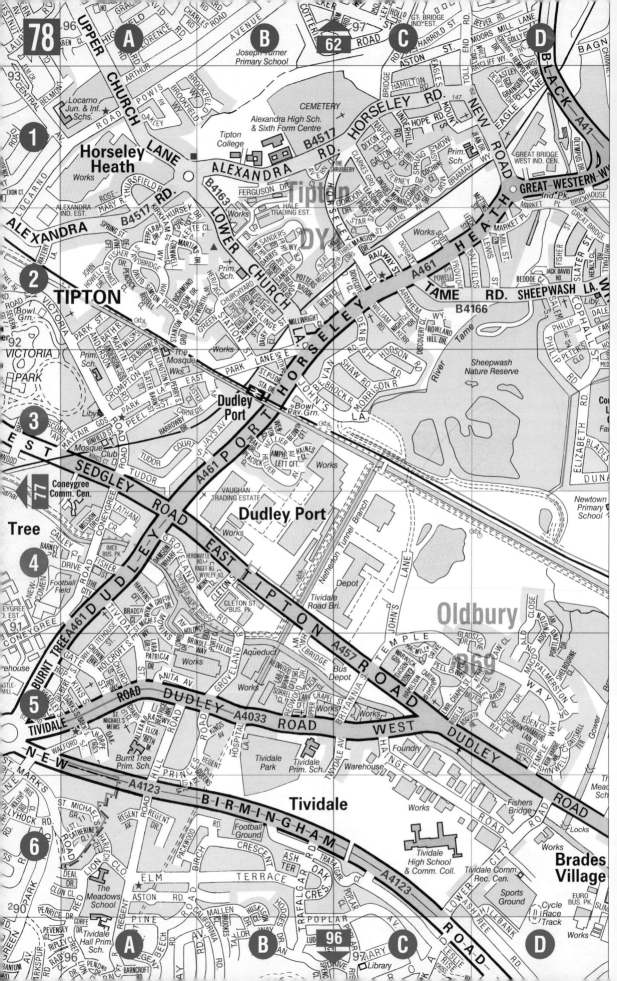

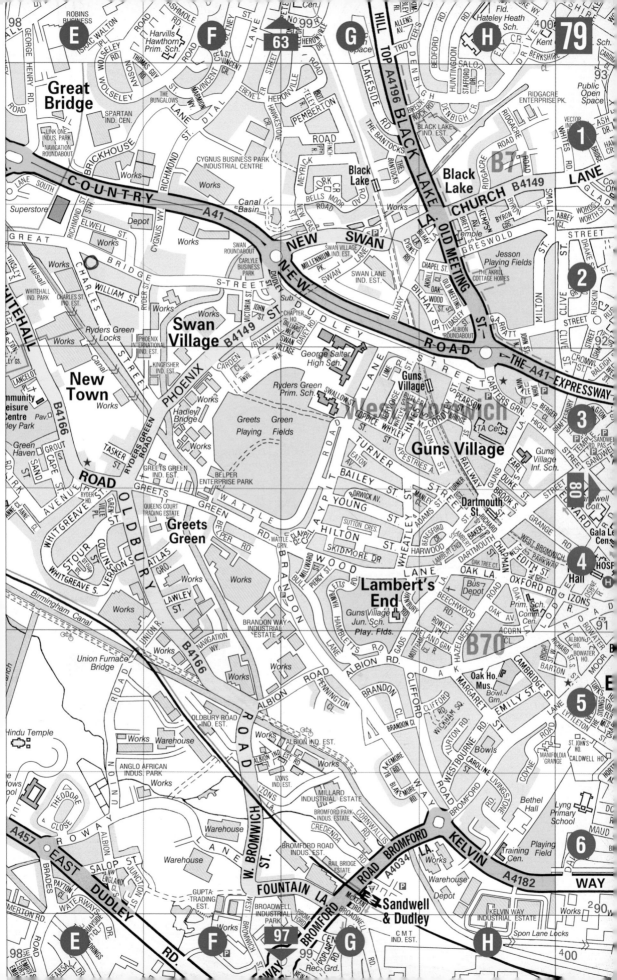

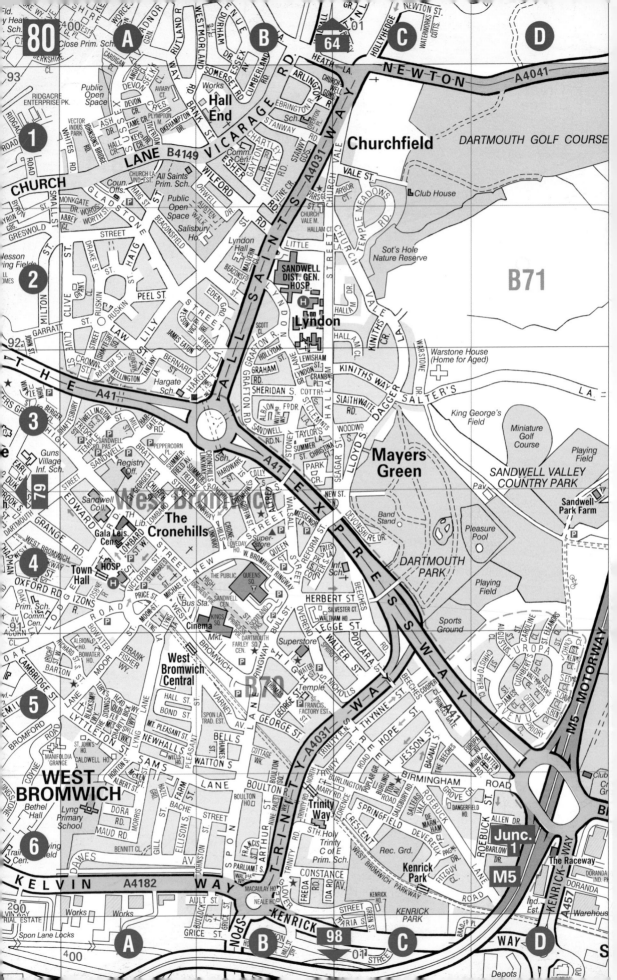

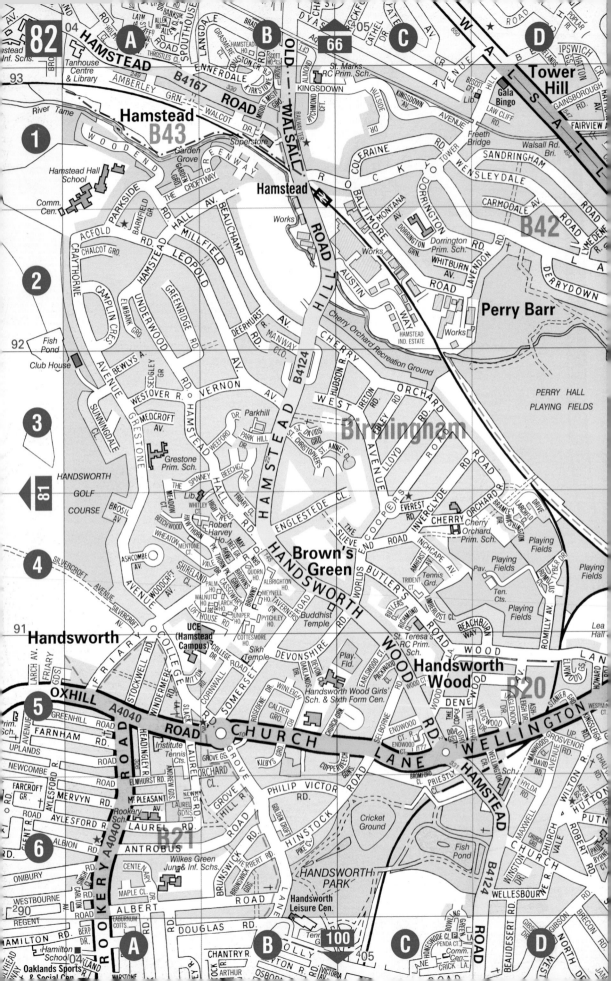

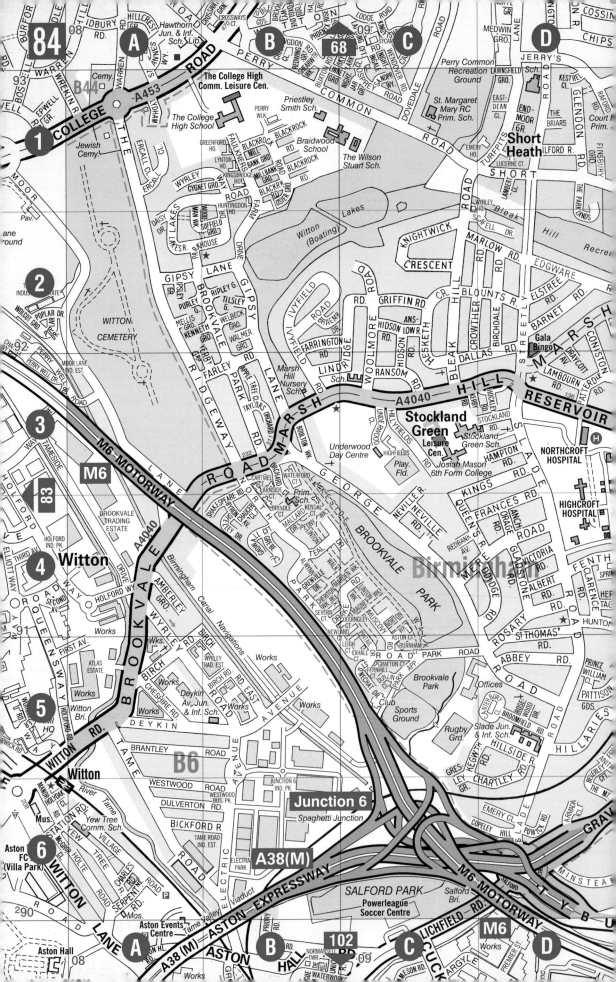

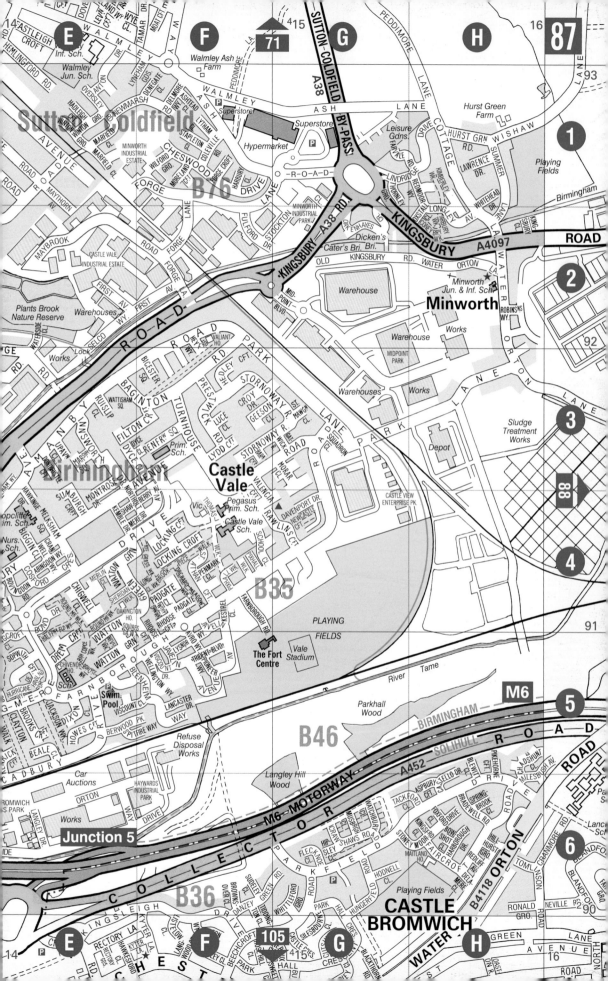

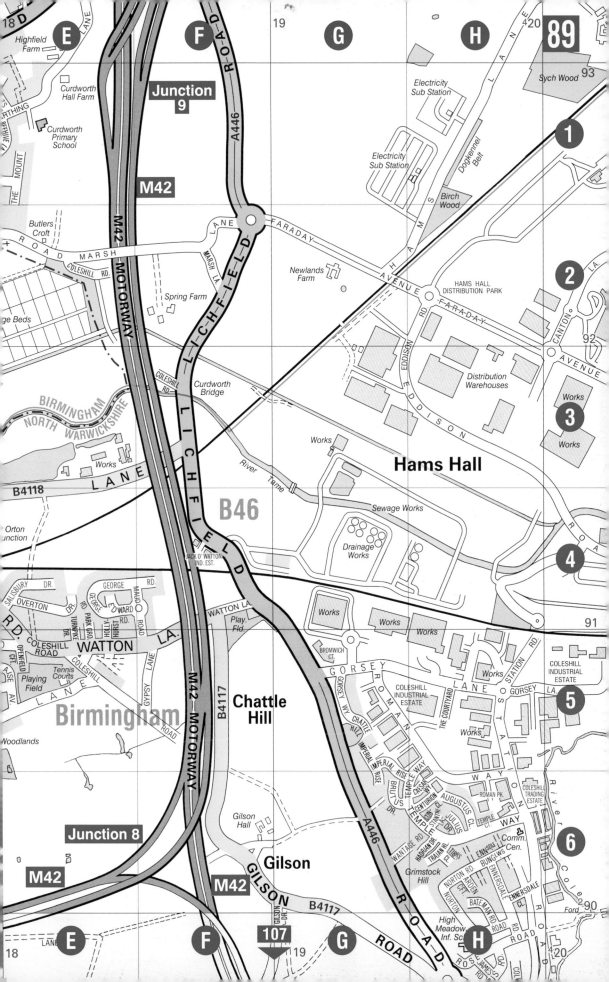

A B ▲ 72 C D

290

HIGHGATE COMMON

COUNTRY PARK

1

Nursery

Chasepool
Lodge

Chasepool
Cottages

Dudley

DY3

My Lady's
Farm

2

COMMON

Camp Farm

89

Black Lands

Square
Covert

EAST

Club
House

3

Pool
Covert

ENVILLE GOLF COURSE

Three
Cornered
Covert

Greensforge

ROAD

Lodge Plantation

4

COMMON

88

ENVILLE

Spittle

The
Spinney

Spittlebrook
Mill

Checkhill Bogs

The
Gorse

Checkhill
Farm

Rickyard
Piece

CHECKHILL

LITTLE

Brook

5

Enville
Towermill

Valley
Field

Stourbridge

LANE

Lower Bog

MILL

6

RUMFORD HILL

87

T H E   M I L L I O N

Hanging
Covert

Cuckoo
Trees

Radway
Cottages

RADWAY HILL

DY7

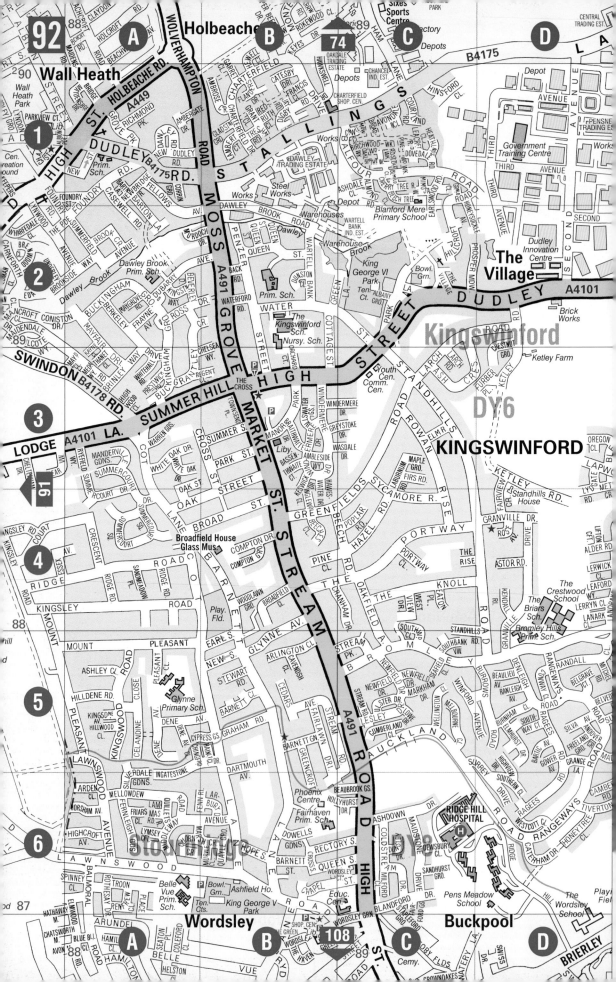

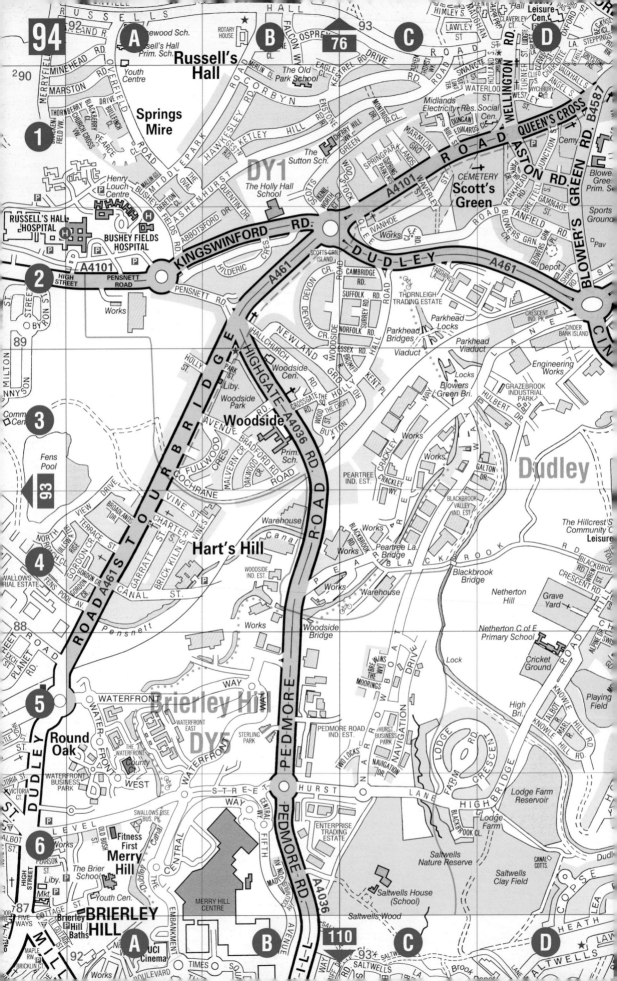

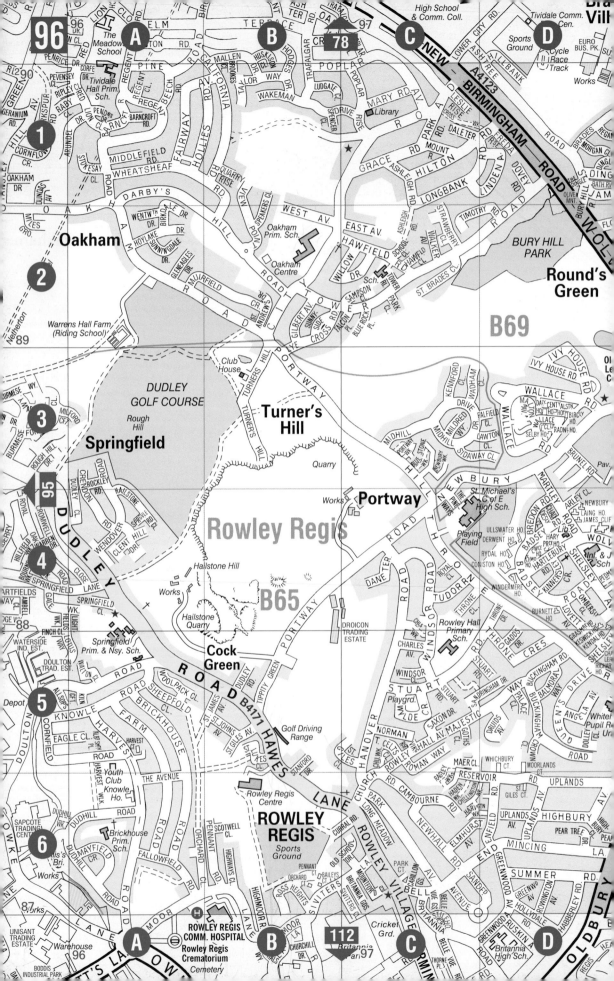

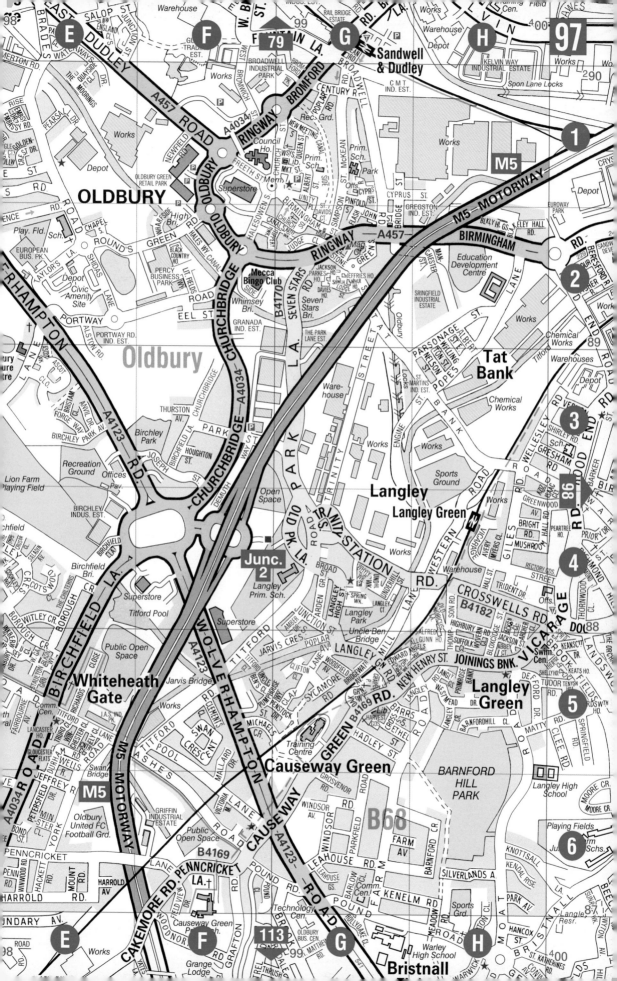

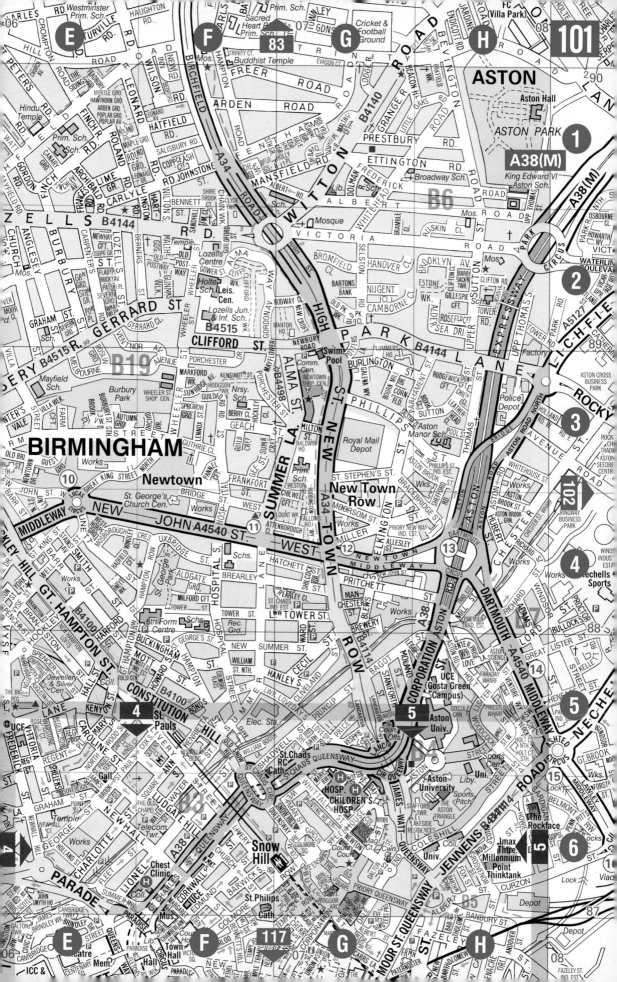

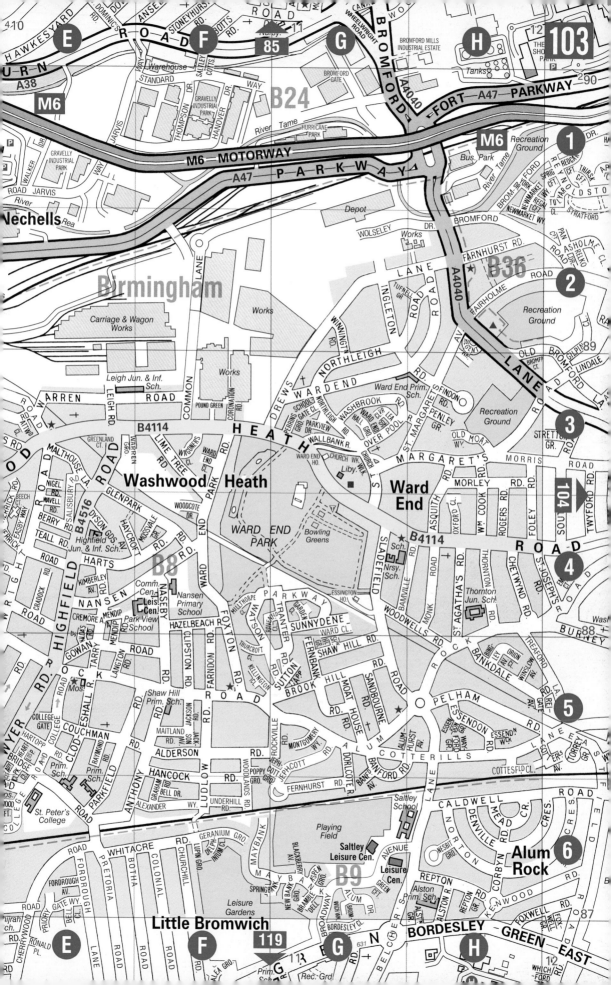

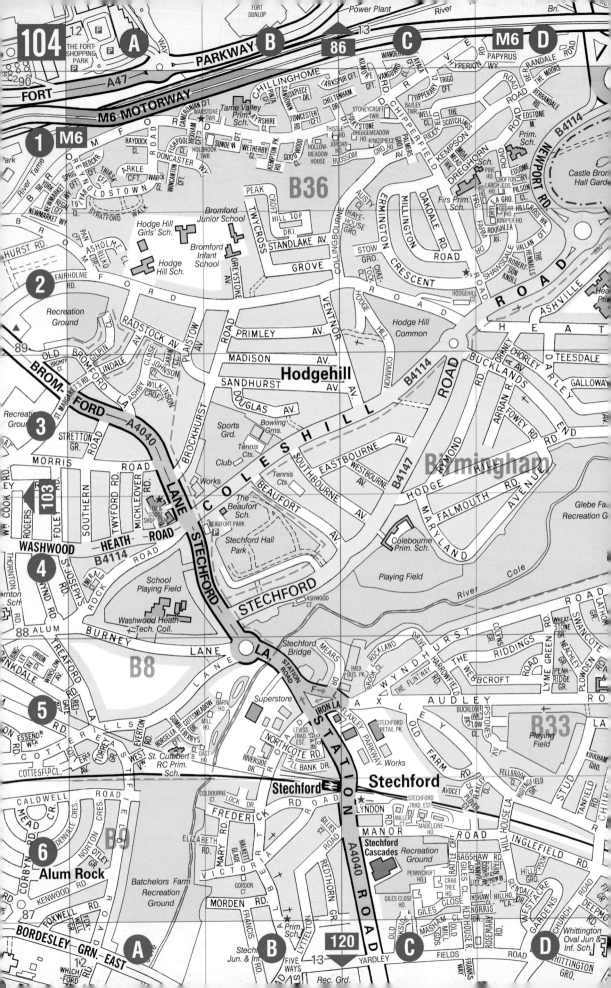

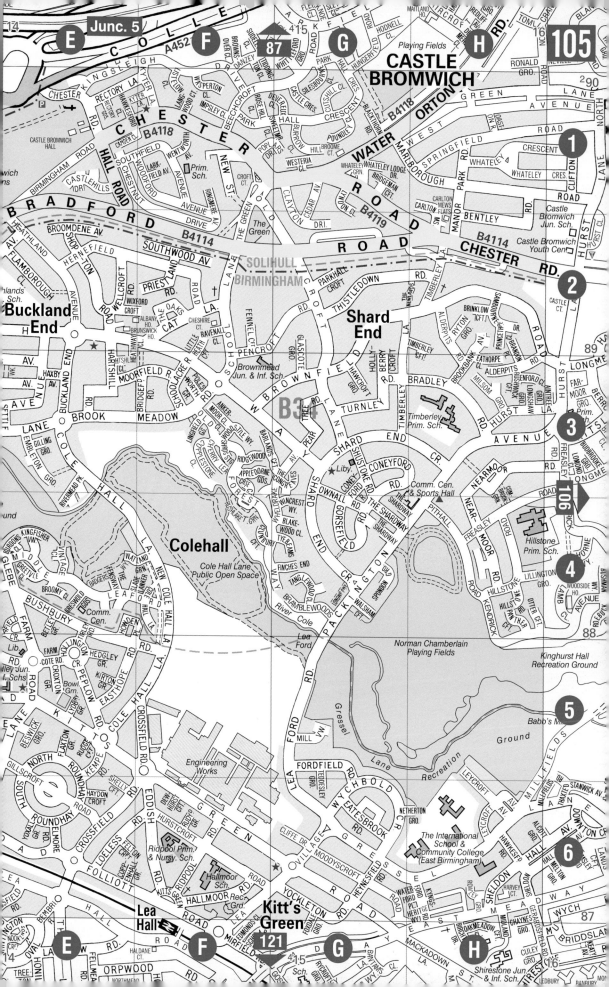

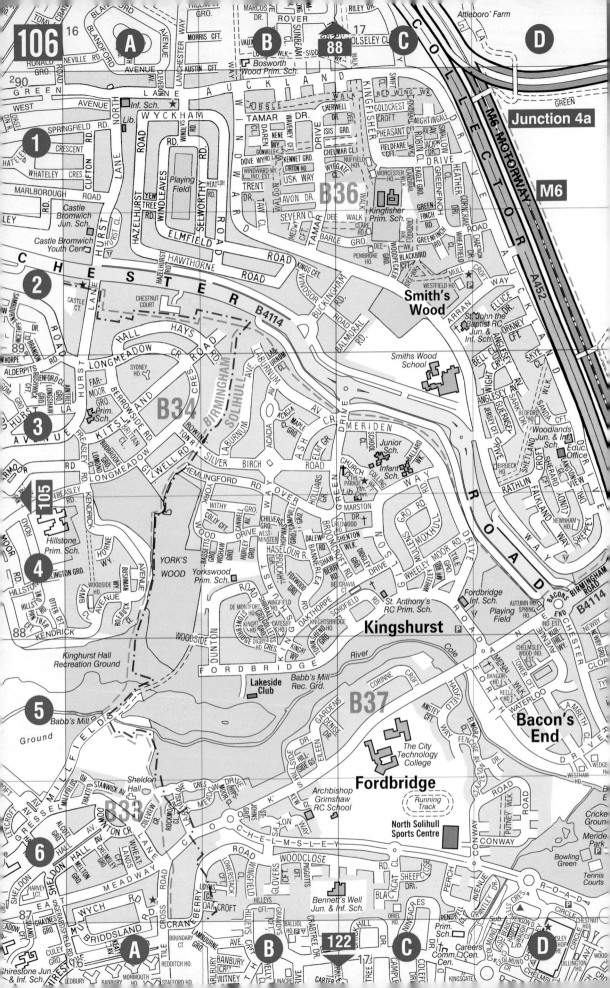

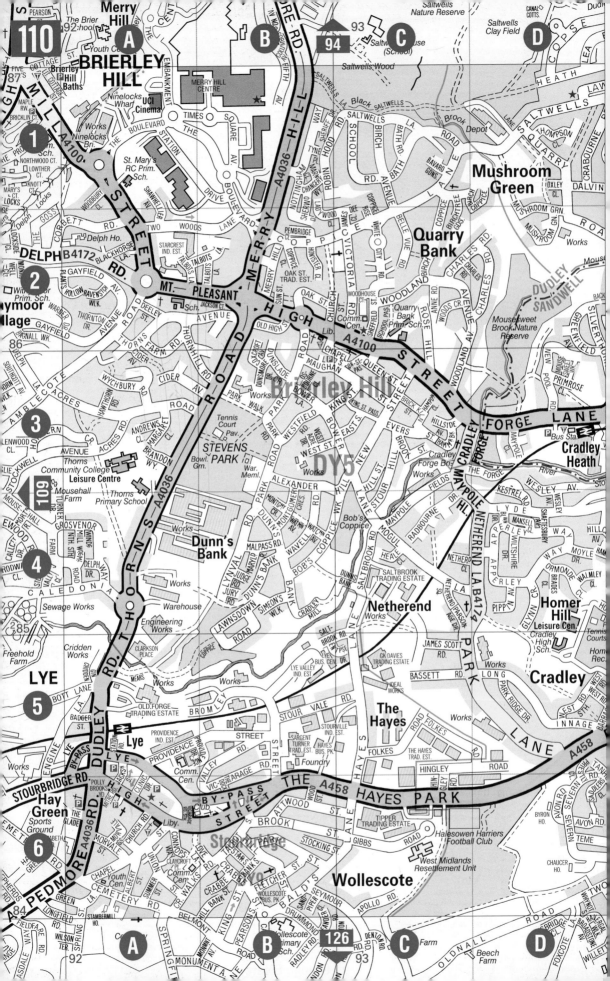

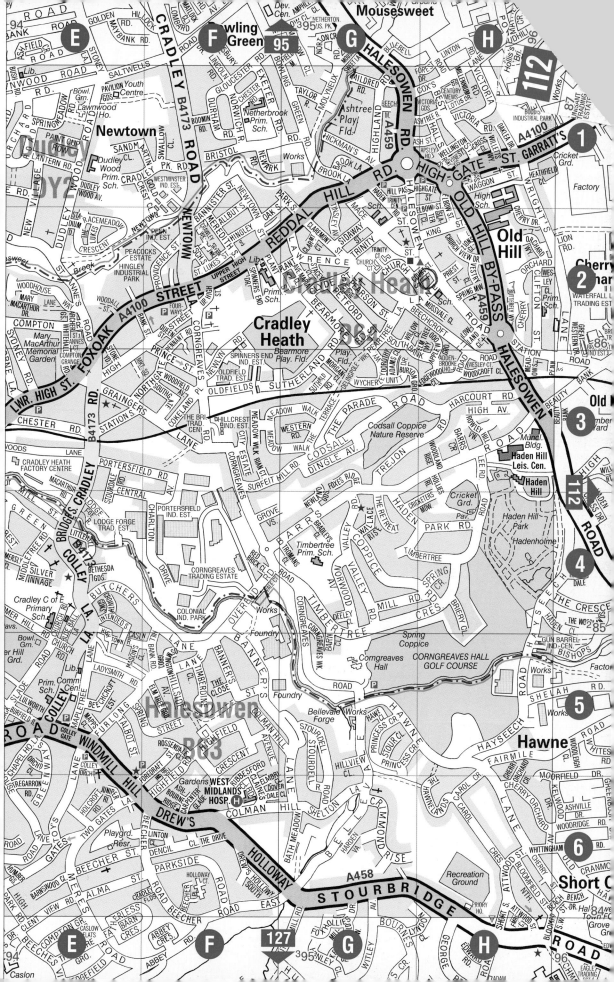

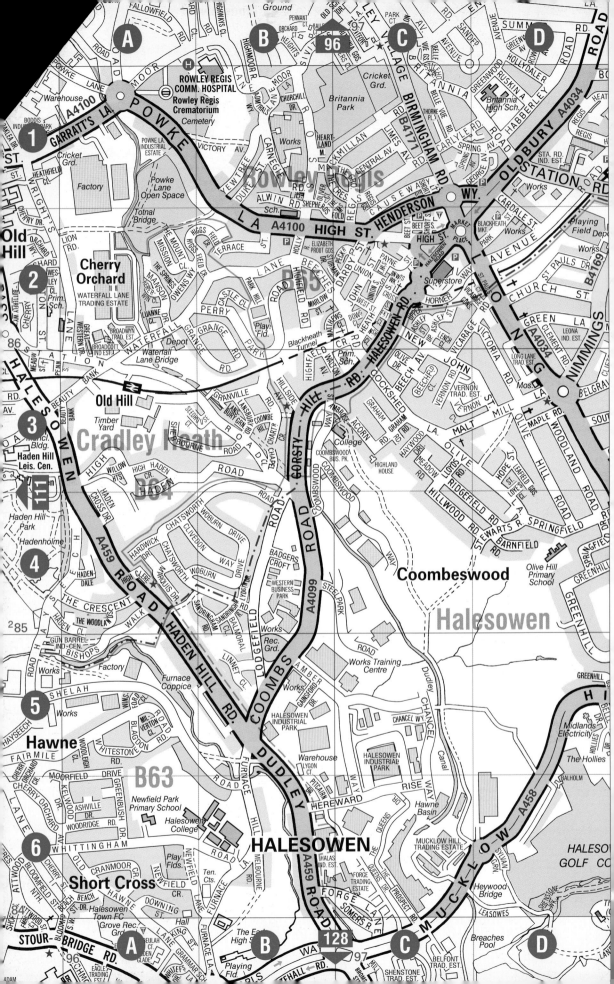

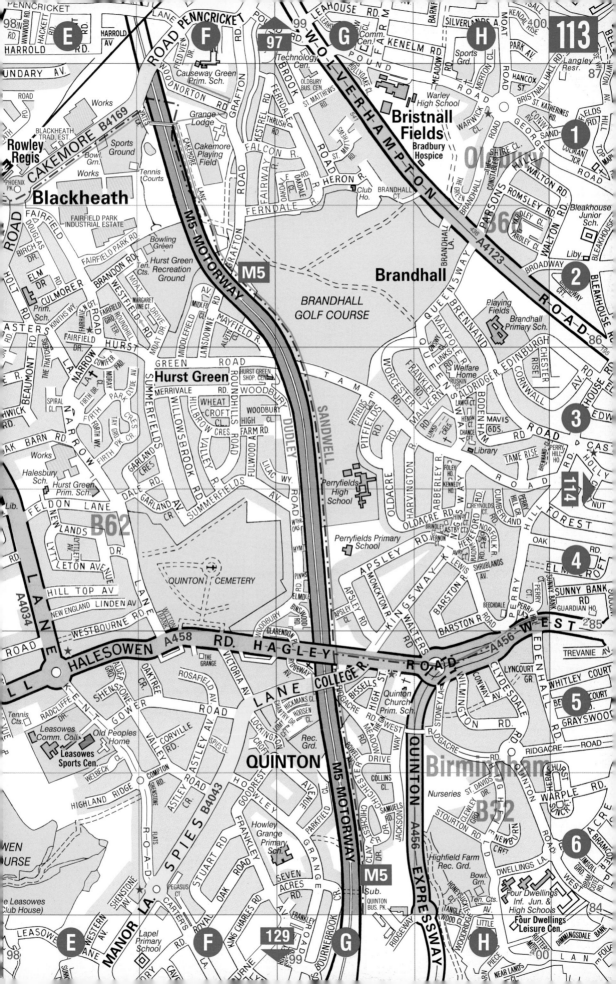

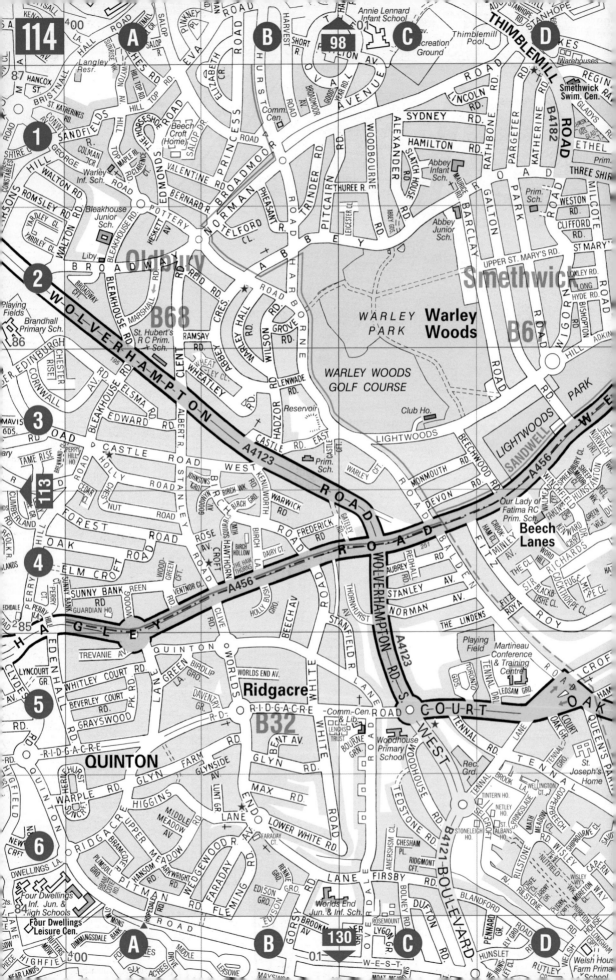

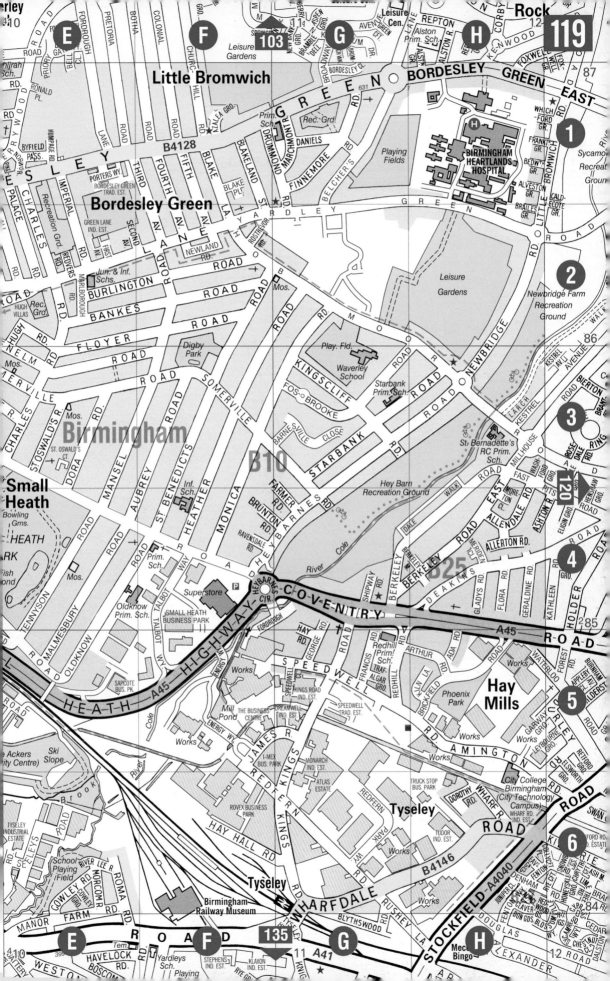

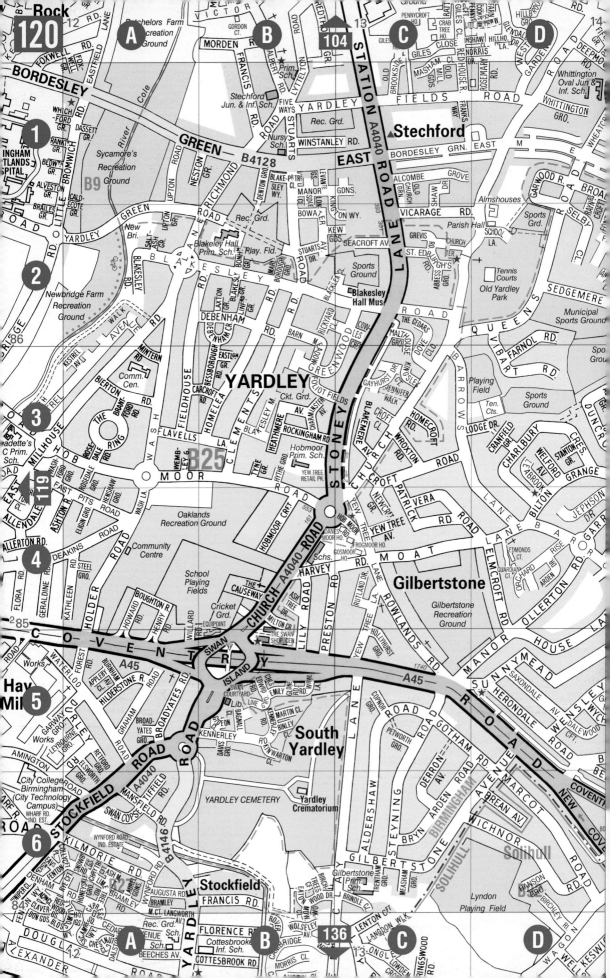

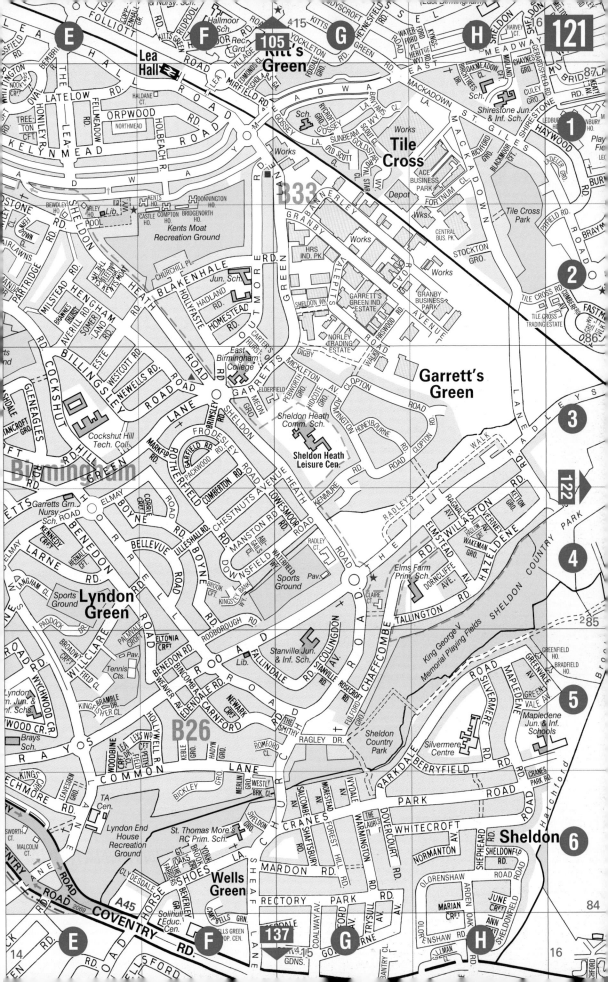

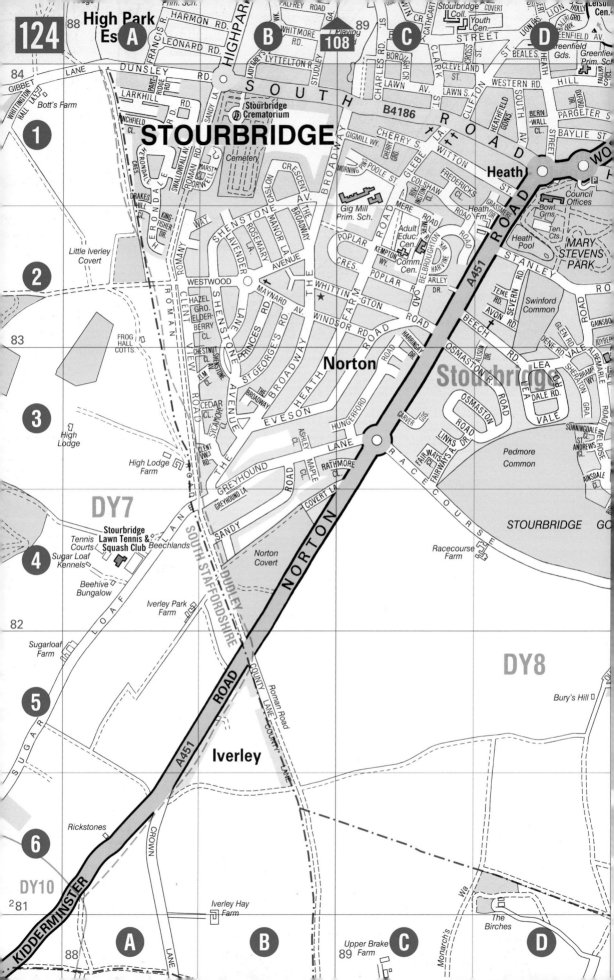

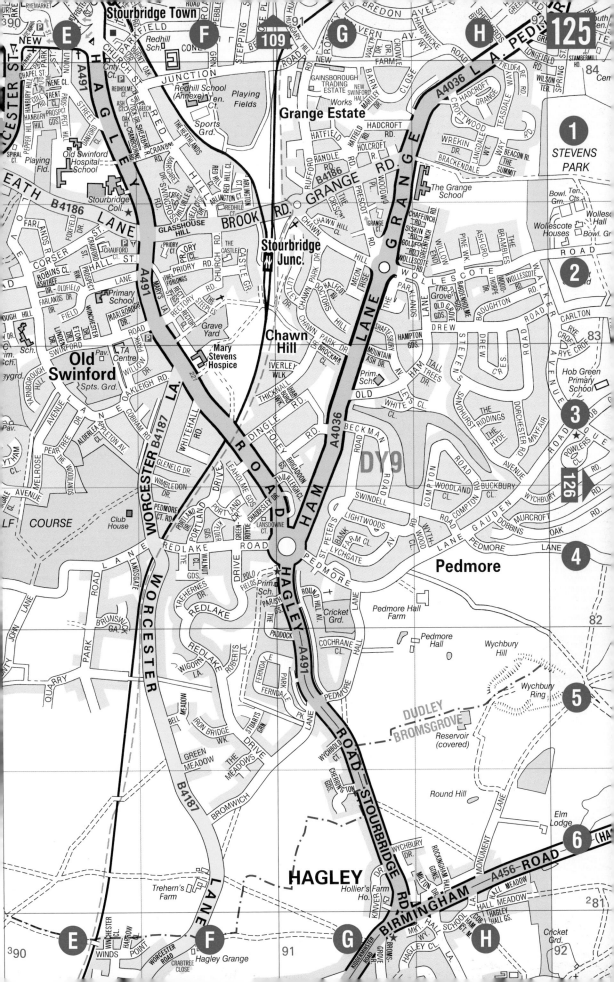

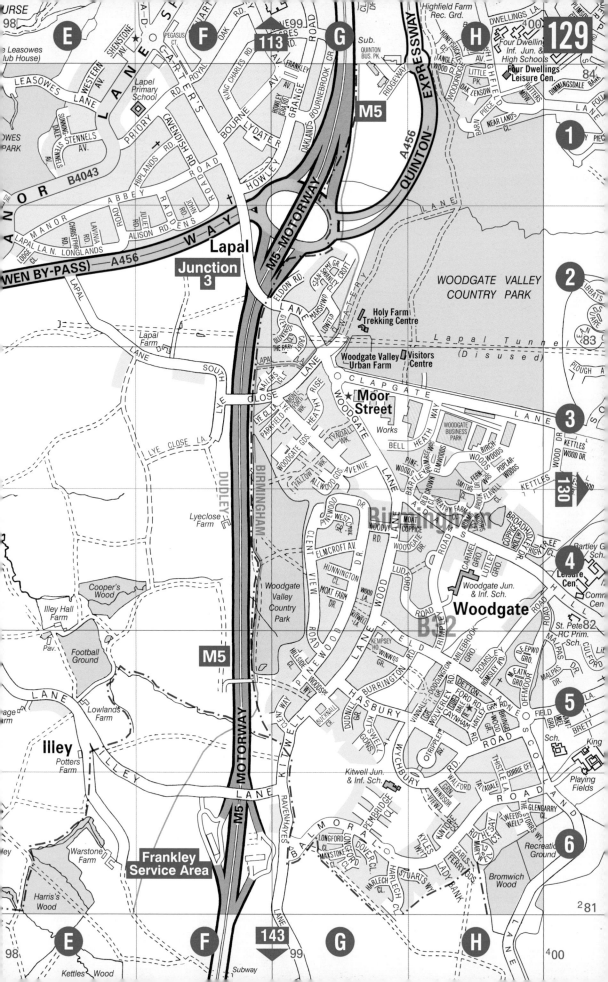

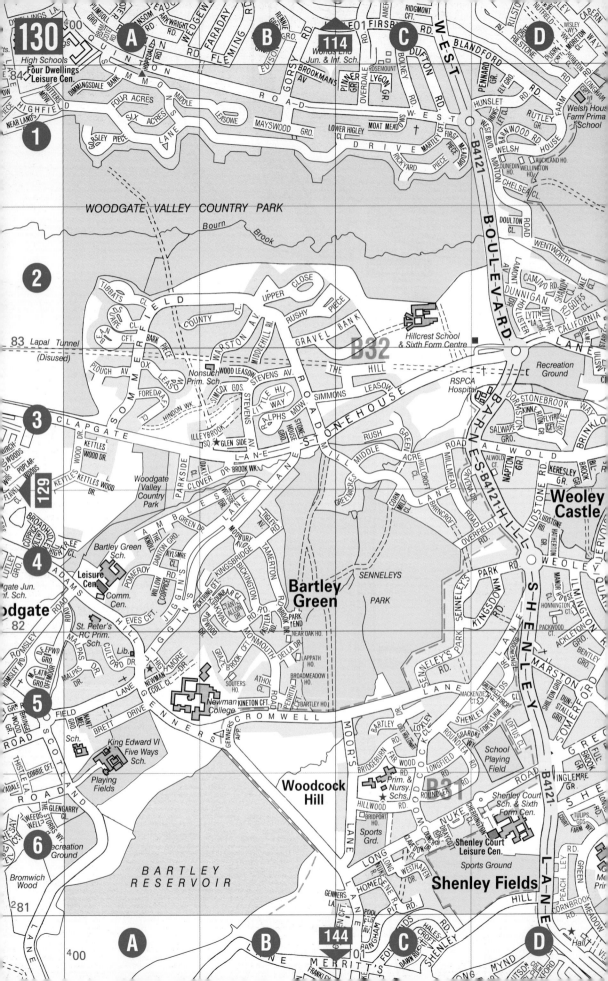

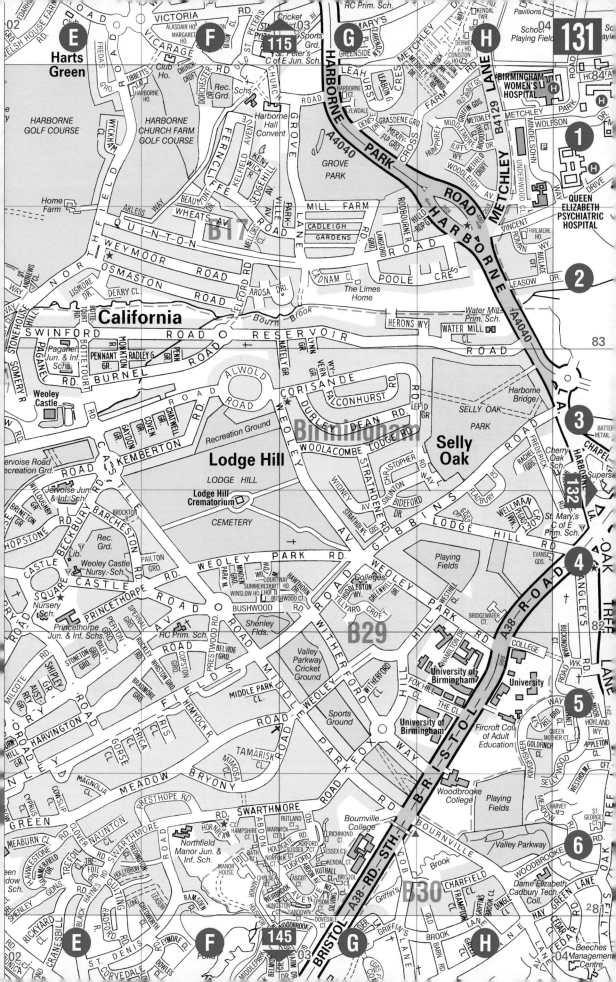

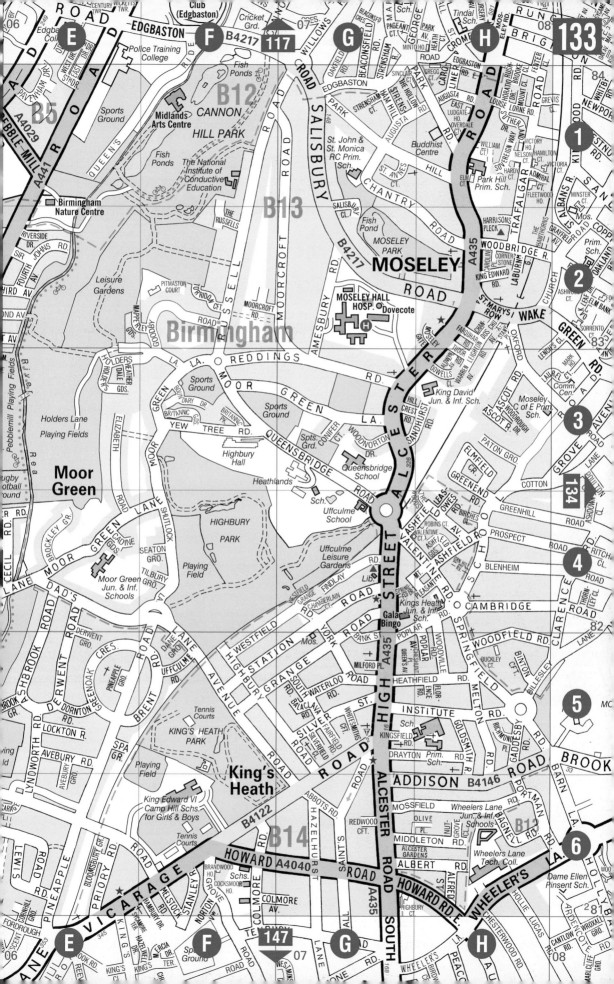

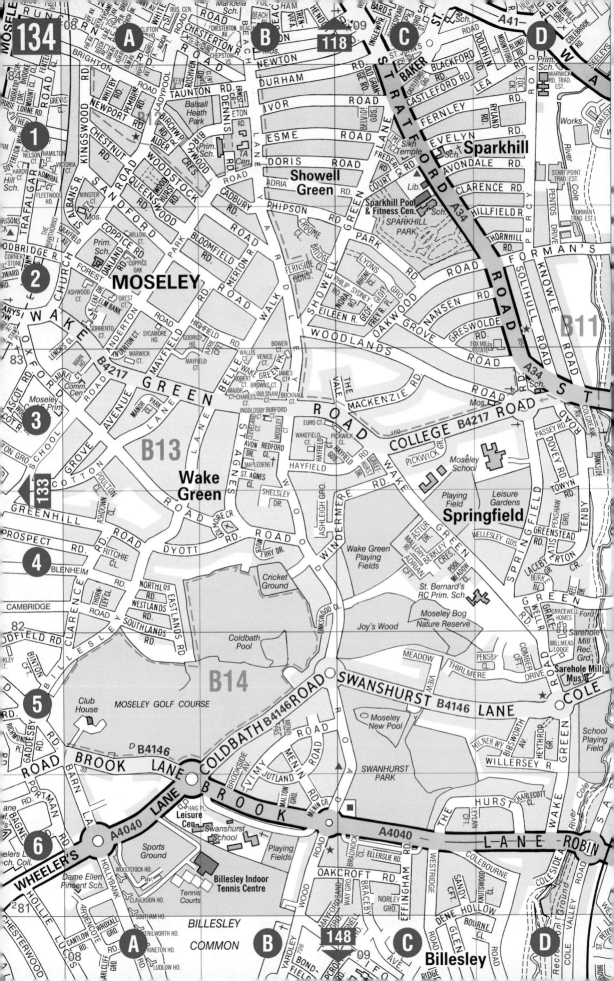

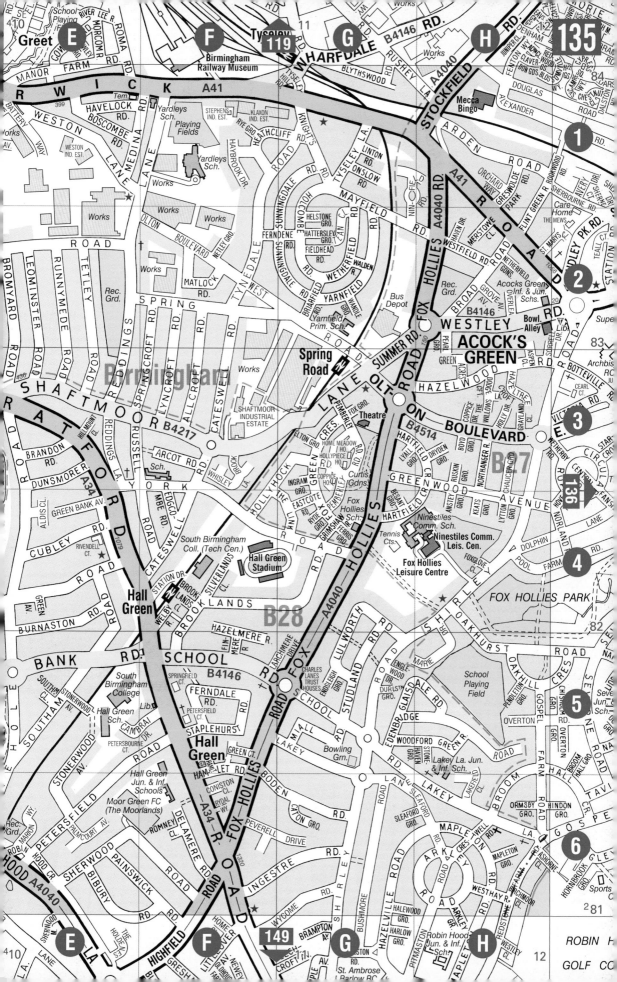

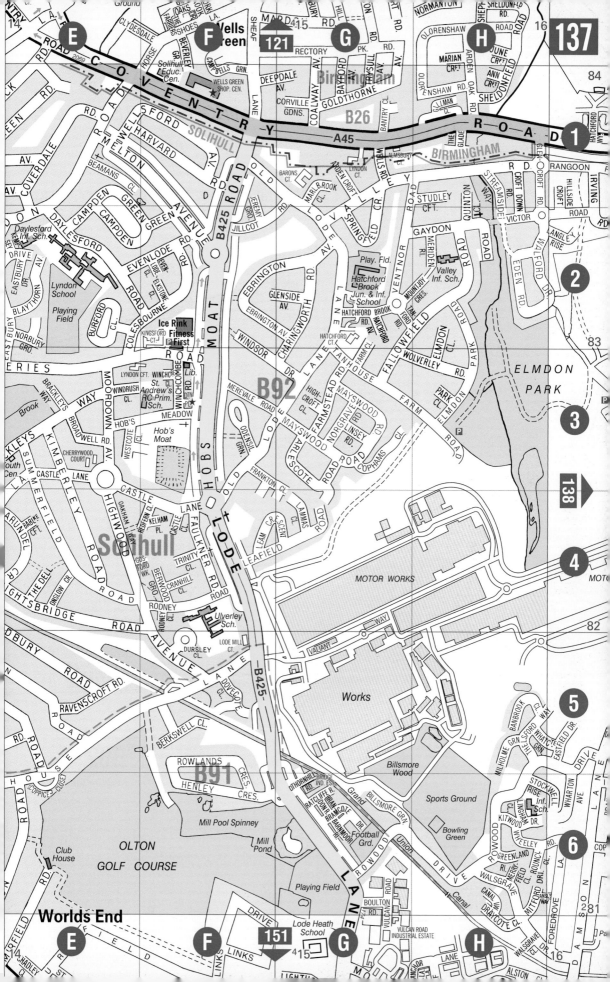

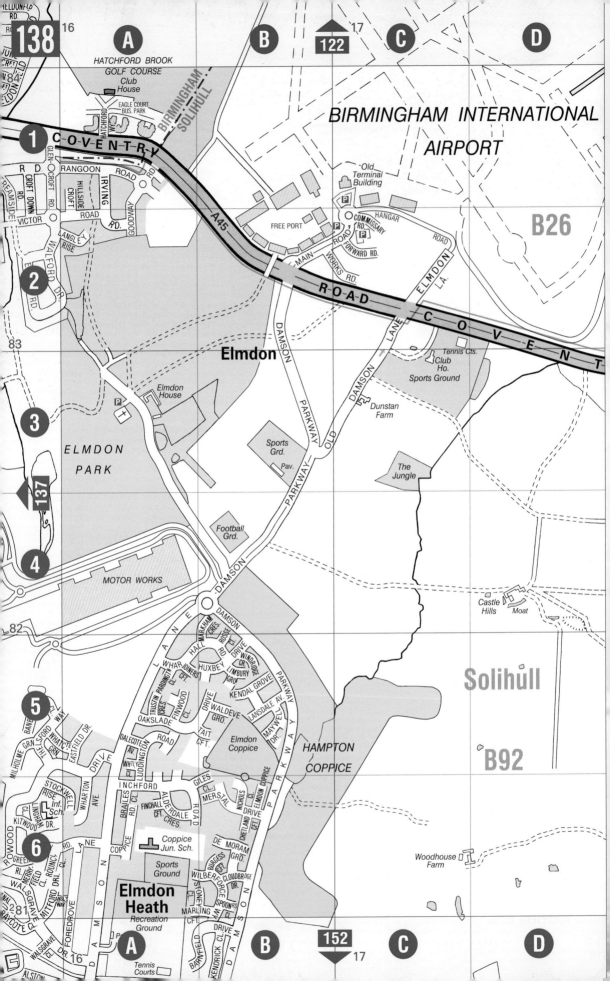

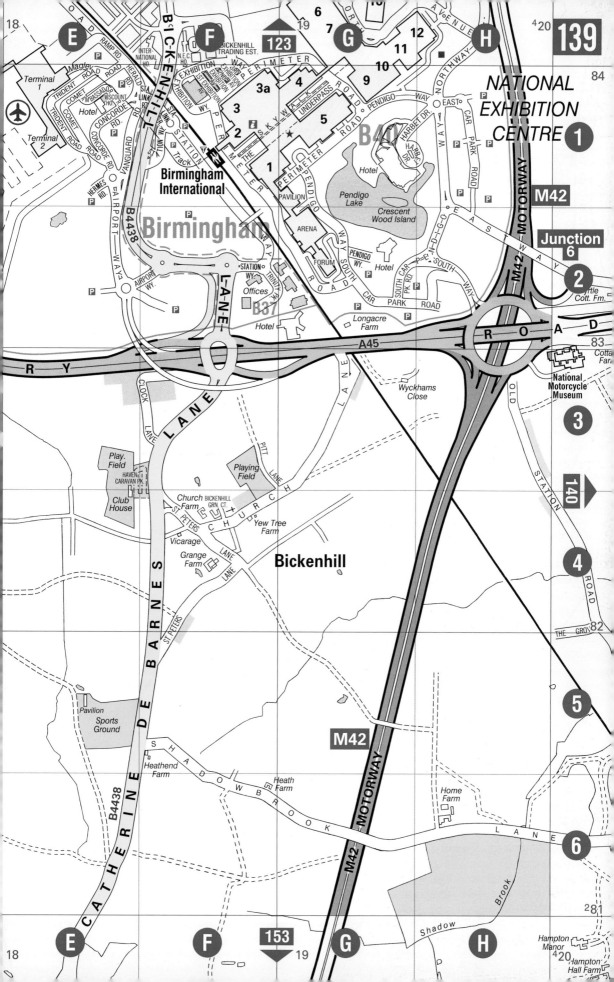

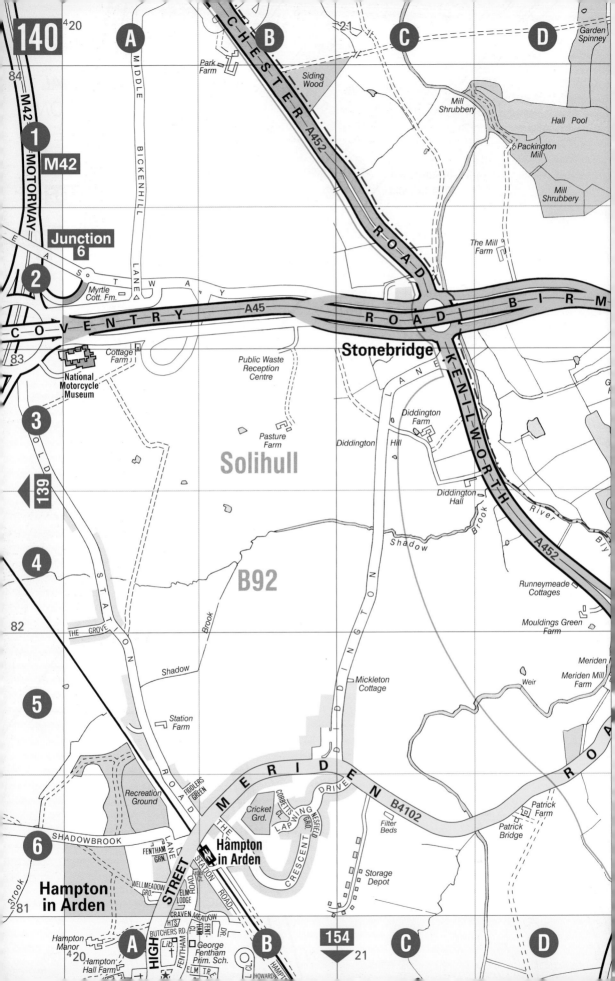

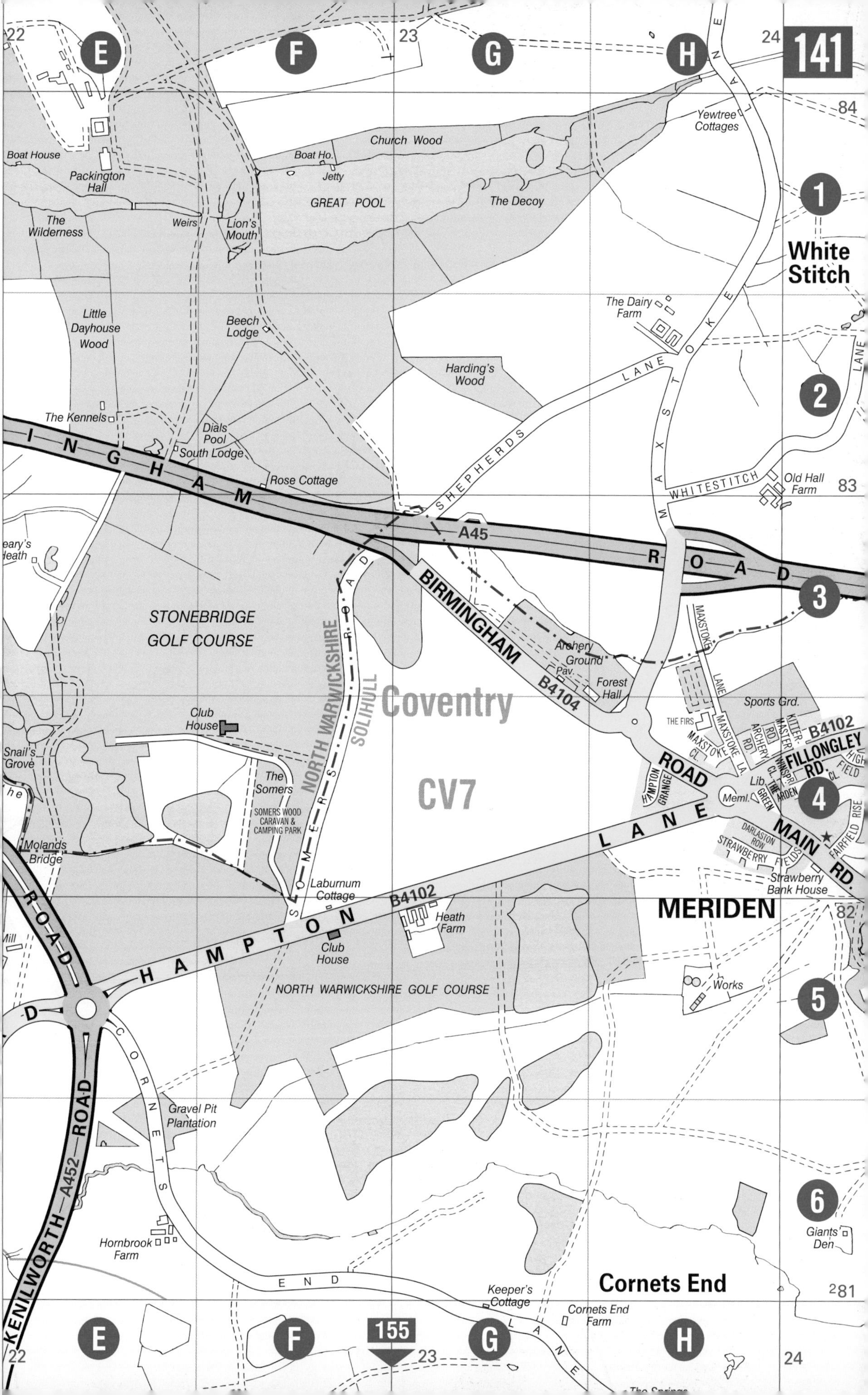

E F 23 G H 24

84

1

White Stitch

2

83

3

Yewtree Cottages

Boat House

Packington Hall

Church Wood

Boat Ho.

Jetty

GREAT POOL

The Decoy

The Dairy Farm

The Wilderness

Weirs

Lion's Mouth

STOKE LANE

FILLONGLEY LANE

Little Dayhouse Wood

Beech Lodge

Harding's Wood

MAXSTOKE ROAD

WHITESTITCH

Old Hall Farm

The Kennels

Dials Pool

South Lodge

Rose Cottage

INGHAM

SHEPHERDS LANE

A45

eary's Heath

STONEBRIDGE GOLF COURSE

NORTH WARWICKSHIRE

SOLIHULL

Coventry

CV7

BIRMINGHAM

B4104

Archery Ground

Pav.

Forest Hall

ROAD

MAXSTOKE

THE FIRS

Sports Grd.

KITTER.

MASTER.

ARCHERY RD.

B4102

FILLONGLEY RD.

HIGH FIELD

4

Club House

Snail's Grove

The Somers

SOMERS WOOD CARAVAN & CAMPING PARK

SOMERS ROAD

MEERS ROAD

Lib

Meml.

THE GREEN

MAIN RD.

FAIRFIELD RISE

82

e

Molands Bridge

ROAD

Laburnum Cottage

B4102

Heath Farm

Club House

HAMPTON LANE

HAMPTON

DARLASTON ROW

STRAWBERRY FIELDS

ORANGE

AMPTON

Strawberry Bank House

MERIDEN

Mill

KENILWORTH—A452—ROAD

D

CORNETS END

NORTH WARWICKSHIRE GOLF COURSE

Works

5

Gravel Pit Plantation

6

Giants Den

Hornbrook Farm

Keeper's Cottage

Cornets End

Cornets End Farm

281

E F 155 23 G H 24

The Springs

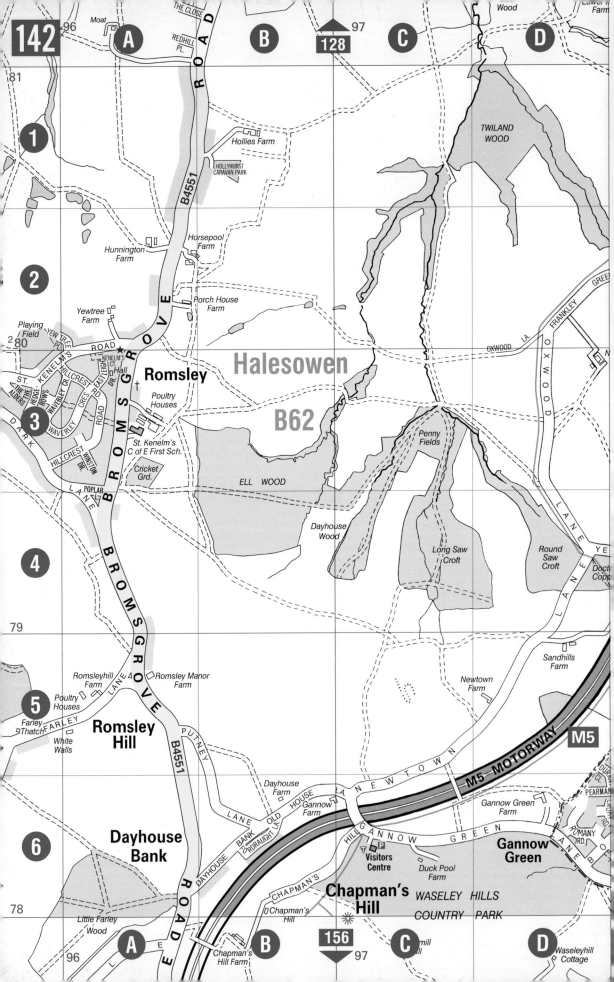

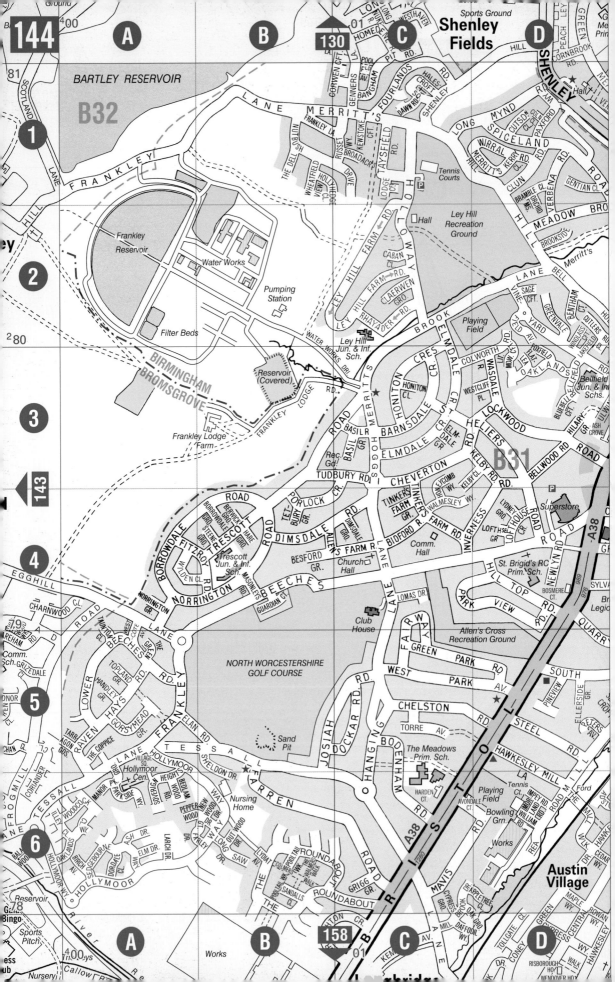

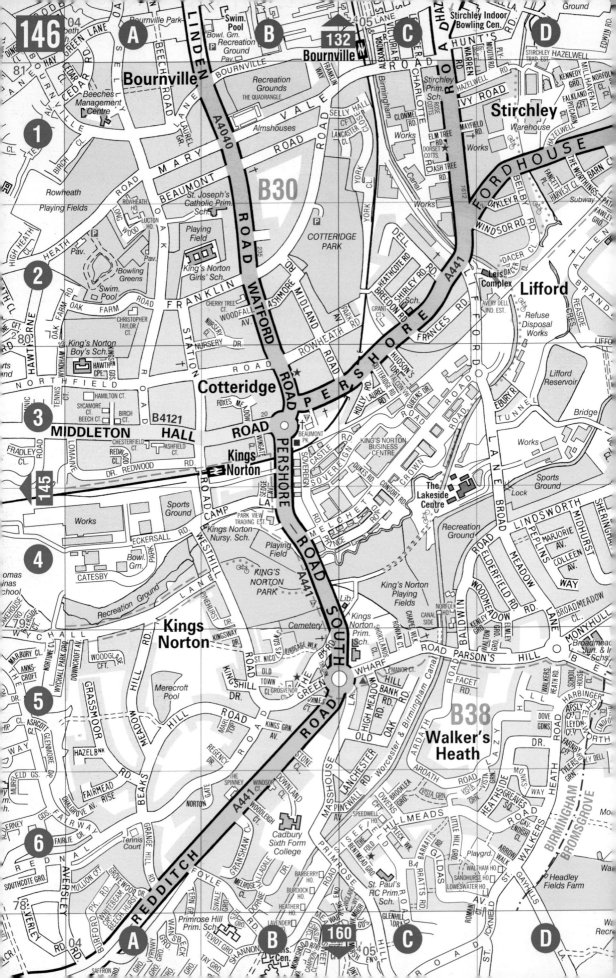

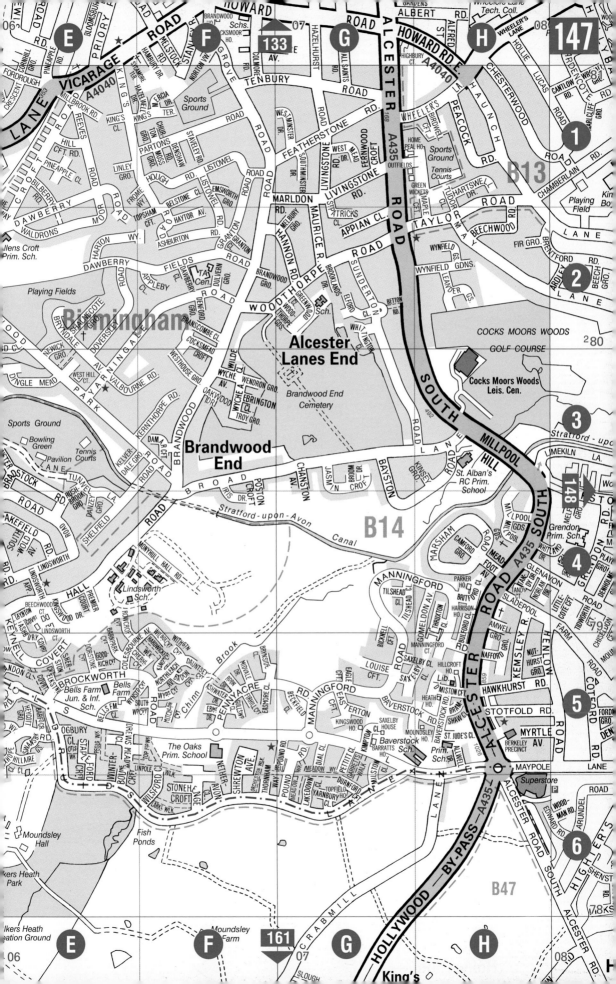

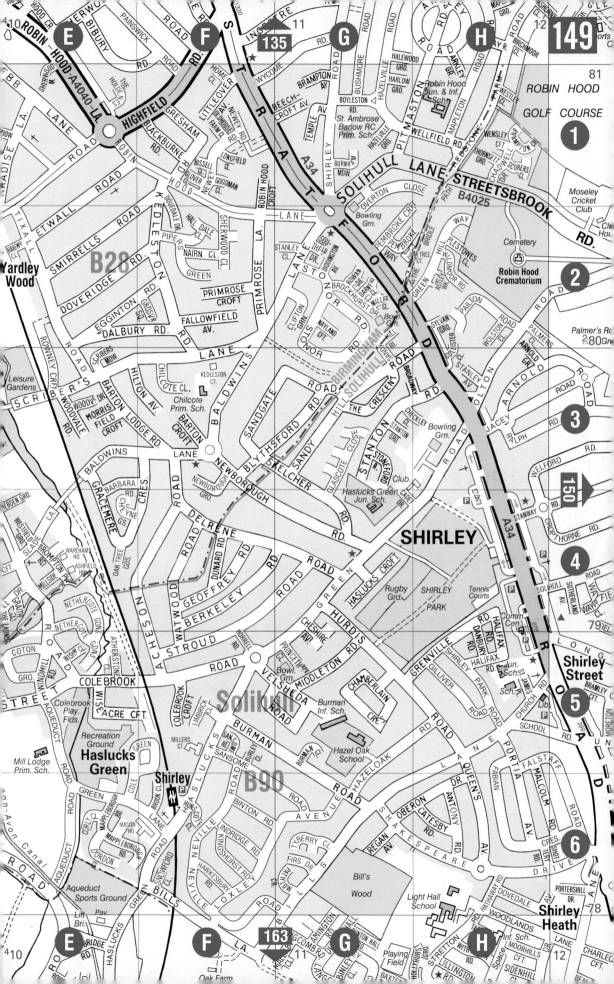

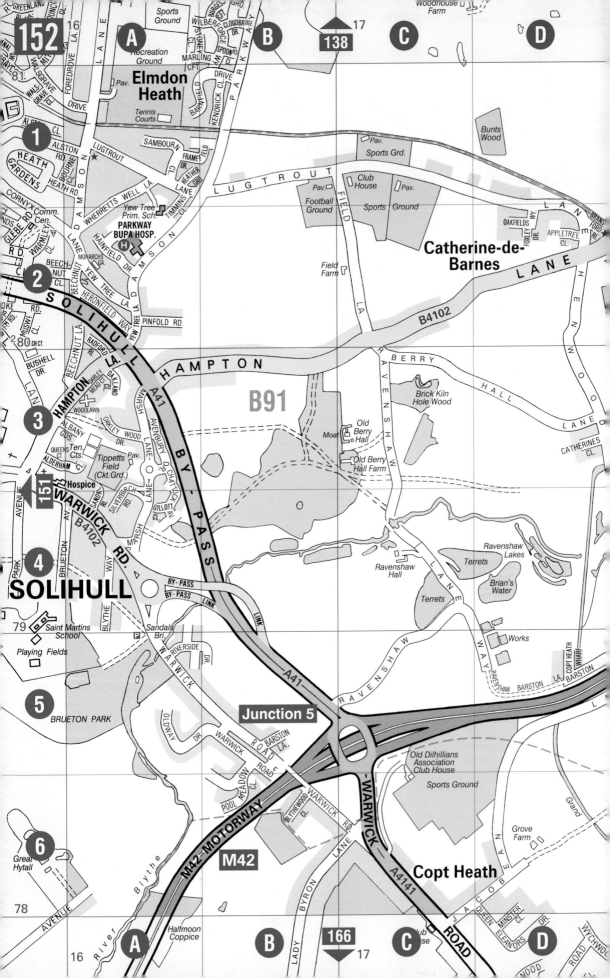

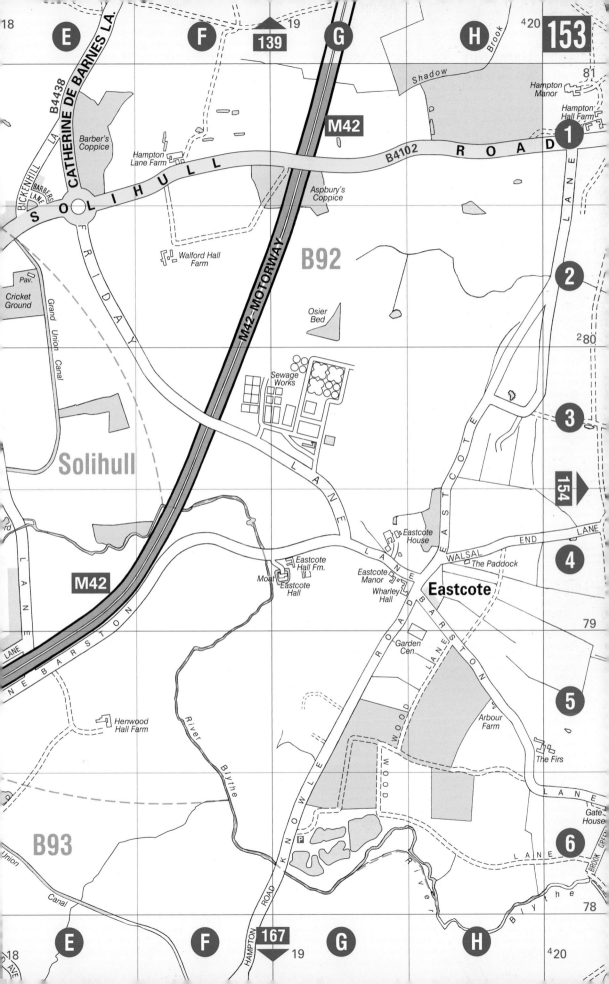

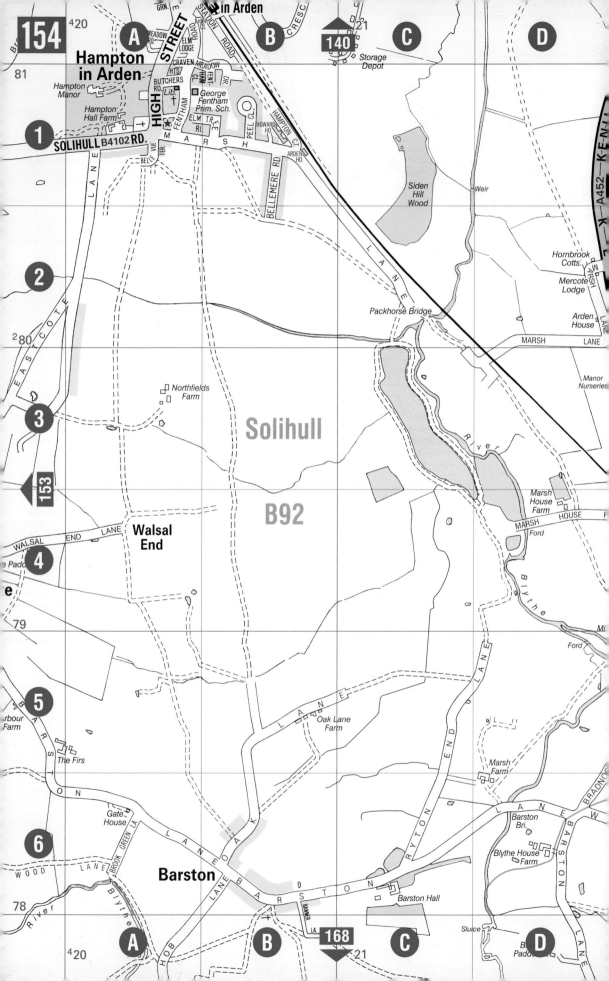

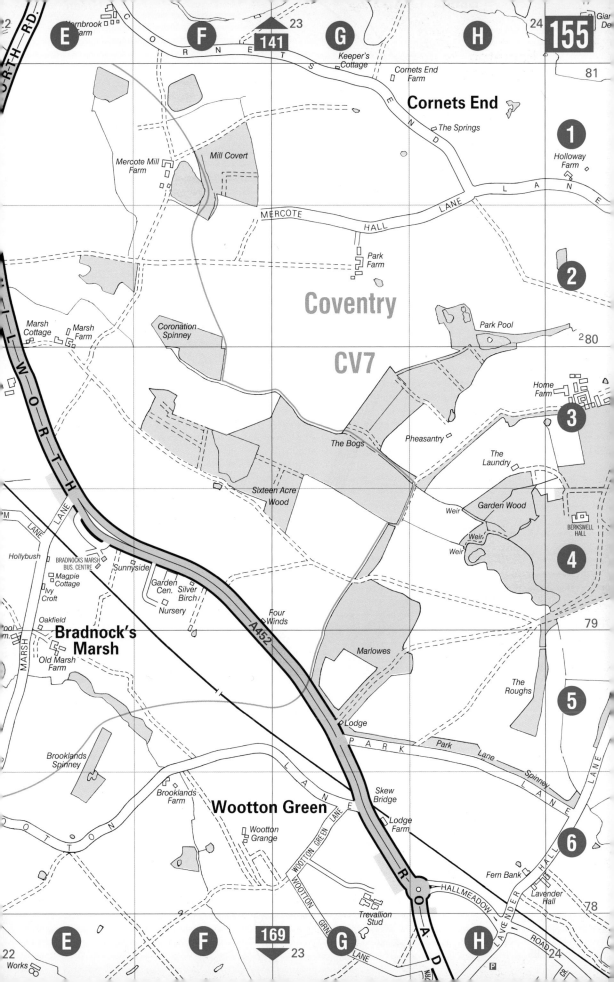

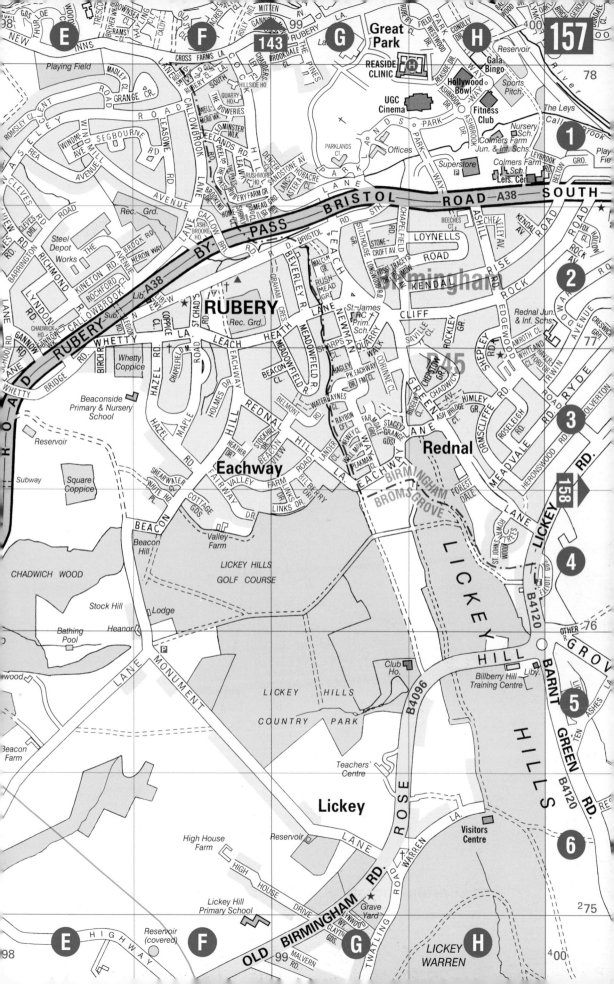

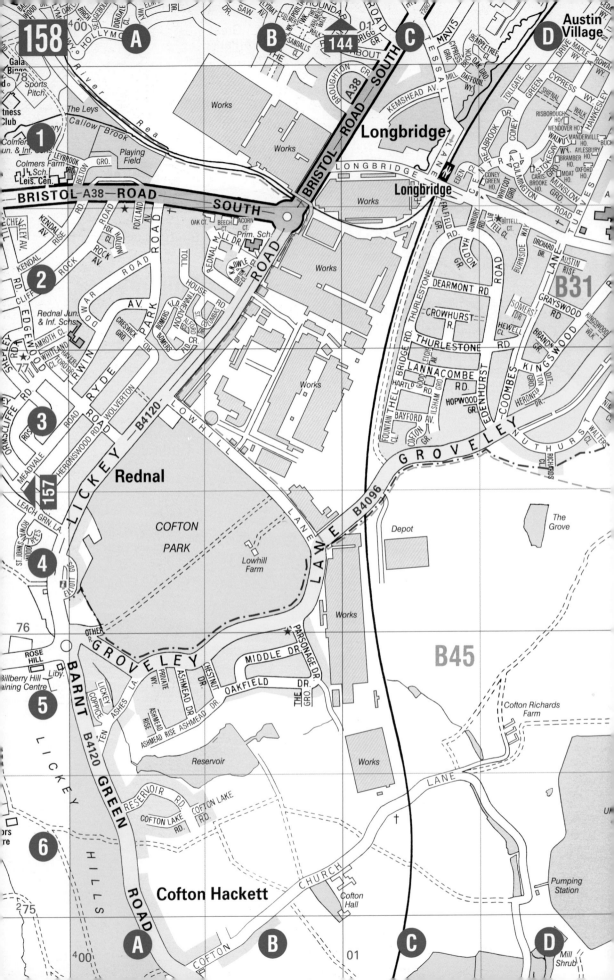

Austin Village

Longbridge

Longbridge

B31

Rednal

COFTON PARK

Lowhill Farm

The Grove

Depot

B45

Cofton Richards Farm

Rose Hill

Billberry Hill Training Centre

Reservoir

Reservoir

Cofton Lake

Cofton Hackett

Cofton Hall

Pumping Station

Mill Shrub

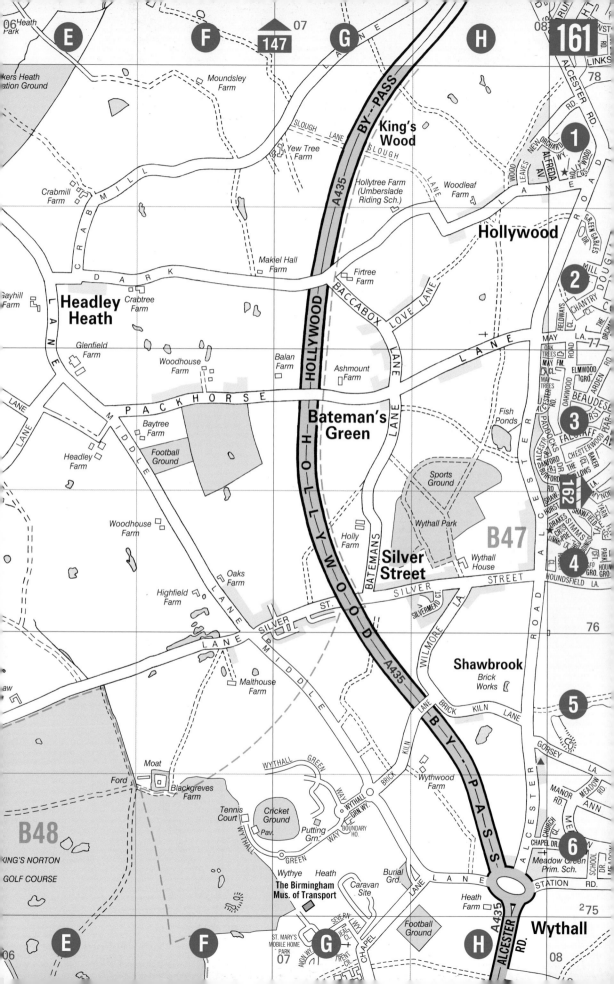

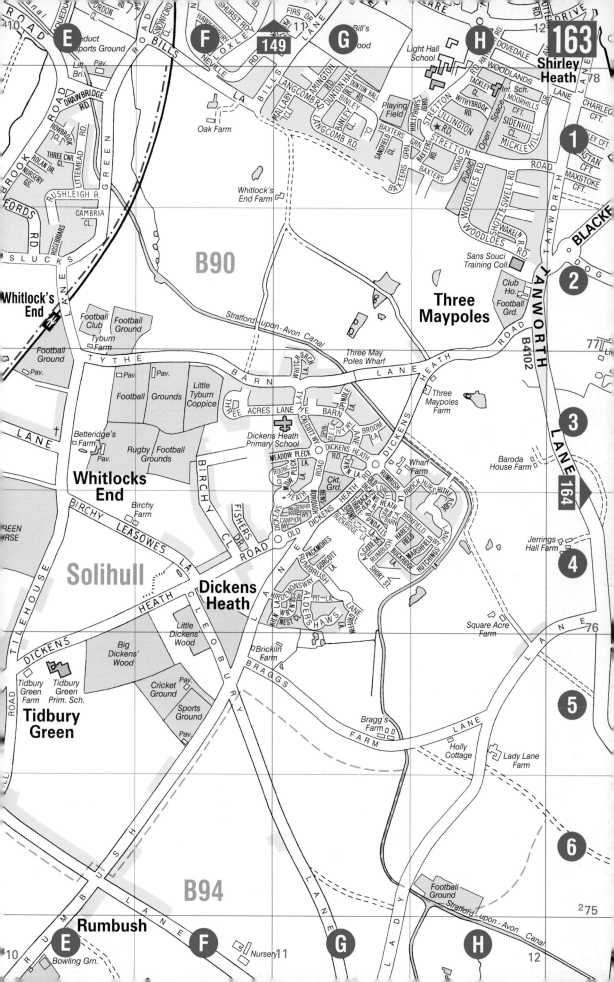

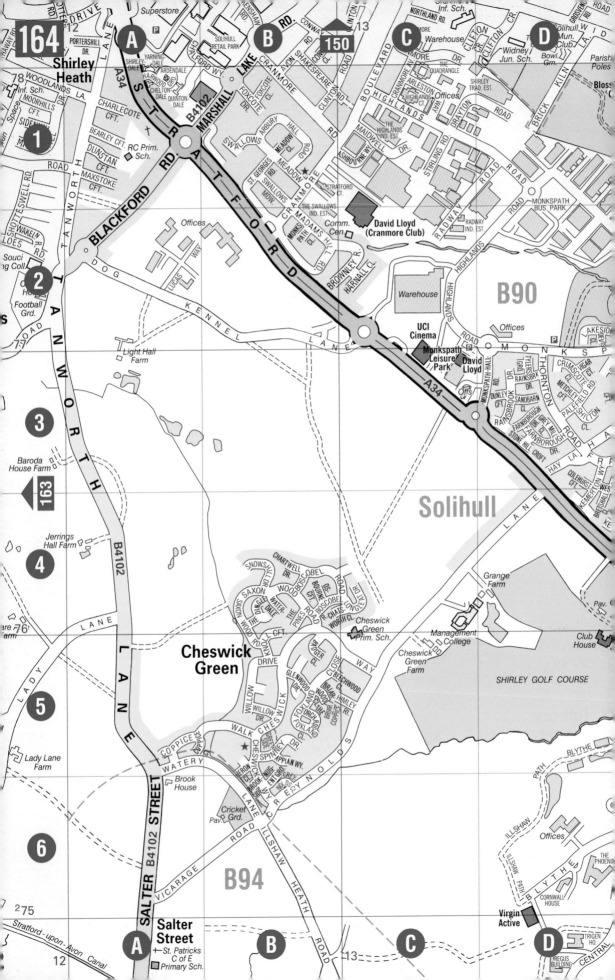

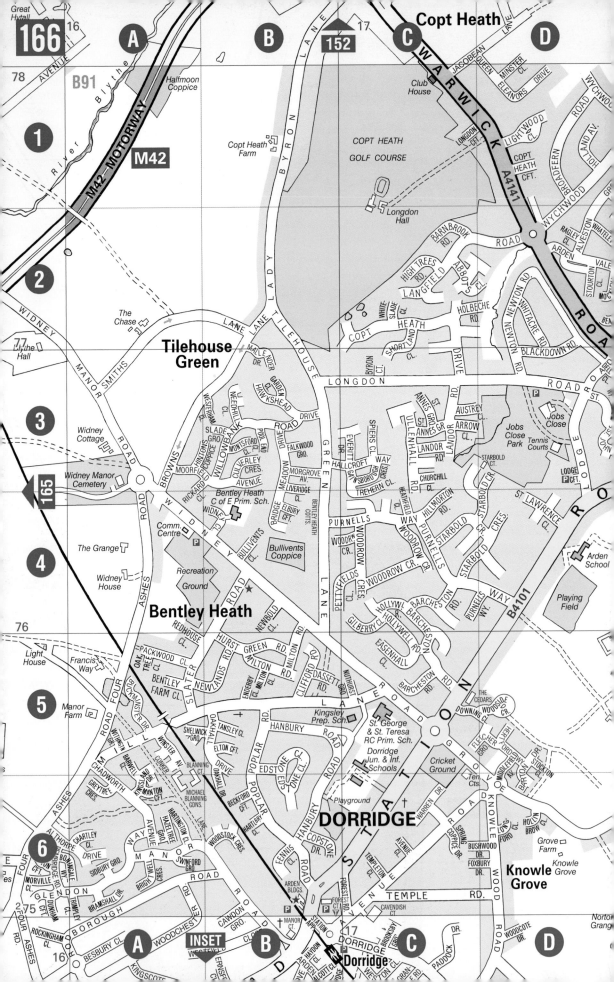

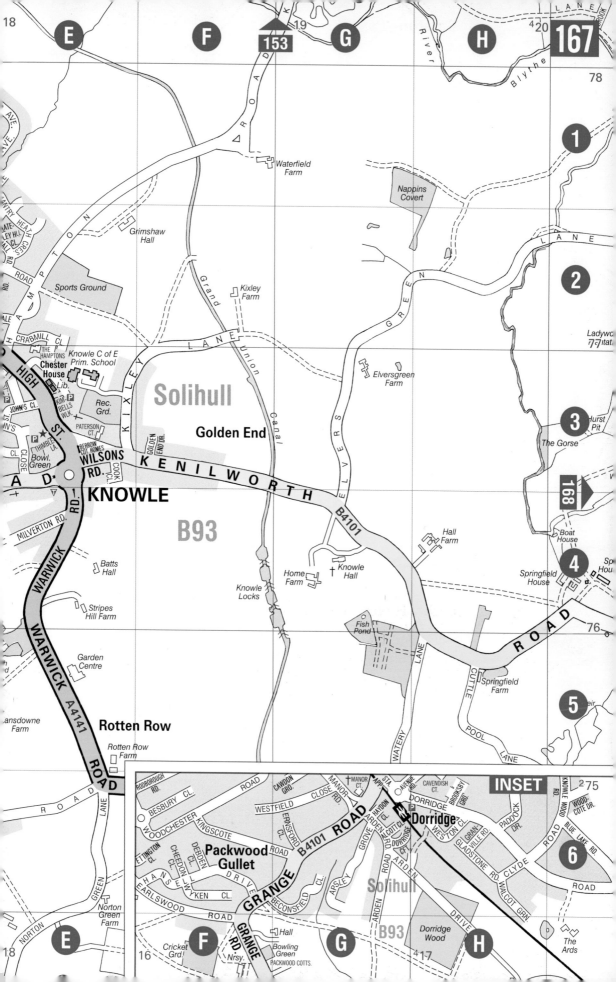

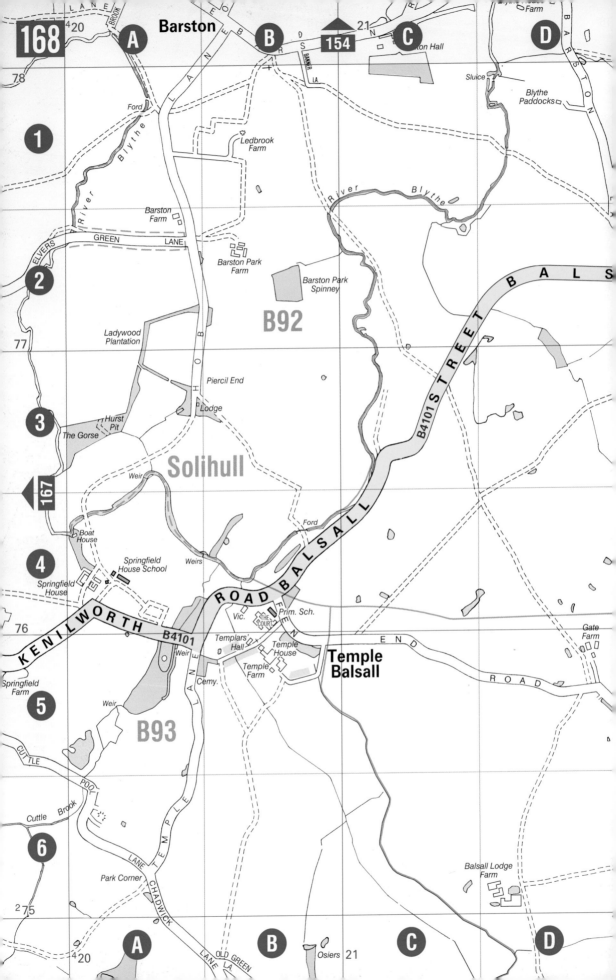

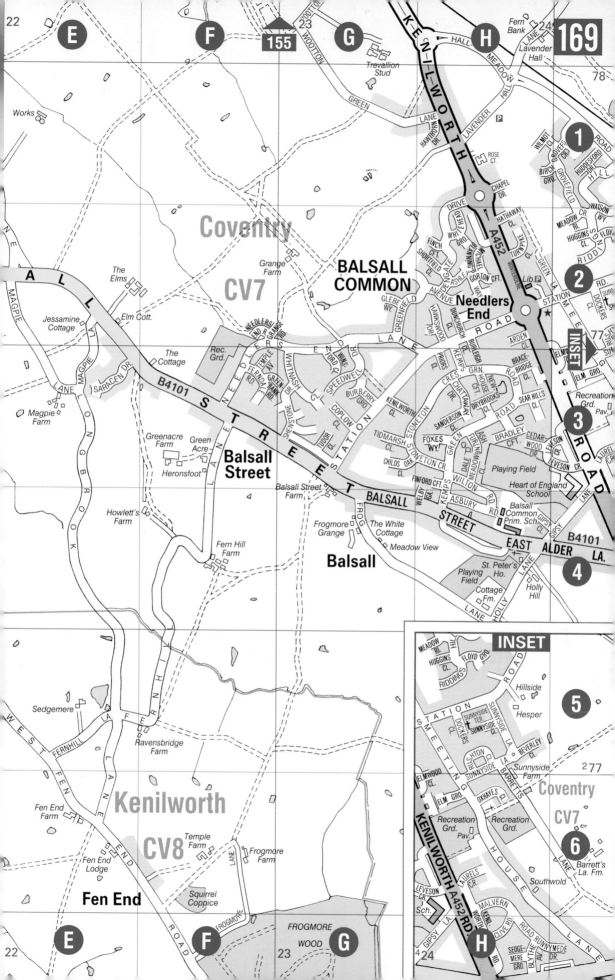

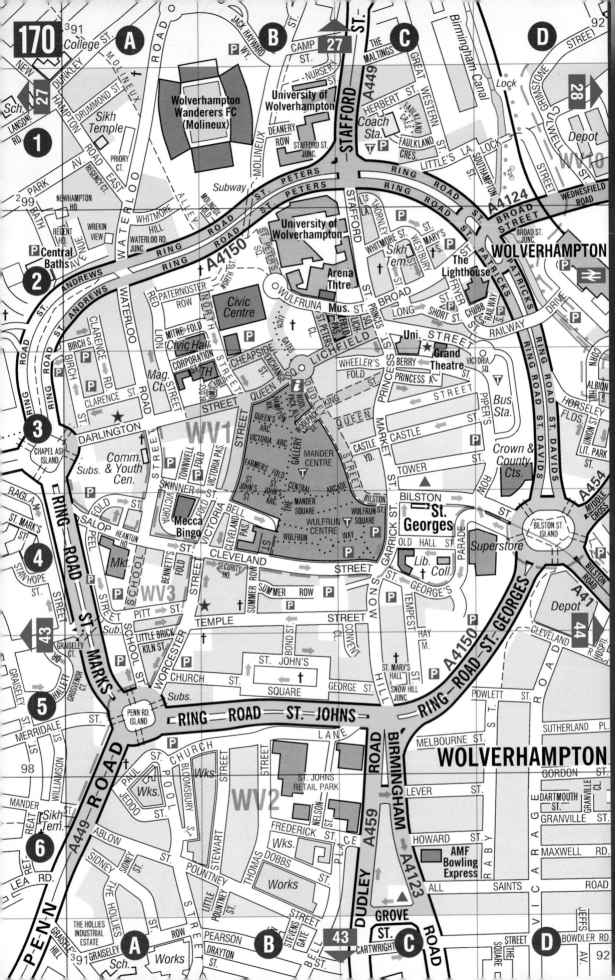

INDEX

Including Streets, Places & Areas, Industrial Estates, Selected Flats & Walkways,
Stations, Junctions and Selected Places of Interest.

HOW TO USE THIS INDEX

1. Each street name is followed by its Postcode District and then by its Locality abbreviation(s) and then by its map reference; e.g. **Abberley Rd.** B68: O'bry . . . .4H **113** is in the B68 Postcode District and the Oldbury Locality and is to be found in square 4H on page **113**. The page number is shown in bold type.

2. A strict alphabetical order is followed in which Av., Rd., St., etc. (though abbreviated) are read in full and as part of the street name; e.g. **Abbeydale Rd.** appears after **Abbey Cres.** but before **Abbey Dr.**

3. Streets and a selection of flats and walkways too small to be shown on the maps, appear in the index with the thoroughfare to which it is connected shown in brackets; e.g. **Abberton Ct.** B23: Erd . . . .5C **84** (off Dunlin Cl.)

4. Addresses that are in more than one part are referred to as not continuous.

5. Places and areas are shown in the index in BLUE TYPE and the map reference is to the actual map square in which the town centre or area is located and not to the place name shown on the map; e.g. **ALDRIDGE** 3D **34**

6. An example of a selected place of interest is **Aston Manor Transport Mus.** 6H **83**

7. An example of a station is **Adderley Park Station (Rail)** . . . .6D **102**. Included are Rail **(Rail)** Stations and Midland Metro **(MM)** Stops.

8. Junction names are shown in the index in BOLD TYPE; e.g. **BURNTWOOD JUNC.** 2B **10**

9. Map references shown in brackets; e.g **Ablow St.** WV2: Wolv . . . .3G **43** (6A **170**) refer to entries that also appear on the large scale pages **4-5** & **170**.

GENERAL ABBREVIATIONS

All. : Alley	**Cott.** : Cottage	**Info.** : Information	**Res.** : Residential
App. : Approach	**Cotts.** : Cottages	**Intl.** : International	**Ri.** : Rise
Arc. : Arcade	**Ct.** : Court	**Junc.** : Junction	**Rd.** : Road
Av. : Avenue	**Cres.** : Crescent	**La.** : Lane	**Rdbt.** : Roundabout
Blvd. : Boulevard	**Cft.** : Croft	**Lit.** : Little	**Shop.** : Shopping
Bri. : Bridge	**Dr.** : Drive	**Lwr.** : Lower	**Sth.** : South
Bldg. : Building	**E.** : East	**Mnr.** : Manor	**Sq.** : Square
Bldgs. : Buildings	**Ent.** : Enterprise	**Mans.** : Mansions	**Sta.** : Station
Bungs. : Bungalows	**Est.** : Estate	**Mkt.** : Market	**St.** : Street
Bus. : Business	**Fld.** : Field	**Mdw.** : Meadow	**Ter.** : Terrace
Cvn. : Caravan	**Flds.** : Fields	**Mdws.** : Meadows	**Twr.** : Tower
C'way. : Causeway	**Gdns.** : Gardens	**M.** : Mews	**Trad.** : Trading
Cen. : Centre	**Ga.** : Gate	**Mt.** : Mount	**Up.** : Upper
Chu. : Church	**Gt.** : Great	**Mus.** : Museum	**Va.** : Vale
Circ. : Circle	**Grn.** : Green	**Nth.** : North	**Vw.** : View
Cir. : Circus	**Gro.** : Grove	**Pde.** : Parade	**Vs.** : Villas
Cl. : Close	**Hgts.** : Heights	**Pk.** : Park	**Vis.** : Visitors
Coll. : College	**Ho.** : House	**Pas.** : Passage	**Wlk.** : Walk
Comn. : Common	**Ho's.** : Houses	**Pl.** : Place	**W.** : West
Cnr. : Corner	**Ind.** : Industrial	**Pct.** : Precinct	**Yd.** : Yard

LOCALITY ABBREVIATIONS

A Grn : **Acock's Green**	Curd : **Curdworth**	Lit A : **Little Aston**	S End : **Shard End**
Alb : **Albrighton**	Darl : **Darlaston**	Lit H : **Little Hay**	Share : **Shareshill**
A'rdge : **Aldridge**	Dic H : **Dickens Heath**	Lit P : **Little Packington**	Sheld : **Sheldon**
A'chu : **Alvechurch**	Dorr : **Dorridge**	Lit W : **Little Wyrley**	S'fld : **Shelfield**
Amb : **Amblecote**	Dray B : **Drayton Bassett**	Longb : **Longbridge**	Shens : **Shenstone**
Aston : **Aston**	Dud : **Dudley**	Lwr G : **Lower Gornal**	Shen W : **Shenstone Woodend**
Bal C : **Balsall Common**	Earls : **Earlswood**	Lwr P : **Lower Penn**	Shir : **Shirley**
Bal H : **Balsall Heath**	Edg : **Edgbaston**	Loz : **Lozells**	Small H : **Small Heath**
B Grn : **Barnt Green**	Env : **Enville**	Lutley : **Lutley**	Smeth : **Smethwick**
Bars : **Barston**	Erd : **Erdington**	L Ash : **Lydiate Ash**	Sol : **Solihull**
Bart G : **Bartley Green**	Ess : **Essington**	Lye : **Lye**	S'brk : **Sparkbrook**
Bass P : **Bassetts Pole**	E'shll : **Ettingshall**	Lynn : **Lynn**	S'hll : **Sparkhill**
Belb : **Belbroughton**	F'stne : **Featherstone**	Maj G : **Major's Green**	Stech : **Stechford**
Ben H : **Bentley Heath**	Fen E : **Fen End**	Marl : **Marlbrook**	Stir : **Stirchley**
Berk : **Berkswell**	Foot : **Footherley**	Mars G : **Marston Green**	Ston : **Stonnall**
Bick : **Bickenhill**	F'bri : **Fordbridge**	Mer : **Meriden**	Stourb : **Stourbridge**
Bilb : **Bilbrook**	F'hses : **Fordhouses**	Midd : **Middleton**	Stourt : **Stourton**
Bils : **Bilston**	Forh : **Forhill**	Min : **Minworth**	S'tly : **Streetly**
Birm : **Birmingham**	Four C : **Four Crosses**	M'path : **Monkspath**	S Cold : **Sutton Coldfield**
Birm A : **Birmingham Int. Airport**	Four O : **Four Oaks**	Mose : **Moseley**	Swind : **Swindon**
B'hth : **Blackheath**	Fran : **Frankley**	Mox : **Moxley**	Tett : **Tettenhall**
Blox : **Bloxwich**	Gorn : **Gornalwood**	Muck C : **Muckley Corner**	Tid G : **Tidbury Green**
Bly P : **Blythe Valley Park**	Gt Barr : **Great Barr**	Nat E C : **National Exhibition Centre**	Tip : **Tipton**
Bold : **Boldmere**	Gt Wyr : **Great Wyrley**	Nech : **Nechells**	Tiv : **Tividale**
Bord G : **Bordesley Green**	Hag : **Hagley**	Neth : **Netherton**	Tres : **Trescott**
B'vlle : **Bournville**	Hale : **Halesowen**	New O : **New Oscott**	Try : **Trysull**
Brie H : **Brierley Hill**	Hall G : **Hall Green**	N'fld : **Northfield**	Tys : **Tyseley**
B'frd : **Brinsford**	Hamm : **Hammerwich**	Nort C : **Norton Canes**	Up Gor : **Upper Gornal**
Bwnhls : **Brownhills**	H Ard : **Hampton in Arden**	Nur : **Nurton**	Wall : **Wall**
Burn : **Burntwood**	Hand : **Handsworth**	Oaken : **Oaken**	W Hth : **Wall Heath**
Bush : **Bushbury**	Harb : **Harborne**	O'bry : **Oldbury**	Walm : **Walmley**
Cann : **Cannock**	Head H : **Headley Heath**	Old H : **Old Hill**	Wals : **Walsall**
Can : **Canwell**	Hilt : **Hilton**	Olton : **Olton**	Wals W : **Walsall Wood**
Cas B : **Castle Bromwich**	Himl : **Himley**	Oxl : **Oxley**	W End : **Ward End**
Cas V : **Castle Vale**	Hints : **Hints**	Patt : **Pattingham**	Wat O : **Water Orton**
Cath B : **Catherine-de-Barnes**	Hock : **Hockley**	Pedm : **Pedmore**	W'bry : **Wednesbury**
Cats : **Catshill**	H'ley H : **Hockley Heath**	Pels : **Pelsall**	Wed : **Wednesfield**
C'wich : **Chadwich**	Hodg H : **Hodge Hill**	Pend : **Pendeford**	W'frd : **Weeford**
Chad E : **Chadwick End**	H'wd : **Hollywood**	Penn : **Penn**	W Cas : **Weoley Castle**
Chase : **Chasetown**	Hopw : **Hopwood**	P'ntt : **Pensnett**	W Brom : **West Bromwich**
Chel W : **Chelmsley Wood**	Hunn : **Hunnington**	P Barr : **Perry Barr**	Wild : **Wildmoor**
C Hay : **Cheslyn Hay**	I'ley : **Iverley**	Pert : **Perton**	W'hall : **Willenhall**
Ches G : **Cheswick Green**	K Hth : **King's Heath**	Quar B : **Quarry Bank**	Win G : **Winson Green**
Clay : **Clayhanger**	K'hrst : **Kingshurst**	Quin : **Quinton**	Wis : **Wishaw**
Clent : **Clent**	K Nor : **King's Norton**	Redn : **Rednal**	Witt : **Witton**
Cod : **Codsall**	K'sdng : **Kingstanding**	R'ley : **Roughley**	Woll : **Wollaston**
Cod W : **Codsall Wood**	K'wfrd : **Kingswinford**	Row R : **Rowley Regis**	W'cte : **Wollescote**
Coft H : **Cofton Hackett**	Kinv : **Kinver**	Rubery : **Rubery**	Wolv : **Wolverhampton**
Col : **Coleshill**	Kitts G : **Kitt's Green**	Rus : **Rushall**	Wom : **Wombourne**
Cose : **Coseley**	Know : **Knowle**	Salt : **Saltley**	Word : **Wordsley**
Coven : **Coven**	Lapw : **Lapworth**	Sed : **Sedgley**	W Grn : **Wylde Green**
Cov H : **Coven Heath**	Lea M : **Lea Marston**	Seis : **Seisdon**	Wyt : **Wythall**
Crad : **Cradley**	Lich : **Lichfield**	S Oak : **Selly Oak**	Yard : **Yardley**
Crad H : **Cradley Heath**	Lick : **Lickey**		Yard W : **Yardley Wood**

3B Business Village B21: Hand 2H **99**	

A

A1 Trad. Est. B66: Smeth 2F **99**	
Aaron Manby Ct. DY4: Tip 5H **61**	
Abberley Cl. B63: Hale 3H **127**	
Abberley Ind. Cen.	
B66: Smeth. 4H **99**	

Abberley Rd. B68: O'bry. 4H **113**
    DY3: Lwr G. 3G **75**
Abberley St. B66: Smeth 4H **99**
    DY2: Dud 1E **95**
Abberton Cl. B63: Hale 2C **128**
Abberton Ct. *B23: Erd 5C **84***
    (off Dunlin Cl.)
Abberton Gro. B90: M'path 2F **165**
Abbess Gro. B25: Yard 2C **120**
Abbey Cl. B71: W Brom 2A **80**
Abbey Ct. B68: O'bry 5H **97**
Abbey Cres. B63: Crad 1F **127**
    B68: O'bry. 3B **114**

Abbeydale Rd. B31: N'fld 5E **145**
Abbey Dr. WS3: Pels 2E **21**
Abbeyfield Rd. B23: Erd 6D **68**
    WV10: Bush 3A **16**
Abbey Gdns.
    B67: Smeth 2C **114**
Abbey Mans. B24: Erd 1H **85**
Abbey Rd. B17: Harb 6H **115**
    B23: Erd 5D **84**
    B63: Crad 1E **127**
    B67: Smeth. 2B **114**
    DY2: Dud. 3F **95**
    DY3: Gorn. 4G **75**

Abbey Sq. WS3: Blox 5E **19**
Abbey St. B18: Hock. 4C **100**
    DY3: Gorn. 4G **75**
Abbey St. Nth.
    B18: Hock. 4C **100**
Abbots Cl. B93: Know. 2C **166**
    WS4: Rus. 3G **33**
Abbotsford Av. B43: Gt Barr 3B **66**
Abbotsford Dr. DY1: Dud 2A **94**
Abbotsford Rd. B11: S'brk 5B **118**
Abbots Rd. B14: K Hth 6G **133**
Abbots Way B18: Hock. 3D **100**
    WV3: Wolv 2C **42**

Abbott Rd.—Amberley Rd.

Abbott Rd. B63: Hale 5E 127
Abbotts M. DY5: Brie H. 2H 109
Abbotts Pl. WS3: Blox. 6B 20
Abbotts Rd. B24: Erd 6F 85
Abbotts St. WS3: Blox. 5B 20
Abdon Av. B29: W Cas. 6F 131
Aberdeen St. B18: Win G 5A 100
Aberford Cl. WV12: W'hall 5D 30
Abigails Cl. B26: Sheld 4F 121
Abingdon Cl. WV1: Wolv 1D 44
Abingdon Rd. B23: Erd 6B 68
DY2: Neth 6F 95
WS3: Blox 5F 19
WV1: Wolv 1D 44
Abingdon Way B35: Cas V 4E 87
WS3: Blox 5F 19
Ablewell St. WS1: Wals 2D 48
Ablow St. WV2: Wolv 3G 43 (6A 170)
Abney Dr. WV14: Cose 4B 60
Abney Gro. B44: K'sdng 3B 68
Aboyne Cl. B5: Edg 5F 117
Ab Row B4: Birm 6H 101 (2H 5)
Acacia Av. B37: K'hrst 3B 106
WS5: Wals 1E 65
Acacia Cl. B37: K'hrst. 3B 106
B69: Tiv 5B 78
DY1: Dud 4C 76
Acacia Cres. WV8: Bilb. 3H 13
Acacia Dr. WV14: Cose 6C 60
Acacia Rd. B30: B'vlle. 5A 132
Acacia Ter. B12: Bal H 6A 118
Accord M. WS10: Darl 4D 46
Ace Bus. Pk. B33: Kitts G 1H 121
Acfold Rd. B20: Hand 2A 82
Acheson Rd.
B90: Hall G, Shir 5F 149
Acheston Rd. B28: Hall G 5F 149
Achilles Cl. WS6: Gt Wyr 4F 7
(not continuous)
Ackers, The (Activity Cen.) 5D 118
Ackleton Gdns.
WV3: Wolv 4D 42
Ackleton Gro. B29: W Cas 5D 130
ACOCKS GREEN 2A 136
Acocks Green Bowl 2H 135
Acocks Green Station (Rail) 1A 136
Acorn Cl. B27: A Grn 6H 119
B30: B'vlle. 5A 132
B70: W Brom 4H 79
WS6: Gt Wyr 4G 7
Acorn Ct. B45: Redn 2B 158
Acorn Gdns. B30: Stir 5C 132
Acorn Gro. B1: Birm 6D 100
DY8: Word 2C 108
WV8: Cod 5E 13
Acorn Rd. B62: B'hth 3C 112
WV11: Wed 6A 18
Acorn St. WV13: W'hall 1C 46
Acre Ri. WV12: W'hall 4B 30
Acres, The WV3: Wolv 2A 42
Acres Rd. DY5: Quar B 3H 109
Acton Dr. DY3: Lwr G 4F 75
Acton Gro. B44: K'sdng 2A 68
WV14: Bils 1D 60
Adam Ct. B63: Hale 1H 127
Adams Brook Dr. B32: Bart G 4H 129
Adams Cl. B66: Smeth 2B 98
DY4: Tip 4H 61
Adams Hill B32: Bart G 4H 129
Adams Rd. WS8: Bwnhls 2C 22
WV3: Wolv 4A 42
Adams St. B7: Birm 4H 101
B70: W Brom 4H 79
WS2: Wals 1B 48
Ada Rd. B9: Birm 1B 118
B25: Yard 5H 119
B66: Smeth 6F 99
Ada Wrighton Cl. WV12: W'hall 2C 30
Addenbrooke Ct. B64: Old H. 3H 111
Addenbrooke Dr. B73: W Grn 3H 69
Addenbrooke Pl. WS10: Darl 4D 46
Addenbrooke Rd. B67: Smeth 6D 98
Addenbrooke St. WS3: Blox 2A 32
WS10: Darl 3D 46
Addenbrook Way DY4: Tip 5D 62
Adderley Gdns. B8: Salt 4D 102
(not continuous)
Adderley Pk. Cl. B8: Salt 5E 103
Adderley Park Station (Rail) 6D 102
Adderley Rd. B8: Salt 6C 102
Adderley Rd. Sth. B8: Salt 6C 102
Adderley St. B9: Birm 2A 118
Adderley Trad. Est. B8: Salt 5C 102
Addington Way B69: Tiv 5D 78
Addison Cl. WS10: W'bry 3C 64
Addison Cft. DY3: Lwr G 2E 75
Addison Gro. WV11: Wed 6D 16
Addison Pl. B46: Wat O 4D 88
WV14: Bils 4A 46
Addison Rd. B7: Nech 1C 102
B14: K Hth 6G 133
DY5: Brie H 1F 109
WS10: W'bry 3C 64
WV3: Wolv 3D 42
Addison St. WS10: W'bry 3F 63
Addison Ter. WS10: W'bry 3F 63
Adelaide Av. B70: W Brom 6G 63
Adelaide St. DY5: Brie H 6H 93
Adelaide Twr. *B34: S End* *4G 105*
(off Packington Av.)
Adelaide Wlk. WV2: Wolv 3A 44
Adelphi Ct. *DY5: Brie H* *1H 109*
(off Promenade, The)
Adey Rd. WV11: Wed 1H 29
Adkins La. B67: Smeth 2D 114
Admington Rd. B33: Sheld 3G 121
Admiral Pl. B13: Mose 1H 133
Admirals Way B65: Row R 1B 112
Adrian Boult Hall 1F 117 (4C 4)
Adrian Ct. B24: Erd 1H 85
Adrian Cft. B13: Mose 4C 134
Adria Rd. B11: S'hll 1B 134
Adshead Rd. DY2: Dud 2E 95
Adstone Gro. B31: N'fld 6D 144
Advent Gdns. *B70: W Brom* *4H 79*
(off Brook St.)
Adwalton Rd. WV6: Pert 6F 25
Agenoria Dr. DY8: Stourb 6D 108
Ainsdale Cl. DY8: Stourb 3D 124
Ainsdale Gdns. B24: Erd 2A 86
B63: Hale 3F 127
Ainsworth Rd. B31: N'fld 5H 145
WV10: Bush 2A 16
Aintree Gro. B34: S End 3A 106
Aintree Rd. WV10: F'hses. 3H 15
Aintree Way DY1: Dud 4A 76
Aire Cft. B31: N'fld 6F 145
Airfield Dr. WS9: A'rdge 6A 34
Air Ministry Cotts. B35: Cas V 5D 86
Airport Way B26: Birm A 1E 139
Ajax Cl. WS6: Gt Wyr 4F 7
Akrill Cl. B70: W Brom 2H 79
Akrill Cott. Homes, The B70: W Brom 2H 79
Alamein Rd. WV13: W'hall 2G 45
Alasdair Ho. B17: Harb 6F 115
Albany Ct. *B62: Quin* *4G 113*
(off Binswood Rd.)
Albany Cres. WV14: Bils 5E 45
Albany Gdns. B91: Sol 3A 152
Albany Gro. DY6: K'wfrd 2C 92
WV11: Ess 6C 18
Albany Ho. B34: S End 2F 105
Albany Rd. B17: Harb 5G 115
WV1: Wolv 1F 43
Albemarle Rd. DY8: Stourb 3D 124
Albermarle Rd. DY6: K'wfrd 4E 93
Albert Av. B12: Bal H 5A 118
Albert Clarke Dr.
WV12: W'hall 2C 30
Albert Cl. WV8: Cod 3E 13
Albert Dr. B63: Hale 3H 127
DY3: Swind 5E 73
Albert Ho. *WS10: Darl* *5C 46*
(off Factory St.)
Albert Rd. B6: Aston 1F 101
B14: K Hth 6G 133
B17: Harb 6F 115
B21: Hand 6A 82
B23: Erd 4D 84
B33: Stech 1B 120
B63: Hale 3H 127
B68: O'bry 3A 114
WV6: Wolv 6D 26
Albert Smith Pl. B65: Row R 5A 96
Albert St. B4: Birm 1G 117 (4F 5)
B5: Birm 6H 101
B69: O'bry 1G 97
B70: W Brom 6A 80
DY4: Tip 5H 61
DY5: P'ntt 2H 93
DY6: W Hth 1H 91
DY8: Stourb 6D 108
DY9: Lye 6A 110
WS2: Wals 1C 48
WS10: W'bry 3F 63
Albert St. E. B69: O'bry 2H 97
Albert Wlk. B17: Harb 6G 115
Albion Av. WV13: W'hall 1C 46
Albion Bus. Pk. B66: Smeth 1C 98
Albion Fld. Dr. B71: W Brom 3B 80
Albion Ho. B70: W Brom 5A 80
Albion Ind. Est. B70: W Brom 5G 79
Albion Ind. Est. Rd. B70: W Brom 5F 79
Albion Pde. DY6: W Hth 1H 91
Albion Rd. B11: S'brk 6D 118
B21: Hand 6H 81
B70: W Brom 5F 79
(not continuous)
B71: W Brom 1F 99
WS8: Bwnhls 5A 10
WV13: W'hall 1B 46
Albion Rdbt. B70: W Brom 3H 79
Albion St. B1: Birm 6D 100 (2A 4)
B69: O'bry 6E 79
DY4: Tip 2H 77
DY5: Brie H 6H 93
DY6: W Hth 6H 73
WV1: Wolv 1H 43 (3D 170)
WV13: W'hall 1C 46
WV14: Bils 5G 45
Albion Ter. *B46: Wat O* *4D 88*
(off St Pauls Ct.)
Alborn Cres. B38: K Nor 1H 159
Albright Ho. *B69: O'bry* *5E 97*
(off Kempsey Cl.)
Albrighton Ho. B20: Hand 4B 82
Albrighton Rd. B63: Hale 2G 127
WV7: Alb 5A 12
Albright Rd. B68: O'bry 5B 98
Albury Wlk. B11: S'brk 4A 118
Albutts Rd. WS8: Nort C 2F 9
Alcester Dr. B73: New O 2D 68
(not continuous)
WV13: W'hall 2F 45
Alcester Gdns. B14: K Hth 6G 133
ALCESTER LANES END 2G 147
Alcester Rd. B13: Mose 3G 133
B47: H'wd 6A 148
B47: Wyt 6H 161
Alcester Rd. Sth. B14: K Hth 6G 133
(not continuous)
Alcester St. B12: Birm 3H 117 (6H 5)
Alcombe Gro. B33: Stech 1C 120
Alcott Cl. B93: Dorr 6G 167
Alcott Gro. B33: Kitts G 6H 105
Alcott La. B37: Mars G 3B 122
Alcove, The WS3: Blox 5B 20
Aldbourne Way B38: K Nor 2H 159
Aldbury Rd. B14: K Hth 5A 148
Aldeburgh Cl. WS3: Blox 4G 19
Aldeford Dr. DY5: Brie H. 3H 109
Alderbrook Cl. DY3: Sed 4F 59
Alderbrook Rd. B91: Sol. 4D 150
Alder Cl. B47: H'wd 3B 162
B76: Walm 6C 70
Alder Coppice DY3: Sed 3G 59
Alder Cres. WS5: Wals 1F 65
Alder Dale WV3: Wolv 2C 42
Alderdale Av. DY3: Sed 2G 59
Alderdale Cres. B92: Sol 6A 138
Alder Dr. B37: Chel W. 2D 122
Alderflat Pl. B7: Birm 4C 102
Alderford Cl. WV8: Pend 1D 26
Alder Gro. B62: Quin. 5E 113
Alderham Cl. B91: Sol 3H 151
Alderhithe Gro. B74: Lit A 6B 36
Alder La. B30: B'vlle 1G 145
CV7: Bal C 4H 169
Alderlea Cl. DY8: Stourb 3E 125
Alderley Cres. WS3: Wals 4C 32
Alderman Bowen Leisure Cen. 6G 103
Alderminster Rd. B91: Sol 6F 151
Aldermore Dr. B75: S Cold 5D 54
Alderney Gdns. B38: K Nor 6H 145
Alderpark Rd. B91: Sol. 4D 150
Alderpits Rd. B34: S End 2H 105
(not continuous)
Alder Rd. B12: Bal H. 1A 134
DY6: K'wfrd 4D 92
WS10: W'bry 5G 47
Alders, The B62: Roms. 3A 142
Aldersea Dr. B6: Aston 2H 101
Aldershaw Rd. B26: Yard 6C 120
Aldershaws B90: Dic H 4G 163
Aldersley Av. WV6: Tett 2C 26
Aldersley Cl. WV6: Tett 2D 26
Aldersley High School Sports Cen. 6B 14
Aldersley Leisure Village 3D 26
Aldersley Rd. WV6: Tett 4C 26
Aldersley Stadium 3D 26
Aldersmead Rd. B31: N'fld 5G 145
Alderson Rd. B8: Salt 5F 103
Alderton Cl. B91: Sol. 6F 151
Alderton Dr. WV3: Wolv 3C 42
Alder Way B74: S'tly 3G 51
Alderwood Pl. B91: Sol 4F 151
Alderwood Pct. DY3: Sed 4G 59
Alderwood Ri. DY3: Up Gor 2H 75
Aldgate Dr. DY5: Brie H 4G 109
Aldgate Gro. B19: Birm 4F 101
Aldis Cl. B28: Hall G 4E 135
WS2: Wals 4G 47
Aldis Rd. WS2: Wals 4G 47
ALDRIDGE 3D 34
Aldridge By-Pass WS9: A'rdge 4D 34
Aldridge Cl. B68: O'bry 5A 98
DY8: Word 3C 108
Aldridge Rd. B44: Gt Barr 3E 67
B68: O'bry 3H 113
B74: Lit A 4H 35
B74: S'tly 2F 51
WS4: Wals 6G 33
WS9: A'rdge 4H 35
Aldridge Sailing Club 1A 34
Aldridge St. WS10: Darl 4D 46
Aldridge Youth Theatre 3D 34
Aldwych Cl. WS9: A'rdge 1D 34
Aldwyck Dr. WV3: Wolv 3G 41
Aldwyn Av. B13: Mose 3H 133
Alexander Gdns. B42: P Barr 4F 83
Alexander Hill DY5: Quar B 3B 110
Alexander Ind. Pk. WV14: Bils 1E 61
Alexander Rd. B27: A Grn 1H 135
B67: Smeth 1C 114
WS2: Wals. 1F 47
WV8: Bilb 4A 14
Alexander Ter. B67: Smeth. 3D 98
Alexander Way B8: Salt. 6F 103
Alexandra Av. B21: Hand 2H 99
Alexandra Ct. *DY3: Gorn* *4G 75*
(off Redhall Rd.)
Alexandra Cres. B71: W Brom 5C 64
Alexandra Ho. B27: A Grn 3B 136
Alexandra Ind. Est. DY4: Tip 1A 78
Alexandra Pl. DY1: Dud 3D 76
WV14: Bils 5F 45
Alexandra Rd. B5: Bal H. 5G 117
B21: Hand. 2H 99
B30: Stir 1C 146
B63: Hale 2H 127
DY4: Tip 2H 77
WS1: Wals 4C 48
WS10: Darl 5E 47
WV4: Penn 6E 43
Alexandra St. DY1: Dud 6D 76
WV3: Wolv 2F 43
Alexandra Theatre 1F 117 (5D 4)
Alexandra Way B69: Tiv 5A 78
WS9: A'rdge 4D 34
Alford Cl. B45: Redn. 2A 158
Alfreda Av. B47: H'wd. 1H 161
Alfred Gunn Ho. B68: O'bry 5H 97
Alfred Rd. B11: S'hll 6B 118
B21: Hand 1A 100
Alfred Squire Rd. WV11: Wed 4E 29
Alfred St. B6: Aston 1B 102
B12: Bal H. 6B 118
B14: K Hth 6H 133
B66: Smeth. 2G 99
B70: W Brom 4B 80
WS3: Blox. 6H 19
WS10: Darl 6C 46
Alfryth Ct. *B15: Edg* *3E 117*
(off Lee Cres.)
Algernon Rd. B16: Edg. 5H 99
Alice St. WV14: Bils 5F 45
Alice Wlk. WV14: Bils. 6F 45
Alison Cl. DY4: Tip 3A 62
Alison Dr. DY8: Stourb 3D 124
Alison Rd. B62: Hale 2F 129
Allan Cl. B66: Smeth. 4F 99
DY8: Word 3D 108
All Angels Wlk. B68: O'bry. 5H 97
Allbut St. B64: Crad H. 2F 111
Allcock St. B9: Birm 2A 118
DY4: Tip 5C 62
Allcroft Rd. B11: Tys. 3F 135
Allenby Cl. DY6: K'wfrd 4E 93
Allen Cl. B43: Gt Barr 6A 66
Allendale Gro. B43: Gt Barr 5A 66
Allendale Rd. B25: Yard 4H 119
B76: Walm 5C 70
Allen Dr. B70: W Brom 6D 80
WS10: Darl 5C 46
Allen Ho. B43: Gt Barr 6A 66
Allen Rd. DY4: Tip 4H 61
WS10: W'bry. 6F 47
WV6: Wolv 6D 26
Allens Av. B18: Hock 3B 100
B71: W Brom 6G 63
Allen's Cl. WV12: W'hall. 4B 30
Allens Cft. Rd. B14: K Hth 2D 146
Allens Farm Rd. B31: N'fld. 4B 144
Allen's La. WS3: Pels 5D 20
Allen's Rd. B18: Hock. 3B 100
Allen St. B70: W Brom 4H 79
Allerdale Rd. WS8: Clay. 6A 10
Allerton Ct. B71: W Brom. 4A 64
Allerton La. B71: W Brom 5A 64
Allerton Rd. B25: Yard 4H 119
Allesley Cl. B74: S Cold 5A 54
Allesley Rd. B92: Olton 5B 136
Allesley St. B6: Aston. 4G 101
Alleston Rd. WV10: Bush. 5H 15
Alleston Wlk. WV10: Bush 5H 15
Alley, The DY3: Lwr G. 4F 75
Alleyne Gro. B24: Erd. 5G 85
Alleyne Rd. B24: Erd 6G 85
Allingham Gro. B43: Gt Barr 1G 67
Allington Cl. WS5: Wals. 3H 49
Allison St. B5: Birm. 1H 117 (5G 5)
Allman Rd. B24: Erd. 3H 85
Allmyn Dr. B74: S'tly. 5A 52
ALL SAINTS 4C 100
All Saints Dr. B74: Four O 1F 53
All Saints Ind. Est. B18: Hock 4C 100
All Saints Rd. B14: K Hth 1G 147
B18: Hock. 4D 100
WS10: Darl 5E 47
WV2: Wolv. 3H 43 (6C 170)
All Saints St. B18: Hock 4C 100
All Saints Way B71: W Brom 3B 80
Allsops Cl. B65: Row R 5H 95
Allwell Dr. B14: K Hth 5H 147
Allwood Gdns. B32: Bart G. 3G 129
Alma Av. DY4: Tip. 6A 62
Alma Cres. B7: Birm. 5B 102
Alma Ind. Est. WS10: Darl 5C 46
Alma Pas. B17: Harb 5H 115
Alma Pl. B12: Bal H 6B 118
DY2: Dud 6E 77
Almar Ct. WV8: Pend 6D 14
Alma St. B19: Hock 3G 101
B63: Crad 6E 111
B66: Smeth. 3G 99
WS2: Wals 5B 32
WS10: Darl 5C 46
WS10: W'bry 2H 63
WV10: Wolv 6B 28
WV13: W'hall 1B 46
Alma Way B19: Loz. 2F 101
Alma Works WS10: Darl. 6D 46
Almond Av. WS2: Wals 5E 31
WS5: Wals 1E 65
Almond Cl. B29: W Cas. 1E 145
WS3: Pels. 5D 20
Almond Cft. B42: Gt Barr 1B 82
Almond Gro. WV6: Wolv. 5G 27
Almond Rd. DY6: K'wfrd. 1C 92
Almsbury Ct. B26: Sheld 1G 137
Alms Ho's. WS1: Wals 3B 48
WV4: Penn 2D 58
Alnwick Ho. B23: Erd 1F 85
Alnwick Rd. WS3: Blox. 3H 19
Alperton Dr. DY9: W'cte 3A 126
Alpha Cl. B12: Bal H. 5G 117
Alpha Twr. B1: Birm. 1E 117 (5B 4)
Alpha Way WS6: Gt Wyr. 5G 7
Alpine Dr. DY2: Neth 5D 94
Alpine Way WV3: Wolv. 1A 42
Alport Cft. B9: Birm. 1B 118
Alston Cl. B74: Four O 1G 53
B91: Sol 1H 151
Alston Gro. B9: Bord G. 6H 103
Alston Ho. B69: O'bry. 3D 96
Alston Rd. B9: Bord G 6H 103
B69: O'bry. 2E 97
B91: Sol 1H 151
Alston St. B16: Birm 1C 116
Althorpe Dr. B93: Dorr 6H 165
Alton Av. WV12: W'hall. 5B 30
Alton Cl. WV10: Bush. 4A 16
Alton Gro. B71: W Brom. 6C 64
DY2: Dud 6G 77
Alton Rd. B29: S Oak 2B 132
Alum Dr. B9: Bord G 6G 103
Alumhurst Av. B8: W End 5G 103
ALUM ROCK 6H 103
Alum Rock Rd. B8: Salt 4D 102
Alumwell Cl. WS2: Wals 2H 47
Alumwell Rd. WS2: Wals 2H 47
Alvaston Cl. WS3: Blox. 4A 20
Alvechurch Highway B60: L Ash. 6C 156
Alvechurch Rd. B31: Longb 1F 159
B63: Hale 3H 127
Alverley Cl. DY6: W Hth. 1H 91
Alverstoke Cl. WV9: Pend. 5E 15
Alveston Gro. B9: Bord G. 1H 119
B93: Know 2D 166
Alveston Rd. B47: H'wd 2A 162
Alvin Cl. B62: B'hth. 2F 113
Alvington Cl. WV12: W'hall 5D 30
Alvis Wlk. B36: Cas B. 6B 88
Alwen St. DY8: Word 1D 108
Alwin Rd. B65: Row R 1B 112
Alwold Ct. B29: W Cas 3D 130
Alwold Rd. B29: W Cas, S Oak. 3D 130
Alwyn Cl. WS6: Gt Wyr. 2F 7
Alwynn Wlk. B23: Erd. 4B 84
Amal Way B6: Witt 5H 83
(not continuous)
Amanda Av. WV4: Penn 1D 58
Amanda Dr. B26: Yard. 2E 121
Amazon Lofts *B1: Birm.* *5D 100*
(off Tenby St.)
Ambassador Rd. B26: Birm A. 1E 139
Ambell Cl. B65: Row R. 4H 95
Amber Dr. B69: O'bry 4G 97
Ambergate Cl. WS3: Blox. 4A 20
Ambergate Dr. DY6: W Hth. 1A 92
Amberley Ct. B29: S Oak 5A 132
Amberley Grn. B43: Gt Barr 1A 82
Amberley Gro. B6: Witt. 4A 84
Amberley Rd. B92: Olton 1D 136

172 A-Z Birmingham Deluxe

Amberley Way—Ash Tree Rd.

Amberley Way B74: S'tly 2G 51
Amber Way B62: Hale 5B 112
Amberwood Cl. WS2: Wals 6D 30
AMBLECOTE 4C 108
Amblecote Av. B44: Gt Barr 3G 67
Amblecote Rd. DY5: Brie H 4G 109
Ambleside B32: Bart G 4A 130
Ambleside Cl. WV14: Bils 2G 61
Ambleside Dr. DY5: Brie H 3G 109
Ambleside Gro. WV12: W'hall 6B 18
Ambleside Way DY6: K'wfrd 3B 92
Ambrose Cl. WV13: W'hall 1G 45
Ambrose Cres. DY6: K'wfrd 1B 92
Ambury Way B43: Gt Barr 5H 65
AMC Cinema 2C 116
Amelas Cl. DY5: Brie H 2E 109
Amersham Cl. B32: Quin 6C 114
Amesbury Rd. B13: Mose 2G 133
Ames Rd. WS10: Darl 4C 46
Amethyst Ct. B92: Olton 4D 136
AMF Bowling
Oxley 3G 27
Wolverhampton 3H 43 (6C 170)
Amherst Av. B20: Hand 4C 82
Amington Cl. B75: R'ley 5B 38
Amington Rd. B25: Yard 5H 119
B90: Shir 1G 163
Amiss Gdns. B10: Small H 3C 118
Amity Cl. B66: Smeth 4F 99
Amos Av. WV11: Wed 2D 28
Amos La. WV11: Wed 2E 29
Amos Rd. DY9: W'cte 3B 126
Amphlett Cft. DY4: Tip 3B 78
Amphletts Cl. DY2: Neth 6G 95
Ampton Rd. B15: Edg 4D 116
Amroth Cl. B45: Redn 2H 157
Amwell Gro. B14: K Hth 4H 147
Anchorage Rd. B23: Erd 4D 84
B74: S Cold 5H 53
Anchor Brook Ind. Pk. WS9: A'rdge 2B 34
Anchor Cl. B16: Edg 2A 116
Anchor Cres. B18: Win G 4B 100
Anchor Hill DY5: Brie H 2G 109
Anchor La. B91: Sol 1H 151
WV14: Cose 3D 60
(not continuous)
Anchor Mdw. WS9: A'rdge 3C 34
Anchor Pde. WS9: A'rdge 3D 34
Anchor Rd. WS9: A'rdge 3D 34
WV14: Cose 3E 61
Andersleigh Dr. WV14: Cose 5C 60
Anderson Cres. B43: Gt Barr 2A 66
Anderson Gdns. DY4: Tip 3A 78
Anderson Rd. B23: Erd 1E 85
B66: Smeth 2E 115
B67: Smeth 2E 115
DY4: Tip 2A 78
Anders Sq. WV6: Pert 5E 25
Anderton Cl. B74: S Cold 4H 53
Anderton Ct. B13: Mose 3A 134
Anderton Pk. Rd. B13: Mose 2A 134
Anderton Rd. B11: S'brk 5B 118
Anderton St. B1: Birm 6D 100
Andover Cres. DY6: K'wfrd 5D 92
Andover St. B5: Birm 1H 117 (4H 5)
Andrew Cl. WV12: W'hall 3D 30
Andrew Ct. B76: Walm 2D 70
Andrew Dr. WV12: W'hall 3D 30
Andrew Gdns. B21: Hand 5A 82
Andrew Rd. B63: Hale 2A 128
B71: W Brom 3D 64
DY4: Tip 4A 62
Andrews Cl. DY5: Quar B 3A 110
Andrews Rd. WS9: Wals W 3D 22
Anerley Gro. B44: Gt Barr 1H 67
Anerley Rd. B44: Gt Barr 1H 67
Angela Av. B65: Row R 5D 96
Angela Pl. WV14: Bils 5F 45
Angelica Cl. WS5: Wals 2E 65
Angelina St. B12: Birm 3H 117
Angel Pas. DY8: Stourb 6E 109
Angel St. DY1: Dud 1D 94
WV13: W'hall 1A 46
Anglesey Av. B36: Cas B 2D 106
Anglesey Cl. WS7: Chase 1A 10
Anglesey Cres. WS8: Bwnhls 3B 10
Anglesey Rd. WS8: Bwnhls 3B 10
Anglesey St. B19: Loz 2E 101
Anglian Rd. WS9: A'rdge 3H 33
Anglo African Ind. Pk. B69: O'bry 5E 79
Angus Cl. B71: W Brom 1A 80
Anita Av. DY4: Tip 5A 78
Anita Cft. B23: Erd 5D 84
Ankadine Rd. DY8: Amb 5F 109
Ankerdine Ct. B63: Hale 2A 128
Ankermoor Cl. B34: S End 3F 105
Annan Av. WV10: Bush 2A 28
Ann Cft. B26: Sheld 1H 137
Anne Cl. B70: W Brom 4E 79
Anne Ct. B76: Walm 2E 71
Anne Gro. DY4: Tip 4B 62
Anne Rd. B66: Smeth 2G 99
DY5: Quar B 2C 110
WV4: Penn 5F 43
Ann Rd. B47: Wyt 6A 162
Annscroft B38: K Nor 5H 145
Ann St. WV13: W'hall 6B 30
Ansbro Cl. B18: Win G 4B 100
Ansculf Rd. DY5: Brie H 2F 109
Ansell Rd. B11: S'brk 5C 118
B24: Erd 6F 85
Ansley Way B92: Sol 6H 137
Anslow Gdns. WV11: Wed 6H 17
Anslow Rd. B23: Erd 2C 84
Anson Cl. WS6: Gt Wyr 4F 7
WV6: Pert 4E 25
Anson Ct. B70: W Brom 6F 63
Anson Gro. B27: A Grn 3B 136
Anson Rd. B70: W Brom 1E 79
WS2: Wals 1E 47
WS6: Gt Wyr 4F 7
Anstey Cft. B37: F'bri 5C 106
Anstey Gro. B27: A Grn 4H 135
Anstey Rd. B44: K'sdng 1G 83
Anston Junc. WS2: Wals 2E 47
Anston Way WV11: Wed 2F 29
Anstree Cl. WS6: C Hay 4D 6
Anstruther Rd. B15: Edg 4H 115
Anthony Rd. B8: Salt 6E 103
Anton Dr. B76: Walm 1E 87
Antony Rd. B90: Shir 6H 149
Antringham Gdns. B15: Edg 3H 115
Antrobus Rd. B21: Hand 6A 82
B73: Bold 4E 69
Anvil Cres. WV14: Cose 3E 61
Anvil Dr. B69: O'bry 3E 97
Anvil Wlk. B70: W Brom 3F 79
Apex Bus. Pk. WS11: Nort C 1D 8
Apex Ind. Pk. DY4: Tip 5D 62
Apex Rd. WS8: Bwnhls 6G 9
Apley Rd. DY8: Woll 4C 108
Apollo Cft. B24: Erd 4B 86
Apollo Rd. B68: O'bry 3A 98
DY9: W'cte 6C 110
Apollo Way B20: Hand 6F 83
B66: Smeth 4G 99
Apperley Way B63: Crad 4D 110
Appian Cl. B14: K Hth 2G 147
Appian Way B90: Ches G 5B 164
Appleby Cl. B14: K Hth 2F 147
Appleby Gdns. WV11: Ess 5C 18
Appleby Gro. B90: M'path 3F 165
Applecross B74: Four O 2F 53
Appledore Cl. WS6: Gt Wyr 2G 7
Appledore Ct. WS3: Blox 1H 31
Appledore Rd. WS5: Wals 3H 49
Appledore Ter. WS5: Wals 3H 49
Appledorne Gdns. B34: S End 3F 105
Applesham Cl. B11: S'brk 5D 118
Appleton Av. B43: Gt Barr 5H 65
DY8: Stourb 3E 125
Appleton Cl. B30: B'vlle 5A 132
Appleton Cres. WV4: Penn 6E 43
Apple Tree Cl. B23: Erd 3B 84
Appletree Cl. B31: Longb 6D 144
B91: Cath B 2D 152
Appletree Gro. WS9: A'rdge 5D 34
WV6: Wolv 4G 27
Applewood Gro. B64: Old H 3H 111
April Cft. B13: Mose 2B 134
Apse Cl. WV5: Wom 6F 57
Apsley Cl. B68: O'bry 4G 113
Apsley Cft. B38: K Nor 5D 146
Apsley Gro. B24: Erd 5G 85
B93: Dorr 6G 167
Apsley Ho. B64: Old H 1H 111
Apsley Rd. B68: O'bry 4G 113
Aqueduct Rd. B90: Shir 5E 149
Aragon Dr. B73: S Cold 5G 53
Arbor Ct. B71: W Brom 1C 80
Arboretum Rd. WS1: Wals 1D 48
Arbor Way B37: Chel W 2E 123
Arbour Ga. WS9: Wals W 3D 22
Arbourtree Ct. WV5: Wom 6H 57
Arbury Dr. DY8: Word 6B 92
Arbury Hall Rd. B90: Shir 1B 164
Arbury Wlk. B76: Min 2H 87
Arcade B31: N'fld 3E 145
Arcade, The DY3: Up Gor 2A 76
WS1: Wals 2C 48
Arcadia B70: W Brom 4A 80
(off W. Bromwich Ringway)
Arcadian Cinema 2G 117
Arcadian Shop. Cen.
B5: Birm 2G 117 (6E 5)
Arcal St. DY3: Sed 6A 60
Arch, The B9: Birm 1A 118
Archer Cl. B68: O'bry 4H 97
WS10: W'bry 2E 63
Archer Ct. DY9: W'cte 3A 126
Archer Gdns. B64: Crad H 2E 111
Archer Rd. B14: Yard W 3C 148
WS3: Blox 3C 32
Archers Cl. B23: Erd 5D 68
(not continuous)
Archery Rd. CV7: Mer 4H 141
Arches, The B10: Small H 3B 118
Arch Hill St. DY2: Neth 4E 95
Archibald Rd. B19: Loz 1E 101
Archway, The WS4: Wals 6D 32
Arcot Rd. B28: Hall G 3F 135
Ardath Rd. B38: K Nor 5C 146
Ardav Rd. B70: W Brom 5F 63
Ardedale B90: Shir 1A 164
Arden Bldgs. B93: Dorr 6B 166
Arden Cl. CV7: Bal C 2H 169
CV7: Mer 4H 141
DY8: Woll 4C 108
DY8: Word 6A 92
Ardencote Rd. B13: Mose 6A 134
Arden Ct. B24: Erd 4H 85
B42: P Barr 3F 83
B92: H Ard 6A 140
DY3: Lwr G 4H 75
(off Chiltern Cl.)
Arden Cft. B46: Col 6H 89
B92: Sol 1G 137
Arden Dr. B26: Yard 4D 120
B73: W Grn 5H 69
B75: S Cold 6F 55
(not continuous)
B93: Dorr 6G 167
Arden Gro. B19: Loz 1E 101
B69: O'bry 4G 97
Arden Ho. B92: H Ard 1B 154
Ardenlea Ct. B91: Sol 2G 151
Arden Oak Rd.
B26: Sheld 6H 121
Arden Pl. WV14: Bils 1B 62
Arden Rd. B6: Aston 1F 101
B8: Salt 6C 102
B27: A Grn 1H 135
B45: Fran 6G 143
B47: H'wd 3A 162
B67: Smeth 5E 99
B93: Dorr 6G 167
Arden Va. Rd. B93: Know 2D 166
Arderne Dr. B37: F'bri 2C 122
Ardingley Wlk. DY5: Brie H 4F 109
Ardley Cl. DY2: Dud 1F 95
Ardley Rd. B14: K Hth 2A 148
Arena B40: Nat E C 2G 139
Arena Theatre 1G 43 (2B 170)
Arena Wlk. B1: Birm 5A 4
Aretha Cl. DY6: K'wfrd 3E 93
Argil Cl. WV11: Wed 1F 29
Argus Cl. B76: Walm 2D 70
Argyle Cl. DY8: Word 2C 108
WS4: Wals 6F 33
Argyle Rd. WS4: Wals 6F 33
WV2: Wolv 5F 43
Argyle St. B7: Nech 1C 102
Argyll Ho. WV1: Wolv 5G 27
Arkle Cft. B36: Hodg H 1A 104
B65: Row R 3H 95
Arkley Gro. B28: Hall G 6H 135
Arkley Rd. B28: Hall G 6H 135
Arkwright Rd. B32: Quin 6A 114
WS2: Wals 4H 31
Arlen Dr. B43: Gt Barr 4H 65
Arlescote Cl. B75: Four O 1A 54
Arlescote Rd. B92: Sol 3G 137
Arless Way B17: Harb 2E 131
Arleston Way B90: Shir 1C 164
Arley Cl. B69: O'bry 4D 96
Arley Ct. DY2: Neth 3E 95
Arley Dr. DY8: Stourb 2C 124
Arley Gro. WV4: Penn 6B 42
Arley Ho. B26: Yard 2E 121
Arley Rd. B8: Salt 4D 102
B29: S Oak 2B 132
B91: Sol 3E 151
Arley Vs. B18: Win G 5H 99
(off Cape St.)
Arlidge Cl. WV14: Bils 1F 61
Arlington Cl. DY6: K'wfrd 5B 92
Arlington Ct. DY8: Stourb 1F 125
Arlington Gro. B14: K Hth 5B 148
Arlington Rd. B14: K Hth 5B 148
B71: W Brom 1B 80
Armada Cl. B23: Erd 6D 84
Armoury Rd. B11: Small H 5D 118
Armoury Trad. Est. B11: Small H 5D 118
Armside Cl. WS3: Pels 3F 21
Armstead Rd. WV9: Pend 4D 14
Armstrong Cl. DY8: Amb 4F 109
Armstrong Dr. B36: Cas B 6B 88
WS2: Wals 5G 31
WV6: Wolv 4E 27
Armstrong Way WV13: W'hall 3B 46
Arnhem Cl. WV11: Wed 1D 28
Arnhem Rd. WV13: W'hall 3G 45
Arnhem Way DY4: Tip 2C 78
Arnold Cl. WS2: Wals 6F 31
Arnold Gro. B30: K Nor 3H 145
B90: Shir 3H 149
Arnold Rd. B90: Shir 3H 149
Arnside Ct. B23: Erd 3B 84
Arnwood Cl. WS2: Wals 1F 47
Arosa Dr. B17: Harb 2F 131
Arps Rd. WV8: Cod 4F 13
Arran Cl. B43: Gt Barr 2A 66
Arran Rd. B34: Hodg H 3D 104
Arran Way B36: Cas B 2C 106
Arras Rd. DY2: Dud 5G 77
Arrow Cl. B93: Know 3C 166
Arrowfield Grn. B38: K Nor 2H 159
Arrow Ind. Est. WV12: W'hall 3C 30
Arrow Rd. WS3: Blox 3C 32
Arrow Wlk. B38: K Nor 6D 146
Arsenal St. B9: Bord G 2C 118
Arter St. B12: Bal H 5H 117
Arthur Gunby Cl. B75: S Cold 4D 54
Arthur Harris Cl. B66: Smeth 6G 99
Arthur Pl. B1: Birm 6D 100 (3A 4)
Arthur Rd. B15: Edg 5D 116
B21: Hand 1B 100
B24: Erd 3H 85
B25: Yard 5H 119
DY4: Tip 1A 78
Arthur St. B10: Small H 2B 118
B70: W Brom 6B 80
WS2: Wals 4H 47
WV2: Wolv 5H 43
WV14: Bils 5F 45
Arthur Terry Sports Cen., The 6G 37
Artillery St. B9: Birm 1B 118
Arton Cft. B24: Erd 5F 85
Arundel Av. WS10: W'bry 2F 63
Arundel Ct. B29: W Cas 6G 131
(off Abdon Av.)
Arundel Cres. B92: Olton 4E 137
Arundel Dr. B69: Tiv 1A 96
Arundel Gro. WV6: Pert 6F 25
Arundel Ho. B23: Erd 1F 85
Arundel Pl. B11: S'brk 5A 118
Arundel Rd. B14: K Hth 6A 148
DY8: Word 1A 108
WV10: Oxl 5F 15
WV12: W'hall 2C 30
Arundel St. WS1: Wals 4C 48
(not continuous)
Arun Way B76: Walm 4E 71
Asbury Ct. B43: Gt Barr 5G 65
Asbury Rd. CV7: Bal C 4H 169
WS10: W'bry 3C 64
Ascot Cl. B16: Birm 1B 116
B69: O'bry 3E 97
Ascot Dr. DY1: Dud 5B 76
WV4: Penn 1E 59
Ascote La. B90: Dic H 4G 163
Ascot Gdns. DY8: Word 1B 108
Ascot Rd. B13: Mose 3H 133
Ascot Wlk. B69: O'bry 3E 97
Ash Av. B12: Bal H 6A 118
Ashborough Dr. B91: Sol 2G 165
Ashbourne Gro. B6: Aston 1G 101
Ashbourne Ridge B63: Crad 6F 111
Ashbourne Rd. B16: Edg 6H 99
WS3: Blox 4A 20
WV1: Wolv 6C 28
WV4: E'shll 2A 60
Ashbourne Way B90: Shir 1C 164
Ash Bridge Ct. B45: Redn 3H 157
Ashbrook Cres. B91: Sol 1G 165
Ashbrook Dr. B45: Redn 1H 157
Ashbrook Gro. B30: Stir 5D 132
Ashbrook Rd. B30: Stir 5E 133
Ashburn Gro. WV13: W'hall 1C 46
Ashburton Rd. B14: K Hth 2F 147
Ashbury Covert B30: K Nor 4E 147
Ashby Cl. B8: W End 3A 104
Ashby Ct. B91: Sol 6G 151
Ash Cl. WV8: Bilb 4G 13
Ashcombe Av. B20: Hand 4A 82
Ashcombe Gdns. B24: Erd 4B 86
Ashcott Cl. B38: K Nor 5H 145
Ash Ct. B66: Smeth 1A 98
DY8: Stourb 1E 125
Ash Cres. B37: K'hrst 3B 106
DY6: K'wfrd 3C 92
Ashcroft B15: Edg 6A 116
B66: Smeth 4G 99
Ashcroft Gro. B20: Hand 5F 83
Ashdale Cl. DY6: K'wfrd 1C 92
Ashdale Dr. B14: K Hth 6B 148
Ashdale Gro. B26: Yard 3E 121
Ashdene Cl. B73: S Cold 2G 69
Ashdene Gdns. DY8: Word 1A 108
Ashdown Cl. B13: Mose 4A 134
B45: Fran 5G 143
Ashdown Dr. DY8: Word 6C 92
Ash Dr. B31: Longb 6A 144
B71: W Brom 1A 80
Ashen Cl. DY3: Sed 2G 59
Ashenden Ri. WV3: Wolv 2G 41
Ashenhurst Rd. DY1: Dud 2A 94
Ashenhurst Wlk. DY1: Dud 1C 94
Ashes Rd. B69: O'bry 5F 97
Ashfern Dr. B76: Walm 6D 70
Ashfield Av. B14: K Hth 4G 133
Ashfield Cl. WS3: Wals 5D 32
Ashfield Ct. B30: K Nor 3A 146
Ashfield Cres. DY2: Neth 6E 95
DY9: W'cte 2B 126
Ashfield Gdns. B14: K Hth 4H 133
Ashfield Gro. B63: Hale 3G 127
WV10: F'hses 4G 15
Ashfield Ho. B28: Hall G 4E 149
Ashfield Rd. B14: K Hth 4H 133
WV3: Wolv 1B 42
WV10: F'hses 4G 15
WV14: Bils 3A 62
Ashford Cl. B24: Erd 3B 86
Ashford Dr. B76: Walm 2D 86
DY3: Sed 6A 60
Ashford Twr. B12: Birm 3A 118
Ash Furlong Cl. CV7: Bal C 3H 169
Ashfurlong Cres. B75: S Cold 4C 54
Ash Grn. DY1: Dud 2C 76
Ash Gro. B12: Bal H 6B 118
B31: N'fld 3D 144
DY3: Gorn 5G 75
DY9: W'cte 2H 125
Ashgrove Ho. B45: Rubery 2E 157
(off Callowbrook La.)
Ashgrove Rd. B44: Gt Barr 3E 67
Ash Hill WV3: Wolv 2B 42
Ashill Rd. B45: Redn 2H 157
Ash La. WS6: Gt Wyr 2G 7
Ashlawn Cres. B91: Sol 2B 150
Ashleigh Dr. B20: Hand 5D 82
Ashleigh Gro. B13: Mose 4B 134
Ashleigh Hgts. B91: Sol 2E 151
Ashleigh Rd. B69: Tiv 1C 96
B91: Sol 3F 151
Ashley Cl. B15: Edg 4E 117
DY6: K'wfrd 5A 92
DY8: Stourb 3B 124
Ashley Gdns. B8: Salt 5D 102
WV8: Cod 3F 13
Ashley Mt. WV6: Tett 4B 26
Ashley Rd. B23: Erd 4E 85
B66: Smeth 5G 99
WS3: Blox 6F 19
WV4: Penn 6C 42
Ashley St. WV14: Bils 5G 45
Ashley Ter. B29: S Oak 4A 132
Ashley Way CV7: Bal C 2H 169
Ashmall WS7: Hamm 1F 11
Ashmead Dr. B45: Coft H 5A 158
Ashmead Gro. B24: Erd 5G 85
Ashmead Ri. B45: Coft H 5A 158
Ash M. B27: A Grn 6A 120
Ashmole Rd. B70: W Brom 6F 63
ASHMOOR LAKE 4B 30
Ashmore Av. WV11: Wed 1A 30
Ashmore Ind. Est. WS2: Wals 6C 32
Ashmore Lake Ind. Est.
WV12: W'hall 5B 30
Ashmore Lake Rd. WV12: W'hall 5B 30
Ashmore Lake Way WV12: W'hall 5B 30
ASHMORE PARK 6A 18
Ashmore Rd. B30: K Nor 2B 146
Ashmores Ind. Est.
DY1: Dud 4G 77
Ashold Farm Rd. B24: Erd 5B 86
Asholme Cl. B36: Hodg H 2A 104
Ashorne Cl. B28: Hall G 6H 135
Ashover Gro. B18: Win G 5A 100
(off Heath Grn. Rd.)
Ashover Rd. B44: Gt Barr 2F 67
Ash Rd. B8: Salt 5D 102
DY1: Dud 4D 76
DY4: Tip 3G 77
WS10: W'bry 6F 47
Ash St. B64: Old H 1H 111
WS3: Blox 6B 20
WV3: Wolv 2E 43
WV14: Bils 2G 61
Ashstead Cl. B76: Walm 1F 87
Ashted Lock B7: Birm 5H 101 (1H 5)
Ashted Wlk. B7: Birm 5B 102
Ash Ter. B69: Tiv 6B 78
Ashton Cft. B91: Sol 6E 151
Ashtoncroft B16: Birm 1C 116
Ashton Dr. WS4: S'fld 4G 21
Ashton Pk. Dr. DY5: Brie H 2G 109
Ashton Rd. B25: Yard 4H 119
Ashtree Cl. DY5: Brie H 3E 109
Ash Tree Dr. B26: Yard 4B 120
Ashtree Dr. DY8: Stourb 2E 125
Ashtree Gro. WV14: Bils 2B 62
Ash Tree Rd. B30: Stir 1C 146

Ashtree Rd.—Barclay Rd.

Ashtree Rd. B64: Old H . . . 1H 111
B69: Tiv . . . 6C 78
WS3: Pels . . . 4E 21
Ashurst Rd. B76: Walm . . . 1D 86
Ashville Av. B34: Hodg H . . . 2D 104
Ashville Dr. B63: Hale . . . 6A 112
Ash Wlk. B76: Walm . . . 3D 70
Ashwater Dr. B14: K Hth . . . 5F 147
Ash Way B23: Erd . . . 5C 68
Ashway B11: S'hll . . . 6B 118
Ashwell Dr. B90: Shir . . . 3B 150
Ashwells Gro. WV9: Pend . . . 5E 15
Ashwin Rd. B21: Hand . . . 2B 100
ASHWOOD . . . 4E 91
Ashwood Av. DY8: Word . . . 1A 108
Ashwood Cl. B74: S'tly . . . 3G 51
Ashwood Ct. B13: Mose . . . 2A 134
B34: Hodg H . . . 4B 104
Ashwood Dr. B37: Chel W . . . 6F 107
Ashwood Gro. WV4: Penn . . . 6E 43
Ashwood Lwr. La. DY6: K'wfrd . . . 4E 91
DY7: Stourt . . . 4E 91
Ashworth Rd. B42: Gt Barr . . . 4D 66
Askew Bri. Rd. DY3: Gorn . . . 4F 75
Askew Cl. DY3: Up Gor . . . 2A 76
Aspbury Cft. B36: Cas B . . . 6H 87
Aspen Cl. B27: A Grn . . . 3H 135
B76: Walm . . . 3D 70
Aspen Dr. B37: Chel W . . . 3E 123
Aspen Gdns. B20: Hand . . . 6D 82
Aspen Gro. B9: Bord G . . . 6G 103
B47: Wyt . . . 4B 162
WV12: W'hall . . . 2E 31
Aspen Ho. B91: Sol . . . 5D 150
Aspen Way WV3: Wolv . . . 2E 43
Asquith Dr. B69: Tiv . . . 5C 78
Asquith Rd. B8: W End . . . 4H 103
Asra Cl. B66: Smeth . . . 1E 99
Asra Ho. *B66: Smeth* . . . *1E 99*
(off Oxford Rd.)
Astbury Av. B67: Smeth . . . 6D 98
Astbury Cl. WS3: Blox . . . 3G 19
WV1: Wolv . . . 2C 44
Astbury Ct. B68: O'bry . . . 4H 113
Aster Wlk. WV9: Pend . . . 4E 15
Aster Way WS5: Wals . . . 2E 65
Astley Av. B62: Quin . . . 5F 113
Astley Cl. DY4: Tip . . . 1D 78
Astley Cres. B62: Quin . . . 6F 113
Astley Pl. WV2: Wolv . . . 5H 43
Astley Rd. B21: Hand . . . 6H 81
Astley Wlk. B90: Shir . . . 2H 149
ASTON . . . 6H 83
Aston Bri. B6: Aston . . . 4H 101
Aston Brook Grn. B6: Aston . . . 4H 101
Aston Brook St. B6: Aston . . . 3H 101
(not continuous)
Aston Brook St. E. B6: Aston . . . 4H 101
Aston Bury B15: Edg . . . 4H 115
Aston Chu. Rd. B7: Nech . . . 2C 102
B8: Salt . . . 2C 102
Aston Chu. Trad. Est. B7: Nech . . . 3D 102
Aston Cl. WV14: Bils . . . 1B 62
Aston Ct. B23: Erd . . . 5C 84
Aston Cross Bus. Pk. B6: Aston . . . 3A 102
Aston Events Cen. . . . 1A 102
Aston Expressway B6: Aston . . . 4H 101
Aston Hall . . . 1H 101
Aston Hall Rd. B6: Aston . . . 1A 102
Aston La. B20: Hand . . . 5F 83
Aston Mnr. Cl. B20: Hand . . . 5G 83
Aston Manor Transport Mus. . . . 6H 83
Aston Newton Pool & Fitness Cen. . . . 3G 101
Aston Rd. B6: Birm . . . 4H 101
(not continuous)
B69: Tiv . . . 6A 78
DY2: Dud . . . 1D 94
WV13: W'hall . . . 1G 45
Aston Rd. Nth. B6: Aston . . . 3H 101
Aston Science Pk. B7: Birm . . . 5H 101 (1H 5)
Aston's Cl. DY5: Brie H . . . 4H 109
Aston Seedbed Cen. B7: Nech . . . 3A 102
Aston's Fold DY5: Brie H . . . 4H 109
Aston Station (Rail) . . . 1B 102
Aston St. B4: Birm . . . 5H 101 (2F 5)
(not continuous)
DY4: Tip . . . 6C 62
WV3: Wolv . . . 3E 43
Aston Students Guild . . . 1G 5
Aston Triangle, The B4: Birm . . . 6H 101 (2G 5)
Aston University . . . 5H 101 (1G 5)
Aston Villa FC . . . 6H 83
Astor Dr. B13: Mose . . . 4C 134
Astoria Cl. WV12: W'hall . . . 6D 18
Astoria Gdns. WV12: W'hall . . . 6D 18
Astor Rd. B74: S'tly . . . 2A 52
DY6: K'wfrd . . . 4D 92
Athelney Ct. WS3: Pels . . . 4E 21
Athelstan Gro. WV6: Pert . . . 4F 25
Atherstone Cl. B90: Shir . . . 5E 149
Atherstone Rd. WV1: Wolv . . . 1D 44
Athlone Rd. WS5: Wals . . . 3G 49
Athol Cl. B32: Bart G . . . 5B 130
Athole St. B12: Birm . . . 4A 118
Atlantic Ct. *WV13: W'hall* . . . *2A 46*
(off Cheapside)
Atlantic Rd. B44: Gt Barr . . . 5H 67
Atlantic Way WS10: W'bry . . . 4E 63
Atlas Cft. WV10: Oxl . . . 3G 27
Atlas Est. B6: Witt . . . 5A 84
B11: Tys . . . 6G 119
Atlas Gro. B70: W Brom . . . 4F 79
Atlas Trad. Est. WV14: Bils . . . 3H 61
Atlas Way B1: Birm . . . 5A 4
Attenborough Cl. B19: Hock . . . 4F 101
Attingham Dr. B43: Gt Barr . . . 3H 65
Attleboro La. B46: Wat O . . . 5C 88
Attlee Cl. B69: Tiv . . . 5D 78
Attlee Cres. WV14: Bils . . . 3G 61
Attlee Rd. WS2: Wals . . . 5E 31
Attwell Pk. WV3: Wolv . . . 4B 42
Attwell Rd. DY4: Tip . . . 4H 61
Attwood Cl. B8: Salt . . . 3E 103
Attwood Gdns. WV4: E'shll . . . 6A 44
Attwood St. B63: Hale . . . 6H 111
DY9: Lye . . . 6B 110
Aubrey Rd. B10: Small H . . . 3F 119
B32: Harb . . . 4C 114
Auchinleck Ho. *B16: Birm* . . . *2D 116*
(off Broad St.)
Auchinleck Sq. *B15: Birm* . . . *2D 116*
(off Islington Row Middleway)
Auckland Dr. B36: Cas B . . . 1B 106
Auckland Ho. B32: Quin . . . 1D 130
Auckland Rd. B11: S'brk . . . 4A 118
B67: Smeth . . . 3C 98
DY6: K'wfrd . . . 5C 92
Auden Ct. WV6: Pert . . . 5F 25
Audleigh Ho. B15: Birm . . . 3E 117
Audlem Wlk. WV10: Wolv . . . 4C 28
Audley Rd. B33: Stech . . . 5C 104
AUDNAM . . . 2D 108
Audnam DY8: Word . . . 2D 108
Augusta Rd. B13: Mose . . . 1G 133
B27: A Grn . . . 6A 120
Augusta Rd. E. B13: Mose . . . 1H 133
Augusta St. B18: Birm . . . 5E 101 (1A 4)
Augustine Gro. B18: Hock . . . 3B 100
B74: Four O . . . 4F 37
Augustus Cl. B46: Col . . . 6H 89
Augustus Ct. B15: Edg . . . 3B 116
Augustus Rd. B15: Edg . . . 3H 115
Augustus St. WS2: Wals . . . 2B 48
Aulton Rd. B75: R'ley . . . 6C 38
Ault St. B70: W Brom . . . 6B 80
Austcliff Dr. B91: Sol . . . 1G 165
Austen Pl. B15: Edg . . . 3D 116
Austen Wlk.
B71: W Brom . . . 2B 80
Austin Cl. B27: A Grn . . . 1B 136
DY1: Dud . . . 5B 76
Austin Ct. B1: Birm . . . 1D 116 (4A 4)
Austin Cft. B36: Cas B . . . 6A 88
Austin Ho. WS4: Wals . . . 6D 32
Austin Ri. B31: Longb . . . 2D 158
Austin Rd. B21: Hand . . . 6G 81
Austin St. WV6: Wolv . . . 5F 27
AUSTIN VILLAGE . . . 6D 144
Austin Way B42: P Barr . . . 2C 82
Austrey Cl. B93: Know . . . 3C 166
Austrey Gro. B29: W Cas . . . 5E 131
Austrey Rd. DY6: K'wfrd . . . 4E 93
Austy Cl. B36: Hodg H . . . 1C 104
Automotive Components Pk.
WS10: W'bry . . . 2C 62
Autumn Berry Gro.
DY3: Sed . . . 1A 76
Autumn Cl. WS4: S'fld . . . 6G 21
Autumn Dr. DY3: Lwr G . . . 3H 75
WS4: S'fld . . . 6G 21
Autumn Gro. B19: Hock . . . 3E 101
Autumn Ho. B37: K'hrst . . . 4D 106
Avalon Cl. B24: Erd . . . 3H 85
Avebury Gro. B30: Stir . . . 6E 133
Avebury Rd. B30: Stir . . . 5E 133
Ave Maria Cl. B64: Old H . . . 2G 111
Avenbury Dr. B91: Sol . . . 3A 152
Avenue, The B27: A Grn . . . 1B 136
B45: Rubery . . . 2E 157
B65: Row R . . . 6A 96
B76: Walm . . . 4C 70
WV3: Wolv . . . 3H 41
WV4: Penn . . . 1C 58
WV10: F'stne . . . 1D 16
WV10: Wolv . . . 4B 28
Avenue Cl. B7: Nech . . . 3A 102
B93: Dorr . . . 6C 166
Avenue Rd. B6: Aston . . . 3H 101
B7: Nech . . . 3H 101
B14: K Hth . . . 5F 133
B21: Hand . . . 5H 81
B23: Erd . . . 3F 85
B65: B'hth, Row R . . . 2D 112
B93: Dorr . . . 6C 166
DY2: Dud . . . 3B 94
WS10: Darl . . . 5D 46
WV3: Wolv . . . 1C 42
WV14: Cose . . . 5E 61
Averill Rd. B26: Yard . . . 2E 121
Avern Cl. DY4: Tip . . . 1B 78
Aversley Rd. B38: K Nor . . . 6H 145
Avery Ct. B68: O'bry . . . 4H 113
Avery Cft. B35: Cas V . . . 5D 86
Avery Dell Ind. Est. B30: K Nor . . . 2D 146
Avery Dr. B27: A Grn . . . 1A 136
Avery Ho. B16: Edg . . . 2C 116
Avery Myers Cl. B68: O'bry . . . 4H 97
Avery Rd. B66: Smeth . . . 3H 99
B73: New O . . . 3C 68
Aviary Ct. B71: W Brom . . . 1A 80
Aviemore Cres. B43: Gt Barr . . . 1D 66
Avington Cl. DY3: Sed . . . 6H 59
Avion Cen. WV6: Wolv . . . 5E 27
Avion Cl. WS1: Wals . . . 4D 48
Avocet Cl. B33: Stech . . . 6C 104
Avon Cl. B14: K Hth . . . 6F 147
DY5: P'ntt . . . 3F 93
WV6: Pert . . . 6F 25
Avon Ct. B73: S Cold . . . 6H 53
Avon Cres. WS3: Pels . . . 6E 21
Avoncroft Ho. B37: Chel W . . . 1C 122
Avondale Cl. DY6: K'wfrd . . . 1C 92
Avondale Ct. B31: N'fld . . . 6C 144
Avondale Rd. B11: S'hll . . . 1C 134
WV6: Wolv . . . 6D 26
Avon Dr. B13: Mose . . . 3B 134
B36: Cas B . . . 1B 106
WV13: W'hall . . . 1C 46
Avon Gro. WS5: Wals . . . 2E 65
Avon Ho. B15: Birm . . . 3F 117
Avon M. DY8: Word . . . 6H 91
Avon Rd. B63: Crad . . . 6D 110
B90: Shir . . . 6B 150
DY8: Stourb . . . 2D 124
WS3: Blox . . . 6C 20
Avon St. B11: S'hll . . . 6C 118
Avon Way B47: Wyt . . . 6G 161
Avro Way B35: Cas V . . . 5F 87
Awbridge Rd. DY2: Neth . . . 6E 95
Awefields Cres. B67: Smeth . . . 5B 98
Awlmakers Gro. WS3: Blox . . . 2A 32
Axcess 10 Bus. Pk. WS10: W'bry . . . 2E 47
Axletree Way WS10: W'bry . . . 5G 47
Ayala Cft. B36: Hodg H . . . 6C 86
Aylesbury Cres. B44: K'sdng . . . 5A 68
Aylesbury Ho. B31: Longb . . . 1D 158
Aylesford Cl. DY3: Sed . . . 3G 59
Aylesford Dr. B37: Mars G . . . 4C 122
B74: Four O . . . 4E 37
Aylesford Rd. B21: Hand . . . 6H 81
Aylesmore Cl. B32: Bart G . . . 4A 130
B92: Olton . . . 5C 136
Aynsley Ct. B90: Shir . . . 5A 150
Ayre Rd. B24: Erd . . . 3H 85
Ayrshire Cl. B36: Hodg H . . . 1B 104
Ayrton Cl. WV6: Pert . . . 5G 25
Azalea Cl. WV8: Bilb . . . 4H 13
Azalea Gro. B9: Bord G . . . 1F 119
Aziz Isaac Cl. B68: O'bry . . . 3H 97

B

Babington Rd. B21: Hand . . . 2A 100
Bablake Cft. B92: Olton . . . 4E 137
Babors Fld. WV14: Cose . . . 2C 60
Babworth Cl. WV9: Pend . . . 5E 15
Baccabox La. B47: H'wd . . . 2G 161
Bacchus Rd. B18: Hock . . . 3B 100
Bache St. B70: W Brom . . . 6A 80
Bach Mill Dr. B28: Hall G . . . 4D 148
Backhouse La.
WV11: Wed . . . 5E 29
Back La. B64: Crad H . . . 2D 110
B90: Dic H . . . 4G 163
WS9: A'rdge . . . 2H 35
WS14: Foot . . . 1E 37
Back Rd. B38: K Nor . . . 5B 146
DY6: K'wfrd . . . 2B 92
BACONS END . . . 5D 106
Bacons End B37: K'hrst . . . 4D 106
Baddesley Rd. B92: Olton . . . 3C 136
Bader Rd. WS2: Wals . . . 1F 47
WV6: Pert . . . 6E 25
Bader Wlk. B35: Cas V . . . 5D 86
Badger Cl. B90: Ches G . . . 5B 164
Badgers Bank Rd.
B74: Four O . . . 4F 37
Badgers Cl. WS3: Pels . . . 2E 21
Badgers Cft. B62: Hale . . . 4B 112
Badger St. DY3: Up Gor . . . 2A 76
DY9: Lye . . . 5A 110
Badgers Way B34: Stech . . . 4E 105
Badminton Cl. DY1: Dud . . . 4B 76
Badon Covert B14: K Hth . . . 5F 147
Badsey Cl. B31: N'fld . . . 3G 145
Badsey Rd. B69: O'bry . . . 4D 96
Baggeridge Cl. DY3: Sed . . . 5E 59
Baggeridge Country Pk. . . . 1C 74
Baggeridge Country Pk. Vis. Cen. . . . 6D 58
Baggott St. WV2: Wolv . . . 4G 43
Baginton Cl. B91: Sol . . . 2F 151
Baginton Rd. B35: Cas V . . . 3E 87
Bagley Ind. Pk. DY2: Neth . . . 5F 95
Bagley's Rd. DY5: Brie H . . . 5G 109
Bagley St. DY9: Lye . . . 6G 109
Bagnall Cl. B25: Yard . . . 5B 120
Bagnall Rd. WV14: Bils . . . 6E 45
Bagnall St. B70: W Brom . . . 5C 80
(Beeches Rd.)
B70: W Brom . . . 6D 62
(Shaw St.)
DY4: Tip . . . 6D 62
(Chimney Rd.)
DY4: Tip . . . 4C 62
(Newman Rd.)
WS3: Blox . . . 3A 32
Bagnall Wlk. DY5: Brie H . . . 2H 109
Bagnell Rd. B13: Mose . . . 6H 133
Bagot St. B4: Birm . . . 5G 101
Bagridge Cl. WV3: Wolv . . . 3H 41
Bagridge Rd. WV3: Wolv . . . 3H 41
Bagshawe Cft. B23: Erd . . . 6D 68
Bagshaw Rd. B33: Stech . . . 6C 104
Bailey Rd. WV14: Bils . . . 4D 44
Baileys Ct. B65: Row R . . . 6B 96
Bailey St. B70: W Brom . . . 3G 79
WV1: Wolv . . . 1A 44
Bakeman Ho. *B25: Yard* . . . *5B 120*
(off Tivoli, The)
Baker Av. WV14: Cose . . . 3B 60
Baker Ho. Gro. B43: Gt Barr . . . 6H 65
Baker Rd. WV14: Bils . . . 2G 61
Bakers Gdns. WV8: Cod . . . 3E 13
Bakers La. B74: S'tly . . . 6H 51
WS9: A'rdge . . . 3D 34
Baker St. B10: Small H . . . 2D 118
B11: S'hll . . . 1C 134
B21: Hand . . . 1B 100
B70: W Brom . . . 4H 79
DY4: Tip . . . 3G 77
(not continuous)
Bakers Way WV8: Cod . . . 3E 13
Bakewell Cl. WS3: Blox . . . 4A 20
Balaams Wood Dr. B31: Longb . . . 6H 143
Balaclava Rd. B14: K Hth . . . 5G 133
Balcaskie Cl. B15: Edg . . . 4A 116
Balden Rd. B32: Harb . . . 4C 114
Baldmoor Lake Rd. B23: Erd . . . 6F 69
Bald's La. DY9: Lye . . . 6B 110
Baldwin Cl. B69: Tiv . . . 5D 78
Baldwin Rd. B30: K Nor . . . 5C 146
Baldwins Ho. *DY5: Quar B* . . . *3B 110*
(off Maughan St.)
Baldwins La. B28: Hall G . . . 3E 149
Baldwin St. B66: Smeth . . . 3F 99
WV14: Bils . . . 1H 61
Baldwin Way DY3: Swind . . . 5E 73
Balfour Ct. B74: Four O . . . 6G 37
WV6: Wolv . . . *5D 26*
(off Balfour Cres.)
Balfour Cres. WV6: Wolv . . . 5D 26
Balfour Dr. B69: Tiv . . . 5C 78
Balfour Ho. B16: Edg . . . 2B 116
Balfour Rd. DY6: K'wfrd . . . 5D 92
Balfour St. B12: Bal H . . . 5G 117
Balham Gro. B44: K'sdng . . . 3A 68
Balholm B62: Hale . . . 6D 112
Balking Cl. WV14: Cose . . . 2D 60
Ballarat Wlk. DY8: Stourb . . . 6D 108
Ballard Cres. DY2: Neth . . . 4F 95
Ballard Rd. DY2: Neth . . . 4F 95
Ballard Wlk. B37: K'hrst . . . 3C 106
Ballfields DY4: Tip . . . 2D 78
Ball Ho. *WS3: Blox* . . . *1H 31*
(off Somerfield Rd.)
Balliol Bus. Pk. WV9: Pend . . . 4B 14
Balliol Ho. B37: F'bri . . . 1B 122
Ball La. WV10: Cov H . . . 1G 15
Ballot St. B66: Smeth . . . 4F 99
BALLS HILL . . . 5G 63
Balls Hill WS1: Wals . . . 1D 48
Balls St. WS1: Wals . . . 2D 48
Balmain Cres. WV11: Wed . . . 1D 28
Balmoral Cl. B62: Hale . . . 4B 112
WS4: Rus . . . 2H 33
Balmoral Ct. B1: Birm . . . 3A 4
Balmoral Dr. WV5: Wom . . . 4G 57
WV12: W'hall . . . 2B 30
Balmoral Rd. B23: Erd . . . 2F 85
B32: Bart G . . . 6G 129
B36: Cas B . . . 2C 106
B74: Four O . . . 4F 37
DY8: Word . . . 6A 92
WV4: Penn . . . 6E 43
Balmoral Vw. DY1: Dud . . . 5A 76
Balmoral Way B65: Row R . . . 5D 96
WS2: Wals . . . 5G 31
BALSALL . . . 4H 169
BALSALL COMMON . . . 3H 169
BALSALL HEATH . . . 6H 117
Balsall Heath Rd. B5: Bal H . . . 4F 117
B12: Bal H . . . 5G 117
BALSALL STREET . . . 3G 169
Balsall St. CV7: Bal C . . . 4B 168
Balsall St. E. CV7: Bal C . . . 4G 169
Baltimore Rd. B42: P Barr . . . 1C 82
Balvenie Way DY1: Dud . . . 4B 76
Bamber Cl. WV3: Wolv . . . 3C 42
Bamford Cl. WS3: Blox . . . 4A 20
Bamford Ho. WS3: Blox . . . 4A 20
Bamford Rd. WS3: Blox . . . 4A 20
WV3: Wolv . . . 3E 43
Bampfylde Pl. B42: Gt Barr . . . 6E 67
Bamville Rd. B8: W End . . . 4G 103
Banbery Dr. WV5: Wom . . . 3F 73
Banbrook Cl. B92: Sol . . . 5H 137
Banbury Cl. DY3: Sed . . . 1A 76
Banbury Cft. B37: F'bri . . . 1B 122
Banbury Ho. B33: Kitts G . . . 1A 122
Banbury St. B5: Birm . . . 6H 101 (3G 5)
Bancroft Cl. WV14: Cose . . . 6D 60
Bandywood Cres. B44: Gt Barr . . . 2H 67
Bandywood Rd. B44: Gt Barr . . . 1G 67
Banfield Av. WS10: Darl . . . 4C 46
Banfield Rd. WS10: Darl . . . 1C 62
Banford Av. B8: W End . . . 5G 103
Banford Rd. B8: W End . . . 5G 103
Bangham Pit Rd. B31: N'fld . . . 1C 144
Bangley La. B78: Hints . . . 3H 39
Bangor Ho. B37: F'bri . . . 5D 106
Bangor Rd. B9: Bord G . . . 1D 118
Bankdale Rd. B8: W End . . . 5H 103
Bankes Rd. B10: Small H . . . 2E 119
Bank Farm Cl. DY9: Pedm . . . 4G 125
Bankfield Rd. DY4: Tip . . . 5C 62
WV14: Bils . . . 6F 45
(not continuous)
Banklands Rd. DY2: Dud . . . 3G 95
Bank Rd. DY2: Neth . . . 3F 95
DY3: Gorn . . . 4G 75
(not continuous)
Bankside B13: Mose . . . 3D 134
B43: Gt Barr . . . 6A 66
WV5: Wom . . . 6F 57
Bankside Cres. B74: S'tly . . . 4H 51
Bankside Way WS9: A'rdge . . . 5D 22
Banks St. WV13: W'hall . . . 1A 46
Bank St. B14: K Hth . . . 5G 133
B64: Crad H . . . 2E 111
B71: W Brom . . . 1A 80
DY5: Brie H . . . 6H 93
DY9: Lye . . . 6B 110
WS1: Wals . . . 2D 48
WV10: Wolv . . . 4A 28
WV14: Bils . . . 2G 61
WV14: Cose . . . 5D 60
Bankwell St. DY5: Brie H . . . 5G 93
Banner La. B92: Bars . . . 6B 154
Bannerlea Rd. B37: K'hrst . . . 4B 106
Bannerley Rd. B33: Sheld . . . 2G 121
Banners Ct. B73: S'tly . . . 2B 68
BANNERS GATE . . . 1B 68
Banners Ga. Rd. B73: S'tly . . . 2B 68
Banners Gro. B23: Erd . . . 1G 85
Banner's La. B63: Crad . . . 5F 111
Banner's St. B63: Crad . . . 5F 111
Banners Wlk. B44: K'sdng . . . 3B 68
Bannington Ct. WV12: W'hall . . . 5D 30
Bannister Rd. WS10: W'bry . . . 3D 62
Bannister St. B64: Crad H . . . 2F 111
Banstead Cl. WV2: Wolv . . . 4A 44
Bantams Cl. B33: Kitts G . . . 1G 121
Bantock Av. WV3: Wolv . . . 3D 42
Bantock Ct. WV3: Wolv . . . 3C 42
Bantock Gdns. WV3: Wolv . . . 2C 42
Bantock House Mus. . . . 2D 42
Bantocks, The B70: W Brom . . . 1G 79
Bantock Way B17: Harb . . . 6H 115
Banton Cl. B23: Erd . . . 5D 68
Bantry Cl. B26: Sheld . . . 1G 137
BAPTIST END . . . 3E 95
Baptist End Rd. DY2: Dud, Neth . . . 4E 95
Barbara Rd. B28: Hall G . . . 3E 149
Barbel Dr. WV10: Wolv . . . 5C 28
Barberry Ho. B38: K Nor . . . 6B 146
Barbers La. B92: Cath B . . . 1E 153
Barbourne Cl. B91: Sol . . . 2F 165
Barbrook Dr. DY5: Brie H . . . 4F 109
Barcheston Rd. B29: W Cas . . . 4E 131
B93: Know . . . 4C 166
Barclay Ct. WV3: Wolv . . . 1E 43
Barclay Rd. B67: Smeth . . . 2C 114

Barcroft—Beech Hill Rd.

Barcroft WV13: W'hall 6B **30**
Bardenholme Gdns. DY9: W'cte 2H **125**
Bardfield Cl. B42: Gt Barr 5B **66**
Bardon Dr. B90: Shir 5A **150**
Bard St. B11: S'hll 6C **118**
Bardwell Cl. WV8: Pend 1D **26**
Barford Cl. B76: Walm 1D **70**
WS10: Darl 3C **46**
Barford Cres. B38: K Nor 5E **147**
Barford Ho. B5: Birm 4G **117**
Barford Rd. B16: Birm 5A **100**
B90: Shir 5B **150**
Barford St. B5: Birm 3G **117**
Bargate Dr. WV6: Wolv 5E **27**
Bargehouse Wlk. B38: K Nor 2A **160**
Bargery Rd. WV11: Wed 6A **18**
Barham Cl. B90: M'path 4E **165**
Barker Rd. B74: S Cold 4H **53**
Barker St. B19: Loz 2D **100**
B68: O'bry 3A **98**
Bark Piece B32: Bart G 2A **130**
Barlands Cft. B34: S End 3F **105**
Barle Gro. B36: Cas B 2B **106**
Barley Cl. DY3: Sed 6B **60**
WS9: A'rdge 1G **51**
WV8: Pend 6C **14**
Barley Cft. WV6: Pert 6D **24**
Barleyfield Ho. *WS1: Wals* *3C 48*
(off Bath St.)
Barleyfield Ri. DY6: W Hth 1G **91**
Barleyfield Row WS1: Wals 3C **48**
Barlow Cl. B45: Fran 5E **143**
B68: O'bry 6G **97**
Barlow Dr. B70: W Brom 6D **80**
Barlow Rd. WS10: W'bry 6G **47**
Barlow's Rd. B15: Edg 6H **115**
Barmouth Cl. WV12: W'hall 3C **30**
Barnabas Rd. B23: Erd 3F **85**
Barnaby Sq. WV10: Bush 3B **16**
Barnard Cl. B37: Chel W 2F **123**
Barnardo's Cen. B7: Birm 4A **102**
Barnard Pl. WV2: Wolv 5A **44**
Barnard Rd. B75: S Cold 4C **54**
WV11: Wed 6H **17**
Barn Av. DY3: Sed 6G **59**
Barnbrook Rd. B93: Know 2C **166**
Barn Cl. B30: Stir 1D **146**
B63: Hale 3G **127**
B64: Crad H 5G **111**
DY9: Lye 1G **125**
Barncroft B32: Bart G 4C **130**
WS6: Gt Wyr 2G **7**
WS7: Chase 1C **10**
Barncroft Rd. B69: Tiv 1A **96**
Barncroft St. B70: W Brom 5G **63**
Barnes Cl. B37: F'bri 1A **122**
Barnes Hill B29: W Cas 3D **130**
Barnesmeadow Pl. WV14: Cose 5D **60**
Barnesville Cl. B10: Small H 3G **119**
Barnet Rd. B23: Erd 2D **84**
Barnett Cl. DY6: K'wfrd 5B **92**
WV14: Bils 1F **61**
Barnett Grn. DY6: K'wfrd 5B **92**
Barnett La. DY6: K'wfrd 4B **92**
DY8: Word 4B **92**
Barnett Rd. WV13: W'hall 2G **45**
Barnetts La. WS8: Bwnhls 5B **10**
Barnett St. B69: Tiv 5A **78**
DY4: Tip 3A **78**
DY8: Word 6B **92**
Barney Cl. DY4: Tip 4H **77**
Barn Farm Cl. WV14: Bils 4A **46**
Barnfield Dr. B92: Sol 1A **152**
Barnfield Gro. B20: Hand 2A **82**
Barnfield Rd. B62: B'hth 4D **112**
DY4: Tip 6G **61**
WV1: Wolv 1C **44**
Barnfield Trad. Est. DY4: Tip 6G **61**
Barnford Cl. B10: Small H 2C **118**
Barnford Cres. B68: O'bry 6H **97**
Barnfordhill Cl. B68: O'bry 5H **97**
Barn Grn. WV3: Wolv 4D **42**
BARN HILL 4C **162**
Barn Ho. B8: W End 5B **104**
Barnhurst La. WV8: Bilb, Pend 4B **14**
Barn La. B13: Mose 6A **134**
B21: Hand 2A **100**
B92: Olton 1C **136**
Barn Mdw. B25: Yard 2B **120**
Barnmoor Ri. B91: Sol 6G **137**
Barn Owl Dr. WS3: Pels 3D **20**
Barn Owl Wlk. DY5: Brie H 5G **109**
Barnpark Covert B14: K Hth 5E **147**
Barn Piece B32: Quin 1H **129**
Barnsbury Av. B72: W Grn 1A **86**
Barns Cl. WS9: Wals W 3B **22**
Barns Cft. B74: Lit A 5B **36**
Barnsdale Cres. B31: N'fld 3C **144**
Barns La. WS4: Rus 2G **33**
WS9: A'rdge 2H **33**
Barnsley Rd. B17: Edg 2E **115**
Barnstaple Rd. B66: Smeth 4F **99**
Barn St. B5: Birm 1H **117** (5H **5**)
Barnswood Cl. B63: Crad 6E **111**
Barnt Grn. Rd. B45: Coft H 5A **158**
Barnt Green Sailing Club 6E **159**
Barnwood Rd. B32: Quin 1D **130**
WV8: Pend 6C **14**
Barons Cl. B17: Harb 5E **115**
Barons Ct. B92: Sol 1G **137**
Barons Ct. Trad. Est. WS9: Wals W 5A **22**
Barrack Cl. B75: S Cold 5E **55**
Barrack La. B63: Crad 5D **110**
Barracks Cl. WS3: Blox 1C **32**
Barracks La. WS3: Blox 1B **32**
WS8: Bwnhls 4E **11**
Barracks Pl. WS3: Blox 1C **32**
Barrack St. B7: Birm 5A **102**
B70: W Brom 5G **63**
Barra Cft. B35: Cas V 3F **87**
Barrar Cl. DY8: Amb 3C **108**
Barratts Cft. DY5: P'ntt 6G **75**
Barratts Ho. B14: K Hth 5G **147**
Barratts Rd. B38: K Nor 6C **146**
BARR COMMON 6D **34**
Barr Comn. Cl. WS9: A'rdge 6D **34**
Barr Comn. Rd. WS9: A'rdge 6D **34**
Barretts La. CV7: Bal C 6H **169**
Barrhill Cl. B43: Gt Barr 3A **66**
Barrington Cl. WS5: Wals 2E **65**
WV10: Oxl 6G **15**
Barrington Rd. B45: Rubery 2E **157**
B92: Olton 3C **136**
Barr Lakes La. WS9: A'rdge 4A **50**
Barron Rd. B31: N'fld 4F **145**
Barrow Hill Rd. DY5: P'ntt 6G **75**
Barrow Ho. *B16: Edg* *2B 116*
(off Meyrick Wlk.)
Barrows La. B26: Yard 3C **120**
(not continuous)
Barrows Rd. B11: S'brk 5C **118**
Barrow Wlk. B5: Birm 4G **117**
(not continuous)
Barrs Cres. B64: Crad H 3H **111**
Barrs Rd. B64: Crad H 4G **111**
Barrs St. B68: O'bry 5G **97**
Barr St. B19: Hock 4E **101**
(not continuous)
DY3: Lwr G 4G **75**
Barry Jackson Twr. B6: Aston 2H **101**
Barry Rd. WS5: Wals 4G **49**
Barsham Cl. B5: Edg 5E **117**
Barsham Dr. DY5: Brie H 3G **109**
BARSTON 6A **154**
Barston La. B91: Sol 5D **152**
(Ravenshaw, not continuous)
B91: Sol 5B **152**
(Warwick Rd.)
B92: Bars, H Ard 4H **153**
CV7: Bal C 6D **154**
Barston Rd. B68: O'bry 4H **113**
Bartholomew Row B5: Birm 6H **101** (3G **5**)
Bartholomew St. B5: Birm 1H **117** (4G **5**)
Bartic Av. DY6: K'wfrd 5D **92**
Bartleet Rd. B67: Smeth 4B **98**
Bartlett Cl. DY4: Tip 4B **62**
Bartley Cl. B92: Olton 3D **136**
Bartley Dr. B31: N'fld 5C **130**
BARTLEY GREEN 4B **130**
Bartley Green Leisure Cen. 4A **130**
Bartley Ho. B32: Bart G 5B **130**
Bartley Woods B32: Bart G 3H **129**
Barton Cft. B28: Hall G 3F **149**
Barton Dr. B93: Know 6D **166**
Barton Ind. Pk. WV14: Bils 4G **45**
Barton La. DY6: W Hth 1A **92**
Barton Lodge Rd. B28: Hall G 3E **149**
Barton Pas. B3: Birm 4C **4**
Barton Rd. WV4: E'shll 1B **60**
Bartons Bank B6: Aston 2G **101**
Barton St. B70: W Brom 5H **79**
Bar Wlk. WS9: A'rdge 6E **23**
Barwell Cl. B93: Dorr 5A **166**
Barwell Ct. B9: Birm 1B **118**
Barwell Rd. B9: Birm 1B **118**
Barwick St. B3: Birm 6F **101** (3D **4**)
Basalt Cl. WS2: Wals 5G **31**
Basil Gro. B31: N'fld 3C **144**
Basil Rd. B31: N'fld 3C **144**
Baslow Cl. B33: Stech 5C **104**
WS3: Blox 4H **19**
Baslow Rd. WS3: Blox 4H **19**
Bason's La. B68: O'bry 4A **98**
Bassano Rd. B65: B'hth 2C **112**
Bassenthwaite Ct. DY6: K'wfrd 3B **92**
Bassett Cl. B76: Walm 1C **70**
WV4: Penn 5A **42**
WV12: W'hall 5D **30**
Bassett Cft. B10: Small H 3B **118**
Bassett Rd. B63: Crad 5C **110**
WS10: W'bry 2A **64**
(not continuous)
Bassetts Gro. B37: K'hrst 4B **106**
BASSETT'S POLE 1F **55**
Bassett St. WS2: Wals 2H **47**
Bassnage Rd. B63: Hale 3G **127**
Batch Cft. WV14: Bils 6F **45**
Batchcroft WS10: Darl 3D **46**
Batchelor Cl. DY8: Amb 3D **108**
Bateman Dr. B73: W Grn 3H **69**
Bateman Rd. B46: Col 6H **89**
BATEMAN'S GREEN 3G **161**
Batemans La. B47: H'wd, Wyt 4G **161**
Bates Cl. B76: Walm 6F **71**
Bates Gro. WV10: Wolv 4C **28**
Bate St. WS2: Wals 6C **32**
WV4: E'shll 2C **60**
Bath Av. WV1: Wolv 1F **43** (2A **170**)
Bath Ct. B15: Birm 2E **117**
B29: W Cas 6F **131**
Batheaston Cl. B38: K Nor 2H **159**
Bath Mdw. B63: Crad 6G **111**
Bath Pas. B5: Birm 2G **117** (6E **5**)
Bath Rd. DY4: Tip 2A **78**
DY5: Quar B 1C **110**
DY8: Stourb 6D **108**
WS1: Wals 3C **48**
WV1: Wolv 1F **43**
Bath Row B15: Birm 2E **117**
B69: O'bry 1D **96**
Bath St. B4: Birm 5G **101** (1E **5**)
DY2: Dud 1E **95**
DY3: Sed 4A **60**
WS1: Wals 2C **48**
WV1: Wolv 2A **44**
WV13: W'hall 2B **46**
WV14: Bils 6G **45**
Bath Wlk. B12: Bal H 6G **117**
Batmans Hill Rd. DY4: Tip 3G **61**
WV14: Bils 3G **61**
Batson Ri. DY5: Brie H 3E **109**
Battenhall Rd. B17: Harb 6E **115**
Battery Retail Pk. B29: S Oak 3A **132**
Battery Way B11: Tys 1E **135**
Battlefield Hill WV5: Wom 6A **58**
Battlefield La. WV5: Wom 1H **73**
Bavaro Gdns. DY5: Quar B 1C **110**
Baverstock Rd. B14: K Hth 5G **147**
Baxterley Grn. B76: Walm 4D **70**
B91: Sol 3B **150**
Baxter Rd. DY5: Brie H 1G **109**
Baxters Grn. B90: Shir 1G **163**
Baxters Rd. B90: Shir 1H **163**
Bayer St. WV14: Cose 5E **61**
Bayford Av. B26: Sheld 1G **137**
B31: Longb 3C **158**
Bayley Cres. WS10: Darl 3C **46**
Bayley Ho. WS8: Bwnhls 1B **22**
Bayleys La. DY4: Tip 5C **62**
Bayley Twr. B36: Hodg H 1C **104**
Baylie Ct. *DY8: Stourb* *6D 108*
(off Green St.)
Baylie St. DY8: Stourb 1D **124**
Baylis Av. WV11: Wed 1H **29**
Bayliss Av. WV4: E'shll 2C **60**
Bayliss Cl. B31: N'fld 2F **145**
WV14: Bils 4E **45**
Baynton Rd. WV12: W'hall 2C **30**
Bayston Av. WV3: Wolv 3C **42**
Bayston Rd. B14: K Hth 3G **147**
Bayswater Rd. B20: Hand 6F **83**
DY3: Lwr G 4H **75**
Bay Tree Cl. B38: K Nor 1H **159**
Baytree Cl. WS3: Blox 5G **19**
Baytree Rd. WS3: Blox 5G **19**
Baywell Cl. B90: M'path 2E **165**
Beach Av. B12: Bal H 6B **118**
WV14: Cose 2B **60**
Beach Brook Cl. B11: S'hll 6B **118**
Beachburn Way B20: Hand 4C **82**
Beach Cl. B31: N'fld 6G **145**
Beachcroft Rd. DY6: W Hth 6A **74**
Beach Dr. B63: Hale 6A **112**
Beach Rd. B11: S'hll 6B **118**
WV14: Bils 4F **45**
Beach St. B63: Hale 6A **112**
Beach Trade Cen. B12: Bal H 6B **118**
Beachwood Av. DY6: W Hth 6A **74**
Beacon Cl. B43: Gt Barr 4B **66**
B45: Rubery 3G **157**
B66: Smeth 2E **99**
Beacon Ct. B43: Gt Barr 4B **66**
B74: S'tly 3H **51**
Beacon Dr. WS1: Wals 3E **49**
Beacon Hgts. WS9: A'rdge 5D **50**
Beacon Hill B6: Aston 1G **101**
B45: Rubery 4F **157**
WS9: A'rdge 2E **51**
Beacon Ho. *B45: Rubery* *2E 157*
(off Callowbrook La.)
Beacon La. B45: Lick 6D **156**
B60: L Ash 6D **156**
DY3: Sed 4A **60**
Beacon M. B43: Gt Barr 4B **66**
Beacon Pas. *DY3: Sed* *5H 59*
(off High St.)
Beacon Ri. DY3: Sed 4A **60**
DY9: W'cte 1H **125**
WS9: A'rdge 6D **34**
Beacon Rd. B43: Gt Barr 3D **50**
B44: K'sdng 1A **68**
B73: Bold 4G **69**
WS5: Wals 6H **49**
WS9: A'rdge 3D **50**
WV12: W'hall 1C **30**
Beaconsfield Av. WV4: E'shll 5H **43**
Beaconsfield Ct. WS1: Wals 3F **49**
Beaconsfield Cres. B12: Bal H 6G **117**
Beaconsfield Dr. WV4: E'shll 5H **43**
Beaconsfield Rd. B12: Bal H 1G **133**
B74: S Cold 4H **53**
Beaconsfield St. B71: W Brom 2A **80**
Beacon St. WS1: Wals 2E **49**
WV14: Cose 4B **60**
Beacon Trad. Est. WS9: A'rdge 3C **34**
Beacon Vw. B45: Rubery 3F **157**
WS2: Wals 1F **47**
(not continuous)
Beacon Vw. Dr. B74: S'tly 6H **51**
Beaconview Ho. B71: W Brom 4D **64**
Beacon Vw. Rd. B71: W Brom 3C **64**
Beacon Way WS9: Wals W 4C **22**
Beakes Rd. B67: Smeth 6D **98**
Beaks Farm Gdns. B16: Edg 1H **115**
Beaks Hill Rd. B38: K Nor 6A **146**
Beak St. B1: Birm 1F **117** (5D **4**)
Beale Cl. B35: Cas V 5E **87**
Beale Ho. B16: Edg 2B **116**
Beales St. B6: Aston 1B **102**
Beale St. DY8: Stourb 6D **108**
Bealeys Av. WV11: Wed 1E **29**
Bealeys Cl. WS3: Blox 4G **19**
Bealeys Fold *WV11: Wed* *4F 29*
(off Nicholls Fold)
Bealeys La. WS3: Blox 4G **19**
Beamans Cl. B92: Olton 1E **137**
Beaminster Rd. B91: Sol 3E **151**
Beamish La. WV8: Cod W 2A **12**
Beamont Cl. DY4: Tip 1G **77**
Bean Cft. B32: Bart G 2A **130**
Bean Rd. DY2: Dud 1F **95**
DY4: Tip 1E **77**
Bean Rd. Ind. Est. DY4: Tip 1E **77**
Beardmore Rd. B72: W Grn 5A **70**
Bearley Cft. B90: Shir 1A **164**
Bearmore Rd. B64: Old H 2G **111**
Bearnett Dr. WV4: Penn 3A **58**
Bearnett La. WV4: Lwr P 4H **57**
WV5: Wom 4H **57**
BEAR WOOD 2E **115**
Bearwood Ho. B66: Smeth 5E **99**
Bearwood Rd. B66: Smeth 2E **115**
Bearwood Shop. Cen. B66: Smeth 2E **115**
Beasley Gro. B43: Gt Barr 4D **66**
Beaton Cl. WV13: W'hall 1G **45**
Beaton Rd. B74: Four O 6G **37**
Beatrice St. WS3: Blox 3A **32**
Beatrice Wlk. B69: Tiv 5A **78**
Beatty Ho. DY4: Tip 5A **62**
Beaubrook Gdns. DY8: Word 6C **92**
Beauchamp Av. B20: Hand 2B **82**
Beauchamp Cl. B37: Chel W 1D **122**
B76: Walm 6F **71**
Beauchamp Rd. B13: Mose 2B **148**
B91: Sol 2F **151**
Beaudesert Cl. B47: H'wd 3A **162**
Beaudesert Rd. B20: Hand 1D **100**
B47: H'wd 3A **162**
Beaufort Av. B34: Hodg H 3B **104**
Beaufort Pk. B8: W End 4B **104**
Beaufort Rd. B16: Edg 2B **116**
B23: Erd 5E **85**
Beaufort Way WS9: A'rdge 5D **34**
Beaulieu Av. DY6: K'wfrd 5D **92**
Beaumaris Cl. DY1: Dud 4B **76**
Beaumont Cl. WS6: Gt Wyr 3F **7**
Beaumont Dr. B17: Harb 1F **131**
DY5: Brie H 4F **109**
Beaumont Gdns. B18: Hock 3B **100**
Beaumont Gro. B91: Sol 2D **150**
Beaumont Pk. B30: K Nor 3B **146**
Beaumont Rd. B30: B'vlle 1A **146**
B62: B'hth 3E **113**
WS6: Gt Wyr 3F **7**
WS10: W'bry 1F **63**
Beaumont Way WS11: Nort C 1E **9**
Beausale Dr. B93: Know 2D **166**
Beauty Bank B64: Crad H 3A **112**
Beauty Bank Cres. DY8: Stourb 5C **108**
Beaver Cl. WV11: Wed 4H **29**
Bebington Cl. WV8: Pend 1D **26**
Beccles Dr. WV13: W'hall 3H **45**
Beckbury Av. WV4: Penn 6A **42**
Beckbury Rd. B29: W Cas 4E **131**
Beck Cl. B66: Smeth 5E **99**
Beckenham Av. B44: K'sdng 4A **68**
Beckensall Cl. DY1: Dud 6D **76**
Becket Cl. B74: Four O 3F **37**
Beckett St. WV14: Bils 5G **45**
Beckfield Cl. B14: K Hth 5G **147**
WS4: S'fld 1G **33**
Beckford Cft. B93: Dorr 6B **166**
Beckman Rd. DY9: Pedm 3G **125**
Beckminster Rd. WV3: Wolv 4D **42**
Beconsfield Cl. B93: Dorr 6G **167**
Becton Gro. B42: Gt Barr 6F **67**
Bedcote Pl. DY8: Stourb 6F **109**
Beddoe Cl. DY4: Tip 2D **78**
Beddow Av. WV14: Cose 6E **61**
Beddows Rd. WS3: Wals 4C **32**
Bedford Dr. B75: S Cold 5C **54**
Bedford Ho. B36: Cas B 3D **106**
WV1: Wolv 5G **27**
Bedford Rd. B11: S'brk 2A **118**
B71: W Brom 6H **63**
B75: S Cold 5C **54**
Bedford St. DY4: Tip 2B **78**
WV1: Wolv 4D **44**
Bedford Ter. B19: Loz 1F **101**
Bedlam Wood Rd. B31: Longb 6A **144**
Bedworth Cft. DY4: Tip 3B **78**
Bedworth Gro. B9: Bord G 1H **119**
Beebee Rd. WS10: W'bry 5F **47**
Beecham Bus. Pk. WS9: A'rdge 1C **34**
Beecham Cl. WS9: A'rdge 1C **34**
Beech Av. B12: Bal H 6A **118**
B32: Quin 4B **114**
B37: Chel W 2D **122**
B62: B'hth 3C **112**
Beech Cl. B75: Four O 5G **37**
DY3: Sed 4A **60**
WV10: Oxl 1F **27**
Beech Ct. B8: Salt 4E **103**
B30: K Nor 3A **146**
B43: Gt Barr 4H **65**
B45: Redn 2B **158**
B66: Smeth 1A **98**
B73: Bold 5F **69**
B91: Sol 2H **151**
DY8: Stourb 1F **125**
WS1: Wals 3E **49**
WS6: Gt Wyr 1G **7**
Beech Cres. DY4: Tip 5C **62**
WS10: W'bry 6F **47**
Beechcroft B15: Edg 4C **116**
Beechcroft Av. B28: Hall G 1G **149**
Beechcroft Ct. B74: Four O 2G **53**
Beechcroft Cres. B74: S'tly 2F **51**
Beechcroft Est. B63: Crad 5E **111**
Beechcroft Pl. WV10: Oxl 2G **27**
Beechcroft Rd. B36: Cas B 1F **105**
B64: Old H 2G **111**
Beechdale B68: O'bry 4H **113**
Beechdale Av. B44: Gt Barr 3G **67**
Beech Dene Gro. B23: Erd 2E **85**
Beecher Pl. B63: Crad 6F **111**
Beecher Rd. B63: Crad 6F **111**
Beecher Rd. E. B63: Crad 6F **111**
Beecher St. B63: Crad 6E **111**
Beeches, The B15: Edg 3E **117**
B70: W Brom 5C **80**
B74: Four O 5D **36**
WV1: Wolv 6E **27**
Beeches Av. B27: A Grn 1A **136**
Beeches Cl. B45: Rubery 2D **156**
DY6: K'wfrd 4B **92**
Beeches Ct. B45: Redn 2H **157**
Beeches Dr. B24: Erd 2A **86**
Beeches Farm Dr.
B31: Longb 2E **159**
Beeches Pl. WS3: Blox 2B **32**
Beeches Rd. B42: Gt Barr 6D **66**
B65: B'hth 2B **112**
B68: O'bry 6A **98**
B70: W Brom 4C **80**
(not continuous)
WS3: Blox 3B **32**
Beeches Vw. Av. B63: Crad 1E **127**
Beeches Wlk. B73: W Grn 2H **69**
Beeches Way B31: Longb 2E **159**
Beechey Cl. B43: Gt Barr 6F **51**
Beech Farm Cft. B31: N'fld 4E **145**
Beechfield Av. B11: S'brk 5B **118**
Beechfield Cl. B62: B'hth 3C **112**
Beechfield Gro.
WV14: Cose 6D **60**
Beechfield Rd. B11: S'brk 5B **118**
B67: Smeth 5D **98**
Beech Gdns. WV8: Cod 5F **13**
Beech Ga. B74: Lit A 4B **36**
Beechglade B20: Hand 3B **82**
Beech Grn. DY1: Dud 2C **76**
Beech Gro. B14: K Hth 2A **148**
Beech Hill Rd. B72: W Grn 6A **70**

Beech Ho.—Birch Ct.

Beech Ho. *B31: N'fld* 4F 145
(off Church Rd.)
B91: Sol 5D 150
Beechhouse La. WV5: Seis 5A 56
Beech Hurst B38: K Nor 1A 160
Beech Hurst Gdns. WV5: Seis 3A 56
BEECH LANES 4D 114
Beech M. B64: Old H 1G 111
Beechmore Rd. B26: Sheld 6D 120
Beechmount Dr. B23: Erd 1G 85
Beechnut Cl. B91: Sol 2H 151
Beechnut La. B91: Sol 3A 152
(not continuous)
Beech Rd. B23: Erd 6F 69
B30: B'vlle 6A 132
B47: H'wd 3B 162
B69: Tiv 1A 96
DY1: Dud 3E 77
DY6: K'wfrd 4C 92
DY8: Stourb 2C 124
WS10: W'bry 6F 47
WV10: Oxl 1F 27
WV13: W'hall 1G 45
Beech St. WV14: Cose 5E 61
Beech Tree Av. WV11: Wed 1E 29
Beech Tree Cl. DY6: K'wfrd 1C 92
Beechtree Rd. WS9: Wals W 4B 22
Beech Wlk. B38: K Nor 1B 160
Beech Way B66: Smeth 4F 99
Beechwood B20: Hand 4A 82
Beechwood Av. WV11: Wed 1D 28
Beechwood Cl. B90: Ches G 5C 164
WS3: Blox 4H 19
Beechwood Ct. B30: K Nor 4E 147
WV6: Tett 6A 26
Beechwood Cft. B74: Lit A 4D 36
Beechwood Dr. WV6: Tett 1G 41
Beechwood Pk. Rd. B91: Sol 1C 150
Beechwood Rd. B14: K Hth 2H 147
B43: Gt Barr 4B 66
B67: Smeth 3C 114
B70: W Brom 4H 79
DY2: Dud 6G 77
Beehive La. B76: Curd 1E 89
Beehive Wlk. DY4: Tip 2G 77
Bee La. WV10: F'hses 4H 15
Beeston Cl. B6: Aston 2A 102
DY5: Brie H 3H 109
Beeton Rd. B18: Win G 3A 100
Beet St. B65: B'hth 2C 112
Beever Rd. DY4: Tip 6D 62
Beggars Bush La. WV5: Wom 2H 73
Beighton Cl. B74: Four O 3F 37
Beilby Rd. B30: Stir 1D 146
Belbroughton Rd. B63: Hale 3H 127
DY8: Stourb 2C 124
Belcher's La. B9: Bord G 1G 119
Beldray Pk. WV14: Bils 5G 45
Beldray Rd. WV14: Bils 5G 45
Belfont Trad. Est. B62: Hale 1C 128
Belfry, The WV6: Pert 5D 24
Belfry Cl. WS3: Blox 4G 19
Belfry Dr. DY8: Woll 5C 108
Belgrade Rd. WV10: Oxl 6F 15
Belgrave Ct. DY6: K'wfrd 5D 92
Belgrave Interchange B5: Birm 4F 117
Belgrave Middleway B5: Birm 4G 117
B12: Birm 4G 117
Belgrave Rd. B62: B'hth 3D 112
Belgrave Ter. B21: Hand 2C 100
Belgrave Wlk. WS2: Wals 6H 31
Belgravia Cl. B5: Bal H 4G 117
Belgravia Cl. Walkway B5: Bal H 4G 117
Belgravia Ct. B37: K'hrst 4C 106
Belgrove Cl. B15: Edg 5A 116
Belinda Cl. WV13: W'hall 6H 29
Bellamy Cl. B90: Shir 6B 150
Bellamy Farm Rd. B90: Shir 6B 150
Bellamy La. WV11: Wed 2E 29
Bell Av. WV13: W'hall 1A 46
Bell Barn Rd. B15: Birm 3E 117
Bell Barn Shop. Cen. B15: Birm 2E 117
Bell Cl. B9: Bord G 1E 119
B36: Cas B 3D 106
WS10: Darl 4D 46
Bellcroft B16: Birm 1D 116
Bell Dr. B8: Salt 6F 103
WS5: Wals 6E 49
Bellefield Av. B18: Win G 5A 100
Bellefield Rd. B18: Win G 5A 100
Belle Isle DY5: Brie H 6G 93
Bellemere Rd. B92: H Ard 2B 154
Bellencroft Gdns. WV3: Wolv 4A 42
Bell End B65: Row R 6C 96
Bellevale B63: Hale 6G 111
Belle Vue DY8: Word 1A 108
Bellevue B5: Bal H 4F 117
Bellevue Av. B16: Edg 5H 99
Belle Vue Dr. B62: Hale 5D 112
Belle Vue Gdns. B65: Row R 6C 96
Belle Vue Rd. B65: Row R 1C 112
DY5: Quar B 2C 110
Bellevue Rd. B26: Sheld 4F 121
WV14: Bils 3A 62
Bellevue St. WV14: Cose 3B 60
Belle Vue Ter. B92: H Ard 1A 154
Belle Wlk. B13: Mose 3B 134
Bellfield B31: N'fld 3D 144
Bellfield Ho. *B14: K Hth* 6F 147
(off Thornham Way)
Bell Flwr Dr. WS5: Wals 2D 64
Bell Fold B68: O'bry 3A 98
BELL GREEN
Birmingham 3D 160
Bell Grn. La. B38: Head H 4D 160
Bell Heather Rd. WS8: Clay 1H 21
Bell Heath Way B32: Bart G 3G 129
Bell Hill B31: N'fld 2E 145
Bell Holloway B31: N'fld 2D 144
Bellington Cft. B90: M'path 3E 165
Bell Inn Shop. Cen., The B31: N'fld 3E 145
Bellis St. B16: Edg 2B 116
Bell La. B31: N'fld 3E 145
B33: Kitts G 2A 122
WS3: Blox 5G 19
WS5: Wals 1D 64
Bellman Cl. WS10: Darl 4D 46
Bell Mdw. DY9: Pedm 5F 125
Bell Mdw. Way B14: K Hth 5G 147
(not continuous)
Bell Pl. WV2: Wolv 3G 43 (6B 170)
Bell Rd. DY2: Neth 4E 95
WS5: Wals 5H 49
WV5: Try 4C 56
Bells Farm Cl. B14: K Hth 5E 147
Bellsize Cl. WS11: Nort C 1D 8
Bells La. B14: K Hth 5D 146
DY8: Word 2B 108
Bells Moor Rd. B70: W Brom 1G 79
Bell St. B70: W Brom 5B 80
DY4: Tip 2G 77
DY5: Brie H 1H 109
DY5: P'ntt 3H 93
(Belmont Rd.)
DY5: P'ntt 2H 93
(Hartland St.)
DY8: Stourb 6D 108
WS10: Darl 4D 46
WV1: Wolv 2G 43 (4B 170)
WV14: Bils 5E 45
WV14: Cose 3E 61
Bell St. Sth. DY5: Brie H 1H 109
Bell Wlk. B37: F'bri 2B 122
Bell Wharf Pl. WS5: Wals 5G 49
Bellwood Rd. B31: N'fld 3D 144
Belmont Cl. DY4: Tip 1H 77
WS9: A'rdge 3C 34
WS11: Cann 1G 7
Belmont Covert B31: N'fld 2F 145
Belmont Cres. B31: N'fld 1F 145
Belmont Gdns. WV14: Bils 1A 62
Belmont Pas. B9: Birm 1A 118
Belmont Rd. B21: Hand 1G 99
B45: Rubery 3G 157
B66: Smeth 1E 115
DY5: P'ntt 3H 93
DY9: W'cte 6A 110
WV4: Penn 6E 43
Belmont Rd. E. B21: Hand 1G 99
Belmont Row B4: Birm 6A 102 (2H 5)
Belmont St. WV14: Bils 1A 62
Belper, The DY1: Dud 6D 76
Belper Ent. Pk. B70: W Brom 3F 79
Belper Rd. B70: W Brom 4F 79
WS3: Blox 4A 20
Belper Row DY2: Neth 5G 95
Belstone Cl. B14: K Hth 1F 147
Belton Av. WV11: Wed 6D 16
Belton Gro. B45: Redn 1A 158
Belvedere Av. WV4: Penn 6F 43
Belvedere Cl. DY6: K'wfrd 5D 92
WS7: Chase 1B 10
Belvedere Gdns. WV6: Tett 2C 26
Belvedere Rd. B24: Erd 5G 85
Belvide Gdns. WV8: Cod 3F 13
Belvide Gro. B29: W Cas 5F 131
Belvidere Gdns. B11: S'hll 1C 134
Belvidere Rd. WS1: Wals 3D 48
Belvoir Cl. DY1: Dud 5A 76
Belwell Dr. B74: Four O 1G 53
Belwell La. B74: Four O 1G 53
Bembridge Cl. WV12: W'hall 1B 30
Bembridge Rd. B33: Yard 6E 105
Benacre Dr. B5: Birm 1H 117 (4H 5)
Benbeck Gro. DY4: Tip 2E 77
Bencroft WV8: Bilb 3H 13
Bendall Rd. B44: K'sdng 3B 68
Benedon Rd. B26: Sheld 4E 121
Benmore Av. B5: Bal H 5F 117
Bennett Av. DY1: Dud 1D 76
Bennett Rd. B74: Four O 1D 52
Bennett's Fold WV3: Wolv 2G 43 (4A 170)
Bennett's Hill B2: Birm 1F 117 (4D 4)
DY2: Dud 1G 95
Bennett's La. WV6: Tres 3A 40
Bennett's Rd. B8: Salt 3D 102
Bennett St. B19: Loz 1F 101
Ben Nevis Way DY8: Amb 5E 109
Bennitt Cl. B70: W Brom 6A 80
Benson Av. WV4: Penn 6G 43
Benson Cl. WV6: Pert 4E 25
Benson Ind. Est. B18: Hock 3C 100
Benson Rd. B14: K Hth 6B 148
B18: Hock 3B 100
Bent Av. B32: Quin 5B 114
Bentham Ct. B31: N'fld 2D 144
BENTLEY 6F 31
Bentley Bridge Leisure Pk. 5D 28
Bentley Bri. Way WV11: Wed 5D 28
Bentley Ct. B76: Walm 5D 70
Bentley Dr. WS2: Wals 1H 47
WV8: Cod 3F 13
Bentley Farm Cl. B93: Ben H 5A 166
Bentley Gro. B29: W Cas 5D 130
BENTLEY HEATH 4B 166
Bentley Heath Cotts. B93: Know 4B 166
Bentley La. WS2: Wals 5G 31
WV12: W'hall 4D 30
Bentley La. Ind. Pk. WS2: Wals 6G 31
Bentley Mill Cl. WS2: Wals 2F 47
Bentley Mill La. WS2: Wals 2F 47
Bentley Mill Way WS2: Wals 2F 47
Bentley New Dr. WS2: Wals 6H 31
Bentley Pl. WS2: Wals 1H 47
Bentley Rd. B36: Cas B 2H 105
WV10: Bush 5A 16
Bentley Rd. Nth. WS2: Wals 2E 47
Bentley Rd. Sth. WS10: Darl 3D 46
Bentmead Gro. B38: K Nor 6C 146
Benton Av. B11: S'hll 5C 118
Benton Cl. WV12: W'hall 5D 30
Benton Cres. WS3: Blox 5B 20
Benton Rd. B11: S'brk 5C 118
Bentons La. WS6: Gt Wyr 4G 7
Bentons Mill Cft. B7: Nech 1C 102
Bent St. DY5: Brie H 5H 93
Ben Willetts Wlk. B65: B'hth 2C 112
Benyon Cen., The WS2: Wals 2G 31
Beoley Cl. B72: W Grn 4A 70
Beoley Gro. B45: Rubery 2F 157
Berberry Cl. B30: B'vlle 1H 145
Beresford Cres. B70: W Brom 4H 79
Beresford Dr. B73: Bold 4G 69
Beresford Rd. B69: O'bry 2A 98
WS3: Blox 1C 32
Berets, The B75: S Cold 5D 54
Bericote Cft. B27: A Grn 2B 136
Berkeley Cl. WV6: Pert 6F 25
Berkeley Dr. DY6: K'wfrd 2A 92
Berkeley M. B25: Yard 4G 119
Berkeley Pct. B14: K Hth 5H 147
Berkeley Rd. B25: Yard 4G 119
B90: Shir 4F 149
Berkeley Rd. E. B25: Yard 4H 119
Berkeley St. WS2: Wals 4H 47
Berkley Cl. WS2: Wals 6F 31
Berkley Ct. B1: Birm 2E 117 (6A 4)
Berkley Cres. B13: Mose 4C 134
Berkley Ho. B23: Erd 1F 85
Berkley St. B1: Birm 1E 117 (5A 4)
Berkshire, The WS3: Blox 4G 19
Berkshire Cl. B71: W Brom 6H 63
Berkshire Cres. WS10: W'bry 1A 64
Berkswell Cl. B74: Four O 5E 37
B91: Sol 5F 137
DY1: Dud 4A 76
Berkswell Hall CV7: Berk 4H 155
Berkswell Rd. B24: Erd 3H 85
Bermuda Cl. DY1: Dud 1D 76
Bernard Pl. B18: Hock 4B 100
Bernard Rd. B17: Edg 1F 115
B68: O'bry 1A 114
DY4: Tip 6B 62
Bernard St. B71: W Brom 3A 80
WS1: Wals 3E 49
Berners St. B19: Loz 2F 101
Bernhard Dr. B21: Hand 1A 100
Bernwall Cl. DY8: Stourb 1D 124
Berrandale Rd. B36: Hodg H 1D 104
Berrington Dr. WV14: Cose 5D 60
Berrington Wlk. B5: Birm 4G 117
Berrow Cott. Homes B93: Know 3E 167
Berrow Dr. B15: Edg 4A 116
Berrowside Rd. B34: S End 3A 106
Berry Av. WS10: Darl 6B 46
Berrybush Gdns. DY3: Sed 6A 60
Berry Cl. B19: Hock 3F 101
Berry Cres. WS5: Wals 1G 65
Berry Dr. B66: Smeth 3E 99
WS9: A'rdge 4A 34
Berryfield Rd. B26: Sheld 5H 121
Berryfields WS9: A'rdge 4A 34
WS9: Ston 2G 23
Berryfields Rd. B76: Walm 2D 70
Berry Hall La. B91: Cath B, Sol 3C 152
Berrymound Vw. B47: H'wd 2C 162
Berry Rd. B8: Salt 4E 103
DY1: Dud 2E 77
Berry St. B18: Hock 3B 100
WV1: Wolv 1H 43 (3C 170)
Bertha Rd. B11: S'brk 6D 118
Bertram Cl. DY4: Tip 4C 62
Bertram Rd. B9: Small H 2D 118
B67: Smeth 3C 98
Berwick Gro. B31: N'fld 4B 144
B43: Gt Barr 1D 66
Berwicks La. B37: Chel W 2D 122
(not continuous)
Berwood Farm Rd. B72: W Grn 1A 86
Berwood Gdns. B24: Erd 2A 86
Berwood Gro. B92: Olton 4F 137
Berwood La. B24: Erd 4C 86
Berwood Pk. B35: Cas V 5E 87
Berwood Rd. B72: W Grn 1B 86
Berwyn Gro. WS6: C Hay 2F 7
Besant Gro. B27: A Grn 4G 135
Besbury Cl. B93: Dorr 6F 167
BESCOT 5A 48
Bescot Cres. WS1: Wals 5B 48
Bescot Cft. B42: Gt Barr 1D 82
Bescot Dr. WS2: Wals 5H 47
Bescot Ind. Est. WS10: W'bry 1D 62
Bescot Rd. WS2: Wals 5H 47
Bescot Stadium 5B 48
Bescot Stadium Station (Rail) 6B 48
Bescot St. WS1: Wals 4B 48
Besford Gro. B31: N'fld 4B 144
B90: M'path 3F 165
Besom Way WS6: C Hay 3C 6
Bessborough Rd. B25: Yard 3B 120
Best Rd. WV14: Bils 4F 45
Best St. B64: Old H 1H 111
Beswick Gro. B33: Kitts G 5E 105
Beta Gro. B14: Yard W 3C 148
Betjeman Pl. WV10: Bush 6C 16
Betley Gro. B33: Stech 4E 105
Betony Cl. WS5: Wals 2E 65
Betsham Cl. B44: K'sdng 4B 68
Bettany Glade WV10: Bush 3A 16
Betteridge Dr. B76: Walm 1C 70
Betton Rd. B14: K Hth 2G 147
Bett Rd. B20: Hand 4B 82
Betty's La. WS11: Nort C 1D 8
Beulah Ct. B63: Hale 1A 128
Bevan Av. WV4: E'shll 1A 60
Bevan Cl. WS4: S'fld 6G 21
WV14: Bils 5H 45
Bevan Ind. Est. DY5: Brie H 1E 109
Bevan Rd. DY4: Tip 3B 78
DY5: Brie H 1E 109
Bevan Way B66: Smeth 1D 98
Beverley Cl. B72: W Grn 6A 70
CV7: Bal C 5H 169
Beverley Ct. Rd. B32: Quin 5A 114
Beverley Cres. WV4: E'shll 1B 60
Beverley Cft. B23: Erd 6D 84
Beverley Dr. DY6: K'wfrd 2A 92
Beverley Gro. B26: Sheld 6F 121
Beverley Rd. B45: Rubery 2G 157
B71: W Brom 4B 64
Beverston Rd. DY4: Tip 3B 62
WV6: Pert 5G 25
Bevington Rd. B6: Aston 6H 83
Bevin Rd. WS2: Wals 6E 31
Bevis Gro. B44: Gt Barr 2H 67
Bewdley Av. B12: Bal H 5A 118
Bewdley Dr. WV1: Wolv 1D 44
Bewdley Ho. B26: Yard 1E 121
Bewdley Rd. B30: Stir 5D 132
Bewdley Vs. *B18: Win G* 5H 99
(off Cape St.)
Bewlay Cl. DY5: Brie H 4F 109
Bewley Rd. WV12: W'hall 5D 30
Bewlys Av. B20: Hand 3A 82
Bexley Gro. B71: W Brom 6C 64
Bexley Rd. B44: K'sdng 5B 68
Bhylls Cres. WV3: Wolv 4A 42
Bhylls La. WV3: Wolv 3H 41
Bibbey's Grn. WV10: Bush 3B 16
Bibsworth Av. B13: Mose 5D 134
Bibury Rd. B28: Hall G 6E 135
BICC & Symphony Hall 1E 117 (4A 4)
Bicester Sq. B35: Cas V 3F 87
BICKENHILL 4F 139
Bickenhill Grn. Ct. B92: Bick 4F 139
Bickenhill La. B37: Mars G 5E 123
(not continuous)
B92: Cath B 1E 153
Bickenhill Pk. Rd. B92: Olton 4B 136
Bickenhill Parkway B40: Nat E C 5F 123
Bickenhill Rd. B37: Mars G 4C 122
Bickenhill Trad. Est. B40: Mars G 6F 123
Bickford Rd. B6: Witt 6A 84
WV10: Wolv 4B 28
Bickington Rd. B32: Bart G 4B 130
Bickley Av. B11: S'brk 5C 118
B74: Four O 4E 37
Bickley Gro. B26: Sheld 6F 121
Bickley Rd. WS4: Rus 2G 33
WV14: Bils 4A 46
Bicknell Cft. B14: K Hth 5G 147
Bickton Cl. B24: Erd 1A 86
Biddings La. WV14: Cose 3D 60
Biddlestone Gro. WS5: Wals 1G 65
Biddlestone Pl. WS10: Darl 4B 46
Biddulph Ct. B73: S Cold 3G 69
Bideford Dr. B29: S Oak 4G 131
Bideford Rd. B66: Smeth 4F 99
Bidford Cl. B90: Shir 5B 150
Bidford Rd. B31: N'fld 4C 144
Bierton Rd. B25: Yard 3A 120
Biggin Cl. B35: Cas V 4E 87
WV6: Pert 4E 25
Big Peg, The B18: Birm 5E 101 (1A 4)
Bigwood Dr. B32: Bart G 4B 130
B75: S Cold 5E 55
Bilberry Cres. B76: Walm 2C 70
Bilberry Dr. B45: Rubery 3G 157
Bilberry Rd. B14: K Hth 1E 147
Bilboe Rd. WV14: Bils 2H 61
BILBROOK 3H 13
Bilbrook Ct. WV8: Bilb 4H 13
Bilbrook Gro. B29: W Cas 3D 130
WV8: Bilb 4H 13
Bilbrook Ho. WV8: Bilb 4H 13
Bilbrook Rd. WV8: Bilb, Cod 3G 13
(not continuous)
Bilbrook Station (Rail) 5H 13
Bilhay La. B70: W Brom 2G 79
Bilhay St. B70: W Brom 2G 79
Billau Rd. WV14: Cose 3F 61
BILLESLEY 1C 148
Billesley Indoor Tennis Cen. 6B 134
Billesley La. B13: Mose 5H 133
Billingham Cl. B91: Sol 1F 165
Billingsley Rd. B26: Yard 3E 121
Bills La. B90: Shir 6F 149
Billsmore Grn. B92: Sol 6G 137
Bills St. WS10: Darl 4E 47
Billy Buns La. WV5: Wom 5G 57
Billy Wright Cl. WV4: Penn 5C 42
Bilport La. WS10: W'bry 5F 63
BILSTON 6H 45
Bilston Central Ind. Est. WV14: Bils 6G 45
Bilston Central (MM) 6F 45
Bilston Craft Gallery & Mus. 5G 45
Bilston Ind. Est. WV14: Bils 6A 46
Bilston Key Ind. Est. WV14: Bils 6H 45
Bilston Leisure Cen. 5F 45
Bilston Rd. DY4: Tip 3B 62
WS10: W'bry 2D 62
WV2: Wolv 2A 44 (4D 170)
WV13: W'hall 4A 46
Bilston St. DY3: Sed 5H 59
WS10: Darl 5D 46
(not continuous)
WV1: Wolv 2H 43 (4C 170)
WV13: W'hall 2A 46
Bilston St. Island
WV1: Wolv 2H 43 (4D 170)
Bilton Grange Rd. B26: Yard 4D 120
Bilton Ind. Est. B38: K Nor 1A 160
Binbrook Rd. WV12: W'hall 5D 30
Bincomb Av. B26: Sheld 5F 121
Binfield St. DY4: Tip 3A 78
Bingley Av. B8: W End 5H 103
Bingley Ent. Cen. *WV3: Wolv* 3E 43
(off Norfolk Rd.)
Bingley St. WV3: Wolv 3E 43
Binley Cl. B25: Yard 5B 120
B90: Shir 1G 163
Binstead Rd. B44: K'sdng 3A 68
Binswood Rd. B62: Quin 4G 113
Binton Cft. B13: Mose 5H 133
Binton Rd. B90: Shir 6F 149
Birbeck Ho. B36: Cas B 3D 106
Birbeck Pl. DY5: P'ntt 3F 93
Birchall St. B12: Birm 2H 117
Birch Av. B31: Longb 6A 144
DY5: Quar B 1C 110
WS8: Bwnhls 5A 10
Birch Cl. B17: Harb 6H 115
B30: B'vlle 1H 145
B76: Walm 3D 70
Birch Coppice DY5: Quar B 2C 110
(not continuous)
WV5: Wom 1E 73
Birchcoppice Gdns.
WV12: W'hall 5E 31
Birch Ct. B30: K Nor 3A 146
B66: Smeth 1B 98
WS4: Wals 5E 33
(off Lichfield Rd.)
WV1: Wolv 5G 27

176 A-Z Birmingham Deluxe

Birch Cres.—Booth Ho.

Birch Cres. B69: Tiv 6A **78**
Birch Cft. B24: Erd 2B **86**
B37: Chel W 2E **123**
WS9: A'rdge 1E **35**
Birchcroft B66: Smeth. 4G **99**
Birch Cft. Rd. B75: S Cold 4B **54**
Birchdale WV14: Bils. 4F **45**
Birchdale Av. B23: Erd 3E **85**
Birchdale Rd. B23: Erd. 2D **84**
Birch Dr. B62: B'hth 2E **113**
B74: Lit A 4D **36**
B75: S Cold 4D **54**
DY8: Stourb 5C **108**
Birches Av. WV8: Bilb 6A **14**
Birches Barn Av. WV3: Wolv 4D **42**
Birches Barn Rd. WV3: Wolv 3D **42**
Birches Cl. B13: Mose 4H **133**
BIRCHES GREEN 5G **85**
Birches Grn. Rd. B24: Erd 5H **85**
Birches Pk. Rd. WV8: Cod 5G **13**
Birches Ri. WV13: W'hall 2A **46**
Birches Rd. WV8: Bilb 5G **13**
BIRCHFIELD 5E **83**
Birchfield Av. WV6: Tett 3H **25**
Birchfield Cl. B63: Hale 3G **127**
Birchfield Cres. DY9: W'cte 2B **126**
Birchfield Gdns. B6: Aston 1F **101**
WS5: Wals 1G **65**
Birchfield La. B69: O'bry 5E **97**
(not continuous)
Birchfield Rd. B19: Loz 1F **101**
B20: Hand 6F **83**
DY9: W'cte 2B **126**
Birchfields Rd. WV12: W'hall 4A **30**
Birchfield Twr. B20: Hand 6F **83**
Birchfield Way WS5: Wals 1F **65**
Birch Ga. DY9: W'cte 1B **126**
Birchglade WV3: Wolv 2B **42**
Birch Gro. B68: O'bry 4B **114**
CV7: Bal C 1H **169**
Birch Hill Av. WV5: Wom 2F **73**
Birch Hollow B15: Edg 5B **116**
B68: O'bry 4B **114**
Birchill Pl. WV5: Wom 2F **73**
Birchills Canal Mus. 5A **32**
Birchills Ho. Ind. Est.
WS2: Wals 5B **32**
Birchills St. WS2: Wals 6A **32**
Birch La. B68: O'bry 4B **114**
WS4: S'fld 6G **21**
WS9: A'rdge 6F **23**
Birchley Ho. B69: O'bry 3D **96**
Birchley Ind. Est. B69: O'bry 4E **97**
Birchley Pk. Av. B69: O'bry 3E **97**
Birchley Ri. B92: Olton 6D **120**
Birchmoor Cl. B28: Hall G 6H **135**
Birchover Rd. WS2: Wals 5G **31**
Birch Rd. B6: Witt 5A **84**
B45: Rubery 3E **157**
B68: O'bry 3B **114**
DY3: Sed 4B **60**
WV11: Wed 6H **17**
Birch Rd. E. B6: Witt 5B **84**
Birch St. B68: O'bry 3A **98**
DY4: Tip 2H **77**
WS2: Wals 6B **32**
WV1: Wolv 1G **43** (2A **170**)
Birch Ter. DY2: Neth 5E **95**
Birch Tree Gdns. WS9: A'rdge 4D **34**
Birchtree Gdns. DY5: Quar B 2C **110**
Birch Tree Gro. B91: Sol 3C **150**
Birchtree Hollow
WV12: W'hall 4D **30**
Birchtrees B24: Erd 3B **86**
Birchtrees Cft. B26: Yard 6B **120**
Birchtrees Dr. B33: Kitts G 1H **121**
Birch Wlk. B68: O'bry 4B **114**
Birchwood Cl. WV11: Ess 4A **18**
Birchwood Cres. B12: Bal H 1B **134**
Birchwood Rd. B12: Bal H 1A **134**
WV4: Penn 6E **43**
Birchwoods B32: Bart G 3H **129**
Birchwood Wlk. DY6: K'wfrd 1C **92**
Birchy Cl. B90: Dic H 3F **163**
Birchy Leasowes La. B90: Dic H 4E **163**
Birdbrook Rd. B44: Gt Barr 4G **67**
Birdcage Wlk. B38: K Nor 5B **146**
DY2: Dud 6F **77**
Bird End B71: W Brom 5D **64**
Birdie Cl. B38: K Nor 6H **145**
Birdlip Gro. B32: Quin 5A **114**
Birds Mdw. DY5: P'ntt 2F **93**
Bird St. DY3: Lwr G 4G **75**
Birdwell Cft. B13: Mose 1H **147**
Birkdale Av. B29: S Oak 4B **132**
Birkdale Cl. DY8: Stourb 4D **124**
WV1: Wolv 1C **44**
Birkdale Dr. B69: Tiv 2A **96**
Birkdale Gro. B29: S Oak 5C **132**
Birkdale Rd. WS3: Blox 4G **19**
Birkenshaw Rd. B44: Gt Barr 5G **67**
Birley Gro. B63: Hale 5E **127**
BIRMINGHAM 1F **117** (5D **4**)
Birmingham Alexander Sports Stadium 1E **83**
Birmingham Botanical Gdns. 4B **116**
Birmingham Bus. Est. B37: Mars G 3G **123**
Birmingham City FC 2C **118**
Birmingham Crematorium
B42: P Barr 2E **83**
Birmingham Hippodrome Theatre
2G **117** (6D **4**)
BIRMINGHAM INTERNATIONAL AIRPORT
1C **138**
Birmingham International Station (Rail)
1F **139**
Birmingham Mus. & Art Gallery
1F **117** (3C **4**)
Birmingham Mus. of Transport, The 6G **161**
Birmingham Nature Cen. 1E **133**
Birmingham New Rd. DY1: Dud 2E **77**
DY4: Tip 2E **77**
WV4: E'shll 6A **44**
WV14: Cose 6A **44**
Birmingham One Bus. Pk. B1: Birm 6D **100**
Birmingham Railway Mus. 6F **119**
Birmingham Repertory Theatre 1E **117** (4B **4**)
Birmingham Rd. B31: Hopw 3F **159**
B36: Cas B 1E **105**
B37: K'hrst 4D **106**
B43: Gt Barr 1A **66**
B45: Rubery 5C **156**
B46: Col 4E **107**
B46: Wat O 5B **88**
B48: Hopw 3F **159**
B61: L Ash, Rubery 5C **156**
B63: Hale 2B **128**
B65: Row R 1C **112**
B69: O'bry 2H **97**
B70: W Brom 6C **80**
B71: W Brom 6E **81**
B72: W Grn 6H **69**
CV7: Mer 2D **140**
DY1: Dud 5G **77**
DY9: Hag 6G **125**
WS1: Wals 2D **48**
WS5: Wals 4F **49**
(not continuous)
WS9: A'rdge 4C **34**
WS14: Shens, Shen W 2G **37**
WV2: Wolv 2H **43** (5C **170**)
Birmingham Sports Cen. 5H **117**
Birmingham Squash Rackets Cen. 1H **115**
Birmingham St. B63: Hale 2B **128**
B69: O'bry 2G **97**
DY2: Dud 6F **77**
DY8: Stourb 6E **109**
DY9: Stourb 6E **109**
WS1: Wals 2D **48**
WS10: Darl 5E **47**
WV13: W'hall 1B **46**
Birmingham Wheels Adventure Pk. 1C **118**
Birnham Cl. DY4: Tip 2F **77**
Birstall Way B38: K Nor 1G **159**
Bisell Way DY5: Brie H 4H **109**
Bishbury Cl. B15: Edg 3A **116**
Bishop Asbury Cottage Mus. 5G **65**
Bishop Asbury Cres. B43: Gt Barr 5G **65**
Bishop Cl. B45: Fran 6E **143**
DY2: Dud 1G **95**
Bishop Rd. WS10: W'bry 3A **64**
Bishop Ryder Ho. B4: Birm 2G **5**
Bishops Cl. B66: Smeth 5G **99**
Bishop's Ct. B31: N'fld 4F **145**
B37: Mars G 3G **123**
Bishops Ga. B31: N'fld 5E **145**
Bishopsgate St. B15: Birm 2D **116** (6A **4**)
Bishops Mdw. B75: R'ley 6C **38**
Bishops Rd. B73: S Cold 2H **69**
Bishop St. B5: Birm 3G **117**
Bishops Wlk. B64: Crad H 5A **112**
Bishops Way B74: Four O 4F **37**
Bishopton Cl. B90: Shir 6A **150**
Bishopton Rd. B67: Smeth 2D **114**
Bishton Gro. DY2: Neth 5F **95**
Bisley Gro. B24: Erd 5G **85**
Bismillah Bldg. B19: Birm 5F **101** (1C **4**)
Bissell Cl. B28: Hall G 1F **149**
Bissell Dr. WS10: W'bry 2H **63**
Bissell St. B5: Birm 3G **117**
B32: Quin 5G **113**
WV14: Bils 6H **45**
Bi-Tec Ind. Pk. WV1: Wolv 2C **44**
Biton Cl. B17: Harb 6F **115**
Bittell Cl. B31: Longb 2D **158**
WV10: Bush 3A **16**
Bittell Ct. B31: Longb 2D **158**
Bittell Farm Rd. B48: Hopw 6F **159**
Bitterne Dr. WV6: Wolv 5E **27**
Bittern Wlk. DY5: Brie H 5G **109**
Blackacre Rd. DY2: Dud 1F **95**
Blackberry Av. B9: Bord G 6G **103**
Blackberry Cl. DY1: Dud 1A **94**
Blackberry La. B63: Hale 3A **128**
B65: Row R 4H **95**
B74: Four O 4E **37**
WS9: Wals W 3D **22**
Blackbird Cft. B36: Cas B 2C **106**
Blackbrook Cl. DY2: Neth 6C **94**
Blackbrook Rd. DY2: Dud, Neth 4C **94**
Blackbrook Valley Ind. Est. DY2: Dud 4C **94**
Blackbrook Way WV10: Bush 3A **16**
Blackburn Av. WV6: Tett 2C **26**
Blackburne Rd. B28: Hall G 1F **149**
Blackbushe Cl. B17: Harb 4D **114**
Blackcat Cl. B37: F'bri 6C **106**
Black Country Ho. B69: O'bry 2F **97**
Black Country Mus. 3F **77**
Black Country New Rd. B70: W Brom 1D **78**
DY4: Tip 1D **78**
WS10: Darl, W'bry 1B **62**
WS10: Tip, W'bry 2D **62**
WV14: Bils 5A **46**
Black Country Route WS2: Wals 4B **46**
WV13: W'hall 4B **46**
WV14: Cose, Bils 2D **60**
Blackdown Cl. B45: Fran 5G **143**
Blackdown Rd. B93: Know 3D **166**
Blackett Ct. B73: S Cold 3G **69**
Blackfirs La. B37: Mars G 4E **123**
Blackford Cl. B63: Hale 3F **127**
Blackford Rd. B11: S'hll 1C **134**
B90: Shir 2A **164**
Blackford St. B18: Win G 4A **100**
Blackhalve La. WV11: Wed, Ess 1D **28**
Blackham Dr. B73: Bold 6G **69**
Blackham Rd. WV11: Wed 1H **29**
Black Haynes Rd. B29: W Cas 1E **145**
BLACKHEATH 2C **112**
Blackheath Mkt. B65: B'hth 2D **112**
Blackheath Trad. Est.
B65: Row R 1E **113**
Blackhorse La. DY5: Brie H 2A **110**
BLACK LAKE 1H **79**
Black Lake B70: W Brom 1G **79**
Black Lake Ind. Est. B70: W Brom 1H **79**
Black Lake Stop (MM) 1G **79**
Blacklea Cl. B25: Yard 2B **120**
Black Mill DY1: Dud 3F **77**
Blackmoor Cft. B33: Kitts G 1H **121**
Blackpit La. WV4: Lwr P 2E **57**
Blackrock Rd. B23: Erd 1B **84**
Blackroot Cl. WS7: Hamm 1F **11**
Blackroot Ho. *B73: New O 3C 68*
(off Welshmans Hill)
Blackroot Rd. B74: S Cold 4G **53**
Blacksmith Dr. B75: R'ley 6C **38**
Blacksmith Way B70: W Brom 5A **80**
Blackthorn Cl. B30: B'vlle 1G **145**
Blackthorne Av. WS7: Chase 1B **10**
Blackthorne Cl. B91: Sol. 3C **150**
DY1: Dud 3B **76**
Blackthorne Rd. B67: Smeth 5B **98**
DY1: Dud 3B **76**
WS5: Wals 6D **48**
Blackthorn Rd. B30: B'vlle 1G **145**
B36: Cas B 1G **105**
DY8: Word 2D **108**
Blackwater Cl. DY5: P'ntt 3E **93**
Blackwell Rd. B72: W Grn 4B **70**
Blackwood Av. WV11: Wed 1D **28**
Blackwood Dr. B74: S'tly 3G **51**
Blackwood Rd. B74: S'tly 2G **51**
Blades Ho. B71: W Brom 5E **65**
Blades Rd. B70: W Brom 3D **78**
Blaenwern Dr. B63: Crad 4D **110**
Blagdon Rd. B63: Hale 5A **112**
Blair Gro. B37: Chel W 2F **123**
Blakedon Rd. WS10: W'bry 2E **63**
Blakedown Rd. B63: Hale 4G **127**
Blakedown Way B69: O'bry 5E **97**
Blake Hall Cl. DY5: Brie H 4G **109**
Blake Ho. *WS2: Wals 3A 48*
(off St Johns Rd.)
Blakeland Rd. B44: K'sdng 1G **83**
Blakeland St. B9: Bord G 1F **119**
Blake La. B9: Bord G 1F **119**
BLAKELEY 2G **73**
Blakeley Av. WV6: Tett 2D **26**
Blakeley Hall Gdns. B69: O'bry 2H **97**
Blakeley Hall Rd. B69: O'bry 2H **97**
Blakeley Heath Dr. WV5: Wom 2G **73**
Blakeley Ri. WV6: Tett 2D **26**
Blakeley Wlk. DY2: Neth 5E **95**
Blakeley Wood Rd. DY4: Tip 5C **62**
Blakemere Av. B25: Yard 3C **120**
Blakemere Ho. *B16: Birm 1C 116*
(off Graston Cl.)
Blakemore Cl. B32: Bart G 2D **130**
Blakemore Dr. B75: S Cold 5D **54**
Blakemore Rd. B70: W Brom 5G **79**
WS9: Wals W 4C **22**
Blakenall Cl. WS3: Blox 1B **32**
BLAKENALL HEATH 1B **32**
Blakenall Heath WS3: Blox 1B **32**
Blakenall La. WS3: Blox 2A **32**
Blakenall Row WS3: Blox 1B **32**
Blakeney Av. B17: Harb 4E **115**
DY8: Woll 5B **108**
Blakeney Cl. DY3: Sed 5G **59**
Blakenhale Rd. B33: Sheld 2F **121**
BLAKENHALL 4G **43**
Blakenhall Gdns. WV2: Wolv 4G **43**
Blakenhall Ind. Est. WV2: Wolv 4F **43**
Blake Pl. B9: Bord G 1F **119**
Blakesley Cl. B76: Walm 2D **86**
Blakesley Gro. B25: Yard 2B **120**
Blakesley Hall Mus. 2C **120**
Blakesley M. B25: Yard 3B **120**
Blakesley Rd. B25: Yard 2A **120**
Blakesley Way B33: Stech 1B **120**
Blake St. B74: Four O 3E **37**
Blake Street Station (Rail) 3F **37**
Blakewood Cl. B34: S End 4G **105**
Blandford Av. B36: Cas B 6A **88**
Blandford Dr. DY8: Word 6C **92**
Blandford Rd. B32: Quin 6C **114**
Blanefield WV8: Pend 5C **14**
Blaney Ct. B93: Dorr 5A **166**
Blay Av. WS2: Wals 1H **47**
Blaydon Av. B75: R'ley 1C **54**
Blaydon Ct. *B17: Harb 1H 131*
(off Metchley La.)
Blaydon Rd. WV9: Pend 5E **15**
Blaythorn Av. B92: Olton 2E **137**
Blaze Hill Rd. DY6: W Hth 1G **91**
Blaze Pk. DY6: W Hth 1H **91**
Bleak Hill Rd. B23: Erd 3C **84**
Bleakhouse Rd. B68: O'bry 2A **114**
Bleak St. B67: Smeth 3D **98**
Blenheim Cl. WS4: Rus 2H **33**
Blenheim Ct. B44: Gt Barr 5H **67**
B91: Sol 3G **151**
Blenheim Dr. B43: Gt Barr 5H **65**
Blenheim Rd. B13: Mose 4H **133**
B90: Shir 5B **150**
DY6: K'wfrd 3D **92**
WS11: Nort C 1F **9**
WV12: W'hall 3B **30**
Blenheim Way B35: Cas V 5F **87**
B44: Gt Barr 5H **67**
DY1: Dud 5A **76**
Bletchley Rd. B24: Erd 3C **86**
Blewitt Cl. B36: Cas B 5H **87**
Blewitt St. DY5: P'ntt 3G **93**
Blews St. B6: Birm 4G **101**
Blithe Cl. DY8: Amb 3E **109**
Blithfield Dr. DY5: Brie H 4F **109**
Blithfield Gro. B24: Erd 2A **86**
Blithfield Rd. WS8: Bwnhls 3F **9**
Blockall WS10: Darl 4D **46**
Blockall Cl. WS10: Darl 5C **46**
BLOOMFIELD 6G **61**
Bloomfield Cl. WV5: Wom 1D **72**
Bloomfield Dr. WV12: W'hall 6D **18**
Bloomfield Pk. DY4: Tip 1F **77**
Bloomfield Pk. Trad. Est.
DY4: Tip 1F **77**
Bloomfield Rd. B13: Mose 2B **134**
DY4: Tip 1G **77**
Bloomfield St. Nth. B63: Hale 6H **111**
Bloomfield St. W. B63: Hale 1H **127**
Bloomfield Ter. DY4: Tip 1F **77**
Bloomsbury Gro. B14: K Hth 6E **133**
Bloomsbury St. WV2: Wolv 3G **43** (5A **170**)
Bloomsbury Wlk. B7: Nech 4B **102**
(not continuous)
Blossom Av. B29: S Oak 3B **132**
BLOSSOMFIELD 5D **150**
Blossomfield Cl. B38: K Nor 1H **159**
DY6: K'wfrd 1C **92**
Blossomfield Club 1E **165**
Blossomfield Ct. B38: K Nor 1H **159**
Blossomfield Gdns. B91: Sol 3E **151**
Blossomfield Rd. B91: Sol 6C **150**
Blossom Gro. B36: Hodg H 1C **104**
B64: Old H 2H 111
(off Cherry Dr.)
Blossom Hill B24: Erd 3G **85**
Blossom Rd. B24: Erd 3A **86**
Blossom's Fold WV1: Wolv 1G **43** (3B **170**)
Blossomville Way B27: A Grn 1H **135**
Blounts Rd. B23: Erd 2C **84**
BLOWER'S GREEN 2D **94**
Blowers Grn. Cres. DY2: Dud 2D **94**
Blowers Grn. Pl. DY2: Dud 2D **94**
Blower's Grn. Rd. DY2: Dud 2D **94**
Bloxcidge St. B68: O'bry 5H **97**
BLOXWICH 6H **19**
Bloxwich Bus. Pk. WS2: Wals 2G **31**
Bloxwich La. WS2: Wals 5G **31**
Bloxwich Library Theatre 6H **19**
Bloxwich North Station (Rail) 4F **19**
Bloxwich Rd. WS2: Wals 2A **32**
WS3: Blox 2A **32**
Bloxwich Rd. Nth. WV12: W'hall 3D **30**
Bloxwich Rd. Sth. WV13: W'hall 6A **30**
Bloxwich Station (Rail) 6G **19**
Bloxwich Swimming Baths & Leisure Cen.
1A **32**
Blucher St. B1: Birm 2F **117** (6C **4**)
Blue Ball La. B63: Crad 5E **111**
Blue Bell Cl. DY8: Word 1A **108**
Bluebell Cres. WV11: Wed 4F **29**
Bluebell Cft. B23: Erd 6C **68**
B31: N'fld 3D **144**
Bluebell La. WS6: Gt Wyr 4G **7**
Bluebell Rd. B64: Old H 6G **95**
DY1: Dud 4D **76**
WS9: Wals W 4D **22**
Bluebellwood Cl. B76: Walm 2E **71**
Blue Bird Pk. B62: Hunn 5A **128**
Bluebird Trad. Est. WV10: Wolv 4A **28**
Blue Cedars DY8: Woll 5A **108**
Blue Lake Rd. B93: Dorr 6H **167**
Blue La. E. WS2: Wals 6B **32**
Blue La. W. WS2: Wals 1B **48**
Blue Rock Pl. B69: Tiv 2C **96**
Blue Stone Wlk. B65: Row R 3C **96**
Blundell Rd. B11: S'hll 6D **118**
Blyth Cl. B92: Olton 6D **136**
Blythe Av. CV7: Bal C 6H **169**
Blythe Ct. B46: Col 2H **107**
B73: S Cold 6H **53**
Blythefield Av. B43: Gt Barr 3G **65**
Blythe Gdns. WV8: Cod 3F **13**
Blythe Gro. B44: Gt Barr 2H **67**
Blythe Rd. B46: Col 2H **107**
BLYTHE VALLEY PARK 6D **164**
Blythe Valley Parkway B90: Bly P 5D **164**
Blythe Way B91: Sol 4A **152**
Blythewood Cl. B91: Sol 6B **152**
Blythsford Rd. B28: Hall G 3F **149**
Blythswood Rd. B11: Tys 1G **135**
Blyton Cl. B16: Birm 6B **100**
Board School Gdns. DY3: Up Gor 1A **76**
Boar Hound Cl. B18: Hock 5C **100**
Boat La. WS14: Muck C 4H **11**
Boatmans La. WS9: Wals W 5A **22**
Bobbington Way DY2: Neth 4F **95**
Bob's Coppice Wlk. DY5: Quar B 4B **110**
Boddis Ind. Pk. B64: Old H 1H **111**
Bodenham Rd. B31: N'fld 5C **144**
B68: O'bry 3H **113**
Boden Rd. B28: Hall G 6F **135**
Bodens La. WS9: A'rdge 4C **50**
Bodiam Ct. WV6: Pert 6G **25**
Bodicote Gro. B75: R'ley 1C **54**
Bodington Rd. B75: Four O 6H **37**
Bodmin Cl. WS5: Wals 4H **49**
Bodmin Ct. DY5: Brie H 1H **109**
Bodmin Gro. B7: Birm 4B **102**
Bodmin Ri. WS5: Wals 4H **49**
Bodmin Rd. DY2: Neth 1F **111**
Bognop Rd. WV11: Ess 3E **17**
BOLDMERE 5F **69**
Boldmere Cl. B73: Bold 6G **69**
Boldmere Ct. *B43: Gt Barr 6A 66*
(off South Vw.)
Boldmere Dr. B73: Bold 5G **69**
Boldmere Gdns. B73: Bold 5F **69**
Boldmere Rd. B73: Bold 3F **69**
Boldmere Ter. B29: S Oak 4A **132**
Boleyn Cl. WS6: C Hay 3D **6**
Boleyn Rd. B45: Fran 6D **142**
Bolney Rd. B32: Quin 6C **114**
Bolton Ct. DY4: Tip 5C **62**
Bolton Ind. Cen. B19: Hock 3D **100**
Bolton Rd. B10: Small H 3B **118**
WV11: Wed 4E **29**
Bolton St. B9: Birm 1B **118**
Bolton Way WS3: Blox 4F **19**
Bomers Fld. B45: Redn 2A **158**
Bond, The B5: Birm 1A **118**
Bond Dr. B35: Cas V 4E **87**
Bondfield Rd. B13: Mose 1B **148**
Bond Sq. B18: Hock 5C **100**
Bond St. B19: Birm 5F **101** (1C **4**)
B30: Stir 6C **132**
B65: Row R 6E **97**
B70: W Brom 5A **80**
WV2: Wolv 2G **43** (5B **170**)
WV14: Cose 5C **60**
Bonham Gro. B25: Yard 2B **120**
Boningale Way B93: Dorr 6H **165**
Bonner Dr. B76: Walm 2D **86**
Bonner Gro. WS9: A'rdge 4B **34**
Bonnington Way B43: Gt Barr 1F **67**
Bonny Stile La. WV11: Wed 3D **28**
Bonsall Rd. B23: Erd 1G **85**
Bonville Gdns. WV10: Bush 3A **16**
Booth Cl. DY6: K'wfrd 3E **93**
WS3: Blox 1B **32**
Booth Ct. DY5: Brie H 1H **109**
Booth Ho. WS4: Wals 6D **32**

A-Z Birmingham Deluxe 177

Booth Rd.—Bridges Cres.

Booth Rd. WS10: W'bry 3A 64
Booth's Farm Rd. B42: Gt Barr 6C 66
Booth's La. B42: Gt Barr 4D 66
(not continuous)
Booth St. B21: Hand 2G 99
B66: Hand, Smeth 2G 99
WS3: Blox 1A 32
WS10: Darl 3D 46
Bordeaux Cl. DY1: Dud 4A 76
Borden Cl. WV8: Pend 1D 26
BORDESLEY
Birmingham 1B 118
Bordesley Cir. B10: Small H 2B 118
Bordesley Cl. B9: Bord G 1G 119
BORDESLEY GREEN 1E 119
Bordesley Grn. B9: Bord G 1D 118
Bordesley Grn. E. B9: Bord G 1H 119
B33: Stech 1A 120
Bordesley Grn. Rd. B8: Salt 1D 118
B9: Bord G 1D 118
Bordesley Grn. Trad. Est.
B9: Bord G 1E 119
Bordesley Middleway
B11: S'brk 3A 118
Bordesley Station (Rail) 2A 118
Bordesley St. B5: Birm 1H 117 (4G 5)
Bordesley Trad. Est. B8: Salt 6D 102
Borneo St. WS4: Wals 5D 32
Borough Cres. B69: O'bry 4E 97
DY8: Stourb 6C 108
Borrowdale Cl. DY5: Brie H 4F 109
Borrowdale Gro. B31: N'fld 4B 144
Borrowdale Rd. B31: N'fld 4A 144
Borrow St. WV13: W'hall 6A 30
Borwick Av. B70: W Brom 4G 79
Bosbury Ter. B30: Stir 6D 132
Boscobel Av. DY4: Tip 3H 77
Boscobel Cl. DY1: Dud 4B 76
Boscobel Cres. WV1: Wolv 5G 27
Boscobel Rd. B43: Gt Barr 3H 65
B90: Ches G 4B 164
WS1: Wals 3F 49
Boscombe Av. B11: S'brk 5C 118
Boscombe Rd. B11: Tys 1E 135
Bosmere Ct. B31: N'fld 4D 144
Bossgate Cl. WV5: Wom 3G 73
Boston Gro. B44: K'sdng 5B 68
Bosty La. WS9: A'rdge 4G 33
Boswell Cl. WS10: Darl 6D 46
WS10: W'bry 4C 62
Boswell Rd. B44: K'sdng 1H 83
B74: S Cold 5A 54
WV14: Bils 4H 45
Bosworth Cl. DY3: Sed 1B 76
Bosworth Ct. B26: Sheld 6E 121
Bosworth Dr. B37: Chel W, F'bri 1B 122
B37: F'bri 1B 122
Bosworth Rd. B26: Yard 1C 136
Botany Dr. DY3: Up Gor 2H 75
Botany Rd. WS5: Wals 6D 48
Botany Wlk. B16: Birm 1C 116
Botha Rd. B9: Bord G 6E 103
Botteley Rd. B70: W Brom 1G 79
Botterham La. DY3: Swind 4E 73
Bottetourt Rd. B29: W Cas 2E 131
(not continuous)
Botteville Rd. B27: A Grn 3A 136
Bott La. DY9: Lye 5H 109
WS1: Wals 2D 48
BOUCHALL 5F 109
Boughton Rd. B25: Yard 4A 120
Boulevard, The B73: W Grn 5H 69
DY5: Brie H 1A 110
Boultbee Rd. B72: W Grn 6A 70
Boulton Ho. B70: W Brom 6B 80
Boulton Ind. Cen. B18: Hock 4D 100
Boulton Middleway B18: Birm 4D 100
Boulton Retreat B21: Hand 2A 100
Boulton Rd. B21: Hand 2A 100
B66: Smeth 3H 99
B70: W Brom 6B 80
B91: Sol 6G 137
Boulton Sq. B70: W Brom 6B 80
Boulton Wlk. B23: Erd 3B 84
Boundary Av. B65: Row R 1E 113
Boundary Cl. WV13: W'hall 2E 45
Boundary Ct. B37: F'bri 1A 122
Boundary Cres. DY3: Lwr G 4G 75
Boundary Dr. B13: Mose 3F 133
Boundary Hill DY3: Lwr G 4G 75
Boundary Ho. B5: Edg 6E 117
B47: Wyt 6G 161
Boundary Ind. Est. WV10: F'hses 2G 15
Boundary Pl. B21: Hand 6G 81
Boundary Rd. B74: S'tly 4H 51
WS9: Wals W 4B 22
Boundary Way WV4: Penn 6A 42
WV6: Tett 1F 41
Bourlay Cl. B45: Fran 5E 143
BOURNBROOK 3B 132
Bournbrook Ct. B5: S Oak 2C 132
Bournbrook Rd. B29: S Oak 2C 132
Bourne Av. B62: Quin 1F 129
DY4: Tip 6C 62
Bournebrook Cl. DY2: Neth 4E 95
Bournebrook Cres. B62: Quin 1G 129
Bourne Cl. B13: Mose 1D 148
B91: Sol 1A 152
Bourne Grn. B32: Quin 5C 114
Bourne Hill Cl. DY2: Neth 6G 95
Bourne Rd. B6: Aston 2B 102
Bournes Cl. B63: Hale 2H 127
Bournes Cres. B63: Hale 1G 127
Bournes Hill B63: Hale 1G 127
Bourne St. DY2: Dud 6F 77
DY3: Sed 6C 60
WV14: Cose 6C 60
Bourne Va. WS9: A'rdge 6F 35
Bourne Wlk. B65: Row R 4H 95
Bourne Way Gdns. B29: S Oak 5C 132
Bourn Mill Dr. B6: Aston 3G 101
BOURNVILLE 6A 132
Bournville La. B30: B'vlle 6H 131
Bournville Station (Rail) 6C 132
Bourton Cl. WS5: Wals 2E 65
Bourton Cft. B92: Olton 5D 136
Bourton Rd. B92: Olton 5D 136
Bovey Cft. B76: Walm 6E 71
Bovingdon Rd. B35: Cas V 4E 87
Bowater Av. B33: Stech 2B 120
Bowater Ho. *B19: Birm 4F 101*
(off Aldgate Gro.)
B70: W Brom 5A 80
Bowater St. B70: W Brom 4A 80
Bowbrook Av. B90: M'path 4E 165
Bowcroft Gro. B24: Erd 1A 86
Bowden Rd. B67: Smeth 3C 98
Bowdler Rd. WV2: Wolv 3H 43 (6D 170)
Bowen Av. WV4: E'shll 2C 60
Bowen-Cooke Av. WV6: Pert 3E 25
Bowen Ct. B13: Mose 2B 134
Bowen St. WV4: E'shll 6A 44
Bowercourt Cl. B91: Sol 6F 151
Bower La. DY5: Quar B 3B 110
Bowes Rd. B45: Rubery 2E 157
Bowker St. WV13: W'hall 2E 45
Bowlas Av. B74: Four O 3H 53
BOWLING GREEN 6F 95
Bowling Grn. Cl. B23: Erd 6E 69
WS10: Darl 4D 46
Bowling Grn. La. B20: Hand 1C 100
Bowling Grn. Rd. DY2: Neth 6F 95
DY8: Stourb 6C 108
Bowlplex
Birmingham 2C 116
Dudley 4G 77
Bowman Rd. B42: Gt Barr 4D 66
Bowmans Ri. WV1: Wolv 6C 28
Bowness Gro. WV12: W'hall 6B 18
Bowood Cres. B31: N'fld 5F 145
Bowood Dr. WV6: Tett 3B 26
Bowood End B76: Walm 2C 70
Bowshot Cl. B36: Cas B 6H 87
Bowstoke Rd. B43: Gt Barr 5G 65
Bow St. B1: Birm 2F 117 (6D 4)
WV13: W'hall 2B 46
WV14: Bils 5G 45
Bowyer Rd. B8: Salt 5E 103
Bowyer St. B10: Small H 2A 118
Boxhill Cl. B6: Aston 3H 101
Box Rd. B37: Chel W 3E 123
Box St. WS1: Wals 2D 48
Box Trees Rd. B93: Dorr 6H 165
Boyd Gro. B27: A Grn 3H 135
Boydon Cl. WV2: E'shll 5C 44
Boyleston Rd. B28: Hall G 1G 149
Boyne Rd. B26: Sheld 4E 121
Boyton Gro. B44: Gt Barr 2H 67
Brabazon Gro. B35: Cas V 4D 86
Brabham Cres. B74: S'tly 5H 51
Bracadale Av. B24: Erd 3G 85
Bracebridge Cl. CV7: Bal C 3H 169
Bracebridge Ct. B17: Harb 6H 115
Bracebridge Rd. B24: Erd 6F 85
B74: Four O 3F 53
Bracebridge St. B6: Aston 3G 101
Braceby Av. B13: Mose 6C 134
Brace St. WS1: Wals 3C 48
(not continuous)
Brackenbury Rd. B44: K'sdng 5B 68
Bracken Cl. WV8: Pend 6C 14
Bracken Cft. B37: Chel W 6E 107
Brackendale Dr. WS5: Wals 2F 65
Brackendale Shop. Cen. WV12: W'hall 5D 30
Brackendale Way DY9: W'cte 1H 125
Bracken Dr. B75: S Cold 6E 55
Brackenfield Rd. B44: Gt Barr 3E 67
B63: Hale 2G 127
Brackenfield Vw. DY1: Dud 1H 93
Bracken Pk. Gdns. DY8: Word 1D 108
Bracken Rd. B24: Erd 5A 86
Bracken Way B38: K Nor 2H 159
B74: S'tly 3H 51
Brackenwood WS5: Wals 6H 49
Brackenwood Dr. WV11: Wed 4H 29
Brackley Av. B20: Hand 6E 83
Brackleys Way B92: Olton 3D 136
Bradbeer Ho. B16: Edg 2C 116
Bradburne Way B7: Birm 4A 102
Bradburn Rd. WV11: Wed 1D 28
Bradbury Cl. WS8: Bwnhls 2B 22
Bradbury Rd. B92: Olton 4D 136
Braden Rd. WV4: Penn 2B 58
Brades Cl. B63: Crad 4D 110
Brades Ri. B69: O'bry 1D 96
Brades Rd. B69: O'bry 6E 79
BRADES VILLAGE 1D 96
Bradewell Rd. B36: Cas B 6H 87
Bradfield Ho. B26: Sheld 5A 122
Bradfield Rd. B42: Gt Barr 6F 67
Bradford Cl. B43: Gt Barr 6B 66
Bradford Ct. B12: Birm 3A 118
Bradford La. WS1: Wals 2C 48
Bradford Mall WS1: Wals 2C 48
Bradford Pl. B11: S'brk 5A 118
B70: W Brom 1C 98
WS1: Wals 2C 48
Bradford Rd. B36: Cas B 1E 105
DY2: Dud 3B 94
WS8: Bwnhls 5A 10
Bradford St. B5: Birm 2H 117 (6G 5)
WS1: Wals 2C 48
Bradgate Cl. WV12: W'hall 3C 30
Bradgate Dr. B74: Four O 4E 37
Bradgate Pl. B12: Bal H 6A 118
BRADLEY 2G 61
Bradley Cft. CV7: Bal C 3H 169
Bradley La. WV14: Bils 2H 61
Bradleymore Rd. DY5: Brie H 6H 93
Bradley Rd. B34: S End 3H 105
DY8: Stourb 5D 108
Bradleys Cl. B64: Crad H 4G 111
Bradley's La. DY4: Tip 5F 61
WV14: Cose 5F 61
Bradley St. DY4: Tip 5H 77
DY5: P'ntt 2F 93
WV14: Bils 1H 61
BRADMORE 3C 42
Bradmore Cl. B91: Sol 1E 165
Bradmore Gro. B29: W Cas 5E 131
Bradmore Rd. WV3: Wolv 3D 42
Bradnock Cl. B13: Mose 6C 134
BRADNOCK'S MARSH 4E 155
Bradnocks Marsh Bus. Cen.
B92: H Ard 4E 155
Bradnocks Marsh La. B92: H Ard 6D 154
Bradshaw Av. B38: K Nor 6H 145
WS10: Darl 6B 46
Bradshaw Cl. DY4: Tip 4A 78
Bradshawe Cl. B28: Hall G 4D 148
Bradshaw St. WV1: Wolv 1A 44
Bradstock Rd. B30: K Nor 3E 147
Bradwell Cft. B75: R'ley 6C 38
Braemar Av. DY8: Word 2A 108
Braemar Cl. DY3: Sed 4G 59
WV12: W'hall 3B 30
Braemar Dr. B23: Erd 2B 84
Braemar Rd. B73: S Cold 3F 69
B92: Olton 4C 136
WS11: Nort C 1E 9
Braeside Cft. B37: Chel W 1F 123
Braeside Way WS3: Pels 4D 20
Bragg Rd. B20: Hand 5F 83
Braggs Farm La. B90: Dic H, Shir 5F 163
Braid Cl. B38: K Nor 6H 145
Brailes Cl. B92: Sol 6A 138
Brailes Dr. B76: Walm 2D 70
Brailes Gro. B9: Bord G 2H 119
Brailsford Cl. WV11: Wed 1G 29
Brailsford Dr. B66: Smeth 4E 99
Braithwaite Dr. DY6: K'wfrd 3B 92
Braithwaite Rd. B11: S'brk 4A 118
Bramah Way DY4: Tip 1C 78
Bramber Dr. WV5: Wom 1F 73
Bramber Ho. B31: Longb 1D 158
Bramber Way DY8: Stourb 3D 124
Bramble Cl. B6: Aston 2G 101
B31: N'fld 1D 144
B46: Col 2H 107
B64: Old H 5H 95
WS8: Clay 2A 22
WV12: W'hall 2C 30
Bramble Dell B9: Bord G 6G 103
Bramble Dr. B26: Sheld 5E 121
Bramble Grn. DY1: Dud 2B 76
Brambles, The B76: Walm 5E 71
DY9: W'cte 2H 125
Brambleside DY8: Word 2D 108
Bramblewood WV5: Wom 6G 57
Bramblewood Dr. WV3: Wolv 3C 42
Bramblewoods B34: S End 4G 105
Brambling Wlk. B15: Edg 4E 117
DY5: Brie H 5G 109
Bramcote Dr. B91: Sol 6G 137
Bramcote Ri. B75: S Cold 4A 54
Bramcote Rd. B32: Quin 6A 114
(not continuous)
Bramdean Wlk. WV4: Penn 5A 42
Bramerton Cl. WV11: Wed 3C 28
Bramford Dr. DY1: Dud 1D 76
Bramley Cl. B43: Gt Barr 2F 67
WS5: Wals 3H 49
Bramley Cft. B90: Shir 5A 150
Bramley Dr. B20: Hand 4D 82
B47: H'wd 3B 162
Bramley M. Ct. B27: A Grn 6A 120
Bramley Rd. B27: A Grn 6A 120
WS5: Wals 1F 65
Brampton Av. B28: Hall G 1G 149
Brampton Cres. B90: Shir 1H 149
Bramshall Dr. B93: Dorr 6A 166
Bramshaw Cl. B14: K Hth 5H 147
Bramshill Ct. B15: Edg 3D 116
Bramstead Av. WV6: Tett 1H 41
Bramwell Dr. WS6: C Hay 4D 6
Branchal Rd. WS9: A'rdge 6E 23
Branch Rd. B38: K Nor 1A 160
BRANDHALL 3H 113
Brandhall Ct. B68: O'bry 1G 113
Brandhall La. B68: O'bry 2H 113
Brandhall Rd. B68: O'bry 1H 113
Brandon Cl. B70: W Brom 5G 79
DY3: Sed 6A 60
WS9: A'rdge 6H 35
Brandon Ct. B31: N'fld 6F 145
Brandon Gro. B31: Longb 2D 158
Brandon Pk. WV3: Wolv 4C 42
Brandon Pas. B16: Birm 6A 100
Brandon Pl. B34: S End 2H 105
Brandon Rd. B28: Hall G 3E 135
B62: B'hth 2E 113
B91: Sol 6G 137
Brandon Thomas Ct. B6: Aston 1B 102
Brandon Way B70: W Brom 4G 79
DY5: Quar B 3A 110
Brandon Way Ind. Est. B70: W Brom 4F 79
BRANDWOOD END 3F 147
Brandwood Gro. B14: K Hth 4E 147
Brandwood Ho. B14: K Hth 6F 133
Brandwood Pk. Rd. B14: K Hth 2D 146
Brandwood Rd. B14: K Hth 3F 147
Branfield Cl. WV14: Cose 4C 60
Branksome Av. B21: Hand 1B 100
Branscombe Cl. B14: K Hth 2F 147
Bransdale Cl. WV6: Wolv 4E 27
Bransdale Rd. WS8: Clay 6A 10
Bransford Ri. B91: Cath B 2D 152
Bransford Twr. B12: Birm 3H 117
Branston Ct. B18: Birm 4E 101
Branston St. B18: Birm 4E 101
Brantford Rd. B25: Yard 3A 120
Branthill Cft. B91: Sol 6F 151
Brantley Av. WV3: Wolv 2A 42
Brantley Rd. B6: Witt 5A 84
Branton Hill La. WS9: A'rdge 4E 35
Brasshouse La. B66: Smeth 3D 98
Brassie Cl. B38: K Nor 6H 145
Brassington Av. B73: S Cold 1H 69
BRATCH, THE 6E 57
Bratch Cl. DY2: Neth 6E 95
Bratch Comn. Rd. WV5: Wom 6E 57
Bratch Hollow WV5: Wom 5G 57
Bratch La. WV5: Wom 5F 57
Bratch Pk. WV5: Wom 5F 57
Bratt St. B70: W Brom 3A 80
Braunston Cl. B76: Walm 3E 71
Brawnes Hurst B26: Yard 2E 121
Brayford Av. DY5: Brie H 4F 109
Bray Ho. WV11: Wed 4E 29
Braymoor Rd. B33: Kitts G 2A 122
Brays Rd. B26: Sheld 5E 121
Bray St. WV13: W'hall 1B 46
Bream Cl. B37: Chel W 1E 123
WV10: Wolv 5D 28
Breamore Cres. DY1: Dud 4B 76
Brean Av. B26: Yard 6D 120
Brearley Cl. B19: Birm 4G 101
Brearley St. B19: Birm 4F 101
B21: Hand 1H 99
Breaside Wlk. B37: Chel W 6E 107
Brecknock Rd.
B71: W Brom 1G 79
Brecon Dr. DY8: Amb 5F 109
Brecon Rd. B20: Hand 1D 100
Bredon Av. DY9: Lye 6G 109
Bredon Ct. B63: Hale 2A 128
Bredon Cft. B18: Hock 4C 100
Bredon Rd. B69: O'bry 4D 96
DY8: Amb 5E 109
Breech Cl. B74: S'tly 4G 51
Breeden Dr. B76: Curd 1D 88
Breedon Rd. B30: K Nor 2C 146
Breedon Ter. *B18: Hock 4C 100*
(off Brookfield Rd.)
Breedon Way WS4: S'fld 6G 21
Breener Ind. Est. DY5: Brie H 2F 109
Breen Rydding Dr. WV14: Cose 4D 60
Brelades Cl. DY1: Dud 5A 76
Brennand Cl. B68: O'bry 3H 113
Brennand Rd. B68: O'bry 2H 113
Brentford Rd. B14: K Hth 2A 148
B91: Sol 4C 150
Brentmill Cl. WV10: Bush 3B 16
Brentnall Dr. B75: Four O 6H 37
Brenton Rd. WV4: Penn 2D 58
Brent Rd. B30: Stir 5F 133
Brentwood Cl. B91: Sol 4C 150
Brentwood Gro. B44: Gt Barr 5G 67
Brenwood Cl. DY6: K'wfrd 2H 91
Brereton Cl. DY2: Dud 1G 95
Brereton Rd. WV12: W'hall 2C 30
Bretby Gro. B23: Erd 1G 85
Bretshall Cl. B90: M'path 4D 164
Brett Dr. B32: Bart G 5A 130
Brettell La. DY5: Brie H 3D 108
DY8: Amb 3D 108
Brettell St. DY2: Dud 1D 94
Bretton Gdns. WV10: Wolv 3B 28
Bretton Rd. B27: A Grn 3B 136
Brett St. B71: W Brom 2H 79
Brevitt Rd. WV2: Wolv 5H 43
Brewer's Dr. WS3: Pels 6E 21
Brewers Ter. WS3: Pels 5E 21
Brewer St. WS2: Wals 5C 32
Brewery St. B6: Birm 4G 101
B21: Hand 1H 99
B67: Smeth 3D 98
DY2: Dud 6G 77
DY4: Tip 3H 77
Brewins Way DY5: Brie H 5C 94
Brewster St. DY2: Neth 4E 95
Breydon Gro. WV13: W'hall 3H 45
Brian Rd. B67: Smeth 3C 98
Briar Av. B74: S'tly 2A 52
Briarbeck WS4: S'fld 1G 33
Briar Cl. B24: Erd 3G 85
Briar Coppice B90: Ches G 5B 164
Briar Ct. *DY5: Brie H 1H 109*
(off Hill St.)
Briarfield Rd. B11: Tys 2G 135
Briarley B71: W Brom 4D 64
Briar Rd. DY1: Dud 2B 76
Briars, The B23: Erd 1D 84
Briars Cl. DY5: Brie H 5G 93
Briarwood Cl. B90: Ches G 5B 164
WV2: E'shll 4C 44
Brickbridge La. WV5: Wom 2E 73
Brickfield Rd. B25: Yard 5H 119
Brickheath Rd. WV1: Wolv 6C 28
Brickhill Dr. B37: F'bri 1C 122
Brickhouse La. B70: W Brom 1E 79
Brickhouse La. Sth. DY4: Tip 1D 78
Brickhouse Rd. B65: Row R 5A 96
Brickiln St. WS8: Bwnhls 6B 10
Brick Kiln La. B44: Gt Barr 1G 83
B47: Wyt 6G 161
B91: Sol 1D 164
DY3: Gorn 4E 75
Brick Kiln St. DY4: Tip 1G 77
DY5: Brie H 4A 94
DY5: Quar B 3C 110
Brickkiln St. WV13: W'hall 2H 45
Bricklin Ct. DY5: Brie H 1H 109
Brick St. DY3: Sed 5H 59
Brickyard Rd. WS9: A'rdge 6B 22
Briddsland Rd. B33: Kitts G 1A 122
Brides Wlk. B38: K Nor 2A 160
Bridge, The WS1: Wals 2C 48
Bridge Av. DY4: Tip 6C 62
WS6: C Hay 1E 7
Bridgeburn Rd. B31: N'fld 5C 130
Bridge Cl. B11: S'hll 2B 134
WS8: Clay 1A 22
Bridge Ct. *B64: Old H 3H 111*
(off Edgewood Cl.)
Bridge Cft. B12: Bal H 5G 117
Bridgefield Wlk. B65: Row R 4H 95
Bridgefoot Wlk. WV8: Pend 6D 14
Bridgeford Rd. B34: S End 3F 105
Bridgehead Wlk. B76: Walm 6D 70
Bridge Ind. Est. B91: Sol 6G 137
Bridgelands Way B20: Hand 6F 83
Bridgeman Cft. B36: Cas B 1G 105
Bridgeman St. WS2: Wals 2B 48
Bridgemary Cl. WV10: Bush 3B 16
Bridge Mdw. Dr. B93: Know 4B 166
Bridgemeadow Ho. B36: Hodg H 1C 104
Bridgend Cft. DY5: P'ntt 3F 93
Bridgenorth Ho. B33: Yard 2F 121
Bridge Piece B31: N'fld 5F 145
Bridge Rd. B8: Salt 5E 103
DY4: Tip 1C 78
WS4: S'fld 6F 21
Bridges Cres. WS11: Nort C 1D 8

178 A-Z Birmingham Deluxe

Bridges Rd.—Brueton Dr.

Bridges Rd. WS11: Nort C 1D 8
Bridge St. B1: Birm 1E 117 (5B 4)
B63: Crad 4E 111
B69: O'bry 2G 97
B70: W Brom 3H 79
DY8: Word 2C 108
WS1: Wals 1C 48
WS8: Clay 1A 22
WS10: W'bry 4F 63
WV10: Wolv 4A 28
WV13: W'hall 2H 45
WV14: Bils 6G 45
WV14: Cose 5E 61
Bridge St. Ind. Est. WS10: W'bry 4F 63
Bridge St. Nth. B66: Smeth 3F 99
Bridge St. Sth. B66: Smeth 3F 99
Bridge St. W. B19: Hock 4F 101
Bridge Trad. Cen., The B64: Crad H 3F 111
Bridge Trad. Est., The B66: Smeth 3F 99
Bridge Wlk. B27: A Grn 2B 136
Bridgewater Av. B69: O'bry 5G 97
Bridgewater Ct. B29: S Oak 4H 131
Bridgewater Cres. DY2: Dud 6G 77
Bridgewater Dr. WV5: Wom 6F 57
WV14: Cose 3E 61
Bridge Way WS8: Clay 1A 22
Bridgnorth Av. WV5: Wom 3F 73
Bridgnorth Gro. WV12: W'hall 3B 30
Bridgnorth Rd. DY3: Himl 4H 73
DY3: Swind 2A 72
DY7: Stourt 4A 108
(not continuous)
DY8: Woll 4A 108
WV5: Wom 2E 73
WV6: Pert, Tett, Tres 5A 40
Bridgwater Cl. WS9: Wals W 4B 22
Bridle Gro. B71: W Brom 5D 64
Bridle La. B74: S'tly 4G 51
WS9: A'rdge 5E 51
Bridle Mead B38: K Nor 1H 159
Bridle Path, The B90: Shir 2H 149
Bridle Rd. DY8: Woll 5B 108
Bridlewood B74: S'tly 3H 51
Bridport Ho. B31: N'fld 6C 130
BRIERLEY HILL 1H 109
Brierley Hill Baths 1H 109
Brierley Hill Rd. DY5: Brie H 1E 109
DY8: Word 1C 108
Brierley La. WV14: Bils, Cose 3G 61
Brierley Trad. Est., The
DY5: Brie H 6G 93
Brier Mill Rd. B63: Hale 2C 128
Briery Cl. B64: Crad H 4H 111
Briery Rd. B63: Hale 2G 127
Briffen Ho. B16: Birm 1D 116
Brigadoon Gdns. DY9: Pedm 3G 125
Brigfield Cres. B13: Mose 2B 148
Brigfield Rd. B13: Mose 2B 148
Brighton Cl. WS2: Wals 6B 32
Brighton Pl. WV3: Wolv 1E 43
Brighton Rd. B12: Bal H 6H 117
Bright Rd. B68: O'bry 4H 97
Brightstone Cl. WV10: Bush 3B 16
Brightstone Rd. B45: Fran 5H 143
Bright St. DY8: Woll 6B 108
WS10: Darl 6D 46
WV1: Wolv 6F 27
Brightwell Cres. B93: Dorr 6A 166
Brimfield Pl. WV6: Wolv 5D 26
(off Newbridge St.)
Brindle Cl. B26: Yard 6C 120
Brindle Ct. B23: Erd 4B 84
Brindlefields Way DY4: Tip 5A 78
Brindle Rd. WS5: Wals 1G 65
Brindley Av. WV11: Wed 6A 18
Brindley Cl. DY8: Word 2C 108
WS2: Wals 4F 31
WV5: Wom 1D 72
Brindley Ct. B68: O'bry 4H 113
DY4: Tip 2G 77
Brindley Dr. B1: Birm 1E 117 (4A 4)
Brindley Pl. B1: Birm 1D 116 (5A 4)
Brindley Point B16: Birm 1D 116
Brindley Rd. B71: W Brom 5G 63
Brindley Way B66: Smeth 4G 99
Brineton Gro. B29: W Cas 4E 131
Brineton Ind. Est. WS2: Wals 2A 48
Brineton St. WS2: Wals 2A 48
Bringewood Gro. B32: Bart G 5H 129
Brinklow Cft. B34: S End 2H 105
Brinklow Rd. B29: W Cas 3D 130
Brinklow Twr. B12: Birm 4H 117
Brinley Way DY6: K'wfrd 3A 92
Brinsford Rd. WV10: F'hses 4G 15
Brinsley Cl. B91: Sol 5F 151
Brinsley Rd. B26: Sheld 3F 121
Brisbane Rd. B67: Smeth 4C 98
Briseley Cl. DY5: Brie H 3G 109
Bristam Cl. B69: O'bry 3E 97
BRISTNALL FIELDS 1H 113
Bristnall Hall Cres. B68: O'bry 6A 98
Bristnall Hall La. B68: O'bry 6A 98
Bristnall Hall Rd. B68: O'bry 1H 113
Bristnall Ho. B67: Smeth 5B 98
Bristol Ct. B29: W Cas 6G 131
Bristol Rd. B5: S Oak 2B 132
B23: Erd 4E 85
B29: S Oak 6H 131
DY2: Neth 1F 111
Bristol Rd. Sth. B31: Longb 1B 158
B45: Redn 1G 157
Bristol St. B5: Birm 3F 117 (6D 4)
Briston Cl. DY5: Brie H 3G 109
Britannia Gdns. B65: Row R 6C 96
Britannia Grn. DY3: Up Gor 2A 76
Britannia Pk. WS10: W'bry 2D 62
Britannia Rd. B65: Row R 1C 112
WS1: Wals 6B 48
WV14: Bils 2H 61
Britannia St. B69: Tiv 5C 78
Britannic Gdns. B13: Mose 3F 133
Britannic Pk. B13: Mose 3F 133
Britford Cl. B14: K Hth 4H 147
Brittan Cl. B34: S End 3A 106
Britton Dr. B72: W Grn 5A 70
Britwell Rd. B73: W Grn 3G 69
Brixfield Way B90: Dic H 4G 163
Brixham Rd. B16: Edg 5H 99
Broadacres B31: N'fld 1C 144
Broadcott Ind. Est. B64: Old H 2A 112
Broad Cft. DY4: Tip 1C 78
Broadfern Rd. B93: Know 1D 166
Broadfield Cl. B71: W Brom 4D 64
DY6: K'wfrd 4B 92
Broadfield House Glass Mus. 4A 92
Broadfields Rd. B23: Erd 6H 69
Broadfield Wlk. B16: Birm 2D 116
Broadheath Dr. WS4: S'fld 1H 33
Broadhidley Dr. B32: Bart G 4H 129
Broadlands WV10: F'hses 2H 15
Broadlands Dr. DY5: Brie H 4A 94
Broad La. B14: K Hth 3F 147
WS3: Blox 4F 19
WS4: S'fld 6G 21
WV3: Wolv 3C 42
WV11: Ess 1C 18
Broad La. Gdns. WS3: Blox 5G 19
Broad La. Nth. WV12: W'hall 3B 30
Broad Lanes WV14: Bils 2E 61
Broad La. Sth. WV11: Wed 4H 29
Broadmeadow DY6: K'wfrd 1C 92
WS9: A'rdge 1D 34
Broadmeadow Cl. B30: K Nor 4D 146
Broad Mdw. Grn. WV14: Bils 4E 45
Broadmeadow Ho. B32: Bart G 5B 130
Broad Mdw. La. B30: K Nor 4D 146
Broadmeadow La. WS6: Gt Wyr 3G 7
Broadmeadows Cl. WV12: W'hall 1E 31
Broadmeadows Rd. WV12: W'hall 1E 31
Broadmoor Av. B67: Smeth 1B 114
B68: O'bry 1B 114
Broadmoor Cl. WV14: Bils 1E 61
Broadmoor Rd. WV14: Bils 1E 61
Broadoaks B76: Walm 5E 71
Broad Oaks Rd. B91: Sol 1D 150
Broad Rd. B27: A Grn 2H 135
Broadstone Av. B63: Crad 1D 126
WS3: Blox 3B 32
Broadstone Cl. WV4: Penn 6H 43
Broadstone Rd. B26: Yard 1D 120
Broad St. B1: Birm 2D 116
B15: Birm 2D 116 (6A 4)
B69: O'bry 4G 97
DY5: P'ntt 3G 93
DY6: K'wfrd 4B 92
WV1: Wolv 1H 43 (2C 170)
WV14: Bils 5E 45
WV14: Cose 5E 61
Broad St. Junc. WV1: Wolv 1H 43 (2D 170)
Broadwalk B1: Birm 2E 117 (6A 4)
Broadwalk Retail Pk.
WS1: Wals 5B 48
Broadwaters Av. WS10: Darl 1C 62
Broadwaters Rd. WS10: Darl 1C 62
Broad Way WS4: S'fld 5G 21
Broadway B68: O'bry 2A 114
B90: Shir 3G 149
WS1: Wals 5D 48
WV3: Wolv 2A 42
WV8: Cod 4E 13
WV10: Bush 5A 16
Broadway, The B20: Hand 5F 83
B71: W Brom 6G 63
DY1: Dud 4C 76
DY8: Stourb 2B 124
WV5: Wom 2G 73
Broadway Av. B9: Bord G 1G 119
B63: Hale 3A 128
Broadway Community Leisure Cen. 5G 83
Broadway Cft. B26: Sheld 5E 121
B68: O'bry 2A 114
Broadway Gdns. WV10: Bush 5A 16
Broadway Nth. WS1: Wals 1D 48
Broadway Plaza 2C 116
Broadway W. WS1: Wals 5A 48
Broadwell Ind. Pk. B69: O'bry 6F 79
Broadwell Rd. B69: O'bry 1G 97
B92: Olton 3E 137
Broadwyn Trad. Est. B64: Old H 2A 112
Broadyates Gro. B25: Yard 5A 120
Broadyates Rd. B25: Yard 5A 120
Brobury Cft. B91: Shir 3B 150
Broches, The WS11: Nort C 1F 9
Brockeridge Cl. WV12: W'hall 6C 18
Brockfield Ho. WV10: Wolv 5B 28
Brockhall Gro. B37: K'hrst 4B 106
Brockhill La. B48: A'chu 6D 160
Brockhurst Cres. WS5: Wals 6C 48
Brockhurst Dr. B28: Hall G 2G 149
WV6: Wolv 5E 27
Brockhurst Ho. WS2: Wals 6B 32
Brockhurst La. B75: Can 3E 39
Brockhurst Pl. WS5: Wals 6D 48
Brockhurst Rd. B36: Hodg H 3A 104
B75: R'ley 2B 54
Brockhurst St. WS1: Wals 5C 48
Brockley Cl. DY5: Brie H 6H 93
Brockley Gro. B13: Mose 4E 133
Brockley Pl. B7: Nech 2C 102
BROCKMOOR 5G 93
Brockmoor Cl. DY9: Pedm 3G 125
Brock Rd. DY4: Tip 3C 78
Brockton Rd. B29: W Cas 4E 131
Brockwell Gro. B44: Gt Barr 1G 67
Brockwell Rd. B44: Gt Barr 1G 67
Brockworth Rd. B14: K Hth 5E 147
Brocton Cl. WS3: Blox 1G 31
WV14: Cose 2D 60
Brogden Cl. B71: W Brom 5D 64
Bromfield Cl. B6: Aston 2G 101
Bromfield Ct. WV6: Tett 1H 41
Bromfield Cres. WS10: W'bry 1A 64
Bromfield Rd. WS10: W'bry 2A 64
BROMFORD 5B 86
Bromford Cl. B20: Hand 6C 82
B23: Erd 2E 85
Bromford Ct. B31: N'fld 6F 145
Bromford Cres. B24: Erd 5G 85
Bromford Dale WV1: Wolv 6E 27
WV6: Wolv 6E 27
Bromford Dell B31: N'fld 3G 145
Bromford Dr. B36: Hodg H 1H 103
Bromford Gdns. B15: Edg 3G 115
Bromford Ga. B24: Erd 1G 103
Bromford Hill B20: Hand 4E 83
Bromford Ho. B73: Bold 3F 69
Bromford La. B8: W End 3H 103
B24: Erd 5G 85
B70: W Brom 6G 79
Bromford Mere B92: Olton 5C 136
Bromford Mills Ind. Est.
B24: Erd 6G 85
Bromford Pk. B69: O'bry 1G 97
Bromford Pk. Ho. B13: Mose 3B 134
(off Wake Grn. Pk.)
Bromford Pk. Ind. Est.
B70: W Brom 6G 79
Bromford Ri. WV3: Wolv 3F 43
Bromford Rd. B36: Hodg H 2H 103
B69: O'bry 1G 97
B70: W Brom 6G 79
DY2: Dud 3C 94
Bromford Rd. Ind. Est. B69: O'bry 6G 79
Bromford Wlk. B43: Gt Barr 4B 66
BROMLEY 4F 93
Bromley DY5: P'ntt 4F 93
Bromley Gdns. WV8: Cod 3G 13
Bromley La. DY6: K'wfrd 5C 92
Bromley Pl. WV4: Penn 6E 43
Bromley St. B9: Birm 2A 118
DY9: Lye 5B 110
WV2: Wolv 4G 43
Brompton Dr. DY5: Brie H 4F 109
Brompton Lawns WV6: Tett 6G 25
Brompton Pool Rd. B28: Hall G 4E 149
Brompton Rd. B44: Gt Barr 1G 67
Bromsgrove Rd.
B62: Hunn, Roms 3A 142
B63: Hale 2C 128
DY9: Clent, Hag 6G 125
Bromsgrove St. B5: Birm 2G 117 (6E 5)
B63: Hale 1C 128
Bromwall Rd. B13: Mose 1B 148
Bromwich Ct. B46: Col 5G 89
Bromwich Dr. B75: S Cold 4A 54
Bromwich La. DY9: Pedm 6F 125
Bromwich Wlk. B9: Bord G 6G 103
Bromwynd Cl. WV2: Wolv 5F 43
Bromyard Av. B76: Walm 5E 71
Bromyard Rd. B11: S'hll 2E 135
Bronte Cl. B90: Shir 6B 150
Bronte Ct. B90: Shir 6B 150
Bronte Farm Rd. B90: Shir 6B 150
Bronte Rd. WV2: E'shll 5B 44
Bronwen Rd. WV14: Cose 6E 61
Brookbank Av. B34: S End 3H 105
Brookbank Gdns. DY3: Gorn 5F 75
Brookbank Rd. DY3: Gorn 5F 75
Brook Cl. B33: Stech 5C 104
B90: Shir 6F 149
WS9: Wals W 4C 22
Brook Cres. DY6: W Hth 2A 92
DY9: W'cte 2B 126
Brook Cft. B26: Sheld 4F 121
B37: Mars G 4D 122
Brookdale DY3: Lwr G 4G 75
Brookdale Cl. B45: Redn 6G 143
Brookdale Dr. WV4: Penn 5C 42
Brook Dr. B32: Bart G 4B 130
Brook End WS7: Chase 1C 10
Brookend Dr. B45: Rubery 1F 157
Brookes Cl. B69: Tiv 1B 96
Brookes Ho. WS1: Wals 2D 48
(off Paddock La.)
Brooke St. DY2: Dud 1E 95
Brook Farm Wlk. B37: Chel W 6F 107
Brookfield Cl. WS9: A'rdge 6C 22
Brookfield Rd. B18: Hock 4C 100
WS9: A'rdge 6C 22
WV8: Bilb 4H 13
BROOKFIELDS 5D 100
Brookfields Rd. B68: O'bry 5A 98
Brookfield Ter. B18: Hock 4C 100
Brookfield Way B92: Olton 6B 136
DY4: Tip 1A 78
Brook Grn. La. B92: Bars 6A 154
Brook Gro. WV8: Bilb 4H 13
Brookhill Cl. WV12: W'hall 6C 18
Brook Hill Rd. B8: W End 5G 103
Brookhill Way WV12: W'hall 6D 18
Brook Holloway DY9: W'cte 1B 126
Brookhouse Cl. WV10: F'stne 1D 16
Brook Ho. La. WV10: F'stne 1A 16
Brookhouse Rd. WS5: Wals 4F 49
Brookhurst La. B90: Dic H 3H 163
Brookhus Farm Rd. B76: Walm 5E 71
Brooking Cl. B43: Gt Barr 1F 67
Brookland Gro. WS9: Wals W 5B 22
Brookland Rd. WS9: Wals W 4B 22
Brooklands DY3: Swind 6E 73
DY8: Word 2D 108
WS5: Wals 2F 65
Brooklands Av. WS6: Gt Wyr 1F 7
Brooklands Cl. B28: Hall G 4F 135
Brooklands Dr. B14: K Hth 2G 147
Brooklands Pde. WV1: Wolv 2C 44
Brooklands Rd. B28: Hall G 4F 135
Brooklands Way B37: Mars G 3D 122
Brook La. B13: Mose 5A 134
B32: Harb 6D 114
B64: Old H 1G 111
B92: Olton 5B 136
WS6: Gt Wyr 2G 7
WS9: Wals W 4B 22
Brooklea Gro. B38: K Nor 6C 146
Brooklyn Av. B6: Aston 2H 101
Brooklyn Gro. DY6: W Hth 1H 91
WV14: Cose 5F 61
Brooklyn Rd. WS7: Chase 1C 10
Brookmans Av. B32: Quin 1B 130
Brook Mdw. Ct. B28: Hall G 1D 148
Brook Mdw. Rd. B34: S End 3E 105
WS4: S'fld 1H 33
Brook Mdws. WV8: Bilb 3H 13
Brookmoor Ind. Est. DY5: Brie H 6E 93
Brookpiece Ho. B14: K Hth 5G 147
(off Milston Cl.)
Brook Piece Wlk. B35: Cas V 4F 87
Brook Rd. B15: Edg 4A 116
B45: Rubery 2E 157
B68: O'bry 1G 113
DY8: Stourb 2F 125
WS6: C Hay 1E 7
WV5: Wom 1F 73
WV13: W'hall 2G 45
Brooksbank Dr. B64: Old H 5H 95
Brooksby Gro. B93: Dorr 6H 167
Brooks Cft. B35: Cas V 5E 87
Brookside B31: N'fld 2D 144
B43: Gt Barr 6H 65
B90: Ches G 6B 164
DY3: Gorn 5H 75
WS10: W'bry 2H 63
Brookside Av. B13: Mose 6B 134
Brookside Cl. B23: Erd 6C 68
B63: Hale 2F 127
WV5: Wom 1E 73
Brookside Ind. Est. WS10: W'bry 2H 63
Brookside Way DY6: W Hth 2H 91
Brooks Rd. B72: W Grn 5A 70
Brook St. B3: Birm 6E 101 (2B 4)
B66: Smeth 3F 99
B70: W Brom 4H 79
DY3: Gorn 4G 75
DY3: Sed 6C 60
DY4: Tip 1G 77
DY5: Quar B 3C 110
DY6: W Hth 6H 73
DY8: Stourb 6C 108
DY8: Word 2D 108
DY9: Lye 6B 110
WS2: Wals 2B 48
WV14: Bils 6G 45
Brook St. Bus. Cen. DY4: Tip 1G 77
Brook Ter. WV14: Bils 6G 45
Brookthorpe Dr. WV12: W'hall 6C 30
Brookvale Gro. B92: Olton 4B 136
Brookvale M. B29: S Oak 3D 132
Brookvale Pk. Rd. B23: Erd 2B 84
Brookvale Rd. B6: Witt 5A 84
B92: Olton 4B 136
Brookvale Trad. Est. B6: Witt 4H 83
Brookview B67: Smeth 6D 98
Brook Vw. Cl. B19: Hock 3E 101
Brook Wlk. B32: Bart G 3B 130
Brookwillow Rd. B63: Hale 4F 127
Brookwood Av. B28: Hall G 2D 148
Broomcroft Rd. B37: K'hrst 4B 106
Broomdene Av. B34: S End 2E 105
Broom Dr. B14: K Hth 3G 147
Broome Av. B43: Gt Barr 6G 65
Broome Cl. B63: Hale 2A 128
Broome Ct. B36: Cas B 1G 105
Broome Gdns. B75: S Cold 6A 54
Broomehill Cl. DY5: Brie H 4G 109
Broome Rd. WV10: Bush 2A 28
Broomfield B67: Smeth 4D 98
Broomfield Rd. B23: Erd 5D 84
Broomfields Av. B91: Sol 2H 151
Broomfields Cl. B91: Sol 2H 151
Broomfields Farm Rd. B91: Sol 2H 151
Broomhall Av. WV11: Wed 3F 29
Broom Hall Cres. B27: A Grn 6H 135
Broom Hall Gro. B27: A Grn 5A 136
Broomhill Cl. B43: Gt Barr 5H 65
Broomhill La. B43: Gt Barr 5H 65
Broomhill Rd. B23: Erd 6B 68
(not continuous)
Broom Ho. B71: W Brom 4D 64
Broomhurst B15: Edg 3A 116
Broomie Cl. B75: S Cold 6B 54
Broom La. B90: Dic H 3G 163
Broomlea Cl. B74: S'tly 3G 51
Broom Rd. DY1: Dud 2C 76
WS5: Wals 2F 65
Broom St. B12: Birm 3A 118
Broomy Cl. B34: Stech 4E 105
Broseley Av. B31: Longb 1F 159
Broseley Brook Cl. B9: Bord G 2C 118
Brosil Av. B20: Hand 4A 82
Brougham St. B19: Loz 2D 100
(not continuous)
Brough Cl. B7: Nech 3B 102
WV4: E'shll 2B 60
Broughton Ct. WV6: Pert 6G 25
Broughton Cres. B31: Longb 1B 158
Broughton Rd. B20: Hand 1C 100
DY9: W'cte 2H 125
WV3: Wolv 2A 42
Brownfield Rd. B34: S End 3G 105
BROWNHILLS 6B 10
Brownhills Bus. Pk. WS8: Bwnhls 2B 22
BROWNHILLS COMMON 5A 10
Brownhills Rd. WS8: Wals W 2B 22
WS11: Nort C 1E 9
BROWNHILLS WEST 3G 9
Brownhills West Station
Chasewater Railway 2G 9
Browning Cl. WV12: W'hall 2E 31
Browning Cres. WV10: F'hses 5G 15
Browning Gro. WV6: Pert 5E 25
Browning Rd. DY3: Lwr G 3E 75
Browning St. B16: Birm 1D 116
Browning Twr. B31: N'fld 4G 145
Brownley Rd. B90: Shir 2B 164
Brown Lion St. DY4: Tip 6G 61
Brown Rd. WS10: Darl 4C 46
Brown's Coppice Av. B91: Sol 2B 150
Browns Ct. B13: Mose 3B 134
Brown's Dr. B73: Bold 5F 69
Brownsea Cl. B45: Fran 6E 143
Brownsea Dr. B1: Birm 2F 117 (6C 4)
BROWN'S GREEN
Birmingham 4B 82
Browns Grn. B20: Hand 4B 82
Brownshore La. WV11: Ess 3A 18
Browns La. B93: Know 3A 166
Brownsover Cl. B36: Cas B 6F 87
Brown St. WV2: Wolv 4H 43
Brownswall Est. DY3: Sed 6F 59
Brownswall Rd. DY3: Sed 6F 59
Broxwood Pk. WV6: Tett 6H 25
Brueton Av. B91: Sol 4H 151
Brueton Dr. B24: Erd 4G 85

A-Z Birmingham Deluxe 179

Brueton Rd. WV14: Bils 4A 46
Bruford Rd. WV3: Wolv 3E 43
Brunel Cl. B12: Bal H 6A 118
Brunel Ct. WS10: Darl 5F 47
WV5: Wom 6G 57
WV14: Cose 5G 61
Brunel Dr. DY4: Tip 4G 61
Brunel Gro. WV6: Pert 3E 25
Brunel Rd. B69: O'bry 3D 96
Brunel St. B2: Birm 1F 117 (5C 4)
Brunel Wlk. WS10: Darl 5F 47
Brunel Way WV2: E'shll 4C 44
Brunslow Cl. WV10: Oxl 6G 15
WV13: W'hall 2C 46
Brunswick Arc. B1: Birm 1D 116
(off Brunswick St.)
Brunswick Ct. WS10: W'bry 2A 64
Brunswick Gdns. B21: Hand 6B 82
WS10: W'bry 1H 63
Brunswick Ga. DY8: Stourb 4E 125
Brunswick Ho. B34: S End 2E 105
B37: Mars G 3B 122
Brunswick Pk. Rd. WS10: W'bry 2G 63
Brunswick Rd. B12: Bal H 6A 118
B21: Hand 6B 82
Brunswick Sq. B1: Birm 1D 116 (5A 4)
Brunswick St. B1: Birm 1D 116 (5A 4)
WS2: Wals 4A 48
Brunswick Ter. WS10: W'bry 2F 63
Brunton Rd. B10: Small H 4F 119
Brushfield Rd. B42: Gt Barr 5F 67
Brutus Dr. B46: Col 6G 89
Bryan Av. WV4: Penn 1B 58
Bryan Rd. WS2: Wals 5A 48
Bryanston Ct. B91: Sol 6D 136
Bryanston Rd. B91: Sol 6D 136
Bryant St. B18: Win G 4A 100
Bryce Rd. DY5: P'ntt 4E 93
(not continuous)
Bryher Wlk. B45: Fran 6E 143
Brylan Cft. B44: K'sdng 1H 83
Brymill Ind. Est. DY4: Tip 6G 61
Bryn Arden Rd. B26: Yard 6C 120
Bryndale Av. B14: K Hth 2E 147
Brynmawr Rd. WV14: Cose 2C 60
Brynside Cl. B14: K Hth 5F 147
Bryony Cft. B23: Erd 6B 68
Bryony Gdns. WS10: Darl 4D 46
Bryony Rd. B29: W Cas 6F 131
BSA Bus. Pk. B11: Small H 5D 118
Buchanan Av. WS4: Wals 6E 33
Buchanan Cl. WS4: Wals 6E 33
Buchanan Rd. WS4: Wals 6E 33
Buckbury Cl. DY9: Pedm 4H 125
Buckbury Cft. B90: M'path 3F 165
Buckingham Cl. WS10: W'bry 1A 64
Buckingham Ct. B29: S Oak 4A 132
Buckingham Dr. WV12: W'hall 2B 30
Buckingham Gro. DY6: K'wfrd 2A 92
Buckingham Ho. B31: Longb 1D 158
Buckingham M. B73: W Grn 2G 69
Buckingham Ri. DY1: Dud 5A 76
Buckingham Rd. B36: Cas B 2B 106
B65: Row R 5D 96
WV4: Penn 1E 59
Buckingham St. B19: Birm 5F 101
BUCKLAND END 2D 104
Buckland End B34: S End 3E 105
Buckland Ho. B15: Edg 4E 117
(off Summer Rd.)
Bucklands End La. B34: Hodg H 3D 104
Buckle Cl. WS1: Wals 3D 48
Buckley Ct. B13: K Hth 5H 133
Buckley Rd. WV4: Penn 6B 42
Bucklow Wlk. B33: Stech 5C 104
Buckminster Dr. B93: Dorr 5A 166
Bucknall Ct. B13: Mose 3B 134
Bucknall Cres. B32: Bart G 5G 129
Bucknall Rd. WV11: Wed 6B 18
Bucknell Cl. B91: Sol 2G 151
BUCKPOOL 1D 108
Buckridge Cl. B38: K Nor 2H 159
Buckridge La. B90: Dic H 4G 163
(not continuous)
Buckton Cl. B75: R'ley 1C 54
Budbrooke Gro. B34: S End 3A 106
Budden Rd. WV14: Cose 6F 61
Bude Rd. WS5: Wals 4H 49
Buffery Rd. DY2: Dud 2F 95
Bufferys Cl. B91: Sol 1F 165
Buildwas Cl. WS3: Blox 5F 19
Bulford Cl. B14: K Hth 5H 147
Bulger Rd. WV14: Bils 4E 45
Bullace Cft. B15: Edg 2H 131
Buller St. WV4: E'shll 6A 44
Bullfields Cl. B65: Row R 4H 95
Bullfinch Cl. DY1: Dud 1A 94
Bullivents Cl. B93: Ben H 4B 166
Bull La. B70: W Brom 4G 79
WS10: Mox 2B 62
WV5: Wom 5G 57
WV14: Bils 2B 62
Bull Mdw. La. WV5: Wom 5G 57
Bullock's Row WS1: Wals 2D 48
Bullock St. B7: Birm 4A 102
B70: W Brom 1B 98
Bullows Rd. WS8: Bwnhls 1G 21
Bull Ring B63: Hale 2B 128
DY3: Sed 5H 59
WV13: W'hall 6A 30
Bullring Shop. Cen. B5: Birm 1G 117 (5F 5)
Bull Ring Trad. Est.
B12: Birm 2H 117 (6H 5)
Bull's La. B76: Walm 2F 71
(not continuous)
Bull St. B4: Birm 6G 101 (3E 5)
B17: Harb 5H 115
B70: W Brom 4B 80
DY1: Dud 1C 94
DY3: Gorn 5G 75
DY5: Brie H 2F 109
(Goldencross Way)
DY5: Brie H 1E 109
(Hawbush Rd.)
WS10: Darl 5E 47
Bull St. Trad. Est. DY5: Brie H 1F 109
Bulrush Cl. WS8: Bwnhls 6A 10
Bulwell Cl. B6: Aston 2A 102
Bulwer St. WV10: Wolv 6H 27
BUMBLE HOLE 4G 95
Bumblehole Mdws. WV5: Wom 6F 57
Bumble Hole Nature Reserve 4G 95
Bunbury Gdns. B30: K Nor 3G 145
Bunbury Rd. B31: N'fld 3F 145
Bundle Hill B63: Hale 2A 128
Bungalows, The B70: W Brom 1F 79
BUNKER'S HILL 4G 45
Bunkers Hill La. WV14: Bils 3G 45
Bunn's La. DY2: Dud 6H 77
Burbage Cl. WV10: Wolv 3B 28
Burberry Ct. DY4: Tip 5A 62
Burberry Gro. CV7: Bal C 3G 169
Burbidge Rd. B9: Bord G 6D 102
Burbury St. B19: Loz 2E 101
Burbury St. Sth. B19: Hock 3E 101
Burcombe Twr. B23: Erd 1H 85
Burcot Av. WV1: Wolv 1C 44
Burcot Ct. B74: Four O 1F 53
Burcote Rd. B24: Erd 4B 86
Burcot Wlk. WV1: Wolv 1C 44
Burdock Cl. WS5: Wals 2E 65
Burdock Ho. B38: K Nor 6B 146
Burdock Rd. B29: W Cas 1E 145
Burdons Cl. B34: Stech 4E 105
Bure Gro. WV13: W'hall 1D 46
Burfield Rd. B63: Crad 5E 111
Burford Cl. B92: Olton 2E 137
WS5: Wals 2E 65
Burford Ct. B13: Mose 3B 134
Burford Pk. Rd. B38: K Nor 1A 160
Burford Rd. B44: K'sdng 6H 67
B47: H'wd 3H 161
Burgess Cft. B92: Sol 6B 138
Burghley Dr. B71: W Brom 3D 64
Burghley Wlk. DY5: Brie H 3F 109
Burgh Way WS2: Wals 4G 31
Burhill Way B37: F'bri 4D 106
Burke Av. B13: Mose 4D 134
Burkitt Dr. DY4: Tip 5C 62
Burland Av. WV6: Tett 2C 26
Burleigh Cl. CV7: Bal C 2H 169
WV12: W'hall 3B 30
Burleigh Cft. WS7: Chase 1C 10
Burleigh Rd. WV3: Wolv 4E 43
Burleigh St. WS1: Wals 2E 49
Burleton Rd. B33: Kitts G 1A 122
Burley Cl. B90: Shir 5F 149
Burley Way B38: K Nor 1G 159
Burlington Arc. B2: Birm 4D 4
Burlington Av. B70: W Brom 6C 80
Burlington Pas. B2: Birm 4D 4
Burlington Rd. B10: Small H 2E 119
B70: W Brom 6C 80
Burlington St. B6: Aston 3G 101
Burlish Av. B92: Olton 4D 136
Burman Cl. B90: Shir 5G 149
Burman Dr. B46: Col 4H 107
Burman Rd. B90: Shir 5F 149
Burmarsh Wlk. WV8: Pend 1D 26
Burmese Way B65: Row R 3H 95
Burnaston Cres. B90: M'path 3G 165
Burnaston Rd. B28: Hall G 4E 135
Burnbank Gro. B24: Erd 3H 85
Burn Cl. B66: Smeth 5E 99
Burncross Way WV10: Wolv 3B 28
Burnell Gdns. WV3: Wolv 3C 42
Burnel Rd. B29: W Cas 3E 131
Burnett Ho. B69: O'bry 4D 96
Burnett Rd. B74: Lit A 1B 52
Burney La. B8: W End 4A 104
Burnfields Way WS9: A'rdge 2C 34
Burnham Av. B25: Yard 5A 120
WV10: Oxl 1F 27
Burnham Cl. DY6: K'wfrd 5D 92
Burnham Ct. B23: Erd 5C 84
DY5: Brie H. 1H 109
(off Hill St.)
Burnham Mdw. B28: Hall G 1G 149
Burnham Rd. B44: Gt Barr 6G 67
Burnhill Gro. B29: W Cas 5E 131
Burnlea Gro. B31: N'fld 6G 145
Burnsall Cl. B37: F'bri 1B 122
WV9: Pend 4E 15
Burns Av. DY4: Tip 5A 62
WV10: F'hses 5H 15
Burns Cl. DY8: Amb 3E 109
Burns Gro. DY3: Lwr G 3E 75
Burnside Ct. B73: W Grn 4G 69
Burnside Gdns. WS5: Wals 5H 49
Burnside Way B31: Longb 2D 158
Burns Pl. WS10: Mox 6A 46
Burns Rd. WS10: Mox 6A 46
Burnthurst Cres. B90: M'path 2E 165
Burnt Oak Dr. DY8: Stourb 6F 109
BURNT TREE 5H 77
Burnt Tree DY4: Tip 5H 77
BURNTWOOD JUNC. 2B 10
Burntwood Rd. WS7: Hamm 1F 11
Burrelton Way B43: Gt Barr 5H 65
Burrington Rd. B32: Bart G 5G 129
Burrowes St. WS2: Wals 6B 32
Burrow Hill Cl. B36: Cas B 1G 105
Burrows Ho. WS2: Wals 6B 32
(off Burrowes St.)
Burrows Rd. DY6: K'wfrd 5D 92
Bursledon Wlk. WV1: Wolv 3E 45
Burslem Cl. WS3: Blox 3G 19
Bursnips Rd. WV11: Ess 5B 18
Burton Av. WS4: Rus 1F 33
Burton Cres. WV10: Wolv 6A 28
Burton Farm Rd. WS4: Wals 6F 33
Burton Gro. B64: Old H 3G 111
Burton Rd. DY1: Dud 3B 76
WV10: Wolv 6A 28
Burton Rd. E. DY1: Dud 3B 76
Burton Wood Dr. B20: Hand 5F 83
Buryfield Rd. B91: Sol 1E 151
Bury Hill Rd. B69: O'bry 2D 96
Bury Mound Ct. B90: Shir 5C 148
Bush Av. B66: Smeth 4G 99
BUSHBURY 6A 16
Bushbury Ct. WV10: Bush 5A 16
Bushbury Crematorium WV10: Bush 4B 16
Bushbury Cft. B37: Chel W 6E 107
Bushbury La. WV10: Oxl, Bush 3G 27
Bushbury Rd. B33: Stech 4E 105
WV10: Wolv 3C 28
Bushbury Swimming Pool 6A 16
Bushell Dr. B91: Sol 3H 151
Bushey Cl. B74: S'tly 1H 51
Bushey Flds. Rd. DY1: Dud 1A 94
Bush Gro. B21: Hand 6G 81
WS3: Pels 5E 21
Bushley Cft. B91: Sol 1F 165
Bushman Way B34: S End 4A 106
Bushmore Rd. B28: Hall G 1G 149
Bush Rd. DY2: Neth 1E 111
DY4: Tip 3G 77
Bush St. WS10: Darl 4D 46
Bushway Cl. DY5: Brie H. 1E 109
Bushwood Ct. B15: Edg 3E 117
B29: S Oak 4G 131
Bushwood Dr. B93: Dorr 6C 166
Bushwood Rd. B29: S Oak 4F 131
(not continuous)
Business Cen., The B11: Tys 5F 119
Bustleholme Av. B71: W Brom 4D 64
Bustleholme Cres.
B71: W Brom 4C 64
Bustleholme La. B71: W Brom 4C 64
(not continuous)
Butchers La. B63: Crad 4E 111
Butchers Rd. B92: H Ard 1A 154
BUTCROFT 5E 47
Butcroft Gdns. WS10: Darl 5E 47
Bute Cl. B45: Fran 6E 143
WV12: W'hall 3B 30
Butler Lane Station (Rail) 6G 37
Butler Rd. B92: Olton 2D 136
Butlers Cl. B20: Hand 4C 82
B23: Erd 4D 68
Butlers La. B74: Four O 6F 37
Butlers Pct. WS1: Wals 1C 48
Butler's Rd. B20: Hand 4C 82
Butler St. B70: W Brom 3G 79
Butlin St. B7: Nech 2C 102
Buttercup Cl. WS5: Wals 2E 65
Butterfield Cl. WV6: Pert 6D 24
Butterfield Ct. DY1: Dud 5C 76
Butterfield Rd. DY5: P'ntt 2F 93
Butterfly Way B64: Old H 2H 111
Buttermere Cl. DY5: Brie H 4F 109
WV6: Tett 1B 26
Buttermere Ct. WV6: Pert 5F 25
Buttermere Dr. B32: Bart G 2D 130
WV11: Ess 5A 18
Buttermere Gro. WV12: W'hall 6B 18
Butter Wlk. B38: K Nor 1G 159
Butterworth Cl. WV14: Cose 4C 60
Buttery Rd. B67: Smeth 3C 98
Buttons Farm Rd. WV4: Penn 2B 58
Buttress Way B66: Smeth 3E 99
Butts, The WS4: Wals 6D 32
Butts Cl. WS11: Nort C 1C 8
Butts La. WS11: Nort C 1C 8
Butts Rd. WS4: Wals 6D 32
WV4: Penn 1D 58
Butts St. WS4: Wals 6D 32
Butts Way WS11: Nort C 1C 8
Buxton Cl. WS3: Blox 4A 20
Buxton Rd. B23: Erd 1B 84
B73: W Grn 4G 69
DY2: Dud 3B 94
WS3: Blox 4A 20
Byeways WS3: Blox 4A 20
Byfield Cl. B33: Kitts G 3A 122
Byfield Pas. B9: Bord G 1E 119
Byfield Way DY3: Sed 6A 60
Byfleet Cl. WV14: Cose 2C 60
Byford Way B37: Mars G 3D 122
Byland Way WS3: Blox 5F 19
By-Pass Link B91: Sol 4A 152
Byrchen Moor Gdns. DY5: P'ntt 2F 93
Byrne Rd. WV2: Wolv 4H 43
Byron Av. B23: Erd 4B 84
Byron Cl. B10: Small H 4D 118
Byron Ct. B74: Four O 4G 37
B93: Know 3C 166
Byron Cres. DY1: Dud 2D 76
Byron Cft. B74: Four O 3F 37
DY3: Lwr G 2E 75
Byron Gdns. B71: W Brom 2H 79
Byron Ho. B63: Crad 6D 110
Byron Rd. B10: Small H 4D 118
WV10: Bush 1C 28
WV12: W'hall 2E 31
Byron St. B71: W Brom 1H 79
DY5: P'ntt 2H 93
Bywater Ho. WS1: Wals 2D 48
(off Paddock La.)

C

Caban Cl. B31: N'fld 2C 144
Cable Dr. WS2: Wals 4A 32
Cabot Gro. WV6: Pert 5E 25
Cadbury Dr. B35: Cas V 6E 87
Cadbury Ho. B19: Birm 4F 101
(off Gt. Hampton Row)
Cadbury Rd. B13: Mose 1B 134
Cadbury Way B17: Harb 6F 115
Cadbury World 6B 132
Caddick Cres. B71: W Brom 6B 64
Caddick Rd. B42: Gt Barr 4D 66
Caddick St. WV14: Cose 5C 60
(not continuous)
Cadet Dr. B90: Shir 4G 149
Cadgwith Gdns. WV14: Bils 3A 62
Cadine Gdns. B13: Mose 4E 133
Cadleigh Gdns. B17: Harb 2G 131
Cadle Rd. WV10: Bush 2A 28
Cadman Cres. WV10: Wolv 3C 28
Cadman's La. WS3: Blox 1B 20
WS6: Gt Wyr 5A 8
(not continuous)
Cadnam Cl. B17: Harb 2G 131
WV13: W'hall 3B 46
Caernarvon Cl. WV12: W'hall 2C 30
Caernarvon Way DY1: Dud 5A 76
Caesar Way B46: Col 6H 89
Cahill Av. WV10: Wolv 5C 28
Cairn Dr. WS2: Wals 1F 47
Cairns St. WS2: Wals 6A 32
Caister Dr. WV13: W'hall 3H 45
Cakemore La. B68: O'bry 1F 113
Cakemore Rd. B65: Row R 1E 113
Cala Dr. B15: Edg 4D 116
Calcot Dr. WV6: Tett 2C 26
Calcutt Way B90: Dic H 3G 163
(not continuous)
Caldecote Gro. B9: Bord G 1A 120
Caldeford Av. B90: M'path 2E 165
Calder Av. WS1: Wals 1E 49
Calder Dr. B76: Walm 5D 70
Calderfields Cl. WS4: Wals 6E 33
Calder Gro. B20: Hand 5B 82
Calder Ri. DY3: Sed 1B 76
Calder Twr. B20: Hand 6F 83
CALDMORE 3C 48
Caldmore Grn. WS1: Wals 3C 48
Caldmore Rd. WS1: Wals 2C 48
Caldwell Ct. B91: Sol 2G 151
Caldwell Gro. B91: Sol 2G 151
Caldwell Ho. B70: W Brom 5A 80
Caldwell Rd. B9: Bord G 6H 103
Caldwell St. B71: W Brom 5B 64
Caldy Wlk. B45: Fran 6F 143
Caledonia DY5: Quar B 4H 109
Caledonia Cl. WS5: Wals 2G 65
Caledonia Rd. WV2: Wolv 3H 43
(not continuous)
Caledonia St. WV14: Bils 5G 45
Caledon Pl. WS2: Wals 4A 48
Caledon St. WS2: Wals 4A 48
(not continuous)
Calewood Rd. DY5: Quar B 4H 109
CALIFORNIA 2D 130
California Ho. B32: Bart G 3C 130
(off Millmead Rd.)
California Rd. B69: Tiv 1B 96
California Way B32: Bart G 2D 130
Callcott Dr. DY5: Quar B 4H 109
Callear Rd. WS10: W'bry 4D 62
Calley Cl. DY4: Tip 4H 77
Callow Bri. Rd. B45: Rubery 2F 157
Callowbrook La. B45: Rubery 1F 157
Calshot Rd. B42: Gt Barr 4B 66
Calstock Rd. WV12: W'hall 5D 30
Calthorpe Cl. WS5: Wals 5A 50
Calthorpe Mans. B15: Edg 2D 116
Calthorpe Rd. B15: Edg 3C 116
B20: Hand 5E 83
WS5: Wals 5H 49
Calver Cres. WV11: Wed 4H 29
Calver Gro. B44: Gt Barr 2F 67
Calverley Rd. B38: K Nor 6H 145
Calverton Gro. B43: Gt Barr 5A 66
Calverton Wlk. WV6: Wolv 4F 27
Calves Cft. WV13: W'hall 6A 30
Calvin Cl. WV5: Wom 2F 73
WV10: F'hses 4H 15
Camberley B71: W Brom 4D 64
Camberley Cres. WV4: E'shll 3A 60
Camberley Dr. WV4: Penn 1E 59
Camberley Gro. B23: Erd 1E 85
Camberley Rd. DY6: K'wfrd 6D 92
Camborne Cl. B6: Aston 2G 101
Camborne Ct. WS5: Wals 4H 49
Camborne Rd. WS5: Wals 4H 49
Cambourne Rd. B65: Row R 6C 96
Cambrai Dr. B28: Hall G 5E 135
Cambria Cl. B90: Maj G 2E 163
Cambridge Av. B73: W Grn 5H 69
B91: Sol 4C 150
Cambridge Cl. WS9: A'rdge 1C 34
Cambridge Cres. B15: Edg 4E 117
Cambridge Dr. B37: Mars G 3B 122
Cambridge Rd. B13: Mose 4H 133
B66: Smeth 2E 99
DY2: Dud 2C 94
Cambridge St. B1: Birm 1E 117 (4A 4)
B70: W Brom 5H 79
WS1: Wals 4C 48
WV10: Wolv 5H 27
Cambridge Twr. B1: Birm 6E 101 (4A 4)
Cambridge Way B27: A Grn 1B 136
Camden Cl. B36: Cas B 1E 105
WS5: Wals 2F 65
Camden Dr. B1: Birm 6D 100 (2A 4)
Camden St. B1: Birm 5C 100 (2A 4)
B18: Hock 5C 100
WS1: Wals 3B 48
WS9: Wals W 3A 22
Camden Way DY6: K'wfrd 6B 74
Camellia Gdns. DY8: Word 1C 108
WV9: Pend 4D 14
Camelot Way B10: Small H 3C 118
Cameo Dr. DY8: Amb 3D 108
Cameronian Cft. B36: Hodg H 1A 104
Cameron Rd. WS4: Wals 6E 33
Camford Gro. B14: K Hth 4H 147
Cam Gdns. DY5: P'ntt 3F 93
Camino Rd. B32: Bart G 2D 130
Camomile Cl. WS5: Wals 2E 65
Campbell Cl. WS4: Wals 6E 33
Campbells Grn. B26: Sheld 1F 137
Campbell St. DY5: Brie H 5G 93
Campden Grn. B92: Olton 2E 137
Camp Hill B12: Birm 3A 118
DY8: Word 2C 108
Camp Hill Cir. B11: S'brk 3A 118
Camp Hill Ind. Est. B12: Birm 4A 118
Camphill La. WS10: W'bry 3F 63
Camphill Pct. WS10: W'bry 3F 63
Campians Av. WS6: C Hay 3D 6
Campion Cl. B38: K Nor 1B 160
WS5: Wals 2E 65
WV5: Wom 1E 73
Campion Ct. DY4: Tip 2F 77
Campion Dr. WV10: F'stne 1C 16
Campion Gro. B63: Hale 2F 127
Campion Ho. B38: K Nor 1A 160
WV10: Wolv 5B 28

Campion Way—Challenor Av.

Campion Way B90: Dic H 4G 163
Camp La. B21: Hand 6F 81
B38: K Nor 4B 146
Camplea Cft. B37: F'bri 1C 122
Camplin Cres. B20: Hand 2A 82
Camp Rd. B75: R'ley 2A 38
WS14: Lit H 2H 37
Camp St. B9: Bord G 2C 118
WS10: W'bry 3F 63
WV1: Wolv 6G 27 (1B 170)
Campville Cres. B71: W Brom 4C 64
Campville Gro. B37: K'hrst 4B 106
Campwood Cl. B30: B'vlle 5A 132
Camrose Cft. B12: Bal H 6H 117
B34: S End 3F 105
Camrose Gdns. WV9: Pend 4E 15
Canal Cotts. DY2: Neth 6D 94
Canal La. B24: Erd 6G 85
Canal Side B30: K Nor 4C 146
B48: Hopw 6G 159
B69: O'bry 2F 97
DY2: Neth 5G 95
Canalside Cl. WS3: Blox 6D 20
WS10: W'bry 3C 64
Canalside Ind. Est. DY5: Brie H 2G 109
Canal St. B69: O'bry 2F 97
DY4: Tip 3F 77
DY5: Brie H 4A 94
DY8: Amb 5D 108
WS2: Wals 1B 48
WV14: Cose 5E 61
Canal Vw. Ind. Est. DY5: Brie H 2F 109
Canary Gro. B19: Loz 1E 101
Canberra Rd. WS5: Wals 6G 49
Canberra Way B12: Birm 3A 118
Canford Cl. B12: Birm 4H 117
Canford Cres. WV8: Cod 4E 13
Canning Cl. WS5: Wals 5H 49
Canning Gdns. B18: Win G 5A 100
Canning Rd. WS5: Wals 5H 49
Cannock Rd.
WV10: Bush, F'stne, Share 2D 16
WV10: Wolv 5H 27
WV12: W'hall 2C 30
Cannon Bus. Pk. WV14: Cose 4E 61
Cannon Dr. WV14: Cose 3E 61
Cannon Hill Gro. B12: Bal H 6G 117
Cannon Hill Pl. B12: Bal H 6G 117
Cannon Hill Rd. B12: Bal H 6F 117
Cannon Raceway 4E 61
Cannon Rd. WV5: Wom 1G 73
Cannon St. B2: Birm 1G 117 (4D 4)
WS2: Wals 5C 32
WV13: W'hall 1B 46
Cannon St. Nth. WS2: Wals 5C 32
Canterbury Av. WV13: W'hall 1D 46
Canterbury Cl. B23: Erd 5D 84
B65: Row R 5E 97
B71: W Brom 5C 64
WS3: Pels 3E 21
Canterbury Dr. B37: Mars G 4C 122
WV6: Pert 5D 24
Canterbury Rd. B20: Hand 6F 83
B71: W Brom 5B 64
WV4: Penn 6C 42
Canterbury Twr. B1: Birm 6D 100
(off St Marks St.)
Cantlow Ho. B12: Birm 4H 117
Cantlow Rd. B13: Mose 1A 148
Canton La. B46: Col 2H 89
Canute Cl. WS1: Wals 4D 48
Canvey Cl. B45: Fran 6E 143
CANWELL 4E 39
Canwell Av. B37: K'hrst 4B 106
Canwell Dr. B75: Can 4E 39
Canwell Gdns. WV14: Bils 1E 61
Canwell Ga. B75: R'ley 5C 38
Capcroft Rd. B13: Mose 1B 148
Cape Cl. WS8: Bwnhls 1C 22
Cape Hill B66: Smeth 5F 99
Cape Hill Retail Cen.
B66: Smeth 5F 99
Capener Rd. B43: Gt Barr 3C 66
Capern Gro. B32: Harb 6D 114
Cape St. B18: Win G 5H 99
B70: W Brom 3E 79
Capethorn Rd. B66: Smeth 6E 99
Capilano Rd. B23: Erd 6C 68
Capponfield Cl. WV14: Cose 2D 60
Capstone Av. B18: Hock 5C 100
WV10: Oxl 1F 27
Captain's Cl. WV3: Wolv 1B 42
Carcroft Rd. B25: Yard 3B 120
Cardale St. B65: B'hth 1D 112
Carden Cl. B70: W Brom 3F 79
Carder Cres. WV14: Bils 1F 61
Carder Dr. DY5: Brie H 1G 109
Cardigan Cl. B71: W Brom 6A 64
Cardigan Dr. WV12: W'hall 3B 30
Cardigan St. B4: Birm 6H 101 (2H 5)
Cardington Av. B42: Gt Barr 4D 66
Cardoness Pl. DY1: Dud 5B 76
Careless Grn. DY9: Lye, W'cte 1B 126
Careynon Ct. WS3: Blox 1H 31
Carhampton Rd. B75: S Cold 5E 55
Carillon Gdns. B65: Row R 6C 96
Carisbrooke Av. B37: Chel W 1E 123
Carisbrooke Cl. WS10: W'bry 3C 64
Carisbrooke Cres. WS10: W'bry 2C 64
Carisbrooke Dr. B62: Hale 1D 128
Carisbrooke Gdns. WV10: Bush 4A 16
Carisbrooke Ho. B31: Longb 1D 158
Carisbrooke Rd. B17: Edg 2F 115
WS10: W'bry 3B 64
WV6: Pert 6G 25
WV10: Bush 4A 16
Carless Av. B17: Harb 4F 115
Carless St. WS1: Wals 3C 48
Carlisle St. B18: Win G 4A 100
Carlson Pk. B17: Harb 6F 115
Carl St. WS2: Wals 4B 32
Carlton Av. B21: Hand 6A 82
B74: S'tly 1H 51
DY9: W'cte 2A 126
WV11: Wed 2C 28
WV14: Bils 4H 45
Carlton Cl. B75: S Cold 4B 54
DY1: Dud 1E 77
Carlton Cft. B74: S'tly 1A 52
Carlton M. B36: Cas B 1H 105
Carlton M. Flats B36: Cas B 1H 105
Carlton Rd. B9: Small H 2D 118
B66: Smeth 1E 99
WV3: Wolv 4E 43
Carlyle Bus. Pk. B70: W Brom 2F 79
Carlyle Gro. WV10: Bush 1C 28
Carlyle Rd. B16: Edg 2A 116
B19: Loz 1E 101
B65: Row R 1C 112
WV10: Bush 1C 28
Carmel Gro. B32: Bart G 4H 129
Carmodale Av. B42: P Barr 1D 82
Carnegie Av. DY4: Tip 3A 78
Carnegie Dr. WS10: W'bry 2G 63
Carnegie Rd. B65: Row R 1B 112
Carnford Rd. B26: Sheld 5F 121
Carnforth Cl. DY6: K'wfrd 2H 91
Carnoustie Cl. B75: S Cold 3A 54
WS3: Blox 4G 19
Carnwath Rd. B73: New O 3E 69
Carol Cres. B63: Hale 6H 111
WV11: Wed 3G 29
Carol Gdns. DY8: Amb 3D 108
Caroline Pl. B13: Mose 2H 133
Caroline Rd. B13: Mose 1H 133
Caroline St. B3: Birm 5E 101 (1B 4)
B70: W Brom 5H 79
DY2: Dud 6G 77
Carpathian, The B18: Birm 1A 4
Carpathian Ct. B18: Birm 5E 101
Carpenter Glade B63: Crad 6F 111
Carpenter Pl. B12: Bal H 5A 118
Carpenter Rd. B15: Edg 4C 116
Carpenters Ct. B12: Birm 3H 117
(off Vaughton St.)
Carpenter's Rd. B19: Loz 2E 101
Carrick Cl. WS3: Pels 2E 21
Carriers Cl. WS2: Wals 2F 47
Carriers Fold WV5: Wom 6H 57
Carrington Rd. WS10: W'bry 3B 64
CARROWAY HEAD 5G 39
Carroway Head Hill
B75: Bass P, Can 6F 39
Carrs La. B4: Birm 1G 117 (4F 5)
Carshalton Gro. WV2: Wolv 4A 44
Carshalton Rd. B44: K'sdng 3A 68
Cartbridge Cres. WS3: Wals 3D 32
(not continuous)
Cartbridge La. WS4: Wals 4E 33
Cartbridge La. Sth. WS4: Wals 5E 33
Cartbridge Wlk. WS3: Wals 3E 33
Carter Av. WV8: Bilb 4H 13
Carter Rd. B43: Gt Barr 3B 66
WV6: Wolv 4F 27
Carters Cl. B37: Mars G 4C 122
B76: Walm 2D 70
Cartersfield La. WS9: Ston 1F 23
Carters Grn. B70: W Brom 3H 79
Carter's Hurst B33: Sheld 2F 121
Carter's La. B62: Quin 6F 113
Cartland Rd. B11: S'brk 4C 118
B14: K Hth 5D 132
B30: Stir 5D 132
Cartmel Ct. B23: Erd 3B 84
Cartway, The WV6: Pert 5D 24
Cartwright Gdns. B69: Tiv 5C 78
Cartwright Ho. WS3: Blox 6H 19
Cartwright Rd. B75: R'ley 6A 38
Cartwright St. WV2: Wolv 3H 43 (6C 170)
Carver Ct. B24: Erd 1A 86
DY4: Tip 4A 62
Carver Gdns. DY8: Stourb 3C 124
Carver St. B1: Birm 5D 100
Casern Vw. B75: S Cold 5E 55
Casewell Rd. DY6: W Hth 1A 92
Casey Av. B23: Erd 5D 68
Cash-Joynson Av. WS10: Darl 3C 46
Caslon Cres. DY8: Stourb 1B 124
Caslon Rd. B63: Crad 5E 111
Caslow Flats B63: Crad 1E 127
Cassandra Cl. DY5: P'ntt 6G 75
Cassowary Rd. B20: Hand 4B 82
Castello Dr. B36: Cas B 6H 87
Castillo Ct. B14: K Hth 2A 148
Castings, The WV14: Cose 3F 61
Castle, The DY8: Stourb 2F 125
Castlebridge Gdns. WV11: Wed 2H 29
Castlebridge Rd. WV11: Wed 3H 29
CASTLE BROMWICH 1F 105
Castle Bromwich Bus. Pk.
B35: Cas V 6D 86
Castle Bromwich Hall B36: Cas B 1E 105
Castle Cl. B64: Old H 2B 112
B92: Olton 4F 137
WS8: Bwnhls 3B 10
Castle Ct. B34: S End 2A 106
Castle Cres. B36: Cas B 1G 105
CASTLECROFT 2G 41
Castle Cft. B68: O'bry 3B 114
Castlecroft WS11: Nort C 1C 8
Castlecroft Av. WV3: Wolv 3G 41
Castlecroft Gdns. WV3: Wolv 3A 42
Castlecroft La. WV3: Wolv 3F 41
Castle Cft. Rd. WV14: Bils 4G 45
Castlecroft Rd. WV3: Wolv 3F 41
Castle Dr. B46: Col 4H 107
WV12: W'hall 4B 30
Castleford Gro. B11: S'hll 1C 134
Castleford Rd. B11: S'hll 1C 134
Castlefort Rd. WS9: Wals W 4C 22
Castlegate Dr. DY1: Dud 5G 77
Castlegate Island DY1: Dud 5G 77
Castlegate Way DY1: Dud 5G 77
Castle Gro. DY8: Stourb 2F 125
Castle Hgts. B64: Old H 3B 112
(off Granville Rd.)
Castle Hill DY1: Dud 5F 77
Castlehill Rd. WS9: Wals W 4D 22
Castlehills Dr. B36: Cas B 1E 105
Castle Ho. B33: Yard 2F 121
Castle La. B92: Olton 4D 136
Castlemill DY4: Tip 5H 77
Castle Mill Rd. DY1: Dud 3E 77
Castle Rd. B29: W Cas 3E 131
B30: K Nor 3B 146
DY4: Tip 3F 77
WS9: Wals W 5C 22
Castle Rd. E. B68: O'bry 3B 114
Castle Rd. W. B68: O'bry 3A 114
Castle Sq. B29: W Cas 4E 131
Castle St. B70: W Brom 5G 63
DY1: Dud 6F 77
DY3: Sed 5H 59
DY4: Tip 2G 77
WS8: Bwnhls 3B 10
WS10: Darl 3D 46
(not continuous)
WV1: Wolv 1H 43 (3C 170)
WV14: Cose 5E 61
Castleton Rd. B42: Gt Barr 6F 67
WS3: Blox 4A 20
Castleton St. DY2: Neth 4E 95
CASTLE VALE 3F 87
Castle Vale Baths 5E 87
Castle Va. Ind. Est. B76: Min 2E 87
Castle Va. Shop. Cen. B35: Cas V 4D 86
Castle Vw. DY1: Dud 5D 76
Castle Vw. Cl. WS10: Mox 1A 62
Castle Vw. Enterprise Pk.
B35: Cas V 4G 87
Castle Vw. Ind. Est. DY4: Tip 4H 77
Castle Vw. Rd. WV14: Bils 1A 62
Castle Vw. Ter. WV14: Cose 5D 60
Castle Yd. WV1: Wolv 1H 43 (3C 170)
Caswell Rd. DY3: Sed 5G 59
Cat & Kittens La. WV10: F'stne 1A 16
Cater Dr. B76: Walm 3D 70
Caterham Dr. DY6: K'wfrd 6D 92
Catesby Dr. DY6: K'wfrd 1B 92
Catesby Ho. B37: K'hrst 4B 106
Catesby Pk. B38: K Nor 4A 146
Catesby Rd. B90: Shir 6H 149
Cateswell Rd. B11: Tys 3F 135
B28: Hall G 4F 135
Cathcart Rd. DY8: Stourb 6C 108
Cathedral Cl. DY4: Tip 2G 77
Cathel Dr. B42: Gt Barr 6C 66
Catherine Ct. B24: Erd 3A 86
CATHERINE-DE-BARNES 2D 152
Catherine de Barnes La.
B92: Bick, Cath B 1E 153
Catherine Dr. B73: S Cold 5G 53
Catherine Rd. WV14: Cose 4C 60
Catherines Cl. B91: Cath B 3D 152
Catherine St. B6: Aston 2A 102
Catherton Cl. DY4: Tip 3C 62
Catholic La. DY3: Sed 1G 75
Catisfield Cres. WV8: Pend 6D 14
Cat La. B34: S End 2F 105
Caton Gro. B28: Hall G 6G 135
Cato St. B7: Birm 5B 102
Cato St. Nth. B7: Nech 4C 102
CATSHILL
Walsall 6C 10
Catshill Rd. WS8: Bwnhls 6C 10
Cattell Dr. B75: S Cold 6F 55
Cattell Rd. B9: Bord G 2C 118
Cattells Gro. B7: Nech 3C 102
Cattermole Gro. B43: Gt Barr 2E 67
Cattock Hurst Dr. B72: W Grn 6B 70
Causeway B65: Row R 1C 112
Causeway, The B25: Yard 4B 120
CAUSEWAY GREEN 6F 97
Causeway Grn. Rd. B68: O'bry 6F 97
Causeway Rd. WV14: Cose 5F 61
Causey Farm Rd. B63: Hale 5E 127
Cavalier Cir. WV10: Bush 3A 16
Cavalier Dr. B63: Hale 2A 128
Cavandale Av. B44: Gt Barr 4G 67
Cavell Cl. WS2: Wals 1B 48
Cavell Rd. DY2: Dud 6H 77
Cavendish Cl. B38: K Nor 6D 146
DY6: K'wfrd 5B 92
Cavendish Ct. B17: Harb 3F 115
B93: Dorr 6C 166
Cavendish Gdns. WS2: Wals 5G 31
WV1: Wolv 2E 45
Cavendish Rd. B16: Edg 6H 99
B62: Hale 1F 129
WS2: Wals 4G 31
WV1: Wolv 2D 44
Cavendish Way WS9: A'rdge 4D 34
Caversham Pl. B73: S Cold 1H 69
Caversham Rd. B44: K'sdng 3A 68
Cawdon Gro. B93: Dorr 6G 167
Cawdor Cres. B16: Edg 2B 116
Cawney Hill DY2: Dud 1G 95
Caxton Ga. B2: Birm 4E 5
Caxton Gate Shop. Cen. B2: Birm 1G 117
Caxton Gro. B44: K'sdng 4C 68
Caynham Rd. B32: Bart G 5H 129
Cayton Gro. B23: Erd 1F 85
Cearl Ct. B27: A Grn 3A 136
Cecil Dr. B69: Tiv 5D 78
Cecil Rd. B24: Erd 4F 85
B29: S Oak 4E 133
Cecil St. B19: Birm 5G 101
DY8: Stourb 6D 108
WS4: Wals 6D 32
Cedar Av. B36: Cas B 1G 105
WS8: Bwnhls 5C 10
WV14: Cose 6D 60
Cedar Bri. Cft. B74: Four O 3H 53
Cedar Cl. B30: B'vlle 1A 146
B68: O'bry 3A 114
DY8: Stourb 3B 124
WS5: Wals 1F 65
Cedar Dr. B24: Erd 2A 86
B31: Longb 2F 159
B74: S'tly 2G 51
Cedar Gro. WS6: Gt Wyr 1H 7
WV3: Wolv 4D 42
WV8: Bilb 4H 13
WV14: Bils 4H 45
Cedar Ho. B36: Hodg H 1D 104
B91: Sol 6D 150
Cedarhurst B32: Harb 6E 115
B91: Sol 4G 151
Cedar Pk. Rd. WV12: W'hall 6C 18
Cedar Rd. B30: B'vlle 1A 146
DY1: Dud 4D 76
(not continuous)
DY4: Tip 2F 77
WS10: W'bry 3G 63
WV13: W'hall 1G 45
Cedars, The B25: Yard 2C 120
B93: Know 5C 166
WV6: Tett 4B 26
WV6: Wolv 6D 26
Cedars Av. B27: A Grn 1A 136
DY6: K'wfrd 5B 92
WV5: Wom 2G 73
Cedar Tree B23: Erd 5E 85
Cedar Wlk. B37: Chel W 1D 122
(off Chelmsley Wood Shop. Cen.)
Cedar Way B31: Longb 6D 144
WV11: Wed 2E 29
Cedarwood B74: Four O 3H 53
Cedarwood Cft. B42: Gt Barr 5B 66
Cedarwood Dr. CV7: Bal C 3H 169
Cedarwood Rd. DY3: Up Gor 2H 75
Celandine Cl. DY6: K'wfrd 5A 92
Celandine Rd. DY1: Dud 3C 76
Celandines, The WV5: Wom 1E 73
Celbury Way B43: Gt Barr 5H 65
Celts Cl. B65: Row R 5C 96
Cemetery La. B18: Birm 4D 100
Cemetery Rd. B66: Smeth 3A 98
B67: Smeth 5D 98
B68: O'bry 3A 98
B75: S Cold 5B 54
DY9: Lye 6H 109
WS10: Darl 3F 47
WV13: W'hall 6A 30
Cemetery St. WS6: C Hay 3C 6
WV14: Bils 5E 45
Cemetery Way WS3: Blox 6H 19
Centenary Cl. B31: N'fld 6E 145
Centenary Dr. B21: Hand 6A 82
Centenary Plaza B1: Birm 1E 117 (5B 4)
Centenary Sq. B1: Birm 1E 117 (4B 4)
Centenary Way B1: Birm 2F 117
(off Blucher St.)
B1: Birm 4B 4
(off Queensway)
Central Arc. WV1: Wolv 1G 43 (3B 170)
Central Av. B31: Longb 1C 158
B64: Crad H 4E 111
B65: Row R 1C 112
DY4: Tip 6H 61
DY9: W'cte 2A 126
WV14: Bils 4G 45
Central Baths 1F 43 (2A 170)
Central Blvd. B90: Bly P 6D 164
Central Bus. Pk. B33: Kitts G 2H 121
Central Cl. WS3: Blox 6G 19
Central Dr. DY3: Gorn 5G 75
WS3: Blox 1F 31
WV14: Cose 6E 61
Central Gro. B27: A Grn 3A 136
Central Links Ind. Est. B7: Nech 3B 102
Central Pk. Dr. B18: Win G 4B 100
Central Pk. Ind. Est. DY2: Neth 6G 95
Central Sq. B1: Birm 1D 116 (5A 4)
B23: Erd 3G 85
Central Trad. Est. DY6: K'wfrd 6D 74
Central Way DY5: Brie H 6A 94
Centre City B5: Birm 6D 4
Centre La. B63: Hale 2B 128
Centreway, The B14: Yard W 3D 148
Centurion Cl. B46: Col 6H 89
Century Ho. B69: O'bry 3D 96
Century Ind. Est. B44: Gt Barr 2G 67
Century Pk. B9: Bord G 1C 118
B37: Mars G 5E 123
Century Rd. B69: O'bry 1G 97
Century Twr. B5: Edg 6E 117
Ceolmund Cres. B37: Chel W 1D 122
Chaceley Gro. B23: Erd 6D 68
Chadbrook Crest B15: Edg 4A 116
Chadbury Cft. B91: Sol 1F 165
Chadbury Rd. B63: Hale 2C 128
Chaddersley Cl. B45: Rubery 6F 143
Chaddesley Cl. B69: O'bry 4D 96
Chaddesley Ct. DY1: Dud 6D 76
Chaddesley Dr. DY9: Pedm 4F 125
Chaddesley Rd. B31: N'fld 5H 145
B63: Hale 3H 127
Chadley Cl. B91: Sol 1E 151
Chad Rd. B15: Edg 3B 116
WV14: Cose 6C 60
Chadshunt Cl. B36: Cas B 5H 87
Chad Sq. B15: Edg 4A 116
Chadstone Cl. B90: M'path 4F 165
CHAD VALLEY 4A 116
Chad Valley Cl. B17: Harb 5H 115
Chadwell Dr. B90: Shir 1H 149
Chadwell Gdns. WV8: Cod 3F 13
Chadwich La. B61: C'wich 2A 156
Chadwick Av. B45: Redn 3H 157
Chadwick Cl. WV4: Penn 5A 42
Chadwick Ct. B43: Gt Barr 5A 66
Chadwick Ho. B45: Rubery 2E 157
Chadwick La. B93: Chad E, Know 6A 168
Chadwick Rd. B75: S Cold 6D 54
Chadworth Av. B93: Dorr 5A 166
Chaffcombe Rd. B26: Sheld 5G 121
Chaffinch Cl. DY3: Sed 3G 59
Chaffinch Dr. B36: Cas B 2D 106
Chaffinch Rd. DY9: W'cte 2H 125
Chainmakers Cl.
WV14: Cose 3F 61
Chain Wlk. B19: Loz 1F 101
Chalcot Gro. B20: Hand 2A 82
Chaldon Cl. WV9: Pend 6E 15
Chale Gro. B14: K Hth 4A 148
Chalfont Pl. DY9: W'cte 3A 126
Chalfont Rd. B20: Hand 5D 82
Chalford Rd. B23: Erd 5C 68
Chalford Way B90: Shir 6A 150
Chalgrove Av. B38: K Nor 6H 145
Chalgrove Cres. B91: Sol 6F 151
Challenge Way WV10: Wolv 4A 28
Challenor Av. WV13: W'hall 1F 45

Chalybeate Cl.—Chillington Dr.

Chalybeate Cl. B45: Fran 6F 143
Chamberlain Clock 5D 100 (1A 4)
Chamberlain Cl. B69: Tiv 5D 78
Chamberlain Ct. B14: K Hth 4G 133
B18: Birm 5E 101
Chamberlain Cres. B90: Shir 5G 149
Chamberlain Hall B15: Edg 5C 116
Chamberlain Ho. *B16: Edg* *2C 116*
(off Skipton Rd.)
Chamberlain Rd. B13: Mose 1H 147
Chamberlains La. WV4: Penn 2C 58
Chamberlain Sq. B3: Birm 1F 117 (4C 4)
(not continuous)
Chamberlain Wlk. B66: Smeth 4F 99
Chance Cft. B68: O'bry 3H 113
Chancel Ind. Est. DY6: K'wfrd 1C 92
WS10: Darl 6D 46
WV1: Wolv 2C 44
WV13: W'hall 1B 46
Chancellors Cl. B15: Edg 3A 116
Chancel Way B6: Witt 2H 83
B62: Hale 5C 112
Chancery Way DY5: Quar B 1B 110
Chandler Dr. WV4: Penn 2B 58
Chandler Ho. B69: O'bry 5D 96
Chandlers Cl. B18: Win G 4B 100
WV9: Pend 6E 15
Chandlers Keep WS8: Bwnhls 1B 22
Chandos Av. B13: Mose 2H 133
Chandos Rd. B12: Birm 3A 118
Channon Dr. DY5: Brie H 3H 109
Chanston Av. B14: K Hth 3G 147
Chanterelle Gdns. WV4: Penn 1E 59
Chantrey Cres. B43: Gt Barr 1F 67
WV14: Bils 4H 45
Chantry Av. WS3: Blox 1A 32
Chantry Cl. B47: H'wd 2A 162
Chantry Dr. B62: Quin 5G 113
Chantry Heath Cres.
B93: Know 1E 167
Chantry Rd. B13: Mose 1G 133
B21: Hand 1B 100
DY7: Stourt 4A 108
Chapel Ash WV3: Wolv 1F 43
Chapel Ash Island WV1: Wolv 1F 43 (3A 170)
Chapel Av. WS8: Bwnhls 3A 10
Chapel Cl. B64: Old H 3B 112
WV5: Wom 2F 73
Chapel Ct. *DY5: Brie H* *1H 109*
(off Promenade, The)
DY5: P'ntt *2G 93*
(off Chapel St.)
Chapel Dr. B47: Wyt 6H 161
CV7: Bal C 1H 169
WS8: Bwnhls 3A 10
Chapelfield M. B45: Rubery 3F 157
DY8: Stourb 1E 125
Chapelfield Rd. B45: Redn 2G 157
Chapel Flds. Rd. B92: Olton 3D 136
Chapel Grn. WV13: W'hall 1B 46
Chapel Ho. La. B63: Crad 5E 111
Chapelhouse Rd. B37: F'bri 1B 122
Chapel Ho. St. B12: Birm 2H 117 (6H 5)
Chapel La. B29: S Oak 3A 132
B43: Gt Barr 2A 66
B47: Wyt 6G 161
DY3: Swind 3C 72
WV8: Cod 4E 13
Chapel Pas. B69: O'bry 5G 97
Chapel Sq. WS6: C Hay 2D 6
Chapel St. B21: Hand 2H 99
B63: Hale 2A 128
B69: O'bry 2E 97
B70: W Brom 2H 79
DY2: Neth 5F 95
DY4: Tip 2G 77
(not continuous)
DY5: P'ntt 2G 93
DY5: Quar B 3B 110
DY6: W Hth 1G 91
DY8: Stourb 1E 125
DY8: Word 6B 92
DY9: Lye 6A 110
WS3: Blox 1B 32
WS3: Pels 4D 20
WS8: Bwnhls 3A 10
WS11: Nort C 1C 8
WV2: Wolv 4H 43
WV5: Wom 2F 73
(not continuous)
WV14: Bils 6H 45
Chapel Vw. B67: Smeth 5D 98
Chapel Wlk. B30: K Nor 4C 146
DY3: Gorn 5G 75
Chapelwood Gro. B42: P Barr 2F 83
Chapman Rd. B10: Small H 3C 118
CHAPMAN'S HILL 6B 142
Chapman's Hill B62: Roms 6B 142
Chapmans Pas. B1: Birm 2F 117 (6C 4)
Chapman St. B70: W Brom 4H 79
Chapter Ho. B70: W Brom 2G 79
Charfield Cl. B30: B'vlle 6H 131
Charingworth Rd. B92: Sol 3G 137
Charity Bick Way B70: W Brom 5A 80
Charlbury Av. B37: F'bri 1B 122
Charlbury Cres. B26: Yard 3D 120
Charlbury Twr. *B5: Birm* *3G 117*
(off Southacre Av.)
Charlecote Cft. B90: Shir 1A 164
Charlecote Dr. B23: Erd 6E 69
DY1: Dud 4A 76
Charlecote Gdns. B73: Bold 5G 69
Charlecote Ri. WV13: W'hall 3H 45
Charlecott Cl. B13: Mose 6D 134
CHARLEMONT 5C 64
Charlemont Av. B71: W Brom 5C 64
Charlemont Cl. WS5: Wals 5G 49
Charlemont Cres. B71: W Brom 5C 64
Charlemont Gdns. WS5: Wals 5G 49
Charlemont Rd. B71: W Brom 5C 64
WS5: Wals 5F 49
Charles Av. B65: Row R 5C 96
WV4: Penn 6F 43
WV11: Ess 3H 17
Charles Cl. B8: Salt 5D 102
WS6: C Hay 4D 6
Charles Ct. B13: Mose 3B 134
B76: Walm *2D 70*
(off Berryfields Rd.)
Charles Cres. WS3: Pels 2E 21
Charlesdale Dr. WS9: A'rdge 5D 34
Charles Edward Rd. B26: Yard 5B 120
Charles Foster St. WS10: Darl 5C 46
Charles Henry St. B12: Birm 3H 117
Charles Holland St. WV13: W'hall 1B 46
Charles Lanes Trust Ho's. B28: Hall G 5G 135
Charles Pearson Ct. *B66: Smeth* *4F 99*
(off Mill Dr.)
Charles Rd. B6: Aston 6A 84
B9: Small H 1E 119
B20: Hand 6E 83
B63: Hale 1H 127
B91: Sol 5C 150
DY4: Tip 6A 62
DY5: Quar B 2C 110
DY8: Stourb 1C 124
Charles St. B66: Smeth 2G 99
B70: W Brom 2E 79
WS2: Wals 1B 48
WV13: W'hall 6C 30
Charles St. Ind. Est. B70: W Brom 2E 79
Charles Wlk. B65: Row R 4C 96
Charles Wesley Ct. *WV3: Wolv* *4E 43*
(off Claremont Rd.)
Charlesworth Av. B90: M'path 3F 165
Charleville Rd. B19: Hock 2D 100
Charlotte Cl. B69: Tiv 5A 78
Charlotte Gdns. B66: Smeth 4F 99
Charlotte Rd. B15: Edg 4E 117
B30: Stir 1C 146
WS10: W'bry 4C 62
Charlotte St. B3: Birm 6E 101 (3B 4)
DY1: Dud 1D 94
WS1: Wals 1E 49
Charlton Dr. B64: Crad H 4F 111
Charlton Pl. B8: Salt 4D 102
Charlton Rd. B44: K'sdng 6A 68
Charlton St. DY1: Dud 6D 76
DY5: Brie H 6E 93
Charminster Av. B25: Yard 3B 120
Charnley Dr. B75: R'ley 1C 54
Charnwood Av. DY3: Sed 3H 59
Charnwood Bus. Pk. WV14: Bils 6E 45
Charnwood Cl. B45: Fran 4H 143
DY5: Brie H 4F 109
WV14: Bils 2B 62
Charnwood Ct. DY9: W'cte 3A 126
Charnwood Rd. B42: Gt Barr 6B 66
WS5: Wals 1E 65
Charter Cl. WS11: Nort C 1C 8
Charter Cres. B64: Old H 3B 112
Charterfield Dr. DY6: K'wfrd 1B 92
Charterfield Shop. Cen. DY6: K'wfrd 1C 92
Charterhouse Dr. B91: Sol 6F 151
Charter Rd. DY4: Tip 4C 62
Charters Av. WV8: Bilb 6H 13
Charters Cl DY4: Tip 2G 77
Charter St. DY5: Brie H 4A 94
Chartist Rd. B8: Salt 3D 102
Chartley Cl. B93: Dorr 6A 166
WV6: Pert 5F 25
Chartley Rd. B23: Erd 6D 84
B71: W Brom 1B 80
Chartway, The WS3: Pels 3E 21
Chartwell Cl. DY1: Dud 1D 76
Chartwell Dr. B74: Four O 5D 36
B90: Ches G 4B 164
WV5: Wom 2F 73
WV10: Bush 6A 16
Chase, The B76: Walm 6B 70
WV6: Wolv 3F 27
Chase Av. WS6: C Hay 2F 7
Chase Gro. B24: Erd 1B 86
Chase Link, The WS8: Bwnhls 4C 10
Chasepool Rd. DY3: Swind 2C 90
Chase Rd. DY3: Gorn 6F 75
DY5: P'ntt 6G 75
WS3: Blox 1G 31
WS8: Bwnhls 4C 10
Chase Sailing Club, The 1H 9
Chase Vw. WV4: E'shll 3A 60
Chasewater Railway Mus.
Chasewater Railway 2H 9
Chasewater Sports Cen. 2G 9
Chassieur Wlk. B46: Col 1H 107
Chater Dr. B76: Walm 4E 71
Chatham Rd. B31: N'fld 4E 145
Chatsworth Av. B43: Gt Barr 4G 65
Chatsworth Cl. B72: W Grn 6B 70
B90: Ches G 4B 164
WV12: W'hall 4B 30
Chatsworth Cres. WS4: Rus 2H 33
Chatsworth Gdns. WV6: Tett 2G 25
Chatsworth M. DY8: Word 6H 91
Chatsworth Rd. B62: Hale 4A 112
Chattaway Dr. CV7: Bal C 3H 169
Chattaway St. B7: Nech 2C 102
CHATTLE HILL 5G 89
Chattle Hill B46: Col 5G 89
Chattock Av. B91: Sol 3A 152
Chattock Cl. B36: Hodg H 2C 104
Chatwell Gro. B29: S Oak 3F 131
Chatwin Pl. WV14: Bils 2G 61
Chatwin St. B66: Smeth 2D 98
Chatwins Wharf DY4: Tip 2H 77
Chaucer Av. DY3: Lwr G 2E 75
DY4: Tip 5B 62
WV12: W'hall 1E 31
Chaucer Cl. B23: Erd 4B 84
DY8: Amb 3E 109
WV14: Cose 5F 61
Chaucer Gro. B27: A Grn 3H 135
Chaucer Ho. B63: Crad 6D 110
Chaucer Rd. WS3: Blox 1C 32
Chauson Gro. B91: Sol 1E 165
Chavasse Rd. B72: S Cold 2A 70
CHAWN HILL 2G 125
Chawn Hill DY9: Pedm 2G 125
Chawn Hill Cl. DY9: Pedm 2G 125
Chawn Pk. Dr. DY9: Pedm 2G 125
Chaynes Gro. B33: Kitts G 6H 105
Cheadle Dr. B23: Erd 5D 68
Cheam Gdns. WV6: Tett 1C 26
Cheapside B5: Birm 2H 117 (6G 5)
B12: Birm 2H 117
WV1: Wolv 1G 43 (3B 170)
WV13: W'hall 2A 46
Cheapside Ind. Est. B12: Birm 2H 117
Cheatham St. B7: Nech 3C 102
Checketts St. WS2: Wals 1A 48
Checkley Cl. B90: Shir 3G 149
Checkley Cft. B76: Walm 5D 70
Cheddar Rd. B12: Bal H 5G 117
Chedworth Cl. B29: W Cas 6F 131
Chedworth Ct. B29: S Oak 5A 132
Cheedon Cl. B93: Dorr 6F 167
Chelford Cres. DY6: K'wfrd 6E 93
Chells Gro. B13: Mose 2B 148
Chelmar Cl. B36: Cas B 1B 106
Chelmar Dr. DY5: P'ntt 3E 93
Chelmarsh Av. WV3: Wolv 2G 41
Chelmorton Rd. B42: Gt Barr 6F 67
Chelmscote Rd. B92: Olton 4D 136
Chelmsley Av. B46: Col 3H 107
Chelmsley Circ. B37: Chel W 1D 122
Chelmsley Gro. B33: Kitts G 6A 106
Chelmsley La. B37: Mars G 3B 122
(not continuous)
Chelmsley Rd. B37: Chel W, F'bri 6B 106
CHELMSLEY WOOD 1D 122
Chelmsley Wood Ind. Est. B37: F'bri 5D 106
Chelmsley Wood Shop. Cen.
B37: Chel W 1D 122
Chelsea *B37: K'hrst* *4B 106*
(off Chilvers Gro.)
Chelsea Cl. B32: Quin 1D 130
Chelsea Ct. B29: W Cas 6F 131
Chelsea Dr. B74: Four O 5F 37
Chelsea Way DY6: K'wfrd 3B 92
Chelston Dr. WV6: Wolv 5C 26
Chelston Rd. B31: N'fld 5C 144
Cheltenham Cl. WV6: Wolv 3F 27
Cheltenham Dr. B36: Hodg H 1B 104
DY6: K'wfrd 3H 91
Chelthorn Way B91: Sol 5G 151
Cheltondale Rd. B91: Sol 1D 150
Chelveston Cres. B91: Sol 6F 151
Chelwood Gdns. WV14: Bils 6D 44
Chelworth Rd. B38: K Nor 5D 146
Chem Rd. WV14: Bils 6E 45
Cheniston Rd. WV12: W'hall 3C 30
Chepstow Cl. WV6: Pert 5F 25
Chepstow Gro. B45: Redn 3H 157
Chepstow Rd. WS3: Blox 6F 19
WV10: F'hses 2H 15
Chepstow Vs. B12: Bal H 6B 118
Chepstow Way WS3: Blox 6F 19
Chequerfield Dr. WV3: Wolv 5E 43
Chequers Av. WV5: Wom 4G 57
Chequer St. WV3: Wolv 5E 43
Cherhill Covert B14: K Hth 5E 147
Cherington Rd. B29: S Oak 5C 132
Cherish Ho. B12: Birm 3A 118
Cheriton Gro. WV6: Pert 6E 25
Cheriton Wlk. B23: Erd 4B 84
Cherrington Cl. B31: N'fld 6C 130
Cherrington Dr. WS6: Gt Wyr 1F 7
Cherrington Gdns. DY9: Pedm 6G 125
WV6: Tett 1H 41
Cherrington Way B91: Sol 6F 151
Cherry Cres. B24: Erd 4F 85
Cherrydale Ct. DY1: Dud 5B 76
Cherry Dr. B9: Birm 2B 118
B64: Old H 2H 111
Cherry Gdns. *B73: W Grn* *6H 69*
(off Emscote Dr.)
Cherry Grn. DY1: Dud 3B 76
Cherry Gro. *B66: Smeth* *4G 99*
(off Rosedale Av.)
DY8: Stourb 1C 124
WV11: Wed 2E 29
Cherry Hill Wlk. DY1: Dud 1C 94
Cherry La. B73: Bold 6G 69
DY3: Himl 4A 74
WS10: W'bry 3G 63
Cherry Lea B34: S End 3F 105
CHERRY ORCHARD 2H 111
Cherry Orchard B64: Old H 2H 111
Cherry Orchard Av. B63: Hale 6H 111
Cherry Orchard Cres.
B63: Hale 5H 111
Cherry Orchard Rd. B20: Hand 2B 82
Cherry Rd. DY4: Tip 6H 61
Cherry St. B2: Birm 1G 117 (4E 5)
B63: Hale 6H 111
DY8: Stourb 1C 124
Cherry Tree Av. WS5: Wals 1E 65
Cherry Tree Ct. B30: K Nor 2B 146
Cherrytree Ct. DY9: W'cte 2A 126
Cherry Tree Cft. B27: A Grn 6A 120
Cherry Tree Gdns. WV8: Bilb 4H 13
Cherry Tree La. B63: Hale 4F 127
WV8: Bilb 4H 13
Cherry Tree Rd. DY6: K'wfrd 1C 92
WS11: Nort C 1F 9
Cherry Wlk. B47: H'wd 4B 162
Cherrywood Cl. WV14: Cose 4E 61
Cherrywood Ct. B92: Olton 3E 137
Cherrywood Cres. B91: Sol 1G 165
Cherrywood Grn. WV14: Bils 3F 45
Cherrywood Ind. Est. B9: Bord G 6D 102
Cherrywood Rd. B9: Bord G 1D 118
B74: S'tly 2F 51
Cherrywood Way B74: Lit A 4D 36
Chervil Cl. B42: Gt Barr 6E 67
Chervil Ri. WV10: Wolv 6B 28
Cherwell Ct. B73: S Cold 6H 53
Cherwell Dr. B36: Cas B 1B 106
WS8: Bwnhls 3G 9
(not continuous)
Cherwell Gdns. B6: Aston 1F 101
Cheshire Av. B90: Shir 4G 149
Cheshire Cl. DY8: Woll 3B 108
Cheshire Ct. B34: S End 2F 105
Cheshire Gro. WV6: Pert 5E 25
Cheshire Rd. B6: Witt 5A 84
B67: Smeth 5E 99
WS2: Wals 1F 47
Cheslyn Dr. WS6: C Hay 2D 6
Cheslyn Gro. B14: K Hth 4A 148
CHESLYN HAY 3D 6
Cheslyn Hay Leisure Cen. 2C 6
Chessetts Gro. B13: Mose 1A 148
Chester Av. WV6: Tett 2D 26
Chester Cl. B37: F'bri 1C 122
WV13: W'hall 1D 46
Chester Ct. *B29: W Cas* *6F 131*
(off Abdon Av.)
B37: Chel W *1F 123*
(off Hedingham Gro.)
Chesterfield Cl. B31: N'fld 5F 145
Chesterfield Ct. B30: K Nor 3A 146
WS9: Wals W 3B 22
Chester Gdns. B73: New O 4E 69
Chestergate Cft. B24: Erd 3B 86
Chester Hayes Ct. B24: Erd 2A 86
Chester House 3E 167
Chester Pl. WS2: Wals 2H 47
Chester Ri. B68: O'bry 3H 113
CHESTER ROAD 6A 70
Chester Rd. B24: Erd 2A 86
B35: Cas V 3C 86
B36: Cas B 1E 105
B37: Chel W, F'bri 4D 106
B46: Col 4H 123
B64: Crad H 3E 111
B71: W Brom 4H 63
B73: New O 4D 68
B74: S'tly 1H 51
CV7: Lit P 1B 140
DY2: Neth 1F 111
WS8: Bwnhls, Wals W 2D 22
WS9: A'rdge, Wals W 4G 35
Chester Rd. Nth. B73: S'tly, New O 6A 52
WS8: Bwnhls 4H 9
Chester Road Station (Rail) 6G 69
Chester St. B6: Aston 4H 101
Chester St. Wharf B6: Aston 4H 101
Chesterton Av. B12: Bal H 6B 118
Chesterton Cl. B91: Sol 2C 150
Chesterton Rd. B12: Bal H 6A 118
WV10: Bush 1C 28
Chesterwood B47: H'wd 3A 162
WS9: A'rdge 1H 51
Chesterwood Gdns. B20: Hand 5F 83
Chesterwood Rd. B13: Mose 1H 147
Chestnut Av. DY1: Dud 4E 77
DY4: Tip 6H 61
Chestnut Cl. B27: A Grn 1A 136
B74: S'tly 6A 36
B92: Olton 5B 136
DY8: Stourb 3B 124
WV8: Cod 5F 13
Chestnut Ct. B36: Cas B 2A 106
Chestnut Dr. B24: Erd 3A 86
B36: Cas B 1E 105
B45: Coft H 5B 158
WS4: S'fld 6F 21
WS6: C Hay 2D 6
WS6: Gt Wyr 2F 7
WV5: Wom 2G 73
Chestnut Gro. B17: Harb 6H 115
B46: Col 2H 107
DY6: K'wfrd 2D 92
WV11: Wed 2E 29
Chestnut Ho. B37: Chel W 1D 122
Chestnut Pl. B14: K Hth 5H 133
WS3: Blox 3B 32
Chestnut Rd. B13: Mose 1A 134
B68: O'bry 4A 114
WS3: Blox 3C 32
WS10: W'bry 4G 63
Chestnuts Av. B26: Sheld 4F 121
Chestnut Wlk. *B37: Chel W* *1D 122*
(off Chelmsley Wood Shop. Cen.)
Chestnut Way WV3: Wolv 3B 42
Chestom Rd. WV14: Bils 5D 44
Chestom Rd. Ind. Est. WV14: Bils 5D 44
Cheston Ind. Est. B7: Nech 3A 102
Cheston Rd. B7: Nech 3A 102
Cheswell Cl. WV6: Tett 1H 41
Cheswick Cl. WV13: W'hall 3H 45
CHESWICK GREEN 5B 164
Cheswick Way B90: Ches G 5B 164
Cheswood Dr. B76: Walm 1F 87
Chetland Cft. B92: Sol 6B 138
Chettle Rd. WV14: Bils 2H 61
Chetton Grn. WV10: F'hses 4F 15
Chetwood Cl. WV6: Wolv 4E 27
Chetwynd Cl. WS2: Wals 6C 30
Chetwynd Rd. B8: W End 4H 103
WV2: Wolv 5F 43
Cheveley Av. B45: Redn 2H 157
Chevening Cl. DY3: Sed 6A 60
Cheveridge Cl. B91: Sol 5F 151
Cheverton Rd. B31: N'fld 3C 144
Cheviot Rd. DY8: Amb 5E 109
WV2: E'shll 4B 44
Cheviot Way B63: Hale 2F 127
Cheylesmore Cl. B73: S Cold 1H 69
Cheyne Ct. *B17: Harb* *6H 115*
(off Greenfield Rd.)
Cheyne Gdns. B28: Hall G 4E 149
Cheyne Pl. B17: Harb 6H 115
Cheyne Wlk. DY5: Brie H 4G 109
Cheyne Way B17: Harb 6H 115
Cheyney Cl. WV6: Wolv 4E 27
Chichester Av. DY2: Neth 5F 95
Chichester Ct. B73: S Cold 6H 53
Chichester Dr. B32: Quin 6G 113
Chichester Gro. B37: Chel W 2C 122
(not continuous)
Chigwell Cl. B35: Cas V 4E 87
Chilcote Cl. B28: Hall G 3F 149
Childs Av. WV14: Cose 3C 60
Childs Oak Cl. CV7: Bal C 3G 169
Chilgrove Gdns. WV6: Tett 4A 26
Chilham Dr. B37: Chel W 1E 123
Chillenden Ct. *WV13: W'hall* *1C 46*
(off Mill St.)
Chillinghome Rd. B36: Hodg H 1B 104
Chillington Cl. WS6: Gt Wyr 4F 7
Chillington Dr. DY1: Dud 4A 76
WV8: Cod 3F 13

Chillington Flds.—Clopton Rd.

Chillington Flds. WV1: Wolv . . . 2C 44
Chillington La. WV8: Cod . . . 2D 12
Chillington Pl. WV14: Bils . . . 6E 45
Chillington Rd. DY4: Tip . . . 4C 62
Chillington Wlk. B65: Row R . . . 6C 96
Chillington Works Ind. Est. WV1: Wolv . . . 2B 44
Chiltern Cl. B63: Hale . . . 3E 127
DY3: Lwr G . . . 4H 75
WS6: C Hay . . . 4D 6
Chiltern Dr. WV13: W'hall . . . 2F 45
Chiltern Rd. DY8: Amb . . . 5F 109
Chilterns, The B69: O'bry . . . 4E 97
Chilton Ct. *B23: Erd . . . 5C 84*
(off Park App.)
Chilton Rd. B14: Yard W . . . 3D 148
Chilvers Gro. B37: K'hrst . . . 4B 106
Chilwell Cl. B91: Sol . . . 6F 151
Chilwell Cft. B19: Hock . . . 4G 101
Chilworth Av. WV11: Wed . . . 2H 29
Chilworth Cl. B6: Aston . . . 3H 101
Chimes Cl. B33: Kitts G . . . 2A 122
Chimney Rd. DY4: Tip . . . 6D 62
Chingford Cl. DY8: Word . . . 5A 92
Chingford Rd. B44: K'sdng . . . 5A 68
Chinley Gro. B44: K'sdng . . . 4C 68
Chinn Brook Rd. B13: Mose . . . 2B 148
Chip Cl. B38: K Nor . . . 5H 145
Chipperfield Rd. B36: Hodg H . . . 1C 104
Chipstead Rd. B23: Erd . . . 6D 68
Chipstone Cl. B91: Sol . . . 1G 165
Chirbury Gro. B31: Longb . . . 6F 145
Chirton Gro. B14: K Hth . . . 1F 147
Chiseldon Cft. B14: K Hth . . . 4A 148
Chisholm Gro. B27: A Grn . . . 5A 136
Chiswell Rd. B18: Win G . . . 5A 100
Chiswick Ct. B23: Erd . . . 5E 85
Chiswick Ho. *B15: Birm . . . 3E 117*
(off Bell Barn Rd.)
Chiswick Wlk. B37: Chel W . . . 1F 123
Chivenor Ho. B35: Cas V . . . 5E 87
Chivington Cl. B90: M'path . . . 3F 165
Chorley Av. B34: Hodg H . . . 3D 104
Chorley Gdns. WV14: Bils . . . 6D 44
Christchurch Cl. B15: Edg . . . 3A 116
Christ Chu. Gro. WS1: Wals . . . 4E 49
Christina Ct. B71: W Brom . . . 3B 80
Christine Cl. DY4: Tip . . . 3C 62
Christopher Ct. *B23: Erd . . . 5D 68*
(off Marshmount Way)
Christopher Rd. B29: S Oak . . . 3G 131
B62: Hale . . . 2E 129
WV2: Wolv . . . 3A 44
Christopher Taylor Ct. B30: B'vlle . . . 2A 146
Chubb St. WV1: Wolv . . . 1H 43 (2D 170)
CHUCKERY, THE . . . 2E 49
Chuckery Rd. WS1: Wals . . . 2E 49
Chudleigh Gro. B43: Gt Barr . . . 5H 65
Chudleigh Rd. B23: Erd . . . 3E 85
Churchacre B23: Erd . . . 5C 68
Church Av. B13: Mose . . . 2H 133
B20: Hand . . . 1E 101
B46: Wat O . . . 4D 88
DY8: Amb . . . 4E 109
CHURCHBRIDGE . . . 1G 7
Churchbridge B69: O'bry . . . 4F 97
(not continuous)
Churchbridge Ind. Est. *B69: O'bry . . . 4F 97*
(off Churchbridge)
Church Cl. B37: K'hrst . . . 3C 106
B47: Wyt . . . 6A 162
Church Ct. B64: Old H . . . 2G 111
Church Cres. WV11: Ess . . . 4H 17
Church Cft. B63: Hale . . . 1A 128
Churchcroft B17: Harb . . . 1F 131
Chu. Cross Vw. DY1: Dud . . . 1A 94
Chu. Dale Rd. B44: Gt Barr . . . 2F 67
Churchdown Ct. *B23: Erd . . . 5C 84*
(off Dunlin Ct.)
Church Dr. B30: Stir . . . 6D 132
CHURCHFIELD . . . 1B 80
Churchfield Av. DY4: Tip . . . 5H 61
Churchfield Cl. B7: Nech . . . 3C 102
Churchfield Rd. WV10: Oxl . . . 1F 27
Churchfields Rd. WS10: W'bry . . . 1F 63
Churchfield St. DY2: Dud . . . 1E 95
Church Gdns. B67: Smeth . . . 5E 99
Church Grn. B20: Hand . . . 5B 82
WV14: Bils . . . 3E 45
Church Gro. B13: Mose . . . 2C 148
B20: Hand . . . 6D 82
CHURCH HILL
Wednesbury . . . 2F 63
Church Hill B31: N'fld . . . 4F 145
(not continuous)
B32: Fran . . . 2G 143
B46: Col . . . 2H 107
B72: S Cold . . . 6A 54
DY5: Brie H . . . 1H 109
WS1: Wals . . . 2D 48
WS10: W'bry . . . 2F 63
(Ethelfleda Ter.)
WS10: W'bry . . . 2F 63
(Walsall St.)
WV4: Penn . . . 2C 58
WV8: Cod . . . 2F 13
Chu. Hill Cl. B91: Sol . . . 5G 151
Chu. Hill Ct. WS10: W'bry . . . 2F 63
Chu. Hill Dr. WV6: Tett . . . 4C 26
Chu. Hill Rd. B20: Hand . . . 6D 82
B91: Sol . . . 4G 151
WV6: Tett . . . 3B 26
Chu. Hill St. B67: Smeth . . . 3D 98
Church Ho. WS2: Wals . . . 4A 48
Church Ho. Dr. B72: S Cold . . . 6A 54
Churchill Cl. B69: Tiv . . . 5C 78
Churchill Dr. B65: Row R . . . 1B 112
DY8: Amb . . . 4E 109
Churchill Gdns. DY3: Sed . . . 6G 59
Churchill Pde. B75: S Cold . . . 6E 55
Churchill Pl. B33: Sheld . . . 2F 121
Churchill Rd. B9: Bord G . . . 6F 103
B63: Hale . . . 3H 127
B73: New O . . . 2D 68
B75: S Cold . . . 6E 55
WS2: Wals . . . 1D 46
Churchill Shop. Pct., The DY2: Dud . . . 6F 77
Churchill Wlk. DY4: Tip . . . 5A 62
Church La. B6: Aston . . . 1A 102
B20: Hand . . . 5B 82
B33: Stech . . . 6D 104
B63: Hale . . . 1B 128
B71: W Brom . . . 1H 79
B76: Curd . . . 1D 88
B92: Bick . . . 4F 139
WS7: Hamm . . . 2F 11
WS9: Ston . . . 3G 23
WV2: Wolv . . . 2G 43 (5A 170)
WV5: Seis, Try . . . 3A 56
(not continuous)
WV8: Cod . . . 3F 13
Church La. Ind. Est. B71: W Brom . . . 1A 80
Church M. DY4: Tip . . . 6H 61
Chu. Moat Way WS3: Blox . . . 1H 31
Churchover Cl. B76: Walm . . . 1B 86
Church Pl. WS3: Blox . . . 1B 32
Church Rd. B6: Aston . . . 2B 102
B13: Mose . . . 2A 134
B15: Edg . . . 4C 116
B24: Erd . . . 3F 85
B25: Yard . . . 4B 120
B26: Sheld . . . 6F 121
B31: N'fld . . . 3E 145
B33: Yard . . . 2C 120
B42: P Barr . . . 2F 83
B63: Crad . . . 4E 111
B65: Row R . . . 6C 96
B67: Smeth . . . 5D 98
B73: Bold . . . 5F 69
B73: S Cold . . . 2H 69
B90: Shir . . . 5H 149
DY2: Neth . . . 4D 94
DY3: Swind . . . 4D 72
DY8: Stourb . . . 2F 125
DY8: Word . . . 1B 108
DY9: Lye . . . 6A 110
WS3: Pels . . . 4E 21
WS8: Bwnhls . . . 6B 10
(not continuous)
WS9: Ston . . . 4G 23
WS11: Nort C . . . 1C 8
WV3: Wolv . . . 4C 42
WV5: Wom . . . 6H 57
WV6: Pert . . . 5E 25
WV6: Tett . . . 4C 26
(Rock, The)
WV6: Tett . . . 6H 25
(School Rd.)
WV8: Cod . . . 3F 13
(not continuous)
WV10: Oxl . . . 6G 15
WV12: W'hall . . . 3D 30
WV14: Cose . . . 4F 61
Churchside Way WS9: A'rdge . . . 5D 22
Church Sq. B69: O'bry . . . 2G 97
Church St. B3: Birm . . . 6F 101 (3D 4)
B19: Loz . . . 2E 101
B62: B'hth . . . 2D 112
B64: Old H . . . 2G 111
B69: O'bry . . . 1G 97
B70: W Brom . . . 3A 80
DY2: Dud . . . 1E 95
DY3: Lwr G . . . 4H 75
DY4: Tip . . . 5A 78
DY5: Brie H . . . 2G 109
DY5: P'ntt . . . 2H 93
DY5: Quar B . . . 2B 110
DY8: Stourb . . . 6E 109
WS1: Wals . . . 2D 48
WS3: Blox . . . 1H 31
WS7: Chase . . . 1A 10
WS8: Clay . . . 1A 22
WS10: Darl . . . 4D 46
(Bell St.)
WS10: Darl . . . 1B 62
(Black Country New Rd.)
WV2: Wolv . . . 2G 43 (5A 170)
WV10: Wolv . . . 5C 28
WV11: Wed . . . 4E 29
WV13: W'hall . . . 1B 46
(not continuous)
WV14: Bils . . . 6F 45
Church Ter. B33: Yard . . . 2C 120
B75: Four O . . . 6H 37
Church Va. B20: Hand . . . 6D 82
B71: W Brom . . . 1B 80
WS11: Nort C . . . 1C 8
Church Va. M. B71: W Brom . . . 2B 80
Church Vw. B11: S'brk . . . 5D 118
WS9: A'rdge . . . 4D 34
WS9: Wals W . . . 4B 22
Church Vw. Cl. WS3: Blox . . . 1A 32
Church Vw. Dr. B64: Old H . . . 2H 111
Church Wlk. B8: W End . . . 3G 103
B46: Col . . . 3H 107
B65: Row R . . . 5C 96
WV3: Wolv . . . 4D 42
WV6: Tett . . . 4C 26
WV13: W'hall . . . 2B 46
Churchward Cl. DY8: Amb . . . 5F 109
Churchward Gro. WV5: Wom . . . 6G 57
Church Way WS4: S'fld . . . 5F 21
Churchwell Ct. B63: Hale . . . 2B 128
Churchwell Gdns.
B71: W Brom . . . 1B 80
Churchyard Rd. DY4: Tip . . . 2B 78
Churnet Gro. WV6: Pert . . . 5F 25
Churn Hill Rd. WS9: A'rdge . . . 5C 34
Churns Hill La. DY3: Himl . . . 4H 73
Churston Cl. WS3: Blox . . . 4G 19
Churton House (Crystal Glass Cen., The)
. . . 3C 108
Churwell Ct. WV5: Wom . . . 1G 73
Cider Av. DY5: Quar B . . . 3A 110
(not continuous)
Cinder Bank DY2: Neth . . . 2D 94
Cinder Bank Island DY2: Dud . . . 2D 94
CINDER HILL . . . 4B 60
Cinder Rd. DY3: Gorn . . . 6F 75
Cinder Way WS10: W'bry . . . 2E 63
Cineworld
Solihull . . . 4G 151
Wednesfield . . . 5D 28
Cinquefoil Leasow DY4: Tip . . . 1C 78
Circle, The B17: Harb . . . 4G 115
Circuit Cl. WV13: W'hall . . . 6B 30
Circular Rd. B27: A Grn . . . 3A 136
Circus Av. B37: Chel W . . . 1E 123
City, The DY4: Tip . . . 4A 78
City Arc. *B2: Birm . . . 4E 5*
(off Corporation St.)
City Est. B64: Crad H . . . 3F 111
City Hgts. B4: Birm . . . 1D 4
City Plaza B2: Birm . . . 4E 5
City Rd. B16: Edg . . . 2F 115
B17: Edg . . . 2F 115
B69: Tiv . . . 2B 96
City Trad. Est. B16: Birm . . . 6C 100
City Vw. B8: Salt . . . 5D 102
City Wlk. B5: Birm . . . 2G 117 (6E 5)
Civic Cl. B1: Birm . . . 1E 117 (4A 4)
Claerwen Gro. B31: N'fld . . . 2C 144
Claines Rd. B31: N'fld . . . 3G 145
B63: Crad . . . 6F 111
Claire Ct. B26: Sheld . . . 4G 121
Clairvaux Gdns. B92: Olton . . . 2B 150
Clandon Cl. B14: K Hth . . . 5E 147
Clanfield Av. WV11: Wed . . . 1H 29
Clapgate Gdns. WV14: Cose . . . 2C 60
Clap Ga. Gro. WV5: Wom . . . 1E 73
Clapgate La. B32: Bart G . . . 3G 129
Clapgate Rd. WV5: Wom . . . 6E 57
Clapton Gro. B44: K'sdng . . . 4B 68
Clare Av. WV11: Wed . . . 6H 17
Clare Ct. B90: Shir . . . 5D 148
Clare Cres. WV14: Cose . . . 3B 60
Clare Dr. B15: Edg . . . 3B 116
Clare Ho. B36: Cas B . . . 2C 106
Clarel Av. B8: Salt . . . 6C 102
Claremont Ct. B64: Old H . . . 2G 111
Claremont M. WV3: Wolv . . . 4E 43
Claremont Pl. B18: Win G . . . 4B 100
Claremont Rd. B11: S'brk . . . 4B 118
B18: Hock . . . 3D 100
B66: Smeth . . . 5F 99
DY3: Sed . . . 5A 60
WV3: Wolv . . . 4E 43
Claremont St. B64: Old H . . . 2G 111
WV14: Bils . . . 5E 45
Claremont Way B63: Hale . . . 2B 128
Clarence Av. B21: Hand . . . 1G 99
Clarence Ct. B68: O'bry . . . 1A 114
Clarence Gdns. B74: Four O . . . 1F 53
Clarence M. B17: Harb . . . 5H 115
Clarence Rd. B11: S'hll . . . 1C 134
B13: K Hth . . . 4A 134
B17: Harb . . . 5H 115
B21: Hand . . . 1G 99
B23: Erd . . . 4D 84
B74: Four O . . . 4E 37
DY2: Dud . . . 3F 95
WV1: Wolv . . . 1G 43 (2A 170)
WV14: Bils . . . 4G 45
Clarence St. DY3: Up Gor . . . 1A 76
WV1: Wolv . . . 1G 43 (3A 170)
Clarenden Pl. B17: Harb . . . 6G 115
Clarendon Dr. DY4: Tip . . . 4D 62
Clarendon Pl. B62: Quin . . . 4F 113
WS3: Pels . . . 3D 20
Clarendon Rd. B16: Edg . . . 2A 116
B67: Smeth . . . 5D 98
B75: R'ley . . . 6A 38
WS4: S'fld . . . 5G 21
Clarendon St. WS3: Blox . . . 6H 19
WV3: Wolv . . . 1E 43
Clarendon Way B91: Sol . . . 4G 151
Clare Rd. WS3: Wals . . . 3E 33
WV10: Bush . . . 2A 28
Clarewell Av. B91: Sol . . . 1F 165
Clarke Ho. WS3: Blox . . . 6H 19
Clarkes Gro. DY4: Tip . . . 1C 78
Clarke's La. B71: W Brom . . . 6A 64
WV13: W'hall . . . 6C 30
Clark Rd. WV3: Wolv . . . 1D 42
Clarkson Pl. DY5: Quar B . . . 5A 110
Clarkson Rd. WS10: W'bry . . . 1G 63
Clark St. B16: Birm . . . 1B 116
DY8: Stourb . . . 6C 108
Clarry Dr. B74: Four O . . . 3F 53
Clary Gro. WS5: Wals . . . 2E 65
CLATTERBATCH . . . 6F 109
Claughton Rd. DY2: Dud . . . 6F 77
Claughton Rd. Nth. DY2: Dud . . . 6F 77
Clausen Cl. B43: Gt Barr . . . 1G 67
Clavedon Cl. B31: N'fld . . . 6C 130
Claverdon Cl. B91: Sol . . . 4C 150
WS8: Bwnhls . . . 5C 10
Claverdon Dr. B43: Gt Barr . . . 5H 65
B74: Lit A . . . 5B 36
Claverdon Gdns. B27: A Grn . . . 6H 119
Claverdon Ho. B13: Mose . . . 6A 134
Claverley Ct. DY1: Dud . . . 6D 76
Claverley Dr. WV4: Penn . . . 6B 42
Claybrook St. B5: Birm . . . 2G 117 (6E 5)
Claycroft Pl. DY9: Lye . . . 6A 110
Claycroft Ter. DY1: Dud . . . 1D 76
Claydon Gro. B14: K Hth . . . 4A 148
Claydon Rd. DY6: W Hth . . . 6A 74
Clay Dr. B32: Quin . . . 6G 113
CLAYHANGER . . . 1A 22
Clayhanger La. WS8: Bwnhls, Clay . . . 6H 9
Clayhanger Rd. WS8: Bwnhls . . . 1B 22
Clay La. B26: Yard . . . 6C 120
B69: O'bry . . . 5G 97
Claypit Cl. B70: W Brom . . . 4G 79
Clay Pit La. B90: Dic H . . . 4G 163
(not continuous)
Claypit La. B70: W Brom . . . 4G 79
Clayton Cl. WV2: Wolv . . . 4G 43
Clayton Dr. B36: Cas B . . . 1G 105
Clayton Gdns. B45: Lick . . . 6G 157
Clayton Ho. B16: Edg . . . 2B 116
Clayton Rd. B8: Salt . . . 4D 102
WV14: Cose . . . 6D 60
Clayton Wlk. B35: Cas V . . . 5E 87
Clear Vw. DY6: K'wfrd . . . 3H 91
Clearwell Gdns. DY1: Dud . . . 4A 76
Clee Hill Dr. WV3: Wolv . . . 2G 41
Clee Hill Rd. DY3: Lwr G . . . 3G 75
Clee Rd. B31: Longb . . . 1E 159
B68: O'bry . . . 5A 98
DY2: Dud . . . 2C 94
DY8: Amb . . . 5E 109
Cleeve Dr. B74: Four O . . . 3F 37
Cleeve Ho. B24: Erd . . . 5G 85
Cleeve Rd. B14: Yard W . . . 3C 148
WS3: Blox . . . 4F 19
Cleeve Way WS3: Blox . . . 5F 19
Clee Vw. Mdw. DY3: Sed . . . 3H 59
Clee Vw. Rd. WV5: Wom . . . 2E 73
Clematis Dr. WV9: Pend . . . 4D 14
Clem Attlee Ct. WV14: Wolv . . . 3E 45
Clement Pl. WV14: Bils . . . 4F 45
Clement Rd. B62: B'hth . . . 2D 112
WV14: Bils . . . 4F 45
Clements Cl. B69: O'bry . . . 5F 97
Clements Rd. B25: Yard . . . 3B 120
Clement St. B1: Birm . . . 6D 100 (3A 4)
WS2: Wals . . . 2B 48
Clemson St. WV13: W'hall . . . 1A 46
Clent Ct. DY1: Dud . . . 6D 76
Clent Hill Dr. B65: Row R . . . 4A 96
Clent Ho. B63: Hale . . . 3A 128
Clent Rd. B21: Hand . . . 6H 81
B45: Rubery . . . 1E 157
B68: O'bry . . . 3A 114
DY8: Amb . . . 5E 109
Clent Vw. B66: Smeth . . . 6F 99
Clent Vw. Rd. B32: Bart G . . . 4G 129
B63: Crad . . . 1E 127
DY8: Stourb . . . 2A 124
(not continuous)
Clent Vs. B12: Bal H . . . 1B 134
Clent Way B32: Bart G . . . 5G 129
Cleobury La. B90: Tid G . . . 4F 163
B94: Earls . . . 4F 163
Cleton St. DY4: Tip . . . 4B 78
Cleton St. Bus. Pk. DY4: Tip . . . 4B 78
Clevedon Av. B36: Cas B . . . 1A 106
Clevedon Rd. B12: Bal H . . . 5G 117
Cleveland Cl. WV11: Wed . . . 6H 17
WV13: W'hall . . . 2F 45
Cleveland Ct. B13: Mose . . . 3B 134
Cleveland Pas. WV1: Wolv . . . 2G 43 (4B 170)
Cleveland Rd. WV2: Wolv . . . 2H 43 (5D 170)
Cleveland St. DY1: Dud . . . 6D 76
DY8: Stourb . . . 1C 124
WV1: Wolv . . . 2G 43 (4B 170)
Cleveland Twr. B1: Birm . . . 6D 4
Cleves Cres. WS6: C Hay . . . 4D 6
Cleves Dr. B45: Rubery . . . 2E 157
Cleves Rd. B45: Rubery . . . 1E 157
Clewley Dr. WV9: Pend . . . 4E 15
Clewley Gro. B32: Quin . . . 6H 113
Clews Cl. WS1: Wals . . . 4C 48
Clewshaw La. B38: Head H . . . 5D 160
Cley Cl. B5: Edg . . . 5F 117
Cliff, The DY8: Stourb . . . 5E 109
Cliffe Dr. B33: Kitts G . . . 6G 105
Clifford Rd. B67: Smeth . . . 2D 114
B70: W Brom . . . 5G 79
B93: Ben H . . . 5B 166
Clifford St. B19: Loz . . . 2F 101
DY1: Dud . . . 1D 94
WV6: Wolv . . . 6E 27
Clifford Wlk. B19: Loz . . . 2F 101
(not continuous)
Cliff Rock Rd. B45: Redn . . . 2H 157
Clift Cl. WV12: W'hall . . . 3C 30
Clifton Av. WS8: Bwnhls . . . 6H 9
WS9: A'rdge . . . 1E 35
Clifton Cl. B6: Aston . . . 2H 101
B69: O'bry . . . 5G 97
Clifton Cres. B91: Sol . . . 6C 150
Clifton Dr. B73: S Cold . . . 5H 53
Clifton Gdns. WV8: Bilb . . . 4A 14
Clifton Grn. B28: Hall G . . . 2G 149
Clifton Ho. B12: Bal H . . . 6A 118
Clifton La. B71: W Brom . . . 5C 64
Clifton Rd. B6: Aston . . . 2H 101
B12: Bal H . . . 6H 117
B36: Cas B . . . 1A 106
B62: B'hth . . . 3D 112
B67: Smeth . . . 5D 98
B73: S Cold . . . 1G 69
WV6: Tett . . . 4B 26
Clifton Rd. Ind. Est. *B12: Bal H . . . 6H 117*
(off Clifton Rd.)
Clifton St. B64: Old H . . . 2H 111
DY8: Stourb . . . 1C 124
WV14: Cose . . . 4B 60
Clifton Ter. B23: Erd . . . 3F 85
Clinic Dr. DY9: Lye . . . 6A 110
Clinton Gro. B90: Shir . . . 6C 150
Clinton Rd. B46: Col . . . 3H 107
B90: Shir . . . 1B 164
WV14: Bils . . . 4A 46
Clinton St. B18: Win G . . . 4A 100
Clipper Vw. B16: Edg . . . 2A 116
Clipston Rd. B8: Salt . . . 5F 103
Clissold Cl. B12: Birm . . . 4G 117
Clissold Pas. B18: Hock . . . 5C 100
Clissold St. B18: Hock . . . 5C 100
Clive Cl. B75: R'ley . . . 1B 54
Cliveden Av. B42: P Barr . . . 3E 83
WS9: A'rdge . . . 6D 22
Cliveden Coppice
B74: Four O . . . 2F 53
Clivedon Way B62: Hale . . . 4A 112
Cliveland St. B19: Birm . . . 5G 101 (1E 5)
Clive Pl. B19: Birm . . . 5F 101 (1D 4)
Clive Rd. B32: Quin . . . 4B 114
CV7: Bal C . . . 6H 169
Clive St. B71: W Brom . . . 2A 80
Clockfields Dr. DY5: Brie H . . . 2E 109
Clock La. B92: Bick . . . 3F 139
Clockmill Av. WS3: Pels . . . 4C 20
Clockmill Pl. WS3: Pels . . . 4D 20
Clockmill Rd. WS3: Pels . . . 4C 20
Clodeshall Rd. B8: Salt . . . 5E 103
Cloister Dr. B62: Hale . . . 2D 128
Cloisters, The WS4: Wals . . . 6D 32
Clonmel Rd. B30: Stir . . . 1C 146
Clopton Cres. B37: F'bri . . . 5D 106
Clopton Rd. B33: Sheld . . . 3G 121

Coppice Way—Crompton Ct.

Coppice Way *B37: Chel W* . . . 1D 122
(off Chelmsley Wood Shop. Cen.)
Copplestone Cl. B34: S End . . . 3F 105
Coppy Hall Gro. WS9: A'rdge . . . 6D 22
Coppy Nook La. WS7: Hamm . . . 1D 10
Copse, The B74: Four O . . . 2F 53
Copse Cl. B31: N'fld . . . 5E 145
Copse Cres. WS3: Pels . . . 3E 21
Copse Rd. DY2: Neth . . . 6D 94
Copstone Dr. B93: Dorr . . . 6B 166
Copston Gro. B29: W Cas . . . 5F 131
Copthall Rd. B21: Hand . . . 5G 81
COPT HEATH . . . 6C 152
Copt Heath Cft. B93: Know . . . 1D 166
Copt Heath Dr. B93: Know . . . 2C 166
Copt Heath Golf Course . . . 1C 166
Copt Heath Wharf B91: Sol . . . 5D 152
Copthorne Av. WS7: Chase . . . 1B 10
Copthorne Rd. B44: Gt Barr . . . 2G 67
WV3: Wolv . . . 4E 43
Coralin Cl. B37: Chel W . . . 1D 122
Corbett Cres. DY8: Amb . . . 4E 109
Corbett Rd. B47: H'wd . . . 2A 162
DY5: Brie H . . . 2H 109
Corbetts Cl. B92: H Ard . . . 6B 140
Corbett St. B66: Smeth . . . 5F 99
Corbridge Av. B44: Gt Barr . . . 4H 67
Corbridge Rd. B73: S Cold . . . 3F 69
Corbyn Rd. B9: Bord G . . . 6H 103
DY1: Dud . . . 1B 94
Corbyn's Cl. DY5: P'ntt . . . 2F 93
Corbyn's Hall La. DY5: P'ntt . . . 2F 93
Corbyn's Hall Rd. DY5: P'ntt . . . 3F 93
Cordley St. B70: W Brom . . . 3H 79
Corfe Cl. B32: Harb . . . 6D 114
WV6: Pert . . . 6F 25
Corfe Dr. B69: Tiv . . . 1A 96
Corfe Rd. WV14: Cose . . . 5C 60
Corfton Dr. WV6: Tett . . . 5A 26
Coriander Cl. B45: Fran . . . 6H 143
Corinne Cl. B45: Redn . . . 3G 157
Corinne Cft. B37: K'hrst . . . 5C 106
Corisande Rd. B29: S Oak . . . 3G 131
Corley Av. B31: N'fld . . . 4F 145
Corley Cl. B90: Shir . . . 6E 149
Cornbow Cen. B63: Hale . . . 2B 128
Cornbrook Rd. B29: W Cas . . . 6D 130
Cornbury Gro. B91: Shir . . . 3B 150
Corncrake Cl. B72: S Cold . . . 3B 70
Corncrake Dr. B36: Cas B . . . 1C 106
Corncrake Rd. DY3: Lwr G . . . 4A 76
Cornel Cl. B37: Chel W . . . 3E 123
Cornerstone B13: Mose . . . 2H 133
Cornerstone Country Club B31: N'fld . . . 2F 145
Cornerway B38: K Nor . . . 2B 160
CORNETS END . . . 1H 155
Cornets End La. CV7: Mer . . . 5E 141
Cornfield WV8: Pend . . . 6C 14
Cornfield Cl. DY6: W Hth . . . 1G 91
Cornfield Cft. B37: Chel W . . . 6F 107
B76: Walm . . . 2D 70
Cornfield Pl. *B65: Row R* . . . *5H 95*
(off Allsops Cl.)
Cornfield Rd. B31: N'fld . . . 3F 145
B65: Row R . . . 5H 95
B76: Walm . . . 4D 70
Cornflower Cl. WV10: F'stne . . . 1C 16
Cornflower Cres. DY2: Dud . . . 1H 95
Cornflower Rd. WS8: Clay . . . 1H 21
Corngreaves, The B34: S End . . . 3G 105
Corngreaves Rd. B64: Crad H . . . 2F 111
Corngreaves Trad. Est. B64: Crad H . . . 4F 111
Corngreaves Wlk. B64: Crad H . . . 4G 111
Corn Hill WS5: Wals . . . 3A 50
WV10: Wolv . . . 1H 43 (3D 170)
Cornhill Gro. B30: Stir . . . 1E 147
Corn Mill Cl. B32: Bart G . . . 4C 130
B76: Walm . . . 4D 70
WS1: Wals . . . 4B 48
Cornmill Gro. WV6: Pert . . . 6D 24
Cornovian Cl. WV6: Pert . . . 4E 25
Corns Gro. WV5: Wom . . . 2F 73
Corns Ho. *WS10: Darl* . . . *5E 47*
(off Birmingham St.)
Corns St. WS10: Darl . . . 6E 47
Cornwall Av. B68: O'bry . . . 3H 113
Cornwall Cl. DY6: K'wfrd . . . 1C 92
WS9: A'rdge . . . 6C 22
WS10: W'bry . . . 2B 64
Cornwall Ga. WV12: W'hall . . . 4B 30
Cornwall Ho. B90: Bly P . . . 6D 164
Cornwallis Rd. B70: W Brom . . . 6G 79
Cornwall Pl. WS2: Wals . . . 6E 31
Cornwall Rd. B20: Hand . . . 5B 82
B45: Fran . . . 6E 143
B66: Smeth . . . 2F 99
DY8: Woll . . . 3B 108
WS5: Wals . . . 4F 49
WV6: Tett . . . 5A 26
Cornwall Rd. Ind. Est. B66: Smeth . . . 2F 99
Cornwall St. B3: Birm . . . 6F 101 (3C 4)
Cornwall Twr. B18: Hock . . . 4D 100
Cornwell Cl. DY4: Tip . . . 2A 78
Cornyx La. B91: Sol . . . 1H 151
Coronation Av. WV13: W'hall . . . 1D 46
Coronation Rd. B8: Salt . . . 3F 103
B29: S Oak . . . 3B 132
B43: Gt Barr . . . 1A 66
DY4: Tip . . . 5A 62
WS4: S'fld . . . 5F 21
WS9: Wals W . . . 4C 22
WS10: W'bry . . . 2A 64
WV10: Wolv . . . 4C 28
WV14: Bils . . . 6E 45
Corporation Rd. DY2: Dud . . . 5G 77
Corporation Sq. B4: Birm . . . 6G 101 (3F 5)
Corporation St. B2: Birm . . . 1G 117 (4E 5)
(not continuous)
B4: Birm . . . 5G 101 (1F 5)
WS1: Wals . . . 3C 48
WS10: W'bry . . . 3G 63
WV1: Wolv . . . 1G 43 (3A 170)
Corporation St. W. WS1: Wals . . . 3B 48
Corrie Cft. B26: Sheld . . . 4F 121
B32: Bart G . . . 5H 129
Corrin Gro. DY6: W Hth . . . 1A 92
Corron Hill *B63: Hale* . . . *1B 128*
(off Cobham Rd.)
Corsers Ct. WV6: Pert . . . 5E 25
Corser St. DY1: Dud . . . 5B 76
DY8: Stourb . . . 2E 125
WV1: Wolv . . . 2B 44
Corsican Cl. WV12: W'hall . . . 2E 31
Corvedale Rd. B29: W Cas . . . 1E 145
Corve Gdns. WV6: Tett . . . 4C 26
Corve Vw. DY3: Sed . . . 4G 59
Corville Gdns. B26: Sheld . . . 1G 137
Corville Rd. B62: Quin . . . 5F 113
Corwen Cft. B31: N'fld . . . 1C 144
Cory Cft. DY4: Tip . . . 2A 78
COSELEY . . . 5E 61
Coseley Baths . . . 4F 61
Coseley Hall WV14: Cose . . . 5E 61
Coseley Leisure Cen. . . . 4D 60
Coseley Rd. WV14: Bils . . . 6E 45
Coseley Station (Rail) . . . 4E 61
Cosford Ct. WV6: Pert . . . 4E 25
Cosford Cres. B35: Cas V . . . 4E 87
Cosford Dr. DY2: Neth . . . 5G 95
Cosgrove Wlk. WV8: Pend . . . 6D 14
Cossington Rd. B23: Erd . . . 6D 68
Costock Cl. B37: Mars G . . . 3D 122
Cotford Rd. B14: K Hth . . . 5A 148
Cotheridge Cl. B90: M'path . . . 3G 165
Cot La. DY6: K'wfrd . . . 3A 92
DY8: Word . . . 4A 92
Cotleigh Gro. B43: Gt Barr . . . 2G 67
Cotman Cl. B43: Gt Barr . . . 2E 67
Coton Gro. B90: Shir . . . 5E 149
Coton La. B23: Erd . . . 3F 85
Coton Rd. WV4: Penn . . . 6F 43
Cotsdale Rd. WV4: Penn . . . 2C 58
Cotsford B91: Sol . . . 4E 151
Cotswold Av. WS6: Gt Wyr . . . 2F 7
Cotswold Cl. B45: Fran . . . 5H 143
B69: O'bry . . . 4E 97
WS9: A'rdge . . . 6E 23
Cotswold Cft. B63: Hale . . . 4E 127
Cotswold Gro. WV12: W'hall . . . 6B 18
Cotswold Rd. DY8: Amb . . . 5F 109
WV2: E'shll . . . 4B 44
Cotsworld Ct. *WV2: Wolv* . . . *5F 43*
(off Goldthorn Hill)
Cottage Cl. WV11: Wed . . . 3E 29
(not continuous)
Cottage Gdns. B45: Rubery . . . 4F 157
Cottage La. B76: Min . . . 1H 87
WV10: F'hses . . . 4H 15
Cottage M. WS9: A'rdge . . . 5G 35
Cottage St. DY5: Brie H . . . 6H 93
DY6: K'wfrd . . . 2B 92
Cottage Vw. WV8: Bilb . . . 3H 13
Cottage Wlk. B70: W Brom . . . 5B 80
COTTERIDGE . . . 3A 146
Cotteridge Rd. B30: K Nor . . . 3C 146
Cotterills Av. B8: W End . . . 5A 104
Cotterills La. B8: W End . . . 5G 103
Cotterills Rd. DY4: Tip . . . 6B 62
Cottesbrook Rd. B27: A Grn . . . 1B 136
Cottesfield Cl. B8: W End . . . 5H 103
Cottesmore Cl. B71: W Brom . . . 5D 64
Cottesmore Ho. B20: Hand . . . 5B 82
Cottle Cl. WS2: Wals . . . 6F 31
Cotton La. B13: Mose . . . 3H 133
Cottrells Cl. B14: Yard W . . . 3C 148
Cottrells M. B46: Wat O . . . 5D 88
Cottrell St. B71: W Brom . . . 3B 80
Cottsmeadow Dr. B8: W End . . . 5A 104
COTWALL END . . . 6G 59
Cotwall End Countryside Cen. . . . 1G 75
Cotwall End Rd. DY3: Lwr G, Sed . . . 3F 75
Cotwall End Valley Local Nature Reserve . . . 3F 75
Cotysmore Rd. B75: S Cold . . . 5B 54
Couchman Rd. B8: Salt . . . 5E 103
Coulter Gro. WV6: Pert . . . 5D 24
Council Cres. WV12: W'hall . . . 5C 30
Counterfield Dr. B65: Row R . . . 4H 95
Countess Dr. WS4: Rus . . . 2H 33
Countess St. WS1: Wals . . . 4B 48
COUNTY BRIDGE . . . 1D 46
County Cl. B30: Stir . . . 1D 146
B32: Bart G . . . 2A 130
County La. DY8: I'ley . . . 5B 124
WV7: Alb . . . 2A 12
WV8: Cod W . . . 2A 12
County Pk. Av. B62: Hale . . . 2C 128
Court, The B93: Know . . . 4B 168
Court Cres. DY6: K'wfrd . . . 4H 91
Courtenay Gdns. B43: Gt Barr . . . 3A 66
Courtenay Rd. B44: Gt Barr . . . 6G 67
Court Farm Rd. B23: Erd . . . 1E 85
Court Farm Way B29: W Cas . . . 6D 130
Courtland Rd. DY6: K'wfrd . . . 1C 92
Courtlands, The WV6: Wolv . . . 5C 26
Courtlands Cl. B5: Edg . . . 5E 117
Court La. B23: Erd . . . 5E 69
Court Oak Gro. B32: Harb . . . 5D 114
Court Oak Rd. B32: Harb . . . 5C 114
Court Pde. WS9: A'rdge . . . 3D 34
Court Pas. DY1: Dud . . . 6E 77
Court Rd. B11: S'hll . . . 1C 134
B12: Bal H . . . 5G 117
WV4: E'shll . . . 2C 60
WV6: Wolv . . . 5D 26
Court St. B64: Old H . . . 2H 111
DY8: Stourb . . . 6E 109
Court Way WS2: Wals . . . 1C 48
Courtway Av. B14: K Hth . . . 6B 148
Courtway Ho. B29: S Oak . . . 4G 131
Court Yd., The *B70: W Brom* . . . *4G 79*
(off Hambletts Rd.)
Courtyard, The B46: Col . . . 5H 89
B91: Sol . . . 3G 151
Coveley Gro. B18: Hock . . . 4C 100
Coven Cl. WS3: Pels . . . 2E 21
Coven Gro. B29: S Oak . . . 3F 131
COVEN HEATH . . . 1H 15
Coven La. WV9: Coven . . . 2D 14
Coventry Rd. B10: Small H . . . 2A 118
B25: Yard . . . 4G 119
B26: Yard, Sheld . . . 5C 120
Coventry Rd. B46: Col . . . 6H 107
B92: Bick . . . 2C 138
Coventry St. B5: Birm . . . 1H 117 (5G 5)
DY8: Stourb . . . 6E 109
WV1: Wolv . . . 1C 44
Cover Cft. B76: Walm . . . 4E 71
Coverdale Rd. B92: Olton . . . 1E 137
Covert, The WV8: Pend . . . 6C 14
Covert La. DY8: Stourb . . . 4B 124
Cowles Cft. B25: Yard . . . 2C 120
Cowley Cl. B36: Cas B . . . 6B 88
Cowley Dr. B27: A Grn . . . 1B 136
DY1: Dud . . . 5B 76
Cowley Gro. B11: Tys . . . 6E 119
Cowley Rd. B11: Tys . . . 6E 119
Cowper Cl. WV12: W'hall . . . 2E 31
Cowslip Cl. B29: W Cas . . . 6E 131
B38: K Nor . . . 1B 160
Cowslip Wlk. DY5: Brie H . . . 5G 109
Coxcroft Av. DY5: Quar B . . . 3B 110
Coxmoor Cl. WS3: Blox . . . 4F 19
Cox Rd. WV14: Cose . . . 4G 61
Cox's La. B64: Old H . . . 1H 111
Cox St. B3: Birm . . . 5F 101 (1C 4)
Coxwell Av. WV10: Wolv . . . 3G 27
Coxwell Gdns. B16: Birm . . . 1B 116
Coyne Cl. DY4: Tip . . . 2F 77
Coyne Rd. B70: W Brom . . . 5H 79
Crabbe St. DY9: Lye . . . 6B 110
Crab La. DY6: K'wfrd . . . 5E 93
WV12: W'hall . . . 6D 18
Crabmill Cl. B38: K Nor . . . 2A 160
B93: Know . . . 2E 167
Crabmill La. B38: Head H . . . 2E 161
Crabourne Rd. DY2: Neth . . . 1D 110
Crabtree Cl. B31: N'fld . . . 5G 145
B71: W Brom . . . 5D 64
DY9: Hag . . . 6F 125
Crabtree Dr. B37: F'bri . . . 1B 122
Crab Tree Ho. B33: Stech . . . 6C 104
Crabtree Rd. B18: Hock . . . 4C 100
WS1: Wals . . . 1E 49
Crackley Way DY2: Dud . . . 3C 94
Craddock Rd. B67: Smeth . . . 3C 98
Craddock St. WV6: Wolv . . . 5E 27
CRADLEY . . . 4E 111
Cradley Cft. B21: Hand . . . 4G 81
Cradley Flds. B63: Crad . . . 6E 111
Cradley Forge DY5: Quar B . . . 3C 110
CRADLEY HEATH . . . 2G 111
Cradley Heath Factory Cen.
B64: Crad H . . . 3E 111
Cradley Heath Station (Rail) . . . 3D 110
Cradley Leisure Cen. . . . 4D 110
Cradley Mill DY5: Quar B . . . 4B 110
Cradley Pk. Rd. DY2: Neth . . . 1E 111
Cradley Rd. B64: Crad H . . . 3E 111
DY2: Neth . . . 5F 95
Cradock Rd. B8: Salt . . . 4E 103
Craig Cft. B37: Chel W . . . 1F 123
Crail Gro. B43: Gt Barr . . . 1D 66
Cramlington Rd. B42: Gt Barr . . . 5C 66
Cramp Hill WS10: Darl . . . 5D 46
Cranbourne Av. WV4: E'shll . . . 2A 60
Cranbourne Cl. B45: Fran . . . 5G 143
Cranbourne Gro. B44: K'sdng . . . 5A 68
Cranbourne Pl. B71: W Brom . . . 3B 80
Cranbourne Rd. B44: K'sdng . . . 5A 68
DY8: Stourb . . . 1E 125
Cranbrook Ct. *WV13: W'hall* . . . *1C 46*
(off Mill St.)
Cranbrook Gro. WV6: Pert . . . 6F 25
Cranbrook Rd. B21: Hand . . . 6G 81
Cranby St. B8: Salt . . . 4C 102
Cranebrook Hill B78: Hints . . . 4H 39
Cranebrook La.
WS14: Hilt, Lynn . . . 1H 23
Crane Ct. WS1: Wals . . . 6E 33
Crane Dr. WS7: Chase . . . 1C 10
Crane Hollow WV5: Wom . . . 2E 73
Cranehouse Rd. B44: K'sdng . . . 3B 68
Cranemoor Cl. B7: Nech . . . 3C 102
Crane Rd. WV14: Bils . . . 2H 61
Cranesbill Rd. B29: W Cas . . . 1E 145
Cranes Pk. Rd. B26: Sheld . . . 6G 121
Crane Ter. WV6: Tett . . . 4C 26
Cranfield Gro. B26: Yard . . . 3D 120
Cranfield Pl. WS5: Wals . . . 1D 64
Cranford Gro. B91: Sol . . . 6F 151
Cranford Rd. WV3: Wolv . . . 3A 42
Cranford St. B66: Smeth . . . 4G 99
Cranford Way B66: Smeth . . . 4G 99
Cranham Dr. DY6: K'wfrd . . . 4C 92
Cranhill Cl. B92: Olton . . . 4F 137
Crankhall La. B71: W Brom . . . 2H 63
WS10: W'bry . . . 2H 63
Cranleigh Cl. WS9: A'rdge . . . 4D 34
WV12: W'hall . . . 6C 18
Cranleigh Ho. B23: Erd . . . 1F 85
Cranleigh Pl. B44: P Barr . . . 2G 83
Cranley Dr. WV8: Cod . . . 3F 13
Cranmer Av. WV12: W'hall . . . 2D 30
Cranmer Cl. WS6: C Hay . . . 4D 6
Cranmere Av. WV6: Tett . . . 3G 25
Cranmere Ct. WV6: Tett . . . 3G 25
Cranmer Gro. B74: Four O . . . 3F 37
Cranmoor Cres. B63: Hale . . . 6A 112
Cranmore Av. B21: Hand . . . 2H 99
B90: Shir . . . 1C 164
Cranmore Blvd. B90: Shir . . . 1B 164
Cranmore Cl. DY4: Tip . . . 5A 62
Cranmore Dr. B90: Shir . . . 6C 150
Cranmore Rd. B36: Cas B . . . 6H 87
B90: Shir . . . 1B 164
WV3: Wolv . . . 6D 26
Cransley Gro. B91: Sol . . . 6E 151
Crantock Cl. WV11: Ess . . . 6C 18
Crantock Rd. B42: P Barr . . . 3E 83
Cranwell Grn. WV5: Wom . . . 2F 73
Cranwell Gro. B24: Erd . . . 4B 86
Cranwell Way B35: Cas V . . . 4E 87
Crathorne Av. WV10: Oxl . . . 6G 15
Crauford Ct. DY8: Stourb . . . 2E 125
Crauford St. DY8: Stourb . . . 2E 125
Craven Hgts. B92: H Ard . . . 6A 140
Craven St. WV2: E'shll . . . 5B 44
Crawford Av. B67: Smeth . . . 4D 98
WS10: Darl . . . 4C 46
WV4: E'shll . . . 2B 60
Crawford Rd. B76: Walm . . . 5D 70
WV3: Wolv . . . 1E 43
Crawford St. B8: Salt . . . 5C 102
Crawley Wlk. B64: Crad H . . . 2F 111
Crawshaws Rd. B36: Cas B . . . 6G 87
Crayford Rd. B44: K'sdng . . . 4A 68
Craythorne Av. B20: Hand . . . 2A 82
Crecy Cl. B76: Walm . . . 1C 70
Credenda Rd. B70: W Brom . . . 6G 79
Credon Gro. B15: Edg . . . 1B 132
Cregoe St. B15: Birm . . . 2E 117
Cremore Av. B8: Salt . . . 4E 103
Cremorne Rd. B75: Four O . . . 1H 53
Cremorne Wlk. B75: Four O . . . 1H 53
Crendon Rd. B65: Row R . . . 3A 96
Crescent, The B18: Hock . . . 3D 100
B37: Mars G . . . 3G 123
B43: Gt Barr . . . 4C 66
(Handsworth Dr.)
B43: Gt Barr . . . 2F 67
(King's Rd.)
B46: Wat O . . . 4D 88
B64: Crad H . . . 4A 112
B65: Row R . . . 1B 112
B90: Shir . . . 3G 149
B91: Sol . . . 3F 151
B92: H Ard . . . 6B 140
DY1: Dud . . . 3G 77
DY9: Lye . . . 1G 125
WS1: Wals . . . 3E 49
WS6: Gt Wyr . . . 3G 7
WS10: W'bry . . . 1G 63
WV6: Tett . . . 6H 25
WV13: W'hall . . . 2C 46
WV14: Bils . . . 5F 45
Crescent Arc. *B91: Sol* . . . *4G 151*
(off Touchwood Shop. Cen.)
Crescent Av. DY5: Brie H . . . 1G 109
Crescent Ind. Pk. DY2: Dud . . . 2D 94
Crescent, The (MM) . . . 5F 45
Crescent Rd. DY2: Neth . . . 4D 94
WS10: Darl . . . 5D 46
WV13: W'hall . . . 1C 46
Crescent Studios B18: Hock . . . 3C 100
Crescent Theatre . . . 1D 116
Crescent Twr. B1: Birm . . . 4A 4
Cressage Av. B31: N'fld . . . 6E 145
Cressett Av. DY5: Brie H . . . 5F 93
Cressett La. DY5: Brie H . . . 5G 93
Cressington Dr. B74: Four O . . . 2G 53
Cresswell Ct. WV9: Pend . . . 4E 15
Cresswell Cres. WS3: Blox . . . 5F 19
Cresswell Gro. B24: Erd . . . 3B 86
Crest, The B31: Longb . . . 2F 159
Crest Vw. B14: K Hth . . . 3B 148
B74: S'tly . . . 3H 51
Crestwood Dr. B44: Gt Barr . . . 6G 67
Crestwood Glen WV6: Tett . . . 2C 26
Creswell Rd. B28: Hall G . . . 6H 135
Creswick Gro. B45: Redn . . . 2A 158
Crew Rd. WS10: W'bry . . . 1G 63
Creynolds Cl. B90: Ches G . . . 6B 164
Creynolds La. B90: Ches G . . . 6B 164
Cricket Cl. WS5: Wals . . . 4F 49
Cricketers Mdw. B64: Crad H . . . 4G 111
Cricket Mdw. DY3: Up Gor . . . 2A 76
WV10: F'hses . . . 3H 15
Cricket St. B70: W Brom . . . 6F 63
Crick La. B20: Hand . . . 1C 100
Cricklewood Dr. B62: Hale . . . 2D 128
Crimmond Ri. B63: Hale . . . 6G 111
Crimscote Cl. B90: M'path . . . 3D 164
Cripps Rd. WS2: Wals . . . 6E 31
Criterion Works WV13: W'hall . . . 3B 46
Crocketts Av. B21: Hand . . . 2H 99
Crockett's La. B66: Smeth . . . 4E 99
Crocketts Rd. B21: Hand . . . 2G 99
Crockett St. DY1: Dud . . . 5C 76
Crockford Dr. B75: Four O . . . 6H 37
Crockford Rd. B71: W Brom . . . 4A 64
Crockington La. WV5: Seis, Try . . . 3A 56
Crocus Cres. WV9: Pend . . . 4E 15
Croft, The B31: N'fld . . . 4F 145
DY2: Dud . . . 3B 94
DY3: Sed . . . 4A 60
WS5: Wals . . . 3A 50
WS6: C Hay . . . 3E 7
WV5: Wom . . . 2D 72
WV12: W'hall . . . 3D 30
Croft Apartments *WV13: W'hall* . . . *1A 46*
(off Croft St.)
Croft Cl. B25: Yard . . . 3C 120
Croft Ct. B36: Cas B . . . 1F 105
Croft Cres. WS8: Bwnhls . . . 6H 9
Cft. Down Rd. B92: Sol . . . 1H 137
Croftdown Rd. B17: Harb . . . 5D 114
Crofters Cl. DY8: Stourb . . . 1F 125
Crofters Ct. B15: Edg . . . 5A 116
Crofters La. B75: R'ley . . . 6C 38
Crofters Wlk. WV8: Pend . . . 6C 14
Croft Ho. *WS1: Wals* . . . *2D 48*
(off Paddock La.)
Croft Ind. Est. B37: Chel W . . . 1F 123
WV13: W'hall . . . 1A 46
Croft La. WV10: Bush . . . 2C 28
Croftleigh Gdns. B91: Sol . . . 5C 150
Croft Pde. WS9: A'rdge . . . 3D 34
Croft Rd. B26: Yard . . . 3C 120
Crofts, The B76: Walm . . . 6E 71
Croft St. WS2: Wals . . . 6B 32
WV13: W'hall . . . 1A 46
(not continuous)
Croftway, The B20: Hand . . . 1A 82
Croftwood Rd. DY9: W'cte . . . 1H 125
Cromane Sq. B43: Gt Barr . . . 6A 66
Cromdale Dr. B63: Hale . . . 2F 127
Cromer Gdns. WV6: Wolv . . . 4D 26
Crome Rd. B43: Gt Barr . . . 2F 67
Cromer Rd. B12: Bal H . . . 6H 117
Crompton Av. B20: Hand . . . 6E 83
Crompton Cl. WS2: Wals . . . 4G 31
Crompton Ct. WV8: Bilb . . . 3H 13

A-Z Birmingham Deluxe 185

Crompton Rd.—Deerhurst Ct.

Crompton Rd. B7: Nech 1C 102
B20: Hand 6E 83
B45: Fran 6D 142
DY4: Tip 3A 78
Cromwell Cl. B65: Row R 4H 95
WS2: Wals 5E 31
Cromwell Ct. WS6: Gt Wyr 4G 7
Cromwell Dr. DY2: Dud 1H 95
Cromwell La. B31: N'fld 5B 130
Cromwell Rd. WV10: Bush 4A 16
Cromwell St. B7: Nech 4B 102
B71: W Brom 3A 80
DY2: Dud 1G 95
Crondal Pl. B15: Edg 4D 116
CRONEHILLS, THE 4A 80
Cronehills Linkway B70: W Brom 3B 80
Cronehills St. B70: W Brom 4B 80
Crooked Ho. La. DY3: Gorn, Himl 5D 74
Crookham Cl. B17: Harb 4D 114
Crookhay La. B71: W Brom 5G 63
Crook La. WS9: A'rdge 4C 50
Croome Cl. B11: S'hll 2B 134
Cropredy Rd. B31: Longb 1E 159
Cropthorne Dr. B47: H'wd 2B 162
Cropthorne Rd. B90: Shir 4A 150
Crosbie Rd. B17: Harb 5F 115
Crosby Cl. B1: Birm 6D 100
WV6: Wolv 4D 26
Cross, The DY6: K'wfrd 3B 92
Cross Cl. B64: Old H 1H 111
Cross Farm Mnr. *B17: Harb 1H 131*
(off Cross Farm Rd.)
Cross Farm Rd. B17: Harb 1G 131
Cross Farms La. B45: Rubery 6F 143
Crossfield Rd. B33: Kitts G 5F 105
Crossgate Rd. DY2: Dud 3B 94
Cross Ho. *WV2: Wolv 4G 43*
(off Blakenhall Gdns.)
Crossings Ind. Est., The *WS3: Blox 1H 31*
(off Fryer's Rd.)
Crosskey Cl. B33: Kitts G 1A 122
Crossland Cres. WV6: Tett 3D 26
Cross La. B43: Gt Barr 4A 66
DY3: Sed 5H 59
WS14: Foot 1E 37
Crossley St. DY2: Neth 5F 95
Cross Pl. DY3: Sed 4A 60
Cross Quays Ind. Est. *B69: Tiv 5B 78*
(off Hallbridge Way)
Cross St. B21: Hand 1G 99
B63: Hale 2A 128
B65: B'hth 2C 112
B66: Smeth 3E 99
B68: O'bry 5G 97
DY1: Dud 6D 76
DY6: K'wfrd 3B 92
DY6: W Hth 1H 91
DY8: Stourb 6C 108
DY8: Word 6B 92
WS3: Pels 6E 21
WS6: C Hay 3D 6
WS10: Darl 4D 46
WS10: W'bry 2E 63
WV1: Wolv 2B 44
WV13: W'hall 2A 46
WV14: Bils 3G 61
(not continuous)
Cross St. Nth. WV1: Wolv 5H 27
Cross St. Sth. WV2: Wolv 4G 43
Cross Wlk. B69: Tiv 1C 96
Cross Walks Rd. DY9: Lye 6A 110
Crossway La. B44: K'sdng 1H 83
Crossways Ct. B44: K'sdng 6B 68
Crossways Grn. B44: K'sdng 6B 68
Crossways Shop. Cen. WV10: Wolv 6C 28
Crosswells Rd. B68: O'bry 4H 97
Crosswell Way WV14: Bils 6G 45
Crowberry Cl. WS8: Clay 1H 21
Crowesbridge M. WV14: Cose 5D 60
Crowhurst Rd. B31: Longb 2C 158
Crowland Av. WV6: Pert 5E 25
Crowle Dr. DY9: Lye 6G 109
Crown Av. B20: Hand 5F 83
Crown Cen., The DY8: Stourb 6E 109
Crown Cl. B65: Row R 5D 96
DY3: Sed 4H 59
Crown Ct. B74: Four O 6E 37
WS10: Darl 3C 46
Crown La. B74: Four O 6E 37
DY8: I'ley 6A 124
DY8: Stourb 6D 108
Crownmeadow Dr. DY4: Tip 6D 62
Crown Rd. B9: Bord G 1D 118
B30: K Nor 3C 146
Crown St. WV1: Wolv 5H 27
Crown Wlk. DY4: Tip 5A 78
Crown Wharf Shop. Pk. WS2: Wals 1B 48
Crows Nest Cl. B76: Walm 2D 70
Crowther Gdns. B63: Crad 4E 111
Crowther Gro. WV6: Wolv 5D 26
Crowther Rd. B23: Erd 2C 84
WV6: Wolv 5C 26
Crowther St. WV10: Wolv 5A 28
Croxall Way B66: Smeth 4F 99
Croxdene Av. WS3: Blox 6F 19
(not continuous)
Croxley Gdns. WV13: W'hall 3H 45
Croxstalls Av. WS3: Blox 1G 31
Croxstalls Cl. WS3: Blox 6G 19
Croxstalls Pl. WS3: Blox 1G 31
Croxstalls Rd. WS3: Blox 6G 19
Croxton Gro. B33: Stech 5E 105
Croyde Av. B42: Gt Barr 6C 66
Croydon Ct. *B29: W Cas 6G 131*
(off Abdon Av.)
Croydon Rd. B24: Erd 6F 85
B29: S Oak 2B 132
Croy Dr. B35: Cas V 3F 87
Crucible, The WV14: Cose 3E 61
Crusader Cl. B69: O'bry 4E 97
Crychan Cl. B45: Fran 5H 143
Cryersoak Cl. B90: M'path 2F 165
Crystal Av. DY8: Word 2D 108
Crystal Dr. B66: Smeth 1A 98
Crystal Ho. B66: Smeth 3F 99
Crystal Leisure Cen. 6D 108
Cubley Rd. B28: Hall G 4E 135
Cuckoo Rd. B7: Aston, Nech 1C 102
Cuin Rd. B66: Smeth 4G 99
Cuin Wlk. *B66: Smeth 4G 99*
(off Cuin Rd.)
Culey Gro. B33: Kitts G 1H 121
Culey Wlk. B37: Chel W 1F 123
Culford Dr. B32: Bart G 5A 130
Culham Cl. B27: A Grn 3B 136
Cullwick St. WV1: Wolv 4C 44
Culmington Rd. B31: Longb 1D 158
Culmore Cl. WV12: W'hall 5D 30
Culmore Rd. B62: B'hth 2E 113
Culverhouse Dr. DY5: Brie H 2E 109
Culverley Cres. B93: Know 3B 166
Culvert Way B66: Smeth 2B 98
Culwell Ind. Est. WV10: Wolv 6A 28
Culwell St. WV10: Wolv 6H 27 (1D 170)
Culwell Trad. Est. WV10: Wolv 5B 28
Cumberford Av. B33: Kitts G 2A 122
Cumberland Av. B5: Birm 4G 117
Cumberland Cl. DY6: K'wfrd 5C 92
Cumberland Ho. WV1: Wolv 5G 27
Cumberland Rd. B68: O'bry 4H 113
B71: W Brom 1B 80
WV13: W'hall 1D 46
WV14: Bils 4F 45
Cumberland St. B1: Birm 1E 117 (5A 4)
Cumberland Wlk. B75: S Cold 6F 55
Cumbrian Cft. B63: Hale 3F 127
Cumbria Way B8: Salt 3D 102
Cunningham Rd. WS2: Wals 1E 47
WV6: Pert 5E 25
Cupfields Av. DY4: Tip 5B 62
Cupfields Cres. DY4: Tip 6C 62
Curbar Rd. B42: Gt Barr 1E 83
Curdale Rd. B32: Bart G 5H 129
CURDWORTH 1D 88
Curlews Cl. B23: Erd 5C 68
Curral Rd. B65: Row R 6B 96
Curtin Dr. WS10: Mox 1B 62
Curtis Cl. B66: Smeth 5G 99
Curzon Circ. B4: Birm 6A 102
Curzon St. B4: Birm 6H 101 (3H 5)
WV2: Wolv 4H 43
Cushman Av. WV5: Wom 6E 57
Custard Factory, The
B9: Birm 2H 117 (6H 5)
Cuthbert Rd. B18: Win G 5A 100
Cutlers Rough Cl. B31: N'fld 2D 144
Cutler St. B66: Smeth 3F 99
Cutsdean Cl. B31: N'fld 1D 144
Cutshill Cl. B36: Cas B 1G 105
Cutting, The WS4: Wals 6D 32
Cuttle Pool La. B93: Know 5H 167
Cutworth Cl. B76: Walm 2E 71
Cwerne Ct. DY3: Gorn 4G 75
Cygnet Cl. WV6: Tett 1A 42
Cygnet Dr. WS8: Bwnhls 6A 10
Cygnet Gro. B23: Erd 1A 84
Cygnet La. DY5: P'ntt 2G 93
Cygnet Rd. B70: W Brom 2G 79
Cygnus Bus. Pk. Ind. Cen.
B70: W Brom 1F 79
Cygnus Way B70: W Brom 2F 79
Cypress Av. DY3: Up Gor 2H 75
Cypress Gdns. B74: S Cold 4G 53
DY6: K'wfrd 5A 92
WS5: Wals 1G 65
Cypress Gro. B31: N'fld 6C 144
Cypress Rd. DY2: Dud 6H 77
WS5: Wals 1G 65
Cypress Sq. B27: A Grn 6A 120
Cypress Way B31: Longb 1D 158
Cyprus Cl. B29: W Cas 6E 131
Cyprus St. B69: O'bry 1G 97
(not continuous)
WV2: Wolv 5G 43
Cyril Rd. B10: Small H 3C 118

D

Dacer Cl. B30: Stir 2D 146
Dace Rd. WV10: Wolv 5D 28
Dadford Vw. DY5: Brie H 1F 109
Dad's La. B13: Mose 4E 133
Daffodil Cl. DY3: Sed 6A 60
Daffodil Pl. WS5: Wals 3H 49
Daffodil Rd. WS5: Wals 3H 49
Daffodil Way B31: Longb 1C 158
Dagger La. B71: W Brom 3C 80
Dagnall Rd. B27: A Grn 2B 136
Dahlia Ct. WV1: Wolv 2E 45
Daimer Cl. B36: Cas B 6B 88
Daimler Rd. B14: Yard W 4D 148
Dainton Gro. B32: Bart G 4A 130
Dairy Cl. DY4: Tip 2B 78
Dairy Ct. B68: O'bry 4B 114
DAISY BANK 3H 49
Daisy Bank Cl. WS3: S'fld 5F 21
Daisy Bank Cres. WS5: Wals 3H 49
Daisy Dr. B23: Erd 2A 84
Daisy Farm Rd. B14: K Hth 5B 148
Daisy Mdw. DY4: Tip 1C 78
Daisy Rd. B16: Edg 1B 116
Daisy St. WV14: Cose 3F 61
Daisy Wlk. WV9: Pend 4E 15
Dakota Apartments *B16: Birm 1D 116*
(off Grosvenor St. W.)
Dalbeg Cl. WV8: Pend 1C 26
Dalbury Rd. B28: Hall G 2E 149
Dalby Rd. WS3: Wals 3D 32
Dale Cl. B43: Gt Barr 4H 65
B66: Smeth 6E 99
DY4: Tip 2D 78
Dalecote Av. B92: Sol 5A 138
Dale End B4: Birm 1G 117 (4F 5)
WS10: Darl 5D 46
(not continuous)
Dale Mdw. Cl. CV7: Bal C 3H 169
Dale Rd. B29: S Oak 2A 132
B62: B'hth 4E 113
DY8: Stourb 3D 124
Dales Cl. WV6: Wolv 3F 27
Dales La. WS9: A'rdge 4G 33
Dalesman Cl. DY6: K'wfrd 2H 91
Dale St. B66: Smeth 6E 99
WS1: Wals 4B 48
(not continuous)
WS10: W'bry 2E 63
WV3: Wolv 2F 43
WV14: Bils 6H 45
Dale Ter. B69: Tiv 1C 96
Daleview Rd. B14: Yard W 3C 148
Dale Wlk. B25: Yard 4H 119
Dalewood Cft. B26: Sheld 5D 120
Dalewood Rd. B37: K'hrst 4B 106
Daley Cl. B1: Birm 6D 100
Daley Rd. WV14: Bils 3H 61
Dalkeith Rd. B73: New O 3D 68
Dalkeith St. WS2: Wals 6A 32
Dallas Rd. B23: Erd 3C 84
Dallimore Cl. B92: Olton 2D 136
Dalloway Cl. B5: Edg 5F 117
Dalston Cl. DY2: Dud 3F 95
Dalston Rd. B27: A Grn 1A 136
Dalton Ct. B23: Erd 4B 84
WV5: Wom 6E 57
Dalton Pl. B92: Olton 3F 137
Dalton Rd. WS2: Wals 6G 31
Dalton St. B4: Birm 6G 101 (3F 5)
WV3: Wolv 3F 43
Dalton Twr. B4: Birm 1G 5
Dalton Way B4: Birm 6G 101 (3E 5)
Dalvine Rd. DY2: Neth 1D 110
Dalwood Cl. WV14: Cose 6D 60
Damar Cft. B14: K Hth 3F 147
Damian Cl. B67: Smeth 4D 98
Damson Cl. WV12: W'hall 3A 30
Damson La. B91: Sol 2A 152
B92: Sol 2A 152
Damson Parkway B91: Sol 2A 152
B92: Sol 2B 138
Damson Wharf DY4: Tip 4A 78
Danbury Cl. B76: Walm 3E 71
Danbury Rd. B90: Shir 5H 149
Danby Gro. B24: Erd 5H 85
Dando Rd. DY2: Dud 1F 95
Dandy Bank Rd. DY6: P'ntt 1E 93
Dandy's Wlk. WS1: Wals 2D 48
Dane Gro. B13: Mose 5F 133
Danehill Wlk. WV8: Pend 1D 26
Danesbury Cres. B44: K'sdng 5A 68
Danes Cl. WV11: Ess 3H 17
Danescourt Rd. WV6: Tett 3A 26
Danesmoor Ho. B25: Yard 4B 120
Daneswood Dr. WS9: Wals W 4B 22
Dane Ter. B65: Row R 4C 96
Daneways Cl. B74: S'tly 3A 52
Danford Cl. DY8: Stourb 1E 125
Danford Gdns. B10: Small H 3C 118
Danford La. B91: Sol 4C 150
Danford Rd. B47: H'wd 3H 161
Danford Way B43: Gt Barr 5H 65
Dangerfield Ho. B70: W Brom 6C 80
Dangerfield La. WS10: Darl 6C 46
Daniels La. WS9: A'rdge 5E 35
Daniels Rd. B9: Bord G 1G 119
Danks St. DY4: Tip 5A 78
Danzey Grn. Rd. B36: Cas B 6F 87
Danzey Gro. B14: K Hth 4E 147
Darby Cl. WV14: Cose 3C 60
DARBY END 5G 95
Darby End Rd. DY2: Neth 5G 95
Darby Ho. *WS2: Wals 4A 48*
(off Caledon St.)
Darby Rd. B68: O'bry 4A 98
WS10: W'bry 2H 63
Darby's Hill Rd. B69: Tiv 1A 96
Darby St. B65: B'hth 2C 112
Darbys Way DY4: Tip 2B 78
Darell Cft. B76: Walm 2C 70
Daren Cl. B36: Cas B 1B 106
Dare Rd. B23: Erd 3E 85
Darfield Wlk. B12: Birm 3H 117
Darges La. WS6: Gt Wyr 1F 7
Darkhouse La. WV14: Cose 3E 61
Darkies, The B31: N'fld 4F 145
(not continuous)
Dark La. B38: Head H 2E 161
B47: H'wd 2E 161
B62: Roms 3A 142
WS6: Gt Wyr 4A 8
DARLASTON 4D 46
Darlaston Central Trad. Est. WS10: Darl 4E 47
DARLASTON GREEN 3D 46
Darlaston La. WV14: Bils 4A 46
Darlaston Rd. WS2: Wals 4F 47
WS10: Darl, W'bry 6D 46
Darlaston Rd. Ind. Est. WS10: Darl 6D 46
Darlaston Row CV7: Mer 4H 141
Darlaston Swimming Pool 4E 47
Darley Av. B34: Hodg H 3D 104
Darleydale Av. B44: Gt Barr 4G 67
Darley Dr. WV6: Wolv 4F 27
Darley Ho. B69: O'bry 3D 96
Darley Mead Ct. B91: Sol 3A 152
Darley Way B74: S'tly 4A 52
Darlington St. WS10: Darl 1D 62
WV1: Wolv 1F 43 (3A 170)
WV3: Wolv 1F 43
Darnel Cft. B10: Small H 2B 118
Darnel Hurst Rd. B75: R'ley 6A 38
Darnford Cl. B28: Hall G 2G 149
B72: W Grn 6B 70
Darnick Rd. B73: New O 2D 68
Darnley Rd. B16: Birm 1C 116
Darris Rd. B29: S Oak 5C 132
Dartford Rd. WS3: Blox 6F 19
Dartmoor Cl. B45: Fran 5G 143
Dartmouth Av. DY8: Word 5B 92
WS3: Wals 4C 32
WV13: W'hall 1A 46
Dartmouth Cir. B6: Birm 4H 101
Dartmouth Cl. WS3: Wals 4C 32
Dartmouth Cres. WV14: Bils 4A 46
Dartmouth Dr. WS9: A'rdge 4B 34
Dartmouth Ho. *WS3: Wals 3D 32*
(off Ryecroft Pl.)
Dartmouth Middleway B6: Birm 4H 101
B7: Birm 4H 101 (1H 5)
Dartmouth Pl. WS3: Wals 3D 32
Dartmouth Rd. B29: S Oak 3B 132
B66: Smeth 1D 98
Dartmouth Sq. B70: W Brom 5B 80
Dartmouth Steet Stop (MM) 4H 79
Dartmouth St. B70: W Brom 4H 79
WV2: Wolv 3H 43 (6D 170)
(not continuous)
Darvel Rd. WV12: W'hall 5D 30
Darwall St. WS1: Wals 1C 48
Darwin Ct. WV6: Pert 5E 25
Darwin Ho. B37: Chel W 2E 123
Darwin Pl. WS2: Wals 3H 31
Darwin Rd. WS2: Wals 4H 31
Dassett Gro. B9: Bord G 1A 120
Dassett Rd. B93: Ben H 5B 166
Dauntsey Covert B14: K Hth 5F 147
Davena Dr. B29: W Cas 3C 130
Davena Gro. WV14: Cose 2F 61
Davenport Dr. B35: Cas V 4G 87
Davenport Rd. WV6: Tett 4H 25
WV11: Wed 3G 29
Daventry Gro. B32: Quin 5A 114
Davey Rd. B20: Hand 6G 83
B70: W Brom 2G 79
David Harman Dr. B71: W Brom 6D 64
David Lloyd Leisure
Birmingham Club 2F 67
Cranmore Club 2C 164
Solihull 3C 164
David Peacock Cl. DY4: Tip 2A 78
David Rd. B20: Hand 5D 82
DY4: Tip 6A 62
Davids, The B31: N'fld 1G 145
Davies Av. WV14: Cose 2F 61
Davies Ho. B69: O'bry 2G 97
WS3: Blox 5H 19
Davis Av. DY4: Tip 3G 77
Davis Gro. B25: Yard 5B 120
Davison Rd. B67: Smeth 6D 98
Davis Rd. WV12: W'hall 1D 30
Davy Cl. WS7: Chase 1B 10
Davy Rd. WS2: Wals 4G 31
Dawberry Cl. B14: K Hth 2F 147
Dawberry Flds. Rd. B14: K Hth 2E 147
Dawberry Rd. B14: K Hth 2E 147
DAW END 3G 33
Daw End WS4: Rus 3G 33
Daw End La. WS4: Rus 2F 33
Dawes Av. B70: W Brom 6A 80
Dawes La. WS8: Bwnhls 4C 10
Dawley Brook Rd. DY6: K'wfrd 2B 92
Dawley Cl. WS2: Wals 4H 47
Dawley Cres. B37: Mars G 2D 122
Dawley Rd. DY6: W Hth 1A 92
Dawley Trad. Est. DY6: K'wfrd 1B 92
Dawlish Rd. B29: S Oak 2B 132
B66: Smeth 4F 99
DY1: Dud 1D 76
Dawn Dr. DY4: Tip 3C 62
Dawney Dr. B75: Four O 5G 37
Dawn Rd. B31: N'fld 1C 144
Dawson Av. WV14: Cose 3C 60
Dawson Ct. B24: Erd 4F 85
Dawson Rd. B21: Hand 1A 100
Dawson Sq. WV14: Bils 6E 45
Dawson St. B66: Smeth 6E 99
WS3: Blox 1B 32
Day Av. WV11: Wed 2G 29
Day Ho. DY4: Tip 5C 62
DAYHOUSE BANK 6B 142
Dayhouse Bank B62: Roms 6B 142
Daylesford Rd. B92: Olton 2E 137
Day St. WS2: Wals 6C 32
Deakin Av. WS8: Bwnhls 4B 10
Deakin Rd. B24: Erd 4F 85
B75: S Cold 4C 54
Deakins Rd. B25: Yard 4H 119
Deal Dr. B69: Tiv 6A 78
Deal Gro. B31: N'fld 3E 145
Deanbrook Cl. B90: M'path 3E 165
Dean Cl. B44: K'sdng 5B 68
B72: W Grn 6H 69
DY8: Amb 5F 109
Dean Ct. *DY5: Brie H 1H 109*
(off Promenade, The)
WV6: Pert 3E 25
Deanery Row WV1: Wolv 6G 27 (1B 170)
Dean Rd. B23: Erd 2F 85
WS4: Rus 2G 33
WV5: Wom 2F 73
Deans Bank Cen., The
WS1: Wals 3B 48
Deansfield Rd. WV1: Wolv 1C 44
Deans Pl. WS3: Wals 3D 32
Dean's Rd. WV1: Wolv 6C 28
Dean St. B5: Birm 2G 117 (6F 5)
DY3: Sed 5H 59
Dearman Rd. B11: S'brk 4B 118
Dearmont Rd. B31: Longb 2C 158
Dearne Ct. DY3: Sed 1C 76
Debden Cl. B93: Dorr 6F 167
Debenham Cres. B25: Yard 2B 120
Debenham Rd. B25: Yard 2B 120
Deblen Dr. B16: Edg 2H 115
Deborah Cl. WV2: Penn 5G 43
Dee Gro. B38: K Nor 1A 160
Deelands Rd. B45: Rubery 1F 157
Deeley Cl. B15: Edg 4E 117
B64: Crad H 4G 111
Deeley Dr. DY4: Tip 1C 78
Deeley Pl. WS3: Blox 1H 31
Deeley St. DY5: Quar B 2A 110
WS3: Blox 1H 31
Deepdale Av. B26: Sheld 1F 137
Deepdale La. DY3: Lwr G 4A 76
Deepdales WV5: Wom 1E 73
DEEPFIELDS 3D 60
Deeplow Cl. B72: S Cold 1A 70
Deepmoor Rd. B33: Yard 6D 104
Deepmore Av. WS2: Wals 6H 31
Deepwood Cl. WS4: S'fld 1F 33
Deepwood Gro. B32: Bart G 5H 129
Deer Cl. WS3: Blox 6A 20
Deerham Cl. B23: Erd 6D 68
Deerhurst Ct. B91: Sol 3H 151

186 A-Z Birmingham Deluxe

Deerhurst Rd. B20: Hand 2B 82
Dee Rd. WS3: Blox 6C 20
Deer Pk. Way B91: Sol 6G 151
Deer Wlk. WV8: Pend 5D 14
Dee Wlk. B36: Cas B 1C 106
(not continuous)
Defford Av. WS4: S'fld 6G 21
Defford Dr. B68: O'bry 5H 97
De Havilland Dr. B35: Cas V 5E 87
Deighton Rd. WS5: Wals 1F 65
Delamere Cl. B36: Cas B 6H 87
Delamere Dr. WS5: Wals 2G 65
Delamere Rd. B28: Hall G 6F 135
WV12: W'hall 2C 30
Delancey Keep B75: S Cold 6E 55
Delhurst Rd. B44: Gt Barr 4F 67
WV4: E'shll 2A 60
Delingpole Wlk. B64: Old H 3G 111
Delius Ho. B16: Birm 1D 116
Dell, The B31: N'fld 1B 144
B36: Cas B 6B 88
B74: Four O 3G 53
B92: Olton 4E 137
DY8: Woll 5C 108
Della Dr. B32: Bart G 5B 130
Dell Farm Cl. B93: Know 3D 166
Dellows Cl. B38: K Nor 2H 159
Dell Rd. B30: K Nor 2C 146
DY5: P'ntt 4F 93
Dell Stadium, The 4F 93
Delmore Way B76: Walm 1F 87
Delph Dr. DY5: Quar B 4A 110
Delphinium Cl. B9: Bord G 6F 103
Delph La. DY5: Brie H 3H 109
Delph Rd. DY5: Brie H 2G 109
Delph Rd. Ind. Est. DY5: Brie H 2G 109
Delrene Rd. B28: Hall G 4F 149
B90: Shir 4F 149
DELVES, THE 6D 48
Delves Cres. WS5: Wals 6E 49
Delves Grn. Rd. WS5: Wals 5E 49
Delves Rd. WS1: Wals 4D 48
Delville Cl. WS10: W'bry 1F 63
Delville Rd. WS10: W'bry 1F 63
Delville Ter. WS10: W'bry 1F 63
De Marnham Cl. B70: W Brom 6C 80
De Montfort Ho. B37: K'hrst 4B 106
De Montfort M. B46: Col 3H 107
De Moram Gro. B92: Sol 6B 138
Demuth Way B69: O'bry 4F 97
Denaby Gro. B14: Yard W 3D 148
Denbigh Cl. DY1: Dud 5B 76
Denbigh Ct. *B29: W Cas 6G 131*
(off Tugford Rd.)
Denbigh Cres. B71: W Brom 1H 79
Denbigh Dr. B71: W Brom 6G 63
WS10: W'bry 1B 64
Denbigh Rd. DY4: Tip 2C 78
Denbigh St. B9: Bord G 1D 118
Denby Cl. B7: Birm 4B 102
Denby Cft. B90: M'path 3F 165
Dencer Cl. B45: Rubery 1F 157
Dencil Cl. B63: Crad 6F 111
Dene Av. DY6: K'wfrd 5A 92
Dene Ct. Rd. B92: Olton 4D 136
Dene Ct. WS3: Blox 6G 19
Denegate Cl. B76: Walm 1F 87
Dene Hollow B13: Mose 1C 148
Dene Rd. DY8: Stourb 2D 124
WV4: Lwr P 1F 57
Denewood Av. B20: Hand 5C 82
Denford Gro. B14: K Hth 2F 147
Dengate Dr. CV7: Bal C 2H 169
Denham Ct. *B23: Erd 5C 84*
(off Park App.)
Denham Gdns. WV3: Wolv 3H 41
Denham Rd. B27: A Grn 6H 119
Denholme Gro. B14: K Hth 4A 148
Denholm Rd. B73: New O 2D 68
Denise Dr. B17: Harb 1G 131
B37: K'hrst 5B 106
WV14: Cose 5D 60
Denleigh Rd. DY6: K'wfrd 5D 92
Denmark Cl. WV6: Wolv 5E 27
Denmead Dr. WV11: Wed 1H 29
Denmore Gdns. WV1: Wolv 1D 44
Dennfield Dr. WS6: C Hay 2C 6
Dennis Hall DY8: Amb 3D 108
Dennis Hall Rd. DY8: Amb 3E 109
Dennis Rd. B12: Bal H 1B 134
Dennis St. DY8: Amb 3D 108
Denshaw Rd. B14: K Hth 1F 147
Denstone Gdns. WV10: Bush 4A 16
Denton Cft. B93: Dorr 6H 165
Denton Gro. B33: Stech 1B 120
B43: Gt Barr 6H 65
Denton Rd. DY9: W'cte 1C 126
Denver Rd. B14: K Hth 5A 148
Denville Cl. WV14: Bils 4G 45
Denville Cres. B9: Bord G 6H 103
Derby Av. WV6: Tett 2C 26
Derby Dr. B37: Chel W 1D 122
Derby St. B9: Birm 1A 118
WS2: Wals 5B 32
Dereham Cl. B8: Salt 5D 102
Dereham Wlk. WV14: Bils 3G 61
Dereton Cl. DY1: Dud 1A 94
DERITEND 2A 118 (6H 5)
Derron Av. B26: Yard 6C 120
Derry Cl. B17: Harb 2E 131
Derrydown Cl. B23: Erd 4E 85
Derrydown Rd. B42: P Barr 2D 82
Derry St. DY5: Brie H 1H 109
WV2: Wolv 3H 43
Derwent Cl. B74: S'tly 1H 51
DY5: P'ntt 3E 93
WV13: W'hall 1C 46
Derwent Ct. B73: S Cold 6H 53
Derwent Gro. B30: Stir 5E 133
Derwent Ho. B17: Harb 6H 115
B69: O'bry 4D 96
Derwent Rd. B30: Stir 5E 133
WV6: Tett 1B 26
Desford Av. B42: Gt Barr 6E 67
Dettonford Rd. B32: Bart G 5H 129
Devereux Cl. B36: Cas B 1G 105
Devereux Rd. B70: W Brom 6C 80
B75: Four O 2A 54
Devey Dr. DY4: Tip 1D 78
Devil's Elbow La. WV11: Wed 2G 29
Devine Cft. DY4: Tip 2A 78
Devitts Cl. B90: M'path 2D 164
Devon Cl. B20: Hand 5B 82
Devon Ct. *B29: W Cas 6F 131*
(off Holdgate Rd.)
Devon Cres. B71: W Brom 1A 80
DY2: Dud 2B 94
WS9: A'rdge 6C 22
Devon Rd. B45: Fran 5E 143
B67: Smeth 4C 114
DY8: Woll 4C 108
WS10: W'bry 1A 64
WV1: Wolv 6F 27
WV13: W'hall 1D 46
Devonshire Av. B18: Hock 3B 100
Devonshire Ct. B74: Four O 1F 53
Devonshire Dr. B71: W Brom 4C 80
Devonshire Rd. B20: Hand 5B 82
B67: Smeth 3C 98
Devonshire St. B18: Hock 3B 100
Devon St. B7: Birm 5C 102
Devoran Cl. WV6: Wolv 5F 27
Dewberry Dr. WS5: Wals 2E 65
Dewberry Rd. DY8: Word 2D 108
Dewhurst Cft. B33: Kitts G 6F 105
Dewsbury Cl. DY8: Word 6C 92
Dewsbury Dr. WV4: Penn 2E 59
Dewsbury Gro. B42: P Barr 2E 83
Deykin Av. B6: Witt 5A 84
Deyncourt Rd. WV10: Wolv 2C 28
Dial Cl. B14: K Hth 5G 147
Dial La. B70: W Brom 1F 79
DY8: Amb 3C 108
Diamond Pk. Dr. DY8: Word 2C 108
Diana Cl. WS9: Wals W 4D 22
Diane Cl. DY4: Tip 3B 62
Dibble Cl. WV12: W'hall 4D 30
Dibble Rd. B67: Smeth 3D 98
Dibdale Ct. *DY3: Lwr G 4H 75*
(off Yorkdale Cl.)
Dibdale Rd. DY1: Dud 4A 76
Dibdale Rd. W. DY1: Dud 4A 76
Dibdale St. DY1: Dud 5B 76
Dice Pleck B31: N'fld 5G 145
Dickens Cl. DY3: Lwr G 2F 75
DICKENS HEATH 4F 163
Dickens Heath Rd.
B90: Dic H, Tid G 5E 163
Dickens Rd. WV10: Bush 1C 28
WV14: Cose 3F 61
Dickinson Av. WV10: Bush 1A 28
Dickinson Dr. B76: Walm 1C 70
WS2: Wals 5A 48
Dickinson Rd. WV5: Wom 3G 73
Dick Sheppard Av. DY4: Tip 5B 62
Diddington Av. B28: Hall G 2G 149
Diddington La. B92: Bick, H Ard 5C 140
Didgley Gro. B37: K'hrst 4C 106
DIGBETH 2H 117 (6H 5)
Digbeth B5: Birm 1G 117 (5F 5)
WS1: Wals 2C 48
Digby Ct. B27: A Grn 2A 136
Digby Cres. B46: Wat O 4D 88
Digby Dr. B37: Mars G 5D 122
Digby Ho. B37: K'hrst 5B 106
Digby Rd. B46: Col 3H 107
B73: S Cold 2G 69
DY6: K'wfrd 1B 92
Digby Wlk. B33: Sheld 3G 121
Dilke Rd. WS9: A'rdge 4B 34
Dilliars Wlk. B70: W Brom 2G 79
Dillington Ho. B37: Chel W 1D 122
Dilloway's La. WV13: W'hall 2G 45
Dimmingsdale Bank B32: Quin. 1A 130
Dimmingsdale Rd. WV4: Lwr P 6E 41
Dimminsdale WV13: W'hall 2A 46
Dimmocks Av. WV14: Cose 5F 61
Dimmock St. WV4: E'shll 6A 44
Dimsdale Gro. B31: N'fld 4C 144
Dimsdale Rd. B31: N'fld 4B 144
Dingle, The B29: S Oak 3A 132
B69: O'bry 1D 96
B90: Ches G 4B 164
WV3: Wolv 2B 42
Dingle Av. B64: Crad H 3G 111
Dingle Cl. B30: B'vlle 6H 131
DY2: Dud 2G 95
Dingle Ct. *B69: O'bry 1E 97*
(off Dingle St.)
B91: Sol 6D 150
Dingle Hollow B69: O'bry 1D 96
Dingle La. B91: Sol 5D 150
WV13: W'hall 5A 30
Dingle Mead B14: K Hth 3E 147
Dingle Mdw. Ct. B69: O'bry 1E 97
Dingle Rd. DY2: Dud 2G 95
DY6: K'wfrd 5E 93
DY9: Pedm 3F 125
WS8: Clay 1A 22
WV5: Wom 1F 73
Dingle St. B69: O'bry 1D 96
Dingle Vw. DY3: Sed 1G 75
Dingley Rd. WS10: W'bry 6G 47
Dingleys Pas. B4: Birm 1G 117 (4F 5)
Dinham Gdns. DY1: Dud 4A 76
Dinmore Av. B31: N'fld 3F 145
Dinsdale Wlk. WV6: Wolv 4E 27
Dippons Dr. WV6: Tett 6G 25
Dippons La. WV6: Pert 3E 25
WV6: Tett 3F 25
Dippons Mill Cl. WV6: Tett 6G 25
DIRCHILLS 1A 48
Dirtyfoot La. WV4: Lwr P 6G 41
Discovery Cl. DY4: Tip 2C 78
Ditch, The WS1: Wals 2D 48
Ditton Gro. B31: Longb 3D 158
Dixon Cl. B35: Cas V 5E 87
DY4: Tip 1C 78
Dixon Ct. B10: Small H 3B 118
Dixon Ho. B16: Edg 2C 116
Dixon Rd. B10: Small H 3B 118
DIXON'S GREEN 1G 95
Dixon's Grn. Ct. *DY2: Dud 1G 95*
(off Dixon's Grn. Rd.)
Dixon's Grn. Rd. DY2: Dud 1F 95
Dixon St. WV2: E'shll 5A 44
Dobbins Oak Rd. DY9: W'cte 4H 125
Dobbs Mill Cl. B29: S Oak 3D 132
Dobbs St. WV2: Wolv 3G 43 (6B 170)
Dock, The DY9: Lye 6B 110
Dockar Rd. B31: N'fld 5C 144
Dockers Cl. CV7: Bal C 5H 169
Dock La. DY1: Dud 6D 76
Dock La. Ind. Est. *DY1: Dud 6D 76*
(off Dock La.)
Dock Mdw. Dr. WV4: E'shll 1C 60
Dock Rd. DY8: Word 1D 108
Doctors Hill DY9: Pedm 2G 125
Doctors La. DY6: K'wfrd 4F 91
Doctor's Piece WV13: W'hall 1B 46
Doddington Gro. B32: Bart G 5H 129
Dodford Cl. B45: Rubery 2F 157
DOE BANK 3H 53
Doe Bank Ct. B74: Four O 3H 53
Doe Bank La. B43: Gt Barr 5E 51
WS9: A'rdge 5E 51
Doe Bank Rd. DY4: Tip 4C 62
Dogge La. Cft. B27: A Grn 3H 135
Dog Kennel La. B68: O'bry 4A 98
B90: Shir 2A 164
WS1: Wals 1D 48
Dogkennel La. B63: Hale 2B 128
Dogpool La. B30: Stir 4D 132
Doidge Rd. B23: Erd 4D 84
Dollery Dr. B5: Edg 6E 117
Dollis Gro. B44: Gt Barr 2H 67
Dolman Rd. B6: Aston 1G 101
Dolobran Rd. B11: S'brk 4B 118
Dolphin Cl. WS3: Blox 6D 20
Dolphin Ct. *WV12: W'hall 2D 30*
(off Huntington Rd.)
Dolphin Ho. WS3: Blox 1D 32
Dolphin La. B27: A Grn 4H 135
(not continuous)
Dolphin Rd. B11: S'hll 6D 118
Dolton Way DY4: Tip 1G 77
Dominic Dr. B30: K Nor 3H 145
Doncaster Way B36: Hodg H 1A 104
Don Cl. B15: Edg 3H 115
Donegal Rd. B74: S'tly 6H 51
Donibristle Cft. B35: Cas V 3E 87
Donnington Ho. B33: Yard 1F 121
Donovan Dr. B73: S Cold 5G 53
Dooley Cl. WV13: W'hall 1G 45
Dora Herbert Ct. B12: Bal H 6G 117
Doran Cl. B63: Hale 4F 127
Doranda Way B71: W Brom 6D 80
Doranda Way Ind. Pk. B71: W Brom 6D 80
Dora Rd. B10: Small H 3E 119
B21: Hand 2A 100
B70: W Brom 6A 80
Dora St. WS2: Wals 4H 47
Dorchester Cl. WV12: W'hall 1C 30
Dorchester Ct. B91: Sol 3E 151
Dorchester Dr. B17: Harb 1F 131
Dorchester Rd. B91: Sol 3E 151
DY9: W'cte 3H 125
WV12: W'hall 1C 30
Dordale Cl. B31: Longb 6A 144
Dordon Cl. B90: Shir 6E 149
Doreen Gro. B24: Erd 5G 85
Doris Rd. B9: Bord G 1D 118
B11: S'hll 1B 134
B46: Col 1H 107
Dorking Ct. *B29: W Cas 6G 131*
(off Abdon Av.)
Dorlcote Rd. B8: Salt 5G 103
Dormie Cl. B38: K Nor 6H 145
Dormington Rd. B44: Gt Barr 2G 67
Dormston Cl. B91: Sol 2G 165
Dormston Dr. B29: W Cas 3D 130
DY3: Sed 5A 60
Dormston Sports & Art Cen. 5A 60
Dormston Trad. Est. DY1: Dud 3A 76
Dormy Dr. B31: Longb 2E 159
Dorncliffe Av. B33: Sheld 4H 121
Dornie Dr. B38: K Nor 6B 146
Dornton Rd. B30: Stir 5E 133
Dorothy Adams Cl. B64: Old H 3G 111
Dorothy Gdns. B20: Hand 5C 82
Dorothy Rd. B11: Tys 6H 119
B67: Smeth 6E 99
Dorothy St. WS1: Wals 4B 48
DORRIDGE 6B 166
Dorridge Cft. B93: Dorr 6G 167
Dorridge Rd. B93: Dorr 6H 167
Dorridge Station (Rail) 6G 167
Dorrington Grn. B42: P Barr 2C 82
Dorrington Rd. B42: P Barr 1C 82
Dorset Cl. B45: Fran 5F 143
Dorset Cotts. B30: Stir 1C 146
Dorset Ct. *B29: W Cas 6F 131*
(off Abdon Av.)
Dorset Dr. WS9: A'rdge 6C 22
Dorset Rd. B17: Edg 6F 99
DY8: Woll 4B 108
Dorset Twr. B18: Hock 5D 100
Dorsett Pl. WS3: Blox 2A 32
Dorsett Rd. WS10: Darl 5C 46
WS10: W'bry 3B 64
Dorsett Rd. Ter. WS10: Darl 5C 46
Dorsheath Gdns. B23: Erd 3F 85
Dorsington Rd. B27: A Grn 4B 136
Dorstone Covert B14: K Hth 5E 147
Dorville Cl. B38: K Nor 1H 159
Douay Rd. B24: Erd 1H 85
Double Row DY2: Neth 5G 95
Doughty St. DY4: Tip 2C 78
Douglas Av. B36: Hodg H 3B 104
B68: O'bry 4B 98
Douglas Davies Cl.
WV12: W'hall 5C 30
Douglas Pl. WV10: Oxl 3G 27
Douglas Rd. B21: Hand 1A 100
B27: A Grn 1H 135
B47: H'wd 2A 162
B62: B'hth 2E 113
B68: O'bry 5B 98
Douglas Rd. B72: S Cold 2A 70
DY2: Dud 1F 95
WV14: Cose 5F 61
Doulton Cl. B32: Quin. 2D 130
Doulton Dr. B66: Smeth 3E 99
Doulton Rd. B64: Old H 6H 95
B65: Row R 6H 95
Doulton Trad. Est.
B65: Row R 5H 95
Dovebridge Cl. B76: Walm 1D 70
Dove Cl. B25: Yard 3C 120
WS1: Wals 2E 49
WS10: W'bry 1G 63
Dovecote 2G 133
Dovecote Cl. B91: Sol 5F 137
DY4: Tip 2C 78
WV6: Tett 5A 26
Dovecotes, The B75: Four O 6H 37
Dovedale Av. B90: Shir 6H 149
WS3: Pels 2E 21
WV12: W'hall 4A 30
Dovedale Ct. B29: W Cas 6G 131
B46: Wat O 4C 88
WV4: E'shll 3B 60
Dovedale Dr. B28: Hall G 1F 149
Dovedale Rd. B23: Erd 5C 68
DY6: K'wfrd 1C 92
WV4: E'shll 2A 60
Dove Dr. DY8: Amb 3E 109
Dove Gdns. B38: K Nor 5D 146
Dove Hollow WS6: Gt Wyr 4F 7
Dove Ho. Ct. B91: Sol 6D 136
Dovehouse La. B91: Sol 6D 136
Dovehouse Pool Rd. B6: Aston 1G 101
Dover Cl. B32: Bart G 6G 129
Dover Ct. *B29: W Cas 6G 131*
(off Abdon Av.)
Dovercourt Rd. B26: Sheld 6G 121
Doverdale Cl. B63: Crad 6F 111
Dover Ho. *WS3: Blox 2A 32*
(off Providence Cl.)
Dove Ridge DY8: Amb 4E 109
Doveridge Cl. B91: Sol 6C 136
Doveridge Pl. WS1: Wals 3D 48
Doveridge Rd. B28: Hall G 2E 149
Doversley Rd. B14: K Hth 2E 147
Dover St. B18: Hock 3C 100
WV14: Bils 5F 45
Dove Way B36: Cas B 1B 106
Dovey Dr. B76: Walm 6E 71
Dovey Rd. B13: Mose 3D 134
B69: Tiv 1D 96
Dovey Twr. B7: Birm 5A 102
Dowar Rd. B45: Redn 2A 158
Dowells Cl. B13: Mose 3H 133
Dowells Gdns. DY8: Word 6B 92
Doweries, The B45: Rubery 1F 157
Dower Rd. B75: Four O 2H 53
Dowles Cl. B29: W Cas 1F 145
Downcroft Av. B38: K Nor 5A 146
Downend Cl. WV10: Bush 3B 16
Downes Ct. DY4: Tip 2G 77
Downey Cl. B11: S'brk 4B 118
Downfield Cl. WS3: Blox 3G 19
Downfield Dr. DY3: Sed 1A 76
Downham Cl. WS5: Wals 2A 50
Downham Pl. WV3: Wolv 3D 42
Downham Wood WS5: Wals 3A 50
Downie Rd. WV8: Bilb 4A 14
Downing Cl. B65: B'hth 2C 112
B93: Know 5C 166
WV11: Wed 2A 30
Downing Ct. B68: O'bry 4H 113
Downing Ho. B37: Chel W 2D 122
Downing St. B63: Hale 6A 112
B66: Smeth 2F 99
Downing St. Ind. Est.
B66: Smeth 2G 99
Downland Cl. B38: K Nor 6B 146
Downs, The WS9: A'rdge 1G 51
WV10: Oxl 3G 27
Downsfield Rd. B26: Sheld 4F 121
Downside Rd. B24: Erd 6E 85
Downs Rd. WV13: W'hall 3C 46
Downton Cres. B33: Kitts G 6A 106
Dowry Ho. *B45: Rubery 1F 157*
(off Rubery La. Sth.)
Dowty Way WV9: Pend 4E 15
Drainage Board Cotts. *B24: Erd 6F 85*
(off Saltley Cotts.)
Drake Cl. WS3: Blox 6H 19
Drake Rd. B23: Erd 4B 84
B66: Smeth 2C 98
WS3: Blox 6H 19
Drakes Cross Pde. B47: H'wd 4A 162
Drakes Grn. WV14: Bils 2H 61
Drakes Hill Cl. DY8: Stourb 1A 124
Drake St. B71: W Brom 2A 80
Drancy Av. WV12: W'hall 3D 30
(not continuous)
Drawbridge Rd. B90: Maj G 1E 163
Draycote Cl. B92: Sol 6H 137
Draycott Av. B23: Erd 3D 84
Draycott Cl. WV4: Penn 6A 42
Draycott Dr. B31: N'fld 6C 130
Draycott Rd. B66: Smeth 2C 98
Drayman Cl. WS1: Wals 3D 48
Drayton Cl. B75: Four O 6H 37
Drayton Rd. B14: K Hth 5G 133
B66: Smeth 2E 115
B90: Shir 1C 164
Drayton St. WS2: Wals 1H 47
WV2: Wolv 3G 43 (6B 170)
Drayton St. E. WS2: Wals 1A 48
Dreadnought Rd. DY5: P'ntt 2F 93
Dreamwell Ind. Est. B11: Tys 5G 119
Dreel, The B15: Edg 4A 116
Dreghorn Rd. B36: Hodg H 1C 104
Drem Cft. B35: Cas V 5E 87
Dresden Cl. WV4: E'shll 1C 60
Drew Cres. DY9: W'cte 3H 125
Drew Rd. DY9: W'cte 2H 125
Drew's Holloway B63: Crad 6F 111
Drew's Holloway Sth. B63: Crad 6F 111
Drews Ho. *B14: K Hth 6F 147*
(off Netheravon Cl.)

Drews La.—Egelwin Cl.

Drews La. B8: W End 3G 103
Drews Mdw. Cl. B14: K Hth 5E 147
DRIFFOLD 1G 69
Driffold B73: S Cold 1H 69
Driffold Vs. B73: S Cold 2H 69
Driftwood Cl. B38: K Nor 2H 159
Drive, The B20: Hand 5C 82
B23: Erd 5E 85
B48: Hopw 6F 159
B63: Crad 6F 111
B63: Hale 2A 128
DY5: Brie H 4G 93
WS3: Blox 5C 20
WS4: S'fld 6G 21
WV6: Tett 4A 26
WV8: Cod 4F 13
Drive Flds. WV4: Lwr P 5H 41
Droicon Trad. Est. B65: Row R 4C 96
Droveway, The WV8: Pend 5C 14
WV9: Pend 5C 14
Droxford Wlk. WV8: Pend 6C 14
Druid Pk. Rd. WV12: W'hall 6C 18
Druids Av. B65: Row R 5D 96
WS9: A'rdge 6E 23
DRUID'S HEATH 6D 22
Druids La. B14: K Hth 5E 147
Druids Wlk. WS9: Wals W 4C 22
Drummond Cl. WV11: Wed 5A 18
Drummond Gro. B43: Gt Barr 2E 67
Drummond Rd. B9: Bord G 1F 119
DY9: W'cte 6B 110
Drummond St. WV1: Wolv 6G 27 (1A 170)
Drummond Way B37: Chel W 1E 123
Drury La. B91: Sol 4G 151
(not continuous)
DY8: Stourb 6E 109
WV8: Cod 3F 13
Drybrook Cl. B38: K Nor 1A 160
Drybrooks Cl. CV7: Bal C 3H 169
Dryden Cl. DY4: Tip 6A 62
WV12: W'hall 1E 31
Dryden Gro. B27: A Grn 3H 135
Dryden Pl. WS3: Blox 2C 32
Dryden Rd. WS3: Blox 2C 32
WV10: Bush 6B 16
Drylea Gro. B36: Hodg H 2D 104
Dubarry Av. DY6: K'wfrd 2A 92
Duchess Pde. B70: W Brom 4B 80
Duchess Pl. B16: Edg 2C 116
Duchess Rd. B16: Edg 2C 116
WS1: Wals 6B 48
Duckhouse Rd. WV11: Wed 2F 29
Duck La. WV8: Bilb 5H 13
WV14: Bils 6G 45
Duddeston Dr. B8: Salt 5D 102
Duddeston Mnr. Rd. B7: Birm 5A 102
Duddeston Mill Rd. B7: Birm 5B 102
B8: Birm, Salt 5C 102
Duddeston Mill Trad. Est. B8: Salt 5C 102
Duddeston Station (Rail) 5B 102
Dudding Rd. WV4: Penn 6H 43
Dudhill Rd. B65: Row R 6A 96
Dudhill Wlk. B65: Row R 6H 95
DUDLEY 6E 77
Dudley Castle 5F 77
Dudley Central Trad. Est. DY2: Dud 1E 95
Dudley Cl. B65: Row R 3A 96
Dudley Cres. WV11: Wed 3G 29
DUDLEY FIELDS 5G 93
Dudley Gro. B18: Win G 5A 100
Dudley Leisure Cen. 6D 76
Dudley Mus. & Art Gallery 6E 77
Dudley Pk. Rd. B27: A Grn 2A 136
DUDLEY PORT 3B 78
Dudley Port DY4: Tip 4A 78
Dudley Port Station (Rail) 3B 78
Dudley Rd. B18: Win G 5H 99
B63: Hale 5B 112
B65: Row R 3H 95
B69: O'bry 6E 79
DY3: Himl 4A 74
DY3: Sed 6A 60
DY4: Tip 2F 77
DY5: Brie H 6H 93
DY6: K'wfrd 2D 92
DY6: W Hth 1A 92
DY9: Lye 5A 110
WV2: Wolv 3H 43 (6C 170)
Dudley Rd. E. B69: O'bry, Tiv 5C 78
Dudley Rd. W. B69: Tiv 5A 78
DY4: Tip 5A 78
Dudley Row DY2: Dud 6F 77
DUDLEY'S FIELDS 1G 31
Dudley Southern By-Pass DY2: Dud 2C 94
Dudley St. B5: Birm 1G 117 (5E 5)
B70: W Brom 2F 79
DY3: Sed 5H 59
WS1: Wals 2C 48
WS10: W'bry 3E 63
WV1: Wolv 1G 43 (3B 170)
WV14: Bils 6F 45
Dudley Wlk. WV4: Penn 6G 43
Dudley Wood Av. DY2: Neth 1E 111
Dudley Wood Rd. DY2: Neth 2E 111
Dudley Zoo 5F 77
Dudmaston Way DY1: Dud 4A 76
Dudnill Gro. B32: Bart G 5G 129
Duffield Cl. WV8: Pend 6D 14
Dufton Rd. B32: Quin 6C 114
Dugdale Cres. B75: Four O 6A 38
Dugdale Ho. B71: W Brom 5E 65
Dugdale St. B18: Win G 5H 99
Dukes Rd. B30: K Nor 3C 146
Duke St. B65: Row R 1B 112
B70: W Brom 3H 79
B72: S Cold 1H 69
DY3: Up Gor 2H 75
DY8: Stourb 5E 109
WV1: Wolv 2A 44
WV3: Wolv 4E 43
WV11: Wed 4F 29
Dulvern Gro. B14: K Hth 2F 147
Dulverton Rd. B6: Witt 6A 84
Dulwich Gro. B44: K'sdng 5B 68
Dulwich Rd. B44: K'sdng 5A 68
Dumbleberry Av. DY3: Sed 6G 59
Dumblederry La. WS9: A'rdge 1A 34
(not continuous)
Dunard Rd. B90: Shir 4F 149
Dunbar Cl. B32: Bart G 4B 130
Dunbar Gro. B43: Gt Barr 1D 66
Duncalfe Dr. B75: Four O 6H 37
Duncan Edwards Cl.
DY1: Dud 1C 94
Duncan Ho. B73: W Grn 4H 69
Dunchurch Cl. CV7: Bal C 2H 169
Dunchurch Cres. B73: New O 2C 68
Dunchurch Dr. B31: N'fld 6C 130
Dunchurch Ho. B5: Birm 3G 117
Duncombe Grn. B46: Col 2H 107
Duncombe Gro. B17: Harb 4D 114
Duncombe St. DY8: Woll 5B 108
Duncroft Rd. B26: Yard 3D 120
Duncroft Wlk. DY1: Dud 1D 76
Duncumb Rd. B75: S Cold 6E 55
Dundalk La. WS6: C Hay 3D 6
Dundas Av. DY2: Dud 1H 95
Dunedin Ho. B32: Quin 1D 130
Dunedin Rd. B44: Gt Barr 2G 67
Dunham Cft. B93: Dorr 6H 165
Dunkirk Av. B70: W Brom 3D 78
Dunkley St. WV1: Wolv 6G 27 (1A 170)
Dunley Ct. *B23: Erd 5C 84*
(off Dunlin Cl.)
Dunley Cft. B90: M'path 3D 164
Dunlin Cl. B23: Erd 5C 84
DY6: K'wfrd 3E 93
Dunlop Way B35: Cas V 6C 86
Dunnerdale Rd. WS8: Clay 1H 21
Dunnigan Rd. B32: Bart G 2D 130
DUNN'S BANK 4B 110
Dunn's Bank DY5: Quar B 4B 110
(Lynval Rd.)
DY5: Quar B 4C 110
(Saltbrook Rd.)
Dunsfold Cl. WV14: Cose 2C 60
Dunsfold Cft. B6: Aston 3H 101
Dunsford Cl. DY5: Brie H 4F 109
Dunsford Rd. B66: Smeth 1E 115
Dunsink Rd. B6: Aston 6H 83
Dunslade Cres. DY5: Quar B 3B 110
Dunslade Rd. B23: Erd 6D 68
Dunsley Dr. DY8: Word 6C 92
Dunsley Gro. WV4: Penn 1E 59
Dunsley Rd. DY8: Woll 1A 124
Dunsmore Dr. DY5: Quar B 3B 110
Dunsmore Gro. B91: Sol 6D 136
Dunsmore Rd. B28: Hall G 3E 135
Dunstall Av. WV6: Wolv 4G 27
Dunstall Gro. B29: W Cas 5D 130
DUNSTALL HILL 4F 27
Dunstall Hill WV6: Wolv 4G 27
Dunstall Hill Trad. Est.
WV6: Wolv 4G 27
Dunstall La. WV6: Wolv 4E 27
Dunstall Pk. 3E 27
Dunstall Pk. WV6: Wolv 3F 27
Dunstall Rd. B63: Hale 2F 127
WV6: Wolv 5F 27
Dunstan Cft. B90: Shir 1A 164
Dunster Cl. B30: K Nor 3D 146
Dunster Gro. WV6: Pert 6F 25
Dunster Rd. B37: Chel W 6E 107
Dunston Cl. DY6: K'wfrd 2B 92
WS6: Gt Wyr 5E 7
Dunton Cl. B75: Four O 5G 37
Dunton Hall Rd. B90: Shir 1G 163
Dunton Rd. B37: K'hrst 5B 106
Dunton Trad. Est. B7: Nech 2D 102
Dunvegan Rd. B24: Erd 3G 85
Durant Cl. B45: Fran 5D 142
Durban Rd. B66: Smeth 5G 99
D'Urberville Cl. *WV2: E'shll 5B 44*
(off D'urberville Rd.)
D'Urberville Rd. WV2: E'shll 4B 44
(not continuous)
Durberville Rd. Ind. Est. WV2: E'shll 4B 44
Durham Av. WV13: W'hall 6C 30
Durham Ct. *B29: W Cas 6G 131*
(off Abdon Av.)
Durham Cft. B37: Chel W 1D 122
Durham Dr. B71: W Brom 6B 64
Durham Ho. WV1: Wolv 5G 27
Durham Pl. WS2: Wals 2F 47
Durham Rd. B11: S'hll 1B 134
B65: Row R 5E 97
DY2: Neth 1F 111
DY8: Woll 3B 108
WS2: Wals 3H 47
WS10: W'bry 1B 64
Durham Twr. B1: Birm 6D 100
Durley Dean Rd. B29: S Oak 3G 131
Durley Dr. B73: New O 2C 68
Durley Rd. B25: Yard 5A 120
Durlston Gro. B28: Hall G 5G 135
Durnford Cft. B14: K Hth 6G 147
Dursley Cl. B92: Olton 5F 137
WV12: W'hall 5D 30
Dutton's La. B75: R'ley 5C 38
Duxford Rd. B42: Gt Barr 5D 66
Dwellings La. B32: Quin 6H 113
Dyas Av. B42: Gt Barr 6B 66
Dyas Rd. B44: Gt Barr 4F 67
B47: H'wd 2A 162
Dyce Cl. B35: Cas V 3E 87
Dymoke St. B12: Birm 3H 117
Dynes Wlk. B67: Smeth 4E 99
Dyott Rd. B13: Mose 4A 134
Dyson Cl. WS2: Wals 6F 31
Dyson Gdns. B8: Salt 4E 103

E

Eachelhurst Rd. B24: Erd 3C 86
B76: Walm 2D 86
Eachus Rd. WV14: Cose 5F 61
EACHWAY 3F 157
Eachway B45: Rubery 3F 157
Eachway Farm Cl. B45: Redn 3G 157
Eachway La. B45: Redn 3G 157
Eadgar Ct. B43: Gt Barr 6H 65
Eagle Cl. B65: Row R 5H 95
DY1: Dud 1B 94
WS6: C Hay 3D 6
Eagle Ct. WV3: Wolv 5E 43
Eagle Ct. Bus. Pk.
B26: Sheld 1A 138
Eagle Cft. B14: K Hth 5G 147
Eagle Gdns. B24: Erd 5G 85
Eagle Gro. B36: Cas B 1C 106
Eagle Ind. Est. DY4: Tip 6E 63
Eagle La. DY4: Tip 1D 78
Eagle St. DY4: Tip 1C 78
WV2: Wolv 3A 44
WV3: Wolv 4E 43
Eagle Trad. Est. B63: Hale 1A 128
Ealing Gro. B44: K'sdng 4A 68
Eanwulf Ct. B15: Edg 3E 117
Earlsbury Gdns. B20: Hand 6F 83
Earls Ct. Rd. B17: Harb 5E 115
Earls Ferry Gdns. B32: Bart G 6H 129
Earlsmead Rd. B21: Hand 1G 99
Earls Rd. WS4: Rus 2G 33
Earlston Way B43: Gt Barr 5H 65
Earl St. B70: W Brom 3H 79
DY6: K'wfrd 5B 92
WS1: Wals 4B 48
WV14: Bils 6F 45
WV14: Cose 5F 61
Earls Way B63: Hale 1B 128
Earlswood Cl. B20: Hand 5C 82
Earlswood Cres. WV9: Pend 4E 15
Earlswood Dr. B74: S Cold 4A 54
Earlswood Ho. *B5: Birm 4G 117*
(off Barrow Wlk.)
Earlswood Rd. B93: Dorr 6F 167
DY6: K'wfrd 2C 92
Easby Way B8: Salt 4E 103
WS3: Blox 5F 19
Easenhall Cl. B93: Know 5C 166
Easmore Cl. B14: K Hth 5F 147
Eastacre WV13: W'hall 2A 46
East Av. B69: Tiv 2C 96
WV11: Wed 3E 29
Eastbourne Av. B34: Hodg H 3B 104
Eastbourne St. WS4: Wals 6D 32
Eastbrook Cl. B76: Walm 1B 70
Eastbury Dri B92: Olton 2E 137
Eastbury Dr. B92: Olton 2E 137
E. Car Pk. Rd. B40: Nat E C 1H 139
EASTCOTE 4H 153
Eastcote Cl. B90: Shir 4B 150
Eastcote La. B92: H Ard 4H 153
Eastcote Rd. B27: A Grn 4G 135
WV10: Wolv 4B 28
East Cft. Rd. WV4: Penn 1A 58
Eastdean Cl. B23: Erd 1D 84
East Dr. B5: Edg 1E 133
Eastern Av. DY5: Brie H 1F 109
Eastern Cl. WS10: Mox 2C 62
Eastern Rd. B29: S Oak 2D 132
B73: W Grn 4H 69
Easterton Cft. B14: K Hth 5G 147
E. Farm Cft. B10: Small H 3D 118
Eastfield Cl. WS9: A'rdge 3C 34
Eastfield Dr. B92: Sol 5A 138
Eastfield Gro. WV1: Wolv 1B 44
Eastfield Retreat WV1: Wolv 1B 44
Eastfield Rd. B8: W End 5A 104
B9: Bord G 5A 104
DY4: Tip 5A 62
WV1: Wolv 1B 44
East Ga. B16: Edg 6A 100
East Grn. WV4: Penn 5B 42
Eastham Rd. B13: Mose 1C 148
East Holme B9: Bord G 1C 118
Easthope Rd. B33: Stech 5E 105
Eastlake Cl. B43: Gt Barr 2F 67
Eastlands Rd. B13: Mose 4A 134
Eastleigh DY3: Sed 5G 59
Eastleigh Cft. B76: Walm 6E 71
Eastleigh Dr. B62: Roms 3A 142
Eastleigh Gro. B25: Yard 3B 120
E. Meadway B33: Kitts G 1H 121
East M. B44: Gt Barr 3F 67
E. Moor Cl. B74: S'tly 1B 52
Eastney Cres. WV8: Pend 1C 26
Easton Gdns. WV11: Wed 4H 29
Easton Gro. B27: A Grn 4A 136
B47: H'wd 2B 162
East Pk. Trad. Est. WV1: Wolv 3B 44
East Pk. Way WV1: Wolv 2D 44
East Pathway B17: Harb 5G 115
East Ri. B75: S Cold 5B 54
East Rd. B24: Erd 5B 86
DY4: Tip 5B 62
WV10: B'frd, F'stne 1C 16
East St. DY2: Dud 1G 95
DY3: Gorn 4H 75
DY5: Quar B 3C 110
WS1: Wals 4D 48
WV1: Wolv 2A 44
East Vw. Rd. B72: S Cold 2B 70
Eastville B31: N'fld 4F 145
Eastward Glen WV8: Bilb 6A 14
East Way B17: Harb 5G 115
Eastway B40: Nat E C 2H 139
B92: Bick 2H 139
Eastwood Rd. B12: Bal H 6F 117
B43: Gt Barr 5A 66
DY2: Dud 3G 95
Eatesbrook Rd. B33: Kitts G 6G 105
Eathorpe Cl. B34: S End 3H 105
Eaton Av. B70: W Brom 3G 79
Eaton Ct. B74: S Cold 4H 53
Eaton Cres. DY3: Gorn 4F 75
Eaton Pl. DY6: K'wfrd 4C 92
Eaton Ri. WV12: W'hall 3B 30
Eaton Wood B24: Erd 4B 86
Eaton Wood Dr. B26: Yard 6B 120
Eaves Ct. Dr. DY3: Sed 4G 59
Eaves Grn. Gdns. B27: A Grn 6H 119
Ebenezer St. B70: W Brom 1F 79
WV14: Cose 5D 60
Ebley Rd. B20: Hand 3C 82
Ebmore Dr. B14: K Hth 5F 147
Ebrington Av. B92: Sol 2F 137
Ebrington Cl. B14: K Hth 3F 147
Ebrington Rd. B71: W Brom 1B 80
Ebrook Rd. B72: S Cold 1A 70
EBSTREE 1C 56
Ebstree Mdw. WV5: Seis 3A 56
Ebstree Rd. WV5: Seis, Try 3A 56
Ebury Rd. B30: K Nor 3D 146
Eccleshall Av. WV10: Oxl 1F 27
Eccleston Cl. B75: S Cold 6D 54
Ecclestone Rd. WV11: Wed 1A 30
Echo Way WV4: E'shll 1C 60
Eckersall Rd. B38: K Nor 4A 146
Eckington Wlk. B38: K Nor 2A 160
Eclipse Ind. Est. DY4: Tip 2G 77
Edale Cl. DY6: K'wfrd 2H 91
WV4: E'shll 2A 60
Edale Rd. B42: Gt Barr 6E 67
Eddish Rd. B33: Kitts G 6F 105
Eddison Rd. B46: Col 3G 89
Edelweiss Cl. WS5: Wals 2F 65
Edenbridge Rd. B28: Hall G 5G 135
Edenbridge Vw. DY1: Dud 4A 76
Eden Cl. B31: Longb 1C 158
B69: Tiv 5D 78
Edencroft B15: Edg 3E 117
Edendale Rd. B26: Sheld 5F 121
Eden Gdns. DY3: Sed 5A 60
Eden Gro. B37: Chel W 2F 123
B71: W Brom 2B 80
Edenhall Rd. B32: Quin 5H 113
Eden Ho. DY8: Stourb 6E 109
Edenhurst Rd. B31: Longb 3D 158
Eden Pl. B3: Birm 1F 117 (4C 4)
Eden Rd. B92: Sol 2H 137
Edensor Cl. WV10: Wolv 5A 28
EDGBASTON 6C 116
Edgbaston 6F 117
Edgbaston Archery & Lawn Tennis Society
4B 116
Edgbaston Pk. Rd. B15: Edg 6C 116
Edgbaston Priory Club 5E 117
Edgbaston Rd. B5: Edg 6F 117
B12: Bal H 6F 117
B66: Smeth 5E 99
Edgbaston Rd. E. B12: Bal H 6H 117
Edgbaston Shop. Cen. B16: Edg 3C 116
Edgbaston St. B5: Birm 2G 117 (6E 5)
Edgcombe Rd. B28: Hall G 4F 135
Edge Hill Av. WV10: Bush 5C 16
Edge Hill Dr. DY3: Sed 3G 59
WV6: Pert 6E 25
Edge Hill Rd. B74: Four O 5D 36
Edgehill Rd. B31: Longb 1E 159
Edgemond Av. B24: Erd 3D 86
Edge St. WV14: Cose 5F 61
Edgewood Cl. B64: Old H 3H 111
Edgewood Rd. B38: K Nor 2A 160
B45: Redn 2H 157
Edgeworth Cl. WV12: W'hall 5C 30
Edgware Rd. B23: Erd 2D 84
Edinburgh Av. WS2: Wals 6E 31
Edinburgh Ct. B24: Erd 3B 86
Edinburgh Cres. DY8: Word 2A 108
Edinburgh Dr. WS4: Rus 2H 33
WV12: W'hall 3B 30
Edinburgh La. WS2: Wals 5G 31
Edinburgh Rd. B68: O'bry 3H 113
DY2: Dud 3F 95
WS5: Wals 3F 49
WV14: Bils 2H 61
Edison Cl. *WV12: W'hall 2D 30*
(off Huntington Rd.)
Edison Gro. B32: Quin 6B 114
Edison Rd. WS2: Wals 4G 31
Edison Wlk. WS2: Wals 4H 31
Edith Pope Ho. B42: Gt Barr 5F 67
Edith Rd. B66: Smeth 6F 99
Edith St. B70: W Brom 4H 79
Edmonds Cl. B33: Kitts G 1F 121
Edmonds Ct. B10: Small H 4D 118
B26: Yard 4D 120
Edmonds Rd. B68: O'bry 1A 114
Edmonton Av. B44: K'sdng 4B 68
Edmonton Ho. B5: Bal H 4F 117
Edmoor Cl. WV12: W'hall 3C 30
Edmund Rd. B8: Salt 5D 102
DY3: Up Gor 1A 76
Edmund St. B3: Birm 6F 101 (3C 4)
Ednam Cl. B71: W Brom 5D 64
Ednam Gro. WV5: Wom 4G 57
Ednam Rd. DY1: Dud 6E 77
WV4: Penn 5G 43
Edsome Way B36: Hodg H 1D 104
Edstone Cl. B93: Dorr 5B 166
Edstone M. B36: Hodg H 1D 104
Edward Av. WS9: A'rdge 2C 34
Edward Cl. WV14: Bils 2G 61
Edward Ct. B16: Edg 2G 115
B76: Walm 2D 70
WS1: Wals 3E 49
Edward Fisher Dr. DY4: Tip 2A 78
Edward Rd. B5: Edg 5F 117
B12: Bal H 5F 117
B14: K Hth 6H 147
B46: Wat O 4E 89
B63: Hale 1H 127
B67: Smeth 5D 98
B68: O'bry 3A 114
DY4: Tip 6A 62
WV6: Pert 4E 25
Edwards Rd. B24: Erd 2G 85
B75: R'ley 6B 38
DY2: Neth 5E 95
Edward St. B1: Birm 1D 116 (4A 4)
B68: O'bry 5G 97
B70: W Brom 4A 80
DY1: Dud 6D 76
WS2: Wals 6H 31
WS10: Darl 5E 47
WV4: E'shll 5B 44
Edwin Phillips Dr. B71: W Brom 5H 63
Edwin Rd. B30: Stir 6D 132
Eel St. B69: O'bry 2F 97
Effingham Rd. B13: Mose 1C 148
Egbert Cl. B6: Aston 1B 102
Egelwin Cl. WV6: Pert 4E 25

Egerton Rd.—Eyston Av.

Egerton Rd. B24: Erd 4B 86
B74: S'tly 2H 51
WV10: Bush 4A 16
EGG HILL 4H 143
Egghill La. B31: N'fld 4A 144
B32: Fran 3G 143
B45: Fran 3G 143
Eggington Rd. DY8: Woll 4B 108
Egginton Rd. B28: Hall G 2E 149
Egmont Gdns. WV11: Wed 3H 29
Eileen Gdns. B37: K'hrst 5B 106
Eileen Rd. B11: S'hll 2B 134
Elan Cl. DY3: Lwr G 4H 75
Elan Rd. B31: Longb 5A 144
DY3: Sed 5G 59
Elbow St. B64: Old H 1H 111
Elbury Cft. B93: Know 4B 166
Elcock Dr. B42: P Barr 2F 83
Eldalade Way WS10: W'bry 3B 64
Elderberry Cl. DY8: Stourb 2A 124
WS5: Wals 2D 64
Elderfield B33: Sheld 3F 121
Elderfield Rd. B30: K Nor 4D 146
Elder Gro. WV5: Wom 1F 73
Eldersfield Gro. B91: Sol 2F 165
Elderside Cl. WS8: Bwnhls 5B 10
Elder Way B23: Erd 5E 85
Eldon Ct. WS1: Wals 2D 48
(off Eldon St.)
Eldon Dr. B76: Walm 6C 70
Eldon Rd. B16: Edg 2B 116
B62: Quin 2G 129
Eldon St. WS1: Wals 2D 48
WS10: Darl 4D 46
Eldridge Cl. WV9: Pend 5D 14
Eleanor Rd. WV14: Bils 5F 45
Electra Pk. B6: Witt 6B 84
Electric Av. B6: Witt 6B 84
Elford Cl. B14: K Hth 2G 147
Elford Gro. B37: Mars G 2D 122
WV14: Bils 1E 61
Elford Rd. B17: Harb 2F 131
B71: W Brom 4C 64
Elgar Ct. B15: Edg 4C 116
Elgar Cres. DY5: P'ntt 2H 93
Elgar Ho. B16: Birm 1D 116
Elgin Cl. DY3: Sed 4A 60
DY8: Amb 4E 109
Elgin Ct. WV6: Pert 5E 25
Elgin Rd. WS3: Blox 3G 19
Eligin Gro. B25: Yard 4A 120
Eliot Cft. WV14: Cose 3F 61
Eliot St. B7: Nech 1C 102
Elizabeth Av. WS10: W'bry 2A 64
WV4: Penn 6F 43
WV14: Bils 2H 61
Elizabeth Ct. B17: Harb 1H 131
(off Metchley La.)
Elizabeth Cres. B68: O'bry 1B 114
Elizabeth Gro. B90: Shir 5A 150
DY2: Dud 2H 95
Elizabeth Ho. B76: Walm 2D 70
DY9: Lye 6H 109
WS5: Wals 4H 49
Elizabeth M. B69: Tiv 5A 78
Elizabeth Prout Gdns.
B65: B'hth 2B 112
Elizabeth Rd. B13: Mose 3E 133
B33: Stech 6A 104
B63: Hale 2H 127
B70: W Brom 3D 78
B73: New O 3C 68
WS5: Wals 4F 49
Elizabeth Wlk. DY4: Tip 4A 62
Elkington Cft. B90: M'path 4E 165
Elkington St. B6: Aston 4G 101
Elkstone Cl. B92: Olton 2F 137
Elkstone Covert B14: K Hth 5E 147
Elland Gro. B27: A Grn 3A 136
Ellards Dr. WV11: Wed 4H 29
Ellen St. B18: Hock 5C 100
(not continuous)
Ellenvale Cl. WV14: Cose 5C 60
Ellerby Gro. B24: Erd 3C 86
Ellerside Gro. B31: N'fld 5D 144
Ellerslie Cl. DY5: Quar B 3H 109
Ellerslie Rd. B13: Mose 6C 134
Ellerton Rd. B44: K'sdng 4B 68
Ellerton Wlk. WV10: Wolv 4B 28
Ellesborough Rd. B17: Harb 3F 115
Ellesmere Rd. B8: Salt 5D 102
Ellice Dr. B36: Cas B 2D 106
Elliott Gdns. B45: Redn 4A 158
Elliott Rd. B29: S Oak 4A 132
Elliotts La. WV8: Cod 4G 13
Elliotts Rd. DY4: Tip 2G 77
Elliott Way B6: Witt 3G 83
Elliot Way B6: Witt 4H 83
Ellis Av. DY5: Brie H 1E 109
Ellison St. B70: W Brom 6A 80
Ellis St. B1: Birm 2F 117 (6C 4)
Elliston Av. B44: Gt Barr 5G 67
Ellowes Rd. DY3: Lwr G 3G 75
Elm Av. B12: Bal H 6A 118
WS10: W'bry 1F 63
WV11: Wed 1D 28
WV14: Bils 5F 45
Elmay Rd. B26: Sheld 4E 121
Elm Bank B13: Mose 2A 134
Elmbank Gro. B20: Hand 2A 82
Elmbank Rd. WS5: Wals 1G 65
Elmbridge Cl. B63: Crad 6F 111
Elmbridge Dr. B90: M'path 3F 165
Elmbridge Rd. B44: K'sdng 1G 83
Elmbridge Way B31: N'fld 5H 145
DY3: Sed 1A 76
Elm Cl. DY3: Gorn 5F 75
DY8: Stourb 3B 124
Elm Ct. B13: Mose 1H 133
B66: Smeth 1A 98
WS1: Wals 3E 49
Elm Cres. DY4: Tip 1H 77
Elm Cft. B68: O'bry 4A 114
Elmcroft B66: Smeth 4G 99
Elmcroft Av. B32: Bart G 4G 129
Elmcroft Gdns. WV10: Bush 4A 16
Elmcroft Rd. B26: Yard 4D 120
Elmdale B62: Quin 4G 113
Elmdale Cres. B31: N'fld 2C 144
Elmdale Dr. WS9: A'rdge 1E 35
Elmdale Gro. B31: N'fld 3C 144
Elmdale Rd. WV4: Penn 6E 43
WV14: Cose 6C 60
ELMDON 3B 138
Elmdon Cl. B92: Sol 3H 137
WV10: Oxl 6E 15
Elmdon Coppice B92: Sol 6B 138
Elmdon Ct. B29: W Cas 6G 131
(off Abdon Av.)
B37: Mars G 4C 122
ELMDON HEATH 1A 152
Elmdon La. B26: Birm A 2C 138
B37: Mars G 4B 122
Elmdon Pk. 3A 138
Elmdon Pk. Rd. B92: Sol 3H 137
Elmdon Rd. B27: A Grn 1B 136
B29: S Oak 3C 132
B37: Mars G 4C 122
Elmdon Rd. WV10: Oxl 6E 15
Elmdon Trad. Est. B37: Mars G 6E 123
Elm Dr. B31: Longb 6A 144
B43: Gt Barr 4H 65
B62: B'hth 2E 113
Elm Farm Av. B37: Mars G 4B 122
Elm Farm Rd. WV2: Wolv 4H 43
Elmfield Av. B24: Erd 3D 86
Elmfield Cres. B13: Mose 3H 133
Elmfield Rd. B36: Cas B 2A 106
Elmfield Vw. DY1: Dud 4C 76
Elm Grn. DY1: Dud 2C 76
Elm Gro. B37: K'hrst 3B 106
CV7: Bal C 6H 169
WV8: Bilb 4G 13
Elmhurst Av. B65: Row R 6C 96
Elmhurst Dr. DY6: K'wfrd 5D 92
WS7: Chase 1C 10
Elmhurst Rd. B21: Hand 6A 82
Elmley Cl. WV14: Cose 6D 60
Elmley Gro. B30: K Nor 5D 146
WV6: Pert 6F 25
Elm Lodge B92: H Ard 6A 140
Elmore Cl. B37: F'bri 5C 106
Elmore Grn. Cl. WS3: Blox 1H 31
Elmore Grn. Rd. WS3: Blox 6G 19
Elmore Rd. B33: Kitts G 6E 105
Elmore Row WS3: Blox 6H 19
Elm Rd. B30: B'vlle 5B 132
B76: Walm 3D 70
DY1: Dud 3E 77
DY6: K'wfrd 3C 92
WS3: Blox 3B 32
WS11: Nort C 1F 9
Elms, The B16: Birm 6B 100
Elms Cl. B38: K Nor 1G 159
B91: Sol 2H 151
Elmsdale WV6: Tett 1G 41
Elmsdale Ct. WS1: Wals 3D 48
Elms Rd. B15: Edg 1B 132
B72: S Cold 2A 70
Elmstead Av. B33: Sheld 4H 121
Elmstead Cl. WS5: Wals 2A 50
Elmstead Twr. B5: Birm 4G 117
(off Berrington Wlk.)
Elmstead Wood WS5: Wals 2A 50
Elm St. WV3: Wolv 2E 43
WV13: W'hall 1C 46
Elm Ter. B69: Tiv 6A 78
Elm Tree Cl. WV5: Wom 2F 73
Elm Tree Gro. B63: Crad 5F 111
Elm Tree Ri. B92: H Ard 1A 154
Elm Tree Rd. B17: Harb 5E 115
B30: Stir 1C 146
Elmtree Rd. B74: S'tly 2F 51
Elm Tree Way B64: Old H 2H 111
Elmwood Av. WV11: Ess 4A 18
Elmwood Cl. B5: Edg 5F 117
CV7: Bal C 6H 169
Elmwood Ct. B73: S'tly 6A 52
Elmwood Gdns. B20: Hand 5D 82
Elmwood Gro. B47: H'wd 3A 162
Elmwood Ri. DY3: Sed 4F 59
Elmwood Rd. B24: Erd 5A 86
B74: S'tly 6A 52
DY8: Word 6A 92
Elmwoods B32: Bart G 3H 129
Elphinstone End B24: Erd 1A 86
Elsma Rd. B68: O'bry 3A 114
Elston Hall La. WV10: Bush 6H 15
Elstree Rd. B23: Erd 2D 84
Elswick Gro. B44: K'sdng 5B 68
Elswick Rd. B44: K'sdng 4B 68
Elsworth Gro. B25: Yard 5A 120
Elsworth Rd. B31: N'fld 5H 145
Eltham Gro. B44: K'sdng 4B 68
Elton Cl. WV10: Bush 3A 16
Elton Cft. B93: Dorr 5B 166
Elton Gro. B27: A Grn 3G 135
Eltonia Cft. B26: Sheld 5F 121
Elva Cft. B36: Cas B 6B 88
Elvers Grn. La. B93: Know 3G 167
Elvetham Rd. Nth. B15: Birm 3E 117
Elviron Dr. WV6: Tett 4H 25
Elwell Cres. DY1: Dud 1B 76
Elwells Cl. WV14: Cose 2C 60
Elwell St. B70: W Brom 2E 79
WS10: W'bry 2H 63
Elwyn Rd. B73: S Cold 2G 69
Ely Cl. B37: Chel W 1D 122
B65: Row R 5E 97
Ely Cres. B71: W Brom 6H 63
Ely Gro. B32: Quin 1D 130
Ely Pl. WS2: Wals 2H 47
Ely Rd. WS2: Wals 2H 47
Emay Cl. B70: W Brom 5F 63
Embankment, The DY5: Brie H 6A 94
Embassy Dr. B15: Edg 3C 116
B69: O'bry 1E 97
Embassy Rd. B69: O'bry 1E 97
Embleton Gro. B34: Hodg H 3E 105
Emerald Ct. B8: W End 4A 104
B92: Olton 4D 136
Emerson Cl. DY3: Lwr G 3E 75
Emerson Gro. WV10: Bush 1B 28
Emerson Rd. B17: Harb 5G 115
WV10: Bush 6B 16
Emery Cl. B23: Erd 6D 84
WS1: Wals 3D 48
Emery Ho. B23: Erd 1C 84
Emery St. WS1: Wals 3D 48
Emily Gdns. B16: Birm 6B 100
Emily Rd. B26: Yard 5B 120
Emily St. B12: Birm 3H 117
B70: W Brom 5H 79
Emmanuel Rd. B73: W Grn 6H 69
Emmeline St. B9: Birm 2B 118
Empire Cl. WS9: A'rdge 1B 34
Empire Ind. Pk. WS9: A'rdge 1B 34
Empress Way WS10: Darl 3D 46
Emscote Dr. B73: W Grn 6H 69
Emscote Grn. B91: Sol 5C 150
Emscote Rd. B6: Aston 6H 83
Emsworth Cres. WV9: Pend 5E 15
Emsworth Gro. B14: K Hth 1F 147
Enderby Cl. B93: Ben H 5B 166
Enderby Dr. WV4: Penn 1D 58
Enderley Cl. WS3: Blox 4H 19
Enderley Dr. WS3: Blox 4H 19
End Hall Rd. WV6: Tett 6G 25
Endhill Rd. B44: K'sdng 1A 68
Endicott Rd. B6: Aston 6H 83
Endmoor Gro. B23: Erd 1D 84
Endsleigh Gro. B28: Hall G 5G 135
Endwood Ct. B20: Hand 5C 82
Endwood Ct. Rd. B20: Hand 5C 82
Endwood Dr. B74: Lit A 5C 36
B91: Sol 5D 150
Energy Way B10: Small H 5F 119
(not continuous)
Enfield Cl. B23: Erd 1F 85
Enfield Ct. B29: W Cas 6G 131
(off Abdon Av.)
Enfield Rd. B15: Edg 3D 116
B65: Row R 6D 96
Enford Cl. B34: S End 3H 105
Engine La. DY9: Lye 5H 109
WS8: Bwnhls 5F 9
WS10: Mox 1A 62
Engine St. B66: Smeth 3F 99
B69: O'bry 3G 97
Englestede Cl. B20: Hand 4B 82
Englewood Dr. B28: Hall G 5G 135
Ennerdale Cl. WS8: Clay 6A 10
Ennerdale Dr. B63: Hale 3F 127
WV6: Pert 5F 25
Ennerdale Rd. B43: Gt Barr 1B 82
WV6: Tett 1B 26
Ennersdale Bungs. B46: Col 6H 89
Ennersdale Cl. B46: Col 6H 89
Ennersdale Rd. B46: Col 6H 89
Ensall Dr. DY8: Word 2C 108
Ensbury Cl. WV12: W'hall 5D 30
Ensdale Row WV13: W'hall 2A 46
Ensdon Gro. B44: K'sdng 4B 68
Ensford Cl. B74: Four O 4E 37
Enstone Rd. B23: Erd 6G 69
DY1: Dud 1B 94
Enterprise Dr. B74: S'tly 4G 51
DY9: Lye 5C 110
Enterprise Gro. WS3: Pels 2F 21
Enterprise Trad. Est.
DY5: Brie H 6B 94
Enterprise Way B7: Birm 5H 101
Enville Cl. B37: Mars G 2D 122
WS3: Blox 4G 19
Enville Comn. Rd. DY7: Env 5A 90
Enville Gro. B11: S'brk 6D 118
Enville Pl. DY8: Stourb 6D 108
(off Short St.)
Enville Rd. DY3: Lwr G 3H 75
DY6: W Hth 1G 91
WV4: Penn 1A 58
Enville St. DY8: Stourb 6D 108
Enville Twr. Mill DY7: Env 5B 90
Epping Cl. B45: Fran 5H 143
WS3: Wals 3D 32
Epping Gro. B44: K'sdng 6A 68
Epsom Cl. WV6: Pert 5F 25
Epsom Ct. B29: W Cas 6G 131
Epsom Gro. B44: K'sdng 5B 68
Epwell Gro. B44: K'sdng 1H 83
Epwell Rd. B44: K'sdng 1H 83
Epworth Ct. DY5: P'ntt 4F 93
Equipoint B25: Yard 4B 120
Erasmus Rd. B11: S'brk 4A 118
Ercall Cl. B23: Erd 1A 84
ERDINGTON 3F 85
Erdington Hall Rd. B24: Erd 5E 85
Erdington Ind. Pk. B24: Erd 3D 86
Erdington Rd. WS9: A'rdge 5D 34
Erdington Sports Club 5F 69
Erdington Station (Rail) 2F 85
Erdington Swimming Pool & Turkish Suite 3G 85
Erica Cl. B29: W Cas 5E 131
Erica Rd. WS5: Wals 2F 65
Ermington Cres.
B36: Hodg H 1C 104
Ermington Rd. WV4: Penn 6H 43
Ernest Clarke Cl.
WV12: W'hall 5C 30
Ernest Rd. B12: Bal H 1B 134
B67: Smeth 3C 98
DY2: Dud 6H 77
Ernest St. B1: Birm 2F 117 (6C 4)
Ernsford Cl. B93: Dorr 6G 167
Erskine St. B7: Birm 5B 102
Esher Rd. B44: Gt Barr 1H 67
B71: W Brom 1B 80
Eskdale Cl. WV1: Wolv 1C 44
Eskdale Wlk. DY5: Brie H 3F 109
Esme Rd. B11: S'hll 1B 134
Esmond Cl. B30: B'vlle 2H 145
Esporta Health & Fitness
Birmingham 2C 116
Broadlands 2H 15
Essendon Gro. B8: W End 5H 103
Essendon Rd. B8: W End 5H 103
Essendon Wlk. B8: W End 5H 103
Essex Av. B71: W Brom 6A 64
DY6: K'wfrd 4H 91
WS10: W'bry 1A 64
Essex Ct. B29: W Cas 6G 131
Essex Gdns. DY8: Woll 4B 108
Essex Ho. WV1: Wolv 5G 27
Essex Rd. B75: R'ley 2B 54
DY2: Dud 3C 94
Essex St. B5: Birm 2F 117 (6D 4)
WS2: Wals 4C 32
ESSINGTON 4A 18
Essington Cl. DY8: Word 2C 108
Essington Ho. B8: W End 4G 103
Essington Ind. Est.
WV11: Ess 3H 17
Essington Rd. WV12: W'hall 5B 18
Essington St. B16: Birm 2D 116
Essington Way WV1: Wolv 2D 44
Este Rd. B26: Yard 3E 121
Estone Wlk. B6: Aston 2H 101
Estria Rd. B15: Edg 4D 116
Estridge La. WS6: Gt Wyr 3G 7
Ethelfleda Ter. WS10: W'bry 2F 63
Ethelred Cl. B74: Four O 6G 37
Ethel Rd. B17: Harb 6H 115
Ethel St. B2: Birm 1F 117 (4D 4)
B67: Smeth 1D 114
B68: O'bry 5G 97
Etheridge Rd. WV14: Bils 4E 45
Eton Cl. DY3: Sed 6B 60
Eton Ct. B74: Four O 1F 53
(off Vesey Cl.)
Eton Dr. DY8: Stourb 2E 125
Eton Rd. B12: Bal H 1B 134
Etruria Way WV14: Bils 4G 45
Etta Gro. B44: Gt Barr 1H 67
ETTINGSHALL 6C 44
ETTINGSHALL PARK 1A 60
Ettingshall Pk. Farm La.
WV4: E'shll 1A 60
Ettingshall Rd. WV2: E'shll 4C 44
WV14: Cose 3C 60
Ettington Cl. B93: Dorr 6F 167
Ettington Rd. B6: Aston 1G 101
Ettymore Cl. DY3: Sed 5H 59
Ettymore Rd. DY3: Sed 5H 59
Ettymore Rd. W. DY3: Sed 5G 59
Etwall Rd. B28: Hall G 2E 149
Euan Cl. B17: Harb 3G 115
Euro Bus. Pk. B69: O'bry 6D 78
Euro Ct. B13: Mose 3B 134
Europa Av. B70: W Brom 5D 80
(not continuous)
European Bus. Pk.
B69: O'bry 2E 97
Euroway Pk. B69: O'bry 1A 98
Evans Cl. DY4: Tip 2E 77
Evans Gdns. B29: S Oak 4H 131
Evans Pl. WV14: Bils 4G 45
Evans St. WV6: Wolv 5E 27
WV13: W'hall 2F 45
WV14: Cose 4B 60
Eva Rd. B18: Win G 3H 99
B68: O'bry 6A 98
Evason Ct. B6: Aston 6G 83
EVE HILL 5D 76
Eve La. DY1: Dud 2B 76
Evelyn Cft. B73: Bold 5G 69
Evelyn Rd. B11: S'hll 1C 134
Evenlode Cl. B92: Olton 2F 137
Evenlode Gro. WV13: W'hall 2D 46
Evenlode Rd. B92: Olton 2E 137
Evered Bardon Ho. B69: O'bry 2E 97
(off Round's Grn. Rd.)
Everest Rd. B20: Hand 4C 82
WS2: Wals 6F 31
Evergreen Cl. WV14: Cose 5D 60
Everitt Dr. B93: Know 3C 166
Eversley Dale B24: Erd 5G 85
Eversley Gro. DY3: Sed 3G 59
WV11: Wed 3E 29
Eversley Rd. B9: Small H 2D 118
(not continuous)
Evers St. DY5: Quar B 3C 110
Everton Rd. B8: W End 5A 104
Eves Cft. B32: Bart G 4A 130
Evesham Cres. WS3: Blox 4F 19
Evesham Ri. DY2: Neth 6F 95
Eveson Rd. DY8: Stourb 3B 124
Ewart Rd. WS2: Wals 6E 31
Ewell Rd. B24: Erd 3H 85
Ewhurst Av. B29: S Oak 4B 132
(Heeley Rd.)
B29: S Oak 5C 132
(Umberslade Rd.)
Ewhurst Cl. WV13: W'hall 3H 45
Exbury Cl. WV9: Pend 5D 14
Excel Cl. B11: S'brk 4B 118
Excelsior Gro. WS3: Pels 2F 21
Exchange, The WS3: Blox 6H 19
Exchange St. DY5: Brie H 5H 93
WV1: Wolv 1G 43 (3B 170)
Exe Cft. B31: Longb 1F 159
Exeter Dr. B37: Mars G 3B 122
Exeter Pas. B1: Birm 2F 117
Exeter Pl. WS2: Wals 2H 47
Exeter Rd. B29: S Oak 3B 132
B66: Smeth 4F 99
DY2: Neth 1F 111
Exeter St. B1: Birm 2F 117 (6D 4)
Exford Cl. DY5: Brie H 4F 109
Exhall Cl. B91: Sol 5C 150
Exhall Ct. B23: Erd 5C 84
Exhibition Way B40: Nat E C 1F 139
Exmoor Grn. WV11: Wed 2E 29
Exon Ct. DY4: Tip 1H 77
Expressway, The
B70: W Brom 3H 79
Exton Cl. WV11: Wed 1H 29
Exton Gdns. B66: Smeth 3H 99
(off Foundry La.)
Exton Way B8: Salt 4D 102
Eyland Gro. WS1: Wals 1D 48
Eymore Cl. B29: W Cas 1F 145
Eyre St. B18: Hock 6C 100
Eyston Av. DY4: Tip 5D 62

A-Z Birmingham Deluxe 189

Eyton Cft.—First Av.

Eyton Cft. B12: Birm . . . 4H 117
Ezekiel La. WV12: W'hall . . . 3C 30

F

Fabian Cl. B45: Fran . . . 5F 143
Fabian Cres. B90: Shir . . . 6H 149
Facet Rd. B38: K Nor . . . 5C 146
Factory Est. B44: P Barr . . . 1G 83
Factory Rd. B18: Hock . . . 3B 100
DY4: Tip . . . 1G 77
Factory St. WS10: Darl . . . 5C 46
Fairbourne Av. B44: Gt Barr . . . 3G 67
B65: Row R . . . 5E 97
Fairbourn Twr. B23: Erd . . . 1G 85
Fairburn Cres. WS3: Pels . . . 2F 21
Faircroft Av. B76: Walm . . . 1D 86
Faircroft Rd. B36: Cas B . . . 6H 87
Fairdene Way B43: Gt Barr . . . 5H 65
Fairfax Rd. B31: Longb . . . 1E 159
B75: S Cold . . . 6D 54
WV10: Bush . . . 5H 15
Fairfield Dr. B62: B'hth . . . 2E 113
WS3: Pels . . . 3F 21
WV8: Cod . . . 3E 13
Fairfield Gro. B62: B'hth . . . 2E 113
Fairfield Mt. WS1: Wals . . . 3D 48
Fairfield Pk. Ind. Est. B62: B'hth . . . 2E 113
Fairfield Pk. Rd. B62: B'hth . . . 2E 113
Fairfield Ri. CV7: Mer . . . 4H 141
DY8: Woll . . . 6A 108
Fairfield Rd. B14: K Hth . . . 5G 133
B62: B'hth . . . 2E 113
B63: Hale . . . 3A 128
DY2: Dud . . . 2F 95
DY8: Word . . . 1D 108
Fairford Cl. B91: Shir . . . 2B 150
Fairford Gdns. DY8: Word . . . 6C 92
Fairford Rd. B44: K'sdng . . . 1H 83
Fairgreen Gdns. DY5: P'ntt . . . 4F 93
Fairgreen Way B29: S Oak . . . 4B 132
B74: S'tly . . . 2A 52
Fair Ground Way WS1: Wals . . . 3B 48
Fairhaven Cft. B62: B'hth . . . 2E 113
Fairhills DY3: Sed . . . 5H 59
Fairhill Way B11: S'brk . . . 4B 118
Fairholme Rd. B36: Hodg H . . . 2H 103
Fairlawn B15: Edg . . . 4C 116
Fairlawn Cl. WV12: W'hall . . . 6C 18
Fairlawn Dr. DY6: K'wfrd . . . 5B 92
Fairlawns B26: Yard . . . 2E 121
B76: Walm . . . 5E 71
Fairlawn Way WV12: W'hall . . . 6C 18
Fairlie Cres. B38: K Nor . . . 6H 145
Fairmead Ri. B38: K Nor . . . 6A 146
Fairmile Rd. B63: Hale . . . 5H 111
Fairoak Dr. WV6: Tett . . . 6H 25
Fair Oaks Dr. WS6: Gt Wyr . . . 5G 7
Fairview Av. B42: Gt Barr . . . 1D 82
Fairview Cl. WS6: C Hay . . . 3D 6
WV11: Wed . . . 3D 28
Fairview Ct. WS2: Wals . . . 1D 46
Fairview Cres. DY6: K'wfrd . . . 4D 92
WV11: Wed . . . 2D 28
Fairview Gro. WV11: Wed . . . 2D 28
Fairview Ind. Est. B76: Curd . . . 1D 88
Fairview Rd. DY1: Dud . . . 4C 76
WV4: Penn . . . 1A 58
WV11: Wed . . . 2D 28
Fairway B31: N'fld . . . 5C 144
WS4: S'fld . . . 6H 21
Fairway, The B38: K Nor . . . 5H 145
Fairway Av. B69: Tiv . . . 1A 96
Fairway Dr. B45: Rubery . . . 3F 157
Fairway Grn. WV14: Bils . . . 4F 45
Fairway Rd. B68: O'bry . . . 1F 113
Fairways Av. DY8: Stourb . . . 3C 124
Fairways Cl. DY8: Stourb . . . 3C 124
Fairyfield Av. B43: Gt Barr . . . 4H 65
Fairyfield Ct. B43: Gt Barr . . . 4H 65
Fakenham Cft. B17: Harb . . . 4D 114
Falcon Cl. WS6: C Hay . . . 3C 6
Falcon Cres. WV14: Cose . . . 3B 60
Falcondale Rd. WV12: W'hall . . . 6C 18
Falconhurst Rd. B29: S Oak . . . 3G 131
FALCON LODGE . . . 6F 55
Falcon Lodge Cres. B75: S Cold . . . 6D 54
Falcon Pl. B69: Tiv . . . 2C 96
Falcon Ri. DY8: Woll . . . 5A 108
Falcon Rd. B68: O'bry . . . 1F 113
Falcons, The B75: S Cold . . . 6F 55
Falcon Vw. B30: K Nor . . . 3C 146
Falcon Way DY1: Dud . . . 6B 76
Falfield Cl. B65: Row R . . . 3D 96
Falfield Gro. B31: Longb . . . 2C 158
Falkland Cft. B30: Stir . . . 1D 146
Falklands Cl. DY3: Swind . . . 5E 73
Falkland Way B36: Cas B . . . 4D 106
Falkwood Gro. B93: Know . . . 3B 166
Fallindale Rd. B26: Sheld . . . 5F 121
FALLINGS HEATH . . . 5F 47
Fallings Heath Cl. WS10: Darl . . . 4F 47
FALLINGS PARK . . . 4B 28
Fallings Pk. Ind. Est. WV10: Wolv . . . 4B 28
Fallow Fld. B74: Lit A . . . 6B 36
Fallowfield B15: Edg . . . 3A 116
WV6: Pert . . . 5D 24
WV8: Pend . . . 5C 14
Fallowfield Av. B28: Hall G . . . 2F 149
Fallowfield Rd. B63: Hale . . . 2F 127
B65: Row R . . . 6A 96
B92: Sol . . . 3G 137
WS5: Wals . . . 3A 50
Fallows Ho. B19: Hock . . . 4G 101
Fallows Rd. B11: S'brk . . . 5C 118
Fallow Wlk. B32: Bart G . . . 3G 129
Falmouth Rd. B34: Hodg H . . . 4C 104
WS5: Wals . . . 4H 49
Falstaff Av. B47: H'wd . . . 3A 162
Falstaff Cl. B76: Walm . . . 6F 71
Falstaff Ct. B75: S Cold . . . 6G 55
Falstaff Rd. B90: Shir . . . 5H 149
Falstone Rd. B73: New O . . . 3D 68
Fancott Rd. B31: N'fld . . . 2E 145
Fancourt Av. WV4: Penn . . . 1B 58
Fane Rd. WV11: Wed . . . 6A 18
Fanshawe Rd. B27: A Grn . . . 4A 136
Fanum Ho. B63: Hale . . . 2B 128
Faraday Av. B32: Quin . . . 6B 114
B46: Col . . . 2H 89
B76: Curd . . . 2G 89
Faraday Ct. B32: Quin . . . 6B 114
Faraday Ho. B15: Birm . . . 3E 117
Faraday Rd. WS2: Wals . . . 3H 31
Faraday Wharf B7: Birm . . . 5H 101
Farbrook Way WV12: W'hall . . . 3B 30
Farclose Ho. B15: Edg . . . 4E 117
Farcroft Av. B21: Hand . . . 1H 99
Farcroft Gro. B21: Hand . . . 6H 81
Farcroft Rd. B21: Hand . . . 6H 81
Fareham Cres. WV4: Penn . . . 5A 42
Farfield Cl. B31: N'fld . . . 5F 145
Far High Dr. DY4: Tip . . . 2B 78
Far Highfield B76: Walm . . . 1B 70
Farhill Cl. B71: W Brom . . . 5D 64
Farlands Dr. DY8: Stourb . . . 2E 125
Farlands Gro. B43: Gt Barr . . . 6B 66
Farlands Rd. DY8: Stourb . . . 2E 125
Farleigh Dr. WV3: Wolv . . . 3G 41
Farleigh Rd. WV6: Pert . . . 6G 25
Farley Cen. B70: W Brom . . . 5B 80
Farley La. B62: Roms . . . 5A 142
Farley Rd. B23: Erd . . . 3B 84
Farley St. DY4: Tip . . . 2D 78
Farlow Cft. B37: Mars G . . . 3B 122
Farlow Rd. B31: N'fld . . . 4G 145
Farlows End B38: K Nor . . . 2H 159
Farmacre B9: Birm . . . 1B 118
Farm Av. B68: O'bry . . . 6G 97
Farmbridge Cl. WS2: Wals . . . 6D 30
Farmbridge Rd. WS2: Wals . . . 6D 30
Farmbridge Way WS2: Wals . . . 6D 30
Farmbrook Av. WV10: F'hses . . . 4H 15
Farm Cl. B92: Sol . . . 3G 137
DY3: Sed . . . 6F 59
WV8: Bilb . . . 5H 13
Farmcote Rd. B33: Stech . . . 5E 105
Farm Cft. B19: Hock . . . 3E 101
Farmcroft Rd. DY9: W'cte . . . 2A 126
Farmdale Gro. B45: Redn . . . 3G 157
Farmer Rd. B10: Small H . . . 4G 119
Farmers Cl. B76: Walm . . . 1C 70
Farmers Ct. B63: Hale . . . 1H 127
Farmers Fold WV1: Wolv . . . 1G 43 (3B 170)
Farmers Wlk. B21: Hand . . . 2H 99
Farmer Way DY4: Tip . . . 4B 62
Farm Ho. La. B75: R'ley . . . 6C 38
Farmhouse Rd. WV12: W'hall . . . 4D 30
Farm Ho. Way B43: Gt Barr . . . 1A 66
Farmhouse Way B90: M'path . . . 2F 165
WV12: W'hall . . . 4E 31
Farmoor Gro. B34: S End . . . 3A 106
Farmoor Way WV10: Bush . . . 3A 16
Farm Rd. B11: S'brk . . . 4B 118
B65: Row R . . . 5A 96
B67: Smeth . . . 6C 98
B68: O'bry . . . 6G 97
DY2: Neth . . . 6C 94
DY4: Tip . . . 6C 62
DY5: Quar B . . . 2A 110
WV3: Wolv . . . 3A 42
Farmside Cl. DY9: W'cte . . . 2B 126
Farmside Grn. WV9: Pend . . . 5D 14
Farmstead Cl. B75: R'ley . . . 6B 38
WS1: Wals . . . 6C 48
Farmstead Rd. B92: Sol . . . 3G 137
Farm St. B19: Hock . . . 3D 100
B70: W Brom . . . 6A 80
WS2: Wals . . . 5C 32
Farnborough Ct. B75: Four O . . . 1H 53
Farnborough Dr. B90: M'path . . . 3D 164
Farnborough Rd. B35: Cas V . . . 5E 87
Farnbury Cft. B38: K Nor . . . 5B 146
Farn Cl. B33: Stech . . . 6D 104
Farncote Dr. B74: Four O . . . 6F 37
Farndale Av. WV6: Wolv . . . 4D 26
Farndale Cl. DY5: Brie H . . . 5F 109
Farndon Av. B37: Mars G . . . 4D 122
Farndon Rd. B8: Salt . . . 5F 103
Farndon Way B23: Erd . . . 5D 68
Farnham Cl. B43: Gt Barr . . . 5B 66
Farnham Rd. B21: Hand . . . 5H 81
Farnhurst Rd. B36: Hodg H . . . 2H 103
Farnol Rd. B26: Yard . . . 3D 120
Farnworth Gro. B36: Cas B . . . 6A 88
Farquhar Rd. B13: Mose . . . 2H 133
B15: Edg . . . 5B 116
Farquhar Rd. E. B15: Edg . . . 5B 116
Farran Way B43: Gt Barr . . . 6A 66
Farren Rd. B31: Longb . . . 6B 144
Farrier Cl. B76: Walm . . . 5D 70
Farrier Rd. B43: Gt Barr . . . 2F 67
Farriers, The B26: Sheld . . . 6F 121
Farriers Mill WS3: Pels . . . 3C 20
Farrier Way DY6: W Hth . . . 2G 91
Farringdon Ho. *WS2: Wals . . . 6B 32*
(off Green La.)
Farringdon St. WS2: Wals . . . 1B 48
Farrington Rd. B23: Erd . . . 2B 84
WV4: E'shll . . . 2H 59
Farrow Rd. B44: Gt Barr . . . 2G 67
Farthing Ct. B1: Birm . . . 6E 101 (2A 4)
Farthing La. B72: S Cold . . . 1H 69
B76: Curd . . . 1E 89
Farthing Pools Cl. B72: S Cold . . . 1A 70
Farthings, The B17: Harb . . . 5H 115
Farthings La. DY2: Dud . . . 2C 94
Farvale Rd. B76: Min . . . 1G 87
Far Vw. WS9: A'rdge . . . 5D 22
Farway Gdns. WV8: Cod . . . 5F 13
Far Wood Rd. B31: N'fld . . . 5C 130
Fashoda Rd. B29: S Oak . . . 4D 132
Fastlea Rd. B32: Bart G . . . 4B 130
Fastmoor Oval B33: Kitts G . . . 2A 122
Fast Pits Rd. B25: Yard . . . 3H 119
Fatherless Barn Cres. B63: Crad . . . 1E 127
Faulkland Cres. WV1: Wolv . . . 6H 27 (1C 170)
Faulkner Cl. DY8: Stourb . . . 1D 124
Faulkner Rd. B92: Olton . . . 4F 137
Faulkners Farm Dr. B23: Erd . . . 1B 84
Faulknor Dr. DY5: P'ntt . . . 2F 93
Faversham Cl. WS2: Wals . . . 6D 30
WV8: Pend . . . 1C 26
Fawdry Cl. B73: S Cold . . . 6H 53
Fawdry St. B9: Birm . . . 1A 118
B66: Smeth . . . 4G 99
WV1: Wolv . . . 6F 27
Fawley Cl. WV13: W'hall . . . 3H 45
Fawley Gro. B14: K Hth . . . 2D 146
Fazeley St. B5: Birm . . . 1H 117 (4G 5)
Fazeley St. Ind. Est. B5: Birm . . . 1A 118 (4H 5)
Fearon Pl. B66: Smeth . . . 4E 99
FEATHERSTONE . . . 1D 16
Featherstone Cl. B90: Shir . . . 5B 150
Featherstone Cres. B90: Shir . . . 5B 150
Featherstone Rd. B14: K Hth . . . 1G 147
Featherston Rd. B74: S'tly . . . 1A 52
FEIASHILL . . . 6B 56
Feiashill Cl. WV5: Try . . . 6B 56
Feiashill Rd. WV5: Try . . . 5B 56
Felbrigg Cl. DY5: Brie H . . . 3G 109
Feldings, The B24: Erd . . . 3A 86
Feldon La. B62: B'hth . . . 4E 113
Felgate Cl. B90: M'path . . . 3E 165
Fellbrook Cl. B33: Stech . . . 5D 104
Fell Gro. B21: Hand . . . 5G 81
Fellmeadow Rd. B33: Yard . . . 1E 121
Fellmeadow Way DY3: Sed . . . 1A 76
Fellows Av. DY6: W Hth . . . 1A 92
Fellows La. B17: Harb . . . 5E 115
Fellows Pk. Gdns. WS2: Wals . . . 5H 47
Fellows Rd. WV14: Bils . . . 4F 45
Fellows St. WV2: Wolv . . . 3G 43
Felsted Way B7: Birm . . . 5A 102
Felstone Rd. B44: Gt Barr . . . 4G 67
Feltham Cl. B33: Kitts G . . . 2A 122
Felton Cft. B33: Kitts G . . . 6E 105
Felton Gro. B91: Sol . . . 6F 151
Fenbourne Cl. WS4: S'fld . . . 1G 33
Fenchurch Cl. WS2: Wals . . . 5B 32
Fencote Av. B37: F'bri . . . 5C 106
FEN END . . . 6F 169
Fen End Rd. CV8: Fen E . . . 6E 169
Fen End Rd. W. B93: Know . . . 4B 168
CV8: Fen E . . . 4B 168
Fenmere Cl. WV4: Penn . . . 6H 43
Fennel Cl. WS6: C Hay . . . 2D 6
Fennel Cft. B34: S End . . . 2F 105
Fennel Rd. DY5: Brie H . . . 4G 109
Fennis Cl. B93: Dorr . . . 6B 166
Fenn Ri. DY8: Word . . . 6B 92
WV12: W'hall . . . 3B 30
Fens Cres. DY5: Brie H . . . 4G 93
Fens Pool Av. DY5: Brie H . . . 4H 93
Fensway, The B34: Stech . . . 4E 105
Fenter Cl. B13: Mose . . . 6H 117
Fentham Cl. B92: H Ard . . . 1B 154
Fentham Ct. B92: Olton . . . 5D 136
Fentham Grn. B92: H Ard . . . 6A 140
Fentham Rd. B6: Aston . . . 1F 101
B23: Erd . . . 4D 84
B92: H Ard . . . 1A 154
Fenton Rd. B27: A Grn . . . 6H 119
B47: H'wd . . . 2A 162
Fenton St. B66: Smeth . . . 2C 98
DY5: Brie H . . . 6H 93
Fenton Way B27: A Grn . . . 1H 135
Fereday Rd. WS9: Wals W . . . 4D 22
Fereday's Cft. DY3: Sed . . . 6H 59
Fereday St. DY4: Tip . . . 5H 61
Ferguson Dr. DY4: Tip . . . 1B 78
Ferguson Rd. B68: O'bry . . . 4B 98
Ferguson St. WV11: Wed . . . 6A 18
Fern Av. DY4: Tip . . . 6H 61
Fern Bank Cl. B63: Hale . . . 3F 127
Fernbank Cres. WS5: Wals . . . 1G 65
Fernbank Rd. B8: W End . . . 5G 103
Ferncliffe Rd. B17: Harb . . . 1F 131
Fern Cl. WS4: S'fld . . . 6G 21
WV14: Cose . . . 5D 60
Ferndale Av. B43: Gt Barr . . . 6B 66
Ferndale Ct. *B17: Harb . . . 1H 131*
(off Metchley La.)
B46: Col . . . 4H 107
Ferndale Cres. B12: Birm . . . 3A 118
Ferndale M. B46: Col . . . 4H 107
Ferndale Pk. DY9: Pedm . . . 5F 125
Ferndale Rd. B28: Hall G . . . 5F 135
B46: Col . . . 4H 107
B68: O'bry . . . 2F 113
B74: S'tly . . . 3H 51
CV7: Bal C . . . 3F 169
WV11: Ess . . . 4B 18
Ferndene Rd. B11: Tys . . . 2F 135
Ferndown Av. DY3: Sed . . . 6G 59
Ferndown Cl. B26: Yard . . . 2E 121
WS3: Blox . . . 3H 19
Ferndown Gdns. WV11: Wed . . . 4H 29
Ferndown Rd. B91: Sol . . . 1F 151
Fern Dr. WS6: Gt Wyr . . . 1G 7
Fernfail Ct. B23: Erd . . . 2E 85
Fernhill Ct. B23: Erd . . . 5C 84
Fernhill Gro. B44: Gt Barr . . . 2H 67
Fernhill La. CV7: Bal C . . . 5F 169
CV8: Fen E . . . 5E 169
Fernhill Rd. B92: Olton . . . 3C 136
Fernhurst Dr. DY5: P'ntt . . . 2F 93
Fernhurst Rd. B8: Salt . . . 6G 103
Fernleigh Ct. B91: Sol . . . 2G 151
Fernleigh Gdns. DY8: Word . . . 6A 92
Fernleigh Rd. WS4: Wals . . . 6F 33
Fernley Av. B29: S Oak . . . 3D 132
Fernley Rd. B11: S'hll . . . 1C 134
Fern Leys WV3: Wolv . . . 2B 42
Fern Rd. B24: Erd . . . 3G 85
DY1: Dud . . . 3E 77
WV3: Wolv . . . 3F 43
Fernside Gdns. B13: Mose . . . 2B 134
Fernside Rd. WV13: W'hall . . . 6F 29
Fernwood Cl. B73: Bold . . . 4E 69
Fernwood Cft. B14: K Hth . . . 1G 147
DY4: Tip . . . 3H 77
Fernwood Rd. B73: Bold . . . 5E 69
Fernwoods B32: Bart G . . . 3H 129
Ferrers Cl. B75: R'ley . . . 1B 54
Ferrie Gro. WS8: Bwnhls . . . 6A 10
Ferris Gro. B27: A Grn . . . 4G 135
Festival Av. WS10: Darl . . . 1C 62
Festival Ct. DY2: Neth . . . 4E 95
Festival Way WV6: Wolv . . . 4F 27
Fibbersley WV11: Wed . . . 5H 29
WV13: W'hall . . . 5H 29
Fibbersley Bank WV13: W'hall . . . 5H 29
Fiddlers Grn. B92: H Ard . . . 6A 140
Field Av. B31: N'fld . . . 2D 144
Field Cl. B26: Sheld . . . 5E 121
DY8: Word . . . 1E 109
WS3: Blox . . . 1A 32
WS4: S'fld . . . 5F 21
Field Cott. Dr. DY8: Stourb . . . 2F 125
Field Ct. WS4: S'fld . . . 5F 21
Fieldfare WS7: Hamm . . . 1F 11
Fieldfare Cl. B64: Old H . . . 5H 95
Fieldfare Cft. B36: Cas B . . . 1C 106
Fieldfare Rd. DY9: W'cte . . . 1H 125
Fieldgate Trad. Est.
WS1: Wals . . . 2D 48
Fld. Head Pl. WV6: Tett . . . 5H 25
Fieldhead Rd. B11: Tys . . . 2G 135
Fieldhouse Rd. B25: Yard . . . 3A 120
WV4: E'shll . . . 1A 60
Field La. B32: Bart G . . . 5G 129
B91: Sol . . . 1C 152
DY8: Stourb . . . 2E 125
WS4: S'fld . . . 5F 21
WS6: Gt Wyr . . . 2F 7
Field M. DY2: Neth . . . 6G 95
Fieldon Cl. B90: Shir . . . 4A 150
Field Rd. DY2: Dud . . . 6G 77
DY4: Tip . . . 5H 61
WS3: Blox . . . 1A 32
Field Rd. Ind. Est. WS3: Blox . . . 1A 32
Fields, The WV8: Bilb . . . 3H 13
Fieldside Wlk. WV14: Bils . . . 3F 45
Fieldstone Vw. DY3: Lwr G . . . 3H 75
Field St. WV10: Wolv . . . 6A 28
WV13: W'hall . . . 1A 46
WV14: Bils . . . 2G 61
Fieldview Cl. WV14: Cose . . . 3G 61
Field Vw. Dr. B65: Row R . . . 6F 97
Field Wlk. WS9: A'rdge . . . 2D 34
Fieldways Cl. B47: H'wd . . . 2A 162
Fifield Gro. B33: Yard . . . 6D 104
Fifth Av. B9: Bord G . . . 1F 119
DY5: Brie H . . . 6B 94
WV10: Bush . . . 2H 27
Filey Rd. WV10: Oxl . . . 5F 15
Fillingham Cl. B37: Chel W . . . 2F 123
Fillongley Rd. CV7: Mer . . . 4H 141
Filton Cft. B35: Cas V . . . 3E 87
Fimbrell Cl. DY5: Brie H . . . 3E 109
Finbury Cl. B92: Olton . . . 4D 136
Finchall Cft. B92: Sol . . . 6A 138
Fincham Cl. WV9: Pend . . . 4E 15
Finch Cl. B65: Row R . . . 5H 95
Finch Cft. CV7: Bal C . . . 2H 169
Finchdene Gro. WV3: Wolv . . . 2B 42
Finch Dr. B74: S'tly . . . 6A 52
Finches End B34: S End . . . 4G 105
Finchfield Cl. DY8: Stourb . . . 1A 124
Finchfield Gdns. WV3: Wolv . . . 2C 42
Finchfield Hill WV3: Wolv . . . 1A 42
(not continuous)
Finchfield La. WV3: Wolv . . . 3A 42
Finchfield Rd. WV3: Wolv . . . 2C 42
Finchfield Rd. W. WV3: Wolv . . . 2B 42
Finchley Av. B19: Loz . . . 1E 101
Finchley Cl. DY3: Lwr G . . . 5H 75
Finchley Rd. B44: K'sdng . . . 3B 68
Finchmead Rd. B33: Kitts G . . . 2A 122
Finchpath Rd. B70: W Brom . . . 1G 79
Finch Rd. B19: Loz . . . 1E 101
Findlay Rd. B14: K Hth . . . 4G 133
Findon Rd. B8: W End . . . 3H 103
Finford Cft. CV7: Bal C . . . 3H 169
Fingerpost Dr. WS3: Pels . . . 2E 21
Finlarigg Dr. B15: Edg . . . 5B 116
Finmere Rd. B28: Hall G . . . 5F 135
Finmere Way B90: Shir . . . 4B 150
Finnemore Rd. B9: Bord G . . . 1G 119
Finneywell Cl. WV14: Cose . . . 2D 60
Finsbury Dr. DY5: Brie H . . . 4G 109
Finsbury Gro. B23: Erd . . . 1D 84
Finstall Cl. B7: Birm . . . 5A 102
B72: W Grn . . . 4A 70
Finwood Cl. B92: Sol . . . 5A 138
Fir Av. B12: Bal H . . . 6A 118
Firbank Cl. B30: B'vlle . . . 6A 132
Firbank Way WS3: Pels . . . 5D 20
Firbarn Cl. B76: Walm . . . 2B 70
Firbeck Gro. B44: K'sdng . . . 4A 68
Firbeck Rd. B44: K'sdng . . . 4A 68
Fir Cft. DY5: Brie H . . . 3G 109
Fircroft B31: N'fld . . . 5D 130
B91: Sol . . . 1D 150
WV14: Bils . . . 2A 62
Fircroft Ho. B37: Chel W . . . 1C 122
Firecrest Cl. B23: Erd . . . 6B 68
Fire Sta. Rd. B26: Birm A . . . 6C 122
Fir Gro. B14: K Hth . . . 2H 147
DY8: Woll . . . 5A 108
WV3: Wolv . . . 2E 43
Firhill Cft. B14: K Hth . . . 5F 147
Firmstone Ct. DY8: Woll . . . 4C 108
Firmstone St. DY8: Woll . . . 4C 108
Firs, The B11: S'brk . . . 5C 118
CV7: Mer . . . 4H 141
Firsbrook Cl. WV6: Wolv . . . 4D 26
Firsbrook Ho. WV6: Wolv . . . 4E 27
Firsby Rd. B32: Quin . . . 6C 114
Firs Cl. B67: Smeth . . . 4E 99
Firs Dr. B90: Shir . . . 6G 149
Firs Farm Dr. B36: Hodg H . . . 1D 104
Firsholm Cl. B73: Bold . . . 6G 69
Firs Ho. B36: Hodg H . . . 1D 104
Firs La. B67: Smeth . . . 4E 99
Firs Rd. DY6: K'wfrd . . . 3C 92
Firs St. DY2: Dud . . . 6F 77
First Av. B6: Witt . . . 5H 83
B9: Bord G . . . 2E 119
B29: S Oak . . . 2D 132
B76: Min . . . 2E 87
DY6: P'ntt . . . 6E 75

First Av.—Frederick St.

First Av. WS8: Bwnhls 5C 10
WV10: Bush 3A 28
First Exhibition Av. B40: Nat E C 1F 139
First Mdw. Piece B32: Quin 1C 130
Fir St. DY3: Sed 6D 58
Firsvale Rd. WV11: Wed 4H 29
Firsway WV6: Tett 1G 41
Firswood Rd. B33: Sheld 2G 121
Firth Dr. B14: Yard W 2B 148
B62: B'hth 3E 113
Firth Pk. Cres. B62: B'hth 3E 113
Firtree Cl. B44: Gt Barr 6G 67
Fir Tree Dr. DY3: Sed 6A 60
WS5: Wals 1F 65
Fir Tree Gro. B73: Bold 4F 69
Fir Tree Rd. WV3: Wolv 3B 42
Firtree Rd. B24: Erd 4H 85
Fisher Cl. B45: Fran 5E 143
Fisher Rd. B69: O'bry 2A 98
WS3: Blox 5F 19
Fishers Dr. B90: Dic H 4F 163
Fisher St. DY2: Dud 6F 77
DY4: Tip 4A 78
(Dudley Port)
DY4: Tip 2D 78
(Great Bridge)
DY5: Brie H 1F 109
WV13: W'hall 1C 46
FISHLEY 4A 20
Fishley Cl. WS3: Blox 3A 20
Fishley La.
WS3: Blox, Lit W 4B 20
Fishpool Cl. B36: Hodg H 1A 104
Fistral Gdns. WV3: Wolv 4D 42
Fithern Cl. DY3: Up Gor 2A 76
Fitness First Health Club
Brierley Hill 6A 94
Mere Green 1H 53
Solihull 2F 137
Stirchley 5D 132
Walsall Wood 3C 22
Wednesbury 3D 62
Wolverhampton *6C 170*
(in AMF Bowling Express)
Fitters Mill Cl. B5: Bal H 5G 117
Fitton Av. DY6: K'wfrd 4E 93
Fitzgerald Pl. DY5: Brie H 5F 109
Fitzguy Cl. B70: W Brom 6C 80
Fitzmaurice Rd. WV11: Wed 2H 29
Fitz Roy Av. B17: Harb 4D 114
Fitzroy Rd. B31: N'fld 4A 144
Five Flds. Rd. WV12: W'hall 4A 30
Five Oaks Rd. WV13: W'hall 3G 45
FIVE WAYS
Birmingham 3E 117
Five Ways B15: Birm 2D 116
B33: Stech 1B 120
DY3: Lwr G 4H 75
DY5: Brie H 1H 109
WV1: Wolv 5G 27
WV3: Penn 4A 42
Five Ways Shop. Cen.
B15: Birm 2D 116
Five Ways Station (Rail) 3D 116
Flackwell Rd. B23: Erd 6E 69
Fladbury Cl. DY2: Neth 6F 95
Fladbury Cres. B29: S Oak 4H 131
Fladbury Gdns. B19: Hand 1E 101
Fladbury Pl. B19: Loz 2E 101
Flamborough Cl. B34: Hodg H 2E 105
Flamborough Way WV14: Cose 6D 60
Flanders Dr. DY6: K'wfrd 1B 92
Flash La. WV4: Lwr P 3E 57
Flash Rd. B69: O'bry 2G 97
Flatlea B31: N'fld 3D 144
Flatts, The WS10: Darl 4E 47
Flavell Av. WV14: Cose 4F 61
Flavell Cl. B32: Bart G 4H 129
Flavells La. B25: Yard 3A 120
DY3: Gorn 5F 75
Flavell St. DY1: Dud 1D 76
Flax Cl. B47: H'wd 4A 162
Flax Gdns. B38: K Nor 1B 160
Flaxhall St. WS2: Wals 3H 47
Flaxley Cl. B33: Stech 6D 104
Flaxley Parkway B33: Stech 5C 104
Flaxley Rd. B33: Stech, Kitts G 5B 104
Flaxton Gro. B33: Kitts G 5E 105
Flaxton Wlk. WV6: Wolv 4E 27
Flecknoe Cl. B36: Cas B 6G 87
Fledburgh Dr. B76: Walm 1B 70
Fleet St. B3: Birm 6E 101 (3B 4)
WV14: Bils 6F 45
Fleetwood Gro. B26: Yard 2E 121
Fleetwood Ho. B13: Mose 1H 133
Fleming Pl. WS2: Wals 3G 31
Fleming Rd. B32: Quin 6B 114
WS2: Wals 3G 31
(not continuous)
Flemmynge Cl. WV8: Cod 3E 13
Fletcher Gro. B93: Know 5C 166
Fletcher Rd. WV12: W'hall 6D 18
Fletcher's La. WV13: W'hall 1C 46
Fletcher St. DY9: Lye 6B 110
Fletchers Wlk. B3: Birm 1E 117 (4B 4)
Fletton Gro. B14: K Hth 4A 148
Flinkford Cl. WS5: Wals 5H 49
Flint Grn. Rd. B27: A Grn 2H 135
Flintham Cl. B27: A Grn 2C 136
Flint Ho. WV1: Wolv 5G 27
Flintway, The B33: Stech 5C 104
Floodgate St. B5: Birm 2H 117 (6H 5)
Flood St. DY2: Dud 1F 95
Flood St. Island DY2: Dud 1F 95
Flora Rd. B25: Yard 4H 119
Florence Av. B11: S'hll 5C 118
B73: W Grn 6H 69
WV4: E'shll 1B 60
Florence Bldgs. B29: S Oak 3B 132
Florence Dr. B73: W Grn 6H 69
Florence Gro. B18: Win G 5A 100
B71: W Brom 4C 64
Florence Rd. B14: K Hth 5H 133
B21: Hand 1H 99
B27: A Grn 1B 136
B66: Smeth 5F 99
Florence Rd. B69: O'bry 2D 96
B70: W Brom 6C 80
B73: W Grn 6H 69
DY4: Tip 6A 62
WV8: Bilb 4A 14
Florence St. B1: Birm 2F 117 (6C 4)
WS1: Wals 2E 49
Florian Gro. WS10: Darl 4E 47
Florida Way DY6: K'wfrd 3E 93
Flowerdale Cl.
WV14: Cose 5D 60
Floyd Gro. CV7: Bal C 5H 169
Floyds La. WS4: Rus 3G 33
Floyer Rd. B10: Small H 2E 119
Flyford Cft. B29: W Cas 3D 130
Foden Rd. B42: Gt Barr 5C 66
Foinavon Cl. B65: Row R 3H 95
Fold, The B38: K Nor 6C 146
WS10: Darl 5D 46
WV4: Penn 1D 58
WV5: Seis 3A 56
WV8: Oaken 5D 12
Fold St. WV1: Wolv 2G 43 (4A 170)
Foldyard Cl. B76: Walm 5E 71
Foley Av. WV6: Tett 6A 26
Foley Chu. Cl. B74: S'tly 1A 52
Foley Ct. B74: S'tly 2H 51
Foley Dr. WV6: Tett 6A 26
Foley Gro. WV5: Wom 2E 73
Foley Ho. B68: O'bry 3H 113
Foley Rd. B8: W End 4H 103
DY9: Pedm 3F 125
Foley Rd. E. B74: S'tly 2H 51
Foley Rd. W. B74: S'tly 2F 51
Foley St. WS10: W'bry 2G 63
Foley Wood Cl. B74: S'tly 2G 51
Foliot Flds. B25: Yard 3B 120
Folkes Rd. DY9: Lye 5C 110
Folkestone Cft. B36: Hodg H 1C 104
Folliott Rd. B33: Kitts G 6E 105
Follyhouse Cl. WS1: Wals 4D 48
Follyhouse La. WS1: Wals 4D 48
Fontley Cl. B26: Yard 2D 120
Fontwell Rd. WV10: F'hses 3H 15
Footherley La.
WS14: Foot, Shen W 1F 37
FORDBRIDGE 6C 106
Fordbridge Rd. B37: K'hrst 5B 106
Ford Brook La. WS3: S'fld 5F 21
Fordbrough, The B74: Four O 2G 53
Forder Gro. B14: K Hth 5A 148
Forde Way Gdns. B38: K Nor 2H 159
Fordfield Rd. B33: Kitts G 5G 105
Fordham Gro. WV9: Pend 4E 15
Fordhouse La. B30: Stir 1D 146
Fordhouse Rd. WV10: Bush 6H 15
Fordhouse Rd. Ind. Est.
WV10: Bush 1H 27
FORDHOUSES 4F 15
Fordraught La. B62: Roms 6B 142
Fordrift, The B37: Mars G 6C 122
Fordrough B25: Yard 4F 119
Fordrough, The B31: N'fld 6F 145
B90: Maj G 1B 162
Fordrough Av. B9: Bord G 6E 103
Fordrough La. B9: Bord G 6E 103
Fords Rd. B90: Maj G 2E 163
Ford St. B18: Hock 4D 100
B67: Smeth 3D 98
WS2: Wals 4A 48
Fordwater Rd. B74: S'tly 5H 51
Foredraft Cl. B32: Bart G 3A 130
Foredraft St. B63: Crad 6F 111
Foredrove La. B92: Sol 1A 152
Forest Av. WS3: Blox 2B 32
Forest Cl. B66: Smeth 2C 98
B74: S'tly 4A 52
Forest Ct. B13: Mose 2A 134
B93: Dorr 6B 166
WV12: W'hall 1C 30
Forest Dale B45: Redn 3H 157
Forest Dr. B17: Harb 5H 115
B64: Old H 1H 111
Foresters Way B75: R'ley 6C 38
Forest Ga. WV12: W'hall 1D 30
Forest Glade WS6: C Hay 3F 7
Forest Hill Rd. B26: Sheld 6G 121
Forest La. WS2: Wals 4B 32
Forest Pk. B76: Walm 1C 70
Forest Pl. WS3: Wals 3C 32
Fore St. B2: Birm 1G 117 (4E 5)
Forest Rd. B13: Mose 2A 134
B25: Yard 5A 120
B68: O'bry 4A 114
B93: Dorr 6C 166
DY1: Dud 3E 77
Forest Way B47: H'wd 3B 162
WS6: Gt Wyr 4G 7
Forfar Wlk. B38: K Nor 5H 145
Forge, The B63: Crad 3D 110
Forge Cl. WS7: Hamm 1F 11
WV8: Pend 6C 14
Forge Cft. B76: Walm 1F 87
Forge La. B62: Hale 6C 112
B64: Crad H 3D 110
B71: W Brom 6E 65
B74: Lit A 3C 36
B76: Min 1F 87
(not continuous)
B76: Walm. *1F 87*
(off Walmley Ash La.)
DY6: W Hth 1G 91
WS9: A'rdge 4C 34
(Birmingham Rd.)
WS9: A'rdge 2H 35
(Mill La.)
WS14: Foot 1B 36
Forge Leys WV5: Wom 1E 73
Forge Mill Nature Reserve 6F 65
Forge Rd. DY8: Stourb 5D 108
(not continuous)
WS3: Pels 2D 20
WS10: Darl 5C 46
WV12: W'hall 5C 30
Forge St. WS10: Darl 1E 63
WV13: W'hall 6B 30
Forge Trad. Est. B62: Hale 6C 112
Forge Valley Way WV5: Wom 1E 73
Forge Way B69: O'bry 3E 97
FORHILL 5C 160
Forman's Rd. B11: S'hll 2D 134
Forman Trad. Est. B11: S'hll 2D 134
Formby Av. WV6: Pert 5D 24
Formby Way WS3: Blox 4G 19
Forrell Gro. B31: Longb 2F 159
Forrest Av. WV11: Ess 3A 18
Forrester St. WS2: Wals 1A 48
Forrester St. Pct. WS2: Wals 1A 48
Forster St. B7: Birm 6A 102
B67: Smeth 2C 98
Forsythia Cl. B31: N'fld 5D 130
Forsythia Gro. WV8: Bilb 4G 13
Fort Cen., The 5F 87
Fort Cres. WS9: Wals W 4C 22
Fort Dunlop 6B 86
Forth Dr. B37: F'bri 5D 106
Forth Gro. B38: K Nor 1A 160
Forth Way B62: B'hth 3E 113
Fort Ind. Est., The B35: Cas V 6C 86
Fortnum Cl. B33: Kitts G 1H 121
Forton Cl. WV6: Tett 1H 41
Fort Parkway B24: Erd 1H 103
B35: Cas V 6C 86
Fort Shop. Pk., The B24: Erd 6H 85
Forum B40: Nat E C 2G 139
Forward Rd. B26: Birm A 2C 138
Fosbrooke Rd. B10: Small H 3G 119
Fosseway Dr. B23: Erd 5E 69
Fossil Dr. B45: Redn 2G 157
Foster Av. WV14: Cose 4D 60
Foster Gdns. B18: Hock 3B 100
Foster Grn. WV6: Pert 6E 25
Foster Pl. DY8: Woll 5C 108
Foster Rd. WV10: Bush 3A 28
Foster St. DY8: Stourb 6E 109
WS3: Blox 1B 32
WS10: Darl 4D 46
Foster St. E. DY8: Stourb 6E 109
Foster Way B5: Edg 6E 117
(not continuous)
Fotherley Brook Rd.
WS9: A'rdge 4H 35
Foundry La. B66: Smeth 2G 99
WS3: Pels 4C 20
Foundry Rd. B18: Win G 4H 99
DY6: W Hth 1H 91
Foundry St. DY4: Tip 5G 61
DY6: W Hth 1A 92
WV14: Bils 1A 62
WV14: Cose 4E 61
Fountain Arc. DY1: Dud 6E 77
Fountain Cl. B31: Longb 3C 158
Fountain Ct. B4: Birm 2E 5
Fountain Ho. B63: Hale 2B 128
Fountain La. B69: O'bry 6F 79
DY4: Tip 5F 61
WV14: Cose 5F 61
Fountain Rd. B17: Edg 2F 115
Fountains Rd. WS3: Blox 5E 19
Fountains Way WS3: Blox 5E 19
Four Acres B32: Quin 1A 130
Four Ashes Rd. B93: Ben H, Dorr 6H 165
Four Crosses Rd. WS4: S'fld 6G 21
Four Dwellings Leisure Cen. 1H 129
Fourlands Av. B72: W Grn 6B 70
Fourlands Rd. B31: N'fld 1C 144
FOUR OAKS
Sutton Coldfield 6G 37
Four Oaks Comn. Rd. B74: Four O 6E 37
Four Oaks Ct. B74: Four O 2H 53
FOUR OAKS PARK 3F 53
Four Oaks Rd. B74: Four O 1G 53
Four Oaks Station (Rail) 3H 53
Four Stones Cl. B91: Sol 6E 151
Four Stones Gro. B5: Bal H 5G 117
Fourth Av. B9: Bord G 1F 119
B29: S Oak 2E 133
WS8: Bwnhls 4C 10
(not continuous)
WV10: Bush 3H 27
Fourways B64: Crad H 2F 111
Four Winds Rd. DY2: Dud 3G 95
Fowey Cl. B76: Walm 6E 71
Fowey Rd. B34: Hodg H 3D 104
Fowgay Dr. B91: Sol 6D 150
Fowler Cl. B66: Smeth 1E 99
WV6: Pert 3E 25
Fowler Rd. B75: S Cold 6E 55
Fowler St. B7: Nech 4B 102
WV2: Wolv 5G 43
Fowlmere Rd. B42: Gt Barr 5D 66
Fox & Goose Shop. Cen. B8: W End 4A 104
Foxbury Dr. B93: Dorr 6C 166
Fox Cl. B75: S Cold 4D 54
FOXCOTE 2C 126
Foxcote Av. B21: Hand 2A 100
Foxcote Cl. B90: Shir 1B 164
Foxcote Dr. B90: Shir 1B 164
Foxcote La. B63: Crad 2D 126
Fox Covert DY8: Stourb 6D 108
Fox Cres. B11: S'hll 1D 134
Foxcroft Cl. WS7: Burn 1C 10
Foxdale Dr. DY5: Brie H 6F 93
Foxdale Gro. B33: Kitts G 1G 121
Foxes Mdw. B30: K Nor 3B 146
B76: Walm 5E 71
Foxes Ridge B64: Crad H 3G 111
Foxes Way CV7: Bal C 3H 169
Foxfield B31: N'fld 3D 144
Foxfield Dr. DY8: Stourb 2E 125
Fox Foot Dr. DY5: Brie H 5G 93
Foxford Cl. B36: Cas B 6H 87
B72: W Grn 6B 70
Foxglove Cl. B27: A Grn 4H 135
WS3: Pels 2E 21
WV11: Wed 4G 29
Foxglove Cres. B37: K'hrst 6A 106
Foxglove Rd. DY1: Dud 3B 76
Foxglove Way B21: Hand 2H 99
B23: Erd 6B 68
Fox Grn. Cres. B27: A Grn 4G 135
Fox Gro. B27: A Grn 3G 135
Fox Hill B29: S Oak 5G 131
Fox Hill Cl. B29: S Oak 5G 131
Fox Hill Rd. B75: R'ley 1C 54
(not continuous)
Foxhills Pk. DY2: Neth 5E 95
Foxhills Rd. DY8: Word 2B 108
WV4: Penn 2A 58
Foxhollies Dr. B63: Hale 1G 127
Fox Hollies Leisure Cen. 4G 135
Fox Hollies Rd. B28: Hall G 6F 135
B76: Walm 5D 70
(not continuous)
Fox Hollow WV6: Tett 1A 42
Fox Hollow Cl. B45: Redn 2A 158
Foxhope Cl. B38: K Nor 5E 147
Foxhunt Rd. B63: Hale 3G 127
Foxland Av. B45: Redn 2A 158
WS6: Gt Wyr 2G 7
Foxland Cl. B37: Chel W 1F 123
B90: Ches G 5B 164
Foxlands Av. WV4: Penn 2B 58
Foxlands Cres. WV4: Penn 2A 58
Foxlands Dr. B72: W Grn 6B 70
DY3: Up Gor 2H 75
WV4: Penn 2A 58
Foxlea Rd. B63: Hale 4F 127
Foxley Dr. B91: Cath B 2D 152
Foxmeadow Cl. DY3: Sed 6A 60
Fox Mill Est. B11: S'hll 2D 134
Foxoak Ent. Cen. *B64: Crad H* *2F 111*
(off Foxoak St.)
Foxoak St. B64: Crad H 2E 111
Fox's La. WV1: Wolv 5G 27
Fox St. B5: Birm 6H 101 (3G 5)
DY1: Dud 1E 77
Foxton Rd. B8: Salt 4F 103
Fox Wlk. WS9: Wals W 4D 22
Foxwell Gro. B9: Bord G 6A 104
Foxwell Rd. B9: Bord G 6H 103
Foxwood Av. B43: Gt Barr 3D 66
Foxwood Gro. B37: K'hrst 4B 106
Foxyards Rd. DY4: Tip 2F 77
Foyle Rd. B38: K Nor 6A 146
Fozdar Cres. WV14: Cose 4D 60
Fradley Cl. B30: K Nor 3H 145
Framefield Dr. B91: Sol 1A 152
Framlingham Gro. WV6: Pert 6G 25
Frampton Cl. B30: B'vlle 6H 131
B37: Chel W 6F 107
Frampton Way B43: Gt Barr 1F 67
Frances Dr. WS3: Blox 5H 19
Frances Rd. B19: Loz 1E 101
B23: Erd 4D 84
B30: K Nor 2C 146
Franchise Gdns. WS10: W'bry 6F 47
Franchise St. B42: P Barr 5G 83
WS10: W'bry 6E 47
Francis Cl. B74: S'tly 3H 51
DY6: K'wfrd 1B 92
Francis Rd. B16: Edg 2C 116
B25: Yard 5G 119
B27: A Grn 6B 120
B33: Stech 1B 120
B67: Smeth 4B 98
DY8: Woll 6A 108
Francis Sharp Ho. WS3: Blox 5G 19
Francis St. B7: Birm 5A 102
B70: W Brom 6B 80
WV1: Wolv 5G 27
Francis Wlk. B31: Longb 2E 159
Francis Ward Cl.
B71: W Brom 5G 63
Frankburn Rd. B74: S'tly 3G 51
Frankfort St. B19: Hock 3F 101
Frankholmes Dr. B90: M'path 3D 164
FRANKLEY 2H 143
Frankley Av. B62: Quin 6F 113
FRANKLEY BEECHES 3G 143
Frankley Beeches Rd.
B31: Longb, N'fld 5A 144
Frankley Community Leisure Cen. 6F 143
FRANKLEY GREEN 2G 143
Frankley Grn. B32: Fran 2D 142
Frankley Grn. La. B32: Fran 2E 143
FRANKLEY HILL 4F 143
Frankley Hill La. B32: Fran 4F 143
Frankley Hill Rd. B45: Fran 4F 143
Frankley Ind. Pk. B45: Fran 5H 143
Frankley La. B31: N'fld 1B 144
B32: Bart G, N'fld 1A 144
Frankley Lodge Rd. B31: Fran 3B 144
Frankley Rd. B68: O'bry 3H 113
Frankley Ter. B17: Harb 6F 115
Franklin Rd. B30: B'vlle 2A 146
Franklin St. B18: Win G 4A 100
Franklin Way B30: B'vlle 1B 146
Franklyn Cl. WV6: Pert 4E 25
Frank Rd. B67: Smeth 3C 98
Frank St. B12: Birm 4H 117
Franks Way B33: Stech 1C 120
Frank Tommey Cl. B65: B'hth 2C 112
Frankton Cl. B92: Sol 3F 137
Frankton Gro. B9: Bord G 1H 119
Fraser Rd. B11: S'brk 6D 118
Fraser St. WV14: Bils 6G 45
(not continuous)
Frayne Av. DY6: K'wfrd 2A 92
Freasley Cl. B90: Shir 5B 150
Freasley Rd. B34: S End 4H 105
Freda Ri. B69: Tiv 1D 96
Freda Rd. B70: W Brom 6B 80
Freda's Gro. B17: Harb 6E 115
Frederick Rd. B6: Aston 1G 101
B11: S'hll 1C 134
B15: Edg 3D 116
B23: Erd 5D 84
B29: S Oak 3H 131
B33: Stech 6B 104
B68: O'bry 4B 114
B73: W Grn 3G 69
WV11: Wed 4E 29
Fredericks Cl. DY8: Stourb 1C 124
Frederick St. B1: Birm 5E 101 (1A 4)
B70: W Brom 3A 80
WS2: Wals 1B 48
WV2: Wolv 3G 43 (6B 170)

A-Z Birmingham Deluxe 191

Frederick William St. WV13: W'hall 1B 46
Fred Smith Cl. WS10: W'bry 6H 47
Freeland Gro. DY6: K'wfrd 5D 92
Freeman Dr. B76: Walm 1D 70
Freeman Pl. WV14: Bils 3G 45
Freeman Rd. B7: Nech 3B 102
WS10: W'bry 2A 64
Freeman St. B5: Birm 1G 117 (4F 5)
WV10: Wolv 1B 44
Freemount Sq. B43: Gt Barr 6A 66
Free Port B26: Birm A 2B 138
Freer Rd. B6: Aston 1F 101
Freer St. WS1: Wals 1C 48
Freeth Rd. WS8: Bwnhls 4C 10
Freeth St. B16: Birm 1B 116
B69: O'bry 1F 97
Freezeland St. WV14: Bils 5D 44
Fremont Dr. DY1: Dud 4A 76
French Rd. DY2: Dud 6G 77
French Walls B66: Smeth 4G 99
Frensham Cl. B37: Chel W 1E 123
WS6: C Hay 1E 7
Frensham Way B17: Harb 5G 115
Frenshaw Gro. B44: Gt Barr 5H 67
Freshwater Dr. DY5: Brie H 3F 109
Friardale Cl. WS10: W'bry 2B 64
FRIAR PARK 3A 64
Friar Pk. Farm WS10: W'bry 1B 64
Friar Pk. Rd. WS10: W'bry 2A 64
Friars Cl. DY8: Word 6A 92
Friars Gorse DY7: Stourt 4A 108
Friar St. WS10: W'bry 2H 63
Friars Wlk. B37: Chel W 1F 123
Friary Av. B90: M'path 3E 165
Friary Cl. B20: Hand 4B 82
Friary Cres. WS4: Rus 3G 33
Friary Dr. B74: Four O 6F 37
Friary Gdns. B21: Hand 5H 81
Friary Rd. B20: Hand 5A 82
Friday La.
B92: Cath B, H Ard 2E 153
Friday Wharf B1: Birm 6A 4
Friesland Dr. WV1: Wolv 6D 28
Friezeland Rd. WS2: Wals 1H 47
Friezland La. WS8: Bwnhls 2B 22
Friezland Way WS8: Bwnhls 2C 22
Frinton Gro. B21: Hand 2G 99
Friston Av. B16: Birm 2D 116
Frobisher Cl. WS6: Gt Wyr 4F 7
Frobisher Way B66: Smeth 2B 98
Frodesley Rd. B26: Sheld 3F 121
Froggatt Rd. WV14: Bils 4F 45
Froggatts Ride B76: Walm 2D 70
Frog Hall Cotts. DY7: I'ley 2A 124
Frog La. CV7: Bal C 4G 169
Frogmill Rd. B45: Fran 6H 143
Frogmoor Ho. B25: Yard 4C 120
Frogmore La. CV8: Fen E 6F 169
Frome Cl. DY3: Lwr G 5H 75
Frome Dr. WV11: Wed 4E 29
Frome Way B14: K Hth 1E 147
Frost St. WV2: E'shll 5C 44
Froxmere Cl. B91: Sol 1F 165
Froyle Cl. WV6: Tett 4A 26
Froysell St. WV13: W'hall 1B 46
Fryer Rd. B31: Longb 2F 159
Fryer's Cl. WS3: Blox 2H 31
Fryer's Rd. WS2: Wals 3G 31
WS3: Blox 3G 31
Fryer St. WV1: Wolv 1H 43 (2C 170)
Fuchsia Dr. WV9: Pend 4D 14
Fugelmere Cl. B17: Harb 4D 114
Fulbrook Gro.
B29: W Cas 5D 130
Fulbrook Rd. DY1: Dud 6C 76
Fulford Dr. B76: Min 2F 87
Fulford Gro. B26: Sheld 5G 121
Fulford Hall La. B90: Tid G 6D 162
Fulford Hall Rd. B94: Earls 6D 162
FULFORD HEATH 6D 162
Fulham Rd. B11: S'hll 6B 118
FULLBROOK 5D 48
Fullbrook Cl. B90: M'path 4E 165
Fullbrook Rd. WS5: Wals 6C 48
Fullelove Rd. WS8: Bwnhls 6C 10
Fuller M. B24: Erd 4F 85
Fullerton Cl. WV8: Pend 6C 14
Fullwood Cres. DY2: Dud 3A 94
Fullwoods End WV14: Cose 4E 61
Fulwell Gro. B44: K'sdng 6A 68
Fulwell M. B37: Mars G 3D 122
Fulwood Av. B62: B'hth 3F 113
Furber Pl. DY6: K'wfrd 3D 92
Furlong, The WS10: W'bry 2F 63
Furlong La. B63: Crad 5E 111
Furlong Mdw. B31: N'fld 5G 145
Furlongs, The
DY8: Stourb 2F 125
WV11: Wed 4D 28
Furlongs Rd. DY3: Sed 1H 75
Furlong Wlk. DY3: Lwr G 3H 75
Furnace Cl. WV5: Wom 2E 73
Furnace Hill B63: Hale 5B 112
Furnace La. B63: Hale 6B 112
Furnace Pde. DY4: Tip 1G 77
Furnace Rd. DY2: Dud 1E 95
Furness Cl. WS3: Blox 4F 19
Furst St. WS8: Bwnhls 5C 10
Furzebank Way WV12: W'hall 5E 31
Furze Way WV5: Wals 3A 50

G

Gables, The B24: Erd 3B 86
DY6: W Hth 1H 91
Gaddesby Rd. B14: K Hth 5H 133
Gadds Dr. B65: Row R 5D 96
Gadsby Av. WV11: Wed 2A 30
Gads Grn. DY2: Neth 4G 95
Gads Grn. Cres. DY2: Dud 3G 95
Gads La. B70: W Brom 5G 79
DY1: Dud 6E 77
Gadwall Cft. B23: Erd 4B 84
Gail Cl. WS9: Wals W 3D 22
Gailey Cft. B44: Gt Barr 2G 67
Gail Pk. WV3: Wolv 4B 42
Gainford Cl. WV8: Pend 6D 14
Gainford Rd. B44: K'sdng 4C 68
Gainsborough Cres. B43: Gt Barr 1F 67
B93: Know 3C 166
Gainsborough Dr. WV6: Pert 5F 25
Gainsborough Hill DY8: Stourb 2D 124
Gainsborough Pl. DY1: Dud 5A 76
Gainsborough Rd. B42: Gt Barr 1D 82
Gainsborough Trad. Est. DY9: Lye 1G 125
Gainsford Dr. B62: Hale 5B 112
Gains La. WS3: Lit W 3A 8
WS11: Lit W 3A 8
Gairloch Rd. WV12: W'hall 6B 18
Gaitskell Ter. B69: Tiv 5D 78
Gaitskell Way B66: Smeth 2D 98
Gala Bingo
Aldridge 3D 34
Bushbury 1H 27
Darlaston 4F 47
Dudley 5F 77
Gala Casino 1F 117 (5D 4)
Great Park 6H 143
Harborne 6G 115
Kings Heath 4G 133
Stockland Green 2D 84
Tower Hill 1D 82
Tyburn 4C 86
Walsall 2B 48
Wednesfield 2H 29
Yardley 5B 120
(off Swan Shop. Cen., The)
Galahad Way WS10: W'bry 3G 63
Gala Leisure Cen. 4A 80
Galbraith Cl. WV14: Cose 5F 61
Galena Way B6: Aston 3G 101
Gale Wlk. B65: Row R 4H 95
Gallagher Ct. *B13: Mose* 3B 134
(off Wake Grn. Pk.)
Gallery, The WV1: Wolv 2G 43 (4B 170)
Gallery Sq. WS2: Wals 1B 48
Galloway Av. B34: Hodg H 3D 104
Galton Cl. B24: Erd 3D 86
DY4: Tip 1C 78
Galton Dr. DY2: Dud 3D 94
Galton Rd. B67: Smeth 1D 114
Galton Twr. B1: Birm 1E 117 (4A 4)
Gamesfield Grn. WV3: Wolv 2D 42
Gammage St. DY2: Dud 1D 94
Gandy Rd. WV12: W'hall 3A 30
Gannah's Farm Cl. B76: Walm 2D 70
GANNOW GREEN 6C 142
Gannow Grn. La. B45: Roms 6C 142
Gannow Mnr. Cres. B45: Fran 5E 143
Gannow Mnr. Gdns. B45: Fran 6F 143
Gannow Rd. B45: Rubery 2E 157
Gannow Shop. Cen. B45: Fran 6E 143
Gannow Wlk. B45: Rubery 2E 157
Ganton Rd. WS3: Blox 3G 19
Ganton Wlk. WV8: Pend 1D 26
Garden Cl. B8: W End 4G 103
B45: Fran 5G 143
B93: Know 3B 166
Garden Cres. WS3: Pels 4D 20
Garden Cft. WS9: A'rdge 2D 34
Gardeners Wlk. B91: Sol 4G 151
Gardeners Way WV5: Wom 3F 73
Garden Gro. B20: Hand 1A 82
Gardens, The B23: Erd 4E 85
B72: W Grn 5H 69
Garden St. WS2: Wals 6C 32
Garden Wlk. DY2: Dud 6E 77
DY3: Gorn 5G 75
(not continuous)
WV14: Bils 5H 45
Garfield Rd. B26: Sheld 3F 121
Garland Cres. B62: B'hth 3E 113
Garlands, The WV11: Wed 2E 29
Garland St. B9: Birm 6C 102
Garland Way B31: N'fld 2F 145
(not continuous)
Garman Cl. B43: Gt Barr 3A 66
Garner Cl. WV14: Cose 2F 61
Garnet Av. B43: Gt Barr 1D 66
Garnet Cl. WS9: Ston 3G 23
Garnet Ct. B92: Olton 4D 136
Garnett Dr. B75: S Cold 5C 54
Garrard Gdns. B73: S Cold 6H 53
Garratt Cl. B68: O'bry 5A 98
Garratt's La. B64: Old H 1H 111
Garratt St. B71: W Brom 2H 79
DY5: Brie H 4A 94
Garret Cl. DY6: K'wfrd 1B 92
GARRETT'S GREEN 3G 121
Garrett's Grn. Ind. Est. B33: Sheld 2G 121
Garretts Grn. La. B26: Sheld 4D 120
Garretts Wlk. B14: K Hth 5G 147
Garrick Cl. DY1: Dud 4B 76
Garrick St. WV1: Wolv 2H 43 (4C 170)
Garrington St. WS10: Darl 4C 46
Garrison Cir. B9: Birm 1A 118
Garrison Ct. *B9: Birm* 1B 118
(off Barwell Rd.)
Garrison La. B9: Birm 1B 118
Garrison St. B9: Birm 1B 118
Garston Way B43: Gt Barr 5H 65
Garth, The B14: Yard W 3D 148
Garway Gro. B25: Yard 5H 119
Garwood Rd. B26: Yard 1D 120
Gas St. B1: Birm 1E 117 (5A 4)
Gatacre St. DY3: Gorn 4H 75
Gatcombe Cl. WV10: Bush 3B 16
Gatcombe Rd. DY1: Dud 5A 76
Gatehouse Fold *DY2: Dud* 6F 77
(off Birmingham St.)
Gatehouse Trad. Est. WS8: Bwnhls 4D 10
Gate La. B73: Bold 3F 69
B93: Dorr 5F 165
B94: H'ley H 5F 165
Gateley Rd. B68: O'bry 4C 114
Gate St. B8: Salt 4D 102
DY3: Sed 6A 60
DY4: Tip 5A 78
Gatis St. WV6: Wolv 5E 27
Gatwick Rd. B35: Cas V 3G 87
Gauden Rd. DY9: W'cte 4H 125
Gavin Way B6: Witt 3H 83
Gaydon Cl. WV6: Pert 4E 25
Gaydon Gro. B29: S Oak 3E 131
Gaydon Pl. B73: S Cold 1H 69
Gaydon Rd. B92: Sol 2H 137
WS9: A'rdge 5C 34
Gayfield Av. DY5: Brie H 2H 109
GAY HILL 2D 160
Gayhill La. B38: Head H 6D 146
Gayhurst Dr. B25: Yard 3C 120
Gayle Gro. B27: A Grn 5A 136
Gayton Rd. B71: W Brom 1B 80
Geach Twr. *B19: Birm* 4F 101
(off Uxbridge St.)
Gedney Cl. B90: Shir 4C 148
Geeson Cl. B35: Cas V 3F 87
Gee St. B19: Hock 3F 101
Gem Ho. B4: Birm 2G 5
Geneva Rd. DY4: Tip 2F 77
Genge Av. WV4: E'shll 1A 60
Genners App. B31: N'fld 5B 130
Genners La. B31: N'fld 6B 130
B32: Bart G 5A 130
Genthorn Cl. WV4: E'shll 1B 60
Gentian B74: Four O 5F 37
Gentian Cl. B31: N'fld 1D 144
Geoffrey Cl. B76: Walm 6F 71
Geoffrey Pl. B11: S'hll 2C 134
Geoffrey Rd. B11: S'hll 2C 134
B90: Shir 4F 149
George Arthur Rd. B8: Salt 5D 102
George Av. B65: Row R 1D 112
George Bird Cl. B66: Smeth 3E 99
George Cl. DY2: Dud 1G 95
George Frederick Rd. B73: S'tly 1A 68
George Henry Rd. DY4: Tip 6E 63
George Rd. B15: Edg 3D 116
B23: Erd 3B 84
B25: Yard 5B 119
B29: S Oak 2A 132
B43: Gt Barr 3B 66
B46: Wat O 4E 89
B63: Hale 1H 127
B68: O'bry 1H 113
B73: New O 4D 68
B91: Sol 4G 151
DY4: Tip 1F 77
WV14: Cose 4F 61
George Rose Gdns. WS10: Darl 5C 46
George St. B3: Birm 6E 101 (3A 4)
B12: Bal H 6G 117
B19: Loz 2D 100
B21: Hand 1G 99
B70: W Brom 5B 80
DY1: Dud 1D 76
DY8: Word 2D 108
WS1: Wals 2C 48
WV2: E'shll 4C 44
WV2: Wolv 2H 43 (5C 170)
WV13: W'hall 5A 30
George St. W. B18: Hock 5C 100
Georgian Gdns. WS10: W'bry 2F 63
Georgina Av. WV14: Cose 2F 61
Geraldine Rd. B25: Yard 4H 119
Gerald Rd. DY8: Woll 4C 108
Geranium Gro. B9: Bord G 6F 103
Geranium Rd. DY2: Dud 1H 95
Gerardsfield Rd. B33: Kitts G 6H 105
Germander Dr. WS5: Wals 2F 65
Gerrard Cl. B19: Loz 2E 101
Gerrard Rd. WV13: W'hall 2G 45
Gerrard St. B19: Loz 2E 101
Gertrude Pl. B18: Hock 4C 100
Gervase Dr. DY1: Dud 4E 77
Geston Rd. DY1: Dud 1B 94
Gibbet La. DY7: Kinv 1A 124
(not continuous)
Gibbins Rd. B29: S Oak 4G 131
Gibbons Gro. WV6: Wolv 5D 26
Gibbons Hill Rd. DY3: Sed 3H 59
Gibbons Ind. Est. DY6: K'wfrd 2E 93
Gibbon's La. DY5: P'ntt 2E 93
Gibbons Rd. B75: Four O 6H 37
WV6: Wolv 5D 26
Gibbs Hill Rd. B31: Longb 2F 159
Gibb Sq. B9: Birm 2A 118 (6H 5)
Gibbs Rd. DY9: Lye 6C 110
Gibbs St. WV6: Wolv 5E 27
Gibb St. B9: Birm 2H 117 (6H 5)
GIB HEATH 3B 100
Gibson Dr. B20: Hand 1D 100
B66: Smeth 3E 99
Gibson Rd. B20: Hand 1D 100
WV6: Pert 6E 25
Gideon Cl. B25: Yard 5B 120
Gideons Cl. DY3: Up Gor 2H 75
Giffard Rd. WV1: Wolv 4D 44
WV10: Bush 4A 16
Gifford Ct. *DY5: Brie H* 1H 109
(off Hill St.)
Giggetty La. WV5: Wom 1E 73
Gigmill Way DY8: Stourb 1C 124
Gilbanks Rd. DY8: Woll 4B 108
Gilberry Cl. B93: Know 4C 166
Gilbert Av. B69: Tiv 2B 96
Gilbert Cl. WV11: Wed 2A 30
Gilbert Ct. *WS4: Wals* 5E 33
(off Lichfield Rd.)
Gilbert Ent. Pk. WV12: W'hall 5B 30
Gilbert La. WV5: Wom 6H 57
Gilbert Rd. B66: Smeth 5F 99
GILBERTSTONE 4C 120
Gilbertstone Av. B26: Yard 6C 120
Gilbert St. DY4: Tip 5H 77
Gilbeys Cl. DY8: Word 2C 108
Gilby Rd. B16: Birm 1C 116
Gilchrist Dr. B15: Edg 3A 116
Gildas Av. B38: K Nor 6C 146
Giles Cl. B33: Stech 6C 104
B92: Sol 6B 138
Giles Cl. Ho. B33: Stech 6C 104
Giles Hill DY8: Stourb 5E 109
Giles Rd. B68: O'bry 4H 97
Gilldown Pl. B15: Edg 4D 116
Gillespie Cft. B6: Aston 2H 101
Gillhurst Rd. B17: Harb 4F 115
Gillies Ct. B33: Stech 6B 104
Gilling Gro. B34: Hodg H 3E 105
Gillingham Cl. WS10: W'bry 6B 48
Gillity Av. WS5: Wals 3F 49
Gillity Cl. WS5: Wals 3F 49
Gillity Ct. WS5: Wals 4H 49
Gilliver Rd. B90: Shir 5H 149
Gillman Cl. B26: Sheld 1H 137
Gillott Cl. B91: Sol 4A 152
Gillott Rd. B16: Edg 2G 115
Gillows Cft. B90: M'path 2E 165
Gillscroft Rd. B33: Kitts G 5E 105
Gill St. B70: W Brom 6A 80
DY2: Neth 5G 95
Gilmorton Cl. B17: Harb 4F 115
B91: Sol 6G 151
Gilpin Cl. B8: W End 2A 104
Gilpin Cres. WS3: Pels 3E 21
Gilpins Cft. WS6: C Hay 4D 6
GILSON 6F 89
Gilson Dr. B46: Col 2F 107
Gilson Rd. B46: Col 6F 89
Gilson St. DY4: Tip 5C 62
Gilson Way B37: K'hrst 4C 106
Gilwell Rd. B34: S End 3A 106
Gimble Wlk. B17: Harb 3E 115
(not continuous)
Gin Cridden DY9: Lye 5A 110
Gipsy Cl. CV7: Bal C 4H 169
Gipsy La. B23: Erd 2A 84
CV7: Bal C 4H 169
WV13: W'hall 2B 46
Girton Ho. B36: Cas B 1B 106
Gisborn Cl. B10: Small H 3B 118
GK Davies Trad. Est. B63: Crad 5C 110
Glade, The B26: Sheld 1H 137
B74: S'tly 2G 51
DY9: Lye 6A 110
WV8: Pend 6C 14
Glades, The WS9: A'rdge 2D 34
Gladeside Cl. WS4: S'fld 1H 33
Gladstone Dr. B69: Tiv 5C 78
DY8: Woll 6B 108
Gladstone Gro. DY6: K'wfrd 1B 92
Gladstone Rd. B11: S'brk 5B 118
B23: Erd 4D 84
B26: Yard 5B 120
B93: Dorr 6H 167
DY8: Woll 5B 108
Gladstone St. B6: Aston 1A 102
B71: W Brom 1A 80
WS2: Wals 5B 32
WS10: Darl 5E 47
Gladys Rd. B25: Yard 4H 119
B67: Smeth 1D 114
Gladys Ter. B67: Smeth 1D 114
Glaisdale Gdns. WV6: Wolv 4E 27
Glaisdale Rd. B28: Hall G 5G 135
Glaisedale Gro. WV13: W'hall 1C 46
Glaisher Dr. WV10: Wolv 3G 27
Glamis Rd. WV12: W'hall 2B 30
Glanville Dr. B75: Four O 5G 37
Glasbury Cft. B38: K Nor 2A 160
Glascote Cl. B90: Shir 3G 149
Glascote Gro. B34: S End 2G 105
Glassford Dr. WV6: Tett 3C 26
Glasshouse Hill DY8: Stourb 2F 125
Glastonbury Cres. WS3: Blox 5E 19
Glastonbury Rd. B14: Yard W 3C 148
B71: W Brom 4B 64
Glastonbury Way WS3: Blox 6E 19
Glaston Dr. B91: Sol 6E 151
Gleads Cft. B62: Quin 2G 129
Gleaston Wlk. WV1: Wolv 3E 45
Gleave Rd. B29: S Oak 4A 132
Glebe Dr. B73: Bold 5F 69
Glebe Farm Rd. B33: Stech 4E 105
Glebe Flds. B76: Curd 1D 88
Glebefields Rd. DY4: Tip 5A 62
Glebeland Cl. B16: Birm 2D 116
Glebe La. DY8: Stourb 1C 124
Glebe Pl. WS10: Darl 5B 46
Glebe Rd. B91: Sol 2H 151
WV13: W'hall 3H 45
Glebe St. WS1: Wals 3C 48
Glebe Way CV7: Bal C 2G 169
Glenavon Rd. B14: K Hth 4H 147
Glen Cl. WS4: Wals 6E 33
Glencoe Rd. B16: Edg 5G 99
Glen Ct. WV3: Wolv 1C 42
WV8: Cod 3G 13
Glencroft Rd. B92: Sol 1H 137
Glendale Cl. B63: Hale 1B 128
WV3: Wolv 3A 42
Glendale Dr. B33: Stech 6D 104
WV5: Wom 1G 73
Glendale Twr. B23: Erd 1H 85
Glendene Cres. B38: K Nor 2G 159
Glendene Dr. B43: Gt Barr 5H 65
Glendevon Cl. B45: Fran 5G 143
Glendon Rd. B23: Erd 1D 84
Glendon Way B93: Dorr 6H 165
Glendower Rd. B42: P Barr 3E 83
WS9: A'rdge 6D 22
Gleneagles Dr. B43: Gt Barr 2A 66
B69: Tiv 2A 96
B75: S Cold 4A 54
Gleneagles Rd. B26: Yard 3E 121
WS3: Blox 4F 19
WV6: Pert 4D 24
Glenelg Dr. DY8: Stourb 3F 125
Glenelg M. WS5: Wals 6H 49
Glenfern Rd. WV14: Cose 5C 60
Glenfield WV8: Pend 5C 14
Glenfield Cl. B76: Walm 2C 70
B91: Sol 1G 165
Glenfield Gro. B29: S Oak 4C 132
Glengarry Cl. B32: Bart G 6H 129
Glengarry Gdns. WV3: Wolv 2D 42
Glenhill Dr. B38: K Nor 1C 160
Glenhurst Cl. WS2: Wals 6D 30
Glenmead Rd. B44: Gt Barr 5F 67
Glenmore Cl. WV3: Wolv 4C 42
Glenmore Dr. B38: K Nor 5H 145
Glen Pk. Rd. DY3: Gorn 5H 75
Glenpark Rd. B8: Salt 4E 103

Glen Ri.—Greenhill Ct.

Glen Ri. B13: Mose 1C 148
Glen Rd. DY3: Up Gor 1A 76
DY8: Stourb 2D 124
Glenroyde B38: K Nor 2A 160
Glen Side B32: Bart G 3B 130
Glenside Av. B92: Sol 2G 137
Glenthorne Dr. WS6: C Hay 2E 7
Glenthorne Rd. B24: Erd 5G 85
Glenthorne Way B24: Erd 5G 85
Glentworth B76: Walm 3E 71
Glentworth Gdns. WV6: Wolv 4F 27
Glenville Dr. B23: Erd 2E 85
Glenwood Cl. DY5: Quar B 3H 109
Glenwood Dr. B90: Ches G 5B 164
Glenwood Ri. WS9: Ston 4F 23
Glenwood Rd. B38: K Nor 1H 159
Globe St. WS10: W'bry 4F 63
Gloucester Flats B65: Row R 5E 97
Gloucester Ho. WV1: Wolv 5G 27
Gloucester Pl. WV13: W'hall 1D 46
Gloucester Rd. DY2: Neth 1F 111
WS5: Wals 3F 49
WS10: W'bry 2A 64
Gloucester St. B5: Birm 2G 117 (6E 5)
WV6: Wolv 5F 27
Gloucester Way B37: Mars G 2C 122
Glover Cl. B28: Hall G 1F 149
Glover Rd. B75: S Cold 6D 54
Glovers Cft. B37: F'bri 6B 106
Glovers Fld. Dr. B7: Nech 2C 102
Glover's Rd. B10: Small H 3C 118
Glover St. B9: Birm 1A 118
B70: W Brom 6B 80
Glovers Trust Homes B73: Bold 5F 69
Glyme Dr. WV6: Tett 4C 26
Glyn Av. WV14: Bils 2B 62
Glyn Dr. WV14: Bils 2B 62
Glyne Ct. B73: S Cold 6H 53
Glyn Farm Rd. B32: Quin 6A 114
Glynn Cres. B63: Crad 4D 110
Glynne Av. DY6: K'wfrd 5B 92
Glyn Rd. B32: Quin 5B 114
Glynside Av. B32: Quin 5B 114
Godrich Ho. B13: Mose 2A 134
Goffs Cl. B32: Bart G 2D 130
Goldborough Cl. WV14: Cose 2F 61
Gold Crest Cl. DY2: Neth 1F 111
Goldcrest Cft. B36: Cas B 1C 106
Goldencrest Dr. B69: O'bry 1E 97
Golden Cft. B20: Hand 6B 82
Goldencross Way DY5: Brie H 2F 109
GOLDEN END 3F 167
Golden End Dr. B93: Know 3F 167
Golden Hillock Rd. B10: Small H 4D 118
B11: S'brk 6D 118
DY2: Neth 6E 95
Goldfinch Cl. B30: B'vlle 5H 131
Goldfinch Rd. DY9: W'cte 2G 125
Goldicroft Rd. WS10: W'bry 1G 63
Goldieslie Cl. B73: W Grn 3H 69
Goldieslie Rd. B73: W Grn 3H 69
Golding St. DY2: Neth 3E 95
GOLDS GREEN 6E 63
Golds Hill Gdns. B21: Hand 2B 100
Golds Hill Rd. B21: Hand 1B 100
Golds Hill Way DY4: Tip 6D 62
Goldsmith Rd. B14: K Hth 5H 133
WS3: Blox 2C 32
Goldstar Way B33: Kitts G 1G 121
Goldthorn Av. WV4: Penn 5F 43
Goldthorn Cres. WV4: Penn 5E 43
Goldthorne Av. B26: Sheld 1G 137
GOLDTHORN HILL 6F 43
Goldthorn Hill WV2: Penn 5E 43
Goldthorn Hill Rd. WV2: Penn 5F 43
GOLDTHORN PARK 1G 59
Goldthorn Rd. WV2: Wolv 5F 43
Goldthorn Ter. WV2: Wolv 4F 43
Goldthorn Wlk. DY5: Brie H 3H 109
Golf Club Dr. WS1: Wals 5E 49
Golf La. WV14: Bils 4F 45
Golson Cl. B75: S Cold 5D 54
Gomeldon Av. B14: K Hth 4H 147
Gomer St. WV13: W'hall 1A 46
Gomer St. W. WV13: W'hall 1A 46
Gonville Ho. B36: Cas B 1B 106
Gooch Cl. DY8: Amb 5E 109
Gooch St. B5: Birm 3G 117
Gooch St. Nth. B5: Birm 2G 117
Goodall Gro. B43: Gt Barr 6G 51
Goodall St. WS1: Wals 2D 48
Goodby Rd. B13: Mose 2F 133
Goode Av. B18: Hock 4C 100
Goode Cl. B68: O'bry 5A 98
Goodeve Wlk. B75: S Cold 6F 55
Goodison Gdns. B24: Erd 2H 85
Goodleigh Av. B31: Longb 3C 158
Goodman Cl. B28: Hall G 1F 149
Goodman St. B1: Birm 6D 100
Goodrest Av. B62: Quin 6F 113
Goodrest Cft. B14: Yard W 3C 148
Goodrest La. B38: Head H 3B 160
(not continuous)
Goodrich Av. WV6: Pert 6G 25
Goodrich Covert B14: K Hth 5E 147
Goodrick Way B7: Nech 3B 102
Goodway Ho. *B4: Birm* *1E 5*
(off Shadwell St.)
Goodway Rd. B44: Gt Barr 5G 67
B92: Sol 2A 138
Goodwood Cl. B36: Hodg H 1B 104
Goodwood Dr. B74: S'tly 4H 51
Goodwyn Av. B68: O'bry 4B 114
Goodyear Av. WV10: Bush 1A 28
Goodyear Rd. B67: Smeth 1B 114
Goosemoor La. B23: Erd 6E 69
Gopsal St. B4: Birm 6A 102 (2H 5)
Gorcott La. B90: Dic H 4G 163
Gordon Av. B19: Loz 2F 101
B71: W Brom 5A 64
WV4: E'shll 2B 60
Gordon Cl. B69: Tiv 5D 78
Gordon Ct. B33: Stech 6B 104
Gordon Cres. DY5: Brie H 4A 94
Gordon Dr. DY4: Tip 1C 78
Gordon Pl. WV14: Bils 6E 45
Gordon Rd. B17: Harb 5H 115
B19: Loz 1E 101
Gordon St. *B9: Birm* *1B 118*
(off Garrison La.)
WS10: Darl 5D 46
WV2: Wolv 3H 43 (6D 170)
Gorey Cl. WV12: W'hall 1B 30
Gorge Rd. DY3: Sed 5A 60
WV14: Cose 5A 60
Gorleston Gro. B14: K Hth 5B 148
Gorleston Rd. B14: K Hth 5B 148
GORNALWOOD 4G 75
Gornal Wood Crematorium DY3: Gorn 5G 75
Gorsebrook Rd. WV6: Wolv 4F 27
WV10: Wolv 4G 27
Gorse Cl. B29: W Cas 5E 131
B37: F'bri 1B 122
Gorse Farm Rd. B43: Gt Barr 5A 66
Gorse Farm Wood Nature Reserve 5B 66
Gorsefield Rd. B34: S End 4G 105
Gorse La. WV5: Try 1A 72
Gorsemoor Way WV11: Ess 4B 18
Gorse Rd. DY1: Dud 3C 76
WV11: Wed 1A 30
Gorsey La. B46: Col 5G 89
B47: Wyt 5A 162
WS3: Lit W 3B 8
WS6: Gt Wyr 4F 7
Gorsey Way B46: Col 5G 89
WS9: A'rdge 4A 34
Gorsly Piece B32: Quin 1A 130
Gorstie Cft. B43: Gt Barr 5A 66
Gorsty Av. DY5: Brie H 6G 93
Gorsty Cl. B71: W Brom 5D 64
Gorsty Hayes WV8: Cod 4F 13
Gorsty Hill Rd. B65: B'hth 3B 112
Gorsymead Gro. B31: Longb 5A 144
Gorsy Rd. B32: Quin 1B 130
Gorton Cft. CV7: Bal C 2H 169
Gorway Cl. WS1: Wals 4D 48
Gorway Gdns. WS1: Wals 4E 49
Gorway Rd. WS1: Wals 4D 48
GOSCOTE 5C 20
Goscote Cl. WS3: Wals 2D 32
Goscote Ind. Est. WS3: Blox 6C 20
Goscote La. WS3: Blox, Wals 6C 20
Goscote Lodge Cres. WS3: Wals 2E 33
Goscote Pl. WS3: Wals 2E 33
Goscote Rd. WS3: Pels 6D 20
Gosford St. B12: Bal H 5H 117
Gosford Wlk. B92: Olton 4F 137
Gosmoor Ho. B26: Yard 4C 120
Gospel End Rd. DY3: Sed 5E 59
Gospel End St. DY3: Sed 6H 59
GOSPEL END VILLAGE 5E 59
Gospel Farm Rd. B27: A Grn 5H 135
Gospel La. B27: A Grn 6A 136
Gospel Oak Rd. DY4: Tip 4B 62
Gosport Cl. WV1: Wolv 4D 44
Goss, The DY5: Brie H 2H 109
Goss Cft. B29: S Oak 4H 131
Gossey La. B33: Kitts G 1G 121
Gosta Grn. B4: Birm 5H 101 (1G 5)
Gotham Rd. B26: Yard 5C 120
GOTHERSLEY 6E 91
Gothersley La. DY7: Stourt 6D 90
Goths Cl. B65: Row R 5C 96
Gough Av. WV11: Wed 1D 28
Gough Rd. B11: S'brk 6D 118
B15: Edg 4E 117
WV14: Cose 4E 61
Gough St. B1: Birm 2F 117 (6C 4)
WV1: Wolv 1A 44
WV13: W'hall 6C 30
Gould Firm La. WS9: A'rdge 3G 35
Gowan Rd. B8: Salt 5E 103
Gower Av. DY6: K'wfrd 5D 92
Gower Ho. *B62: Quin* *5F 113*
(off Lockington Cft.)
Gower Rd. B62: Quin 5E 113
DY3: Sed 5F 59
Gower St. B19: Loz 2F 101
WS2: Wals 4H 47
WV2: Wolv 3A 44
(not continuous)
WV13: W'hall 1A 46
Gozzard St. WV14: Bils 6G 45
Gracechurch Cen. B72: S Cold 6H 53
Gracemere Cres. B28: Hall G 4E 149
Grace Rd. B11: S'brk 4C 118
B69: Tiv 1C 96
DY4: Tip 6A 62
Gracewell Homes B13: Mose 4D 134
Gracewell Rd. B13: Mose 4D 134
Grafton Ct. WV6: Wolv 5D 26
Grafton Dr. WV13: W'hall 3F 45
Grafton Gdns. DY3: Lwr G 4F 75
Grafton Gro. B19: Loz 2E 101
Grafton Pl. WV14: Bils 4G 45
Grafton Rd. B11: S'brk 4B 118
B21: Hand 6H 81
B68: O'bry 2F 113
B71: W Brom 3B 80
B90: Shir 5C 148
Graham Cl. DY4: Tip 4B 62
Graham Cres. B45: Rubery 2G 157
Graham Rd. B8: Salt 6F 103
B25: Yard 5A 120
B62: B'hth 3C 112
B71: W Brom 3B 80
DY8: Word 5B 92
Graham St. B1: Birm 6E 101 (2A 4)
B19: Loz 2E 101
Grainger Cl. DY4: Tip 1D 78
Graingers La. B64: Crad H 3E 111
Grainger St. DY2: Dud 2F 95
Graiseley Ct. WV3: Wolv 2G 43 (5A 170)
Graiseley Hill WV2: Wolv 3G 43 (6A 170)
Graiseley La. WV11: Wed 4D 28
Graiseley Recreation Cen. 3G 43
Graiseley Row WV2: Wolv 3G 43 (6A 170)
Graiseley St. WV3: Wolv 2F 43 (5A 170)
Graith Cl. B28: Hall G 4E 149
Grammar School La. B63: Hale 1A 128
Grampian Rd. DY8: Amb 5E 109
Granada Ind. Est. B69: O'bry 2F 97
Granary, The WS9: A'rdge 2D 34
Granary Cl. DY6: W Hth 1G 91
Granary La. B76: Walm 2D 70
Granary Rd. WV8: Pend 6C 14
Granbourne Rd. WS2: Wals 5D 30
Granby Av. B33: Sheld 2G 121
Granby Bus. Pk. B33: Sheld 2H 121
Granby Cl. B92: Olton 6C 136
Grandborough Dr. B91: Sol 6E 151
Grand Cl. B66: Smeth 6F 99
Grand Junc. Way WS1: Wals 5B 48
Grand Theatre 1H 43 (3C 170)
Grandys Cft. B37: F'bri 6B 106
Grange, The B62: Quin 5F 113
WV5: Wom 6G 57
Grange Av. B75: Four O 6A 38
WS9: A'rdge 5C 22
Grange Ct. DY1: Dud 6C 76
DY9: Lye 2G 125
WS2: Wals 1D 46
WV3: Wolv 2F 43
Grange Cres. B45: Rubery 1E 157
B63: Hale 2B 128
WS4: S'fld 1F 33
GRANGE ESTATE 1G 125
Grange Farm Dr. B38: K Nor 6H 145
Grangefield Cl. WV8: Pend 6D 14
Grange Hill B62: Hale 3C 128
Grange Hill Rd. B38: K Nor 6A 146
Grange La. B75: R'ley 6A 38
DY6: K'wfrd 5D 92
DY9: Lye 2G 125
Grange Ri. B38: K Nor 2B 160
Grange Rd. B6: Aston 1G 101
B10: Small H 2D 118
B14: K Hth 5F 133
B24: Erd 2H 85
B29: S Oak 2B 132
B63: Hale 2B 128
B64: Old H 2A 112
B66: Smeth 6E 99
B70: W Brom 4H 79
B91: Sol 6C 136
B93: Dorr 6F 167
CV7: Bal C 2F 169
DY1: Dud 6D 76
DY9: Lye 1G 125
WV2: Wolv 5F 43
WV6: Tett 4A 26
WV14: Cose 6D 60
Grange St. DY1: Dud 6D 76
WS1: Wals 4D 48
Grangewood B73: Bold 6G 69
Grangewood Ct. B92: Olton 6C 136
Granmore Ho. B90: Shir 6C 150
Granshaw Cl. B38: K Nor 6B 146
Grant Cl. B71: W Brom 2A 80
DY6: K'wfrd 1B 92
Grant Ct. B30: K Nor 2C 146
Grantham Rd. B11: S'brk 4B 118
B66: Smeth 6F 99
Grantley Cres. DY6: K'wfrd 3A 92
Grantley Dr. B37: F'bri 6D 106
Granton Cl. B14: K Hth 2F 147
Granton Rd. B14: K Hth 2F 147
Grantown Gro. WS3: Blox 3G 19
Grant St. B15: Birm 3F 117
WS3: Blox 1H 31
Granville Cl. WV2: Wolv 3H 43 (6D 170)
Granville Dr. DY6: K'wfrd 4D 92
Granville Rd. B64: Old H 3B 112
B93: Dorr 6H 167
Granville Sq. B15: Birm 2E 117 (6A 4)
Granville St. B1: Birm 2E 117 (6A 4)
WV2: Wolv 3H 43 (6D 170)
WV13: W'hall 6A 30
Grasdene Gro. B17: Harb 1G 131
Grasmere Av. B74: Lit A 1A 52
WV6: Pert 6F 25
Grasmere Cl. B43: Gt Barr 6B 66
DY6: K'wfrd 2H 91
WV6: Tett 1C 26
WV11: Wed 2E 29
Grasmere Ho. B69: O'bry 5D 96
Grasmere Rd. B21: Hand 2B 100
Grassington Dr. B37: F'bri 2B 122
Grassmere Ct. WS6: C Hay 2D 6
Grassmere Dr. DY8: Stourb 1D 124
Grassmoor Rd. B38: K Nor 5A 146
Grassy La. WV11: Wed 6D 16
Graston Cl. B16: Birm 1C 116
Gratham Cl. DY5: Brie H 4F 109
Grattidge Rd. B27: A Grn 3B 136
Gravel Bank B32: Bart G 2B 130
Gravel Hill WV5: Wom 1H 73
GRAVELLY HILL 5E 85
Gravelly Hill B23: Erd 6D 84
Gravelly Hill Nth. B23: Erd 5E 85
Gravelly Hill Station (Rail) 5E 85
Gravelly Ind. Pk. B24: Erd 1E 103
(Jarvis Way)
B24: Erd 1F 103
(Thompson Dr.)
Gravelly La. B23: Erd 2F 85
WS9: Ston 5G 23
Graydon Ct. B74: S Cold 4H 53
Grayfield Av. B13: Mose 2A 134
Grayland Cl. B27: A Grn 3H 135
Grayling Cl. WS10: Mox 2B 62
Grayling Rd. DY9: Lye 5G 109
Grayling Wlk. B37: Chel W 6E 107
WV10: Wolv 5D 28
Grayshott Cl. B23: Erd 2E 85
Grays Rd. B17: Harb 5H 115
Gray St. B9: Birm 1B 118
Grayswood Pk. Rd. B32: Quin 5A 114
Grayswood Rd. B31: Longb 2D 158
Grazebrook Cft. B32: Bart G 5B 130
Grazebrook Ind. Pk. DY2: Dud 3D 94
Grazebrook Rd. DY2: Dud 2E 95
Grazewood Cl. WV12: W'hall 1B 30
Greadier St. WV12: W'hall 4C 30
Gt. Arthur St. B66: Smeth 2D 98
GREAT BARR 1A 66
Great Barr Leisure Cen. 4F 67
Gt. Barr St. B9: Birm 1A 118
Gt. Brickkiln St. WV3: Wolv 2E 43
GREAT BRIDGE 1E 79
Great Bri. DY4: Tip 2D 78
Gt. Bridge Ind. Est. DY4: Tip 6C 62
Gt. Bridge Rd. WV14: Bils 1A 62
Gt. Bridge St. B70: W Brom 2E 79
Gt. Bridge W. Ind. Cen.
DY4: Tip 1D 78
Gt. Brook St. B7: Birm 5A 102 (1H 5)
Gt. Charles St. WS8: Bwnhls 5B 10
Gt. Charles St. Queensway
B3: Birm 6F 101 (3C 4)
Gt. Colmore St. B15: Birm 3F 117
Gt. Cornbow B63: Hale 2B 128
Great Cft. Ho. *WS10: Darl* *5D 46*
(off Lawrence Way)
Gt. Farley Dr. B31: Longb 6A 144
Gt. Francis St. B7: Birm 5B 102
Gt. Hampton Row B19: Birm 5E 101
Gt. Hampton St. B18: Birm 4E 101
WV1: Wolv 6F 27
(not continuous)
Great Hill DY1: Dud 6D 76
Gt. King St. B19: Birm 4E 101
(not continuous)
Gt. King St. Nth. B19: Hock 3E 101
Gt. Lister St. B7: Birm 5H 101
Great Mdw. DY4: Tip 2B 78
Gt. Moor Rd. WV6: Patt 1A 40
Great Oaks B26: Sheld 6F 121
Greatorex Ct. B71: W Brom 5H 63
GREAT PARK 6H 143
Gt. Stone Rd. B31: N'fld 4E 145
Gt. Tindal St. B16: Birm 1C 116
Gt. Western Arc. B2: Birm 6G 101 (3E 5)
Gt. Western Cl. B18: Win G 3A 100
Gt. Western Dr. B64: Old H 2A 112
Gt. Western Ind. Est.
B18: Win G 3A 100
Gt. Western St. WS10: W'bry 3E 63
WV1: Wolv 6H 27 (1C 170)
Gt. Western Way DY4: Tip 1D 78
Gt. Wood Rd. B10: Small H 2C 118
GREAT WYRLEY 2E 7
Greaves, The B76: Min 1B 88
Greaves Av. WS5: Wals 4G 49
Greaves Cl. WS5: Wals 3G 49
Greaves Cres. WV12: W'hall 1C 30
Greaves Rd. DY2: Neth 4F 95
Greaves Sq. B38: K Nor 6D 146
Grebe Cl. B23: Erd 4B 84
Greek Cathedral 3A 4
Green, The B23: Erd 2G 85
B31: Longb 5A 144
B32: Quin 5G 113
B36: Cas B 2F 105
B38: K Nor 5B 146
B68: O'bry 1H 113
B72: W Grn 4B 70
B91: Sol 2H 151
CV7: Mer 4H 141
DY8: Word 1B 108
WS3: Blox 6H 19
(not continuous)
WS9: A'rdge 3D 34
(not continuous)
WS10: Darl 4D 46
WV5: Try 5C 56
Greenacre Dr. WV8: Bilb 5H 13
Greenacre Rd. DY4: Tip 4A 62
Green Acres B27: A Grn 3H 135
DY3: Sed 4F 59
WV5: Wom 2F 73
Greenacres B32: Bart G 4C 130
B76: Walm 5E 71
WV6: Tett 4H 25
Greenacres Av. WV10: Bush 5D 16
Greenacres Cl. WS9: A'rdge 1G 51
Grn. Acres Rd. B38: K Nor 1H 159
Greenaleigh Rd. B14: Yard W 3D 148
Green Av. B28: Hall G 4E 135
Greenaway Cl. B43: Gt Barr 2E 67
Greenaway Ct. *WV10: F'stne* *1E 17*
(off Avenue, The)
Grn. Bank Av. B28: Hall G 4E 135
Greenbank Gdns. DY8: Word 1C 108
Greenbank Rd. CV7: Bal C 3F 169
Grn. Barns La. WS14: Lit H 1H 37
Greenbush Dr. B63: Hale 6A 112
Green Cl. B47: Wyt 6A 162
Green Ct. B24: Erd 5E 85
B28: Hall G 5F 135
Green Cft. B9: Bord G 6G 103
WV14: Bils 5F 45
Greencroft DY6: K'wfrd 5B 92
Green Dr. B32: Bart G 4A 130
WV10: Oxl 2G 27
Greenend Rd. B13: Mose 3H 133
Greenfels Ri. DY2: Dud 1H 95
Greenfield Av. B64: Crad H 2D 110
CV7: Bal C 2G 169
DY8: Stourb 6D 108
Greenfield Cft. WV14: Cose 3F 61
Greenfield Ho. B26: Sheld 5H 121
Greenfield La. WV10: F'hses 2H 15
Greenfield Rd. B17: Harb 6G 115
B43: Gt Barr 6G 65
B67: Smeth 5C 98
Green Flds. WS9: A'rdge 2C 34
Greenfields Rd. DY6: K'wfrd 4B 92
WS4: S'fld 5H 21
WV5: Wom 2G 73
Greenfield Vw. DY3: Sed 6F 59
Greenfinch Rd. B36: Cas B 1C 106
DY9: W'cte 2H 125
Greenford Ho. B23: Erd 1B 84
B70: W Brom *1C 98*
(off Maria St.)
Greenford Rd. B14: K Hth 4B 148
Green Gables B74: S Cold 4H 53
Grn. Gables Dr. B47: H'wd 2A 162
Greenhill WV5: Wom 1H 73
Grn. Hill Av. B14: K Hth 4H 133
Greenhill Cl.
WV12: W'hall 4B 30
Greenhill Ct. WV5: Wom 2H 73

Greenhill Dr.—Halfcot Av.

Greenhill Dr. B29: S Oak 4G 131
Greenhill Gdns. B43: Gt Barr 3A 66
B62: Hale 5D 112
WV5: Wom 2H 73
Greenhill Rd. B13: Mose 4H 133
B21: Hand 5H 81
B62: B'hth 4D 112
B72: W Grn 5H 69
DY3: Up Gor 2A 76
Greenhill Wlk. WS1: Wals 3D 48
Grn. Hill Way B90: Shir 2H 149
Greenhill Way WS9: A'rdge 6D 22
Greenholm Rd. B44: Gt Barr 6G 67
Greening Dr. B15: Edg 4C 116
Greenland Cl. DY6: K'wfrd 1C 92
Greenland Ct. B8: Salt 3E 103
Greenland Ri. B92: Sol 6H 137
Greenland Rd. B29: S Oak 4C 132
Greenlands WV5: Wom 6F 57
Greenlands Rd. B37: Chel W 1D 122
Green La. B9: Small H 2C 118
B21: Hand 1G 99
B32: Quin 5A 114
B36: Cas B 1H 105
B38: K Nor 1A 160
B43: Gt Barr 5H 65
B46: Col 4H 107
(Castle Dr., not continuous)
B46: Col 1D 106
(Collector Rd., not continuous)
B46: Col 5F 107
(Ryeclose Cft.)
B62: B'hth 2D 112
B90: Shir 6E 149
CV7: Bal C 2H 169
DY3: Up Gor 2B 76
DY6: K'wfrd 2B 92
DY9: Lye 6H 109
WS2: Wals 3A 32
WS3: Blox 2A 32
WS3: Pels 3E 21
WS4: S'fld 6G 21
WS7: Hamm 3C 10
WS8: A'rdge 4G 35
WS9: Wals W 6G 21
WV6: Tett 2C 26
Green La. Ind. Est. B9: Bord G 2E 119
GREEN LANES 4E 45
Green Lanes B73: W Grn 6H 69
WV14: Bils 4E 45
Green La. Wlk. B38: K Nor 1B 160
Greenleas Gdns. B63: Hale 2C 128
Green Leigh B23: Erd 5F 69
Greenleighs DY3: Sed 2H 59
Greenly Rd. WV4: Penn, E'shll 6H 43
Grn. Man Entry DY1: Dud 6F 77
Green Mdw. DY9: Pedm 5F 125
WV11: Wed 4G 29
Green Mdw. Cl. WV5: Wom 2E 73
Green Mdw. Rd. B29: W Cas 6D 130
WV12: W'hall 2B 30
Greenoak Cres. B30: Stir 5E 133
WV14: Cose 6C 60
Grn. Oak Rd. WV8: Bilb 5H 13
Green Pk. Av. WV14: Bils 3E 45
Green Pk. Dr. WV14: Bils 3E 45
Green Pk. Rd. B31: N'fld 5C 144
DY2: Dud 1H 95
Greenridge Rd. B20: Hand 2A 82
Green Rd. B13: Mose 4D 134
DY2: Dud 2F 95
Grn. Rock La. WS3: Blox 6B 20
Greenroyde DY9: Pedm 4F 125
Greens, The *WV6: Pert* *6E 25*
(off Edge Hill Dr.)
Greensand WV14: Cose 3F 61
GREENSFORGE 3D 90
Greensforge La. DY7: Stourt 6E 91
Greens Health & Fitness Club 1H 157
Greenside B17: Harb 6G 115
B90: Ches G 5B 164
Greenside Gdns. WS5: Wals 1F 65
Greenside Rd. B24: Erd 2A 86
Greenside Way WS5: Wals 1D 64
Greensill Av. DY4: Tip 5H 61
Greenslade Cft. B31: N'fld 5E 145
Greenslade Rd. B90: Shir 5C 148
DY3: Sed 3F 59
WS5: Wals 4G 49
Greensleeves B74: Four O 2F 53
Greenstead Rd. B13: Mose 4D 134
Green St. B12: Birm 2H 117 (6H 5)
B67: Smeth 4D 98
B69: O'bry 2G 97
B70: W Brom 6C 80
DY8: Stourb 6D 108
WS2: Wals 6A 32
WV14: Cose 5E 61
Greensway WV11: Wed 1D 28
Greenvale B31: N'fld 2D 144
Greenvale Av. B26: Sheld 5H 121
Green Wlk. B17: Harb 4D 114
Greenway B20: Hand 1B 82
DY3: Sed 4A 60
WS9: A'rdge 5D 22
Greenway, The B37: Mars G 5C 122
B73: S'tly 2B 68
Greenway Av. DY8: Word 2C 108
Greenway Dr. B73: S'tly 2B 68
Greenway Gdns. B38: K Nor 2A 160
DY3: Sed 4A 60
Greenway Rd. WV14: Bils 1G 61
Greenways B31: N'fld 5D 130
B63: Crad 6E 111
DY8: Word 2A 108
Greenway St. B9: Bord G 2C 118
Greenway Wlk. B33: Kitts G 2A 122
Green Wickets B14: K Hth 1H 147
Greenwood B25: Yard 3B 120
Greenwood Av. B27: A Grn 3G 135
B65: Row R 6D 96
B68: O'bry 4H 97
Greenwood Cl. B14: K Hth 2G 147
Greenwood Cotts. *DY1: Dud* *2C 76*
(off Maple Grn.)
Greenwood Pk. WS9: A'rdge 5E 23
Greenwood Pl. B44: K'sdng 4B 68
Greenwood Rd. B71: W Brom 5H 63
WS9: A'rdge 5C 22
WV10: Oxl 2F 27
Greenwoods, The DY8: Stourb 6C 108
Greenwood Sq. *B37: Chel W* *1D 122*
(off Chelmsley Wood Shop. Cen.)
Greenwood Way *B37: Chel W* *1D 122*
(off Chelmsley Wood Shop. Cen.)
GREET 6D 118
Greethurst Dr. B13: Mose 3C 134
GREETS GREEN 4F 79
Greets Grn. Ind. Est. B70: W Brom 3F 79
Greets Grn. Rd. B70: W Brom 4F 79
Greetville Cl. B34: Stech 4E 105
Gregg Ct. B12: Bal H 1H 133
Gregory Av. B29: W Cas 5D 130
Gregory Cl. WS10: W'bry 3F 63
Gregory Ct. WV11: Wed 4F 29
Gregory Dr. DY1: Dud 5C 76
Gregory Rd. DY8: Woll 6A 108
Gregston Ind. Est. B69: O'bry 2H 97
Grendon Dr. B73: New O 2D 68
Grendon Gdns. WV3: Penn 5B 42
Grendon Rd. B14: K Hth 4A 148
B92: Olton 5C 136
Grenfell Ct. B72: W Grn 4H 69
Grenfell Dr. B15: Edg 3B 116
Grenfell Rd. WS3: Blox 4B 20
Grenville Cl. WS2: Wals 6D 30
Grenville Dr. B23: Erd 4B 84
B66: Smeth 1B 98
Grenville Pl. B70: W Brom 4E 79
Grenville Rd. B90: Shir 5H 149
DY1: Dud 6A 76
Gresham Rd. B28: Hall G 1F 149
B68: O'bry 3A 98
Gresham Twr. B12: Birm 3H 117
Gresley Cl. B75: Four O 5G 37
Gresley Gro. B23: Erd 5C 84
Gressel La. B33: Kitts G 6G 105
Grestone Av. B20: Hand 3A 82
Greswolde Dr. B24: Erd 3H 85
Greswolde Pk. Rd. B27: A Grn 1H 135
Greswolde Rd. B11: S'hll 2C 134
B91: Sol 1C 150
Greswold Gdns. B34: Stech 4E 105
Greswold St. B71: W Brom 2H 79
Gretton Cres. WS9: A'rdge 4A 34
Gretton Rd. B23: Erd 6D 68
WS9: A'rdge 4B 34
Greville Dr. B15: Edg 5E 117
Grevis Cl. B13: Mose 1H 133
Grevis Rd. B25: Yard 2C 120
Greyfort Cres. B92: Olton 4D 136
Greyfriars Cl. B92: Olton 1B 150
DY1: Dud 4A 76
Greyhound La. DY8: Stourb 3B 124
WV4: Lwr P 6E 41
Greyhurst Cft. B91: Sol 1G 165
Grey Mill Cl. B90: M'path 3D 164
Greystoke Av. B36: Hodg H 2B 104
Greystoke Dr. DY6: K'wfrd 3B 92
Greystone Pas. DY1: Dud 6D 76
Greystone St. DY1: Dud 6E 77
Greytree Cres. B93: Dorr 6A 166
Grice St. B70: W Brom 1A 98
Griffin Cl. B31: N'fld 1F 145
Griffin Gdns. B17: Harb 1H 131
Griffin Ind. Est. B65: Row R 6F 97
Griffin La. B90: Dic H 4G 163
Griffin Rd. B23: Erd 2C 84
Griffin's Brook Cl. B30: B'vlle 6H 131
Griffin's Brook La. B30: B'vlle 1G 145
Griffin St. B70: W Brom 4B 80
DY2: Neth 5E 95
WV1: Wolv 2B 44
Griffiths Dr. WV5: Wom 2G 73
WV11: Wed 1H 29
Griffiths Rd. B71: W Brom 4A 64
DY1: Dud 1C 76
WV12: W'hall 1D 30
Griffiths St. DY4: Tip 2G 77
Grigg Gro. B31: Longb 6C 144
Grimley Rd. B31: N'fld 5H 145
Grimpits La. B38: Head H 2C 160
Grimshaw Rd. B27: A Grn 4G 135
Grimstone St. WV10: Wolv 6H 27 (1D 170)
Grindleford Rd. B42: Gt Barr 6F 67
Gristhorpe Rd. B29: S Oak 4C 132
Grizedale Cl. B45: Fran 5H 143
Grocott Rd. WS10: Mox 1B 62
Grosmont Av. B12: Bal H 5A 118
Grosvenor Av. B20: Hand 5E 83
B74: S'tly 2H 51
Grosvenor Cl. B75: R'ley 2A 54
WV10: Bush 5H 15
Grosvenor Ct. B20: Hand 5E 83
B38: K Nor 5B 146
DY3: Lwr G 5H 75
DY9: Pedm *4F 125*
(off Redlake Rd.)
WV3: Wolv 2G 43 (5A 170)
WV11: Wed 4F 29
Grosvenor Cres. WV10: Bush 5H 15
Grosvenor Ho. B23: Erd 2G 85
Grosvenor Pk. WV4: Penn 6D 42
Grosvenor Rd. B6: Aston 1B 102
B17: Harb 5E 115
B20: Hand 5E 83
B68: O'bry 6G 97
B91: Sol 6D 150
DY3: Lwr G 5H 75
WV4: E'shll 2A 60
WV10: Bush 5H 15
Grosvenor Rd. Sth. DY3: Gorn 5H 75
Grosvenor Shop. Cen. B31: N'fld 3E 145
Grosvenor Sq. B28: Hall G 2F 149
Grosvenor St. B5: Birm 6H 101 (3G 5)
Grosvenor St. W. B16: Birm 2D 116
Grosvenor Ter. B15: Birm 2D 116
Grosvenor Way DY5: Quar B 4A 110
Grotto La. WV6: Tett 4C 26
Groucutt St. WV14: Cose 5E 61
Grounds Dr. B74: Four O 6F 37
Grounds Rd. B74: Four O 6F 37
Grout St. B70: W Brom 3E 79
Grove, The B8: Salt 5C 102
B31: Longb 1F 159
B43: Gt Barr 1A 66
B45: Coft H 5B 158
B46: Col 5H 107
B65: Row R 1C 112
B74: Lit A 4D 36
B92: H Ard 4A 140
DY5: Brie H 3G 109
WS5: Wals 2F 65
WV4: E'shll 6A 44
WV11: Wed 3D 28
Grove Av. B13: Mose 3A 134
B21: Hand 1B 100
B27: A Grn 2H 135
B29: S Oak 4A 132
B63: Hale 2H 127
Grove Av. B91: Sol 2G 151
Grove Cott. Rd. B9: Small H 1D 118
Grove Cotts. WS3: Blox 1H 31
Grove Ct. B42: Gt Barr 1B 82
Grove Cres. B70: W Brom 6C 80
DY5: Brie H 4G 93
WS3: Pels 4D 20
GROVE END 2H 71
Grove Farm Dr. B75: S Cold 6D 54
Grovefield Cres. CV7: Bal C 1H 169
Grove Gdns. B20: Hand 5B 82
Grove Hill WS5: Wals 3A 50
Grove Hill Rd. B21: Hand 6B 82
Groveland Rd. DY4: Tip 4A 78
Grovelands Cres. WV10: F'hses 4H 15
Grove La. B17: Harb 1G 131
B20: Hand 5B 82
B21: Hand 1B 100
B66: Smeth 4G 99
(not continuous)
WS3: Lit W 4C 8
WV6: Tett 1H 41
Groveley La. B31: Longb 3C 158
B45: Coft H 5A 158
Grove M. B31: Longb 1F 159
Grove Pk. DY6: W Hth 1A 92
Grove Rd. B11: S'hll 2C 134
B14: K Hth 6F 133
B68: O'bry 2B 114
B91: Sol 2G 151
B93: Know 5C 166
DY9: W'cte 1B 126
Groveside Way WS3: Pels 2E 21
Grove St. B66: Smeth 5H 99
DY2: Dud 1G 95
WV2: Wolv 3H 43 (6C 170)
WV10: Wolv 6B 28
Grove Ter. WS1: Wals 2D 48
GROVE VALE 4H 65
Grove Va. Av. B43: Gt Barr 4G 65
Grove Vs. B64: Crad H 4F 111
Grove Way B74: S'tly 4H 51
Grovewood Dr. B38: K Nor 6A 146
Guardian Ct. B26: Yard 4D 120
B31: N'fld 4B 144
B91: Sol 4H 151
Guardian Ho. B68: O'bry 4A 114
Guardians Way B31: N'fld 5C 130
Guernsey Dr. B36: Cas B 3D 106
Guest Av. WV11: Wed 1E 29
Guest Gro. B19: Hock 3E 101
Guild Av. WS3: Blox 2B 32
Guild Cl. B16: Birm 1C 116
Guildford Ct. *B29: W Cas* *6G 131*
(off Abdon Av.)
Guildford Cft. B37: Mars G 3B 122
Guildford Dr. B19: Hock 3F 101
Guildford St. B19: Loz 2F 101
Guildhall M., The *WS1: Wals* *2D 48*
(off Goodall St.)
Guillemard Ct. B37: Chel W 2D 122
Guiting Rd. B29: W Cas 6E 131
Gullane Cl. B38: K Nor 6H 145
Gullswood Cl. B14: K Hth 5F 147
Gumbleberrys Cl. B8: W End 5A 104
Gun Barrel Ind. Est. B64: Crad H 5H 111
Gunmakers Wlk. B19: Loz 2F 101
Gunner Gro. B75: S Cold 5E 55
Gunner La. B45: Rubery 2D 156
Gunns Way B92: Olton 6B 136
Guns La. B70: W Brom 3H 79
Gunstock Cl. B74: S'tly 4G 51
GUNSTONE 1G 13
Gunstone La. WV8: Cod, Cod W 2F 13
(not continuous)
GUNS VILLAGE 3H 79
Guns Village Stop (MM) 3H 79
Gunter Rd. B24: Erd 4C 86
Gupta Trad. Est. B69: O'bry 6F 79
Gurnard Cl. WV12: W'hall 6B 18
Gurney Pl. WS2: Wals 4G 31
Gurney Rd. WS2: Wals 4G 31
Guthram Cl. B23: Erd 5E 69
Guthrie Cl. B19: Hock 3F 101
Guthrum Cl. WV6: Pert 4F 25
Guy Av. WV10: Bush 3H 27
Guy's Cliffe Av. B76: Walm 4D 70
Guy's La. DY3: Gorn 5F 75
Guys Motors Ind. Pk. WV10: Wolv 4B 28
Gwalia Gro. B23: Erd 3F 85
Gwendoline Way WS9: Wals W 3D 22
GWS Ind. Est. WS10: W'bry 4D 62
Gypsy La. B46: Wat O 5F 89

H

Habberley Cft. B91: Sol 6F 151
Habberley Rd. B65: Row R 1D 112
Habitat Ct. B24: Erd 2A 86
B76: Walm 2D 70
Hackett Cl. WV14: Cose 4B 60
Hackett Ct. *B69: O'bry* *2G 97*
(off Canal St.)
Hackett Dr. B66: Smeth 2B 98
Hackett Rd. B65: Row R 6E 97
Hackett St. DY4: Tip 6C 62
Hackford Rd. WV4: E'shll 1B 60
Hack St. B9: Birm 2A 118
Hackwood Ho. B69: O'bry 4D 96
Hackwood Rd. WS10: W'bry 3H 63
Hadcroft Grange DY9: W'cte 1H 125
Hadcroft Rd. DY9: Lye 1G 125
Haddock Rd. WV14: Bils 4E 45
Haddon Cres. WV12: W'hall 2C 30
Haddon Cft. B63: Hale 4E 127
Haddon Rd. B42: Gt Barr 6F 67
Haddon Twr. B5: Birm 3F 117
Haden Cir. B7: Birm 5A 102 (1H 5)
Haden Cl. B64: Crad H 4H 111
DY8: Word 1B 108
Haden Ct. *B12: Birm* *4H 117*
(off Belgrave Middleway)
Haden Cres. WV11: Wed 3A 30
Haden Cross Dr. B64: Crad H 4A 112
Hadendale B64: Crad H 4A 112
Haden Hill 3H 111
Haden Hill WV3: Wolv 1E 43
Haden Hill Leisure Cen. 3H 111
Haden Hill Rd. B63: Hale 5A 112
Haden Pk. Rd. B64: Crad H 4G 111
Haden Rd. B64: Old H 1G 111
DY4: Tip 4A 62
Haden St. B12: Bal H 5H 117
Haden Wlk. B65: Row R 6C 96
Haden Way B12: Bal H 5H 117
Hadfield Cl. B24: Erd 4B 86
Hadfield Cft. B19: Birm 4E 101
Hadfield Way B37: F'bri 5C 106
Hadland Rd. B33: Sheld 2F 121
Hadleigh Cft. B76: Walm 1E 87
Hadley Cl. B47: Wyt 4A 162
Hadley Ct. B16: Edg 2H 115
Hadley Cft. B66: Smeth 2E 99
Hadley Pl. WV14: Bils 4E 45
Hadley Rd. WS2: Wals 3F 31
WV14: Bils 4E 45
Hadleys Cl. DY2: Neth 5G 95
Hadley Stadium 6E 99
Hadley St. B68: O'bry 5G 97
Hadley Way WS2: Wals 3F 31
Hadlow Cft. B33: Sheld 4H 121
Hadrian Dr. B46: Col 6H 89
Hadyn Gro. B26: Sheld 5F 121
Hadzor Rd. B68: O'bry 3B 114
Hafren Cl. B45: Fran 5H 143
Hafton Gro. B9: Small H 2D 118
Haggar St. WV2: Wolv 5G 43
HAGLEY 6G 125
Hagley C'way. DY9: Hag 6B 126
Hagley Cl. DY9: Hag 6G 125
Hagley Hall Gdns. DY9: Hag 6H 125
Hagley Hill DY9: Hag 6A 126
Hagley Mall B63: Hale 2B 128
Hagley Pk. Dr. B45: Redn 3G 157
Hagley Rd. B16: Edg 2E 115
B63: Hale 5E 127
DY8: Pedm, Stourb 1E 125
DY9: Pedm 4G 125
Hagley Rd. W. B17: Harb 4A 114
B32: Quin 5G 113
B62: Quin 5G 113
B68: O'bry 5G 113
Hagley St. B63: Hale 2B 128
Hagley Vw. Rd. DY2: Dud 1E 95
Hagley Vs. *B12: Bal H* *1B 134*
(off Taunton Rd.)
B12: S'hll *6B 118*
(off Taunton Rd.)
Hagley Wood La. DY9: Hag 5D 126
Haig Cl. B75: S Cold 4A 54
Haig Pl. B13: Mose 6A 134
Haig Rd. DY2: Dud 6H 77
Haig St. B71: W Brom 2A 80
Hailes Pk. Cl. WV4: Wolv 5A 44
Hailsham Rd. B23: Erd 2F 85
Hailstone Cl. B65: Row R 4A 96
Haines Cl. DY4: Tip 3B 78
Haines St. B70: W Brom 5B 80
Hainfield Dr. B91: Sol 2A 152
Hainge Rd. B69: Tiv 5C 78
Hainult Cl. DY8: Word 5B 92
Halas Ind. Est. B62: Hale 6B 112
Halberton St. B66: Smeth 5H 99
Haldane Ct. B33: Yard 1F 121
Haldon Gro. B31: Longb 2C 158
Halecroft Av. WV11: Wed 4F 29
Hale Gro. B24: Erd 3B 86
Halesbury Ct. *B63: Hale* *3H 127*
(off Ombersley Rd.)
Hales Cres. B67: Smeth 6C 98
Halescroft Sq. B31: N'fld 1C 144
Hales Gdns. B23: Erd 5C 68
Hales La. B67: Smeth 5C 98
Halesmere Way B63: Hale 2C 128
HALESOWEN 2B 128
Halesowen By-Pass B62: Hale 2D 128
B62: Roms, Hale 4H 127
Halesowen Ind. Pk. B62: Hale 5B 112
(Coombs Rd.)
B62: Hale 5C 112
(Hereward Ri.)
Halesowen Leisure Cen. 2B 128
Halesowen Rd. B61: L Ash 6C 156
B62: Quin 5E 113
B64: Crad H 3H 111
B64: Old H 1G 111
B65: B'hth 3C 112
DY2: Neth 4E 95
(Baptist End Rd.)
DY2: Neth 5F 95
(Cradley Rd.)
Halesowen St. B69: O'bry 2F 97
Hales Rd. B63: Hale 2A 128
(Highfield La.)
B63: Hale 1A 128
(Islington)
WS10: W'bry 1G 63
Hales Way B69: O'bry 2F 97
Halesworth Rd. WV9: Pend 6D 14
Hale Trad. Est. DY4: Tip 1B 78
Halewood Gro. B28: Hall G 6G 135
Haley St. WV12: W'hall 4C 30
Halfcot Av. DY9: Pedm 2G 125

Halford Cres.—Havelock Rd.

Halford Cres. WS3: Wals 4D 32
Halford Gro. B24: Erd 3C 86
Halford Rd. B91: Sol 1C 150
Halford's La. B66: Smeth 2E 99
B71: W Brom 1E 99
Halford's La. Ind. Est. B66: Smeth 1E 99
Halfords Pk. B66: Smeth 1E 99
Halfpenny Fld. Wlk. B35: Cas V 5E 87
Halfway Cl. B44: Gt Barr 1G 83
Halifax Ho. B5: Bal H 4F 117
Halifax Rd. B90: Shir 4H 149
Haliscombe Gro. B6: Aston 1G 101
Halkett Glade B33: Stech 6B 104
Halladale B38: K Nor 6B 146
Hallam Cl. B71: W Brom 2C 80
Hallam Ct. B71: W Brom 2B 80
Hallam Cres. WV10: Wolv 3A 28
Hallam Dr. B71: W Brom 2C 80
Hallam St. B12: Bal H 6G 117
B71: W Brom 3B 80
Hallbridge Cl. WS3: Pels 5D 20
Hallbridge Way B69: Tiv 5B 78
Hallchurch Rd. DY2: Dud 2B 94
Hall Cres. B71: W Brom 1A 80
Hallcroft Cl. B72: W Grn 6A 70
Hallcroft Way B93: Know 3C 166
WS9: A'rdge 4E 35
Hall Dale Cl. B28: Hall G 2F 149
Hall Dr. B37: Mars G 4C 122
HALL END
West Bromwich 1B 80
Hall End WS10: W'bry 2F 63
Hallens Dr. WS10: W'bry 2D 62
Hallett Dr. WV3: Wolv 2F 43 (5A 170)
Hallewell Rd. B16: Edg 6H 99
HALL GREEN
Bilston 3G 61
Birmingham 5F 135
West Bromwich 4A 64
Hall Green Little Theatre 3G 135
Hall Grn. Rd. B71: W Brom 4A 64
Hall Green Stadium 4F 135
Hall Green Station (Rail) 4F 135
Hall Grn. St. WV14: Bils 2G 61
Hall Gro. WV14: Cose 5E 61
Hall Hays Rd. B34: S End 2A 106
Hall La. DY2: Neth 3E 95
DY4: Tip 5B 62
DY9: Hag 6H 125
WS3: Pels 4D 20
WS6: Gt Wyr 1F 7
WS7: Hamm 1F 11
WS9: Wals W 3A 22
WS14: Muck C 3H 11
WV14: Cose 4B 60
Hall Mdw. DY9: Hag 6H 125
Hallmeadow Rd. CV7: Bal C 6H 155
Hallmoor Rd. B33: Kitts G 6F 105
Hall of Memory, The 1E 117 (4B 4)
Hallot Cl. B23: Erd 5D 68
Halloughton Rd. B74: S Cold 4G 53
Hall Pk. St. WV2: E'shll 5D 44
Hall Rd. B8: Salt 5D 102
B20: Hand 1C 100
B36: Cas B 1E 105
B67: Smeth 5C 98
Hall Rd. Av. B20: Hand 1C 100
Hallstead Rd. B13: Mose 2B 148
Hall St. B18: Birm 5E 101 (1B 4)
B64: Old H 1H 111
B68: O'bry 4H 97
B70: W Brom 5A 80
DY2: Dud 6F 77
DY3: Sed 5H 59
DY4: Tip 2G 77
DY8: Stourb 2E 125
WS2: Wals 6B 32
WS10: Darl 4B 46
WV11: Wed 4E 29
WV13: W'hall 2B 46
WV14: Bils 6G 45
Hall St. E. WS10: Darl 4C 46
Hall St. Sth. B70: W Brom 1B 98
Hallswelle Gro. B43: Gt Barr 1G 67
Hall Wlk. B46: Col 4G 107
(not continuous)
Halow Cl. B31: N'fld 5H 145
Halsbury Gro. B44: K'sdng 5B 68
Halstead Gro. B91: Sol 1E 165
Halton Rd. B73: New O 2D 68
Halton St. DY2: Neth 4E 95
Hamar Way B37: Mars G 2D 122
Hamberley Ct. B18: Win G 5H 99
Hamble Cl. DY5: P'ntt 3E 93
Hamble Ct. B73: S Cold 6H 53
Hambledon Cl. WV9: Pend 5E 15
Hamble Gro. WV6: Pert 6E 25
Hamble Rd. B42: Gt Barr 4B 66
WV4: Penn 5A 42
Hambleton Rd. B63: Hale 3F 127
Hambletts Rd. B70: W Brom 4G 79
Hambrook Cl. WV6: Wolv 4E 27
Hambury Dr. B14: K Hth 6F 133
Hamilton Av. B17: Harb 3E 115
B62: Hale 2C 128
DY8: Woll 5B 108
Hamilton Cl. DY3: Sed 6G 59
DY8: Word 1A 108
Hamilton Ct. B13: Mose 1H 133
B30: K Nor 3A 146
Hamilton Dr. B29: S Oak 5H 131
B69: Tiv 5C 78
DY8: Word 1A 108
Hamilton Gdns. WV10: Bush 4A 16
Hamilton Ho. B66: Smeth 4G 99
WS3: Blox 6A 20
Hamilton Rd. B21: Hand 1H 99
B67: Smeth 1C 114
DY4: Tip 1C 78
Hamilton St. WS3: Blox 6A 20
Ham La. DY6: K'wfrd 6C 74
DY9: Pedm 4G 125
Hamlet, The WS11: Nort C 1C 8
Hamlet Gdns. B28: Hall G 5F 135
Hamlet Rd. B28: Hall G 5F 135
Hammer Bank DY5: Quar B 3C 110
Hammersley Cl. B63: Crad 4D 110
HAMMERWICH 1F 11
Hammerwich Link WS7: Hamm 2H 11
Hammond Av. WV10: Bush 1A 28
Hammond Dr. B23: Erd 2F 85
Hammond Way DY8: Amb 4E 109
Hampden Cl. DY5: Quar B 3C 110
Hampden Retreat B12: Bal H 5G 117
Hampshire Ct. B29: W Cas 6F 131
Hampshire Dr. B15: Edg 3A 116
Hampshire Rd. B71: W Brom 5G 63
Hampson Cl. B11: S'brk 5B 118
Hampstead Glade B63: Hale 3C 128
Hampton Cl. B73: New O 3C 68
Hampton Ct. B15: Edg 3D 116
(off George Rd.)
B71: W Brom 4A 64
B92: H Ard 1B 154
Hampton Ct. WV10: Bush 5D 16
Hampton Ct. Rd. B17: Harb 5D 114
Hampton Dr. B74: Four O 3H 53
Hampton Gdns. DY9: Pedm 2G 125
Hampton Grange CV7: Mer 4H 141
Hampton Gro. WS3: Pels 3D 20
HAMPTON IN ARDEN 1A 154
Hampton in Arden Station (Rail) 6B 140
Hampton La. B91: Cath B, Sol 3H 151
(not continuous)
CV7: Mer 5E 141
Hampton Pl. WS10: Darl 3C 46
Hampton Rd. B6: Aston 6F 83
B23: Erd 3D 84
B93: Know 2E 167
WV10: Oxl 6F 15
Hamptons, The B93: Know 3E 167
Hampton St. B19: Birm 5F 101 (1C 4)
DY2: Neth 4E 95
WV14: Cose 5D 60
Hampton Vw. WV10: Wolv 5B 28
Hampton Wlk. WV1: Wolv 1G 43 (3B 170)
HAMS HALL 3H 89
Hams Hall Distribution Pk. B46: Col 2H 89
Hams La. B76: Lea M 2G 89
Hams Rd. B8: Salt 5D 102
HAMSTEAD 6B 66
Hamstead Cl. WV11: Wed 3F 29
Hamstead Hall Av. B20: Hand 2A 82
Hamstead Hall Rd. B20: Hand 3A 82
Hamstead Hill B20: Hand 4B 82
Hamstead Ho. B43: Gt Barr 6B 66
Hamstead Ind. Est. B42: P Barr 6D 66
Hamstead Rd. B20: Hand 6D 82
B43: Gt Barr 5G 65
Hamstead Station (Rail) 1B 82
Hamstead Ter. WS10: W'bry 3G 63
Hanam Cl. B75: S Cold 5D 54
Hanbury Cl. B63: Hale 3H 127
Hanbury Ct. DY8: Stourb 1E 125
(off College Rd.)
Hanbury Cres. WV4: Penn 5C 42
Hanbury Cft. B27: A Grn 2C 136
Hanbury Dr. B69: O'bry 5E 97
Hanbury Hill DY8: Stourb 1E 125
Hanbury Pas. DY8: Stourb 6E 109
Hanbury Rd. B70: W Brom 4G 79
B93: Dorr 5B 166
WS8: Bwnhls 3A 10
Hanch Pl. WS1: Wals 3D 48
Hancock Rd. B8: Salt 5F 103
Hancox St. B68: O'bry 1H 113
Handley Gro. B31: Longb 5A 144
Handley St. WS10: W'bry 1G 63
HANDSWORTH 6A 82
Handsworth Booth Street Stop (MM) 2G 99
Handsworth Cl. B21: Hand 2H 99
Handsworth Dr. B43: Gt Barr 2C 66
Handsworth Horticultural Institute 5A 82
(off Oxhill Rd.)
Handsworth Leisure Cen. B20: Hand 6B 82
Handsworth New Rd. B18: Win G 3A 100
HANDSWORTH WOOD 5C 82
Handsworth Wood Rd. B20: Hand 4B 82
Hangar Rd. B26: Birm A 2C 138
Hanging La. B31: N'fld 5C 144
Hangleton Dr. B11: S'brk 5D 118
Hanley Cl. B63: Hale 1G 127
Hanley St. B19: Birm 5F 101 (1E 5)
Hannafore Rd. B16: Edg 6H 99
Hannah Rd. WV14: Bils 2A 62
Hanney Hay Rd. WS7: Chase, Hamm 1C 10
Hannon Rd. B14: K Hth 2G 147
Hanover Cl. B6: Aston 2G 101
Hanover Ct. WS2: Wals 2E 47
WV6: Tett 5A 26
Hanover Dr. B24: Erd 1F 103
Hanover Rd. B65: Row R 5C 96
Hansell Dr. B93: Dorr 6F 167
Hansom Rd. B32: Quin 6A 114
Hanson Gro. B92: Olton 6D 120
Hansons Bri. Rd. B24: Erd 2D 86
Hanwell Cl. B76: Walm 6F 71
Hanwood Cl. B12: Birm 3H 117
Harald Cl. WV6: Pert 4E 25
Harbeck Av. B44: Gt Barr 5H 67
Harbet Dr. B40: Nat E C 1G 139
Harbinger Rd. B38: K Nor 5D 146
HARBORNE 5F 115
Harborne Ct. B17: Harb 1G 131
Harborne Ho. B17: Harb 1E 131
Harborne La. B17: Harb, S Oak 2H 131
B29: S Oak 3A 132
Harborne Pk. Rd. B17: Harb 6G 115
Harborne Pool & Fitness Cen. 6F 115
Harborne Rd. B15: Edg 5A 116
B68: O'bry 2B 114
Harborough Ct. B74: Four O 1G 53
Harborough Dr. B36: Cas B 6H 87
WS9: A'rdge 4C 34
Harborough Wlk. DY9: Pedm 3G 125
Harbours Hill B61: Wild 4A 156
Harbour Ter. WV3: Wolv 2E 43
Harbury Cl. B76: Walm 1F 87
Harbury Rd. B12: Bal H 6F 117
Harby Cl. B37: Mars G 3D 122
Harcourt Dr. B74: Four O 5F 37
DY3: Gorn 5H 75
Harcourt Rd. B23: Erd 1E 85
B64: Crad H 3H 111
WS10: W'bry 1F 63
HARDEN 2C 32
Harden Cl. WS3: Blox 2C 32
Harden Ct. B31: N'fld 6C 144
Harden Gro. WS3: Blox 2C 32
Harden Keep B66: Smeth 5E 99
Harden Mnr. Ct. B63: Hale 2C 128
Harden Rd. WS3: Blox, Wals 2B 32
Harden Va. B63: Hale 6G 111
Harding St. WV14: Cose 3F 61
Hardon Rd. WV4: E'shll 6B 44
Hardware St. B70: W Brom 3B 80
HARDWICK 2G 51
Hardwick Ct. B74: S'tly 1H 51
Hardwick Dr. B62: Hale 4A 112
Hardwick Wlk. B14: K Hth 5F 147
Hardwicke Way DY9: Lye 6H 109
Hardwick Rd. B26: Yard 1C 136
B74: S'tly 1H 51
B92: Olton 1C 136
Hardy Ct. B13: Mose 1H 133
Hardy Rd. WS3: Blox 1C 32
WS10: W'bry 2G 63
Hardy Sq. WV2: E'shll 5B 44
Harebell Cl. WS5: Wals 2E 65
Harebell Cres. DY1: Dud 3C 76
Harebell Gdns. B38: K Nor 1B 160
Harebell Wlk. B37: Chel W 1F 123
Hare Gro. B31: N'fld 4B 144
Haresfield B90: Dic H 4G 163
Hare St. WV14: Bils 6H 45
(not continuous)
Harewell Dr. B75: R'ley 2A 54
Harewood Av. B43: Gt Barr 3G 65
WS10: W'bry 2A 64
Harewood Cl. B28: Hall G 2E 149
Harford St. B19: Birm 5E 101
Hargate La. B70: W Brom 3A 80
B71: W Brom 3A 80
Hargrave Cl. B46: Wat O 4D 88
Hargrave Rd. B90: Shir 5C 148
Hargreave Cl. B76: Walm 6D 70
Hargreaves St. WV1: Wolv 4C 44
Harland Rd. B74: Four O 6G 37
Harlech Cl. B32: Bart G 6G 129
B69: Tiv 6A 78
Harlech Ho. WS3: Blox 3A 32
(off Providence Cl.)
Harlech Rd. WV12: W'hall 3C 30
Harlech Twr. B23: Erd 1G 85
Harlech Way DY1: Dud 5B 76
Harleston Rd. B44: Gt Barr 5H 67
Harley Cl. WS8: Bwnhls 1C 22
Harley Dr. WV14: Bils 1D 60
Harlow Gro. B28: Hall G 1G 149
Harlstones Cl. DY8: Amb 3E 109
Harlyn Cl. WV14: Bils 3A 62
Harman Rd. B72: W Grn 6H 69
Harmon Rd. DY8: Woll 6A 108
Harmony Ho. B10: Small H 2C 118
Harnall Cl. B90: Shir 2C 164
Harness Cl. WS5: Wals 1D 64
Harold Rd. B16: Edg 2B 116
B67: Smeth 6C 98
Harper Av. WV11: Wed 2E 29
Harper Rd. WV14: Bils 5F 45
Harpers Rd. B14: K Hth 6A 148
B31: N'fld 6E 145
Harper St. WV13: W'hall 1A 46
Harpur Cl. WS4: Wals 5E 33
Harpur Rd. WS4: Wals 5E 33
Harrier Rd. B27: A Grn 3B 136
Harrier Way B42: P Barr 4F 83
Harriet Cl. DY5: P'ntt 4F 93
Harringay Dr. DY8: Stourb 2C 124
Harringay Rd. B44: K'sdng 3H 67
Harrington Cft. B71: W Brom 6D 64
Harringworth Ct. WS4: S'fld 1G 33
Harriots Hayes Rd. WV8: Cod W 1A 12
Harris Ct. B18: Hock 3C 100
Harris Dr. B42: Gt Barr 5C 66
B66: Smeth 6F 99
Harrison Cl. WS3: Blox 6A 20
WS6: C Hay 4D 6
Harrison Ct. DY8: Amb 2E 109
Harrison Ho. B14: K Hth 4H 147
Harrison Rd. B24: Erd 3F 85
B74: Four O 4E 37
DY8: Word 2E 109
WS4: S'fld 5G 21
Harrison's Fold DY2: Neth 4E 95
Harrisons Grn. B15: Edg 5A 116
Harrisons Pleck B13: Mose 2H 133
Harrison's Rd. B15: Edg 5A 116
Harrison St. WS3: Blox 6H 19
Harrold Av. B65: Row R 6E 97
Harrold Rd. B65: Row R 6E 97
Harrold St. DY4: Tip 6C 62
Harrop Way DY8: Amb 3C 108
Harrowby Dr. DY4: Tip 3A 78
Harrowby Pl. WV13: W'hall 2D 46
WV14: Bils 1A 62
Harrowby Rd. WV10: F'hses 4F 15
WV14: Bils 1A 62
Harrow Cl. DY9: Hag 6E 125
Harrowfield Rd. B33: Stech 5C 104
Harrow Rd. B29: S Oak 2B 132
DY6: K'wfrd 6B 74
Harrow St. WV1: Wolv 5F 27
Harry Mitchell Leisure Cen. 4D 98
Harry Perks St. WV13: W'hall 6A 30
Harry Price Ho. B69: O'bry 4D 96
Hart Dr. B73: Bold 5G 69
Hartfield Cres. B27: A Grn 3G 135
Hartfields Way B65: Row R 4H 95
Hartford Cl. B17: Harb 4E 115
Hartill Rd. WV4: Penn 2B 58
Hartill St. WV13: W'hall 3B 46
Hartington Cl. B93: Dorr 6A 166
Hartington Rd. B19: Loz 1F 101
Hartland Av. WV14: Cose 5C 60
Hartland Rd. B31: Longb 3C 158
B71: W Brom 5D 64
DY4: Tip 2F 77
Hartland St. DY5: P'ntt 2H 93
Hartlebury Cl. B93: Dorr 6B 166
Hartlebury Rd. B63: Hale 3H 127
B69: O'bry 4D 96
Hartledon Rd. B17: Harb 6F 115
Hartley Dr. WS9: A'rdge 5D 34
Hartley Gro. B44: K'sdng 2B 68
Hartley Pl. B15: Edg 3B 116
Hartley Rd. B44: K'sdng 2B 68
Hartley St. WV3: Wolv 1E 43
Harton Way B14: K Hth 2E 147
Hartopp Rd. B8: Salt 5E 103
B74: Four O 2F 53
Hart Rd. B24: Erd 2G 85
WV11: Wed 5F 29
Hartsbourne Dr.
B62: Hale 1D 128
Harts Cl. B17: Harb 5H 115
HARTS GREEN 6E 115
Harts Grn. Rd. B17: Harb 6E 115
HART'S HILL 4A 94
Hartshill Cl. B34: S End 3E 105
Hartshill Rd. B27: A Grn 3B 136
B34: S End 3E 105
Hartshorn St. WV14: Bils 6F 45
Hartside Cl. B63: Hale 3F 127
Harts Rd. B8: Salt 4E 103
Hart St. WS1: Wals 3C 48
Hartswell Dr. B13: Mose 1H 147
Hartwell Cl. B91: Sol 6F 151
Hartwell La. WS6: Gt Wyr 2G 7
Hartwell Rd. B24: Erd 5H 85
Hartwood Cres. WV4: Penn 6D 42
Harvard Cl. DY1: Dud 3B 76
Harvard Rd. B92: Olton 1F 137
Harvest Cl. B30: Stir 1D 146
DY3: Up Gor 2A 76
Harvest Ct. B65: Row R 5A 96
Harvesters Cl. WS9: A'rdge 1G 51
Harvesters Rd. WV12: W'hall 4D 30
Harvesters Wlk. WV8: Pend 6C 14
Harvesters Way WV12: W'hall 4D 30
Harvester Way DY6: W Hth 1G 91
Harvest Flds. Way B75: R'ley 5B 38
Harvest Gdns. B68: O'bry 5G 97
Harvest Rd. B65: Row R 5A 96
B67: Smeth 6B 98
Harvest Wlk. B65: Row R 5A 96
Harvey Ct. B33: Kitts G 6H 105
Harvey Dr. B75: R'ley 1A 54
Harvey M. B30: B'vlle 6A 132
Harvey Rd. B26: Yard 4B 120
WS2: Wals 4H 31
Harvey's Ter. DY2: Neth 5F 95
HARVILLS HAWTHORN 6F 63
Harvills Hawthorn B70: W Brom 6F 63
Harvine Wlk. DY8: Stourb 2C 124
Harvington Dr. B90: M'path 3F 165
Harvington Rd. B29: W Cas 5E 131
B63: Hale 3H 127
B68: O'bry 4G 113
WV14: Cose 5D 60
Harvington Wlk. B65: Row R 6C 96
Harvington Way B76: Walm 5E 71
Harwin Cl. WV6: Tett 2D 26
Harwood Gro. B90: Shir 1A 164
Harwood St. B70: W Brom 4H 79
HASBURY 3G 127
Hasbury Cl. B63: Hale 3G 127
Hasbury Rd. B32: Bart G 5G 129
Haseley Rd. B21: Hand 2A 100
B91: Sol 1C 150
Haselor Rd. B73: New O 4E 69
Haselour Rd. B37: K'hrst 4B 106
Haskell St. WS1: Wals 4D 48
Haslucks Cft. B90: Shir 4G 149
HASLUCKS GREEN 6E 149
Haslucks Grn. Rd. B90: Maj G 2E 163
Hassop Rd. B42: Gt Barr 6F 67
Hastings Ct. DY1: Dud 5A 76
Hastings Rd. B23: Erd 6B 68
(not continuous)
Hastingwood Ind. Pk. B24: Erd 6H 85
Haswell Rd. B63: Hale 2F 127
Hatcham Rd. B44: K'sdng 3C 68
Hatchett St. B19: Birm 4G 101
Hatchford Av. B92: Sol 2G 137
Hatchford Brook Rd. B92: Sol 2G 137
Hatchford Ct. B92: Sol 2G 137
Hatchford Wlk. B37: Chel W 2D 122
Hatchford Way B26: Sheld 1A 138
Hatch Heath Cl. WV5: Wom 6F 57
Hateley Dr. WV4: E'shll 1A 60
HATELEY HEATH 6A 64
Hatfield Cl. B23: Erd 6D 68
Hatfield Rd. B19: Loz 1F 101
DY9: Lye 1G 125
Hathaway Cl. CV7: Bal C 2H 169
WV13: W'hall 3H 45
Hathaway M. DY8: Word 6H 91
Hathaway Rd. B75: Four O 5G 37
B90: Shir 6H 149
Hatherden Dr. B76: Walm 3E 71
Hathersage Rd. B42: Gt Barr 6F 67
Hatherton Gdns.
WV10: Bush 5A 16
Hatherton Gro. B29: W Cas 4D 130
Hatherton Pl. WS9: A'rdge 2C 34
Hatherton Rd. WS1: Wals 1C 48
WV14: Bils 5H 45
Hatherton St. WS1: Wals 1C 48
WS6: C Hay 3C 6
Hattersley Gro. B11: Tys 2G 135
Hatton Cres. WV10: Wolv 2C 28
Hatton Gdns. B42: Gt Barr 6D 66
Hatton Rd. WV6: Wolv 6D 26
Hattons Gro. WV8: Bilb 5H 13
Hatton St. WV14: Bils 1G 61
Haughton Rd. B20: Hand 6E 83
Haunch La. B13: Mose 1H 147
Haunchwood Dr. B76: Walm 6D 70
Havacre La. WV14: Cose 3E 61
Havelock Cl. WV3: Wolv 3C 42
Havelock Rd. B8: Salt 4D 102
B11: Tys 1E 135
B20: Hand 6E 83

A-Z Birmingham Deluxe 195

Haven, The—Heron Ct.

Haven, The B14: Yard W 3D 148
DY8: Word 1B 108
WV2: Wolv 3G 43
Haven Cvn. Pk. B92: Bick 3E 139
Haven Cft. B43: Gt Barr 5H 65
Haven Dr. B27: A Grn 2H 135
Haverford Dr. B45: Redn 3H 157
Havergal Wlk. B63: Crad 1D 126
Haverhill Cl. WS3: Blox 4G 19
Hawbridge Cl. B90: M'path 3F 165
HAWBUSH 1E 109
Hawbush Gdns. DY5: Brie H 2E 109
Hawbush Rd. DY5: Brie H 1E 109
WS3: Blox 3B 32
Hawbush Urban Farm Vis. Cen. 1F 109
Hawcroft Gro. B34: S End 3G 105
Hawes Cl. WS1: Wals 5D 48
Hawes La. B65: Row R 5B 96
Hawes Rd. WS1: Wals 5D 48
Haweswater Dr. DY6: K'wfrd 3B 92
Hawfield Cl. B69: Tiv 2C 96
Hawfield Gro. B72: W Grn 6A 70
Hawfield Rd. B69: Tiv 2C 96
Hawker Dr. B35: Cas V 5D 86
Hawkesbury Rd. B90: Shir 6F 149
Hawkes Cl. B30: Stir 5C 132
Hawkesford Cl. B36: Cas B 1E 105
B74: Four O 2H 53
Hawkesford Rd. B33: Kitts G 6H 105
Hawkeshaw Path B90: Bly P 5E 165
(not continuous)
Hawkes La. B70: W Brom 6G 63
HAWKESLEY 2A 160
Hawkesley Cres. B31: Longb 6D 144
Hawkesley Dr. B31: Longb 1D 158
Hawkesley End B38: K Nor 2A 160
Hawkesley Mill La. B31: N'fld 5D 144
Hawkesley Rd. DY1: Dud 1B 94
Hawkesley Sq. B38: K Nor 2A 160
Hawkes St. B10: Small H 3D 118
Hawkestone Cres. B70: W Brom 1F 79
Hawkestone Rd. B29: W Cas 6E 131
Hawkeswell Cl. B92: Olton 4C 136
Hawkesyard Rd. B24: Erd 6E 85
Hawkhurst Rd. B14: K Hth 5H 147
Hawkinge Dr. B35: Cas V 4E 87
Hawkins Cl. B5: Bal H 5G 117
Hawkins Cft. DY4: Tip 4A 78
Hawkins Dr. WS11: Cann 1C 6
Hawkins Pl. WV14: Bils 2H 61
Hawkins St. B70: W Brom 5G 63
Hawkley Cl. WV1: Wolv 1D 44
Hawkley Rd. WV1: Wolv 1D 44
Hawkmoor Gdns. B38: K Nor 1C 160
Hawks Cl. WS6: C Hay 3D 6
Hawksford Cres. WV10: Bush 2H 27
Hawkshead Dr. B93: Know 3B 166
Hawksmill Ind. Est. B9: Small H 2C 118
Hawksmoor Dr. WV6: Pert 6D 24
Hawkstone Ct. WV6: Pert 4D 24
Hawkswell Av. WV5: Wom 2G 73
Hawkswell Dr. DY6: K'wfrd 1B 92
WV13: W'hall 2H 45
Hawkswood Dr. CV7: Bal C 2H 169
WS10: Mox 2B 62
Hawkswood Gro. B14: K Hth 4B 148
Hawley Cl. WS4: Wals 5D 32
Hawley Ct. B43: Gt Barr 4A 66
Hawnby Gro. B76: Walm 3E 71
HAWNE 5G 111
Hawne Cl. B63: Hale 5G 111
Hawnelands, The B63: Hale 6H 111
Hawne La. B63: Hale 5G 111
Hawthorn Av. WS6: Gt Wyr 4G 7
Hawthorn Brook Way B23: Erd 5E 69
Hawthorn Cl. B23: Erd 6F 69
Hawthorn Coppice B30: K Nor 3A 146
Hawthorn Cft. B68: O'bry 4B 114
Hawthornden Ct. B76: Walm 6B 70
Hawthorn Dr. B47: H'wd 3B 162
CV7: Bal C 1H 169
Hawthorne Cft. B30: K Nor 2H 145
Hawthorne Gro. DY3: Gorn 5H 75
Hawthorne Ho. WV10: Wolv 6B 28
Hawthorne La. WV8: Cod 5F 13
Hawthorne Rd. B15: Edg 4A 116
B30: K Nor 3H 145
B36: Cas B 2A 106
B63: Hale 3G 127
DY1: Dud 3E 77
WS5: Wals 6D 48
WS6: C Hay 1E 7
WV2: Wolv 5H 43
WV11: Ess 3A 18
WV11: Wed 4H 29
WV12: W'hall 2D 30
Hawthorn Gro. B19: Loz 1E 101
Hawthorn Pk. B20: Hand 4A 82
Hawthorn Pk. Dr. B20: Hand 4B 82
Hawthorn Pl. WS2: Wals 6E 31
Hawthorn Rd. B44: K'sdng 5H 67
B72: W Grn 4A 70
B74: S'tly 2A 52
DY4: Tip 5A 62
DY5: Quar B 3A 110
WS4: S'fld 6F 21
WS10: W'bry 1F 63
WV1: Wolv 3D 44
Hawthorns, The 6F 81
Hawthorns, The B13: Mose 2H 133
B68: O'bry 4B 114
Hawthorns Bus. Cen. B66: Smeth 1E 99
Hawthorns Ind. Est. B21: Hand 6F 81
Hawthorns Station, The (Rail & MM) 1F 99
Hawthorn Ter. WS10: W'bry 1F 63
Haxby Av. B34: Hodg H 3E 105
Haybarn, The B76: Walm 5E 71
Haybrook Dr. B11: Tys 1F 135
Haycock Pl. WS10: Darl 4C 46
Haycroft Av. B8: Salt 4E 103
Haycroft Dr. B74: Four O 5G 37
Haydn Sanders Sq. WS1: Wals 3C 48
Haydock Cl. B36: Hodg H 1A 104
WV6: Wolv 3F 27
Haydon Cl. B93: Dorr 6G 167
Haydon Cft. B33: Kitts G 6E 105
Hayehouse Gro. B36: Hodg H 2C 104
HAYES, THE 5C 110
Hayes, The B31: Birm 2G 159
DY9: Lye 6B 110
WV12: W'hall 3B 30
Hayes Bus. Pk. DY9: Lye 5B 110
Hayes Cres. B68: O'bry 4B 98
Hayes Cft. B38: K Nor 2A 160
Hayes Dr. B24: Erd 2B 86
Hayes Gro. B24: Erd 1B 86
Hayes La. DY9: Lye 5C 110
Hayes Mdw. B72: W Grn 6B 70
Hayes Rd. B68: O'bry 4B 98
Hayes St. B70: W Brom 3G 79
Hayes Trad. Est., The DY9: Lye 5C 110
Hayes Vw. Dr. WS6: C Hay 1E 7
Hayfield Ct. B13: Mose 3B 134
Hayfield Gdns. B13: Mose 3C 134
Hayfield Rd. B13: Mose 3B 134
HAY GREEN 6H 109
Hay Grn. DY9: Lye 6H 109
Hay Grn. Cl. B30: B'vlle 1H 145
Hay Grn. La. B30: B'vlle 2G 145
Hay Gro. WS8: Bwnhls 5B 10
Hay Hall Rd. B11: Tys 6F 119
Hay Head Wood (Nature Reserve) 6A 34
Hay Hill WS5: Wals 3A 50
Hayland Rd. B23: Erd 1E 85
Hay La. B90: M'path 3D 164
Hayle Cl. B38: K Nor 5D 146
Hayley Ct. B24: Erd 1A 86
HAYLEY GREEN 4F 127
Hayley Grn. Rd. B32: Bart G 5H 129
Hayley Pk. Rd. B63: Hale 5E 127
Hayling Cl. B45: Fran 6F 143
Hayling Gro. WV2: Wolv 5F 43
Haylofts, The B63: Hale 4E 127
Haymarket, The WV8: Pend 6C 14
HAY MILLS 5H 119
Haynes La. WS5: Wals 1F 65
Hay Pk. B5: Bal H 5F 117
Haypits Cl. B71: W Brom 6C 64
Hayrick Dr. DY6: W Hth 2G 91
Hay Rd. B25: Yard 4G 119
Hayseech B64: Crad H 4H 111
Hayseech Rd. B63: Hale 5H 111
Hays Kent Moat, The B26: Yard 2E 121
Haytor Av. B14: K Hth 2F 147
Haywain Cl. WV9: Pend 5E 15
Hayward Ind. Pk. WS9: A'rdge 2C 34
Hayward Rd. B75: S Cold 3A 54
Haywards Cl. B23: Erd 2E 85
WS3: Pels 4D 20
Haywards Ind. Est. B35: Cas V 6F 87
Hayward St. WV14: Cose 5D 60
Hayway, The WS2: Wals 6G 31
Haywharf Rd. DY5: P'ntt 4F 93
Haywood Dr. B62: B'hth 3C 112
WV6: Tett 5A 26
Haywood Rd. B33: Kitts G 1A 122
Haywood's Farm B71: W Brom 3D 64
Hazel Av. B73: New O 4C 68
WS10: W'bry 1G 63
Hazelbank B38: K Nor 5A 146
Hazelbeach Rd. B8: Salt 4F 103
Hazelbeech Rd. B70: W Brom 5H 79
Hazel Cft. B31: N'fld 4E 145
B37: Chel W 2D 122
Hazeldene Gro. B6: Aston 1G 101
Hazeldene Rd. B33: Sheld 4H 121
B63: Hale 3G 127
Hazel Dr. B47: H'wd 4B 162
Hazeley Cl. B17: Harb 4D 114
Hazel Gdns. B27: A Grn 1A 136
WV8: Cod 3G 13
Hazelglen Gro. *B18: Win G 5A 100*
(off Heath Grn. Rd.)
Hazel Gro. B70: W Brom 6A 80
DY8: Stourb 2A 124
WV5: Wom 6G 57
WV11: Wed 2E 29
WV14: Bils 4G 45
Hazelhurst Rd. B14: K Hth 1G 147
B36: Cas B 2A 106
Hazel La. WS6: Gt Wyr 3H 7
Hazelmead Ct. B73: Bold 6G 69
Hazelmere Dr. WS7: Chase 1B 10
WV3: Wolv 2G 41
Hazelmere Rd. B28: Hall G 4F 135
Hazeloak Rd. B90: Shir 6G 149
Hazel Rd. B45: Rubery 3F 157
DY1: Dud 5E 77
DY4: Tip 4C 62
DY6: K'wfrd 4C 92
WV3: Wolv 4C 42
Hazelton Cl. B91: Sol 6F 151
Hazeltree Cft. B27: A Grn 3H 135
Hazeltree Gro. B93: Dorr 6A 166
Hazelville Gro. B28: Hall G 1G 149
Hazelville Rd. B28: Hall G 1G 149
Hazelwell Cres. B30: Stir 1D 146
Hazelwell Dr. B14: K Hth 1F 147
Hazelwell Fordrough B30: Stir 6D 132
Hazelwell La. B30: Stir 6C 132
Hazelwell Rd. B30: Stir 1C 146
Hazelwell St. B30: Stir 6C 132
Hazelwood Cl. WS6: C Hay 3D 6
Hazelwood Dr. WV11: Wed 4C 28
Hazelwood Gro. WV12: W'hall 4D 30
Hazelwood Rd. B27: A Grn 3H 135
B74: S'tly 2F 51
DY1: Dud 2B 76
Hazlemere Dr. B74: Four O 3G 53
Hazlitt Gro. B30: K Nor 3H 145
Headborough Wlk. WS9: A'rdge 6D 22
Headingley Rd. B21: Hand 5A 82
Headland Dr. B8: Salt 4D 102
Headland Rd. WV3: Wolv 2F 41
Headlands, The B74: Lit A 6C 36
Headley Cft. B38: K Nor 1H 159
HEADLEY HEATH 3E 161
Headley Heath La. B38: Head H 2D 160
Headley Ri. B90: Shir 5B 150
Headway Rd. WV10: F'hses 4G 15
Heale Cl. B63: Crad 4C 110
Heanor Cft. B6: Aston 1B 102
Heantum Cft. WV10: Wolv 4C 28
Heantun Ho. WV3: Wolv 2G 43 (4A 170)
Heantun Mill Ct. WS10: W'bry 4D 62
Heantun Ri. WV1: Wolv 5G 27
Heartland M. B65: Row R 1B 112
Heartlands High Community Leisure Cen. 5A 102
Heartlands Parkway B7: Nech 4C 102
Heartlands Pl. B8: Salt 5E 103
HEATH
Stourbridge 1D 124
Heath Acres WS10: Darl 1C 62
Heath Bri. Cl. WS4: Rus 1E 33
Heathbrook Av. DY6: W Hth 2H 91
Heathcliff Rd. B11: Tys 1F 135
DY2: Dud 2H 95
Heath Cl. B30: B'vlle 2H 145
B75: S Cold 5D 54
DY4: Tip 2B 78
WS9: Ston 2G 23
Heathcote Av. B91: Sol 4C 150
Heathcote Ho. *B17: Harb 6G 115*
(off Vivian Cl.)
Heathcote Rd. B30: K Nor 2C 146
Heath Cft. B31: Longb 2E 159
Heath Cft. Rd. B75: R'ley 2A 54
HEATH END
Walsall 5E 21
Heather Av. WS5: Wals 1F 65
Heather Cl. B36: Cas B 1C 106
WS3: Blox 1G 31
WV11: Wed 4G 29
Heather Ct. Gdns. B74: Four O 3H 53
Heather Cft. B44: Gt Barr 4H 67
Heather Dale B13: Mose 3E 133
Heather Dr. B45: Rubery 3F 157
Heather Gro. B91: Sol 1A 152
WV12: W'hall 5E 31
Heather Ho. B38: K Nor 6B 146
Heatherleigh Rd. B36: Cas B 1B 106
Heather Rd. B10: Small H 4F 119
B43: Gt Barr 5G 65
B67: Smeth 3C 98
DY1: Dud 3E 77
WS3: Blox 1G 31
Heath Farm Rd. DY8: Stourb 3B 124
WV8: Bilb 5H 13
Heathfield Av. B20: Hand 1D 100
Heathfield Cl. B64: Old H 1H 111
B93: Know 4C 166
Heathfield Ct. B19: Loz 2D 100
Heathfield Dr. B74: Four O 6F 37
WS3: Blox 5H 19
Heathfield Gdns. DY8: Stourb 1D 124
Heathfield La. WS10: Darl 5C 46
Heathfield La. W. WS10: Darl 6B 46
Heathfield Rd. B14: K Hth 5G 133
B19: Hand 1D 100
B63: Hale 2G 127
Heathfields WV8: Cod 6E 13
Heath Gdns. B91: Sol 1H 151
Heath Grn. DY1: Dud 2B 76
Heathgreen Cl. B37: Chel W 6F 107
Heath Grn. Gro. *B18: Win G 5A 100*
(off Heath Grn. Rd.)
Heath Grn. Rd. B18: Win G 5A 100
Heath Gro. WV8: Bilb 4H 13
Heath Hill Rd. WV6: Tett 2E 41
Heath Ho. B14: K Hth 5H 147
Heath Ho. Dr. WV5: Wom 2D 72
Heath Ho. La. WV8: Cod 1E 25
Heathland Av. B34: S End 2E 105
Heathlands, The B65: B'hth 2C 112
DY8: Stourb 1F 125
WS2: Wals 6G 31
WV5: Wom 2D 72
Heathlands Cl. DY6: K'wfrd 1C 92
Heathlands Cres. B73: Bold 4F 69
Heathlands Gro. B31: N'fld 6E 145
Heathlands Rd. B73: Bold 3F 69
Heath La. B71: W Brom 6B 64
DY8: Stourb 1E 125
Heathleigh Rd. B38: K Nor 1G 159
Heathmere Av. B25: Yard 3B 120
Heathmere Dr. B37: F'bri 1B 122
Heath Mill Cl. WV5: Wom 3D 72
Heath Mill La. B9: Birm 2A 118 (6H 5)
Heath Mill Rd. WV5: Wom 3D 72
Heath Pk. WV10: Cov H 1G 15
Heath Ri. B14: K Hth 6A 148
Heath Rd. B30: B'vlle 2G 145
B47: H'wd 2A 162
B91: Sol 1H 151
DY2: Neth 1D 110
WS10: Darl 3E 47
WV12: W'hall 1C 30
Heath Rd. Sth. B31: N'fld 3E 145
Heathside Dr. B38: K Nor 6D 146
WS3: Pels 3E 21
Heath St. B18: Win G 4H 99
B65: B'hth 2C 112
B66: Smeth 4H 99
DY8: Stourb 6D 108
Heath St. Ind. Est. B66: Smeth 4H 99
Heath St. Sth. B18: Win G 5B 100
HEATH TOWN 5D 28
Heath Town Leisure Cen. 5C 28
Heath Trad. Pk. B66: Smeth 4H 99
Heath Vw. WS2: Wals 6F 31
Heath Way B34: Hodg H, S End 2D 104
Heathway Cl. B34: S End 3E 105
Heathy Farm Cl. B32: Bart G 4H 129
Heathy Ri. B32: Bart G 3G 129
Heaton Cl. WV10: Bush 2A 16
Heaton Dr. B15: Edg 3A 116
B74: Four O 3F 53
Heaton Rd. B91: Sol 1D 150
Heaton St. B18: Hock 4D 100
Hebden Gro. B28: Hall G 4E 149
WV12: W'hall 6B 18
Heddon Pl. B7: Birm 6A 102
Hedera Cl. WS5: Wals 2F 65
Hedgefield Gro. B63: Crad 1E 127
Hedgerow Dr. DY6: K'wfrd 6B 74
Hedgerows, The B62: Roms 3A 142
Hedgerow Wlk. WV8: Pend 6C 14
Hedges, The WV5: Wom 1E 73
Hedgetree Cft. B37: Chel W 1E 123
Hedgings, The *B34: S End 3F 105*
(off Meadow Rd.)
Hedgley Gro. B33: Stech 5E 105
Hedingham Gro. B37: Chel W 1F 123
Hedley Cft. B35: Cas V 3F 87
Hednesford Rd. WS8: Bwnhls 2G 9
Heeley Rd. B29: S Oak 3A 132
Hefford Dr. B66: Smeth 3E 99
Helena Pl. B66: Smeth 2A 98
Helena St. B1: Birm 6E 101 (3A 4)
Helenny Cl. WV11: Wed 4C 28
Helford Cl. DY4: Tip 2F 77
Hellaby Cl. B72: S Cold 1H 69
Hellaby Ct. B73: Bold 6G 69
Hellaby Ho. B74: Four O 6F 37
Hellier Av. DY4: Tip 3B 78
Hellier Dr. WV5: Wom 6E 57
Hellier Rd. WV10: Bush 5A 16
Hellier St. DY2: Dud 1E 95
Helming Dr. WV1: Wolv 6D 28
Helmsdale Way DY3: Sed 6C 60
Helmsley Cl. DY5: Brie H 3G 109
Helmsley Rd. WV11: Wed 1E 29
Helmswood Dr. B37: Chel W 3E 123
Helston Cl. DY8: Word 1A 108
WS5: Wals 4H 49
Helstone Gro. B11: Tys 2G 135
Helston Rd. WS5: Wals 4H 49
Hembs Cres. B43: Gt Barr 5G 65
Hemlingford Cft. B37: Mars G 4C 122
Hemlingford Rd. B37: K'hrst 3A 106
B76: Walm 6E 71
Hemmings Cl. DY8: Stourb 6D 108
Hemmings St. WS10: Darl 3C 46
Hemplands Rd. DY8: Stourb 6D 108
Hempole La. DY4: Tip 6D 62
Hemyock Rd. B29: W Cas 5F 131
Henbury Rd. B27: A Grn 2B 136
Henderson Ct. B68: O'bry 3H 113
Henderson Wlk. DY4: Tip 5B 62
Henderson Way B65: B'hth 2C 112
Hendon Cl. DY3: Lwr G 5H 75
WV10: Bush 1A 28
Hendon Rd. B11: S'hll 6B 118
Heneage Pl. B7: Birm 5A 102
Heneage St. B7: Birm 5A 102
Heneage St. W. B7: Birm 5H 101 (1H 5)
(not continuous)
Henfield Cl. WV11: Wed 2F 29
Hengham Rd. B26: Yard 2E 121
Henley Cl. B73: W Grn 5H 69
DY4: Tip 2D 78
WS3: Blox 6C 20
Henley Cres. B91: Sol 6F 137
Henley Dr. B75: Four O 6G 37
Henley Rd. WV10: Oxl 6F 15
Henley St. B11: S'brk 4A 118
Henley Vs. *B12: Bal H 6B 118*
(off Chesterton Rd.)
Henlow Cl. DY4: Tip 2F 77
Henlow Rd. B14: K Hth 5H 147
Hennalls, The B36: Hodg H 2D 104
Henn Dr. DY4: Tip 5G 61
Henne Dr. WV14: Cose 4E 61
Henn St. DY4: Tip 5A 62
Henrietta St. B19: Birm 5F 101 (1C 4)
Henry Rd. B25: Yard 4A 120
Henry St. WS2: Wals 2B 48
Hensborough B90: Dic H 4G 163
Hensel Dr. WV3: Wolv 3A 42
Henshaw Gro. B25: Yard 4A 120
Henshaw Rd. B10: Small H 3D 118
Henstead St. B5: Birm 3F 117
Henwood Cl. WV6: Tett 6A 26
Henwood La. B91: Cath B 2D 152
Henwood Rd. WV6: Tett 1A 42
Hepburn Cl. WS9: A'rdge 5C 34
Hepburn Edge B24: Erd 3H 85
Hepworth Cl. WV6: Pert 5F 25
Herald Ct. DY1: Dud 6E 77
Herald Rd. B26: Birm A 1E 139
Herbert Rd. B10: Small H 2C 118
B21: Hand 6B 82
B67: Smeth 2E 115
B91: Sol 4F 151
WS9: A'rdge 6C 22
Herberts Pk. Rd. WS10: Darl 5B 46
Herbert St. B70: W Brom 4B 80
WV1: Wolv 6H 27 (1C 170)
WV14: Bils 5D 44
Herbhill Cl. WV4: Penn 1H 59
Hereford Av. B12: Bal H 5A 118
Hereford Cl. B45: Fran 5G 143
WS9: A'rdge 1C 34
Hereford Ho. WV1: Wolv 6G 27
Hereford Pl. B71: W Brom 6H 63
Hereford Rd. B68: O'bry 4H 113
DY2: Neth 6G 95
Hereford St. WS2: Wals 5C 32
Hereford Wlk. B37: Mars G 2B 122
Hereward Ri. B62: Hale 6B 112
Heritage, The *WS1: Wals 3C 48*
(off Sister Dora Gdns.)
Heritage Cl. B68: O'bry 5A 98
Heritage Ct. B18: Birm 1A 4
Heritage Way B33: Kitts G 6H 105
DY4: Tip 2B 78
Hermes Ct. B74: Four O 6F 37
Hermes Rd. B26: Birm A 1E 139
Hermitage, The B91: Sol 1G 151
Hermitage Dr. B76: Walm 2D 70
Hermitage Rd. B15: Edg 2G 115
B23: Erd 4D 84
B91: Sol 2G 151
Hermit St. DY3: Up Gor 2H 75
Hermon Row B11: S'brk 6D 118
Hernall Cft. B26: Sheld 4E 121
Hernefield Rd. B34: S End 2E 105
Hernehurst B32: Quin 6H 113
Hern Rd. DY5: Brie H 5G 109
Heron Cl. B90: Ches G 5B 164
WS8: Bwnhls 6A 10
Heron Ct. *B73: W Grn 6H 69*
(off Florence Av.)

Herondale Cres.—Hingley St.

Herondale Cres. DY8: Stourb . . . 1A 124
Herondale Rd. B26: Sheld . . . 5D 120
Heronfield Dr. B31: Longb . . . 3D 158
Heronfield Way B91: Sol . . . 2A 152
Heron Mill WS3: Pels . . . 4C 20
Heron Rd. B68: O'bry . . . 1G 113
Heronry, The WV6: Tett . . . 1F 41
Heronsdale Rd. DY8: Stourb . . . 2A 124
Herons Way B29: S Oak . . . 2G 131
Heronswood Dr. DY5: Brie H . . . 2H 109
Heronswood Rd. B45: Redn . . . 3H 157
Heronville Dr. B70: W Brom . . . 6G 63
Heronville Ho. DY4: Tip . . . 4B 78
Heronville Rd. B70: W Brom . . . 1F 79
Heron Way B45: Rubery . . . 2F 157
Herrick Rd. B8: Salt . . . 4E 103
Herrick St. WV3: Wolv . . . 2F 43
Herringshaw Cft. B76: Walm . . . 2C 70
Hertford St. B12: Bal H . . . 6A 118
Hertford Way B93: Know . . . 5D 166
Hervey Gro. B24: Erd . . . 1B 86
Hesketh Cres. B23: Erd . . . 2C 84
Heskett Av. B68: O'bry . . . 2A 114
Hessian Cl. WV14: Cose . . . 3D 60
Hestia Dr. B29: S Oak . . . 5A 132
Heston Av. B42: Gt Barr . . . 5C 66
Hever Av. B44: K'sdng . . . 4A 68
Hever Cl. DY1: Dud . . . 4A 76
Hewell Cl. B31: Longb . . . 2D 158
DY6: K'wfrd . . . 6B 74
Hewitson Gdns. B67: Smeth . . . 1D 114
Hewitt St. WS10: Darl . . . 5C 46
Hexham Cft. B36: Hodg H . . . 1A 104
Hexham Way DY1: Dud . . . 5B 76
Hexton Cl. B90: Shir . . . 5D 148
Heybarnes Cir. B10: Small H . . . 4F 119
Heybarnes Rd. B10: Small H . . . 4F 119
Heycott Gro. B38: K Nor . . . 5E 147
Heydon Rd. DY5: P'ntt . . . 4F 93
Heyford Gro. B91: Sol . . . 1G 165
Heyford Way B35: Cas V . . . 2F 87
Heygate Way WS9: A'rdge . . . 5D 22
Heynesfield Rd. B33: Kitts G . . . 6G 105
Heythrop Gro. B13: Mose . . . 5D 134
Hickman Av. WV1: Wolv . . . 2C 44
Hickman Gdns. B16: Edg . . . 2B 116
Hickman Pl. WV14: Bils . . . 5E 45
Hickman Rd. B11: S'brk . . . 5B 118
DY4: Tip . . . 5H 61
DY5: Brie H . . . 5G 93
WV14: Bils . . . 6E 45
Hickman's Av. B64: Old H . . . 1G 111
Hickmans Cl. B62: Quin . . . 5G 113
Hickman St. DY9: Lye . . . 5G 109
Hickmerelands La. DY3: Sed . . . 5H 59
Hickory Dr. B17: Edg . . . 1E 115
Hidcote Av. B76: Walm . . . 5E 71
Hidcote Gro. B33: Sheld . . . 3G 121
B37: Mars G . . . 4C 122
Hidson Rd. B23: Erd . . . 2C 84
Higgins Av. WV14: Cose . . . 3F 61
Higgins La. B32: Quin . . . 6A 114
Higgins Wlk. B66: Smeth . . . 3F 99
Higgs Fld. Cres. B64: Old H . . . 2A 112
Higgs Rd. WV11: Wed . . . 6A 18
Highams Cl. B65: Row R . . . 6B 96
Higham Way WV10: Wolv . . . 3A 28
High Arcal Dr. DY3: Sed . . . 6B 60
High Arcal Rd. DY3: Lwr G . . . 4D 74
High Av. B64: Crad H . . . 3H 111
High Beeches B43: Gt Barr . . . 4H 65
HIGHBRIDGE . . . 2E 21
Highbridge Rd. B73: Bold . . . 4F 69
DY2: Neth . . . 6C 94
High Brink Rd. B46: Col . . . 2H 107
Highbrook Cl. WV9: Pend . . . 5E 15
High Brow B17: Harb . . . 4F 115
High Bullen WS10: W'bry . . . 2F 63
Highbury Av. B21: Hand . . . 1B 100
B65: Row R . . . 6D 96
Highbury Cl. B65: Row R . . . 6D 96
Highbury Ct. B13: Mose . . . 6G 133
Highbury Little Theatre . . . 6G 69
Highbury Rd. B14: K Hth . . . 5F 133
B66: Smeth . . . 2B 98
B68: O'bry . . . 4H 97
B74: Four O . . . 6C 36
High Clere B64: Crad H . . . 4A 112
Highcrest Cl. B31: Longb . . . 2E 159
High Cft. B43: Gt Barr . . . 4G 65
WS3: Pels . . . 2F 21
Highcroft WS9: A'rdge . . . 5D 22
Highcroft Av. DY8: Word . . . 6A 92
Highcroft Cl. B92: Sol . . . 3G 137
Highcroft Dr. B74: Four O . . . 6E 37
Highcroft Rd. B23: Erd . . . 4E 85
Highdown Cres. B90: M'path . . . 3E 165
HIGH ERCAL . . . 1G 109
High Ercal Av. DY5: Brie H . . . 1G 109
High Farm Rd. B62: B'hth . . . 3F 113
B63: Hale . . . 2G 127
Highfield CV7: Mer . . . 4H 141
Highfield Av. WS4: S'fld . . . 1G 33
WV10: Bush . . . 5C 16
Highfield Cl. B28: Hall G . . . 2D 148
Highfield Ct. B73: W Grn . . . 4H 69
Highfield Cres. B63: Crad . . . 5F 111
B65: B'hth . . . 3B 112
WV11: Wed . . . 3D 28
Highfield Dr. B73: Bold . . . 6F 69
Highfield La. B32: Quin . . . 5H 113
B63: Hale . . . 2H 127
Highfield M. B63: Crad . . . 5F 111
Highfield Pas. WS1: Wals . . . 3C 48
Highfield Pl. B14: Yard W . . . 2D 148
Highfield Rd. B8: Salt . . . 5E 103
B13: Mose . . . 2B 134
B14: Yard W . . . 2D 148
B15: Edg . . . 3C 116
B28: Hall G . . . 2D 148
B43: Gt Barr . . . 6G 65
B63: Crad . . . 6F 111
B65: B'hth . . . 2B 112
B67: Smeth . . . 4D 98
DY2: Dud . . . 6G 77
DY3: Sed . . . 4H 59
Highfield Rd. DY4: Tip . . . 6A 62
DY8: Word . . . 1E 109
WS3: Pels . . . 3E 21
Highfield Rd. Nth. WS3: Pels . . . 2D 20
HIGHFIELDS . . . 1B 10
Highfields B23: Erd . . . 3C 84
Highfields, The WV6: Tett . . . 1G 41
Highfields Av. WV14: Bils . . . 1G 61
Highfields Ct. WV4: Penn . . . 5A 42
Highfields Dr. WV5: Wom . . . 2G 73
WV14: Cose . . . 2F 61
Highfields Grange WS6: C Hay . . . 4D 6
Highfields Pk. WS6: C Hay . . . 4D 6
Highfields Rd. WS7: Chase . . . 1B 10
WV14: Bils, Cose . . . 2E 61
Highfield Ter. B18: Hock . . . 4C 100
Highfield Way WS9: A'rdge . . . 5D 22
HIGHGATE . . . 3H 117
Highgate B74: S'tly . . . 2A 52
DY3: Up Gor . . . 2A 76
Highgate Av. WS1: Wals . . . 3D 48
WV4: Penn . . . 5B 42
Highgate Bus. Cen. B12: Bal H . . . 5B 118
Highgate Cl. B12: Birm . . . 4H 117
WS1: Wals . . . 4D 48
Highgate Common Country Pk. . . . 1A 90
Highgate Comn. E. DY3: Swind . . . 2A 90
DY7: Env . . . 2A 90
Highgate Dr. WS1: Wals . . . 4D 48
Highgate Ho. *B5: Birm . . . 3G 117*
(off Southacre Av.)
Highgate Middleway B12: Birm . . . 4H 117
Highgate Pl. B12: Birm . . . 4A 118
Highgate Rd. B12: Bal H . . . 5A 118
DY2: Dud . . . 3B 94
WS1: Wals . . . 3D 48
Highgate Sq. B12: Birm . . . 4H 117
Highgate St. B12: Birm . . . 4H 117
B64: Old H . . . 1H 111
(not continuous)
Highgate Trad. Est. B12: Birm . . . 4A 118
Highgrove WV6: Tett . . . 6A 26
Highgrove Cl. WV12: W'hall . . . 2B 30
Highgrove Pl. DY1: Dud . . . 5B 76
High Haden Cres.
B64: Crad H, Old H . . . 3A 112
High Haden Rd. B64: Crad H, Old H . . . 3A 112
HIGH HEATH
Sutton Coldfield . . . 3F 55
Walsall . . . 5G 21
High Heath Cl. B30: B'vlle . . . 2H 145
High Hill WV11: Ess . . . 5A 18
High Holborn DY3: Sed . . . 6H 59
High Ho. Dr. B45: Lick . . . 6F 157
Highland Ho. B62: B'hth . . . 3C 112
Highland M. WV14: Cose . . . 4F 61
Highland Ridge B62: Quin . . . 6E 113
Highland Rd. B23: Erd . . . 2F 85
B43: Gt Barr . . . 2A 66
B64: Old H . . . 1G 111
DY1: Dud . . . 4C 76
WS9: Wals W . . . 4D 22
Highlands Ct. B90: Shir . . . 1C 164
Highlands Ind. Est., The B90: Shir . . . 1C 164
Highlands Rd. B90: Shir . . . 1C 164
WV3: Wolv . . . 3B 42
High Leasowes B63: Hale . . . 1A 128
High Mdw. Rd. B38: K Nor . . . 5C 146
High Mdws. WV5: Wom . . . 1G 73
WV6: Tett . . . 1A 42
Highmoor Cl. WV12: W'hall . . . 2B 30
WV14: Cose . . . 2F 61
Highmoor Rd. B65: Row R . . . 6B 96
Highmore Dr. B32: Bart G . . . 5A 130
High Oak DY5: P'ntt . . . 2G 93
Highover Dr. B75: Four O . . . 5G 37
Highpark Av. DY8: Woll . . . 6B 108
High Pk. Cl. B66: Smeth . . . 4F 99
DY3: Sed . . . 4H 59
High Pk. Cres. DY3: Sed . . . 4H 59
HIGH PARK ESTATE . . . 6A 108
High Pk. Rd. B63: Crad . . . 6E 111
High Pk. St. B7: Nech . . . 3B 102
High Point B15: Edg . . . 5A 116
High Ridge WS9: A'rdge . . . 4B 34
High Ridge Cl. WS9: A'rdge . . . 4A 34
WS10: Mox . . . 1A 62
High Rd. WV12: W'hall . . . 4C 30
High St. B4: Birm . . . 1G 117 (4E 5)
B6: Aston . . . 2G 101
B8: Salt . . . 4C 102
B14: K Hth . . . 5G 133
B17: Harb . . . 6G 115
B23: Erd . . . 3F 85
B32: Quin . . . 5G 113
B46: Col . . . 1H 107
B63: Hale . . . 1B 128
B64: Crad H . . . 3E 111
B65: B'hth . . . 2B 112
B66: Smeth . . . 3D 98
B70: W Brom . . . 3H 79
(not continuous)
B72: S Cold . . . 5A 54
B90: Shir . . . 5C 148
B91: Sol . . . 3G 151
B92: H Ard . . . 1A 154
B93: Know . . . 3E 167
DY1: Dud . . . 1E 95
DY3: Sed . . . 4H 59
DY3: Swind . . . 5E 73
DY4: Tip . . . 5G 61
(Princes End)
DY4: Tip . . . 2G 77
(Tipton)
DY5: Brie H . . . 1H 109
(Brierley Hill)
DY5: Brie H . . . 5F 93
(Brockmoor)
DY5: P'ntt . . . 2E 93
DY5: Quar B . . . 2B 110
DY6: K'wfrd . . . 3B 92
DY6: W Hth . . . 1H 91
DY8: Stourb . . . 6E 109
DY8: Woll . . . 5C 108
DY8: Word . . . 6C 92
DY9: Lye . . . 6A 110
High St. WS1: Wals . . . 2C 48
WS3: Blox . . . 1H 31
WS3: Pels . . . 3E 21
WS6: C Hay . . . 3D 6
WS7: Chase . . . 1B 10
(not continuous)
WS8: Bwnhls . . . 6B 10
WS8: Clay . . . 1A 22
WS9: A'rdge . . . 3D 34
(not continuous)
WS9: Wals W . . . 4B 22
WS10: Mox . . . 1A 62
WV5: Wom . . . 1H 73
WV6: Tett . . . 5B 26
WV11: Wed . . . 4E 29
WV14: Bils . . . 6F 45
High St. Amblecote DY8: Amb . . . 3D 108
High St. Bordesley B12: Birm . . . 2A 118
High St. Deritend B12: Birm . . . 2H 117 (6H 5)
Highters Cl. B14: K Hth . . . 5B 148
HIGHTER'S HEATH . . . 5A 148
Highter's Heath La. B14: K Hth . . . 6A 148
Highters Rd. B14: K Hth . . . 4A 148
High Timbers B45: Fran . . . 6F 143
High Town B63: Crad . . . 5E 111
Hightree Cl. B32: Bart G . . . 4H 129
High Trees B20: Hand . . . 4B 82
High Trees Rd. B93: Know . . . 2C 166
High Vw. WV14: Cose . . . 4B 60
Highview *WS1: Wals . . . 3D 48*
(off Highgate Rd.)
Highview Dr. DY6: K'wfrd . . . 5D 92
Highview St. DY2: Dud . . . 6G 77
Highwood Av. B92: Olton . . . 4E 137
High Wood Cl. DY6: K'wfrd . . . 3A 92
Highwood Cft. B38: K Nor . . . 6H 145
Hiker Gro. B37: Chel W . . . 1F 123
Hilary Cres. DY1: Dud . . . 1D 76
Hilary Dr. B76: Walm . . . 2E 71
WS9: A'rdge . . . 4C 34
WV3: Wolv . . . 4B 42
Hilary Gro. B31: N'fld . . . 3D 144
Hilden Rd. B7: Birm . . . 5A 102
Hilderic Cres. DY1: Dud . . . 2B 94
Hilderstone Rd. B25: Yard . . . 5A 120
Hildicks Cres. WS3: Wals . . . 2D 32
Hildicks Pl. WS3: Wals . . . 2D 32
HILL . . . 5G 37
Hill, The B32: Bart G . . . 3C 130
Hillaire Cl. B38: K Nor . . . 5E 147
Hillaries Rd. B23: Erd . . . 5D 84
Hillary Av. WS10: W'bry . . . 2A 64
Hillary Crest DY3: Up Gor . . . 2A 76
Hillary St. WS2: Wals . . . 4A 48
Hill Av. WV4: E'shll . . . 2B 60
Hill Bank DY9: Lye . . . 6B 110
Hillbank B69: Tiv . . . 6D 78
Hill Bank Dr. B33: Stech . . . 5B 104
Hill Bank Rd. B38: K Nor . . . 5C 146
B63: Crad . . . 5F 111
Hillborough Rd. B27: A Grn . . . 3C 136
Hillbrook Gro. B33: Stech . . . 6D 104
Hillbrow Cres. B62: B'hth . . . 3F 113
Hillbury Dr. WV12: W'hall . . . 1B 30
Hill Cl. B31: N'fld . . . 6F 145
DY3: Sed . . . 4A 60
Hillcrest DY3: Lwr G . . . 3G 75
Hillcrest Av. B43: Gt Barr . . . 3A 66
B63: Crad . . . 4D 110
DY5: Brie H . . . 2G 109
WV10: Bush . . . 6A 16
Hillcrest Bus. Pk. DY2: Neth . . . 2E 95
Hillcrest Cl. DY2: Neth . . . 4E 95
Hillcrest Community Leisure Cen. . . . 4D 94
Hillcrest Gdns. WV12: W'hall . . . 4D 30
Hillcrest Gro. B44: K'sdng . . . 6A 68
Hillcrest Ind. Est. B64: Crad H . . . 3F 111
Hillcrest Ri. WS7: Burn . . . 1D 10
Hill Crest Rd. B13: Mose . . . 3G 133
Hillcrest Rd. B43: Gt Barr . . . 3A 66
B62: Roms . . . 3A 142
B72: W Grn . . . 5A 70
DY2: Dud . . . 6G 77
Hillcroft Ho. B14: K Hth . . . 5H 147
Hill Cft. Rd. B14: K Hth . . . 1E 147
Hillcroft Rd. DY6: K'wfrd . . . 2C 92
Hillcross Wlk. B36: Hodg H . . . 1D 104
Hilldene Rd. DY6: K'wfrd . . . 5A 92
Hilldrop Gro. B17: Harb . . . 2H 131
Hilleys Cft. B37: F'bri . . . 6B 106
HILLFIELD . . . 6F 151
Hillfield M. B91: Sol . . . 1F 165
Hillfield Rd. B11: S'hll . . . 2D 134
B91: Sol . . . 1F 165
(not continuous)
Hillfields B67: Smeth . . . 6B 98
Hillfields Rd. DY5: Brie H . . . 4F 109
Hillfield Wlk. B65: Row R . . . 4H 95
Hill Gro. B20: Hand . . . 5E 83
HILL HOOK . . . 4E 37
Hill Hook Nature Reserve . . . 4F 37
Hill Hook Rd. B74: Four O . . . 4E 37
Hill Ho. La. B33: Stech . . . 6D 104
(not continuous)
Hillhurst Gro. B36: Cas B . . . 6H 87
Hillhurst Rd. B73: New O . . . 2B 68
Hilliards Cft. B42: Gt Barr . . . 5C 66
Hillingford Av. B43: Gt Barr . . . 2E 67
Hill La. B43: Gt Barr . . . 3A 66
B75: Bass P . . . 1F 55
Hillman Dr. DY2: Dud . . . 2G 95
Hillman Gro. B36: Cas B . . . 6A 88
Hillmeads Dr. DY2: Dud . . . 2G 95
Hillmeads Rd. B38: K Nor . . . 6C 146
Hillmorton B74: Four O . . . 6F 37
Hill Morton Rd. B74: Four O . . . 5F 37
Hillmorton Rd. B93: Know . . . 4C 166
Hillmount Cl. B28: Hall G . . . 3E 135
Hill Pk. WS9: Wals W . . . 3C 22
Hill Pas. B64: Old H . . . 1G 111
Hill Pl. WV11: Wed . . . 6A 18
Hill Rd. B69: Tiv . . . 5A 78
WV13: W'hall . . . 3F 45
Hillside DY3: Lwr G . . . 3G 75
WS8: Bwnhls . . . 1C 22
WV5: Wom . . . 6E 57
Hillside Av. B63: Crad . . . 5F 111
B65: B'hth . . . 3B 112
DY5: Quar B . . . 3C 110
Hillside Cl. B32: Bart G . . . 5G 129
WS8: Bwnhls . . . 1C 22
Hillside Ct. B43: Gt Barr . . . 3H 65
Hillside Cres. WS3: Pels . . . 5D 20
Hillside Cft. B92: Sol . . . 1A 138
Hillside Dr. B37: K'hrst . . . 5B 106
B42: Gt Barr . . . 1C 82
B74: S'tly . . . 4H 51
Hillside Gdns. B37: K'hrst . . . 5B 106
WV1: Wolv . . . 6C 28
Hillside Ho. B45: Rubery . . . 1F 157
Hillside Rd. B23: Erd . . . 5D 84
B43: Gt Barr . . . 3H 65
B74: Four O . . . 5G 37
DY1: Dud . . . 2C 76
Hillside Wlk. WV1: Wolv . . . 6C 28
Hillstone Gdns. WV10: Bush . . . 1B 28
Hillstone Rd. B34: S End . . . 4H 105
Hill St. B2: Birm . . . 1F 117 (4C 4)
B5: Birm . . . 1F 117 (4C 4)
B63: Hale . . . 2A 128
B66: Smeth . . . 3E 99
DY2: Neth . . . 4D 94
DY3: Up Gor . . . 2H 75
DY4: Tip . . . 3H 77
DY5: Brie H . . . 1H 109
DY5: Quar B . . . 3C 110
DY8: Amb . . . 3D 108
DY8: Stourb . . . 1D 124
DY9: Lye . . . 6B 110
WS1: Wals . . . 2D 48
WS6: C Hay . . . 3C 6
WS10: Darl . . . 5E 47
WV11: Ess . . . 4H 17
WV14: Bils . . . 2G 61
HILL TOP
West Bromwich . . . 6G 63
Hill Top B70: W Brom . . . 5G 63
Hilltop DY9: W'cte . . . 2A 126
Hill Top Av. B62: B'hth . . . 4E 113
Hill Top Cl. B44: Gt Barr . . . 1G 83
Hill Top Dr. B36: Hodg H . . . 2B 104
Hill Top Ind. Est. B70: W Brom . . . 5F 63
(Bilport La.)
B70: W Brom . . . 5E 63
(Pikehelve St.)
Hill Top Rd. B31: N'fld . . . 4D 144
B68: O'bry . . . 1A 114
Hilltop Rd. DY2: Dud . . . 1G 95
Hill Top Wlk. WS9: A'rdge . . . 6E 23
Hillview WS9: A'rdge . . . 5D 22
Hillview Cl. B63: Hale . . . 5G 111
Hillview Rd. B45: Rubery . . . 1E 157
Hill Village Rd. B75: Four O . . . 4G 37
Hillville Gdns. DY8: Stourb . . . 2F 125
HILL WOOD . . . 5A 38
Hillwood WS3: Pels . . . 5D 20
Hillwood Av. B90: M'path . . . 3E 165
Hillwood Cl. DY6: K'wfrd . . . 5A 92
Hillwood Comn. Rd. B75: Four O . . . 5H 37
Hillwood Rd. B31: N'fld . . . 6C 130
B62: B'hth . . . 4C 112
B75: Four O, R'ley . . . 5H 37
Hillyfields Rd. B23: Erd . . . 3C 84
Hilly Rd. WV14: Bils . . . 3G 61
Hilsea Cl. WV8: Pend . . . 6D 14
Hilston Av. B63: Hale . . . 1H 127
WV4: Penn . . . 1A 58
HILTON . . . 5H 11
Hilton Av. B28: Hall G . . . 3E 149
Hilton Cl. WS3: Blox . . . 5F 19
Hilton Cross WV10: F'stne . . . 2D 16
Hilton Cross Bus. Pk. WV10: F'stne . . . 2D 16
Hilton Dr. B72: W Grn . . . 5A 70
Hilton La. WS6: Gt Wyr . . . 3F 7
WV11: Ess . . . 6A 6
Hilton Main Ind. Est. WV10: F'stne . . . 2E 17
Hilton Pk. WV11: Ess . . . 1G 17
Hilton Pl. WV14: Bils . . . 6H 45
Hilton Rd. B69: Tiv . . . 1C 96
WV4: E'shll . . . 6B 44
WV10: F'stne . . . 1D 16
WV12: W'hall . . . 1C 30
Hilton St. B70: W Brom . . . 4G 79
WV10: Wolv . . . 6A 28
Hilton Trad. Est. WV4: E'shll . . . 6B 44
Hilton Way WV12: W'hall . . . 1C 30
Himbleton Cft. B90: M'path . . . 2E 165
HIMLEY . . . 4H 73
Himley Av. DY1: Dud . . . 5B 76
Himley By-Pass DY3: Himl . . . 4G 73
Himley Cl. B43: Gt Barr . . . 3G 65
WV12: W'hall . . . 4B 30
Himley Ct. *DY3: Lwr G . . . 4A 76*
(off Peak Dr.)
Himley Cres. WV4: Penn . . . 6F 43
Himley Gdns. DY3: Lwr G . . . 3D 74
Himley Gro. B45: Redn . . . 3H 157
Himley House & Model Village . . . 4A 74
Himley La. DY3: Himl, Swind . . . 5E 73
(not continuous)
Himley Ri. B90: Ches G . . . 5C 164
Himley Rd. DY1: Dud . . . 5G 75
DY3: Gorn . . . 4D 74
Himley St. DY1: Dud . . . 6C 76
Himley Wood Nature Reserve . . . 4G 73
Hinbrook Rd. DY1: Dud . . . 6A 76
Hinchliffe Av. WV14: Cose . . . 3D 60
Hinckes Rd. WV6: Tett . . . 4H 25
Hinckley Ct. B68: O'bry . . . 4H 113
Hinckley St. B5: Birm . . . 2F 117 (6D 4)
Hincks St. WV2: E'shll . . . 4C 44
Hindhead Rd. B14: Yard W . . . 3C 148
Hindlip Cl. B63: Hale . . . 3H 127
Hindlow Cl. B7: Birm . . . 5B 102
Hindon Gro. B27: A Grn . . . 6A 136
Hindon Sq. B15: Edg . . . 3B 116
Hindon Wlk. B32: Bart G . . . 3A 130
Hingeston St. B18: Hock . . . 5D 100
Hingley Cft. WS9: A'rdge . . . 6H 35
Hingley Ind. Pk. B64: Crad H . . . 2E 111
Hingley Rd. B63: Crad . . . 5C 110
Hingley St. B64: Crad H . . . 2F 111

Hinksford—Howard Rd. E.

HINKSFORD 1F 91
Hinksford Gdns. DY3: Swind. 5E 73
Hinksford La. DY3: Swind. 5E 73
DY6: K'wfrd. 5E 73
Hinksford Pk. Res. Mobile Homes
DY6: K'wfrd. 1E 91
Hinsford Cl. DY6: K'wfrd. 1C 92
Hinstock Cl. WV4: Penn 1E 59
Hinstock Rd. B20: Hand 6B 82
Hintlesham Av. B15: Edg 6H 115
Hinton Gro. WV11: Wed 4H 29
Hintons Coppice B93: Know 3A 166
Hipkins St. DY4: Tip 6G 61
Hiplands Rd. B62: Hale 1F 129
Hipsley Cl. B36: Cas B 6G 87
Hipsmoor Cl. B37: K'hrst 6B 106
Hirdemonsway B90: Dic H 4G 163
Histons Dr. WV8: Cod 5F 13
Histons Hill WV8: Cod. 5F 13
Hitchcock Cl. B67: Smeth 4B 98
Hitches La. B15: Edg 4D 116
Hitherside B90: Dic H. 4H 163
Hive Development Cen. B18: Hock 2C 100
HMP Birmingham B18: Win G 4A 100
Hobacre Cl. B45: Rubery 1G 157
Hobart Ct. B74: Four O 6G 37
Hobart Cft. B7: Birm 5A 102
Hobart Dr. WS5: Wals. 5G 49
Hobart Rd. DY4: Tip 4G 61
Hobbis Ho. B38: K Nor 2G 159
HOBBLE END 6G 7
Hobble End La. WS6: Gt Wyr. 1G 19
Hobgate Cl. WV10: Wolv 5B 28
Hobgate Rd. WV10: Wolv. 5B 28
Hob Grn. Rd. DY9: W'cte 3A 126
Hobhouse Cl. B42: Gt Barr 6B 66
Hob La. B92: Bars. 3A 168
Hobley St. WV13: W'hall. 1C 46
Hobmoor Cft. B25: Yard 4B 120
Hob Moor Rd. B10: Small H 2F 119
B25: Yard 3A 120
Hobnock Rd. WV11: Ess. 3A 18
Hobs Hole La. WS9: A'rdge 2D 34
Hob's Mdw. B92: Olton 3E 137
Hobs Moat Rd. B92: Olton, Sol. 3F 137
Hobson Cl. B18: Hock. 4C 100
Hobson Rd. B29: S Oak 4D 132
Hobs Rd. WS10: W'bry. 1G 63
HOCKLEY
Birmingham 4D 100
Hockley Brook Trad. Est.
B18: Hock. 3C 100
Hockley Cen. *B18: Birm* *1A 4*
(off Big Pen, The)
Hockley Cir. B19: Hock. 3D 100
Hockley Cl. B19: Hock. 3F 101
Hockley Flyover B19: Hock. 3D 100
Hockley Hill B18: Birm 4D 100
Hockley Hill Ind. Est. B18: Hock 4D 100
Hockley Ind. Est. B18: Hock. 4D 100
Hockley La. DY2: Neth 6D 94
Hockley Pool Cl. B18: Hock 4D 100
Hockley Rd. B23: Erd. 3D 84
WV14: Cose 6C 60
Hockley St. B18: Birm. 5E 101
B19: Birm 5E 101
Hodder Gro. B71: W Brom 6D 64
HODGEHILL 3B 104
Hodge Hill Av. DY9: W'cte 2A 126
Hodge Hill Comn. B36: Hodg H 2C 104
Hodgehill Ct. B36: Hodg H. 2C 104
Hodge Hill Rd. B34: Hodg H. 3C 104
Hodges Dr. B69: Tiv 6B 78
Hodgetts Cl. B67: Smeth 6B 98
Hodgetts Dr. B63: Hale 5F 127
Hodgkins Cl. WS8: Bwnhls. 1C 22
Hodgson Twr. B19: Hock. 3F 101
Hodnell Cl. B36: Cas B. 6G 87
Hodnet Cl. WV14: Bils 6D 44
Hodnet Dr. DY5: P'ntt 3G 93
Hodson Av. WV13: W'hall 2C 46
Hodson Cl. WV11: Wed 1H 29
Hoff Beck Ct. B9: Birm 1B 118
Hogarth Cl. B43: Gt Barr 6F 51
WV13: W'hall 1G 45
Hogarth Ho. B15: Birm 3E 117
Hogg's La. B31: N'fld 3C 144
HOLBEACHE 6A 74
Holbeache La. DY6: K'wfrd 6A 74
Holbeache Rd. DY6: W Hth 1A 92
Holbeach Rd. B33: Yard 1F 121
Holbeche Rd. B75: S Cold. 6F 55
B93: Know 2C 166
Holberg Gro. WV11: Wed. 4H 29
Holborn Cen., The DY3: Sed 6H 59
Holborn Hill B6: Aston 1B 102
Holbrook Gro. B37: Mars G 2D 122
Holbrook Twr. B36: Hodg H 1A 104
Holbury Cl. WV9: Pend. 5E 15
Holcombe Rd. B11: Tys 1G 135
Holcroft Rd. B63: Crad 6E 111
DY6: W Hth. 6A 74
DY9: Lye. 1G 125
Holcroft St. DY4: Tip. 5A 78
WV2: E'shll 4C 44
Holden Cl. B23: Erd 5E 85
Holden Cres. WS3: Wals 4C 32
Holden Cft. DY4: Tip. 4A 78
Holden Pl. WS3: Wals 5C 32
Holden Rd. WS10: W'bry 3G 63
WV4: Penn 2B 58
Holdens, The B28: Hall G 1E 149
Holden Way B75: Four O 1H 53
Holder Rd. B11: S'brk. 5C 118
B25: Yard 4A 120
Holders Gdns. B13: Mose 3E 133
Holders La. B13: Mose. 3E 133
Holdford Rd. B6: Witt. 5H 83
Holdgate Rd. B29: W Cas 6F 131
Hole Farm Rd. B31: N'fld 3G 145
Hole Farm Way B38: K Nor 2B 160
Hole La. B31: N'fld 1G 145
Holendene Way WV5: Wom 6E 57
Holford Av. WS2: Wals 5A 48
Holford Dr. B6: Witt 3G 83
B42: P Barr. 3G 83
Holford Ind. Pk. B6: Witt 4H 83
Holford Way B6: Witt 3H 83
Holifast Rd. B72: W Grn. 6H 69
Holland Av. B68: O'bry 5B 98
B93: Know 1D 166
Holland Ho. *B19: Birm* *4F 101*
(off Gt. Hampton Row)
Holland Ind. Pk. WS10: Darl 3D 46
Holland Rd. B43: Gt Barr 6H 65
B72: S Cold 2H 69
WV14: Bils 4G 45
Holland Rd. W. B6: Aston 3H 101
Hollands Pl. WS3: Blox 6B 20
Hollands Rd. WS3: Blox 6B 20
Holland St. B3: Birm 6E 101 (3A 4)
B72: S Cold 1H 69
DY1: Dud 1D 94
DY4: Tip 6C 62
Hollands Way WS3: Pels 3D 20
Hollemeadow Av. WS3: Blox 2B 32
Holliars Gro. B37: K'hrst 4B 106
Holliday Pas. B1: Birm 2E 117 (6B 4)
Holliday Rd. B21: Hand 2B 100
B24: Erd 3G 85
Holliday St. B1: Birm. 2E 117 (6A 4)
Holliday Wharf B1: Birm 2E 117 (6B 4)
Hollie Lucas Rd. B13: Mose. 6H 133
Hollies, The B6: Aston 1B 102
B16: Birm 6B 100
WV2: Wolv. 3G 43 (6A 170)
WV5: Wom 6H 57
Hollies Cft. B5: Edg. 6E 117
Hollies Dr. B62: Hale 5D 112
WS10: W'bry. 2F 63
Hollies Ind. Est., The
WV2: Wolv. 3G 43 (6A 170)
Hollies La. WV6: Nur 5A 24
Hollies Ri. B64: Crad H 3H 111
Hollies Rd. B69: Tiv 1A 96
Hollies St. DY5: P'ntt 2H 93
Hollin Brow Cl. B93: Know. 6D 166
Hollingberry La. B76: Walm. 2D 70
Hollings Gro. B91: Sol 1F 165
Hollington Cres. B33: Stech 5E 105
Hollington Rd. WV1: Wolv 3D 44
Hollington Way B90: M'path. 2G 165
Hollinwell Cl. WS3: Blox 4G 19
Hollister Dr. B32: Bart G. 2D 130
Hollow, The B13: Mose 1G 133
Holloway B31: N'fld 1C 144
Holloway, The DY3: Swind. 6D 72
DY8: Amb 4D 108
WV6: Tett 1A 42
Holloway Bank B70: W Brom 4F 63
WS10: W'bry. 4F 63
Holloway Bank Trad. Est. WS10: W'bry 4F 63
Holloway Cir. Queensway
B1: Birm. 2F 117 (6D 4)
Holloway Ct. B63: Crad. 6F 111
Holloway Dr. WV5: Wom 2E 73
HOLLOWAY END 5F 109
Holloway Head B1: Birm 2F 117 (6C 4)
Holloway St. DY3: Lwr G, Up Gor 3H 75
WV1: Wolv 4C 44
Holloway St. W. DY3: Lwr G 2H 75
Hollow Cft. B31: N'fld 4F 145
Hollowcroft Rd. WV12: W'hall 1B 30
Hollowmeadow Ho. B36: Hodg H. 1B 104
Holly Av. B12: Bal H 6A 118
B29: S Oak. 4D 132
HOLLY BANK 4C 22
Hollybank Av. WV11: Ess 4A 18
Hollybank Cl. WS3: Blox 5G 19
Hollybank Gro. B63: Hale 4F 127
Hollybank Rd. B13: Mose. 6A 134
Hollyberry Av. B91: Sol. 1E 165
Hollyberry Cl. B63: Hale. 2A 128
Hollyberry Cft. B34: S End 3G 105
Hollybrow B29: W Cas 6E 131
Holly Bush Gro. B32: Quin 4B 114
Holly Bush La. WV10: Share 5A 6
(not continuous)
Hollybush La. DY8: Amb 4D 108
WV4: Penn 1B 58
WV8: Oaken 5D 12
Holly Bush Wlk. B64: Crad H 2F 111
Holly Cl. B76: Walm 3D 70
WV12: W'hall 3C 30
Hollycot Gdns. B12: Bal H 5H 117
Holly Ct. B23: Erd. 2G 85
WS5: Wals 1E 65
Hollycroft Gdns. WV6: Tett. 4H 25
Hollycroft Rd. B21: Hand 6H 81
Hollydale Rd. B24: Erd. 4A 86
B65: Row R 6D 96
Holly Dell B38: K Nor. 5D 146
Holly Dr. B27: A Grn. 3H 135
B47: H'wd. 2B 162
Hollyfaste Rd. B33: Sheld. 2E 121
Hollyfield Av. B91: Sol 4C 150
Hollyfield Ct. B75: S Cold. 6C 54
Hollyfield Cres. B75: S Cold. 1C 70
Hollyfield Dr. B75: S Cold. 6C 54
Hollyfield Rd. B75: S Cold 6C 54
Hollyfield Rd. Sth. B76: Walm. 1D 70
Holly Gro. B19: Hand 1D 100
B29: S Oak 3B 132
(not continuous)
B30: B'vlle. 5B 132
DY8: Stourb 6D 108
WV3: Wolv 4D 42
Holly Hall Rd. DY2: Dud. 3C 94
Hollyhedge Cl. B31: N'fld 1B 144
WS2: Wals 1A 48
Hollyhedge La. WS2: Wals. 6A 32
Hollyhedge Rd. B71: W Brom 6C 64
Holly Hill B45: Fran. 6F 143
WS6: Gt Wyr. *5E 7*
(off Holly La.)
Holly Hill Rd. B45: Fran 5G 143
Holly Hill Shop. Cen. B45: Fran. 6G 143
Hollyhock Rd. B27: A Grn 4F 135
DY2: Dud 6H 77
Hollyhurst B46: Wat O. 4E 89
Hollyhurst Cvn. Pk. B62: Hunn. 1B 142
Hollyhurst Dr. DY8: Word. 6B 92
Hollyhurst Gro. B26: Yard. 5C 120
B90: Shir 1H 163
Hollyhurst Rd. B73: S'tly 2B 68
Holly La. B24: Erd 2H 85
B37: Mars G 3B 122
B66: Smeth. 2C 98
B67: Smeth. 4B 98
B74: Four O 6G 37
B75: Four O 6G 37
B76: Wis. 2H 71
CV7: Bal C 4H 169
WS6: Gt Wyr. 5E 7
WS9: A'rdge 1H 35
WS9: Wals W 3C 22
(not continuous)
Holly Lodge Wlk. B37: F'bri 1B 122
Hollymoor Way B31: Longb 5A 144
Holly Mt. B16: Edg 2H 115
Hollymount B62: Quin. 4G 113
Hollyoak Cft. B31: Longb 1F 159
Hollyoake Cl. B68: O'bry 1G 113
Hollyoak Gro. B91: Sol 6E 151
Hollyoak Rd. B74: S'tly. 5H 51
Hollyoak St. B71: W Brom 3B 80
Holly Pk. Dr. B24: Erd 3H 85
Holly Pk. Ind. Est. B24: Erd 5A 86
Hollypiece Ho. B27: A Grn 3G 135
Holly Pl. B6: Aston 1G 101
B29: S Oak 3D 132
Holly Rd. B16: Edg. 2G 115
B20: Hand. 1B 100
B30: K Nor 3C 146
B65: B'hth. 2B 112
B68: O'bry. 3A 114
B71: W Brom 5C 64
DY1: Dud 4C 76
WS10: W'bry 6F 47
Holly St. B67: Smeth 4D 98
DY1: Dud 3A 94
Holly Vw. WV11: Ess 4A 18
Hollywell Rd. B26: Sheld 5F 121
B93: Know 4C 166
Hollywell St. WV14: Cose. 4C 60
HOLLYWOOD 1A 162
Holly Wood B43: Gt Barr. 4C 66
Hollywood Bowl 1H 157
Hollywood By-Pass B38: Head H 3G 161
B47: H'wd. 3G 161
Hollywood Cft. B42: Gt Barr 5B 66
Hollywood Dr. B47: H'wd 1A 162
Hollywood Gdns. B47: H'wd. 1A 162
Hollywood La. B47: H'wd 1A 162
Hollywood Nature Reserve. 4C 66
Holman Cl. WV13: W'hall 1G 45
Holman Rd. WV13: W'hall. 1F 45
Holman Way WV13: W'hall. 1G 45
Holmbridge Gro. WS4: S'fld. 5H 21
Holme Mill WV10: F'hses 3H 15
Holmes, The WV10: F'hses 4H 15
Holmes Cl. B43: Gt Barr 6A 66
Holmes Dr. B45: Rubery 3F 157
Holmesfield Rd. B42: Gt Barr 6E 67
Holmes Rd. WV12: W'hall 2D 30
Holme Way WS4: Rus. 2F 33
Holmwood Rd. B10: Small H 2D 118
Holt Ct. Nth. B7: Birm. 5H 101 (1H 5)
Holt Ct. Sth. B7: Birm 5H 101 (1H 5)
Holte Community Leisure Cen. 2F 101
Holte Dr. B75: R'ley 1B 54
Holte Rd. B6: Aston 6A 84
B11: S'brk. 6D 118
Holtes Wlk. B6: Aston. 1B 102
Holt Rd. B62: B'hth. 2E 113
Holtshill La. WS1: Wals 1D 48
Holt St. B7: Birm. 5H 101 (1G 5)
Holy Farm Trekking Cen. 2G 129
Holyhead Community Leisure Cen. 1H 99
Holyhead Rd. B21: Hand. 6F 81
WS10: Darl 1C 62
WS10: W'bry 2D 62
WV8: Cod, Oaken 5B 12
Holyhead Rd. Ind. Est. WS10: W'bry. 2D 62
Holyhead Way B21: Hand. 1H 99
Holyoak Cl. B6: Aston. 6H 83
Holyrood Gro. B6: Aston. 1G 101
Holy Well Cl. B16: Edg. 1C 116
Holywell La. B45: Rubery 3D 156
Home Cl. B28: Hall G 1F 149
Homecroft Rd. B25: Yard 3C 120
Homedene Rd. B31: N'fld 6C 130
Homefield Rd. WV8: Bilb 4H 13
Homelands B42: Gt Barr. 6D 66
Homelands Pk. WV10: Cov H 1G 15
Homelea Rd. B25: Yard 3B 120
Homemead Gro. B45: Rubery. 2F 157
Home Mdw. Ho. B27: A Grn. 3G 135
Home Peal Ho. B14: K Hth. 1G 147
HOMER HILL 4D 110
Homer Hill Rd. B63: Crad. 4E 111
Homer Rd. B75: R'ley 1A 54
B91: Sol 4F 151
Homers Fold WV14: Bils. 6F 45
Homer St. B12: Bal H 6H 117
Homerton Rd. B44: K'sdng 4B 68
Homestead Cl. DY3: Up Gor. 2A 76
Homestead Dr. B75: R'ley. 6A 38
Homestead Rd. B33: Sheld 2F 121
Home Twr. B7: Birm 4B 102
Homewood Cl. B76: Walm 2C 70
Honesty Cl. WS8: Clay 1H 21
Honeswode Cl. B20: Hand 1C 100
Honeyborne Rd. B75: S Cold 4B 54
Honeybourne Cl. B63: Hale. 2A 128
Honeybourne Cres. WV5: Wom 2F 73
Honeybourne Rd. B33: Sheld. 3G 121
B63: Hale 2C 128
Honeybourne Way WV13: W'hall 1C 46
Honeycomb Way B31: N'fld 4C 144
Honeysuckle Av. DY6: K'wfrd 2C 92
Honeysuckle Cl. B32: Quin. 6H 113
Honeysuckle Dr. WS5: Wals 2E 65
Honeysuckle Gro. B27: A Grn. 6A 120
Honeysuckle Way WS6: Gt Wyr 1H 7
Honeytree Cl. DY6: K'wfrd 6D 92
Honiley Dr. B73: New O 3C 68
Honiley Rd. B33: Yard. 1E 121
Honister Cl. DY5: Quar B 2B 110
Honiton Cl. B31: N'fld. 3C 144
Honiton Cres. B31: N'fld. 3C 144
Honiton Wlk. B66: Smeth 4F 99
Honiton Way WS9: A'rdge. 4B 34
Honnington Ct. B29: W Cas 4D 130
Honor Av. WV4: Penn. 6G 43
Hood Gro. B30: K Nor. 3H 145
Hook Dr. B74: Four O 5F 37
Hooper St. B18: Win G 5B 100
Hoosen Cl. B62: Quin. 5G 113
Hopedale Rd. B32: Quin. 6A 114
Hope Pl. B29: S Oak. 3B 132
Hope Rd. DY4: Tip 1C 78
Hope St. B5: Birm 3F 117
B62: B'hth 3D 112
B70: W Brom 5C 80
DY2: Dud 1E 95
DY8: Word 6B 92
WS1: Wals 3C 48
Hope Ter. DY2: Neth 4E 95
WS10: Darl. 1D 62
Hopkins Ct. WS10: W'bry. 2G 63
Hopkins Dr. B71: W Brom. 6C 64
Hopkins St. DY4: Tip. 5A 78
Hopstone Gdns. WV4: Penn. 6D 42
Hopstone Rd. B29: W Cas. 4E 131
Hopton Cl. DY4: Tip 3C 62
WV6: Pert 6F 25
Hopton Cres. WV11: Wed. 3G 29
Hopton Gdns. DY1: Dud 4C 76
Hopton Gro. B13: Mose 2C 148
Hopwas Gro. B37: K'hrst 4B 106
HOPWOOD 6G 159
Hopwood Cl. B63: Hale. 3A 128
Hopwood Gro. B31: Longb 3C 158
Hopyard Cl. DY3: Gorn. 4F 75
Hopyard Gdns. WV14: Cose. 2D 60
Hopyard La. DY3: Gorn. 5F 75
Hopyard Rd. WS2: Wals 1E 47
Horace Partridge Rd. WS10: Mox 6A 46
Horace St. WV14: Cose 5C 60
Horatio Dr. B13: Mose 1H 133
Hordern Cl. WV6: Wolv 4D 26
Hordern Cres. DY5: Quar B 3H 109
Hordern Gro. WV6: Wolv 4D 26
Hordern Pk. WV10: Cov H 1G 15
Hordern Rd. WV6: Wolv 4D 26
Hornbeam Cl. B29: W Cas 6F 131
Hornbeam Wlk. WV3: Wolv 2E 43
Hornbrook Gro. B92: Olton 6A 136
Hornby Gro. B14: Yard W 3C 148
Hornby Rd. WV4: Penn. 1G 59
Horner Way B65: B'hth 2C 112
Horne Way B34: S End 4A 106
Horning Dr. WV14: Bils. 2E 61
Hornsey Gro. B44: K'sdng. 3A 68
Hornsey Rd. B44: K'sdng 3A 68
Hornton Cl. B74: Lit A. 4D 36
Horrell Rd. B26: Sheld 4E 121
B90: Shir 5F 149
Horsecroft Dr. *B71: W Brom* *5E 65*
(off Tompstone Rd.)
Horse Fair B5: Birm 2F 117 (6D 4)
Horsehills Dr. WV3: Wolv. 1C 42
Horselea Cft. B8: W End. 5A 104
Horseley Flds. WV1: Wolv 1H 43 (3D 170)
HORSELEY HEATH 1C 78
Horseley Heath DY4: Tip 3B 78
Horseley Rd. DY4: Tip 1C 78
Horseshoe, The B68: O'bry 1A 114
Horseshoe Cl. *WS2: Wals* *4H 47*
(off Wellington St.)
Horse Shoes La. B26: Sheld 6F 121
Horseshoe Wlk. *DY4: Tip.* *2G 77*
(off New Cross St.)
Horsfall Rd. B75: S Cold. 6E 55
Horsham Av. DY8: Word. 6A 92
Horsley Rd. B43: Gt Barr. 1F 67
B74: Lit A 1B 52
Horton Cl. DY3: Sed 5G 59
WS10: Darl 4D 46
Horton Gro. B90: M'path. 4E 165
Horton Pl. WS10: Darl 4D 46
Horton Sq. B12: Birm 4G 117
Horton St. B70: W Brom. 5A 80
DY4: Tip 2D 78
WS10: Darl. 4D 46
Hospital Dr. B15: Edg. 1A 132
Hospital La. B69: Tiv 5B 78
WS6: C Hay 2B 6
WV14: Cose 6D 60
Hospital Rd. WS7: Burn 1C 10
Hospital St. B19: Birm, Hock. 4F 101 (1D 4)
(not continuous)
WS2: Wals. 5B 32
WV2: Wolv 2H 43 (5D 170)
Hothersall Dr. B73: Bold 5F 69
Hotspur Rd. B44: K'sdng 4H 67
Hough Pl. WS2: Wals. 4H 47
Hough Rd. B14: K Hth. 1F 147
WS2: Wals 4G 47
Houghton Ct. B28: Hall G. 3D 148
Houghton St. B69: O'bry. 3F 97
B70: W Brom 1B 98
Houldey Rd. B31: N'fld. 6F 145
Houliston Cl. WS10: W'bry. 6H 47
Houndsfield Cl. B47: H'wd 3C 162
Houndsfield Ct. B47: Wyt. 4A 162
Houndsfield Gro. B47: Wyt. 4A 162
(not continuous)
Houndsfield La. B47: H'wd. 3C 162
B47: Wyt. 4A 162
B90: Dic H 3C 162
Houndsfield M. B47: Wyt 4B 162
Houx, The DY8: Amb 3C 108
Hove Rd. B27: A Grn. 4A 136
Howard Ho. B92: H Ard 1B 154
Howard Rd. B14: K Hth. 6F 133
B20: Hand. 5D 82
B25: Yard 4A 120
B43: Gt Barr 5G 65
B92: Olton. 2C 136
WV11: Wed. 1H 29
WV14: Bils 2H 61
Howard Rd. E. B13: Mose 6H 133

198 A-Z Birmingham Deluxe

Howard St.—Jiggin's La.

Howard St. B19: Birm 5F 101 (1C 4)
B70: W Brom 6F 63
DY4: Tip 2B 78
WV2: Wolv 3H 43 (6C 170)
Howard St. Ind. Est. B70: W Brom 6F 63
Howarth Way B6: Aston 2A 102
Howden Pl. B33: Stech 4E 105
Howdle's La. WS8: Bwnhls 3B 10
Howe Cres. WV12: W'hall 3C 30
Howell Rd. WV2: Wolv 4A 44
Howes Cft. B35: Cas V 5E 87
Howe St. B4: Birm 6H 101 (2H 5)
Howford Gro. B7: Birm 5B 102
Howland Cl. WV9: Pend 5D 14
Howley Av. B44: Gt Barr 4G 67
Howley Grange Rd. B62: Quin 6F 113
Howl Pl. DY4: Tip 2H 77
Hoylake Cl. WS3: Blox 4H 19
Hoylake Dr. B69: Tiv 2A 96
Hoylake Rd. WV6: Pert 4D 24
Hoyland Way B30: B'vlle 5A 132
HRS Ind. Pk. B33: Sheld 2G 121
Hubert Cft. B29: S Oak 3B 132
Hubert Rd. B29: S Oak 3B 132
Hubert St. B6: Aston 4H 101
Hucker Cl. WS2: Wals 4G 47
Hucker Rd. WS2: Wals 4G 47
Huddesford Dr. CV7: Bal C 1H 169
Huddlestone Cl. WV10: F'stne 1D 16
Huddleston Way B29: S Oak 4G 131
Huddocks Vw. WS3: Pels 2D 20
Hudson Av. B46: Col 3H 107
Hudson Gro. WV6: Pert 4E 25
Hudson Rd. B20: Hand 3B 82
DY4: Tip 3C 78
Hudson's Dr. B30: K Nor 3C 146
Hudswell Dr. DY5: Brie H 3H 109
Huggins Cl. CV7: Bal C 5H 169
Hughes Av. WV3: Wolv 3D 42
Hughes Pl. WV14: Bils 4F 45
Hughes Rd. WS10: Mox 6A 46
WV14: Bils 4F 45
Hugh Gaitskell Ct. WV14: Wolv 3E 45
Hugh Porter Way WV6: Tett 2D 26
Hugh Rd. B10: Small H 2E 119
B67: Smeth 4B 98
Hugh Vs. B10: Small H 2E 119
Hulbert Dr. DY2: Dud 3D 94
Hulland Pl. DY5: Brie H 6G 93
Hullbrook Rd. B13: Mose 2C 148
Humber Av. B76: Walm 6E 71
Humber Gdns. B63: Crad 6E 111
Humber Gro. B36: Cas B 6B 88
Humber Rd. WV3: Wolv 2E 43
Humberstone Rd. B24: Erd 3C 86
Humber Twr. B7: Birm 5A 102
Hume St. B66: Smeth 5F 99
(not continuous)
Humpage Rd. B9: Bord G 1E 119
Humphrey Middlemore Dr.
B17: Harb 1H 131
Humphrey's Rd. WV10: Bush 2H 27
Humphrey St. DY3: Lwr G 4H 75
Humphries Cres. WV14: Bils 4H 61
Humphries Ho. WS8: Bwnhls 6B 10
Hundred Acre Rd. B74: S'tly 4H 51
Hungary Cl. DY9: Lye 6G 109
Hungary Hill DY9: Lye 6G 109
Hungerfield Rd. B36: Cas B 6G 87
Hungerford Rd. DY8: Stourb 3C 124
Hunningham Gro. B91: Sol 1F 165
HUNNINGTON 6B 128
Hunnington Cl. B32: Bart G 4G 129
Hunnington Cres. B63: Hale 3B 128
Hunscote Cl. B90: Shir 6F 149
Hunslet Cl. B32: Quin 1D 130
Hunslet Rd. B32: Quin 1D 130
Hunstanton Av. B17: Harb 4D 114
Hunstanton Cl. DY5: Brie H 4G 109
Hunter Ct. B5: Edg 6F 117
Hunter Cres. WS3: Blox 3D 32
Hunters Cl. WV14: Bils 4A 46
Hunters Ride DY7: Stourt 6H 91
Hunters Ri. B63: Hale 4F 127
Hunter's Rd. B19: Hock 2D 100
Hunter St. WV6: Wolv 5E 27
Hunters Wlk. B23: Erd 5C 68
Huntingdon Ho. B23: Erd 1B 84
Huntingdon Rd. B71: W Brom 1H 79
Huntington Rd. WV12: W'hall 2D 30
Huntingtree Rd. B63: Hale 1G 127
Huntlands Rd. B63: Hale 3G 127
Huntley Dr. B91: Sol 5F 151
Huntly Rd. B16: Edg 2C 116
Hunton Ct. *B23: Erd* *5E 85*
(off Gravelly Hill N.)
Hunton Hill B23: Erd 4D 84
Hunton Rd. B23: Erd 4E 85
Hunt's La. WV12: W'hall 3D 30
Huntsman Cl. WV14: Cose 3F 61
Hunts Mill Dr. DY5: P'ntt 6G 75
Hunt's Rd. B30: Stir 6C 132
Hurdis Rd. B90: Shir 4G 149
Hurdlow Av. B18: Hock 4D 100
Hurley Cl. B72: W Grn 3A 70
WS5: Wals 5H 49
Hurley Gro. B37: K'hrst 4B 106
Hurley's Fold DY2: Neth 4D 94
Hurlingham Rd. B44: K'sdng 3A 68
Hurricane Pk. B24: Erd 1G 103
Hurricane Way B35: Cas V 5E 87
Hursey Dr. DY4: Tip 2A 78
Hurst, The B13: Mose 6C 134
B47: H'wd 3A 162
Hurstbourne Cres. WV1: Wolv 2D 44
Hurst Cl. B36: Cas B 2A 106
Hurstcroft Rd. B33: Kitts G 6F 105
Hurst Grn. Rd. B62: B'hth 2E 113
B76: Min 1H 87
B93: Ben H 5B 166
Hurst Grn. Shop. Cen. B62: B'hth 3F 113
HURST HILL 5C 60
Hurst Hill Ct. *WV14: Cose* *5C 60*
(off Caddick St.)
WV14: Cose 5C 60
(Hartland Av.)
Hurst La. B34: S End 3H 105
DY4: Tip 2F 77
DY5: Brie H 6B 94
Hurst La. Nth. B36: Cas B 2A 106
Hurst Rd. B67: Smeth 6B 98
WV14: Cose 4C 60
Hurst St. B5: Birm 2G 117 (6E 5)
(not continuous)
Hurstway, The B23: Erd 5C 68
Hurstwood Rd. B23: Erd 5C 68
Huskison Cl. B69: Tiv 6B 78
Husphins La. WV8: Cod, Cod W 2A 12
Hussey Rd. WS8: Bwnhls 5A 10
Hutchings La. B90: Dic H 4H 163
Hut Hill La. WS6: Gt Wyr 1G 7
Hutton Av. B8: Salt 4D 102
Hutton Rd. B8: Salt 4D 102
B20: Hand 6D 82
Huxbey Dr. B92: Sol 5B 138
Huxley Cl. WV9: Pend 4E 15
Hyacinth Cl. WS5: Wals 2D 64
Hyatt Sq. DY5: Brie H 4G 109
Hyatts Wlk. B65: Row R 4H 95
Hyde, The DY9: W'cte 3H 125
Hyde Rd. WV11: Wed 3F 29
Hydes Rd. B71: W Brom 4A 64
WS10: W'bry 2G 63
Hyett Way WV14: Bils 3B 62
Hylda Rd. B20: Hand 6D 82
Hylstone Cres. WV11: Wed 3F 29
Hylton St. B18: Birm 4E 101
Hyperion Dr. WV4: Penn 2E 59
Hyperion Rd. B36: Hodg H 6C 86
DY7: Stourt 4A 108
Hyron Hall Rd. B27: A Grn 3A 136
Hyssop Cl. B7: Birm 4A 102
Hytall Rd. B90: Shir 5C 148
Hythe Gro. B25: Yard 3B 120

I

Ibberton Rd. B14: K Hth 4B 148
Ibis Gdns. DY6: K'wfrd 3E 93
Ibstock Dr. DY8: Stourb 1E 125
Icknield Cl. B74: S'tly 2A 52
Icknield Port Rd. B16: Birm 5A 100
Icknield Sq. B16: Birm 6C 100
Icknield St. B18: Birm 5D 100
(not continuous)
B38: Forh 6C 160
B38: Head H, K Nor 1C 160
Ida Rd. B70: W Brom 6B 80
WS2: Wals 2H 47
Idbury Rd. B44: K'sdng 6A 68
Ideal Works DY9: Lye 5C 110
Idmiston Cft. B14: K Hth 5H 147
Idonia Rd. WV6: Pert 4E 25
Ikon Gallery 1E 117 (5A 4)
Ilford Rd. B23: Erd 1D 84
Iliffe Way B17: Harb 1H 131
Ilkley Gro. B37: F'bri 1B 122
ILLEY 5E 129
Illeybrook Sq. B32: Bart G 3B 130
Illey Cl. B31: Longb 6H 143
Illey La. B32: Fran 5E 129
B62: Hunn 4C 128
Illshaw WV9: Pend 4F 15
Illshaw Heath Rd. B94: H'ley H 6B 164
Illshaw Path B90: Bly P 6D 164
Ilmington Dr. B73: New O 2C 68
Ilmington Rd. B29: W Cas 4D 130
Ilsham Gro. B31: Longb 3C 158
Ilsley Rd. B23: Erd 3E 85
Imax Theatre 6H 101 (2H 5)
Imex Bus. Pk. B9: Bord G 1D 118
B11: Tys 5F 119
B33: Stech 5C 104
DY4: Tip 4A 78
WV2: Wolv 4G 43
Imperial Ri. B46: Col 5G 89
Imperial Rd. B9: Bord G 1E 119
Impey Rd. B31: N'fld 6D 144
Impsley Cl. B36: Cas B 1F 105
Ince Rd. WS10: Darl 4C 46
Inchcape Av. B20: Hand 4C 82
Inchford Rd. B92: Sol 6A 138
Inchlaggan Rd. WV10: Wolv 3B 28
Infantry Pl. B75: S Cold 5E 55
Ingatestone Dr. DY8: Word 6A 92
Ingestre Cl. WS3: Blox 4F 19
Ingestre Dr. B43: Gt Barr 4H 65
Inge St. B5: Birm 2G 117 (6D 4)
Ingestre Rd. B28: Hall G 6F 135
WV10: Oxl 6G 15
Ingham Way B17: Harb 3E 115
Ingleby Gdns. WV6: Wolv 4D 26
Ingledew Cl. WS2: Wals 6D 30
Inglefield Rd. B33: Stech 6D 104
Inglemere Gro. B29: W Cas 6D 130
Inglenook Dr. B20: Hand 5D 82
Ingleside Vs. *B11: S'hll* *6C 118*
(off Warwick Rd.)
Ingleton Rd. B8: W End 2G 103
Inglewood Av. WV3: Wolv 3D 42
Inglewood Cl. DY6: K'wfrd 4B 92
Inglewood Gro. B74: S'tly 1H 51
Inglewood Rd. B11: S'hll 6C 118
Ingoldsby Ct. B13: Mose 3B 134
Ingoldsby Rd. B31: N'fld 3C 144
Ingot Cl. WS2: Wals 3H 31
Ingram Gro. B27: A Grn 3G 135
Ingram Pl. WS3: Blox 6B 20
Ingram Rd. WS3: Blox 6A 20
Inhedge, The DY1: Dud 6E 77
Inhedge St. DY3: Up Gor 2A 76
Inkberrow Cl. B69: O'bry 5E 97
Inkberrow Rd. B63: Hale 3H 127
Inkerman Gro. WV10: Wolv 1B 44
Inkerman Ho. *B19: Hock* *3G 101*
(off Newtown Shop. Cen.)
Inkerman St. WV10: Wolv 6B 28
Inland Rd. B24: Erd 5H 85
Innage, The B47: H'wd 4A 162
Innage Rd. B31: N'fld 3F 145
Innisfree Cl. B47: Wyt 5C 162
Innsworth Dr. B35: Cas V 3E 87
Inshaw Cl. B33: Stech 6C 104
Institute Rd. B14: K Hth 5H 133
Instone Rd. B63: Hale 2H 127
Instow Cl. WV12: W'hall 1B 30
Insull Av. B14: K Hth 6B 148
Intended St. B63: Crad 4E 111
International Ho. B37: Mars G 6F 123
International Sq. B37: Mars G 5E 123
Intown WS1: Wals 1D 48
Intown Row WS1: Wals 1D 48
Inverclyde Rd. B20: Hand 4C 82
Inverness Ho. WV1: Wolv 6G 27
Inverness Rd. B31: N'fld 4C 144
Inworth WV9: Pend 4F 15
Ipsley Gro. B23: Erd 2A 84
Ipstones Av. B33: Stech 5D 104
Ipswich Cres. B42: Gt Barr 6D 66
Ipswich Wlk. B37: Chel W 1D 122
Ireland Grn. Rd.
B70: W Brom 5H 79
Ireton Rd. B20: Hand 3C 82
WV10: Bush 4A 16
Iris Cl. B29: W Cas 5F 131
DY2: Dud 6H 77
Iris Dr. B14: K Hth 3F 147
Irnham Rd. B74: Four O 1G 53
Iron Bri. Wlk. DY9: Pedm 5F 125
Iron La. B33: Stech 5B 104
Irvan Av. B70: W Brom 2F 79
Irvine Cl. WS3: Blox 2H 31
Irvine Rd. WS3: Blox 1H 31
Irving Cl. DY3: Lwr G 3E 75
Irving Rd. B92: Sol 1A 138
WV14: Bils 4A 62
Irving St. B1: Birm 2F 117
Irwin Av. B45: Redn 3A 158
Isaac Walton Pl. B70: W Brom 6E 63
Isbourne Way B9: Birm 1B 118
Isis Gro. B36: Cas B 1B 106
WV13: W'hall 1C 46
Island Rd. B21: Hand 6G 81
Islington B63: Hale 1A 128
Islington Row Middleway B15: Birm 2D 116
Ismere Rd. B24: Erd 5H 85
Itchen Gro. WV6: Pert 6E 25
Ithon Gro. B38: K Nor 1A 160
Ivanhoe Rd. B43: Gt Barr 2D 66
WV2: E'shll 5C 44
Ivanhoe St. DY2: Dud 2C 94
Ivatt Cl. WS4: Rus 2F 33
IVERLEY 5B 124
Iverley Rd. B63: Hale 1C 128
Iverley Wlk. DY9: Pedm 3G 125
Ivor Rd. B11: S'hll 1B 134
Ivy Av. B12: Bal H 6A 118
(Clifton Rd.)
B12: Bal H 6A 118
(Runcorn Rd.)
Ivybridge Gro. B42: P Barr 4E 83
Ivy Cl. WS8: Wals W 3C 22
Ivy Cft. WV9: Pend 4D 14
Ivydale Av. B26: Sheld 6G 121
Ivyfield Rd. B23: Erd 2B 84
Ivy Gro. *B18: Win G* *5A 100*
(off Heath Grn. Rd.)
Ivyhouse La. WV14: Cose 5D 60
Ivy Ho. Rd. B69: O'bry 3D 96
Ivyhouse Rd. B38: K Nor 1G 159
Ivy Lodge Cl. B37: Mars G 4C 122
Ivy Pl. B29: S Oak 3B 132
Ivy Rd. B21: Hand 2C 100
B30: Stir 1C 146
B73: Bold 3F 69
DY1: Dud 3C 76
DY4: Tip 6H 61
Ivy Way B90: Dic H 3G 163
Izons Ind. Est. B70: W Brom 6F 79
Izons La. B70: W Brom 6F 79
Izons Rd. B70: W Brom 4A 80

J

Jacey Rd. B16: Edg 1H 115
B90: Shir 3H 149
Jack David Ho. DY4: Tip 2D 78
Jackdaw Cl. DY3: Sed 3G 59
Jackdaw Dr. B36: Cas B 1C 106
Jack Hayward Way
WV1: Wolv 6G 27 (1B 170)
Jack Holden Av. WV14: Cose 3C 60
Jack Newell Ct. *WV14: Cose* *5E 61*
(off Castle St.)
Jack O'Watton Ind. Est. B46: Wat O 4F 89
Jackson Av. B8: Salt 5F 103
Jackson Cl. B11: S'brk 4B 118
B68: O'bry 4H 97
DY4: Tip 4B 62
WS11: Nort C 1C 8
WV10: F'stne 1C 16
Jackson Ct. DY5: Quar B 2B 110
Jackson Dr. B67: Smeth 4B 98
Jackson Ho. B69: O'bry 2G 97
Jackson Rd. B8: Salt 5F 103
Jackson St. B68: O'bry 5H 97
DY9: Lye 6A 110
WV6: Wolv 5F 27
Jackson Wlk. B35: Cas V 5E 87
Jackson Way B32: Quin 6G 113
Jacmar Cres. B67: Smeth 3C 98
Jacobean La. B91: Sol 6C 152
B93: Know 6C 152
Jacob's Hall La.
WS6: Gt Wyr 4G 7
Jacoby Pl. B5: Edg 6E 117
Jaffray Cres. B24: Erd 4F 85
Jaffray Rd. B24: Erd 4F 85
Jakeman Rd. B12: Bal H 6G 117
Jamaica Row B5: Birm 2G 117 (6F 5)
James Bri. Cl. WS2: Wals 4H 47
James Brindley Wlk.
B1: Birm 1E 117 (4A 4)
James Clift Ho. B69: O'bry 4D 96
James Cl. B67: Smeth 4E 99
WS10: Darl 5F 47
James Ct. B13: Mose 3B 134
B38: K Nor 5B 146
James Dee Cl. DY5: Quar B 2C 110
James Eaton Cl. B71: W Brom 2A 80
James Ho. *B17: Harb* *6F 115*
(off Cadbury Way)
B19: Hock *3E 101*
(off Newtown Dr.)
James Lloyd Trust Flats B30: B'vlle 2G 145
James Memorial Homes *B7: Nech* *2C 102*
(off Stuart St.)
Jameson Rd. B6: Aston 1C 102
Jameson St. WV6: Wolv 5F 27
James Rd. B11: Tys 5F 119
B43: Gt Barr 6A 66
B46: Col 1H 107
James Row B69: O'bry 1D 96
James Samuel Pl. B12: Birm 4H 117
James Scott Rd. B63: Crad 5C 110
James St. B3: Birm 6E 101 (2B 4)
WV13: W'hall 6A 30
WV14: Bils 5G 45
James Turner St. B18: Win G 3A 100
James Watt Dr. B19: Hand 1D 100
James Watt Ho. B66: Smeth 4F 99
James Watt Ind. Pk. B66: Smeth 3G 99
James Watt Queensway
B4: Birm 6G 101 (2F 5)
James Watt St. *B4: Birm* *3F 5*
(off Dalton St.)
B71: W Brom 5H 63
(not continuous)
Jane La. Cl. WS2: Wals 5F 31
Janice Gro. B14: Yard W 3C 148
Janine Av. WV11: Wed 2G 29
Jaques Cl. B46: Wat O 5D 88
Jardine Rd. B6: Aston 6H 83
Jarratt Hall B29: S Oak 2A 132
Jarvis Cres. B69: O'bry 5F 97
Jarvis Rd. B23: Erd 1F 85
Jarvis Way B24: Erd 1E 103
J A S Ind. Pk. B65: Row R 5E 97
Jasmin Cft. B14: K Hth 3G 147
Jasmine Cl. WV9: Pend 4D 14
Jasmine Gro. WV8: Bilb 4H 13
Jasmine Rd. DY2: Dud 6H 77
Jasmine Way WS10: Darl 4D 46
Jason Rd. DY9: W'cte 1B 126
Javelin Av. B35: Cas V 4F 87
Jayne Cl. B71: W Brom 4C 64
WV11: Wed 2F 29
Jay Rd. DY6: K'wfrd 1B 92
Jay's Av. DY4: Tip 3B 78
Jayshaw Av. B43: Gt Barr 4A 66
Jeal Cl. B47: Wyt 6G 161
Jean Dr. DY4: Tip 1D 78
Jeavons Pl. WV14: Bils 6E 45
Jedburgh Av. WV6: Pert 5E 25
Jeddo St. WV2: Wolv 3G 43 (6A 170)
Jeffcock Rd. WV3: Wolv 3D 42
Jefferson Cl. B71: W Brom 5H 63
Jeffrey Av. WV4: E'shll 6B 44
Jeffrey Rd. B65: Row R 6E 97
Jeffries Ho. B69: O'bry 2G 97
Jeffs Av. WV2: Wolv 3H 43 (6D 170)
Jenkins Cl. WV14: Bils 6E 45
Jenkinson Rd.
WS10: W'bry 4D 62
Jenkins St. B10: Small H 3C 118
Jenks Av. WV10: Bush 1A 28
Jenks Rd. WV5: Wom 2F 73
Jennens Rd. B4: Birm 6H 101 (3G 5)
B7: Birm 6H 101 (2H 5)
Jenner Cl. WS2: Wals 3G 31
Jenner Ho. WS2: Wals 3F 31
Jenner Rd. WS2: Wals 3F 31
Jenner St. WV2: Wolv 2A 44
Jennifer Wlk. B25: Yard 3C 120
Jennings St. B64: Old H 1H 111
Jenny Cl. WV14: Bils 4G 61
Jennyns Ct. WS10: W'bry 2F 63
Jenny Walkers La. WV6: Pert 3D 40
Jephcott Gro. B8: Salt 5G 103
Jephcott Rd. B8: Salt 5G 103
Jephson Dr. B26: Yard 4D 120
Jeremy Gro. B92: Sol 1F 137
Jeremy Rd. WV4: Penn 6G 43
Jerome Ct. B74: S'tly 2H 51
Jerome K Jerome Birthplace Mus. *2C 48*
(off Bradford St.)
Jerome Retail Pk. WS1: Wals 2B 48
Jerome Rd. B72: S Cold 1B 70
WS2: Wals 2H 47
Jerrard Ct. B75: S Cold 6A 54
Jerrard Dr. B75: S Cold 6A 54
Jerry's La. B23: Erd 6D 68
Jersey Cft. B36: Cas B 3D 106
Jersey Rd. B8: Salt 5D 102
Jervis Cl. DY5: P'ntt 2G 93
Jervis Ct. *WS1: Wals* *1D 48*
(off Dog Kennel La.)
Jervis Cres. B74: Four O 6D 36
Jervis Pk. B74: Lit A 5C 36
Jervis Ter. B21: Hand 1H 99
Jervoise Dr. B31: N'fld 2F 145
Jervoise La. B71: W Brom 4C 64
Jervoise Rd. B29: W Cas 4D 130
Jervoise St. B70: W Brom 3G 79
Jesmond Gro. B24: Erd 3C 86
Jessel Rd. WS2: Wals 1A 48
Jessie Rd. WS9: A'rdge 6C 22
Jesson Cl. WS1: Wals 4E 49
Jesson Ct. WS1: Wals 3E 49
Jesson Rd. B75: S Cold 6E 55
DY3: Sed 1C 76
WS1: Wals 3D 48
Jesson St. B70: W Brom 5C 80
Jevons Dr. DY4: Tip 2B 78
Jevons Rd. B73: New O 2C 68
Jevon St. WV14: Cose 5D 60
(not continuous)
JEWELLERY QUARTER 5D 100 (1A 4)
Jewellery Quarter Station (Rail & MM)
5D 100
Jew's La. DY3: Up Gor 3A 76
Jiggin's La. B32: Bart G 5A 130

Jill Av.—Kingsbury Av.

Jill Av. B43: Gt Barr 5G 65
Jillcot Rd. B92: Sol 2F 137
Jinnah Cl. B12: Birm 3H 117
Joan St. WV2: E'shll 5A 44
Jockey Fld. DY3: Up Gor 1A 76
Jockey La. WS10: W'bry 1G 63
Jockey Rd. B73: New O 3C 68
Joe Jones Ct. DY3: Sed 4A 60
Joey's La. WV8: Bilb 3A 14
John Bright Cl. DY4: Tip 5H 61
John Bright St. B1: Birm 1F 117 (5D 4)
John F Kennedy Wlk. DY4: Tip 5A 62
John Fletcher Cl.
WS10: W'bry 1H 63
John Harper St. WV13: W'hall 1B 46
John Howell Dr. DY4: Tip 2A 78
John Kempe Way B12: Birm 4A 118
John Riley Dr. WV12: W'hall 1C 30
John Rd. B62: Hale 2F 129
Johns Gro. B43: Gt Barr 5G 65
Johns La. B69: Tiv 4C 78
DY4: Tip 3B 78
WS6: Gt Wyr 2F 7
John Smyth Ho. B1: Birm 6E 101 (3A 4)
Johnson Av. WV11: Wed 2H 29
Johnson Cl. B8: W End 3A 104
B11: S'hll 6C 118
WS10: Darl 6D 46
Johnson Dr. B35: Cas V 4D 86
Johnson Pl. WV14: Bils 4H 45
Johnson Rd. B23: Erd 2F 85
WS10: Darl 6D 46
WS10: W'bry 3A 64
WV12: W'hall 2D 30
Johnson Row WV14: Cose 4B 60
Johnsons Bri. Rd. B71: W Brom 1A 80
Johnsons Gro. B68: O'bry 3A 114
Johnson St. B7: Nech 3C 102
WV2: Wolv 4H 43
WV14: Cose 4B 60
Johnstone St. B19: Loz 1F 101
Johnston St. B70: W Brom 6B 80
John St. B19: Loz 2D 100
B65: B'hth 2C 112
B69: O'bry 2G 97
B70: W Brom 3H 79
(Guns La.)
B70: W Brom 2F 79
(Phoenix St.)
DY5: Brie H 5H 93
DY8: Word 2D 108
WS2: Wals 6C 32
WV2: E'shll 5C 44
WV13: W'hall 2B 46
John St. Nth. B71: W Brom 2H 79
John Wilmott Community Leisure Cen.
1D 70
John Wooton Ho. *WS10: Darl* 5D 46
(off Lawrence Way)
Joiners Cft. B92: Sol 5A 138
Joinings Bank B68: O'bry 5H 97
Jones Fld. Cres. WV1: Wolv 1C 44
Jones Ho. WS2: Wals 6B 32
Jones Rd. WV10: Oxl 3G 27
WV12: W'hall 6D 18
Jones's La. WS6: Gt Wyr 4G 7
Jones Wood Cl. B76: Walm 6D 70
Jonfield Gdns. B43: Gt Barr 4B 66
Jordan Cl. B66: Smeth 4F 99
B75: Four O 2H 53
Jordan Ho. B36: Hodg H 1B 104
Jordan Leys DY4: Tip 2B 78
Jordan Pl. WV14: Bils 2G 61
Jordan Rd. B75: Four O 2H 53
Jordan Way WS9: A'rdge 6D 22
Joseph St. B69: O'bry 3F 97
Josiah Rd. B31: N'fld 5B 144
Jowett's La. B71: W Brom 5H 63
Joyberry Dr. DY8: Stourb 2D 124
Joynson St. WS10: Darl 6E 47
Jubilee Av. B71: W Brom 6H 63
Jubilee Cl. WS3: Wals 3C 32
WS6: Gt Wyr 3F 7
Jubilee Ct. B27: A Grn 3A 136
B31: N'fld 6F 145
Jubilee Gdns. B23: Erd 6B 68
Jubilee Rd. B45: Fran 5E 143
DY4: Tip 6A 62
WV14: Bils 1A 62
Jubilee St. B71: W Brom 6B 64
Jubilee Trad. Cen. B5: Birm 2G 117
Judge Cl. B69: O'bry 2G 97
Judge Rd. DY5: Quar B 4B 110
Julia Av. B24: Erd 3D 86
Julia Gdns. B71: W Brom 5D 64
Julian Cl. WS6: Gt Wyr 2G 7
WV1: Wolv 1D 44
Julian Rd. WV1: Wolv 1D 44
Julie Cft. WV14: Bils 4G 61
Juliet Rd. B62: Hale 2F 129
Julius Dr. B46: Col 6H 89
Junction, The DY8: Word 3C 108
Junction 6 Ind. Pk. B6: Witt 6B 84
Junction Ind. Est.
B66: Smeth 1D 98
Junction Rd. B21: Hand 1G 99
DY8: Stourb 1F 125
DY8: Word 3C 108
DY9: Stourb 1G 125
WV2: E'shll 4D 44
Junction St. B69: O'bry 6E 79
DY2: Dud 1D 94
WS1: Wals 3B 48
Junction St. Sth. B69: O'bry 4G 97
Junc. Two Ind. Est. *B69: O'bry* 4F 97
(off Demuth Way)
June Cft. B26: Sheld 6H 121
Juniper Cl. B27: A Grn 6H 119
B76: Walm 2D 70
Juniper Dr. B76: Walm 6E 71
WS5: Wals 1F 65
Juniper Ho. B20: Hand 4B 82
B36: Hodg H 2D 104
Juniper Ri. B63: Crad 6E 111
Jupiter B16: Birm 1D 116
(not continuous)
Jury Rd. DY5: Quar B 4B 110
Jutland Rd. B13: Mose 6B 134

K

Karen Way DY5: Brie H 3H 109
KATE'S HILL 6H 77
Katherine Ho. *B17: Harb* 6F 115
(off Cadbury Way)
Katherine Rd. B67: Smeth 1D 114
Kathleen Rd. B25: Yard 4A 120
B72: S Cold 1A 70
Katie Rd. B29: S Oak 4A 132
Kayne Cl. DY6: K'wfrd 3A 92
Keanscott Dr. B68: O'bry 5A 98
Keasdon Gro. WV13: W'hall 6C 30
Keating Gdns. B75: Four O 5G 37
Keatley Av. B33: Kitts G 1A 122
Keats Av. B10: Small H 4D 118
Keats Cl. B74: Four O 3F 37
DY3: Lwr G 2E 75
DY8: Amb 3E 109
Keats Dr. WV14: Cose 3F 61
Keats Gro. B27: A Grn 4H 135
WV10: Bush 1C 28
Keats Ho. B68: O'bry 5A 98
Keats Rd. WS3: Blox 2C 32
WV10: Bush 5C 16
WV12: W'hall 2E 31
Keble Gro. B26: Sheld 5F 121
WS1: Wals 4E 49
Keble Ho. B37: F'bri 1C 122
Kedleston Cl. WS3: Blox 4G 19
Kedleston Ct. B28: Hall G 3F 149
Kedleston Rd. B28: Hall G 1F 149
Keegan Wlk. WS2: Wals 5F 31
Keel Dr. B13: Mose 4D 134
Keele Ho. B37: F'bri 5D 106
Keeley St. B9: Birm 1B 118
Keelinge St. DY4: Tip 2B 78
Keen St. B66: Smeth 5H 99
Keepers Cl. B18: Win G 4B 100
B46: Col 5H 107
DY6: W Hth 1H 91
WS9: Wals W 4B 22
Keepers Ga. Cl. B74: S Cold 4A 54
Keepers Ho. *B73: New O* 3C 68
(off Welshmans Hill)
Keepers La. WV6: Tett 5G 13
WV8: Cod 5G 13
Keepers Rd. B74: Lit A 4C 36
Keer Ct. B9: Birm 1B 118
Kegworth Rd. B23: Erd 5C 84
Keir Hardie Wlk. B69: Tiv 5D 78
Keir Pl. DY8: Amb 3C 108
Keir Rd. WS10: W'bry 3A 64
Kelby Cl. B31: N'fld 3C 144
Kelby Rd. B31: N'fld 3D 144
Keldy Cl. WV6: Wolv 4D 26
Kelfield Av. B17: Harb 1F 131
Kelham Pl. B92: Olton 4F 137
Kelia Dr. B67: Smeth 3D 98
Kellett Rd. B7: Birm 5A 102
Kelling Cl. DY5: Brie H 3G 109
Kellington Cl. B8: W End 5F 103
Kelmarsh Dr. B91: Sol 6F 151
Kelmscott Rd. B17: Harb 4F 115
Kelsall Cl. WV1: Wolv 1D 44
Kelsall Cft. B1: Birm 6D 100
Kelsey Cl. B7: Birm 5B 102
Kelso Gdns. WV6: Pert 5D 24
Kelsull Cft. B37: F'bri 1C 122
Kelton Ct. B15: Edg 4C 116
Kelvedon Gro. B91: Sol 3G 151
Kelverdale Gro. B14: K Hth 3E 147
Kelverley Gro. B71: W Brom 4E 65
Kelvin Ho. DY1: Dud 5F 77
Kelvin Pl. WS2: Wals 3H 31
Kelvin Rd. B31: N'fld 6E 145
WS2: Wals 3G 31
Kelvin Way B70: W Brom 6H 79
Kelvin Way Ind. Est. B70: W Brom 6H 79
Kelway Av. B43: Gt Barr 2D 66
Kelwood Dr. B63: Hale 6A 112
Kelynmead Rd. B33: Yard 1E 121
Kemberton Cl. WV3: Wolv 2A 42
Kemberton Rd. B29: S Oak 3E 131
WV3: Wolv 2A 42
Kemble Cl. WV12: W'hall 6D 30
Kemble Cft. B5: Bal H 4G 117
Kemble Dr. B35: Cas V 4E 87
Kemelstowe Cres. B63: Hale 5E 127
Kemerton Way B90: M'path 4D 164
Kempe Rd. B33: Kitts G 5E 105
Kempsey Cl. B63: Hale 1G 127
B69: O'bry 5E 97
B92: Olton 2E 137
Kempsey Covert B38: K Nor 2A 160
Kempsey Ho. B32: Bart G 5G 129
Kemps Grn. Rd. CV7: Bal C 3H 169
Kempson Av. B71: W Brom 2H 79
B72: W Grn 4A 70
Kempson Rd. B36: Hodg H 1C 104
Kempsons Gro. WV14: Cose 2D 60
Kempthorne Av. WV10: Bush 6A 16
Kempthorne Gdns. WS3: Blox 5G 19
Kempthorne Rd. WV14: Bils 5H 45
Kempton Dr. WS6: Gt Wyr 3F 7
Kempton Pk. Rd.
B36: Hodg H 1B 104
Kempton Way DY8: Stourb 2C 124
Kemsey Dr. WV14: Bils 2H 61
Kemshead Av. B31: Longb 1C 158
Kemsley Rd. B14: K Hth 5H 147
Kendal Av. B45: Redn 2H 157
B46: Col 2H 107
Kendal Cl. WV6: Tett 3D 26
Kendal Ct. B23: Erd 4B 84
B29: W Cas 6G 131
WS9: Wals W 3B 22
Kendal Gro. B92: Sol 5B 138
Kendal Ho. B69: O'bry 5D 96
Kendall Ri. DY6: K'wfrd 4D 92
Kendal Ri. B68: O'bry 6H 97
WV6: Tett 3D 26
Kendal Ri. Rd. B45: Redn 2H 157
Kendal Rd. B11: S'brk 4B 118
Kendal Twr. B17: Harb 6H 115
Kendrick Av. B34: S End 4A 106
Kendrick Cl. B92: Sol 1B 152
Kendrick Pl. WV14: Bils 1A 62
Kendrick Rd. B76: Walm 2D 86
WV10: Bush 3A 28
WV14: Bils 1A 62
Kendricks Rd. WS10: Darl 4F 47
Kendrick St. WS10: W'bry 2G 63
Keneggy M. B29: S Oak 3B 132
Kenelm Rd. B10: Small H 3E 119
B68: O'bry 6G 97
B73: S Cold 1H 69
WV14: Cose 4E 61
Kenelm's Ct. B62: Roms 3A 142
Kenilworth Cl. B74: Four O 3G 53
CV7: Bal C 3G 169
DY4: Tip 3F 77
DY8: Word 1B 108
Kenilworth Ct. B16: Edg 3B 116
B24: Erd 5E 85
DY1: Dud 1B 94
Kenilworth Cres. WS2: Wals 5G 31
WV4: E'shll 1A 60
Kenilworth Ho. B13: Mose 1A 148
WS3: Blox 3A 32
(off Providence La.)
Kenilworth Rd. B20: Hand 6G 83
B46: Col 2H 123
B68: O'bry 3B 114
B92: H Ard 1D 154
B93: Know 3F 167
CV7: Bal C 2E 155
CV7: Mer 3C 140
WV6: Pert 5F 25
Kenley Gro. B30: K Nor 4D 146
Kenley Way B91: Shir 3B 150
Kenmare Way WV11: Wed 5E 29
Kenmure Rd. B33: Sheld 4G 121
Kennedy Cl. B72: S Cold 1A 70
Kennedy Ct. DY8: Stourb 6D 108
Kennedy Cres. DY3: Lwr G 3H 75
WS10: Darl 4C 46
Kennedy Cft. B26: Sheld 4E 121
Kennedy Gro. B30: Stir 1D 146
Kennedy Ho. B68: O'bry 3H 113
Kennedy Rd. WV10: Wolv 6H 27
Kennedy Twr. B4: Birm 2E 5
Kennerley Rd. B25: Yard 5B 120
Kennet Cl. WS8: Bwnhls 3G 9
Kennet Gro. B36: Cas B 1B 106
Kenneth Gro. B23: Erd 2A 84
Kennford Cl. B65: Row R 3C 96
Kennington Rd. WV10: Wolv 4B 28
Kenrick Cft. B35: Cas V 5E 87
Kenrick Ho. B70: W Brom 6C 80
Kenrick Park Stop (MM) 6C 80
Kenrick Way B70: W Brom 1B 98
B71: W Brom 6D 80
Kensington Av. B12: Bal H 1A 134
Kensington Dr. B74: Four O 4F 37
Kensington Gdns. DY8: Word 2A 108
Kensington Rd. B29: S Oak 3C 132
WV12: W'hall 2B 30
Kensington St. B19: Hock 3F 101
Kenswick Dr. B63: Hale 3A 128
Kent Av. WS2: Wals 6H 31
Kent Cl. B71: W Brom 6H 63
WS2: Wals 4C 32
WS9: A'rdge 6D 22
Kentish Rd. B21: Hand 1G 99
Kentmere Twr. B23: Erd 1H 85
Kenton Av. WV6: Wolv 5D 26
Kenton Wlk. B29: S Oak 3B 132
Kent Pl. DY2: Dud 3C 94
Kent Rd. B45: Fran 6F 143
B62: Quin 5E 113
DY8: Woll 4B 108
WS2: Wals 6F 31
WS10: W'bry 1A 64
WV2: Wolv 4A 44
Kents Cl. B92: Olton 2D 136
Kents Ho. B33: Yard 1F 121
Kent St. B5: Birm 3G 117
DY3: Up Gor 2A 76
WS2: Wals 4C 32
Kent St. Nth. B18: Hock 4B 100
Kenward Cft. B17: Harb 4D 114
Kenway B47: H'wd 2A 162
Kenwick Rd. B17: Harb 1F 131
Kenwood Rd. B9: Bord G 6H 103
Kenyon Cl. DY8: Amb 4E 109
Kenyon St. B18: Birm 5E 101 (1B 4)
Kerby Rd. B23: Erd 3C 84
Kererwin Cl. B64: Old H 2A 112
Keresley Cl. B91: Sol 2G 151
Keresley Gro. B29: W Cas 3D 130
Kernthorpe Rd. B14: K Hth 3F 147
Kerr Dr. DY4: Tip 5G 61
Kerria Ct. B15: Birm 3F 117
Kerridge Cl. WV9: Pend 5E 15
Kerrison Ride B73: Bold 4F 69
Kerry Cl. B31: N'fld 1D 144
DY5: Brie H 5G 93
Kerry Ct. WS1: Wals 3E 49
Kersley Gdns. WV11: Wed 3H 29
Kerswell Dr. B90: M'path 4D 164
Kesterton Rd. B74: Four O 4E 37
Kesteven Cl. B15: Edg 5D 116
Kesteven Rd. B71: W Brom 6A 64
Keston Rd. B44: Gt Barr 1H 67
Kestrel Av. B25: Yard 3H 119
Kestrel Cl. B23: Erd 1D 84
B35: Cas V 4F 87
Kestrel Dr. B74: Four O 4F 37
Kestrel Gro. B30: B'vlle 5H 131
WV12: W'hall 1C 30
Kestrel Ri. WV6: Tett 2D 26
Kestrel Rd. B63: Crad 4D 110
B68: O'bry 1F 113
DY1: Dud 1B 94
Kestrel Way WS6: C Hay 3C 6
Keswick Dr. DY6: K'wfrd 3B 92
Keswick Gro. B74: S'tly 1H 51
Keswick Ho. B69: O'bry 5D 96
Keswick Rd. B92: Olton 1D 136
Ketley Cft. B12: Birm 4H 117
Ketley Flds. DY6: K'wfrd 4E 93
Ketley Hill Rd. DY1: Dud 1B 94
Ketley Rd. DY6: K'wfrd 3D 92
(not continuous)
Kettlebrook Rd. B90: M'path 3F 165
Kettlehouse Rd. B44: Gt Barr 2H 67
Kettles Bank Rd. DY3: Gorn 5G 75
(not continuous)
Kettles Wood Dr. B32: Bart G 3H 129
Kettlewell Way B37: F'bri 1B 122
Ketton Gro. B33: Sheld 4H 121
Kew Cl. B37: K'hrst 6B 106
Kew Dr. DY1: Dud 5C 76
Kew Gdns. B33: Stech 2B 120
Kewstoke Cl. WV12: W'hall 6B 18
Kewstoke Cft. B31: N'fld 1C 144
Kewstoke Rd. WV12: W'hall 6B 18
Key Bus. Pk. B24: Erd 4C 86
Keyes Dr. DY6: K'wfrd 6B 74
Key Hill B18: Birm 4D 100
Key Hill Cir. B18: Birm 4D 100
Key Hill Dr. B18: Birm 4D 100
Key Ind. Pk. WV13: W'hall 6F 29
Keynell Covert B30: K Nor 4E 147
Keynes Dr. WV14: Bils 5G 45
Keys Cres. B71: W Brom 1A 80
Keyse Rd. B75: S Cold 4D 54
Keyte Cl. DY4: Tip 2A 78
Keyway, The WV13: W'hall 2H 45
Keyway Retail Pk. WV13: W'hall 3B 46
Keyworth Cl. DY4: Tip 2A 78
Khalsa Ind. Est. B66: Smeth 5H 99
Khyber Cl. WS10: Darl 4C 46
Kidd Cft. DY4: Tip 3C 62
Kidderminster Rd.
DY6: K'wfrd, W Hth 6G 91
DY7: I'ley 6A 124
DY7: Stourt 6G 91
DY9: Hag 6G 125
DY10: I'ley 6A 124
Kielder Cl. WS5: Wals 2G 65
Kielder Gdns. DY9: Pedm 4F 125
Kier's Bri. Cl. DY4: Tip 4A 78
Kilburn Dr. DY6: K'wfrd 6C 74
Kilburn Gro. B44: Gt Barr 2H 67
Kilburn Pl. DY2: Dud 3F 95
Kilburn Rd. B44: Gt Barr 2H 67
Kilby Av. B16: Birm 1C 116
(not continuous)
Kilbys Gro. B20: Hand 5B 82
Kilcote Rd. B90: Shir 5C 148
Kilmet Wlk. B67: Smeth 4E 99
Kilmore Cft. B36: Hodg H 6C 86
Kilmorie Rd. B27: A Grn 6A 120
Kiln Cft. B65: Row R 5A 96
Kiln La. B25: Yard 5H 119
B90: Dic H 4G 163
Kilsby Gro. B91: Sol 1G 165
Kilvert Rd. WS10: W'bry 3H 63
Kimbells Wlk. B93: Know 3E 167
Kimberley Av. B8: Salt 4E 103
Kimberley Cl. B74: S'tly 6A 36
Kimberley Pl. WV14: Cose 6D 60
Kimberley Rd. B66: Smeth 2E 99
B92: Olton 3E 137
Kimberley St. WV3: Wolv 2E 43
Kimberley Wlk. B76: Min 1H 87
Kimble Gro. B24: Erd 4B 86
Kimbley Ri. B71: W Brom 6G 63
Kimpton Cl. B14: K Hth 5G 147
Kimsan Cft. B74: S'tly 4A 52
Kinchford Cl. B91: Sol 1G 165
Kineton Cft. B32: Bart G 5B 130
Kineton Grn. Rd. B92: Olton 5B 136
Kineton Ho. B13: Mose 1A 148
Kineton Ri. DY3: Sed 3G 59
Kineton Rd. B45: Rubery 2E 157
B73: New O 4E 69
Kinfare Dr. WV6: Tett 5H 25
Kinfare Ri. DY3: Up Gor 3A 76
King Charles Av. WS2: Wals 1E 47
King Charles Ct. B44: K'sdng 3B 68
King Charles Rd. B62: Quin 1F 129
King Edmund St. DY1: Dud 5D 76
(not continuous)
King Edward VI Ho. *B4: Birm* 6H 101
(off Aston St.)
King Edward Ct. B63: Hale 1A 128
King Edward Rd. B13: Mose 2H 133
King Edwards Cl. B20: Hand 1D 100
King Edwards Dr. B16: Birm 1D 116
King Edwards Gdns. B20: Hand 2D 100
King Edwards Rd. B1: Birm 6C 100
(Ladywood Middleway)
B1: Birm 1D 116 (4A 4)
(Summer Hill St.)
King Edward's Row WV2: Wolv 3G 43
King Edwards Sq. B73: S Cold 5A 54
King Edward St. WS10: Darl 5D 46
King Edwards Wharf
B16: Birm 1D 116
Kingfield Rd. B90: Shir 5C 148
Kingfisher Cl. B26: Sheld 5E 121
DY3: Sed 3G 59
WS8: Bwnhls 6A 10
Kingfisher Dr. B36: Cas B 1C 106
DY8: Stourb 2A 124
Kingfisher Gro. WV12: W'hall 1B 30
Kingfisher Ind. Est. B70: W Brom 3F 79
Kingfisher Rd. B23: Erd 6C 68
Kingfisher Vw. B34: Stech 4E 105
Kingfisher Way B30: B'vlle 5H 131
King George VI Av. WS1: Wals 3G 49
King George Cres. WS4: Rus 3F 33
King George Pl. WS4: Rus 3F 33
Kingham Cl. DY3: Gorn 5G 75
Kingham Covert B14: K Hth 5F 147
Kings Av. B69: Tiv 5B 78
Kingsbridge Ho. B23: Erd 1B 84
Kingsbridge Rd. B32: Bart G 4B 130
Kingsbridge Wlk. B66: Smeth 4F 99
Kingsbrook Dr. B91: Sol 1F 165
Kingsbury Av. B24: Erd 4B 86

Kingsbury Bus. Pk.—Langton Rd.

Kingsbury Bus. Pk. B76: Min 1A 88
Kingsbury Cl. B76: Min 2H 87
WS4: Wals 5F 33
Kingsbury Leisure Cen. 5F 85
Kingsbury Pl. B24: Erd 3H 85
Kingsbury Rd. B24: Erd 5E 85
B35: Cas V 5B 86
B76: Min, Curd 2G 87
DY4: Tip 5A 62
Kings Bus. Pk. B44: Gt Barr 2G 67
Kings Cinema 4B 80
Kingsclere Wlk. WV4: Penn 5A 42
Kingscliff Rd. B10: Small H 3G 119
King's Cl. B14: K Hth 1E 147
Kingscote Rd. B15: Edg 5H 115
B93: Dorr 6F 167
Kings Ct. B37: Mars G 2G 123
B1: Birm 2E 117 (6B 4)
B3: Birm 2E 117 (1C 4)
B75: Four O 6H 37
DY4: Tip 3A 78
WS10: W'bry 2E 63
Kings Cft. B26: Sheld 6E 121
B36: Cas B 2B 106
Kingscroft Cl. B74: S'tly 4A 52
Kingscroft Rd. B74: S'tly 3A 52
Kingsdene Av. DY6: K'wfrd 5A 92
Kingsdown Av. B42: Gt Barr 1B 82
Kingsdown Rd. B31: N'fld 4D 130
Kingsfield Rd. B14: K Hth 5G 133
Kingsford Cl. B36: Cas B 6H 87
Kingsford Ct. B92: Olton 2F 137
Kingsford Nouveau DY6: K'wfrd 4E 93
Kings Gdns. B30: K Nor 3A 146
Kingsgate Ho. B37: Chel W 1C 122
Kings Grn. Av. B38: K Nor 5B 146
Kingshayes Rd. WS9: A'rdge 5D 22
KING'S HEATH 5G 133
KING'S HILL 6D 46
Kings Hill Bus. Pk. WS10: W'bry 1E 63
Kings Hill Cl. WS10: Darl 6E 47
Kingshill Dr. B38: K Nor 5B 146
Kings Hill Fld. WS10: Darl 6E 47
Kings Hill M. WS10: Darl 6D 46
KINGSHURST 4B 106
Kingshurst Ho. B37: K'hrst 4B 106
Kingshurst Rd. B31: N'fld 4E 145
B90: Shir 6F 149
Kingshurst Way B37: K'hrst 5B 106
Kingsland Dr. B93: Dorr 6A 166
Kingsland Rd. B44: Gt Barr 1G 67
Kingslea Rd. B91: Sol 5C 150
Kingsleigh Cft. B75: Four O 1H 53
Kingsleigh Dr. B36: Cas B 1E 105
Kingsleigh Rd. B20: Hand 5D 82
Kingsley Av. WV6: Tett 5H 25
Kingsley Bank Way B26: Sheld 4F 121
Kingsley Ct. B25: Yard 3C 120
Kingsley Gdns. WV8: Cod 4E 13
Kingsley Gro. DY3: Lwr G 2E 75
Kingsley Rd. B12: Bal H 5A 118
B30: K Nor 3H 145
DY6: K'wfrd 4H 91
Kingsley St. DY2: Neth 4E 95
WS2: Wals 4H 47
Kingslow Av. WV4: Penn 5B 42
Kingsmere Cl. B24: Erd 5E 85
KINGS NORTON 5H 145
King's Norton Bus. Cen. B30: K Nor 3C 146
Kings Norton Community Leisure Cen. 1B 160
Kings Norton Station (Rail) 3B 146
Kingsoak Gdns. DY2: Dud 2G 95
Kings Pde. B4: Birm 4F 5
Kingspiece Ho. B36: Hodg H 1C 104
Kings Rd. B14: K Hth 1E 147
B44: Gt Barr, K'sdng 2G 67
B73: New O 3A 68
DY3: Sed 5A 60
B11: Tys 6G 119
B23: Erd 3C 84
WS4: Rus 2G 33
Kings Rd. Ind. Est. B11: Tys 5G 119
Kings Sq. B70: W Brom 4B 80
WV14: Cose 5C 60
King's Standing Ancient Monument 1H 67
KINGSTANDING 4B 68
Kingstanding Cen., The B44: Gt Barr 2H 67
Kingstanding Leisure Cen. 5A 68
Kingstanding Rd. B44: K'sdng 1H 83
King's Ter. B14: K Hth 1F 147
Kingsthorpe Rd. B14: K Hth 4A 148
Kingston Ct. B29: W Cas 6F 131
B74: S Cold 4H 53
Kingston Ind. Est. *B9: Birm* *2B 118*
(off Glover St.)
Kingston Rd. B9: Birm 2B 118
B75: S Cold 5D 54
Kingston Row B1: Birm 1E 117 (4A 4)
Kingston Way DY6: K'wfrd 2A 92
King St. B11: S'brk 4A 118
B63: Hale 1A 128
B64: Old H 2H 111
B66: Smeth 2F 99
DY2: Dud 1E 95
DY5: Quar B 3C 110
DY8: Woll 5C 108
DY9: Lye 1B 126
WS1: Wals 4B 48
WS7: Chase 1B 10
WS9: Wals W 5B 22
WS10: W'bry 2E 63
WV1: Wolv 1G 43 (3B 170)
WV13: W'hall 1B 46
WV14: Bils 2G 61
WV14: Cose 5C 60
King St. Pas. DY2: Dud 6E 77
DY5: Quar B 3C 110
King St. Pct. WS10: Darl 5D 46
Kingsway B68: O'bry 4G 113
DY8: Woll 3B 108
WV10: Wolv 3C 28
WV11: Ess 3A 18
Kingsway Av. DY4: Tip 5A 62
Kingsway Dr. B38: K Nor 5B 146
Kingsway Nth. WS9: A'rdge 3A 34
Kingsway Rd. WV10: Wolv 3C 28
Kingsway Sth. WS9: A'rdge 3A 34
Kingswear Av. WV6: Pert 6F 25
KINGSWINFORD 3B 92
Kingswinford Rd. DY1: Dud 2A 94
KING'S WOOD 1G 161
KINGSWOOD
Wolverhampton 5A 12
Kingswood Cl. B90: Shir 6B 150
Kingswood Cft. B7: Nech 2C 102
Kingswood Dr. B30: K Nor 4E 147
B74: S'tly 1H 67
WS6: Gt Wyr 1G 7
Kingswood Gdns. WV4: Penn 5D 42
Kingswood Ho. B14: K Hth 5G 147
Kingswood Rd. B13: Mose 1A 134
B31: Longb 3D 158
DY6: K'wfrd 5A 92
Kingswood Wlk. B31: Longb 2D 158
Kington Cl. WV12: W'hall 1B 30
Kington Gdns. B37: F'bri 2B 122
Kington Way B33: Stech 1B 120
King William St. DY8: Amb 3D 108
Kiniths Cres. B71: W Brom 2C 80
Kiniths Way B62: B'hth 2E 113
B71: W Brom 3C 80
Kinlet Cl. WV3: Wolv 3G 41
Kinlet Gro. B31: N'fld 5G 145
Kinloch Dr. DY1: Dud 4B 76
Kinnerley St. WS1: Wals 2E 49
Kinnersley Cres. B69: O'bry 4D 96
Kinnerton Cres.
B29: W Cas 3D 130
Kinross Cres. B43: Gt Barr 1D 66
Kinsey Gro. B14: K Hth 3H 147
Kinsham Dr. B91: Sol 1F 165
Kintore Cft. B32: Bart G 6H 129
Kintyre Cl. B45: Fran 6E 143
Kinver Av. WV12: W'hall 4B 30
Kinver Cres. WS9: A'rdge 6E 23
Kinver Cft. B12: Bal H 4G 117
B76: Walm 5E 71
Kinver Dr. DY9: Hag 6G 125
WV4: Penn 6A 42
Kinver M. B37: Mars G 3C 122
Kinver Rd. B31: N'fld 5H 145
Kinver St. DY8: Word 2B 108
Kinwarton Cl. B25: Yard 5B 120
Kipling Av. WV14: Cose 4D 60
Kipling Cl. DY4: Tip 5A 62
Kipling Rd. B30: K Nor 3G 145
DY3: Lwr G 2E 75
WV10: F'hses 5H 15
WV12: W'hall 2E 31
Kirby Cl. WV14: Bils 2G 61
Kirby Dr. DY1: Dud 4A 76
Kirby Rd. B18: Win G 3A 100
Kirkby Grn. B73: S Cold 2H 69
Kirkham Gdns. DY5: P'ntt 3G 93
Kirkham Gro. B33: Stech 5D 104
Kirkham Way DY4: Tip 2A 78
Kirkside Gro. WS8: Bwnhls 6B 10
Kirkstall M. WS8: Bwnhls 6B 10
Kirkstall Cl. WS3: Blox 5F 19
Kirkstall Cres. WS3: Blox 5F 19
Kirkstone Ct. DY5: Brie H 4F 109
Kirkstone Cres.
B43: Gt Barr 1B 82
WV5: Wom 1F 73
Kirkstone Way DY5: Brie H 4F 109
Kirkwall Rd. B32: Bart G 4B 130
Kirkwood Av. B23: Erd 6F 69
Kirmond Wlk. WV6: Wolv 4F 27
Kirstead Gdns. WV6: Tett 6H 25
Kirton Gro. B33: Stech 5E 105
B91: Sol 6E 151
WV6: Tett 4A 26
Kitchener Rd. B29: S Oak 4D 132
DY2: Dud 6H 77
Kitchener St. B66: Smeth 3H 99
Kitchen La. WV11: Wed 6G 17
Kitebrook Cl. B90: M'path 2E 165
Kitsland Rd. B34: S End 3A 106
Kitswell Gdns. B32: Bart G 5G 129
Kittermaster Rd. CV7: Mer 4H 141
Kittiwake Dr. DY5: Brie H 4G 109
Kittoe Rd. B74: Four O 6F 37
KITT'S GREEN 6G 105
Kitts Grn. B33: Kitts G 6F 105
Kitts Grn. Rd. B33: Kitts G 5E 105
Kitwell La. B32: Bart G 5G 129
Kitwood Dr. B92: Sol 6H 137
Kixley La. B93: Know 3E 167
Klaxon Ind. Est. B11: Tys 1F 135
Knarsdale Cl. DY5: Brie H 3G 109
Knaves Castle Av. WS8: Bwnhls 3B 10
Knebworth Cl. B44: Gt Barr 5G 67
Knightcote Dr. B91: Sol 1F 165
Knight Ct. B75: S Cold 6G 55
Knightley Rd. B91: Sol 5D 150
Knightlow Rd. B17: Harb 3E 115
Knighton Cl. B74: Four O 6F 37
Knighton Dr. B74: Four O 1F 53
Knighton Rd. B31: N'fld 3G 145
B74: Four O 4D 36
DY2: Neth 5F 95
Knights Av. WV6: Tett 3B 26
Knightsbridge Cl. B74: Four O 5F 37
Knightsbridge Ho. B37: K'hrst 4B 106
Knightsbridge La. WV12: W'hall 3C 30
Knightsbridge Rd. B92: Olton 4D 136
Knights Cl. B23: Erd 5E 85
Knights Ct. WS11: Nort C 1E 9
Knights Cres. WV6: Tett 2C 26
Knightsfield Cl. B73: New O 2C 68
Knights Hill WS9: A'rdge 6D 34
Knight's Rd. B11: Tys 1G 135
Knightstowe Av. B18: Hock 5C 100
Knightswood Cl. B75: S Cold 4B 54
Knightwick Cres. B23: Erd 2C 84
Knipersley Rd. B73: Bold 1G 85
Knoll, The B32: Bart G 4A 130
DY6: K'wfrd 4C 92
Knoll Cl. WS7: Chase 1C 10
Knoll Cft. B90: Ches G 5B 164
WS9: A'rdge 6E 23
Knollcroft B16: Birm 1C 116
Knott Ct. DY5: Brie H 1H 109
Knottsall La. B68: O'bry 6H 97
Knotts Farm Rd. DY6: K'wfrd 5E 93
Knowlands Rd. B90: M'path 2E 165
KNOWLE 3E 167
Knowle Cl. B45: Redn 2B 158
KNOWLE GROVE 6C 166
Knowle Hill Rd. DY2: Neth 5D 94
Knowle Rd. B11: S'hll 2D 134
B65: Row R 5H 95
B92: H Ard 6G 153
Knowles Dr. B74: Four O 4G 53
Knowles Rd. WV1: Wolv 2B 44
Knowles St. WS10: W'bry 2G 63
Knowle Wood Rd. B93: Dorr 6D 166
Knox Rd. WV2: Wolv 5H 43
Knoyle Ct. *DY8: Stourb* *5D 108*
(off Scott's Rd.)
Knutsford St. B12: Bal H 5H 117
Knutswood Cl. B13: Mose 6D 134
Kohima Dr. DY8: Stourb 6C 108
Kossuth Rd. WV14: Cose 4C 60
Kyle Cl. WV10: Oxl 6F 15
Kyles Way B32: Bart G 6H 129
Kynaston Cres. WV8: Cod 5H 13
Kyngsford Rd. B33: Kitts G 6H 105
Kyotts Lake Rd. B11: S'brk 4A 118
Kyrwicks La. B11: S'brk 5A 118
Kyter La. B36: Cas B 1F 105

L

Laburnum Av. B37: K'hrst 3B 106
B67: Smeth 5C 98
Laburnum Cl. B37: K'hrst 3B 106
B47: H'wd 4A 162
DY8: Woll 4C 108
WS3: Pels 5E 21
Laburnum Cotts. B21: Hand 1A 100
Laburnum Cft. B69: Tiv 5B 78
Laburnum Dr. B76: Walm 2E 71
Laburnum Gro. B13: Mose 2H 133
WS2: Wals 6F 31
Laburnum Ho. B30: B'vlle 6B 132
Laburnum Rd. B30: B'vlle 5B 132
DY1: Dud 3D 76
DY4: Tip 6H 61
DY6: K'wfrd 3C 92
WS5: Wals 1G 65
WS9: Wals W 4C 22
WS10: W'bry 1H 63
WV1: Wolv 3D 44
WV4: E'shll 2A 60
Laburnum St. DY8: Woll 4C 108
WV3: Wolv 2E 43
Laburnum Trees *B47: H'wd* *3A 162*
(off May Farm Cl.)
Laburnum Vs. B11: S'hll 6C 118
Laburnum Way B31: Longb 6E 145
Laceby Gro. B13: Mose 4D 134
Ladbroke Dr. B76: Walm 3D 70
Ladbroke Gro. B27: A Grn 5A 136
Ladbrook Gro. DY3: Lwr G 4E 75
Ladbrook Rd. B91: Sol 4G 151
Ladbury Gro. WS5: Wals 1D 64
Ladbury Rd. WS5: Wals 1E 65
Ladeler Gro. B33: Kitts G 1A 122
Ladies Wlk. DY3: Sed 5H 59
Lady Bank B32: Bart G 6H 129
Lady Bracknell M. B31: N'fld 3G 145
Lady Byron La. B93: Know 2B 166
Ladycroft B16: Birm 1C 116
Lady Grey's Wlk. DY8: Stourb 1B 124
Lady La. B90: Shir 6G 163
B94: Earls 6G 163
Ladymoor Rd. WV14: Bils 2E 61
Ladypool Av. B11: S'brk 5B 118
Ladypool Cl. B62: Hale 1C 128
WS4: Wals 4E 33
Ladypool Rd. B12: Bal H 1A 134
Ladysmith Rd. B63: Crad 5E 111
Ladywell Cl. WV5: Wom 5G 57
Ladywell Wlk. B5: Birm 2G 117 (6E 5)
LADYWOOD 1D 116
Ladywood Arts & Leisure Cen. 1B 116
Ladywood Cir. B16: Birm 1C 116
Ladywood Cl. DY5: Quar B 2B 110
Ladywood Middleway B1: Birm 6C 100
B16: Birm 6C 100
Ladywood Rd. B16: Edg 2B 116
B74: Four O 4G 53
LA Fitness 6G 69
Laing Ho. B69: O'bry 4D 96
Lake Av. WS5: Wals 4F 49
Lake Cl. WS5: Wals 4G 49
Lakedown Cl. B14: K Hth 6G 147
Lakefield B31: N'fld 3D 144
Lakefield Cl. B28: Hall G 6H 135
Lakefield Rd. WV11: Wed 4G 29
Lakehouse Ct. B23: Erd 5E 69
Lakehouse Gro. B38: K Nor 4H 145
Lakehouse Rd. B73: Bold 5E 69
Laker Cl. DY8: Amb 4E 109
Lakeside B74: Lit A 4B 36
Lakeside Cen., The 4C 146
Lakeside Cl. WV13: W'hall 6G 29
Lakeside Club 5B 106
Lakeside Ct. DY5: Brie H 3F 109
Lakeside Dr. B90: M'path 2D 164
Lakeside Residences B4: Birm 6H 101 (2F 5)
Lakeside Rd. B70: W Brom 1G 79
Lakeside Wlk. B23: Erd 3B 84
Lakes Rd. B23: Erd 2A 84
Lake St. DY3: Lwr G 4H 75
Lakewood Dr. B45: Redn 6H 143
Lakey La. B28: Hall G 5G 135
Lambah Cl. WV14: Bils 4H 45
Lamb Cl. B34: S End 4A 106
Lamb Cres. WV5: Wom 1F 73
(not continuous)
Lambert Cl. B23: Erd 1D 84
Lambert Ct. DY6: K'wfrd 1B 92
Lambert End B70: W Brom 4H 79
Lambert Fold DY2: Dud 1G 95
Lambert Rd. WV10: Wolv 3B 28
LAMBERT'S END 4H 79
Lambert St. B70: W Brom 4H 79
Lambeth Cl. B37: F'bri 5D 106
Lambeth Rd. B44: Gt Barr 2G 67
WV14: Bils 4D 44
Lambourn Cl. WS3: Blox 5A 20
Lambourne Cl. WS6: Gt Wyr 2F 7
Lambourne Way DY5: Brie H 3F 109
WS11: Nort C 1E 9
Lambourn Rd. B23: Erd 3D 84
WV13: W'hall 2D 46
Lambscote Cl. B90: Shir 5C 148
Lamgley Rd. WV3: Penn 6E 41
Lammas Cl. B92: Sol 4G 137
Lammas Rd. DY8: Word 6A 92
Lammermoor Av. B43: Gt Barr 3B 66
Lamont Av. B32: Bart G 2D 130
Lamorna Cl. WV3: Wolv 3H 41
Lanark Cl. DY6: K'wfrd 4D 92
Lanark Cft. B35: Cas V 4D 86
Lancaster Av. B45: Rubery 1G 157
WS9: A'rdge 1D 34
WS10: W'bry 2A 64
Lancaster Cir. Queensway
B4: Birm 5G 101 (1F 5)
Lancaster Cl. B30: B'vlle 1C 146
Lancaster Dr. B35: Cas V 5F 87
Lancaster Gdns. WV4: Penn 6C 42
Lancaster Ho. B65: Row R 5E 97
Lancaster Pl. WS3: Blox 5A 20
Lancaster Rd. DY5: Brie H 1G 109
Lancaster St. B4: Birm 5G 101 (1F 5)
Lancelot Cl. B8: Salt 6E 103
Lancelot Pl. DY4: Tip 3E 79
Lanchester Rd. B38: K Nor 6C 146
Lanchester Way B36: Cas B 6A 88
Lander Cl. B45: Rubery 3G 157
Landgate Rd. B21: Hand 5G 81
Land La. B37: Mars G 4C 122
Landor Rd. B93: Know 3C 166
Landor St. B8: Birm, Salt 6B 102
Landport Rd. WV2: Wolv 3B 44
Landrail Wlk. B36: Cas B 1C 106
(not continuous)
Landrake Rd. DY6: K'wfrd 4D 92
Landseer Gro. B43: Gt Barr 1F 67
Landsgate DY8: Stourb 4E 125
Landswood Cl. B44: K'sdng 4A 68
Landswood Rd. B68: O'bry 5A 98
LANDYWOOD 3G 7
Landywood Ent. Pk. WS6: Gt Wyr 5F 7
Landywood Grn. WS6: C Hay 3E 7
Landywood La. WS6: C Hay, Gt Wyr 3D 6
Landywood Station (Rail) 3F 7
Lane Av. WS2: Wals 6H 31
Lane Cl. WS2: Wals 6H 31
Lane Ct. WV1: Wolv 5G 27
Lane Cft. B76: Walm 5E 71
LANE GREEN 4H 13
Lane Grn. Av. WV8: Bilb 6A 14
Lane Grn. Ct. WV8: Bilb 4H 13
Lane Grn. Rd. WV8: Bilb 4H 13
Lane Grn. Shop. Pde WV8: Bilb 4H 13
LANE HEAD 3C 30
Lane Rd. WV4: E'shll 2C 60
Lanes Cl. WV5: Wom 2E 73
LANESFIELD 1B 60
Lanesfield Dr. WV4: E'shll 1C 60
Lanesfield Ind. Est. WV4: E'shll 1C 60
Laneside Av. B74: S'tly 4H 51
Laneside Gdns. WS2: Wals 1H 47
Lanes Shop. Cen., The B72: W Grn 6H 69
Lane St. WV14: Bils, Cose 2F 61
LANEY GREEN 3A 6
Langcomb Rd. B90: Shir 1G 163
Langdale Cl. WS8: Clay 1A 22
Langdale Cft. B21: Hand 2A 100
Langdale Dr. WV14: Bils 4F 45
Langdale Rd. B43: Gt Barr 6B 66
Langdale Way DY9: W'cte 1H 125
Langdon St. B9: Birm 1B 118
Langdon Wlk. B26: Yard 1C 136
Langfield Rd. B93: Know 2C 166
Langford Av. B43: Gt Barr 5A 66
Langford Cl. WS1: Wals 2E 49
Langford Cft. B91: Sol 5G 151
Langford Gro. B17: Harb 2G 131
Langham Cl. B26: Sheld 4E 121
Langham Grn. B74: S'tly 2H 51
Langholme Dr. B44: K'sdng 4D 68
Langland Dr. DY3: Sed 5G 59
LANGLEY 4G 97
Langley Av. WV14: Cose 5E 61
Langley Cl. WS9: Wals W 3C 22
Langley Ct. B69: O'bry 4G 97
WV4: Penn 5B 42
Langley Cres. B68: O'bry 5H 97
Langley Dr. B35: Cas V 6E 87
Langley Gdns. B68: O'bry 5H 97
WV3: Wolv 4B 42
LANGLEY GREEN 5H 97
Langley Grn. Rd. B69: O'bry 5G 97
Langley Green Station (Rail) 4H 97
Langley Gro. B10: Small H 3D 118
Langley Hall Dr. B75: S Cold 6F 55
Langley Hall Rd. B75: S Cold 6F 55
B92: Olton 6A 136
Langley Heath Dr. B76: Walm 2D 70
Langley High St. B69: O'bry 4G 97
LANGLEY MILL JUNC.
LITTLEWORTH END 2G 55
FALCON LODGE 5H 55
Langley Pk. Way B75: S Cold 5D 54
Langley Ri. B92: Sol 2A 138
Langley Rd. B10: Small H 3D 118
B68: O'bry 5H 97
WV4: Lwr P 6E 41
Langleys Rd. B29: S Oak 4A 132
Langley Swimming Cen. 5H 97
Langmead Cl. WS2: Wals 6D 30
Langstone Rd. B14: K Hth 5B 148
DY1: Dud 6A 76
Langton Cl. B36: Cas B 3D 106
Langton Pl. WV14: Bils 5A 46
Langton Rd. B8: Salt 5E 103

Langtree Av.—Lighthouse, The

Langtree Av. B91: Sol 6F 151
Langwood Ct. B36: Cas B 1F 105
Langworth Av. B27: A Grn 6A 120
Lannacombe Rd. B31: Longb 3C 158
Lansbury Av. WS10: Darl 1C 62
Lansbury Grn. B64: Old H 3B 112
Lansbury Rd. B64: Old H 3B 112
Lansbury Wlk. DY4: Tip 5A 62
Lansdale Av. B92: Sol 5B 138
Lansdowne Av. WV8: Cod 5E 13
Lansdowne Cl. WV14: Cose 6C 60
Lansdowne Ct. DY9: Pedm 4F 125
Lansdowne Ho. B15: Birm 3F 117
Lansdowne Rd. B21: Hand 2C 100
B24: Erd 4F 85
B62: B'hth 3F 113
B63: Hale 3F 127
DY2: Dud 3H 95
WV1: Wolv 6F 27 (1A 170)
WV14: Bils 4G 45
Lansdowne St. B18: Win G 5B 100
(not continuous)
Lansdown Pl. B18: Win G 4B 100
Lantern Rd. DY2: Neth 1E 111
LAPAL 2F 129
Lapal La. B62: Bart G 3F 129
Lapal La. Nth. B62: Hale 2E 129
Lapal La. Sth. B62: Hale 2E 129
Lapley Cl. WV1: Wolv 1D 44
Lappath Ho. B32: Bart G 5B 130
Lapper Av. WV4: E'shll 2B 60
Lapwing Cl. WS6: C Hay 4C 6
Lapwing Cft. B23: Erd 6C 68
Lapwing Dr. B92: H Ard 6B 140
Lapwood Av. DY6: K'wfrd 3D 92
Lapworth Dr. B73: New O 2C 68
Lapworth Gro. B12: Bal H 5H 117
Lapworth Ho. B5: Birm 4G 117
Lapworth Mus. 2B 132
Lara Cl. B17: Harb 3F 115
Lara Gro. DY4: Tip 5A 78
Larch Av. B21: Hand 5H 81
Larch Cft. B37: Chel W 1D 122
B69: Tiv 5B 78
Larch Dr. B31: Longb 6A 144
Larches La. WV3: Wolv 1E 43
Larches St. B11: S'brk 5A 118
Larchfield Cl. B20: Hand 4D 82
Larch Gro. DY3: Sed 6A 60
Larch Ho. B20: Hand 4B 82
B36: Hodg H 1D 104
Larchmere Dr. B28: Hall G 5F 135
WV11: Ess 4B 18
Larch Rd. DY6: K'wfrd 3C 92
Larch Wlk. B25: Yard 3H 119
Larchwood Cres. B74: S'tly 3G 51
Larchwood Grn. WS5: Wals 1F 65
Larchwood Rd. WS5: Wals 1E 65
Larcombe Dr. WV4: Penn 6H 43
Large Av. WS10: Darl 1C 62
Lark Cl. B14: K Hth 5A 148
Larkfield Av. B36: Cas B 1F 105
Larkhill Rd. DY8: Stourb 1A 124
Larkhill Wlk. B14: K Hth 6F 147
Larkin Cl. WV10: Bush 6C 16
Lark Mdw. Dr. B37: K'hrst 6A 106
Larksfield *B66: Smeth* *5F 99*
(off Windmill La.)
Larksfield M. DY5: Brie H 4G 109
Larks Mill WS3: Pels 3C 20
Larkspur Av. WS7: Burn 1C 10
Larkspur Cft. B36: Hodg H 1B 104
Larkspur Rd. DY2: Dud 1H 95
Larkspur Way WS8: Clay 1H 21
Larkswood Dr. DY3: Sed 6H 59
WV4: Penn 2A 58
Larne Rd. B26: Sheld 4E 121
Lashbrooke Ho. B45: Rubery 2F 157
Latches Cl. WS10: Darl 5E 47
Latelow Rd. B33: Yard 1E 121
Latham Av. B43: Gt Barr 6A 66
Latham Cres. DY4: Tip 4A 78
Lath La. B66: Smeth 1B 98
Lathom Gro. B33: Stech 4D 104
Latimer Gdns. B15: Edg 4F 117
Latimer Pl. B18: Win G 3A 100
Latimer St. WV13: W'hall 6B 30
Latymer Cl. B76: Walm 6E 71
Lauder Cl. DY3: Sed 4G 59
WV13: W'hall 2F 45
Lauderdale Cl. WS8: Clay 1A 22
Lauderdale Gdns. WV10: Bush 4A 16
Laughton Cl. B31: Longb 2F 159
Launceston Cl. WS5: Wals 4H 49
Launceston Rd. WS5: Wals 4H 49
Launde, The B28: Hall G 4E 149
Laundry Rd. B66: Smeth 6G 99
Laureates Wlk. B74: Four O 2G 53
Laurel Av. B12: Bal H 6A 118
Laurel Cl. DY1: Dud 4C 76
Laurel Ct. B13: Mose 3H 133
Laurel Dr. B66: Smeth 1E 99
B74: S'tly 3G 51
Laurel Gdns. B21: Hand 6A 82
B27: A Grn 6A 120
Laurel Gro. B30: B'vlle 1A 146
WV3: Wolv 5C 42
WV14: Bils 1A 62
Laurel La. B63: Hale 2B 128
Laurel Rd. B21: Hand 6A 82
B30: K Nor 3C 146
DY1: Dud 3B 76
DY4: Tip 6H 61
WS5: Wals 1F 65
Laurels, The *B16: Birm* *6B 100*
(off Marroway St.)
B26: Sheld 6G 121
Laurels Cres. CV7: Bal C 6H 169
Laurel Ter. B6: Aston 6H 83
Laurence Ct. B31: N'fld 2F 145
Laurence Gro. WV6: Tett 2C 26
Lauriston Cl. DY1: Dud 4B 76
Lavender Cl. WS5: Wals 2D 64
WV9: Pend 4D 14
Lavender Ct. *B71: W Brom* *6A 64*
(off Sussex Av.)
Lavender Gdns. B23: Erd 6B 68
Lavender Gro. WS3: Wals 4C 32
WV14: Bils 5H 45
Lavender Hall La. CV7: Bal C 1H 169
Lavender Ho. B38: K Nor 1B 160
Lavender La. DY8: Stourb 2B 124
Lavender Rd. DY1: Dud 4D 76
Lavendon Rd. B42: P Barr 2D 82
Lavinia Rd. B62: Hale 2E 129
Law Cliff Rd. B42: Gt Barr 1D 82
Law Cl. B69: Tiv 5D 78
Lawden Rd. B10: Small H 3B 118
Lawford Cl. B7: Birm 6A 102
Lawford Gro. B5: Birm 3G 117
B90: Shir 5D 148
Lawfred Av. WV11: Wed 4F 29
Lawley, The B63: Hale 4F 127
Lawley Cl. WS4: S'fld 6F 21
Lawley Middleway B4: Birm 5A 102
Lawley Rd. WV14: Bils 5D 44
Lawley St. B70: W Brom 4F 79
DY1: Dud 6C 76
Lawn Av. DY8: Stourb 1C 124
Lawn La. WV9: Coven 2D 14
Lawn Oaks Cl. WS8: Bwnhls 3H 9
Lawn Rd. WV2: E'shll 5B 44
Lawnsdale Cl. B46: Col 2H 107
Lawnsdown Rd. DY5: Quar B 4B 110
Lawnsfield Gro. B23: Erd 1D 84
Lawnside Grn. WV14: Bils 3F 45
Lawn St. DY8: Stourb 1C 124
LAWNS WOOD 6G 91
Lawnswood B76: Walm 5E 71
DY7: Stourt 5G 91
Lawnswood Av. B90: Shir 4B 150
DY8: Word 5A 92
WS7: Chase 1B 10
WV4: E'shll 1A 60
WV6: Tett 1C 26
Lawnswood Dr. DY7: Stourt 6G 91
WS9: Wals W 4C 22
Lawnswood Gro. B21: Hand 6G 81
Lawnswood Ri. WV6: Tett 1D 26
Lawnswood Rd. DY3: Up Gor 2H 75
DY8: Word 6A 92
Lawnwood Rd. DY2: Neth 1D 110
Lawrence Av. WV10: Wolv 5C 28
WV11: Wed 3H 29
Lawrence Ct. B68: O'bry 3H 113
Lawrence Dr. B76: Min 1H 87
Lawrence La. B64: Old H 2G 111
Lawrence St. DY9: Lye 5G 109
WV13: W'hall 6A 30
Lawrence Twr. B4: Birm 2G 5
Lawrence Wlk. B43: Gt Barr 1F 67
Lawson Cl. WS9: A'rdge 5D 34
Lawson St. B4: Birm 5G 101 (1F 5)
Law St. B71: W Brom 2A 80
Lawton Av. B29: S Oak 3D 132
Lawton Cl. B65: Row R 3D 96
Lawyers Wlk. WS1: Wals 2D 48
Laxey Rd. B16: Edg 6H 99
Laxford Cl. B12: Bal H 5G 117
Laxton Cl. DY6: K'wfrd 4E 93
Laxton Gro. B25: Yard 2B 120
Lazy Hill B38: K Nor 5D 146
WS9: A'rdge 5E 23
Lazy Hill Rd. WS9: A'rdge 1D 34
WS9: Ston 4F 23
Lea, The B33: Yard 1E 121
Lea Av. WS10: W'bry 4D 62
Lea Bank WV3: Wolv 1A 42
Lea Bank Rd. DY2: Neth 6D 94
Leabon Gro. B17: Harb 1G 131
Leabrook B26: Yard 3D 120
Leabrook Rd. DY4: Tip 4C 62
WS10: W'bry 4D 62
Leabrook Rd. Nth. WS10: W'bry 4D 62
Leach Grn. La. B45: Redn 2G 157
Leach Heath La. B45: Rubery 2F 157
Leacliffe Way WS9: A'rdge 6H 35
Leacote Dr. WV6: Tett 5A 26
Leacroft WV12: W'hall 2C 30
Leacroft Av. WV10: Bush 1A 28
Leacroft Cl. WS9: A'rdge 6D 22
Leacroft Gro. B71: W Brom 5H 63
Leacroft La. WS11: Cann 1F 7
Leacroft Rd. DY6: K'wfrd 1C 92
Leadbeater Ho. *WS3: Blox* *1H 31*
(off Somerfield Rd.)
Lea Dr. B26: Sheld 5E 121
LEA END 6B 160
Lea End La. B38: Forh 6A 160
B48: Hopw 5G 159
Leafield Cres. B33: Stech 4E 105
Leafield Gdns. B62: B'hth 3D 112
Leafield Rd. B92: Sol 4F 137
Lea Ford Rd. B33: Kitts G 5G 105
Leaford Way DY6: K'wfrd 4D 92
Leafy Glade B74: S'tly 6A 36
Leafy Ri. DY3: Lwr G 3H 75
Lea Gdns. WV3: Wolv 3F 43
Lea Grn. Av. DY4: Tip 2E 77
Lea Grn. Dr. B47: Wyt 5C 162
Lea Grn. La. B47: Wyt 3C 162
Lea Hall Rd. B33: Yard 6E 105
Lea Hall Station (Rail) 1F 121
Leahill Cft. B37: F'bri 1B 122
Lea Hill Rd. B20: Hand 5E 83
Leaholme Gdns. DY9: Pedm 3F 125
Leahouse Gdns. B68: O'bry 6G 97
Lea Ho. Rd. B30: Stir 6C 132
Leahouse Rd. B68: O'bry 6G 97
Leahurst Cres. B17: Harb 1G 131
Lea La. WS6: Gt Wyr 2G 7
Lea Mnr. Dr. WV4: Penn 2C 58
Leam Cres. B92: Sol 4F 137
Leamington Rd. B12: Bal H 6A 118
LEAMORE 4H 31
Leamore Cl. WS2: Wals 2G 31
Leamore Ent. Pk. WS2: Wals 3G 31
(Fryer's Rd.)
WS2: Wals 2G 31
(Willenhall La., not continuous)
Leamore Ind. Est.
WS2: Wals 3H 31
Leamore La. WS2: Wals 2G 31
WS3: Blox 2G 31
Leamount Dr. B44: K'sdng 3C 68
Leander Cl. WS6: Gt Wyr 4F 7
Leander Gdns. B14: K Hth 2H 147
Leander Rd. DY9: W'cte 1B 126
Leandor Dr. B74: S'tly 4A 52
Lea Rd. B11: S'hll 1D 134
WV3: Wolv 4E 43 (6A 170)
Lear Rd. WV5: Wom 5H 57
Leason La. WV10: Bush 1C 28
Leasow, The WS9: A'rdge 4A 34
Leasow Dr. B15: Edg 2H 131
Leasowe Dr. WV6: Pert 5D 24
Leasowe Rd. B45: Rubery 1F 157
DY4: Tip 3G 77
Leasowes Country Pk., The 1D 128
Leasowes Ct. B63: Hale 3A 128
Leasowes Dr. WV4: Penn 5B 42
Leasowes La. B62: Hale 6D 112
Leasowes Rd. B14: K Hth 4H 133
Leasowes Sports Cen. 5E 113
Leatherhead Cl. B6: Aston 3H 101
Leather Mus., The 6C 32
Lea Va. Rd. DY8: Stourb 3D 124
Leavesden Gro. B26: Sheld 6E 121
Lea Vw. WS9: A'rdge 4A 34
WV12: W'hall 4A 30
Lea Wlk. B45: Rubery 1F 157
Lea Yield Cl. B30: Stir 6C 132
Lechlade Rd. B43: Gt Barr 5A 66
Leckie Rd. WS2: Wals 5C 32
Ledbury Cl. B16: Birm 1C 116
WS9: A'rdge 6E 23
Ledbury Ct. *B29: W Cas* *6G 131*
(off Ruthall Cl.)
WV12: W'hall 5B 30
Ledbury Dr. WV1: Wolv 2D 44
Ledbury Ho. B33: Kitts G 1A 122
Ledbury Way B76: Walm 5E 71
Ledsam Gro. B32: Harb 5D 114
Ledsam St. B16: Birm 1C 116
Ledwell B90: Dic H 3G 163
LEE BANK 3E 117
Lee Bank Middleway B15: Birm 3E 117
Leebank Rd. B63: Hale 3G 127
Leech St. DY4: Tip 2C 78
Lee Ct. WS9: Wals W 4B 22
Lee Cres. B15: Edg 3E 117
Lee Gdns. B67: Smeth 4C 98
Lee Rd. B47: H'wd 2A 162
B64: Crad H 3H 111
Leeson Wlk. B17: Harb 1H 131
Lees Rd. WV14: Bils 2H 61
Lees St. B18: Hock 4B 100
Lees Ter. WV14: Bils 2H 61
Lee St. B70: W Brom 5G 63
Legge La. B1: Birm 6D 100 (2A 4)
WV14: Cose 3F 61
Legge St. B4: Birm 5H 101
B70: W Brom 4B 80
WV2: E'shll 5A 44
Legion Rd. B45: Rubery 2E 157
Legs La. WV10: Bush 3A 16
Leicester Cl. B67: Smeth 2C 114
Leicester Pl. B71: W Brom 6A 64
Leicester Sq. WV6: Wolv 6E 27
Leicester St. WS1: Wals 1C 48
WV6: Wolv 5F 27
Leigham Dr. B17: Harb 4E 115
Leigh Cl. WS4: Wals 5E 33
Leigh Ct. B23: Erd 5C 84
WS4: Wals 6E 33
Leigh Rd. B8: Salt 3E 103
B75: S Cold 6F 55
WS4: Wals 6E 33
Leighs Cl. WS4: S'fld 6G 21
Leighs Rd. WS4: S'fld 6F 21
LEIGHSWOOD 1C 34
Leighswood Av. WS9: A'rdge 2C 34
Leighswood Ct. WS9: A'rdge 3D 34
Leighswood Gro. WS9: A'rdge 2C 34
Leighswood Ind. Est. WS9: A'rdge 6B 22
(Brickyard Rd.)
WS9: A'rdge 2C 34
(Phoenix Dr.)
Leighswood Rd. WS9: A'rdge 2C 34
Leighton Cl. B43: Gt Barr 2E 67
DY1: Dud 5A 76
Leighton Rd. B13: Mose 3H 133
WV4: Penn 5D 42
WV14: Bils 1A 62
Leith Gro. B38: K Nor 1A 160
Lelant Gro. B17: Harb 6E 115
Lellow St. B71: W Brom 5H 63
Lemar Ind. Est. B30: Stir 4D 132
Le More B74: Four O 1G 53
Lemox Rd. B70: W Brom 5G 63
Lench Cl. B62: B'hth 2C 112
Lenches, The *B69: O'bry* *4E 97*
(off Shelsley Av.)
Lench's Cl. B13: Mose 3H 133
Lenchs Grn. B5: Bal H 4G 117
Lench St. B4: Birm 5G 101 (1F 5)
Lenchs Trust B32: Quin 5B 114
Lench's Trust Ho's. B12: Birm 4H 117
(Conybere St.)
B12: Birm 3A 118
(Ravenhurst St.)
B16: Birm *2C 116*
(off Ladywood Middleway)
Len Davis Rd. WV12: W'hall 2B 30
Lennard Gdns. B66: Smeth 3H 99
Lennox Gdns. WV3: Wolv 3E 43
Lennox Gro. B73: Bold 6G 69
Lenton Cft. B26: Yard 1C 136
Lenwade Rd. B68: O'bry 3B 114
Leofric Ct. B15: Edg 3E 117
Leominster Ct. *B45: Rubery* *1F 157*
(off Deelands Rd.)
Leominster Ho. B33: Kitts G 1A 122
Leominster Rd. B11: S'hll 2E 135
Leominster Wlk. B45: Rubery 1F 157
Leona Ind. Est. B62: B'hth 2D 112
Leonard Av. B19: Loz 1F 101
Leonard Gro. B19: Loz 1E 101
Leonard Rd. B19: Loz 1E 101
DY8: Woll 6A 108
Leopold Av. B20: Hand 2A 82
Leopold St. B12: Birm 3H 117
Lepid Gro. B29: S Oak 3H 131
Lerryn Cl. DY6: K'wfrd 4D 92
Lerwick Cl. DY6: K'wfrd 4D 92
Lesley Dr. DY6: K'wfrd 5C 92
Leslie Bentley Ho. B1: Birm 3A 4
Leslie Dr. DY4: Tip 4A 62
Leslie Ri. B69: Tiv 1C 96
Leslie Rd. B16: Edg 1B 116
B20: Hand 5F 83
B74: Lit A 1B 52
WV10: Wolv 4B 28
Lesscroft Cl. WV9: Pend 4E 15
Lester Gro. WS9: A'rdge 1G 51
Lester St. WV14: Bils 6H 45
Levante Gdns. B33: Stech 1B 120
Leve La. WV13: W'hall 1B 46
Level St. DY5: Brie H 6H 93
Leven Cft. B76: Walm 6E 71
Leven Dr. WV12: W'hall 6B 18
Levenwick Way DY6: K'wfrd 4E 93
Leverretts, The B21: Hand 5G 81
Lever St. WV2: Wolv 3H 43 (6C 170)
Leverton Ri. WV10: Oxl 3G 27
Leveson Av. WS6: C Hay 3E 7
Leveson Cl. DY2: Dud 1G 95
Leveson Ct. WV13: W'hall 1A 46
Leveson Cres. CV7: Bal C 6H 169
Leveson Dr. DY4: Tip 1G 77
Leveson Rd. WV11: Wed 1H 29
Leveson St. WV13: W'hall 1A 46
Leveson Wlk. DY2: Dud 1G 95
Levington Cl. WV6: Pert 5F 25
Levis's Trad. Est. B33: Stech 5B 104
Lewis Av. WV1: Wolv 6D 28
Lewis Cl. WV12: W'hall 4D 30
Lewis Gro. WV11: Wed 3F 29
Lewisham Ind. Est. B66: Smeth 2E 99
Lewisham Rd. B66: Smeth 2E 99
WV10: Oxl 5F 15
Lewisham St. B71: W Brom 3B 80
Lewis Rd. B30: Stir 6E 133
B68: O'bry 4H 113
DY9: Lye 6H 109
Lewis St. DY4: Tip 2D 78
WS2: Wals 5B 32
WV14: Bils 5G 45
Lewthorn Ri. WV4: Penn 1H 59
Lexington Grn. DY5: Brie H 4G 109
Leybourne Cres. WV9: Pend 5D 14
Leybourne Gro. B25: Yard 5H 119
Leybrook Rd. B45: Redn 1H 157
Leyburn Cl. WS2: Wals 5D 30
Leycester Cl. B31: Longb 2E 159
Leycroft Av. B33: Kitts G 5H 105
Leydon Cft. B38: K Nor 5D 146
LEY HILL 2G 53
Ley Hill Farm Rd. B31: N'fld 2C 144
Ley Hill Rd. B75: Four O 2A 54
Leylan Cft. B13: Mose 6C 134
Leyland Av. WV3: Wolv 2D 42
Leyland Cft. WS3: Pels 3D 20
Leyland Dr. DY2: Dud 1F 95
Leyman Cl. B14: Yard W 3C 148
Ley Ri. DY3: Sed 4G 59
Leys, The B31: N'fld 2F 145
WS10: Darl 5C 46
Leys Cl. DY9: Pedm 3G 125
Leys Cres. DY5: Brie H 6F 93
Leysdown Gro. B27: A Grn 5A 136
Leysdown Rd. B27: A Grn 5A 136
Leys Rd. DY5: Brie H 6E 93
Leys Wood Cft. B26: Sheld 5E 121
Leyton Cl. DY5: Brie H 3G 109
Leyton Gro. B44: K'sdng 4A 68
Leyton Rd. B21: Hand 1B 100
Libbards Ga. B91: Sol 1G 165
Libbards Way B91: Sol 1F 165
Liberty Ct. WS6: C Hay 2D 6
Liberty Pl. B16: Birm 1D 116
Library, Theatre and Solihull Arts Complex 4G 151
Library Way B45: Rubery 2F 157
Lich Av. WV11: Wed 2G 29
Lichen Gdns. B38: K Nor 2H 159
Lichfield Ct. B90: Shir 5D 148
WS4: Wals *5E 33*
(off Lichfield Rd.)
Lichfield Pas. WV1: Wolv 1H 43 (2C 170)
Lichfield Rd. B6: Aston 3A 102
B46: Col, Wat O 3F 89
B74: Four O 4F 37
B76: Curd, Wis 2F 89
WS3: Blox 5H 19
WS3: Pels 2E 21
WS4: Rus, S'fld, Wals 5E 33
WS8: Bwnhls 5B 10
WS9: Wals W, Bwnhls 4B 22
WV11: Wed 4F 29
WV12: W'hall 2A 30
Lichfield St. DY4: Tip 5H 61
WS1: Wals 1D 48
WV1: Wolv 1G 43 (3B 170)
WV14: Bils 5F 45
Lich Gates WV1: Wolv 1G 43 (2B 170)
Lichwood Rd. WV11: Wed 2H 29
LICKEY 6G 157
Lickey Coppice B45: Coft H 5A 158
Lickey Hills Country Pk. 5G 157
Lickey Hills Vis. Cen. 6H 157
Lickey Rd. B45: Redn 4A 158
DY8: Amb 5F 109
Liddiard Ct. DY8: Woll 5C 108
Liddon Gro. B27: A Grn 5A 136
Liddon Rd. B27: A Grn 5A 136
LIFFORD 2D 146
Lifford Cl. B14: K Hth 2D 146
Lifford La. B30: K Nor 2C 146
Lifton Cft. DY6: K'wfrd 4D 92
Lightfields Wlk. B65: Row R 4A 96
Lighthorne Av. B16: Birm 1C 116
Lighthorne Rd. B91: Sol 1G 151
Lighthouse, The 1H 43 (2C 170)

Lightning Way—Longley Av.

Lightning Way B31: Longb 2F 159
Lightwood Cl. B93: Know 1D 166
Lightwood Rd. DY1: Dud 4C 76
Lightwoods Hill B67: Smeth 3C 114
Lightwoods Rd. B67: Smeth 1E 115
DY9: Pedm 4G 125
Lilac Av. B12: Bal H 6A 118
B44: Gt Barr 6G 67
B74: S'tly 3G 51
DY4: Tip 6G 61
WS5: Wals 1E 65
Lilac Dr. WV5: Wom 1F 73
Lilac Gro. WS2: Wals 6E 31
WS10: W'bry 3G 63
Lilac La. WS6: Gt Wyr 5F 7
Lilac Rd. DY1: Dud 3D 76
WV1: Wolv 3D 44
WV12: W'hall 2E 31
Lilac Way B62: B'hth 3F 113
Lilian Gro. WV14: Bils 4G 61
Lilleshall Cres. WV2: Wolv 4H 43
Lilleshall Rd. B26: Sheld 4F 121
Lilley La. B31: Longb 1F 159
Lillington Cl. B75: S Cold 1E 71
Lillington Gro. B34: S End 4H 105
Lillington Rd. B90: Shir 1H 163
Lillycroft La. B38: Head H 2C 160
Lily Rd. B26: Yard 5B 120
Lily St. B71: W Brom 2A 80
Limberlost Cl. B20: Hand 4C 82
Limbrick Cl. B90: Shir 5F 149
Limbury Gro. B92: Sol 5B 138
Lime Av. B29: S Oak 3B 132
WS2: Wals 6E 31
Lime Cl. B47: H'wd 4A 162
B70: W Brom 3G 79
DY4: Tip 2G 77
WS2: Wals 6E 31
WS6: Gt Wyr 1F 7
Lime Ct. B11: S'hll 1C 134
Lime Gro. B10: Small H 3D 118
B12: Bal H 6H 117
B19: Loz 1E 101
B26: Yard 5B 120
B37: Chel W 2D 122
B66: Smeth 6F 99
(Edith Rd.)
B66: Smeth 5F 99
(Windmill La.)
B73: W Grn 6H 69
WS4: Rus 3G 33
WV14: Bils 4E 45
Limehurst Av. WV3: Wolv 3A 42
Limehurst Rd. WS4: Rus 4G 33
Lime Kiln Cl. B38: K Nor 2H 159
Limekiln La. B14: K Hth 3A 148
Lime Kiln Wlk. DY1: Dud 5F 77
Lime La. WS3: Lit W 3D 8
Limepit La. DY1: Dud 4C 76
Lime Pitts Nature Reserve 4G 33
Limerick Cl. DY3: Gorn 5F 75
Lime Rd. DY3: Sed 4B 60
WS10: W'bry 1F 63
Limes, The B11: S'brk 5C 118
B16: Birm 6B 100
B24: Erd 4F 85
DY3: Himl 4H 73
WS1: Wals 1E 49
WS4: Rus 2H 33
Limes Av. B65: Row R 1C 112
DY5: Brie H 4G 93
Limescroft Cl. WS4: Rus 2F 33
Limes Rd. DY1: Dud 4D 76
WV6: Tett 5A 26
Lime St. WS1: Wals 2D 48
WV3: Wolv 3E 43
WV14: Cose 5C 60
Limes Vw. DY3: Sed 6H 59
Lime Ter. B6: Aston 6H 83
Lime Tree Av. WV6: Tett 6G 25
Lime Tree Gdns. WV8: Bilb 4H 13
Lime Tree Gro. B31: N'fld 5F 145
Lime Tree Rd. B8: Salt 3F 103
B27: A Grn 6A 120
WS5: Wals 1E 65
WV8: Bilb 4H 13
Limetree Rd. B74: S'tly 2F 51
Lime Wlk. B38: K Nor 1A 160
Linacre Ho. B37: F'bri 1B 122
Linchmere Rd. B21: Hand 5G 81
Lincoln Av. WV13: W'hall 6D 30
Lincoln Cl. B27: A Grn 2C 136
Lincoln Ct. *B29: W Cas* *6G 131*
(off Tugford Rd.)
Lincoln Grn. WV10: Bush 5H 15
Lincoln Gro. B37: Mars G 2C 122
Lincoln Rd. B27: A Grn 3B 136
B67: Smeth 1C 114
B71: W Brom 4B 64
DY2: Neth 6F 95
WS1: Wals 1E 49
Lincoln Rd. Nth. B27: A Grn 2C 136
Lincoln Rd. Wharf B92: Olton 3C 136
Lincoln St. B12: Bal H 6G 117
WV10: Wolv 6A 28
Lincoln Twr. *B16: Birm* *2C 116*
(off Morville St.)
Lindale Av. B36: Hodg H 3A 104
Lindale Cres. DY5: Brie H 5F 109
Lindale Dr. WV5: Wom 1F 73
Linden Av. B43: Gt Barr 5H 65
B62: B'hth 4E 113
B69: Tiv 1D 96
Linden Cl. WS2: Wals 1D 46
Linden Dr. DY8: Stourb 2E 125
Linden Glade B63: Hale 1A 128
Linden La. WV12: W'hall 2E 31
Linden Lea WV3: Wolv 2B 42
Linden Rd. B30: B'vlle 5A 132
B66: Smeth 1E 115
DY1: Dud 4D 76
Linden Road Instruction Pool 6B 132
Lindens, The B32: Harb 4C 114
WV6: Wolv 6C 26
Lindens Dr. B74: S'tly 6H 51
Linden Ter. B12: Bal H 6B 118
Lindenwood B73: S Cold 5H 53
Lindford Way B38: K Nor 5D 146
Lindley Av. DY4: Tip 4H 77
Lindon Cl. WS8: Bwnhls 1C 22
Lindon Dr. WS8: Bwnhls 6B 10
Lindon Rd. WS8: Bwnhls 2B 22
Lindon Vw. WS8: Bwnhls 2C 22
Lindrick Cl. WS3: Blox 4F 19
Lindridge Dr. B76: Min 1G 87
Lindridge Rd. B23: Erd 3B 84
B75: S Cold 3D 54
B90: Shir 6F 149
Lindrosa Rd. B74: S'tly 6H 35
Lindsay Rd. B42: Gt Barr 4D 66
Lindsey Av. B31: N'fld 3G 145
Lindsey Pl. DY5: Brie H 6G 93
Lindsey Rd. B71: W Brom 6A 64
Lindsworth App. B30: K Nor 4E 147
Lindsworth Ct. B30: K Nor 4E 147
Lindsworth Rd. B30: K Nor 4D 146
Linfield Gdns. DY3: Sed 4G 59
Linford Gro. B25: Yard 2B 120
Linforth Dr. B74: S'tly 4A 52
Lingard Cl. B7: Nech 4B 102
Lingard Ho. B76: Walm 5D 70
Lingard Rd. B75: S Cold 6D 54
Lingfield Av. B44: Gt Barr 4G 67
WV10: F'hses 2H 15
Lingfield Cl. WS6: Gt Wyr 3F 7
Lingfield Ct. B43: Gt Barr 6H 65
Lingfield Dr. WS6: Gt Wyr 3F 7
Lingfield Gdns. B34: S End 3F 105
Lingfield Grange B74: S'tly 2A 52
Lingfield Gro. WV6: Pert 5F 25
Lingfield Rd. WS11: Nort C 1E 9
Lingfield Way DY6: K'wfrd 4E 93
Lingham Cl. B92: Sol 6H 137
Ling Ho. WV10: Wolv 6B 28
Lingmoor Gro. WS9: A'rdge 2C 34
Linhope Dr. DY6: K'wfrd 4E 93
Link, The B27: A Grn 4G 135
Link One Ind. Pk. DY4: Tip 1E 79
Link Rd. B16: Edg 6A 100
WS9: Wals W 4D 22
WV5: Wom 6G 57
Links Av. WV6: Tett 2B 26
Links Cres. B68: O'bry 3H 113
Links Dr. B45: Rubery 4G 157
B91: Sol 1F 151
DY8: Stourb 3C 124
Links Rd. B14: K Hth 6A 148
B68: O'bry 3H 113
WV4: Penn 2E 59
Links Side Way WS9: A'rdge 1E 35
Links Vw. B62: Hale 1D 128
B74: S'tly 2B 52
Linkswood Cl. B13: Mose 4B 134
Linkwood Ind. Est. DY8: Woll 5C 108
Linley Cl. WS9: A'rdge 4A 34
Linley Dr. WV10: Bush 6A 16
Linley Gro. B14: K Hth 1E 147
DY3: Gorn 5F 75
Linley Lodge Ind. Est. WS9: A'rdge 2A 34
Linley Rd. WS4: Rus 2H 33
Linley Wood Rd. WS9: A'rdge 4A 34
Linnet Cl. B30: B'vlle 5A 132
B62: Hale 5B 112
(Lodgefield Rd.)
B62: Hale 4G 127
(Manor Way)
Linnet Gro. B23: Erd 1B 84
WV12: W'hall 1B 30
Linpole Wlk. B14: K Hth 5E 147
Linsey Rd. B92: Sol 3G 137
Linslade Cl. WV4: Penn 1H 59
Linthouse La. WV11: Wed 1F 29
Linton Av. B91: Sol 6E 151
Linton Cl. B63: Crad 6F 111
Linton Cft. WV14: Bils 6F 45
Linton Rd. B11: Tys 1G 135
B43: Gt Barr 1E 67
B64: Old H 6H 95
WV4: Penn 6C 42
Linton Wlk. B23: Erd 4B 84
Linwood Ct. B23: Erd 4E 85
Linwood Rd. B21: Hand 1A 100
B91: Sol 2B 150
DY1: Dud 2D 76
Lionel St. B3: Birm 6E 101 (3B 4)
Lion Ind. Pk. WS9: A'rdge 1C 34
Lion Pas. DY8: Stourb 6D 108
Lion Rd. B64: Old H 2A 112
Lion's Den WS7: Hamm 3G 11
Lion St. DY8: Stourb 6D 108
Liskeard Rd. WS5: Wals 4H 49
Lisko Cl. DY5: Brie H 3E 109
Lismore Cl. B45: Fran 6E 143
Lismore Dr. B17: Harb 2E 131
Lissimore Dr. DY4: Tip 5A 78
Lissimore Ho. *B70: W Brom* *1C 98*
(off Maria St.)
Lisson Gro. B44: Gt Barr 1H 67
Listelow Cl. B36: Cas B 1F 105
Lister Cl. DY4: Tip 3A 78
WS2: Wals 4H 31
Lister Rd. DY2: Dud 2E 95
WS2: Wals 4H 31
Lister St. B7: Birm 5H 101 (1G 5)
WV13: W'hall 2B 46
Listowel Rd. B14: K Hth 1F 147
Lisures Dr. B76: Walm 1B 70
Lit. Albert St. WS2: Wals 1C 48
Lit. Ann St. B5: Birm 1H 117 (5H 5)
LITTLE ASTON 4C 36
Little Aston Golf Course 5C 36
Lit. Aston Hall Dr. B74: Lit A 4A 36
Lit. Aston La. B74: Lit A 3C 36
Lit. Aston Pk. Rd. B74: Lit A 6A 36
Lit. Aston Rd. WS9: A'rdge 3D 34
Lit. Barr St. B9: Birm 1A 118
Little Birches WV3: Wolv 3D 42
LITTLE BLOXWICH 4B 20
Lit. Brick Kiln St. WV3: Wolv 2G 43 (5A 170)
LITTLE BROMWICH 1F 119
Lit. Bromwich Rd. B9: Bord G 2H 119
Lit. Caldmore WS1: Wals 3C 48
Lit. Checkhill La. DY7: Stourt 5D 90
Lit. Clothier St. WV13: W'hall 6A 30
Lit. Clover Cl. B7: Nech 3C 102
Little Comn. WS3: Pels 3E 21
Lit. Cornbow B63: Hale 2B 128
Littlecote Cft. B14: K Hth 4A 148
Littlecote Dr. B23: Erd 6F 69
Lit. Cottage St. DY5: Brie H 1H 109
Little Cft. B43: Gt Barr 4G 65
Lit. Cross St. WS10: Darl 4C 46
Lit. Edward St. B9: Birm 1A 118
Lit. Fields Way B69: O'bry 2F 97
Lit. Francis Gro. B7: Birm 4B 102
Lit. Gorway WS1: Wals 4D 48
Lit. Green La. B9: Small H 2C 118
Lit. Green Lanes B73: W Grn 6H 69
Lit. Hall Rd. B7: Birm 5B 102
Lit. Hardwick Rd. WS9: A'rdge 1E 51
LITTLE HAY 1H 37
Lit. Hay La. WS14: Lit H, W'frd 2H 37
Lit. Heath Cft. B34: S End 2F 105
Little Hill WS10: W'bry 2F 63
Lit. Hill Gro. B38: K Nor 6C 146
Lit. Hill Ho. B24: Erd 1B 86
Lit. Hill Way B32: Bart G 3B 130
Lit. Johnsons La. WS9: A'rdge 3D 50
Lit. John St. DY5: Brie H 5H 93
Little La. B71: W Brom 2B 80
WV12: W'hall 2D 30
Lit. Lawns Cl. WS8: Wals W 3C 22
LITTLE LONDON 6A 30
Little London WS1: Wals 4C 48
Lit. London Ho. WS1: Wals 4D 48
Littlemead Av. B31: N'fld 6G 145
Lit. Meadow Cft. B31: N'fld 3D 144
Lit. Meadow Wlk. B33: Stech 6C 104
Littlemead Rd. B90: Maj G 1E 163
Lit. Moor Hill B67: Smeth 4D 98
Lit. Newport St. *WS1: Wals* *2C 48*
(off Newport St.)
Lit. Oaks Rd. B6: Aston 1G 101
Littleover Av. B28: Hall G 1F 149
Little Pk. B32: Quin 1H 129
Lit. Park St. WV1: Wolv 1H 43 (3D 170)
Lit. Pitts Cl. B24: Erd 2B 86
Lit. Potter St. DY5: Brie H 1H 109
Lit. Pountney St. WV2: Wolv 3G 43 (6B 170)
Lit. Shadwell St. B4: Birm 5G 101 (1E 5)
Littleshaw Cft. B47: Wyt 5C 162
Littleshaw La. B47: Wyt 5C 162
Little's La. WV1: Wolv 1H 43 (1C 170)
(not continuous)
Lit. Station St. WS2: Wals 1C 48
Little St. DY2: Dud 6F 77
LITTLE SUTTON 1A 54
Lit. Sutton La. B75: S Cold 4A 54
Lit. Sutton Rd. B75: R'ley 1A 54
Littleton Cl. B76: Walm 3E 71
Littleton Cft. B91: Sol 1G 165
Littleton Rd. WV12: W'hall 2C 30
Littleton St. E. WS1: Wals 1D 48
Littleton St. W. WS2: Wals 1C 48
LITTLEWOOD 1E 7
Littlewood Cl. B91: Sol 1F 165
Littlewood La. WS6: C Hay 1E 7
Littlewood Rd. WS6: C Hay 1E 7
Lit. Wood St. WV13: W'hall 1A 46
Littleworth Av. DY1: Dud 1D 76
LITTLEWORTH END 3G 55
Littleworth Gro. B76: Walm 1D 70
LITTLE WYRLEY 5C 8
Liveridge Cl. B93: Know 3B 166
Liverpool Cft. B37: Mars G 3B 122
Liverpool St. B9: Birm 1A 118
Livery St. B3: Birm 5F 101 (1C 4)
(not continuous)
Livingstone Av. WV6: Pert 4E 25
Livingstone Rd. B14: K Hth 1G 147
B20: Hand 6E 83
B70: W Brom 6H 79
WS3: Blox 5C 20
WV14: Bils 6D 44
Living Well Heath Club 3D 68 (5A 4)
Lizafield Cl. B66: Smeth 2C 98
Lloyd Dr. WV4: Penn 3A 58
Lloyd Hill WV4: Penn 2A 58
Lloyd Ho. *B19: Hock* *3E 101*
(off Newtown Dr.)
Lloyd Rd. B20: Hand 3C 82
WV6: Tett 4B 26
Lloyd Sq. B15: Edg 3B 116
Lloyds Rd. B62: B'hth 3C 112
Lloyd St. B10: Small H 3D 118
B71: W Brom 3C 80
DY2: Dud 1F 95
WS10: W'bry 2E 63
WV6: Wolv 5D 26
Locarno Rd. DY4: Tip 2H 77
Lochalsh Gro. WV12: W'hall 6B 18
Lochranza Cft. B43: Gt Barr 3A 66
Lock Dr. B33: Stech 6B 104
Lock Pl. B7: Birm 6A 102
Locket Cl. WS2: Wals 5F 31
Lockfield Cl. DY8: Word 2D 108
Lockhart Dr. B75: R'ley 2A 54
Locking Cft. B35: Cas V 4F 87
Lockington Cft. B62: Quin 5F 113
Lock Keepers Cl. WS11: Nort C 1D 8
Lockley Cl. WV10: Wolv 5B 28
Lock Mus. 2A 46
Lock Side DY4: Tip 2G 77
Lockside WS9: A'rdge 2B 34
WV5: Wom 6E 57
Lockside Cl. DY5: Brie H 2H 109
Locksmith Cl. WV13: W'hall 1B 46
Lock St. WV1: Wolv 6H 27 (1D 170)
(not continuous)
Locks Vw. DY8: Word 2C 108
Lockton Rd. B30: Stir 5E 133
Lockwood Rd. B31: N'fld 3D 144
LODE HEATH 2H 151
Lode La. B91: Sol 3F 151
B92: Olton, Sol 4F 137
Lode Mill Ct. B92: Olton 5F 137
Lodge Cl. B62: Hale 2E 129
WS5: Wals 5H 49
Lodge Cres. DY2: Neth 5C 94
Lodge Cft. B31: N'fld 1C 144
B93: Know 3D 166
Lodge Dr. B26: Yard 3D 120
Lodge Farm Cl. B76: Walm 2D 70
Lodgefield Rd. B62: Hale 5B 112
Lodge Forge Rd. B64: Crad H 4E 111
Lodge Forge Trad. Est. B64: Crad H 4E 111
Lodge Gro. WS9: A'rdge 4C 34
LODGE HILL 3F 131
Lodge Hill Crematorium B29: S Oak 4F 131
Lodge Hill Rd. B29: S Oak 4H 131
Lodge La. DY6: K'wfrd 3G 91
WS11: Cann 1C 6
Lodge Pool Cl. B44: Gt Barr 1G 83
Lodge Rd. B6: Aston 1G 101
B18: Win G, Hock 3A 100
(not continuous)
B67: Smeth 2C 98
B70: W Brom 4H 79
B93: Know 3D 166
WS4: S'fld 6F 21
WS5: Wals 6H 49
(not continuous)
WS10: Darl 6D 46
WV10: Oxl 1F 27
WV14: Bils 1H 61
Lodge St. B69: O'bry 2G 97
WV12: W'hall 4C 30
Lodge Ter. B17: Harb 6G 115
Lodge Vw. WS6: C Hay 2C 6
Loeless Rd. B33: Kitts G 6E 105
Lofthouse Cres. B31: N'fld 4D 144
Lofthouse Gro. B31: N'fld 4D 144
Lofthouse Rd. B20: Hand 4A 82
Loftus Cl. B29: W Cas 5D 130
Logan Cl. WV10: Oxl 3G 27
Lomaine Dr. B30: K Nor 3A 146
Lomas Dr. B31: N'fld 4C 144
Lomas St. WV1: Wolv 5G 27
Lombard Av. DY2: Neth 6F 95
Lombard St. B12: Birm 3H 117
B70: W Brom 4A 80
Lombard St. W. B70: W Brom 4A 80
Lombardy Cft. B62: Quin 5G 113
Lombardy Gdns. WV12: W'hall 2E 31
Lomond Cl. B34: S End 3A 106
Lomond Rd. DY3: Sed 4G 59
LONDONDERRY 5B 98
Londonderry Gro. B67: Smeth 4D 98
Londonderry Ho. B4: Birm 3F 5
Londonderry La. B67: Smeth 5B 98
Londonderry Rd. B68: O'bry 5B 98
LONDON FIELDS 5B 76
London Hgts. DY1: Dud 5C 76
London Rd. B20: Hand 5G 83
B75: Bass P 6F 39
B75: Can 4E 39
B78: Midd 1G 55
WS14: W'frd 1D 38
London St. B66: Smeth 4G 99
London St. Ind. Est. B66: Smeth 4H 99
Lones Rd. B71: W Brom 1F 99
Long Acre B7: Nech 3B 102
WV8: Cod 5F 13
Longacre WV13: W'hall 3A 46
Long Acre Ind. Est. B7: Nech 2B 102
(not continuous)
Longacre Ind. Est. B7: Nech 1C 102
Longacres B74: Lit A 5C 36
Long Acre St. WS2: Wals 6B 32
Longbank Rd. B69: Tiv 1C 96
Longboat La. DY8: Word 3C 108
Longboat Quay DY2: Neth 5F 95
Longbow Rd. B29: W Cas 6D 130
LONGBRIDGE 1D 158
Longbridge La. B31: Longb 1C 158
Longbridge Station (Rail) 1C 158
Longbrook La. CV7: Bal C 3E 169
CV8: Fen E 3E 169
Long Cl. Wlk. B35: Cas V 4F 87
Longcroft, The B63: Hale 2G 127
WS4: Rus 2G 33
Longcroft Av. WS10: W'bry 2G 63
Longcroft Cl. B35: Cas V 5D 86
Longdales Rd. B38: K Nor 2H 159
Longdon Av. WV4: Penn 6H 43
Longdon Cft. B93: Know 1C 166
Longdon Dr. B74: Four O 5E 37
Longdon Rd. B93: Know 3C 166
Longfellow Rd. B30: K Nor 3H 145
DY3: Lwr G 2E 75
Longfield Cl. B28: Hall G 1F 149
Longfield Dr. B74: Lit A 5D 36
Longfield Ho. WV10: Wolv 6B 28
Longfield Rd. B31: N'fld 5C 130
DY9: Lye 6H 109
Longford Cl. B32: Bart G 6G 129
B93: Dorr 6D 166
WV5: Wom 2D 72
Longford Gro. B44: K'sdng 2A 68
Longford Rd. B44: K'sdng 2A 68
WV10: Wolv 5B 28
Long Furrow WV8: Pend 6C 14
Longham Cft. B32: Harb 1D 130
Longhurst Cft. B31: Longb 2F 159
Long Hyde Rd. B67: Smeth 2D 114
Long Innage B63: Crad 5D 110
Long Knowle La. WV11: Wed 1D 28
Longlake Av. WV6: Tett 6G 25
Longlands, The WV5: Wom 1G 73
Longlands Cl. *B38: K Nor* *1G 159*
(off Nearhill Rd.)
Longlands Rd. B62: Hale 2E 129
Long La. B62: B'hth 2D 112
B65: B'hth 2D 112
WS6: Ess, Gt Wyr 2D 18
WS11: Nort C 1D 8
Long La. Trad. Est. B62: B'hth 3D 112
Long Leasow B29: W Cas 6E 131
Longleat B43: Gt Barr 3H 65
Longleat Dr. B90: Ches G 4C 164
DY1: Dud 5A 76
Longleat Rd. WS9: A'rdge 6C 22
Long Ley WV10: Wolv 6B 28
Longley Av. B76: Min 2H 87

Longley Cres.—Malvern Av.

Longley Cres. B26: Yard 1C 136
Long Leys Ct. B46: Wat O 4D 88
Longleys Cft. B46: Wat O 5D 88
Longley Wlk. B37: Chel W 1E 123
Long Mdw. B65: Row R 6C 96
Longmeadow Cl. B75: S Cold 6D 54
Longmeadow Cres. B34: S End 3A 106
Long Mdw. Dr. DY3: Sed 3F 59
Longmeadow Gro. B31: Longb 3E 159
Longmeadow Rd. WS5: Wals 3A 50
Long Mill Av. WV11: Wed 2D 28
Long Mill Nth. WV11: Wed 2D 28
Long Mill Sth. WV11: Wed 2D 28
Longmoor Cl. WV11: Wed 4H 29
Longmoor Rd. B63: Hale 2G 127
B73: S'tly 2B 68
Longmore Av. WS2: Wals 2F 47
Longmore Cl. B73: S'tly 6A 52
Longmore Rd. B90: Shir 5A 150
Longmore St. B12: Bal H 4G 117
WS10: W'bry 2F 63
Long Mynd B63: Hale 4F 127
Long Mynd Cl. WV12: W'hall 6B 18
Long Mynd Rd. B31: N'fld 1C 144
Long Nuke Rd. B31: N'fld 6C 130
Long Saw Dr. B31: Longb 6B 144
Longshaw Gro. B34: S End 3H 105
Longstone Cl. B90: M'path 3F 165
Longstone Rd. B42: Gt Barr 6E 67
Long St. B11: S'brk 5A 118
WS2: Wals 2B 48
WV1: Wolv 1H 43 (2C 170)
Long Wood B30: B'vlle 2A 146
Longwood La. WS4: Wals 1A 50
WS5: Wals 1A 50
Longwood Pathway B34: S End 4G 105
Longwood Ri. WV12: W'hall 4D 30
Longwood Rd. B45: Redn 2G 157
WS9: A'rdge 6D 34
Lonicera Cl. WS5: Wals 2F 65
Lonsdale Cl. B33: Stech 1B 120
WV12: W'hall 4B 30
Lonsdale Ct. B17: Harb 5G 115
Lonsdale Rd. B17: Harb 5F 115
B66: Smeth 2B 98
WS5: Wals 5G 49
WV3: Wolv 4F 43
WV14: Bils 5H 45
Lords B17: Harb 5F 115
Lords Dr. WS2: Wals 6C 32
Lordsmore Cl. WV14: Cose 4G 61
Lord St. B7: Birm 5H 101
WS1: Wals 4B 48
(not continuous)
WV3: Wolv 1F 43
(not continuous)
WV14: Bils 2G 61
Lord St. W. WV14: Bils 2G 61
Lordswood Rd. B17: Harb 3E 115
Lordswood Sq. B17: Harb 4F 115
Lorimer Way B43: Gt Barr 6F 51
Lorne St. DY4: Tip 5H 61
Lorrainer Av. DY5: Brie H 3E 109
Lothians Rd. WS3: Pels 2E 21
WV6: Tett 3C 26
Lottie Rd. B29: S Oak 4A 132
Lotus Ct. B16: Edg 2A 116
Lotus Cft. B67: Smeth 5D 98
Lotus Dr. B64: Old H 1H 111
Lotus Wlk. B36: Cas B 6B 88
Lotus Way B65: Row R 5A 96
Loughton Gro. B63: Hale 1H 127
Louisa Pl. B18: Hock 4C 100
Louisa St. B1: Birm 6E 101 (3A 4)
Louis Ct. B67: Smeth 4D 98
Louise Ct. B27: A Grn 2A 136
B91: Sol 6C 150
Louise Cft. B14: K Hth 5G 147
Louise Lorne Rd. B13: Mose 1H 133
Louise Rd. B21: Hand 2B 100
Louise St. DY3: Gorn 4F 75
Lount Wlk. B19: Hock 4G 101
Lovatt Cl. DY4: Tip 4C 62
Lovatt St. WV1: Wolv 1F 43
Loveday Ho. B70: W Brom 4B 80
Loveday St. B4: Birm 5G 101 (1E 5)
(not continuous)
Lovelace Av. B91: Sol 1H 165
Love La. B7: Birm 5H 101
B47: H'wd 2G 161
B69: Tiv 6A 78
DY8: Stourb 2E 125
DY9: Lye 6A 110
WS1: Wals 4C 48
WS6: Gt Wyr 2G 7
WV6: Tett 3B 26
Lovell Cl. B29: W Cas 1F 145
Loveridge Cl. WV8: Cod 4F 13
Lovers Wlk. B6: Aston 1B 102
WS10: W'bry 2F 63
Lovett Av. B69: O'bry 4D 96
Low Av. B43: Gt Barr 3B 66
Lowbridge Cl. WV12: W'hall 4C 30
Lowbrook La. B90: Tid G 5D 162
Lowcroft Gdns. WV10: Bush 1A 28
Lowden Cft. B26: Yard 1C 136
Lowe Av. WS10: Darl 4B 46
Lowe Dr. B73: New O 2D 68
DY6: K'wfrd 5C 92
Lwr. Beeches Rd. B31: Longb 5A 144
LOWER BRADLEY 2A 62
Lwr. Chapel St. B69: Tiv 5C 78
Lwr. Church La. DY4: Tip 2B 78
Lwr. City Rd. B69: Tiv 6C 78
Lowercroft Way B74: Four O 4E 37
Lwr. Dartmouth St. B9: Birm 1B 118
Lwr. Derry St. DY5: Brie H 1H 109
Lwr. Essex St. B5: Birm 2G 117
Lwr. Forster St. WS1: Wals 1D 48
LOWER GORNAL 4H 75
Lower Grn. DY4: Tip 2G 77
WS10: Darl 3D 46
WV6: Tett 4C 26
Lwr. Ground Cl. *B6: Aston 6H 83*
(off Emscote Rd.)
Lwr. Hall La. WS1: Wals 2C 48
Lwr. Hall St. *WV13: W'hall 2B 46*
(off Walsall St.)
Lwr. High St. B64: Crad H 3E 111
DY8: Stourb 5D 108
WS10: W'bry 3F 63
Lwr. Higley Cl. B32: Quin 1B 130
Lwr. Lichfield St. WV13: W'hall 1A 46
Lwr. Loveday St. B19: Birm 5F 101 (1D 4)
Lwr. Mall & Up. Mall
B5: Birm 1G 117 (5F 5)
Lower Moor B30: B'vlle 5A 132
Lower Nth. St. WS4: Wals 6D 32
Lower Pde., The B72: S Cold 6A 54
LOWER PENN 6G 41
Lwr. Prestwood Rd.
WV11: Wed 2E 29
Lwr. Queen St. B72: S Cold 1A 70
Lwr. Reddicroft B73: S Cold 6A 54
Lwr. Rushall St. WS1: Wals 1D 48
Lwr. Severn St. B1: Birm 1F 117 (5D 4)
Lowerstack Cft. B37: F'bri 6B 106
LOWER STONNALL 3H 23
Lower St. WV6: Tett 4C 26
Lwr. Temple St. B2: Birm 1F 117 (4D 4)
Lwr. Tower St. B19: Birm 4G 101
Lwr. Trinity St. B9: Birm 2A 118
B70: W Brom 6B 80
(off Glover St.)
Lwr. Valley Rd. DY5: Brie H 1E 109
Lwr. Vauxhall WV1: Wolv 1E 43
Lwr. Villiers St. WV2: Wolv 4G 43
Lwr. White Rd. B32: Quin 6B 114
Lowesmoor Rd. B26: Sheld 4G 121
Lowe St. WV6: Wolv 5E 27
Loweswater Dr. DY3: Lwr G 4H 75
Loweswater Ho. B38: K Nor 6C 146
Lowfield Cl. B62: Quin 2G 129
LOW HILL 2A 28
Low Hill Cres. WV10: Bush 1A 28
Lowhill La. B45: Redn 3A 158
Lowland Cl. B64: Old H 2H 111
Lowlands Av. B74: S'tly 3F 51
WV6: Tett 3C 26
Lowlands Ct. WV6: Tett 3C 26
Lowndes Rd. DY8: Woll 5C 108
Lowry Cl. B67: Smeth 3D 98
WV6: Pert 5F 25
WV13: W'hall 1G 45
Low St. WS6: C Hay 2D 6
Low Thatch B38: K Nor 2A 160
Lowther Ct. DY5: Brie H 1H 109
Low Town B69: O'bry 2G 97
Low Wood Rd. B23: Erd 2D 84
LOXDALE 1H 61
Loxdale Ind. Est. WV14: Bils 1G 61
Loxdale Sidings WV14: Bils 1H 61
Loxdale St. WS10: W'bry 3F 63
WV14: Bils 1H 61
Loxley Av. B14: Yard W 4C 148
B90: Shir 6F 149
Loxley Cl. B31: N'fld 5C 130
Loxley Rd. B67: Smeth 2D 114
B75: R'ley 5B 38
Loxley Sq. B92: Olton 5B 136
Loxton Cl. B74: Lit A 4D 36
Loxton Ct. B7: Birm 4B 102
Loynells Rd. B45: Redn 2H 157
Loyns Cl. B37: F'bri 6B 106
LOZELLS 2D 100
Lozells Rd. B19: Loz 2D 100
Lozells St. B19: Loz 2E 101
Lozells Wood Cl. B19: Loz 2D 100
Luanne Cl. B64: Old H 2A 112
Lucas Cir. B19: Birm 4E 101
Lucas Way B90: Shir 2A 164
Luce Cl. B35: Cas V 3F 87
Lucerne Ct. B23: Erd 1D 84
Luce Rd. WV10: Bush 3A 28
Lucknow Rd. WV12: W'hall 5B 30
Lucton Ho. B30: B'vlle 2A 146
Luddington Rd. B92: Sol 5A 138
Ludford Cl. B75: S Cold 4C 54
Ludford Rd. B32: Bart G 4G 129
Ludgate Cl. B46: Wat O 4C 88
B69: Tiv 1B 96
Ludgate Ct. WS5: Wals 4H 49
Ludgate Hill B3: Birm 6F 101 (2C 4)
Ludgate Ho. B13: Mose 1H 133
Ludgate Loft Apartments B3: Birm 2C 4
Ludgate St. DY1: Dud 6D 76
Ludlow Cl. B37: Chel W 1E 123
WV12: W'hall 3B 30
Ludlow Ct. B11: S'brk 5B 118
Ludlow Ho. B13: Mose 1A 148
WS3: Blox 3A 32
(off Providence La.)
Ludlow La. WS2: Wals 5G 31
Ludlow Rd. B8: Salt 6F 103
Ludlow Way DY1: Dud 5A 76
Ludmer Way B20: Hand 5E 83
Ludstone Av. WV4: Penn 6B 42
Ludstone Rd. B29: W Cas 4D 130
Ludworth Av. B37: Mars G 2D 122
Lugtrout La. B91: Cath B, Sol 1A 152
Lukes, The DY2: Neth 2E 111
Lulworth Cl. B63: Crad 5E 111
Lulworth Rd. B28: Hall G 5G 135
Lulworth Wlk. WV4: Penn 5A 42
Lumley Gro. B37: Chel W 1F 123
Lumley Rd. WS1: Wals 2E 49
Lundy Vw. B36: Cas B 4D 106
LUNT, THE 4A 46
Lunt Gro. B32: Quin 6B 114
Lunt Pl. WV14: Bils 5A 46
Lunt Rd. WV14: Bils 5H 45
Lupin Gro. B9: Bord G 6F 103
WS5: Wals 1F 65
Lupin Rd. DY2: Dud 6H 77
Lusbridge Cl. B63: Crad 1D 126
LUTLEY 2E 127
Lutley Av. B63: Hale 1F 127
Lutley Cl. WV3: Wolv 4C 42
Lutley Dr. DY9: Pedm 2G 125
Lutley Gro. B32: Bart G 4H 129
Lutley La. B63: Hale, Lutley 2D 126
(not continuous)
Lutley Mill Rd. B63: Hale 1G 127
Luton Rd. B29: S Oak 2B 132
Luttrell Rd. B74: Four O 3F 53
Lyall Gdns. B45: Fran 6E 143
Lyall Gro. B27: A Grn 3G 135
Lychgate Av. DY9: Pedm 4G 125
Lydate Rd. B62: Quin 1F 129
Lydbrook Covert B38: K Nor 1A 160
Lydbury Gro. B33: Kitts G 5E 105
Lyd Cl. WV11: Wed 4D 28
Lydd Cft. B35: Cas V 3F 87
Lyddington Dr. B62: Hale 4B 112
Lyde Grn. B63: Crad 4D 110
Lydford Gro. B24: Erd 5G 85
Lydford Rd. WS3: Blox 5H 19
Lydgate Rd. DY6: K'wfrd 3D 92
Lydget Gro. B23: Erd 6D 68
Lydham Cl. B44: K'sdng 1A 84
WV14: Bils 1D 60
Lydia Cft. B74: Four O 3E 37
Lydiat Av. B31: Longb 6B 144
LYDIATE ASH 6C 156
Lydiate Ash Rd. B61: L Ash 6B 156
(not continuous)
Lydiates Cl. DY3: Sed 6F 59
Lydney Cl. WV12: W'hall 6D 30
Lydney Gro. B31: N'fld 4D 144
LYE 6A 110
Lye Av. B32: Bart G 3G 129
Lye Bus. Cen. DY9: Lye 5B 110
Lye By-Pass DY9: Lye 5A 110
Lye Cl. La. B32: Bart G 3F 129
B62: Hale 3F 129
Lyecroft Av. B37: Chel W 1F 123
Lye Cross Rd. B69: Tiv 2B 96
Lye Station (Rail) 5A 110
Lye Valley Ind. Est. DY9: Lye 5B 110
Lygon Ct. B62: Hale 5B 112
Lygon Gro. B32: Quin 1C 130
Lymedene Rd. B42: P Barr 2D 82
Lyme Grn. Rd. B33: Stech 5D 104
Lymer Rd. WV10: Oxl 6G 15
Lymington Rd. WV13: W'hall 1D 46
Lymsey Cft. DY8: Word 6A 92
Lynbrook Cl. B47: H'wd 2A 162
DY2: Neth 3F 95
Lyncourt Gro. B32: Quin 5H 113
Lyncroft Rd. B11: Tys 3F 135
Lyndale Dr. WV11: Wed 3G 29
Lyndale Rd. DY2: Dud 3G 95
DY3: Sed 3F 59
Lyndhurst Dr. DY8: Word 2D 108
Lyndhurst Rd. B24: Erd 5F 85
B71: W Brom 6C 64
WV3: Wolv 4E 43
LYNDON 2B 80
Lyndon B71: W Brom 2B 80
Lyndon Cl. B20: Hand 5E 83
B36: Cas B 1G 105
B63: Hale 1G 127
DY3: Sed 4A 60
Lyndon Ct. B26: Sheld 1G 137
Lyndon Cft. B37: Mars G 4D 122
B92: Olton 3E 137
LYNDON GREEN 4E 121
Lyndon Gro. B71: W Brom 3B 80
DY6: W Hth 1H 91
Lyndon Ho. B31: N'fld 4F 145
Lyndon Rd. B33: Stech 6C 104
B45: Rubery 2E 157
B73: S Cold 6H 53
B92: Olton 3D 136
Lyndworth Rd. B30: Stir 6E 133
Lyneham Gdns. B76: Walm 1E 87
Lyneham Way B35: Cas V 4D 86
Lynfield Cl. B38: K Nor 2B 160
Lyng La. B70: W Brom 4A 80
(not continuous)
Lynmouth Cl. WS9: A'rdge 4C 34
LYNN 2H 23
Lynn Gro. B29: S Oak 2G 131
Lynn La. WS14: Lynn, Shens 2H 23
Lynton Av. B66: Smeth 3E 99
B71: W Brom 6A 64
WV6: Tett 2C 26
Lynton Ho. B23: Erd 1B 84
Lynton Rd. B6: Aston 2A 102
Lynval Rd. DY5: Quar B 4B 110
Lynwood Av. DY6: W Hth 2H 91
Lynwood Cl. WV12: W'hall 1E 31
Lynwood Wlk. B17: Harb 1H 131
Lynwood Way B45: Lick 6G 157
Lyon Ct. *B72: S Cold 6A 54*
(off Midland Dr.)
Lyons Gro. B11: S'hll 2C 134
Lysander Rd. B45: Fran 5G 143
Lysander Way B35: Cas V 5F 87
Lysways St. WS1: Wals 3D 48
Lytham Cl. B76: Walm 1F 87
DY8: Stourb 3E 125
Lytham Cft. B15: Birm 3F 117
Lytham Gro. WS3: Blox 3G 19
Lytham Rd. WV6: Pert 5D 24
Lythwood Dr. DY5: Brie H 3G 109
Lyttelton Rd. B16: Edg 2H 115
B33: Stech 1B 120
DY8: Stourb 6B 108
Lyttleton Av. B62: B'hth 4E 113
Lyttleton Cl. DY2: Neth 5E 95
Lyttleton Ho. B63: Hale 3A 128
Lyttleton St. B70: W Brom 5A 80
Lytton Av. WV4: Penn 1B 58
Lytton Gro. B27: A Grn 4H 135
Lytton La. B32: Bart G 2D 130

M

Maas Rd. B31: N'fld 4E 145
Macarthur Rd. B64: Crad H 3E 111
Macaulay Ho. B70: W Brom 6B 80
McBean Rd. WV6: Wolv 5D 26
Macdonald Cl. B69: Tiv 5D 78
McDougall Rd. WS10: W'bry 2A 64
Mace St. B64: Old H 2G 111
McGregor Cl. B6: Aston 6H 83
Machin Rd. B23: Erd 3F 85
Mackadown La. B33: Kitts G, Sheld 1H 121
Mackay Rd. WS3: Blox 5B 20
McKean Rd. B69: O'bry 6G 79
McKen Ct. B70: W Brom 6A 80
Mackenzie Ct. B31: N'fld 5C 130
Mackenzie Rd. B11: S'hll 3C 134
Mackmillan Rd. B65: Row R 1B 112
McLean Rd. WV10: Oxl 5G 15
Macmillan Cl. B69: Tiv 5C 78
Macrome Rd. WV6: Tett 1C 26
Madams Hill Rd. B90: Shir 2B 164
Maddocks Hill B72: W Grn 3A 70
Madehurst Rd. B23: Erd 1E 85
Madeira Av. WV8: Cod 5G 13
Madeleine Ho. B33: Stech 6C 104
Madeley Rd. B11: S'brk 6C 118
DY6: K'wfrd 5D 92
Madin Rd. DY4: Tip 3G 77
Madison Av. B36: Hodg H 3B 104
DY5: Brie H 6B 94
WS2: Wals 1H 47
Madley Cl. B45: Rubery 1E 157
Madresfield Dr. B63: Hale 3B 128
Maer Cl. B65: Row R 5C 96
Mafeking Rd. B66: Smeth 2E 99
Magdala St. B18: Win G 4A 100
Magdalen Cl. DY1: Dud 5C 76
Magdalen Ct. *B16: Edg 2A 116*
(off Vernon Ct.)
Magdalene Rd. WS1: Wals 4E 49
Magna Cl. WS6: C Hay 2E 7
Magness Cres. WV12: W'hall 4C 30
Magnet Wlk. B23: Erd 4C 84
Magnolia Cl. B29: W Cas 6E 131
Magnolia Dr. WS5: Wals 1D 64
Magnolia Gro. WV8: Bilb 4G 13
WV12: W'hall 5B 30
Magnolia Way DY8: Word 3D 108
Magnum Cl. B74: S'tly 4H 51
Magpie Cl. DY2: Neth 6G 95
Magpie La. CV7: Bal C 2E 169
Magreal Ind. Est. B16: Birm 6B 100
Maidendale Rd. DY6: K'wfrd 2H 91
Maidensbridge Dr. DY6: W Hth 1A 92
Maidensbridge Gdns.
DY6: W Hth 6H 73
Maidensbridge Rd. DY6: W Hth 6H 73
Maidstone Dr. DY8: Word 6C 92
Maidstone Rd. B20: Hand 6G 83
Maidwell Dr. B90: Shir 1C 164
Mailbox, The B1: Birm 1F 117 (6C 4)
Mailbox Sq. B1: Birm 1F 117 (5C 4)
Main Rd. B26: Birm A 2B 138
CV7: Mer 4H 141
Mainstream 47 Ind. Pk.
B7: Birm 4C 102
Mainstream Way B7: Birm 5C 102
Main St. B11: S'brk 4A 118
WS9: Ston 4F 23
Main Ter. B11: S'brk 4A 118
Mainwaring Dr. B75: R'ley 1C 54
Maitland Ho. B36: Cas B 6H 87
Maitland Rd. B8: Salt 5F 103
DY1: Dud 6A 76
Majestic Way B65: Row R 5C 96
Major Ct. B13: Mose 3B 134
MAJOR'S GREEN 1D 162
Majuba Rd. B16: Edg 5G 99
Malcolm Av. B24: Erd 2A 86
Malcolm Ct. B26: Sheld 6E 121
WV1: Wolv 6E 27
Malcolm Gro. B45: Redn 2G 157
Malcolm Rd. B90: Shir 6H 149
Malcolmson Cl. B15: Edg 3B 116
Malfield Dr. B27: A Grn 2C 136
Mali Jenkins Ho. WS1: Wals 2F 49
Malins Rd. B17: Harb 6H 115
WV4: E'shll 6A 44
Malkit Cl. WS2: Wals 5F 31
Mallaby Cl. B90: Shir 1G 163
Mallard Cl. B27: A Grn 2A 136
DY5: Brie H 4G 109
WS3: Pels 1E 21
Mallard Dr. B23: Erd 4B 84
B69: O'bry 5F 97
Mallards Reach B92: Olton 5C 136
Mallender Dr. B93: Know 3B 166
Mallen Dr. B69: Tiv 6B 78
Mallin Gdns. DY1: Dud 1A 94
Mallin St. B66: Smeth 2B 98
Mallory Cres. WS3: Blox 5B 20
Mallory Ri. B13: Mose 4C 134
Mallory Rd. WV6: Pert 6E 25
Mallow Cl. WS5: Wals 2E 65
Mallow Ct. WV6: Wolv 4F 27
Mallow Ri. B23: Erd 6B 68
Mallows Cl. WS10: Darl 5D 46
Malmesbury Pk. B15: Edg 4A 116
Malmesbury Rd. B10: Small H 5E 119
Malpas Dr. B32: Bart G 5A 130
Malpass Gdns. WV8: Cod 3E 13
Malpass Rd. DY5: Quar B 4B 110
Malpas Wlk. WV10: Wolv 4C 28
Malt Cl. B17: Harb 5H 115
Malthouse B66: Smeth 2C 98
Malthouse Cft. B6: Aston 1G 101
Malthouse Dr. DY1: Dud 5C 76
Malthouse Gdns. B19: Loz 2F 101
Malthouse Gro. B25: Yard 2C 120
Malt Ho. La. WV13: W'hall 1A 46
Malthouse La. B8: Salt 3E 103
B42: Gt Barr 5F 67
B61: C'wich 4B 156
(not continuous)
WV6: Tett 3C 26
Malthouse Rd. DY4: Tip 2G 77
Malt Ho. Row B37: Mars G 3C 122
Maltings, The B1: Birm 2E 117 (6B 4)
WS9: A'rdge 3E 35
WV1: Wolv 6H 27 (1C 170)
WV5: Wom 1G 73
Malt Mill La. B62: B'hth 3C 112
Malton Av. B69: O'bry 3D 96
Malton Gro. B13: Mose 6B 134
Malvern Av. DY9: Lye 6G 109

Malvern Cl.—Mayfield Cres.

Malvern Cl. B15: Edg 3G 115
B71: W Brom 2B 80
WV12: W'hall 5B 30
Malvern Ct. B27: A Grn 1A 136
WV10: Bush 1H 27
Malvern Cres. DY2: Dud 3B 94
Malvern Dr. B76: Walm 5E 71
WS9: A'rdge 6E 23
WV1: Wolv 2D 44
Malvern Hill Rd. B7: Nech 2C 102
Malvern Ho. *B63: Hale 2A 128*
(off Pickersleigh Cl.)
Malvern Pk. Rd. B91: Sol 4H 151
Malvern Rd. B21: Hand 6G 81
B27: A Grn 1A 136
B45: Lick 6G 157
B68: O'bry 3H 113
CV7: Bal C 6H 169
Malvern St. B12: Bal H 6A 118
Malvern Vw. Rd. DY3: Lwr G 3H 75
Mamble Rd. DY8: Stourb 6C 108
Mammouth Dr. WV10: Wolv 4H 27
Manby Cl. WV6: Wolv 5F 27
Manby Rd. B35: Cas V 3E 87
Manby St. DY4: Tip 5H 61
Mancetter Rd. B90: Shir 4A 150
Manchester St. B6: Birm 4G 101
B69: O'bry 2H 97
Mancroft Cl. DY6: K'wfrd 2H 91
Mancroft Gdns. WV6: Tett 4A 26
Mancroft Rd. WV6: Tett 4A 26
Mandale Rd. WV10: Wolv 3B 28
Mander Cen. WV1: Wolv 1G 43 (3B 170)
Manderley Cl. DY3: Sed 3G 59
Manders Ind. Est. WV1: Wolv 6B 28
Mander Sq. WV1: Wolv 2G 43 (4B 170)
Manderston Cl. DY1: Dud 4A 76
Mander St. WV3: Wolv 3F 43 (6A 170)
Manderville Gdns. DY6: K'wfrd 3A 92
Manderville Ho. B31: Longb 1D 158
Mandeville Gdns. WS1: Wals 3D 48
MANEY 1A 70
Maney Cnr. B72: S Cold 1H 69
Maney Hill Rd. B72: W Grn 2H 69
Manfield Rd. WV13: W'hall 6E 29
Manifoldia Grange B70: W Brom 5H 79
Manilla Rd. B29: S Oak 4D 132
Manitoba Cft. B38: K Nor 1B 160
Manley Cl. B70: W Brom 4H 79
Manlove St. WV3: Wolv 3E 43
Manningford Ct. B14: K Hth 5H 147
Manningford Rd. B14: K Hth 5G 147
Mnr. Abbey Rd. B62: Hale 2E 129
Manor Av. WS6: Gt Wyr 1G 7
Manor Cl. WV4: Penn 1D 58
WV8: Bilb 3H 13
WV13: W'hall 6A 30
Manor Ct. B27: A Grn 3B 136
B30: K Nor 5C 146
B62: Quin 4G 113
(off Binswood Rd.)
B93: Dorr 6G 167
DY2: Neth 5E 95
WS2: Wals 1A 48
Manor Dr. B73: S Cold 1H 69
DY3: Gorn 4F 75
DY3: Swind 5E 73
Manor Farm Dr. WV12: W'hall 4D 30
Manor Farm Rd. B11: Tys 1E 135
Manor Fold WV8: Oaken 5D 12
Manorford Av. B71: W Brom 4E 65
Manor Gdns. B33: Stech 1B 120
WS10: W'bry 1F 63
WV5: Wom 6H 57
Manor Hill B73: S Cold 1H 69
Manor Ho. B31: N'fld 6F 131
Manor Ho., The *B44: Gt Barr 3G 67*
(off Amblecote Av.)
Manor Ho. Cl. B29: W Cas 4D 130
Manor Ho. Dr. B31: N'fld 6F 131
Manor Ho. La. B26: Yard 5D 120
B46: Wat O 4D 88
Manor Ho. Pk. WV8: Bilb 3H 13
Manor Ho. Rd. WS10: W'bry 2F 63
Manorial Rd. B75: R'ley 6C 38
Manor Ind. Est. WS2: Wals 2A 48
Manor La. B61: C'wich, L Ash 4C 156
B62: Hale 2E 129
DY8: Stourb 2B 124
Manor Pk. DY6: K'wfrd 3B 92
Manor Pk. Cl. B13: Mose 3A 134
Manor Pk. Gro. B31: Longb 6A 144
Manor Pk. Rd. B36: Cas B 2H 105
Manor Rd. B6: Aston 6H 83
B16: Edg 2H 115
B33: Stech 6C 104
B47: Wyt 6A 162
B67: Smeth 4B 98
B73: S Cold 6H 53
B74: S'tly 3A 52
B91: Sol 2F 151
B93: Dorr 6A 166
DY4: Tip 3H 77
DY8: Word 1C 108
WS2: Wals 1A 48
WS10: W'bry 3B 64
WV4: E'shll 6C 44
WV4: Penn 1D 58
WV10: Oxl 2G 27
Manor Rd. Nth. B16: Edg 2H 115
Manor Rd. Pct. WS2: Wals 1A 48
Manor Sq. B91: Sol 4G 151
Manor St. WV6: Tett 4A 26
Manor Wlk. B91: Sol 4G 151
Manor Way B62: Hale 4G 127
B73: S Cold 1H 69
Mansard Cl. WV3: Wolv 3D 42
WV11: Bush 1D 28
Mansard Ct. B46: Col 2H 107
Mansell Cl. B63: Crad 4D 110
Mansell Rd. DY4: Tip 5A 62
Mansel Rd. B10: Small H 4E 119
Mansfield Ho. B37: Chel W 6E 107
Mansfield Rd. B6: Aston 1F 101
B25: Yard 6A 120
Mansion Cl. DY1: Dud 4C 76
Mansion Ct. *WV5: Wom 2D 72*
(off Heath Ho. Dr.)
Mansion Cres. B67: Smeth 5C 98
Mansion Dr. DY4: Tip 2C 78
WS7: Hamm 1F 11
Manson Dr. B64: Old H 2A 112
Manston Dr. WV6: Pert 4E 25
Manston Rd. B26: Sheld 4F 121
Manton Cft. B93: Dorr 6A 166
Manton Ho. B19: Loz 2G 101
Manway Cl. B20: Hand 2B 82
Manwoods Cl. B20: Hand 5D 82
Maple Av. WS10: W'bry 1A 64
Maple Bank B15: Edg 4C 116
Maplebeck Ct. B91: Sol 2G 151
Maple Bus. Pk. B7: Nech 3B 102
Maple Cen., The WS10: Mox 2B 62
Maple Cl. B21: Hand 6A 82
DY8: Stourb 3B 124
WV14: Cose 6C 60
Maple Ct. *B24: Erd 4F 85*
(off Coppice Cl.)
B66: Smeth 1B 98
Maple Cft. B13: Mose 1H 147
Mapledene B13: Mose 3B 134
Mapledene Rd. B26: Sheld 5H 121
Maple Dr. B44: K'sdng 5B 68
DY3: Gorn 5F 75
WS4: S'fld 1F 33
WS5: Wals 1F 65
WS10: Mox 1B 62
Maple Grn. DY1: Dud 2C 76
Maple Gro. B19: Loz 1E 101
B37: K'hrst 3B 106
DY6: K'wfrd 3C 92
WV3: Wolv 1A 42
WV14: Bils 1H 61
Maple Leaf Dr. B37: Mars G 3D 122
Maple Leaf Ind. Est. WS2: Wals 6G 31
Maple Leaf Rd. WS10: W'bry 4C 62
Maple Ri. B68: O'bry 1A 114
Maple Rd. B30: B'vlle 5A 132
B45: Rubery 3F 157
B62: B'hth 3D 112
B72: S Cold 2A 70
DY1: Dud 4E 77
WS3: Pels 5D 20
WV3: Wolv 4C 42
Maple Row DY5: Brie H 1H 109
Maple St. WS3: Blox 5B 20
Mapleton Gro. B28: Hall G 6H 135
Mapleton Rd. B28: Hall G 6H 135
Maple Tree La. B63: Crad 5E 111
Maple Wlk. *B37: Chel W 1D 122*
(off Chelmsley Wood Shop. Cen.)
Maple Way B31: Longb 6D 144
Maplewood B76: Walm 5E 71
Mapperley Gdns. B13: Mose 2E 133
Mappleborough Rd. B90: Shir 6E 149
Marans Cft. B38: K Nor 2H 159
Marbury Cl. B38: K Nor 5H 145
Marbury M. DY5: Brie H 2H 109
Marchant Rd. WV3: Wolv 1D 42
WV14: Bils 4E 45
March Cl. WS6: C Hay 4D 6
MARCH END 4G 29
March End Rd. WV11: Wed 4F 29
(not continuous)
Marchmont Rd. B9: Bord G 1G 119
Marchmount Rd. B72: W Grn 5A 70
March Way WS9: A'rdge 6E 23
Marcliff Cres. B90: Shir 5C 148
Marcos Dr. B36: Cas B 6B 88
Marcot Rd. B92: Olton 6D 120
Marden Cl. WV13: W'hall 2H 45
Marden Gro. B31: Longb 2E 159
Marden Wlk. B23: Erd 4B 84
Mardon Rd. B26: Sheld 6F 121
Maree Gro. WV12: W'hall 6B 18
Marfield Cl. B76: Walm 1E 87
Margam Cres. WS3: Blox 5F 19
Margam Ter. WS3: Blox 5F 19
Margam Way WS3: Blox 5F 19
Margaret Av. B63: Hale 1H 127
Margaret Cl. DY5: Quar B 3A 110
Margaret Dr. DY8: Stourb 1F 125
Margaret Gdns. B67: Smeth 4C 98
Margaret Gro. B17: Harb 4G 115
Margaret Ho. B17: Harb 6F 115
Margaret Rd. B17: Harb 6G 115
B73: New O 4D 68
WS2: Wals 6E 31
WS10: Darl 1C 62
Margarets Ho. B76: Walm 2D 70
Margaret St. B3: Birm 6F 101 (3C 4)
B70: W Brom 5H 79
Margaret Va. DY4: Tip 4C 62
Margaret Vine Ct. B62: B'hth 2F 113
Marholm Cl. WV9: Pend 5D 14
Marian Cft. B26: Sheld 6H 121
Maria St. B70: W Brom 1C 98
Marie Dr. B27: A Grn 5H 135
Marigold Cres. DY1: Dud 3C 76
Marine Cres. DY8: Word 2C 108
Marine Dr. B44: K'sdng 1G 83
Marine Gdns. DY8: Word 2C 108
Mariner Av. B16: Edg 2A 116
Marion Cl. DY5: Quar B 1B 110
Marion Rd. B67: Smeth 3B 98
Marion Way B28: Hall G 6E 135
Marita Cl. DY2: Neth 6G 95
Marjoram Cl. B38: K Nor 1B 160
Marjorie Av. B30: K Nor 4D 146
Mark Av. WS10: W'bry 2E 63
Markby Rd. B18: Win G 3A 100
Mark Ct. WS1: Wals 6E 33
Market La. WV4: Lwr P 5F 41
Market Pl. B65: B'hth 2C 112
B69: O'bry 1G 97
(off Market St.)
DY2: Dud 6E 77
DY2: Neth 4E 95
DY4: Tip 2D 78
WS3: Blox 6H 19
WS10: W'bry 3F 63
WV13: W'hall 2A 46
Market Sq. B64: Crad H 3E 111
Market St. B69: O'bry 1G 97
DY6: K'wfrd 3B 92
DY8: Stourb 6E 109
WV1: Wolv 1H 43 (3C 170)
Market Way DY9: Hag 6G 125
WV14: Bils 6F 45
Markfield Rd. B26: Sheld 3F 121
Markford Wlk. B19: Hock 3F 101
Markham Cres. B92: Sol 4B 138
Markham Cft. WV9: Pend 5E 15
Markham Dr. DY6: K'wfrd 5C 92
Markham Rd. B73: New O 2C 68
Mark Ho. B13: Mose 3A 134
Marklew Cl. WS8: Bwnhls 2C 22
Marklin Av. WV10: Oxl 6H 15
Mark Rd. WS10: W'bry 2E 63
Marksbury Cl. WV6: Wolv 4E 27
Marlbank Rd. DY8: Word 2E 109
Marlborough Cl. B74: Four O 3E 37
Marlborough Ct. *B74: Four O 1F 53*
(off Vesey Cl.)
Marlborough Dr. DY8: Stourb 2E 125
Marlborough Gdns. DY8: Word 1A 108
WV6: Wolv 5C 26
Marlborough Gro. B25: Yard 2B 120
Marlborough Rd. B10: Small H 2E 119
B36: Cas B 1G 105
B66: Smeth 6E 99
DY3: Sed 6B 60
Marlborough St. WS3: Blox 6H 19
Marlbrook Cl. B92: Sol 1G 137
Marlbrook Dr. WV4: Penn 5F 43
Marlbrook La. B60: Marl 6D 156
Marlburn Way WV5: Wom 1E 73
Marlcliff Gro. B13: Mose 1A 148
Marldon Rd. B14: K Hth 1G 147
Marlene Cft. B37: Chel W 2E 123
Marley Rd. DY6: K'wfrd 5E 93
Marling Cft. B92: Sol 6A 138
Marlow Cl. DY2: Neth 6G 95
Marlowe Dr. WV12: W'hall 2A 30
Marlow Rd. B23: Erd 2D 84
Marlow St. B65: B'hth 2B 112
WS2: Wals 5C 32
Marlpit La. B75: R'ley 1B 54
Marlpit Ri. B75: R'ley 6C 38
Marlpool Dr. WS3: Pels 6E 21
Marl Rd. DY2: Neth 5D 94
Marl Top B38: K Nor 5B 146
Marmion Dr. B43: Gt Barr 3B 66
Marmion Gro. DY1: Dud 1C 94
Marmion Way B70: W Brom 1F 79
Marnel Dr. WV3: Wolv 3B 42
Marquis Dr. B62: Hale 4A 112
Marriott Rd. B66: Smeth 2B 98
DY2: Neth 5E 95
Marroway St. B16: Birm 6B 100
Marrowfat La. B21: Hand 2B 100
Mars Cl. WV14: Cose 4C 60
Marsden Cl. B92: Olton 4C 136
Marsh, The WS10: W'bry 2E 63
Marshall Cl. WS9: A'rdge 5D 34
Marshall Gro. B44: Gt Barr 6H 67
Marshall Ho. *WS2: Wals 3A 48*
(off St Quentin St.)
Marshall Lake Rd. B90: Shir 1B 164
Marshall Rd. B68: O'bry 2A 114
WV13: W'hall 2E 45
Marshalls Ind. Est. WV2: Wolv 4G 43
Marshall St. B1: Birm 2F 117 (6C 4)
B67: Smeth 2B 98
Marsham Ct. Rd. B91: Sol 6D 136
Marsham Rd. B14: K Hth 4H 147
Marshbrook Cl. B24: Erd 3C 86
Marsh Cl. B23: Erd 2F 85
Marsh Cres. DY8: Word 6A 92
Marsh End B38: K Nor 1C 160
Marshfield B90: Dic H 4H 163
Marshfield Gdns. B24: Erd 5E 85
Marsh Gro. DY3: Swind 5E 73
Marsh Hill B23: Erd 3B 84
Marsh Ho. Farm La. B92: H Ard 4D 154
Marshland Way WS2: Wals 2E 47
Marsh La. B23: Erd 2D 84
B46: Wat O 4D 88
B71: W Brom 6A 64
B76: Curd 2E 89
B91: Sol 3A 152
B92: H Ard 1A 154
(not continuous)
WS2: Wals 1B 48
WV10: F'hses 4F 15
Marsh La. Pde. WV10: Oxl 5G 15
Marshmont Way B23: Erd 5D 68
Marsh St. WS2: Wals 1B 48
Marshwood Cft. B62: Quin 2G 129
Marsland Cl. B17: Edg 2G 115
Marsland Rd. B92: Olton 6C 136
Marston Av. WS10: Darl 5C 46
Marston Cl. DY8: Stourb 1B 124
Marston Cft. B37: Mars G 4B 122
Marston Dr. B37: K'hrst 4C 106
MARSTON GREEN 3B 122
Marston Green Station (Rail) 4B 122
Marston Gro. B43: Gt Barr 5G 65
Marston Rd. B29: W Cas 5D 130
B73: Bold 6G 69
DY1: Dud 1H 93
WV2: Wolv 4F 43
Marston Rd. Ind. Est.
WV2: Wolv 4G 43
Marston St. WV13: W'hall 1C 46
Martham Dr. WV6: Tett 1H 41
Martin Cl. B25: Yard 5B 120
WV14: Cose 6F 61
Martindale Wlk. DY5: Brie H 5F 109
Martin Dr. WV12: W'hall 4C 30
Martineau Pl. B2: Birm 1G 117 (4E 5)
Martineau Twr. *B19: Birm 4F 101*
(off Uxbridge St.)
Martineau Way *B2: Birm 4E 5*
(off Union St.)
Martingale Cl. WS5: Wals 1D 64
Martin Hill St. DY2: Dud 1E 95
Martin Ri. B37: Mars G 3B 122
Martin Rd. DY4: Tip 2A 78
WS5: Wals 3G 49
WV14: Bils 2H 61
Martin St. WV4: E'shll 6B 44
Martlesham Sq. B35: Cas V 3E 87
Martley Cft. B32: Quin 1C 130
B91: Sol 1F 165
Martley Dr. DY9: Lye 1G 125
Martley Rd. B69: O'bry 3D 96
WS4: S'fld 6G 21
Marwood Cft. B74: S'tly 1A 52
Mary Ann St. B3: Birm 5F 101 (1C 4)
WV1: Wolv 2A 44
Maryland Av. B34: Hodg H 4C 104
Maryland Dr. B31: N'fld 2F 145
Maryland Rd. DY5: Quar B 4B 110
Marylebone Cl. DY8: Amb 4E 109
Mary Macarthur Dr.
B64: Crad H 2E 111
Mary Rd. B21: Hand 2A 100
B33: Stech 6B 104
B69: Tiv 1C 96
B70: W Brom 6B 80
Mary St. B3: Birm 5E 101 (1B 4)
B12: Bal H 6G 117
WS2: Wals 6B 32
Maryvale Ct. WS1: Wals 2C 48
Mary Va. Rd. B30: B'vlle 1A 146
Marywell Cl. B32: Bart G 6H 129
Masefield Av. DY1: Dud 6E 61
Masefield Cl. WV14: Bils 3H 61
Masefield M. WV10: Bush 6C 16
Masefield Ri. B62: Hale 2D 128
Masefield Rd. DY3: Lwr G 3E 75
WS3: Blox 2C 32
WV10: Bush 6C 16
Masefield Sq. B31: N'fld 3G 145
Masham Cl. B33: Stech 1C 120
Mashie Gdns. B38: K Nor 6H 145
Maslen Pl. B63: Hale 2B 128
Maslin Dr. WV14: Cose 4C 60
Mason Ct. B27: A Grn 3C 136
Mason Cres. WV4: Penn 6C 42
Mason Hall B15: Edg 5C 116
Mason Ho. B90: Shir 6E 149
Masonleys Rd. B31: N'fld 4B 144
Mason Rd. B24: Erd 3G 85
WS2: Wals 4H 31
Mason's Cl. B63: Crad 5E 111
Masons Cotts. B24: Erd 2H 85
Mason St. B70: W Brom 3H 79
WV2: Wolv 4G 43
WV14: Cose 6D 60
Mason's Way B92: Olton 3C 136
Massbrook Gro.
WV10: Wolv 3B 28
Massbrook Rd. WV10: Wolv 3B 28
Masshouse La. B38: K Nor 6B 146
Masters La. B62: B'hth 2E 113
Matchlock Cl. B74: S'tly 4G 51
Matfen Av. B73: S Cold 3F 69
Math Mdw. B32: Harb 6D 114
Matlock Cl. DY2: Neth 6F 95
WS3: Blox 4A 20
Matlock Rd. B11: Tys 2F 135
WS3: Blox 4A 20
Matlock Vs. *B12: Bal H 6B 118*
(off Chesterton Rd.)
Matthews Cl. B65: B'hth 2B 112
Mattox Rd. WV11: Wed 3F 29
Matty Rd. B68: O'bry 5H 97
Maud Rd. B46: Wat O 4F 89
B70: W Brom 6A 80
Maughan St. DY1: Dud 6C 76
DY5: Quar B 3B 110
Maurice Gro. WV10: Wolv 3C 28
Maurice Rd. B14: K Hth 2G 147
B67: Smeth 1C 114
Mavis Gdns. B68: O'bry 3H 113
Mavis Rd. B31: N'fld 6C 144
Maw St. WS1: Wals 5D 48
Maxholm Rd. B74: S'tly 3G 51
Max Rd. B32: Quin 6B 114
Maxstoke Cl. B32: Bart G 6G 129
B73: New O 3E 69
CV7: Mer 4H 141
WS3: Blox 4G 19
Maxstoke Cft. B90: Shir 1A 164
Maxstoke La. CV7: Mer 3H 141
(not continuous)
Maxstoke Rd. B73: New O 3E 69
Maxstoke St. B9: Birm 1B 118
Maxted Rd. B23: Erd 5C 68
Maxwell Av. B20: Hand 6D 82
Maxwell Rd. WV2: Wolv 3H 43 (6D 170)
Mayall Dr. B75: R'ley 5A 38
May Av. B12: Bal H 6A 118
Maybank B9: Bord G 6F 103
Maybank Pl. B44: P Barr 1G 83
Maybank Rd. DY2: Neth 6E 95
Mayberry Cl. B14: K Hth 5B 148
Maybridge Dr. B91: Sol 1F 165
Maybrook Ho. B63: Hale 1A 128
Maybrook Ind. Est.
WS8: Bwnhls 2B 22
(not continuous)
Maybrook Rd. B76: Min 2E 87
WS8: Bwnhls 3B 22
Maybury Cl. WV8: Cod 3E 13
Maybush Gdns. WV10: Oxl 6G 15
Maydene Cft. B12: Bal H 5H 117
MAYERS GREEN 3C 80
Mayfair *B37: K'hrst 4B 106*
(off Haselour Rd.)
DY9: W'cte 3H 125
Mayfair Cl. B44: K'sdng 6B 68
DY1: Dud 5C 76
Mayfair Dr. DY6: K'wfrd 2A 92
Mayfair Gdns. DY4: Tip 3A 78
WV3: Wolv 1B 42
Mayfair Pde. B44: K'sdng 6B 68
May Farm Cl. B47: H'wd 3A 162
Mayfield Av. B29: S Oak 3D 132
Mayfield Cl. B91: Sol 6G 151
Mayfield Ct. B13: Mose 3A 134
Mayfield Cres. B65: Row R 6A 96

Mayfield Rd.—Milldale Cres.

Mayfield Rd. B11: Tys 1G 135
B13: Mose 3A 134
B19: Hand 1E 101
B27: A Grn 2G 135
B30: Stir 1C 146
B62: B'hth 2F 113
B63: Hale 3F 127
B73: W Grn 3G 69
B74: S'tly 3H 51
DY1: Dud 2D 76
WV1: Wolv 2D 44
Mayfields Dr. WS8: Bwnhls 3F 9
Mayflower Cl. B19: Loz 3F 101
Mayflower Dr. DY5: P'ntt 2E 93
Mayford Gro. B13: Mose 1B 148
Maygrove Rd. DY6: K'wfrd 2A 92
Mayhurst Cl. B47: H'wd 2C 162
DY4: Tip 5A 62
Mayhurst Rd. B47: H'wd 2B 162
Mayland Dr. B74: S'tly 6H 51
Mayland Rd. B16: Edg 1G 115
May La. B14: K Hth 2H 147
B47: H'wd 2A 162
Maynard Av. DY8: Stourb 2B 124
Mayou Ct. WS3: Pels 3E 21
Maypole Cl. B64: Crad H 3D 110
Maypole Ct. WV5: Wom 1G 73
Maypole Dr. DY8: Stourb 6C 108
Maypole Flds. B63: Crad 4C 110
Maypole Gro. B14: K Hth 5B 148
Maypole Hill B63: Crad 3C 110
Maypole La. B14: K Hth 5H 147
Maypole Rd. B68: O'bry 2H 113
Maypole St. WV5: Wom 6H 57
May St. WS3: Blox 3A 32
Mayswood Dr. WV6: Tett 2F 41
Mayswood Gro. B32: Quin 1B 130
Mayswood Rd. B92: Sol 3G 137
Maythorn Av. B76: Walm 1E 87
Maythorn Gdns. WV6: Tett 6A 26
WV8: Bilb 3G 13
Maythorn Gro. B91: Sol 1F 165
Maytree Cl. B37: F'bri 1C 122
May Tree Gro. B20: Hand 4B 82
May Trees B47: H'wd 3H 161
Maywell Dr. B92: Sol 5B 138
Maywood Cl. DY6: K'wfrd 3A 92
Meaburn Cl. B29: W Cas 6E 131
Mead, The DY3: Sed 5F 59
Mead Cl. WS9: A'rdge 3D 34
Mead Cres. B9: Bord G 6H 103
Meadfoot Av. B14: K Hth 4H 147
Meadfoot Dr. DY6: K'wfrd 2H 91
Meadlands, The WV5: Wom 1E 73
Meadow Av. B71: W Brom 4D 64
Meadowbank Grange
WS6: Gt Wyr 1E 7
Meadowbrook Gdns. WV8: Bilb 3H 13
Mdw. Brook Rd. B31: N'fld 2D 144
Meadowbrook Rd. B63: Hale 2F 127
Meadow Cl. B17: Harb 3F 115
B74: S'tly 1H 51
B76: Walm 4D 70
B90: Shir 1B 164
WS4: S'fld 1G 33
WV12: W'hall 1C 30
Meadow Ct. B17: Edg 2F 115
B20: Hand 4A 82
Meadow Cft. B47: Wyt 6A 162
WV6: Pert 6D 24
Meadow Dr. B92: H Ard 1B 154
Meadowfield Rd. B45: Rubery 2G 157
Meadowfields Cl. DY8: Word 1C 108
Mdw. Grange Dr. WV12: W'hall 2C 30
Meadow Gro. B92: Olton 4B 136
WS6: Gt Wyr 3G 7
Meadow Hill Dr. DY8: Word 1C 108
Meadow Hill Rd. B38: K Nor 5A 146
Meadowlands Dr. WS4: S'fld 1H 33
Meadow La. WV5: Wom 5G 57
WV10: Cov H 1G 15
WV12: W'hall 4A 30
WV14: Cose 3D 60
(not continuous)
Meadow Pk. Rd. DY8: Woll 3B 108
Mdw. Pleck La. B90: Dic H 3G 163
Meadow Ri. B30: B'vlle 6H 131
CV7: Bal C 5H 169
Meadow Rd. B17: Harb 2F 115
B32: Quin 5G 113
B47: Wyt 6A 162
B62: B'hth 3C 112
B67: Smeth 5E 99
B68: O'bry 1H 113
DY1: Dud 3C 76
WS9: A'rdge 5C 34
WV3: Wolv 3A 42
Meadows, The DY9: Pedm 5F 125
WS9: A'rdge 4A 34
Meadowside Cl. B43: Gt Barr 4A 66
Meadowside Rd. B74: Four O 5F 37
Meadow St. B64: Old H 3H 111
WS1: Wals 3B 48
Meadowsweet Av. B38: K Nor 1B 160
Meadowsweet Way DY6: K'wfrd 3E 93
Meadow Va. WV8: Bilb 5H 13
Meadow Vw. B13: Mose 5C 134
DY3: Sed 4G 59
WV6: Tett 5C 26
Meadow Vw. Mobile Home Pk.
WV10: Cov H 1G 15
Meadow Vw. Ter. WV6: Tett 5C 26
(not continuous)
Meadow Vw. Wharf WV6: Tett 5C 26
Meadow Wlk. B14: K Hth 6G 147
B64: Crad H 3F 111
Meadow Way DY8: Word 1A 108
WV8: Cod 5E 13
Mead Ri. B15: Edg 5B 116
Meadthorpe Rd. B44: Gt Barr 5F 67
Meadvale Rd. B45: Redn 3H 157
Meadway B33: Yard 1D 120
Meadway, The WV6: Tett 4G 25
Meadwood Ind. Est.
WV14: Bils 6G 45
Mears Cl. B23: Erd 5D 68
Mears Coppice DY5: Quar B 5A 110
DY9: Lye 5A 110
Mears Dr. B33: Stech 5B 104
Mease Cft. B9: Birm 1B 118
Measham Gro. B26: Yard 6C 120
Measham Way WV11: Wed 2G 29
Meaton Gro. B32: Bart G 5H 129
Mecca Bingo
Acocks Green 1H 135
Bilston 1E 61
Brierley Hill 1H 109
Great Barr 2H 67
Oldbury 2F 97
Wednesbury 3E 63
Wolverhampton 2G 43 (4A 170)
Medcroft Av. B20: Hand 3A 82
Medina Cl. WV10: Bush 3B 16
Medina Rd. B11: Tys 1E 135
Medina Way DY6: K'wfrd 3A 92
Medley Gdns. DY4: Tip 3D 78
Medley Rd. B11: S'brk 6D 118
Medlicott Rd. B11: S'brk 5C 118
Medway Cl. DY5: P'ntt 3E 93
Medway Ct. B73: S Cold 6H 53
Medway Cft. B36: Cas B 2B 106
Medway Gro. B38: K Nor 1A 160
Medway Rd. WS8: Bwnhls 3G 9
Medway Twr. B7: Nech 4B 102
Medway Wlk. WS8: Bwnhls 3G 9
Medwin Gro. B23: Erd 6D 68
Meerash La. WS7: Hamm 2D 10
Meer End B38: K Nor 2H 159
Meerhill Av. B90: M'path 3E 165
Meeting Ho. La. CV7: Bal C 5H 169
Meetinghouse La. B31: N'fld 3E 145
Meeting La. DY5: Brie H 2F 109
(not continuous)
Meeting La. Ind. Est. DY5: Brie H 2F 109
Meeting St. DY2: Neth 4E 95
DY4: Tip 1D 78
WS10: W'bry 2E 63
Megabowl
Birmingham 2G 117 (6F 5)
Brierley Hill 1H 109
Nechells *1D 102*
(in Star City)
Melbourne Av. B19: Hock 3E 101
B66: Smeth 2F 99
Melbourne Cl. B70: W Brom 6G 63
DY6: K'wfrd 5C 92
Melbourne Gdns. WS5: Wals 5F 49
Melbourne Rd. B63: Hale 6B 112
B66: Smeth 2E 99
Melbourne St. WV2: Wolv 2H 43 (5C 170)
Melbury Cl. WV3: Wolv 2E 43
Melbury Gro. B14: K Hth 2G 147
Melchett Rd. B30: K Nor 4B 146
Melcote Gro. B44: Gt Barr 5G 67
Meldon Dr. WV14: Bils 3A 62
Melford Cl. DY3: Sed 3G 59
Melford Hall Rd. B91: Sol 6D 136
Melfort Gro. B14: K Hth 4A 148
Melksham Sq. B35: Cas V 4E 87
Mellis Gro. B23: Erd 2A 84
Mellish Ct. *WS4: Wals 6E 33*
(off Mellish Rd.)
Mellish Dr. WS4: Wals 6F 33
Mellish Rd. WS4: Wals 6E 33
Mellor Dr. B74: Four O 6E 37
Mellors Cl. B17: Harb 2F 131
Mellowdew Rd. DY8: Word 6A 92
Mell Sq. B91: Sol 3G 151
Melplash Av. B91: Sol 3E 151
Melrose Av. *B11: S'hll 5C 118*
(off Walford Rd.)
B12: Bal H 5A 118
B71: W Brom 5B 64
B73: S Cold 3E 69
DY8: Stourb 3D 124
Melrose Cl. B38: K Nor 6B 146
Melrose Cotts. WS14: Muck C 4H 11
Melrose Dr. WV6: Pert 5D 24
Melrose Gro. B19: Loz 2D 100
Melrose Pl. B66: Smeth 1B 98
Melrose Rd. B20: Hand 6G 83
Melstock Cl. DY4: Tip 2F 77
Melstock Rd. B14: K Hth 6F 133
Melton Av. B92: Olton 1E 137
Melton Dr. B15: Edg 4E 117
Melton Gro. B33: Kitts G 6A 106
Melton Rd. B14: K Hth 5H 133
Melverley Gro. B44: K'sdng 5H 67
Melverton Av. WV10: Bush 1H 27
Melville Hall B16: Edg 2G 115
Melville Rd. B16: Edg 2G 115
Melvina Rd. B7: Birm 5B 102
Membury Rd. B8: Salt 3D 102
Memorial Cl. WV13: W'hall 1A 46
Memory La. WS10: Darl 3D 46
WV11: Wed 4D 28
Menai Cl. WV12: W'hall 3C 30
Menai Wlk. B37: F'bri 5D 106
Mendip Av. B8: Salt 4E 103
Mendip Cl. B63: Hale 4F 127
DY3: Lwr G 4H 75
WV2: E'shll 5B 44
Mendip Rd. B8: Salt 5E 103
B63: Hale 4F 127
DY8: Amb 5F 109
Menin Cres. B13: Mose 6B 134
Menin Pas. B13: Mose 5B 134
Menin Rd. B13: Mose 5B 134
DY4: Tip 2F 77
Mentone Ct. B20: Hand 4A 82
Meon Gro. B33: Sheld 3F 121
WV6: Pert 5F 25
Meon Ri. DY9: Pedm 2G 125
Meon Way WV11: Wed 2H 29
Meranti Cl. WV12: W'hall 1C 30
Mercer Av. B46: Wat O 4C 88
Mercer Gro. WV11: Wed 2G 29
Merchants Way WS9: A'rdge 2C 34
Mercia Dr. B14: K Hth 1F 147
WV6: Pert 4E 25
Mercote Hall La. CV7: Mer 2G 155
Mere Av. B35: Cas V 4E 87
Mere Cl. WV12: W'hall 4A 30
Merecote Rd. B92: Olton 6B 136
Mere Cft. WS11: Nort C 1D 8
Meredith Rd. DY3: Lwr G 2E 75
WV11: Wed 1E 29
Merediths Pool Cl. B18: Hock 3B 100
Meredith St. B64: Crad H 2F 111
MERE GREEN 6A 38
Mere Grn. Cl. B75: Four O 1A 54
Mere Grn. Rd. B75: Four O 1H 53
Mere Oak Rd. WV6: Pert 4E 25
Mere Pool Rd. B75: R'ley 1B 54
Mere Rd. B23: Erd 4C 84
DY8: Stourb 2C 124
Mereside Way B92: Olton 5C 136
Meres Rd. B63: Crad 6E 111
Merevale Rd. B92: Sol 3F 137
Mere Vw. WS4: S'fld 1G 33
MERIDEN 4H 141
Meriden Av. DY8: Woll 5B 108
Meriden Cl. B25: Yard 4H 119
DY8: Woll 5B 108
Meriden Dr. B37: K'hrst 3C 106
Meriden Ri. B92: Sol 2H 137
Meriden Rd. B92: H Ard 6B 140
CV7: Mer 6B 140
WV10: Oxl 1E 27
Meriden St. B5: Birm 1H 117 (6G 5)
Merino Av. B31: Longb 1E 159
Merlin Cl. B35: Cas V 4E 87
DY1: Dud 1B 94
Merlin Gro. B26: Sheld 6F 121
Merrick Cl. B63: Hale 3F 127
Merrick Rd. WV11: Wed 3A 30
MERRIDALE 2D 42
Merridale Av. WV3: Wolv 2D 42
Merridale Ct. WV3: Wolv 2D 42
Merridale Cres. WV3: Wolv 1E 43
Merridale Gdns. WV3: Wolv 2E 43
Merridale Gro. WV3: Wolv 2C 42
(not continuous)
Merridale La. WV3: Wolv 1E 43
Merridale Rd. WV3: Wolv 2D 42
Merridale St. WV3: Wolv 2F 43 (5A 170)
Merridale St. W. WV3: Wolv 3E 43
Merrill Cl. WS6: C Hay 3E 7
Merrill's Hall La. WV11: Wed 5G 29
Merrington Cl. B91: Sol 1G 165
Merrions Cl. B43: Gt Barr 1A 66
Merrishaw Rd. B31: Longb 1E 159
Merritts Brook Cl. B29: W Cas 2E 145
Merritt's Brook La. B31: N'fld 3C 144
Merritt's Hill B31: N'fld 1B 144
Merrivale Rd. B62: B'hth 3F 113
B66: Smeth 1E 115
Merryfield Cl. B92: Sol 6H 137
Merryfield Gro. B17: Harb 1G 131
Merryfield Rd. DY1: Dud 1H 93
MERRY HILL
Brierley Hill 6A 94
Wolverhampton 4B 42
Merry Hill DY5: Brie H, Quar B 2B 110
Merry Hill Cen. DY5: Brie H 6B 94
Merry Hill Ct. B66: Smeth 3H 99
Merryhill Dr. B18: Hock 3B 100
Merryhills Ent. Pk. WV10: Wolv 4B 28
Mersey Gro. B38: K Nor 1A 160
Mersey Pl. WS3: Blox 6C 20
Mersey Rd. WS3: Blox 6C 20
Merstal Dr. B92: Sol 6B 138
Merstone Cl. WV14: Bils 5E 45
Merstowe Cl. B27: A Grn 2H 135
Merton Cl. B68: O'bry 1H 113
Merton Ho. B37: F'bri 1B 122
Merton Rd. B13: Mose 2B 134
Mervyn Pl. WV14: Bils 2H 61
Mervyn Rd. B21: Hand 6A 82
WV14: Bils 2H 61
Meryhurst Rd. WS10: W'bry 6G 47
Messenger La. B70: W Brom 4B 80
Messenger Rd. B66: Smeth 3F 99
MESTY CROFT 2H 63
Metchley Abbey B17: Harb 6H 115
Metchley Ct. B17: Harb 1H 131
Metchley Cft. B90: M'path 3D 164
Metchley Dr. B17: Harb 6G 115
Metchley Gro. *B18: Win G 5A 100*
(off Heath Grn. Rd.)
Metchley Ho. B17: Harb 6H 115
Metchley La. B17: Harb 1H 131
Metchley Pk. Rd. B15: Edg 1H 131
Metfield Cft. B17: Harb 1H 131
DY6: K'wfrd 3D 92
Metric Wlk. B67: Smeth 4E 99
Metropolitan Ho. *B16: Birm 2C 116*
(off Hagley Rd.)
Metropolitan Lofts *DY1: Dud 6E 77*
(off Parson's St.)
Metro Triangle B7: Nech 2D 102
Metro Way B66: Smeth 2G 99
Mews, The B27: A Grn 2H 135
B44: K'sdng 6B 68
B65: Row R 1B 112
Meynell Ho. B20: Hand 4B 82
Meyrick Rd. B70: W Brom 1G 79
Meyrick Wlk. B16: Edg 2B 116
Miall Pk. Rd. B91: Sol 2C 150
Miall Rd. B28: Hall G 5G 135
Michael Blanning Gdns. B93: Dorr 6A 166
Michael Blanning Ho. *B13: Mose 3B 134*
(off Wake Grn. Pk.)
Michael Blanning Pl. CV7: Bal C 2H 169
Michael Ct. B5: Edg 5F 117
Michael Dr. B15: Edg 4E 117
Michael Rd. B67: Smeth 3C 98
WS10: Darl 4B 46
Michelle Cl. B13: Mose 2A 148
Micklehill Dr. B90: Shir 1H 163
Mickle Mdw. B46: Wat O 4D 88
Mickleover Rd. B8: W End 4A 104
Mickleton Av. B33: Sheld 3G 121
Mickleton Rd. B92: Olton 5B 136
Mickley Av. WV10: Wolv 4A 28
Midacre WV13: W'hall 2A 46
Middle Acre Rd. B32: Bart G 3C 130
Middle Av. WV13: W'hall 3G 45
Middle Bickenhill La. B92: Bick 1A 140
Middle Cres. WS3: Wals 2E 33
Middle Cross WV1: Wolv 2H 43 (4D 170)
Middle Dr. B45: Coft H 5B 158
Middlefield WV8: Pend 5C 14
Middlefield Av. B62: B'hth 3F 113
B93: Know 5D 166
Middlefield Cl. B62: B'hth 2F 113
Middlefield Gdns. *B62: B'hth 3F 113*
(off Hurst Grn. Rd.)
Middlefield Ho. *B14: K Hth 4H 147*
(off Britford Cl.)
Middle Fld. Rd. B31: N'fld 5G 145
Middlefield Rd. B69: Tiv 1A 96
Middle Gdns. WV13: W'hall 1B 46
MIDDLE HILL JUNC. 1A 6
Middlehill Ri. B32: Bart G 3B 130
Middle La. B38: Head H 3E 161
B47: Wyt 5G 161
WV8: Oaken 5C 12
WV9: Coven 3D 14
Middle Leaford B34: Stech 4E 105
Middle Leasowe B32: Quin 1A 130
Middle Mdw. DY4: Tip 2B 78
Middle Mdw. Av. B32: Quin 6A 114
Middlemist Gro. B43: Gt Barr 1B 82
Middlemore Bus. Pk. WS9: A'rdge 4H 33
Middlemore Ind. Est. B21: Hand 1F 99
Middlemore La. WS9: A'rdge 3B 34
Middlemore La. W. WS9: A'rdge 3H 33
Middlemore Rd. B21: Hand 2F 99
B31: N'fld 5F 145
B66: Hand, Smeth 2F 99
B71: W Brom 2F 99
Middle Pk. Cl. B29: W Cas 5F 131
Middle Pk. Dr. B31: N'fld 1F 145
Middle Pk. Rd. B29: W Cas 5F 131
Middlepark Rd. DY1: Dud 1A 94
Middle Rd. B61: Wild 5A 156
Middleton Cl. WS5: Wals 6D 48
(not continuous)
Middleton Gdns. B30: K Nor 3H 145
Middleton Grange B31: N'fld 3G 145
Middleton Hall Rd. B30: K Nor 3H 145
Middleton Rd. B14: K Hth 6G 133
B74: S'tly 2A 52
B90: Shir 5G 149
WS8: Bwnhls 4C 10
Middleton Trad. Est. WV13: W'hall 1G 45
Middletree Rd. B63: Crad 4E 111
Middle Vauxhall WV1: Wolv 1E 43
Middleway B15: Birm 3D 116
Middleway Av. DY8: Word 6A 92
Middleway Grn. WV14: Bils 3E 45
Middleway Ind. Est. *B12: Birm 4H 117*
(off Moseley Rd.)
Middleway Rd. WV14: Bils 3E 45
Middleway Vw. B18: Hock 6C 100
Midgley Dr. B74: Four O 1G 53
Midhill Dr. B65: Row R 3C 96
Midhurst Gro. WV6: Tett 4A 26
Midhurst Rd. B30: K Nor 4D 146
Midland Cl. B21: Hand 2C 100
Midland Ct. *B3: Birm 5E 101*
(off Cox St.)
Midland Cft. B33: Kitts G 1H 121
Midland Dr. B72: S Cold 6A 54
Midland Karting 5B 32
Midland Rd. B30: K Nor 2B 146
B74: S Cold 4G 53
WS1: Wals 2B 48
WS10: Darl 3C 46
Midland Sailing Club 6A 100
Midlands Art Cen. 1F 133
Midland St. B8: Birm 6C 102
Midpoint Blvd. B76: Min 2G 87
Midpoint Pk. B76: Min 3G 87
Midvale Dr. B14: K Hth 5F 147
Milburn Rd. B44: K'sdng 2A 68
Milcote Dr. B73: New O 2C 68
WV13: W'hall 2F 45
Milcote Rd. B29: W Cas 5E 131
B67: Smeth 1D 114
B91: Sol 3F 151
Milcote Way DY6: K'wfrd 2H 91
Mildenhall Rd. B42: Gt Barr 4C 66
Mildred Rd. B64: Old H 1G 111
Mildred Way B65: Row R 3C 96
Milebrook Gro. B32: Bart G 5H 129
Mile Flat DY6: K'wfrd 3E 91
Mile Oak Ct. B66: Smeth 3F 99
Milesbush Av. B36: Cas B 6H 87
Miles Gro. DY2: Dud 2H 95
Miles Mdw. Cl. WV12: W'hall 1C 30
Milestone Ct. WV6: Tett 6G 25
Milestone La. B21: Hand 1H 99
Milestone Way WV12: W'hall 1B 30
Milford Av. B12: Bal H 5A 118
WV12: W'hall 4A 30
Milford Cl. DY8: Word 6C 92
Milford Copse B17: Harb 6F 115
Milford Cft. B19: Birm 4F 101
B65: Row R 3H 95
Milford Gro. B90: M'path 2G 165
Milford Pl. B14: K Hth 5G 133
Milford Rd. B17: Harb 6F 115
WV2: Wolv 4G 43
Milholme Grn. B92: Sol 5H 137
MILKING BANK 5A 76
Milking Bank DY1: Dud 5H 75
Milk St. B5: Birm 2H 117 (6H 5)
Millard Ind. Est. B70: W Brom 6G 79
Millard Rd. WV14: Cose 4D 60
Mill Bank DY3: Sed 5H 59
Millbank Gro. B23: Erd 1B 84
(not continuous)
Millbank St. WV11: Wed 6H 17
Mill Brook Dr. B31: Longb 1C 158
Millbrook Rd. B14: K Hth 1E 147
Millbrook Way DY5: Brie H 3F 109
Mill Burn Way B9: Birm 1B 118
Mill Cl. B47: H'wd 2A 162
Mill Cft. WV14: Bils 5G 45
Millcroft Cl. B32: Bart G 3C 130
Millcroft Rd. B74: S'tly 3A 52
Milldale Cres. WV10: F'hses 3H 15

206 A-Z Birmingham Deluxe

Milldale Rd.—Mossvale Cl.

Milldale Rd. WV10: F'hses . . . 3H 15
Mill Dr. B66: Smeth . . . 4F 99
Millenium Gdns. B64: Old H . . . 1H 111
Millennium Apartments
B3: Birm . . . 2C 4
Millennium Cl. WS3: Pels . . . 4E 21
Millennium Pk.
B70: W Brom . . . 2G 79
Millennium Point . . . 6H 101 (3H 5)
Millennium Way WV8: Bilb . . . 3H 13
Miller Ct. B33: Stech . . . 6C 104
Miller Cres. WV14: Cose . . . 4C 60
Millers Cl. WS2: Wals . . . 2F 47
Millers Ct. *B66: Smeth . . . 4F 99*
(off Corbett St.)
B90: Shir . . . 5F 149
Millersdale Dr. B71: W Brom . . . 3D 64
Millers Grn. Dr. DY6: W Hth . . . 1G 91
Miller St. B6: Aston . . . 4G 101
Millers Va. WV5: Wom . . . 2D 72
Millers Wlk. WS3: Pels . . . 4C 20
Mill Farm Rd. B17: Harb . . . 2G 131
Millfield B31: N'fld . . . 3E 145
Millfield Av. WS3: Blox . . . 5B 20
WS4: S'fld . . . 6F 21
Millfield Ct. *DY1: Dud . . . 5C 76*
(off Pelham Dr.)
Millfield Rd. B20: Hand . . . 2A 82
WS8: Bwnhls . . . 6C 10
Millfields B33: Kitts G . . . 6H 105
(not continuous)
Millfields Cl. B71: W Brom . . . 4H 63
Millfields Rd. B71: W Brom . . . 4H 63
WV4: E'shll . . . 6C 44
WV14: Bils . . . 6C 44
Millfields Way WV5: Wom . . . 1E 73
Millfield Vw. B63: Hale . . . 1G 127
Millford Cl. B28: Hall G . . . 2G 149
Mill Gdns. B14: Yard W . . . 2D 148
B67: Smeth . . . 6D 98
MILL GREEN . . . 2A 36
Mill Grn. WV10: F'hses . . . 3H 15
Mill Gro. WV8: Bilb . . . 4A 14
Millhaven Av. B30: Stir . . . 1D 146
Mill Hill B67: Smeth . . . 6D 98
Mill Ho. B8: W End . . . 5B 104
Mill Ho. La. B75: Can . . . 1D 38
Millhouse Rd. B25: Yard . . . 3H 119
Millicent Pl. B12: Bal H . . . 5A 118
Millichip Rd. WV13: W'hall . . . 2G 45
Millington Rd. B36: Hodg H . . . 1C 104
DY4: Tip . . . 4H 61
WV10: Bush . . . 3A 28
Millison Gro. B90: M'path . . . 2E 165
Mill La. B5: Birm . . . 2H 117 (6G 5)
B31: N'fld . . . 6D 144
B32: Bart G . . . 3B 130
B61: Wild . . . 6A 156
B63: Hale . . . 1C 128
B69: O'bry . . . 5G 97
B91: Sol . . . 4G 151
B93: Dorr . . . 5A 166
DY3: Swind . . . 4D 72
DY7: Env, Stourt . . . 6A 90
WS3: Wals . . . 5D 32
WS4: Wals . . . 5D 32
WS7: Hamm . . . 2F 11
WS9: A'rdge . . . 2H 35
WS9: Ston . . . 3H 23
WV5: Wom . . . 6H 57
WV6: Tett . . . 6G 25
WV8: Cod . . . 1E 13
WV11: Wed . . . 2C 28
WV12: W'hall . . . 4C 30
Mill La. Arc. *B91: Sol . . . 4G 151*
(off Touchwood Shop. Cen.)
Millmead Lodge B13: Mose . . . 5D 134
Mill Mdw. DY8: Amb . . . 5E 109
Millmead Rd. B32: Bart G . . . 3C 130
Mill Pl. WS3: Wals . . . 5C 32
Millpool, The WV5: Seis . . . 3A 56
Mill Pool Cl. WV5: Wom . . . 2D 72
Millpool Gdns. B14: K Hth . . . 4H 147
Millpool Hill B14: K Hth . . . 3H 147
Millpool Way B66: Smeth . . . 5E 99
Mill Race La. DY8: Amb . . . 5E 109
Mill Rd. B64: Crad H . . . 4G 111
WS4: S'fld . . . 6F 21
WS8: Bwnhls . . . 6C 10
Mills Av. B76: Walm . . . 1C 70
Mills Cl. WV11: Wed . . . 1D 28
Mills Cres. WV2: Wolv . . . 3A 44
Millside B28: Hall G . . . 4E 149
WV5: Wom . . . 2E 73
Mills Rd. WV2: Wolv . . . 3A 44
Millstone Cl. B76: Walm . . . 4D 70
Mill Stream Cl. WV8: Bilb . . . 3H 13
Mill St. B6: Birm . . . 4H 101
B63: Crad . . . 4E 111
B70: W Brom . . . 3A 80
B72: S Cold . . . 6A 54
DY4: Tip . . . 2D 78
DY5: Brie H . . . 1H 109
DY8: Word . . . 1C 108
WS2: Wals . . . 6C 32
WS10: Darl . . . 5C 46
WV13: W'hall . . . 1C 46
WV14: Bils . . . 6E 45
Millsum Ho. *WS1: Wals . . . 2D 48*
(off Paddock La.)
Mills Wlk. DY4: Tip . . . 6H 61
Millthorpe Cl. B8: W End . . . 4F 103
Mill Vw. B33: Kitts G . . . 5G 105
Mill Wlk., The B31: N'fld . . . 6D 144
Millwalk Dr. WV9: Pend . . . 4E 15
Millward St. B9: Small H . . . 2C 118
B70: W Brom . . . 4G 79
Millwright Cl. DY4: Tip . . . 2B 78
Milner Rd. B29: S Oak . . . 4C 132
Milner Way B13: Mose . . . 5D 134
Milnes Walker Ct.
B44: Gt Barr . . . 4G 67
Milsom Gro. B34: S End . . . 3H 105
Milstead Rd. B26: Yard . . . 2E 121
Milston Cl. B14: K Hth . . . 6G 147
Milton Av. B12: Bal H . . . 5A 118
Milton Cl. B93: Ben H . . . 5B 166
DY8: Amb . . . 4E 109
WS1: Wals . . . 5B 48
WV12: W'hall . . . 2E 31
Milton Ct. B66: Smeth . . . 2E 115
WV6: Pert . . . 5E 25
Milton Cres. B25: Yard . . . 4B 120
DY3: Lwr G . . . 2E 75
Milton Dr. DY9: Hag . . . 6H 125
Milton Gro. B29: S Oak . . . 2B 132
Milton Pl. WS1: Wals . . . 5B 48
Milton Rd. B67: Smeth . . . 4B 98
B93: Ben H . . . 5B 166
WV10: Wolv . . . 4C 28
WV14: Cose . . . 5F 61
Milton St. B71: W Brom . . . 2H 79
DY5: P'ntt . . . 3H 93
WS1: Wals . . . 3B 48
Milverton Cl. B63: Hale . . . 5A 112
B76: Walm . . . 6D 70
Milverton Ct. *B62: Quin . . . 4G 113*
(off Binswood Rd.)
Milverton Rd. B23: Erd . . . 3E 85
B93: Know . . . 4E 167
Mimosa Cl. B29: W Cas . . . 5F 131
Mimosa Wlk. DY6: K'wfrd . . . 1C 92
Mincing La. B65: Row R . . . 6D 96
Mindelsohn Way B15: Edg . . . 1H 131
Minden Gro. B29: S Oak . . . 4F 131
Minehead Rd. DY1: Dud . . . 1H 93
WV10: Oxl . . . 5F 15
Miner St. WS2: Wals . . . 6A 32
Minerva Cl. WV12: W'hall . . . 5E 31
Minewood Cl. WS3: Blox . . . 4F 19
Minith Rd. WV14: Cose . . . 5F 61
Miniva Dr. B76: Walm . . . 4E 71
Minivet Dr. B12: Bal H . . . 5G 117
Minley Av. B17: Harb . . . 4D 114
Minories B4: Birm . . . 6G 101 (3E 5)
Minories, The DY2: Dud . . . 6E 77
Minstead Rd. B24: Erd . . . 6D 84
Minster, The WV3: Wolv . . . 4D 42
Minster Cl. B65: Row R . . . 6E 97
B93: Know . . . 1D 166
Minster Ct. B13: Mose . . . 1A 134
B29: W Cas . . . 6G 131
(off Abdon Av.)
Minster Dr. B10: Small H . . . 4D 118
Minsterley Cl. WV3: Wolv . . . 3C 42
Mintern Rd. B25: Yard . . . 3A 120
Minto Ho. B12: Bal H . . . 6G 117
Minton Cl. WV1: Wolv . . . 2C 44
Minton Rd. B32: Quin . . . 1D 130
MINWORTH . . . 2H 87
Minworth Ind. Est. B76: Min . . . 1E 87
Minworth Ind. Pk. B76: Min . . . 1G 87
Minworth Rd. B46: Wat O . . . 4C 88
Miranda Cl. B45: Fran . . . 4G 143
Mirfield Cl. WV9: Pend . . . 4E 15
Mirfield Rd. B33: Kitts G . . . 1F 121
B91: Sol . . . 1E 151
Mission Cl. B64: Old H . . . 2A 112
Mission Dr. DY4: Tip . . . 4A 78
Mistletoe Dr. WS5: Wals . . . 2F 65
Mitcham Ct. *B29: W Cas . . . 6G 131*
(off Abdon Av.)
Mitcham Gro. B44: K'sdng . . . 4B 68
Mitcheldean Covert B14: K Hth . . . 5F 147
Mitchell Av. WV14: Cose . . . 4D 60
Mitchells Art & Craft Cen. . . . 1C 54
Mitchel Rd. DY6: K'wfrd . . . 5D 92
Mitford Dr. B92: Sol . . . 6H 137
Mitre Cl. WV11: Ess . . . 4A 18
WV12: W'hall . . . 2D 30
Mitre Ct. B74: S Cold . . . 5A 54
Mitre Fold WV1: Wolv . . . 1G 43 (2A 170)
Mitre Rd. DY9: Lye . . . 6A 110
WS6: C Hay . . . 3C 6
Mitten Av. B45: Fran . . . 6F 143
Mitton Rd. B20: Hand . . . 5A 82
Moatbrook Av. WV8: Cod . . . 3E 13
Moatbrook La. WV8: Cod . . . 2C 12
Moat Coppice B32: Bart G . . . 4H 129
Moat Cft. B37: F'bri . . . 1C 122
B76: Walm . . . 6F 71
Moat Dr. B62: B'hth . . . 2E 113
Moat Farm Dr. B32: Bart G . . . 4G 129
Moat Farm Way WS3: Pels . . . 2E 21
Moatfield Ter. WS10: W'bry . . . 2G 63
Moat Grn. Av. WV11: Wed . . . 2G 29
Moat Ho. B31: Longb . . . 1D 158
Moat Ho. La. E. WV11: Wed . . . 2F 29
Moat Ho. La. W. WV11: Wed . . . 2F 29
Moat Ho. Rd. B8: W End . . . 5G 103
Moat La. B5: Birm . . . 1G 117 (6F 5)
B26: Yard . . . 4C 120
B91: Sol . . . 1G 151
WS6: Gt Wyr . . . 3G 7
Moat Mdws. B32: Quin . . . 1C 130
Moatmead Wlk. B36: Hodg H . . . 1C 104
Moat Rd. B68: O'bry . . . 1H 113
DY4: Tip . . . 6A 62
WS2: Wals . . . 1H 47
Moatside Cl. WS3: Pels . . . 2E 21
Moat St. WV13: W'hall . . . 1A 46
Moatway, The B38: K Nor . . . 2A 160
Mobberley Rd. WV14: Cose . . . 4C 60
Mob La. WS4: S'fld . . . 5G 21
Mockleywood Rd. B93: Know . . . 2D 166
Modbury Av. B32: Bart G . . . 4B 130
Moden Cl. DY3: Up Gor . . . 2H 75
Moden Hill DY3: Sed . . . 1G 75
Mogul La. B63: Crad . . . 4C 110
Moilliett Ct. B66: Smeth . . . 3G 99
Moilliett St. B18: Win G . . . 5H 99
Moira Cres. B14: Yard W . . . 3C 148
Moises Hall Rd. WV5: Wom . . . 6H 57
Moland St. B4: Birm . . . 5G 101
Mole St. B11: S'brk . . . 5B 118
Molineux . . . 6G 27 (1A 170)
Molineux All. WV1: Wolv . . . 6G 27 (1A 170)
(not continuous)
Molineux Fold WV1: Wolv . . . 6G 27 (1B 170)
Molineux St. WV1: Wolv . . . 6G 27 (1B 170)
Mollington Cres. B90: Shir . . . 4A 150
Molyneux Rd. DY2: Neth . . . 1G 111
Monaco Ho. B5: Birm . . . 3F 117
Monarch Dr. DY4: Tip . . . 1C 78
Monarch Ind. Est. B11: Tys . . . 5G 119
Monarchs Ga. B91: Sol . . . 2A 152
Monarch Way DY2: Neth . . . 5E 95
Mona Rd. B23: Erd . . . 2F 85
Monastery Dr. B91: Sol . . . 1B 150
Monckton Rd. B68: O'bry . . . 4G 113
Moncrieffe Cl. DY2: Dud . . . 1G 95
Moncrieffe St. WS1: Wals . . . 2E 49
Money La. B61: C'wich . . . 4A 156
Monica Rd. B10: Small H . . . 4F 119
Monins Av. DY4: Tip . . . 4A 78
Monk Cl. DY4: Tip . . . 4B 78
Monk Rd. B8: W End . . . 4H 103
Monks Cl. WV5: Wom . . . 1E 73
Monkseaton Rd. B72: W Grn . . . 3H 69
Monksfield Av. B43: Gt Barr . . . 4H 65
Monkshood M. B23: Erd . . . 6B 68
Monkshood Retreat B38: K Nor . . . 1B 160
Monks Kirby Rd. B76: Walm . . . 2D 70
MONKSPATH . . . 3E 165
Monkspath B76: Walm . . . 5D 70
Monkspath Bus. Pk. B90: Shir . . . 1D 164
Monkspath Cl. B90: Shir . . . 2B 164
Monkspath Hall Rd. B90: M'path . . . 3D 164
B91: Sol . . . 1F 165
Monkspath Leisure Pk. . . . 3C 164
Monksway B38: K Nor . . . 6D 146
Monkswell Cl. B10: Small H . . . 4D 118
DY5: Brie H . . . 2H 109
Monkswood Rd. B31: N'fld . . . 5G 145
Monkton Rd. B29: W Cas . . . 2E 131
Monmar Ct. WV12: W'hall . . . 4B 30
Monmer Cl. WV13: W'hall . . . 6B 30
Monmer Cl. Ind. Est. WV13: W'hall . . . 6C 30
Monmer La. WV12: W'hall . . . 5B 30
WV13: W'hall . . . 5B 30
Monmore Bus. Pk. WV2: Wolv . . . 4B 44
MONMORE GREEN . . . 3A 44
Monmore Green Stadium . . . 3C 44
Monmore Pk. Ind. Est. WV2: E'shll . . . 4B 44
Monmore Rd. WV1: Wolv . . . 3C 44
Monmouth Dr. B71: W Brom . . . 6H 63
B73: New O, S Cold . . . 2C 68
Monmouth Ho. B33: Kitts G . . . 1A 122
Monmouth Rd. B32: Bart G . . . 5B 130
B67: Smeth . . . 3C 114
WS2: Wals . . . 6E 31
Monsal Av. WV10: Wolv . . . 5A 28
Monsaldale Cl. WS8: Clay . . . 1H 21
Monsal Rd. B42: Gt Barr . . . 6E 67
Mons Rd. DY2: Dud . . . 6G 77
Montague Rd. B16: Edg . . . 2A 116
B21: Hand . . . 1B 100
B24: Erd . . . 6G 85
B66: Smeth . . . 6F 99
Montague St. B6: Aston . . . 1B 102
B9: Birm . . . 1A 118
Montana Av. B42: P Barr . . . 2C 82
Monteagle Dr. DY6: K'wfrd . . . 6B 74
Montford Gro. DY3: Sed . . . 6H 59
Montfort Rd. B46: Col . . . 4H 107
WS2: Wals . . . 5H 47
Montfort Wlk. B32: Bart G . . . 3G 129
Montgomery Cres. DY5: Quar B . . . 4B 110
Montgomery Cft. B11: S'brk . . . 4C 118
Montgomery Rd. WS2: Wals . . . 1E 47
Montgomery St. B11: S'brk . . . 4B 118
Montgomery St. Bus. Cen.
B11: S'brk . . . 4C 118
Montgomery Wlk. B71: W Brom . . . 3B 80
Montgomery Way B8: Salt . . . 5G 103
Montpelier Rd. B24: Erd . . . 6G 85
Montpellier Gdns. DY1: Dud . . . 5A 76
Montpellier St. B12: Birm . . . 5A 118
Montreal Ho. B5: Bal H . . . 4F 117
Montrose Dr. B35: Cas V . . . 4E 87
DY1: Dud . . . 1C 94
Montsford Cl. B93: Know . . . 3B 166
Monument Av. DY9: W'cte . . . 1A 126
Monument La. B45: Lick . . . 5F 157
DY3: Sed . . . 4A 60
DY9: Hag . . . 6H 125
Monument Rd. B16: Edg . . . 2B 116
(not continuous)
Monway Ind. Est. WS10: W'bry . . . 2E 63
Monway Ter. WS10: W'bry . . . 2E 63
Monwood Gro. B91: Sol . . . 5D 150
Monyhull Hall Rd. B30: K Nor . . . 5D 146
Moodyscroft Rd. B33: Kitts G . . . 6G 105
Moons La. WS6: C Hay . . . 3D 6
Moor, The B76: Walm . . . 5E 71
Moor Cen., The DY5: Brie H . . . 6H 93
Moorcroft WV14: Bils . . . 2A 62
Moorcroft Dr. WS10: W'bry . . . 3C 62
Moorcroft Pl. B7: Birm . . . 5A 102
Moorcroft Rd. B13: Mose . . . 2G 133
Moordown Av. B92: Olton . . . 3E 137
Moore Cl. B74: Four O . . . 3F 37
WV6: Pert . . . 5F 25
Moore Cres. B68: O'bry . . . 6A 98
Moorend Av. B37: Chel W, Mars G . . . 3B 122
Moor End La. B24: Erd . . . 3G 85
Moore Rd. WV12: W'hall . . . 1D 30
Moore's Row B5: Birm . . . 2H 117 (6H 5)
Moore St. WV1: Wolv . . . 2B 44
Moorfield Av. B93: Know . . . 3A 166
Moorfield Dr. B63: Hale . . . 5H 111
B73: Bold . . . 5F 69
Moorfield Rd. B34: S End . . . 3E 105
WV2: Wolv . . . 4G 43
Moorfoot Av. B63: Hale . . . 4E 127
MOOR GREEN . . . 3F 133
Moor Grn. La. B13: Mose . . . 4E 133
Moor Hall Dr. B75: R'ley . . . 3A 54
Moorhills Cft. B90: Shir . . . 1H 163
Moor Ho. *B14: K Hth . . . 5E 147*
(off Druids La.)
Moorings, The B18: Win G . . . 4B 100
B69: O'bry . . . 1E 97
DY5: Brie H . . . 5C 94
WV9: Pend . . . 5D 14
Moorland Av. WV10: Oxl . . . 3G 27
Moorland Rd. B16: Edg . . . 2H 115
WS3: Blox . . . 1G 31
Moorlands, The B74: Four O . . . 3F 53
Moorlands Cl. B75: S Cold . . . 5D 54
Moorlands Ct. B65: Row R . . . 5D 96
Moorlands Dr. B90: Shir . . . 4A 150
Moorlands Rd. B71: W Brom . . . 4A 64
Moor La. B6: Witt . . . 1H 83
B65: Row R . . . 1A 112
Moor La. Ind. Est. B6: Witt . . . 3A 84
Moor Leasow B31: N'fld . . . 5G 145
Moor Mdw. Rd. B75: S Cold . . . 4B 54
Moor Pk. WS3: Blox . . . 4H 19
WV6: Pert . . . 4D 24
Moorpark Rd. B31: Longb . . . 6E 145
Moor Pool Av. B17: Harb . . . 5G 115
Moorpool Ter. B17: Harb . . . 5G 115
Moors, The B36: Hodg H . . . 1D 104
Moors Cft. B32: Bart G . . . 4H 129
Moorside Gdns. WS2: Wals . . . 6H 31
Moorside Rd. B14: Yard W . . . 3C 148
Moor's La. B31: N'fld . . . 5C 130
Moors Mill La. DY4: Tip . . . 6D 62
Moorsom St. B6: Aston . . . 4G 101
MOOR STREET . . . 3G 129
Moor St. B5: Birm . . . 5F 5
B70: W Brom . . . 5A 80
DY5: Brie H . . . 6E 93
WS10: W'bry . . . 3H 63
Moor St. Ind. Est. DY5: Brie H . . . 1G 109
Moor St. Queensway
B4: Birm . . . 1G 117 (4F 5)
Moor St. Sth. WV2: Wolv . . . 4G 43
Moor Street Station (Rail) . . . 1G 117 (4F 5)
Moorville Wlk. B11: S'brk . . . 4A 118
Morar Cl. B35: Cas V . . . 3G 87
Moray Cl. B62: B'hth . . . 3E 113
Morcom Rd. B11: Tys . . . 6E 119
Mordaunt Dr. B75: R'ley . . . 1C 54
Morden Rd. B33: Stech . . . 6B 104
Morefields Cl. WS9: A'rdge . . . 2C 34
Moreland Cft. B76: Walm . . . 1F 87
Morelands, The B31: N'fld . . . 6F 145
Morestead Av. B26: Sheld . . . 6G 121
Moreton Av. B43: Gt Barr . . . 2E 67
WV4: E'shll . . . 1A 60
Moreton Cl. B25: Yard . . . 4H 119
B32: Harb . . . 6D 114
(not continuous)
DY4: Tip . . . 3B 62
Moreton Rd. B90: Shir . . . 5A 150
WV10: Bush . . . 6H 15
Moreton St. B1: Birm . . . 5D 100
Morford Rd. WS9: A'rdge . . . 2C 34
Morgan Cl. B64: Old H . . . 3G 111
B69: O'bry . . . 1D 96
WV12: W'hall . . . 5B 30
Morgan Ct. B24: Erd . . . 1A 86
Morgan Dr. WV14: Cose . . . 5D 60
Morgan Gro. B36: Cas B . . . 6B 88
Morgans Bus. Pk. WS11: Nort C . . . 1D 8
Morgrove Av. B93: Know . . . 3B 166
Morjon Dr. B43: Gt Barr . . . 3B 66
Morland Rd. B31: N'fld . . . 6D 144
B43: Gt Barr . . . 1E 67
Morley Gro. WV6: Wolv . . . 5G 27
Morley Rd. B8: W End . . . 3H 103
Morlich Ri. DY5: Brie H . . . 3F 109
Morning Pines DY8: Stourb . . . 1C 124
Morningside B73: S Cold . . . 5H 53
Mornington Ct. B46: Col . . . 2H 107
Mornington Rd. B66: Smeth . . . 2F 99
Morris Av. WS2: Wals . . . 1E 47
Morris Cl. B27: A Grn . . . 1B 136
Morris Cft. B36: Cas B . . . 6A 88
Morris Fld. Cft. B28: Hall G . . . 3E 149
Morrison Av. WV10: Bush . . . 1H 27
Morrison Rd. DY4: Tip . . . 3C 78
Morris Rd. B8: W End . . . 3H 103
Morris St. B70: W Brom . . . 6A 80
Mortimers Cl. B14: K Hth . . . 6B 148
Morton Rd. DY5: Quar B . . . 4H 109
Morvale Gdns. DY9: Lye . . . 6A 110
Morvale St. DY9: Lye . . . 6A 110
Morven Rd. B73: S Cold . . . 3F 69
Morville Cl. B93: Dorr . . . 6H 165
Morville Cft. WV14: Bils . . . 1D 60
Morville Rd. DY2: Neth . . . 5F 95
Morville St. B16: Birm . . . 2C 116
(not continuous)
Mosborough Cres. B19: Birm . . . 4E 101
Mosedale Dr. WV11: Wed . . . 4H 29
MOSELEY
B13 . . . 2H 133
WV10 . . . 3C 16
WV13 . . . 1E 45
Moseley Bog Nature Reserve . . . 4C 134
Moseley Ct. B13: Mose . . . 3B 134
WV11: Ess . . . 4H 17
WV13: W'hall . . . 2F 45
Moseley Dr. B37: Mars G . . . 3B 122
Moseley Ga. B13: Mose . . . 2H 133
Moseley Old Hall WV10: F'stne . . . 2C 16
Moseley Old Hall La.
WV10: F'stne . . . 2C 16
Moseley Pk. Sports Cen. . . . 3G 45
Moseley Rd. B12: Bal H, Birm . . . 6H 117
(not continuous)
WV10: Bush . . . 2B 16
WV13: W'hall . . . 2F 45
Moseley Road Swimming Pool . . . 6H 117
Moseley RUFC . . . 2B 132
Moseley St. B5: Birm . . . 2H 117
B12: Birm . . . 2H 117
DY4: Tip . . . 6C 62
WV10: Wolv . . . 5G 27
Moss Cl. WS4: Wals . . . 6E 33
WS9: A'rdge . . . 4C 34
Mossdale Way DY3: Sed . . . 6A 60
Moss Dr. B72: W Grn . . . 2A 70
Mossfield Rd. B14: K Hth . . . 6G 133
Moss Gdns. WV14: Cose . . . 2D 60
Moss Gro. B14: K Hth . . . 1F 147
DY6: K'wfrd . . . 2B 92
Moss Ho. Cl. B15: Birm . . . 2D 116
Mossley Cl. WS3: Blox . . . 6F 19
Mossley La. WS3: Blox . . . 5F 19
Mossvale Cl. B64: Old H . . . 2H 111

Mossvale Gro.—New Oscott

Mossvale Gro. B8: Salt 4F 103
Moss Way B74: S'tly 4H 51
Mostyn Cres. B71: W Brom 6H 63
Mostyn Rd. B16: Edg 1B 116
B21: Hand 1B 100
Mostyn St. WV1: Wolv 5F 27
Mother Teresa Ho. *B70: W Brom* *4H 79*
(off Baker St.)
Motorway Trad. Est. B6: Birm 4H 101
Mott Cl. DY4: Tip 5C 62
Mottram Cl. B70: W Brom 5G 79
Mottrams Cl. B72: W Grn 3A 70
Mott St. B19: Birm 5F 101 (1C 4)
Mott St. Ind. Est. B19: Birm 5F 101
Motts Way B46: Col 4H 107
Mounds, The B38: K Nor 1A 160
Moundsley Gro. B14: K Hth 4A 148
Moundsley Ho. B14: K Hth 5G 147
Mount, The B23: Erd 6D 84
B64: Old H 2A 112
B76: Curd 1E 89
Mountain Ash Dr. DY9: Pedm 3G 125
Mountain Ash Rd. WS8: Clay 2A 22
Mount Av. DY5: Brie H 5G 93
Mountbatten Cl. B70: W Brom 5D 80
Mountbatten Rd. WS2: Wals 1F 47
Mount Cl. B13: Mose 1H 133
DY3: Gorn 5G 75
WS6: C Hay 3E 7
WV5: Wom 6G 57
Mount Ct. WV6: Tett 1H 41
Mount Dr. WV5: Wom 6G 57
Mountfield Cl. B14: K Hth 5A 148
Mountford Cl. B65: Row R 6C 96
Mountford Cres. WS9: A'rdge 1E 35
Mountford Dr. B75: Four O 3H 53
Mountford Ho. *B70: W Brom* *6C 80*
(off Glover St.)
Mountford La. WV14: Bils 4F 45
Mountford Rd. B90: Shir 6D 148
Mountford St. B11: S'hll 6D 118
Mount Gdns. WV8: Cod 3F 13
Mountjoy Cres. B92: Sol 2G 137
Mount La. DY3: Gorn 5G 75
Mt. Pleasant B10: Small H 2B 118
B14: K Hth 4H 133
DY5: Quar B 2A 110
DY6: K'wfrd 4H 91
WS6: C Hay 3D 6
WV14: Bils 5G 45
Mt. Pleasant Av. B21: Hand 6A 82
WV5: Wom 6F 57
Mt. Pleasant Ct. B10: Small H 2B 118
Mt. Pleasant St. B70: W Brom 5A 80
WV14: Cose 5D 60
Mountrath St. WS1: Wals 2C 48
Mount Rd. B21: Hand 1H 99
B65: Row R 6E 97
B69: Tiv 1C 96
DY8: Stourb 6F 109
DY8: Word 1B 108
WS3: Pels 3E 21
WV4: E'shll 3B 60
WV4: Penn 6E 43
WV5: Wom 6G 57
WV6: Tett 1G 41
WV13: W'hall 3G 45
Mounts Rd. WS10: W'bry 3F 63
Mount St. B7: Nech 3C 102
B63: Hale 3A 128
DY4: Tip 1C 78
DY8: Stourb 6E 109
WS1: Wals 3C 48
Mount St. Bus. Cen. B7: Nech 3C 102
Mount St. Ind. Est. B7: Nech 2D 102
Mounts Way B7: Nech 2C 102
Mount Vw. B75: S Cold 1C 70
Mountwood Covert WV6: Tett 6H 25
Mousehall Farm Rd. DY5: Quar B 3H 109
Mouse Hill WS3: Pels 4D 20
MOUSESWEET 6G 95
Mousesweet Brook Nature Reserve 2D 110
Mousesweet Cl. DY2: Neth 5G 95
Mousesweet La. DY2: Neth 6G 95
Mousesweet Wlk. B64: Crad H 3D 110
Mowbray Cl. B45: Fran 5G 143
Mowbray St. B5: Birm 3G 117
Mowe Cft. B37: Mars G 4C 122
Moxhull Cl. WV12: W'hall 6C 18
Moxhull Dr. B76: Walm 5C 70
Moxhull Gdns. WV12: W'hall 6C 18
Moxhull Rd. B37: K'hrst 4C 106
MOXLEY 1B 62
Moxley Ct. WS10: Mox 1A 62
Moxley Ind. Cen. WS10: Mox 1C 62
Moxley Rd. WS10: Darl 1B 62
Moyle Dr. B63: Crad 4D 110
Moyses Cft. B66: Smeth 1E 99
Muchall Rd. WV4: Penn 6E 43
MUCKLEY CORNER 4H 11
Mucklow Hill B62: Hale 1C 128
Mucklow Hill Trad. Est. B62: Hale 6C 112
Muirfield Cl. WS3: Blox 4G 19
Muirfield Cres. B69: Tiv 2A 96
Muirfield Gdns. B38: K Nor 6H 145
Muirhead Ho. B5: Edg 5E 117
Muirville Cl. DY8: Word 6B 92
Mulberry Dr. B13: Mose 4B 134
Mulberry Grn. DY1: Dud 2B 76
Mulberry Pl. WS3: Blox 6F 19
Mulberry Rd. B30: B'vlle 2G 145
WS3: Blox 6F 19
Mulberry Wlk. B74: S'tly 3G 51
Mull Cl. B45: Fran 6E 143
Mull Cft. B36: Cas B 2C 106
Mullens Gro. Rd. B37: K'hrst 4C 106
Mullett Rd. WV11: Wed 2D 28
Mullett St. DY5: P'ntt 4F 93
Mulliners Cl. B37: Chel W 1E 123
Mullion Cft. B38: K Nor 6A 146
Mulroy Rd. B74: S Cold 5H 53
Mulwych Rd. B33: Kitts G 6A 106
Munslow Gro. B31: Longb 1D 158
Muntz Ho. B16: Edg 2C 116
Muntz St. B10: Small H 3D 118
Murcroft Rd. DY9: W'cte 4H 125
Murdoch Dr. DY6: K'wfrd 2A 92
Murdoch Rd. WV14: Bils 5A 46
Murdock Ct. *WV12: W'hall* *2D 30*
(off Huntington Rd.)
Murdock Gro. B21: Hand 2A 100
Murdock Pl. *B66: Smeth* *5F 99*
(off Corbett St.)
Murdock Rd. B21: Hand 1A 100
B66: Smeth 3H 99
Murdock Way WS2: Wals 3F 31
(not continuous)
Murray Ct. B73: S Cold 2G 69
Murrell Cl. B5: Bal H 4F 117
Musborough Cl. B36: Cas B 6G 87
Muscott Gro. B17: Harb 6F 115
Muscovy Rd. B23: Erd 4C 84
Mus. of the Jewellery Quarter *4E 101*
(off Vyse St.)
Musgrave Cl. B76: Walm 2C 70
Musgrave Rd. B18: Hock 3B 100
MUSHROOM GREEN 1D 110
Mushroom Grn. DY2: Neth 2D 110
Mushroom Hall Rd.
B68: O'bry 4H 97
Musk La. DY3: Lwr G 4F 75
Musk La. W. DY3: Lwr G 4F 75
Muswell Cl. B91: Sol 2H 151
Muxloe Cl. WS3: Blox 4G 19
Myatt Av. WS9: A'rdge 4B 34
WV2: E'shll 5A 44
Myatt Cl. WV2: E'shll 5A 44
Myatt Way WS9: A'rdge 4B 34
Myddleton St. B18: Hock 5C 100
Myles Ct. DY5: Brie H 5H 93
Mynors Cres. B47: H'wd 4A 162
Myring Dr. B75: S Cold 5D 54
Myrtle Av. B12: Bal H 6A 118
B14: K Hth 5H 147
Myrtle Cl. WV12: W'hall 2E 31
Myrtle Gro. B19: Hand 1E 101
WV3: Wolv 5C 42
Myrtle Pl. B29: S Oak 3D 132
Myrtle Rd. DY1: Dud 4D 76
Myrtle St. WV2: E'shll 5B 44
Myrtle Ter. DY4: Tip 3B 62
Myton Dr. B90: Shir 5D 148
Mytton Cl. DY2: Dud 6G 77
Mytton Gro. DY4: Tip 2G 77
Mytton Rd. B30: B'vlle 2G 145
B46: Wat O 4C 88
Myvod Rd. WS10: W'bry 6G 47

N

Naden Rd. B19: Hock 3D 100
Nadin Rd. B73: W Grn 5G 69
Nafford Gro. B14: K Hth 5H 147
Nagersfield Rd. DY5: Brie H 6E 93
Nailers Cl. B32: Bart G 3F 129
Nailers Row WV5: Wom 2F 73
Nailors Fold WV14: Cose 3F 61
Nailstone Cres. B27: A Grn 5A 136
Nairn Cl. B28: Hall G 2F 149
Nairn Rd. WS3: Blox 3G 19
Nally Dr. WV14: Cose 3C 60
Nanaimo Way DY6: K'wfrd 5E 93
Nansen Rd. B8: Salt 4E 103
B11: S'hll 2C 134
Nantmel Gro. B32: Bart G 5A 130
Naomi Way WS9: Wals W 3D 22
Napier Dr. DY4: Tip 1C 78
Napier Rd. WS2: Wals 4G 31
WV2: Wolv 4H 43
Napton Gro. B29: W Cas 3D 130
Narraway Gro. DY4: Tip 5D 62
Narrowboat Way DY2: Dud 4C 94
DY5: Brie H 5C 94
Narrow La. B62: B'hth 3E 113
WS2: Wals 4H 47
WS8: Bwnhls 5B 10
Naseby Dr. B63: Hale 3F 127
Naseby Rd. B8: Salt 4F 103
B91: Sol 1F 151
WV6: Pert 6F 25
Nash Av. WV6: Pert 6E 25
Nash Cl. B65: B'hth 2C 112
Nash Cft. B37: Mars G 3D 122
Nash Sq. B42: P Barr 3F 83
Nash Wlk. *B66: Smeth* *4G 99*
(off Poplar St.)
Nately Gro. B29: S Oak 3G 131
Nathan Cl. B75: S Cold 3H 53
National Exhibition Cen. 6F 123
National Indoor Arena 1D 116 (4A 4)
National Motorcycle Mus. 3A 140
National Sea Life Cen. 1D 116 (4A 4)
Naunton Cl. B29: W Cas 6E 131
Naunton Rd. WS2: Wals 6G 31
Navenby Cl. B90: Shir 4C 148
Navigation Dr. DY5: Brie H 5C 94
Navigation La. WS10: W'bry 3D 64
Navigation Rdbt. DY4: Tip 1E 79
Navigation St. B2: Birm 1F 117 (5C 4)
WS2: Wals 1B 48
WV1: Wolv 2A 44
Navigation Way B18: Win G 4B 100
B70: W Brom 5F 79
Nayland Cft. B28: Hall G 2G 149
Naylors Gro. DY3: Up Gor 3A 76
NEACHELL 1F 45
Neachells La. WV11: Wed 4F 29
WV13: W'hall 1F 45
Neachells La. Ind. Est. WV11: Wed 5F 29
Neachless Av. WV5: Wom 2G 73
Neachley Gro. B33: Stech 5D 104
Neale Ho. B70: W Brom 6B 80
WV2: Wolv *4G 43*
(off Blakenhall Gdns.)
Neale St. WS2: Wals 1A 48
Nearhill Rd. B38: K Nor 1G 159
Near Lands Cl. B32: Quin 1H 129
Nearmoor Rd. B34: S End 3H 105
Near Oak Ho. B32: Bart G 5B 130
Neasden Gro. B44: K'sdng 5B 68
Neath Rd. WS3: Blox 5F 19
Neath Way DY3: Sed 1C 76
WS3: Blox 5F 19
Nebsworth Cl. B90: Shir 2B 150
NECHELLS 2D 102
Nechells Community Sports Cen. 4A 102
NECHELLS GREEN 4B 102
Nechells Pk. Rd. B7: Nech 3B 102
Nechell's Parkway B7: Birm 5A 102
Nechells Pl. B7: Nech 3B 102
NEC House B40: Nat E C 6F 123
Needham St. B7: Nech 2C 102
Needhill Cl. B93: Know 3B 166
NEEDLERS END 2H 169
Needlers End La. CV7: Bal C 3F 169
Needlers End Rd. CV7: Bal C 2F 169
Needless All. B2: Birm 1F 117 (4D 4)
Needwood Cl. WV2: Wolv 5F 43
Needwood Dr. WV4: E'shll 1B 60
Needwood Gro. B71: W Brom 4C 64
Needwood Ho. B27: A Grn 2B 136
Nelson Av. WV14: Bils 4E 45
Nelson Ct. B13: Mose 1H 133
Nelson Ho. DY4: Tip 6A 62
Nelson Rd. B6: Aston 6H 83
DY1: Dud 6D 76
Nelson St. B1: Birm 6D 100
B69: O'bry 3H 97
B71: W Brom 2A 80
WV2: Wolv 3G 43 (6B 170)
WV13: W'hall 6B 30
Nene Cl. DY8: Stourb 1E 125
Nene Way B36: Cas B 1B 106
Neptune Ind. Est. WV13: W'hall 3B 46
Neptune St. DY4: Tip 2G 77
Nesbit Gro. B9: Bord G 6H 103
Nesfield Cl. B38: K Nor 6G 145
Nesfield Gro. B92: H Ard 6B 140
Nesscliffe Gro. B23: Erd 6D 68
Nest Comn. WS3: Pels 2D 20
(not continuous)
Neston Gro. B33: Stech 1A 120
Netheravon Cl. B14: K Hth 5F 147
Netherby Rd. DY3: Sed 5G 59
Nethercote Gdns. B90: Shir 4E 149
Netherdale Cl. B72: W Grn 6A 70
Netherdale Rd. B14: K Hth 6A 148
NETHEREND 4C 110
Netherend Cl. B63: Crad 4C 110
Netherend La. B63: Crad 4D 110
Netherend Sq. B63: Crad 4C 110
Netherfield Gdns. B27: A Grn 2H 135
Nethergate DY3: Up Gor 2B 76
Netherstone Gro. B74: Four O 4F 37
Netherton Bus. Pk. DY2: Neth 5F 95
(not continuous)
Netherton Gro. B33: Kitts G 6H 105
Netherton Hill DY2: Neth 4E 95
Netherton Lodge DY2: Neth 4E 95
Netherwood Cl. B91: Sol 1C 150
Nethy Dr. WV6: Tett 4H 25
Netley Gro. B11: Tys 2F 135
Netley Ho. B32: Harb 6D 114
Netley Rd. WS3: Blox 5E 19
Netley Way WS3: Blox 5E 19
Network Pk. B8: Salt 5C 102
Nevada Way B37: Chel W 2E 123
Neve Av. WV10: Bush 6B 16
Neve's Opening WV1: Wolv 1B 44
Neville Av. WV4: Penn 6H 43
Neville Rd. B23: Erd 4C 84
B36: Cas B 6A 88
B90: Shir 6F 149
Neville Wlk. B35: Cas V 5E 87
Nevin Gro. B42: P Barr 2E 83
Nevis Ct. WV3: Wolv 1C 42
Nevis Gro. WV12: W'hall 6B 18
Nevison Gro. B43: Gt Barr 1D 66
Newark Cft. B26: Sheld 5F 121
Newark Rd. DY2: Neth 1F 111
WV12: W'hall 2C 30
New Art Gallery Walsall, The 1C 48
New Bank Gro. B9: Bord G 6G 103
New Bartholomew St. B5: Birm 1H 117 (4G 5)
New Birmingham Rd. B69: Tiv 5H 77
DY2: Dud 5H 77
Newbold Cl. B93: Ben H 4B 166
Newbold Ct. B63: Hale 2B 128
NEWBOLDS 3C 28
Newbolds Rd. WV10: Wolv 3C 28
Newbolt Rd. WV14: Bils 5G 45
Newbolt St. WS5: Wals 6C 48
New Bond St. B9: Birm 2B 118
DY2: Dud 1F 95
Newborough Gro. B28: Hall G 3F 149
Newborough Rd. B28: Hall G 3F 149
B90: Shir 3F 149
NEWBRIDGE 6C 26
Newbridge Av. WV6: Wolv 6C 26
Newbridge Cres. WV6: Wolv 5C 26
Newbridge Dr. WV6: Wolv 5C 26
Newbridge Gdns. WV6: Wolv 5C 26
Newbridge M. WV6: Wolv 5D 26
Newbridge Rd. B9: Bord G 3H 119
DY6: W Hth 1A 92
Newbridge St. WV6: Wolv 5D 26
Newburn Cft. B32: Quin 6H 113
Newbury Cl. B62: Hale 2D 128
WS6: Gt Wyr 2F 7
Newbury Ho. B69: O'bry 4D 96
Newbury La. B69: O'bry 3C 96
Newbury Rd. B19: Hock 2G 101
DY8: Word 1A 108
WS11: Nort C 1E 9
WV10: F'hses 5G 15
Newbury Wlk. B65: Row R 3C 96
Newby Gro. B37: F'bri 4D 106
New Canal St. B5: Birm 1H 117 (5G 5)
New Cannon Pas. B2: Birm 1G 117 (4E 5)
Newcastle Cft. B35: Cas V 4G 87
Newchurch Gdns. B24: Erd 5E 85
New Church Rd. B73: Bold 5G 69
New Cole Hall La. B34: Stech 4F 105
New Coll. Cl. WS1: Wals 4E 49
Newcombe Rd. B21: Hand 5H 81
Newcome Cl. B24: Erd 3B 86
Newcomen Ct. WS4: Rus 2F 33
Newcomen Dr. DY4: Tip 4H 77
Newcott Cl. WV9: Pend 5D 14
New Ct. *DY5: Brie H* *1H 109*
(off Promenade, The)
New Coventry Rd. B26: Sheld 6D 120
New Cft. B19: Loz 2G 101
Newcroft Gro. B26: Yard 4C 120
NEW CROSS 4C 28
New Cross Av. WV10: Wolv 5D 28
WV11: Wed 5D 28
New Cross Ind. Est. WV1: Wolv 6C 28
New Cross St. DY4: Tip 2G 77
WS10: Darl 6D 46
Newdigate Rd. B75: S Cold 6E 55
New Dudley Rd. DY6: W Hth 1A 92
Newells Dr. DY4: Tip 6D 62
Newells Rd. B26: Yard 3E 121
New England B62: B'hth 4E 113
New England Cl. B69: O'bry 6E 79
Newent Cl. WV12: W'hall 6D 30
New Ent. Cen. WV1: Wolv 3C 44
New Enterprise Workshops
B18: Hock 4C 100
Newent Rd. B31: N'fld 3G 145
Newey Bus. Pk. DY4: Tip 1F 77
Newey Cl. B45: Redn 3G 157
Newey Rd. B28: Hall G 1F 149
WV11: Wed 1A 30
Newey St. DY1: Dud 5C 76
New Farm Rd. DY9: Lye 1G 125
Newfield Cl. B91: Sol 1H 151
WS2: Wals 3A 32
Newfield Cres. B63: Hale 6A 112
Newfield Dr. DY6: K'wfrd 5C 92
Newfield La. B63: Hale 6A 112
Newfield Rd. B69: O'bry 1F 97
New Forest Rd. WS3: Wals 4C 32
New Gas St. B70: W Brom 2G 79
Newhall Ct. B3: Birm 6E 101 (2A 4)
New Hall Dr. B76: Walm 1B 70
(not continuous)
Newhall Farm Cl. B76: Walm 1B 70
Newhall Hill B1: Birm 6E 101 (2A 4)
Newhall Ho. *WS1: Wals* *3C 48*
(off Newhall St.)
New Hall Pl. WS10: W'bry 2G 63
Newhall Pl. B3: Birm 2A 4
Newhall Rd. B65: Row R 6C 96
New Hall St. WV13: W'hall 1A 46
Newhall St. B3: Birm 6E 101 (2B 4)
B70: W Brom 5A 80
DY4: Tip 5G 61
WS1: Wals 3C 48
Newhall Wlk. B72: S Cold 1A 70
Newhampton Ho. WV1: Wolv 6F 27 (1A 170)
New Hampton Lofts B18: Birm 4E 101
New Hampton Rd. E.
WV1: Wolv 6F 27 (1A 170)
New Hampton Rd. W. WV6: Wolv 5D 26
Newhaven Cl. B7: Birm 4A 102
Newhay Cft. B19: Loz 2E 101
New Heath Cl. WV11: Wed 4D 28
New Henry St. B68: O'bry 5G 97
New High Dr. DY4: Tip 2B 78
Newhope Cl. B15: Birm 3F 117
New Hope Rd. B66: Smeth 5G 99
New Horse Rd. WS6: C Hay 2E 7
Newhouse Cres. CV7: Bal C 3H 169
Newhouse Farm Cl. B76: Walm 2D 70
New Ho. Farm Dr. B31: N'fld 1F 145
Newick Av. B74: Lit A 6B 36
Newick Gro. B14: K Hth 3E 147
Newick St. DY2: Neth 5E 95
Newington Rd. B37: Mars G 3D 122
New Inn Rd. B19: Loz 6F 83
New Inns Cl. B21: Hand 1H 99
New Inns La. B45: Fran 6E 143
NEW INVENTION 2D 30
New John St. B6: Birm 4G 101
B62: B'hth 2C 112
New John St. W. B19: Hock 3E 101
New King St. DY2: Dud 6E 77
Newland Cl. WS4: S'fld 5G 21
Newland Ct. B23: Erd 4B 84
Newland Gdns. B64: Crad H 4G 111
Newland Gro. DY2: Dud 2F 95
Newland Rd. B9: Small H 2F 119
Newlands, The B34: S End 2G 105
Newlands Cl. WV13: W'hall 2A 46
Newlands Dr. B62: B'hth 4E 113
Newlands Grn. B66: Smeth 5E 99
Newlands La. B37: Mars G 5C 122
Newlands Rd. B30: Stir 6D 132
B93: Ben H 5B 166
Newlands Wlk. *B68: O'bry* *5H 97*
(off Jackson St.)
New Landywood La. WV11: Ess 1E 19
New Leasow B76: Walm 6E 71
Newlyn Rd. B31: N'fld 4D 144
B64: Crad H 3F 111
Newman Av. WV4: E'shll 1B 60
Newman Coll. Cl. B32: Bart G 5A 130
Newman Ct. B21: Hand 6A 82
Newman Pl. WV14: Bils 4H 45
Newman Rd. B24: Erd 3F 85
DY4: Tip 4C 62
WV10: Bush 6C 16
Newmans Cl. B66: Smeth 5G 99
Newman Way B45: Redn 2G 157
Newmarket Cl. WV6: Wolv 4E 27
Newmarket Rd. WS11: Nort C 1E 9
New Mkt. St. B3: Birm 6F 101 (3C 4)
Newmarket Way B36: Hodg H 1H 103
Newmarsh Rd. B76: Walm 1E 87
New Mdw. Cl. B31: N'fld 5F 145
New Meeting St. B4: Birm 1G 117 (4F 5)
B69: O'bry 1G 97
New Mills St. WS1: Wals 4B 48
New Mill St. DY2: Dud 6E 77
Newmore Gdns. WS5: Wals 6G 49
New Moseley Rd. B12: Birm 3A 118
Newnham Gro. B23: Erd 1E 85
Newnham Ho. B36: Cas B 4D 106
Newnham Ri. B90: Shir 4B 150
Newnham Rd. B16: Edg 1G 115
NEW OSCOTT 4C 68

208 A-Z Birmingham Deluxe

New Pool Rd.—Oak La.

New Pool Rd. B64: Crad H 3D 110
Newport Rd. B12: Bal H 1A 134
B36: Hodg H 1D 104
Newport St. WS1: Wals 2C 48
WV10: Wolv 5A 28
Newquay Cl. WS5: Wals 4A 50
Newquay Rd. WS5: Wals 4H 49
New Railway St. WV13: W'hall 1B 46
New Rd. B18: Win G 3A 100
B45: Rubery 2F 157
B46: Wat O 4D 88
B47: H'wd 1H 161
B63: Hale 1B 128
B91: Sol 4G 151
DY2: Dud, Neth 3E 95
DY3: Swind 4A 72
DY4: Tip 1D 78
DY8: Stourb 6E 109
WS8: Bwnhls 6B 10
WS9: A'rdge 4C 34
WS10: Darl 5D 46
WV6: Wolv 5C 26
WV10: Bush 1D 28
WV13: W'hall 2A 46
New Rowley Rd. DY2: Dud 2G 95
New Royal Briery Experience, The 4F 77
New Shipton Cl. B76: Walm 4D 70
New Spring St. B18: Hock 5C 100
New Spring St. Nth. B18: Hock 4C 100
Newstead Rd. B44: K'sdng 2A 68
New St. B2: Birm 1F 117 (4D 4)
B23: Erd 2F 85
B36: Cas B 1F 105
B45: Fran 5F 143
B66: Smeth 3E 99
B70: W Brom 6G 63
(Norbury Rd.)
B70: W Brom 4B 80
(St Michael St.)
DY1: Dud 6E 77
DY3: Gorn 4G 75
DY4: Tip 2H 77
DY5: Quar B 3C 110
DY6: K'wfrd 5B 92
DY6: W Hth 1A 92
DY8: Stourb 6D 108
DY8: Word 1B 108
WS1: Wals 2D 48
WS3: Blox 6H 19
WS4: Rus 2F 33
WS4: S'fld 6H 21
WS6: Gt Wyr 3G 7
WS10: Darl 5D 46
WS10: W'bry 4F 63
WV2: E'shll 5C 44
WV3: Wolv 4B 42
WV4: E'shll 6A 44
WV11: Ess 4A 18
WV13: W'hall 2G 45
New St. Nth. B71: W Brom 4B 80
New Street Station (Rail) 1F 117 (5D 4)
New Summer St. B19: Birm 5F 101
New Swan La. B70: W Brom 2G 79
New Swinford Hall DY9: Lye 1G 125
NEWTON 5G 65
Newton Av. B74: S Cold 4H 53
Newton Chambers *B2: Birm 4D 4*
(off Cannon St.)
Newton Cl. B43: Gt Barr 4G 65
Newton Ct. WV9: Pend 4D 14
Newton Gdns. B43: Gt Barr 5G 65
Newton Gro. B29: S Oak 3B 132
Newton Ho. WV13: W'hall 2B 46
Newton Ind. Est.
B9: Bord G 1D 118
Newton Mnr. Cl.
B43: Gt Barr 5H 65
Newton Pl. B18: Hock 2B 100
WS2: Wals 3H 31
Newton Rd. B11: S'hll 6B 118
B43: Gt Barr 5G 65
B71: W Brom 1C 80
B93: Know 2D 166
WS2: Wals 4H 31
Newton Sq. B43: Gt Barr 4A 66
Newton St. B4: Birm 6G 101 (2F 5)
B71: W Brom 6C 64
NEW TOWN
Brownhills 4D 10
West Bromwich 3E 79
NEWTOWN
Birmingham 3F 101
Great Wyrley 2G 19
Netherton 1E 111
New Town DY5: Brie H 5G 93
(not continuous)
Newtown DY2: Neth 2E 111
Newtown Dr. B19: Hock 3E 101
Newtown La. B62: Roms 6C 142
B64: Crad H 2F 111
Newtown Middleway B6: Birm 4G 101
NEW TOWN ROW 3G 101
New Town Row B6: Aston 3G 101
Newtown Shop. Cen. B19: Hock 3G 101
Newtown St. B64: Crad H 1F 111
New Village DY2: Neth 2E 111
New Villas WV11: Wed 4C 28
New Wood Cl. DY7: Stourt 3A 108
New Wood Dr. B31: Longb 6B 144
New Wood Gro. WS9: Wals W 4C 22
Next Generation Health Club 5H 93
Ney Ct. DY4: Tip 5H 77
Niall Cl. B15: Edg 3A 116
Nicholas Rd. B74: S'tly 3G 51
Nicholds Cl. WV14: Cose 4D 60
Nicholls Fold WV11: Wed 4F 29
Nicholls Rd. DY4: Tip 4G 61
Nicholls St. B70: W Brom 5C 80
Nichols Cl. B92: Sol 6B 138
Nigel Av. B31: N'fld 2E 145
Nigel Ct. B16: Edg 2A 116
Nigel Rd. B8: Salt 3E 103
DY1: Dud 5C 76
Nightingale Av. B36: Cas B 1C 106
Nightingale Cl. B23: Erd 6C 68
Nightingale Ct. B91: Sol 3G 151
Nightingale Cres. DY5: Brie H 4H 109
WV12: W'hall 1B 30
Nightingale Dr. DY4: Tip 2C 78
Nightingale Pl. WV14: Bils 5F 45
Nightingale Wlk. B15: Edg 4E 117
Nightjar Gro. B23: Erd 1C 84
Nighwood Dr. B74: S'tly 4H 51
Nijon Cl. B21: Hand 6G 81
Nimmings Cl. B31: Longb 3D 158
Nimmings Rd. B62: B'hth 3D 112
Nineacres Dr. B37: F'bri 1C 122
Nine Elms La. WV10: Wolv 4A 28
Nine Leasowes B66: Smeth 2C 98
Nine Locks Ridge DY5: Brie H 1H 109
Nine Pails Wlk. B70: W Brom 6B 80
Ninestiles Community Leisure Cen. 4H 135
Nineveh Av. B21: Hand 2B 100
Nineveh Rd. B21: Hand 2A 100
Ninfield Rd. B27: A Grn 2G 135
Nith Pl. DY1: Dud 5D 76
Noakes Ct. WS10: Darl 4F 47
Nocke Rd. WV11: Wed 6H 17
Nock St. DY4: Tip 6C 62
Noddy Pk. WS9: A'rdge 2D 34
Noddy Pk. Rd. WS9: A'rdge 2D 34
Noel Av. B12: Bal H 5A 118
Noel Rd. B16: Edg 2B 116
Nolton Cl. B43: Gt Barr 5H 65
Nook, The DY5: P'ntt 4F 93
WS6: C Hay 4C 6
Nooklands Cft. B33: Yard 1E 121
Noose Cres. WV13: W'hall 1G 45
Noose La. WV13: W'hall 1G 45
Nora Rd. B11: S'hll 2C 134
Norbiton Rd. B44: K'sdng 5A 68
Norbreck Cl. B43: Gt Barr 4H 65
Norbury Av. WS3: Pels 4D 20
Norbury Cres. WV4: E'shll 1B 60
Norbury Dr. DY5: Brie H 2H 109
Norbury Gro. B92: Olton 2E 137
Norbury Rd. B44: Gt Barr 2H 67
B70: W Brom 6G 63
WV10: Wolv 3B 28
WV14: Bils 5H 45
Norcombe Gro. B90: M'path 4E 165
Nordley Rd. WV11: Wed 4E 29
Nordley Wlk. WV11: Wed 3E 29
Norfolk Av. B71: W Brom 6B 64
Norfolk Cl. B30: Stir 1D 146
Norfolk Ct. B16: Edg 2H 115
B29: W Cas 6F 131
Norfolk Cres. WS9: A'rdge 1D 34
Norfolk Dr. WS10: W'bry 1D 62
Norfolk Gdns. B75: S Cold 3H 53
Norfolk Gro. WS6: Gt Wyr 4F 7
Norfolk Ho. B23: Erd 2F 85
B30: K Nor 4C 146
Norfolk New Rd. WS2: Wals 5G 31
Norfolk Pl. WS2: Wals 4B 32
Norfolk Rd. B15: Edg 4H 115
B23: Erd 2F 85
B45: Fran 5F 143
B68: O'bry 4H 113
B75: S Cold 4H 53
DY2: Dud 2C 94
DY8: Woll 3B 108
WV3: Wolv 3E 43
Norfolk Twr. B18: Hock 4D 100
Norgrave Rd. B92: Sol 3G 137
Norlan Dr. B14: K Hth 4H 147
Norland Rd. B27: A Grn 2H 135
Norley Gro. B13: Mose 6C 134
Norley Trad. Est. B33: Sheld 2G 121
Norman Av. B32: Harb 4C 114
Normandy Rd. B20: Hand 6F 83
Norman Green Athletics Cen. 4E 151
Norman Rd. B31: N'fld 4F 145
B67: Smeth 2B 114
WS5: Wals 3G 49
Normansell Twr. B6: Aston 1B 102
Norman St. B18: Win G 4A 100
DY2: Dud 1F 95
Norman Ter. B65: Row R 5C 96
Normanton Av. B26: Sheld 6H 121
Normanton Twr. B23: Erd 1G 85
Normid Ct. *B31: N'fld 3G 145*
(off Bunbury Rd.)
Norrington Gro. B31: N'fld 4A 144
Norrington Rd. B31: N'fld 4A 144
Norris Dr. B33: Stech 6D 104
Norris Rd. B6: Aston 6H 83
Norris Way B75: S Cold 6B 54
Northampton St. B18: Birm 5E 101
Northam Wlk. WV6: Wolv 5F 27
Northanger Rd. B27: A Grn 3H 135
North Av. B40: Nat E C 6G 123
WV11: Wed 3E 29
Northbrook Ct. B90: Shir 2A 150
Northbrook Rd. B90: Shir 2A 150
Northbrook St. B16: Birm 5B 100
Northcote Rd. B33: Stech 5B 104
Northcote St. WS2: Wals 5B 32
Northcott Rd. DY2: Neth 5F 95
WV14: Bils 1G 61
North Cres. WV10: F'stne 1D 16
North Dale WV6: Tett 5H 25
Northdown Rd. B91: Sol 6D 150
North Dr. B5: Edg 6E 117
B20: Hand 1D 100
B75: S Cold 5A 54
NORTHFIELD 4E 145
Northfield Gro. WV3: Wolv 4A 42
Northfield Pool & Fitness Cen. 4E 145
Northfield Rd. B17: Harb 2E 131
B30: K Nor 3H 145
DY2: Neth 4F 95
Northfield Station (Rail) 5E 145
Northfields Way WS8: Clay 1H 21
North Ga. B17: Harb 4G 115
Northgate B64: Crad H 3F 111
WS9: A'rdge 5C 22
Northgate Way WS9: A'rdge 1C 34
North Grn. WV4: Penn 5B 42
North Holme B9: Bord G 1C 118
Northicote Recreation & Community Cen. 4A 16
Northland Rd. B90: Shir 6C 150
Northlands Rd. B13: Mose 4A 134
Northleach Av. B14: K Hth 5F 147
Northleigh Rd. B8: W End 3G 103
Northmead B33: Yard 1E 121
Northolt Dr. B35: Cas V 4E 87
Northolt Gro. B42: Gt Barr 4B 66
North One M. DY3: Sed 4G 59
North Oval DY3: Up Gor 2A 76
Northover Cl. WV9: Pend 5E 15
North Pk. Rd. B23: Erd 3B 84
North Pathway B17: Harb 4F 115
North Rd. B17: Harb 5H 115
B20: Hand 5G 83
B29: S Oak 2B 132
DY4: Tip 5B 62
WV1: Wolv 5G 27
North Roundhay B33: Kitts G 5E 105
Northside Bus. Cen.
B18: Win G 4A 100
Northside Dr. B74: S'tly 3H 51
North Solihull Sports Cen. 6C 106
Nth. Springfield DY3: Sed 4A 60
North St. B67: Smeth 4D 98
DY2: Dud 6F 77
DY5: Brie H 1G 109
WS2: Wals 5C 32
WS10: W'bry 1F 63
WV1: Wolv 1G 43 (2B 170)
(not continuous)
North St. Ind. Est. DY5: Brie H 1G 109
Northumberland St. B7: Birm 6A 102
North Vw. Dr. DY5: Brie H 4H 93
North Wlk. B31: N'fld 6G 145
Nth. Warwick St. B9: Small H 2D 118
Northway B40: Nat E C 5H 123
DY3: Sed 2G 59
(Alderdale Av.)
DY3: Sed 4F 59
(Sunningdale Rd.)
Nth. Western Arc. B2: Birm 6G 101 (3E 5)
Nth. Western Rd. B66: Smeth 3D 98
Nth. Western Ter. B18: Hock 2B 100
Northwick Cres. B91: Sol 6F 151
Northwood Ct. DY5: Brie H 1H 109
Northwood Pk. Cl. WV10: Bush 4H 15
Northwood Pk. Rd.
WV10: Bush 4A 16
Northwood St. B3: Birm 5E 101 (2B 4)
Northwood Way DY5: Brie H 3F 109
North Yd. B9: Birm 6H 5
Northycote Farm Country Pk. 4C 16
Northycote La. WV10: Bush 3B 16
NORTON 3C 124
NORTON CANES 1E 9
Norton Cl. B31: N'fld 4E 145
B66: Smeth 4G 99
WV4: Penn 2A 58
Norton Cres. B9: Bord G 6H 103
DY2: Neth 6G 95
WV14: Cose 4F 61
Norton Dr. B47: Wyt 5C 162
Norton E. Rd. WS11: Nort C 1E 9
Norton Ga. B38: K Nor 6A 146
Norton Grange WS11: Nort C 1D 8
Norton Grange Cres. WS11: Nort C 1D 8
NORTON GREEN 2D 8
Norton Grn. La. B93: Know 6E 167
WS11: Nort C 1C 8
Norton Hall La. WS11: Nort C 1B 8
Norton La. B47: Tid G, Wyt 5C 162
B94: Earls 6E 163
WS6: Gt Wyr 1G 7
WS11: Cann, Nort C 1B 8
Norton Rd. B46: Col 6H 89
DY8: Stourb 4B 124
WS3: Pels 1E 21
Norton St. B18: Hock 4C 100
Norton Ter. *B30: Stir 1D 146*
(off Warren Rd.)
Norton Twr. B1: Birm 4A 4
Norton Vw. B14: K Hth 6F 133
Norton Wlk. B23: Erd 4C 84
Nortune Cl. B38: K Nor 5H 145
Norwich Cft. B37: Mars G 2B 122
Norwich Dr. B17: Harb 3D 114
Norwich Rd. DY2: Neth 1F 111
WS2: Wals 2H 47
Norwood Av. B64: Crad H 4G 111
Norwood Gro. B19: Hock 2D 100
Norwood Rd. B9: Bord G 1E 119
DY5: Brie H 5G 93
Nottingham Dr. WV12: W'hall 2C 30
Nottingham New Rd.
WS2: Wals 4G 31
Nottingham Way DY5: Quar B 1B 110
Nova Ct. B43: Gt Barr 4D 66
Nova Scotia St. B4: Birm 6H 101 (3G 5)
Nowell St. WS10: Darl 6E 47
Nuffield Ho. B36: Cas B 1C 106
Nugent Cl. B6: Aston 2G 101
Nugent Gro. B90: Ches G 6B 164
Number 9 The Gallery 5A 4
Nursery Av. B12: Bal H 6H 117
WS9: A'rdge 4D 34
Nursery Cl. B30: K Nor 2B 146
Nursery Dr. B30: K Nor 2B 146
WV5: Wom 3F 73
Nursery Gdns. B90: Maj G 1E 163
DY8: Word 2D 108
WV8: Cod 3F 13
Nursery La. B74: Four O 1G 53
Nursery Rd. B15: Edg 5H 115
B19: Loz 3D 100
WS3: Blox 1H 31
Nursery St. WV1: Wolv 6G 27 (1B 170)
Nursery Vw. Cl. WS9: A'rdge 1G 51
Nursery Wlk. WV6: Tett 5B 26
NURTON 6A 24
Nurton Bank WV6: Nur 6A 24
Nutbush Dr. B31: N'fld 1B 144
Nutfield Wlk. B32: Harb 6D 114
Nutgrove Cl. B14: K Hth 6H 133
Nuthatch Dr. DY5: Brie H 4G 109
Nuthurst B75: S Cold 1F 71
Nuthurst Dr. WS11: Cann 1F 7
Nuthurst Gro. B14: K Hth 5H 147
B93: Ben H 5C 166
Nuthurst Rd. B31: Longb 3D 158
Nutley Dr. DY4: Tip 5D 62
Nutmeg Gro. WS1: Wals 1E 49
Nuttall Gro. B21: Hand 2G 99

O

Oak Av. B12: Bal H 6A 118
B70: W Brom 4H 79
WS2: Wals 6E 31
WS6: Gt Wyr 4G 7
Oak Bank B18: Hock 3C 100
Oak Barn Rd. B62: B'hth 3E 113
Oak Cl. B17: Harb 5E 115
DY4: Tip 4A 62
Oak Ct. B45: Redn 2A 158
B63: Hale 3H 127
B66: Smeth 1A 98
DY8: Stourb 1E 125
WS5: Wals 1E 65
Oak Cres. B69: Tiv 6B 78
WS3: Blox 3B 32
Oak Cft. B37: F'bri 6B 106
Oakcroft Rd. B13: Mose 6B 134
Oakdale Cl. B68: O'bry 1G 113
DY5: P'ntt 2F 93
Oakdale Rd. B36: Hodg H 1C 104
B68: O'bry 1G 113
Oakdale Trad. Est.
DY6: K'wfrd 6B 74
Oakdene Cl. WS6: C Hay 3D 6
Oak Dr. B23: Erd 6C 68
WV5: Seis 3A 56
OAKEN 5D 12
Oaken Covert WV8: Cod 5E 13
Oaken Dr. B91: Sol 2D 150
WV8: Cod, Oaken 5D 12
WV12: W'hall 2E 31
Oaken Grange WS6: Gt Wyr 4F 7
Oaken Gro. WV8: Cod 5E 13
Oakenhayes Cres. B76: Min 2G 87
WS8: Bwnhls 4B 10
Oakenhayes Dr.
WS8: Bwnhls 4B 10
Oaken La. WV8: Oaken 4C 12
Oaken Lanes WV8: Cod 4E 13
Oaken Pk. WV8: Cod 5G 13
Oakenshaw Rd. B90: Shir 6B 150
Oakeswell St. WS10: W'bry 2G 63
Oakeywell St. DY2: Dud 6F 77
OAKFARM 6C 74
Oak Farm Cl. B76: Walm 6E 71
Oak Farm Rd. B30: B'vlle 2H 145
Oakfield Av. B11: S'brk 5C 118
B12: Bal H 5A 118
B21: Hand 2H 99
DY1: Dud 6D 60
DY6: K'wfrd 4C 92
Oakfield Cl. B66: Smeth 3G 99
DY8: Word 2D 108
Oakfield Ct. *DY5: Brie H 1H 109*
(off Promenade, The)
Oakfield Dr. B45: Coft H 5B 158
WS3: Pels 2F 21
Oakfield Rd. B12: Bal H 6G 117
B24: Erd 4F 85
B29: S Oak 2C 132
B66: Smeth 3G 99
DY8: Word 2E 109
DY9: W'cte 3B 126
WV8: Bilb 5H 13
Oakfields Way B91: Cath B 2D 152
Oak Grn. DY1: Dud 2C 76
WV6: Tett 6H 25
Oak Grn. Way B68: O'bry 5G 97
Oak Gro. B31: Longb 6C 144
WV11: Wed 2D 28
Oakhall Dr. B93: Dorr 5B 166
OAKHAM 2B 96
Oakham Av. DY2: Dud 2G 95
Oakham Ct. DY2: Dud 1G 95
Oakham Cres. DY2: Dud 2G 95
Oakham Dr. DY2: Dud 1H 95
Oakham Rd. B17: Harb 4F 115
B69: Tiv 1G 95
DY2: Dud 1G 95
Oakham Way B92: Olton 4E 137
Oak Hill WV3: Wolv 3A 42
Oakhill Cl. B17: Harb 3F 115
Oakhill Cres. B27: A Grn 5H 135
Oak Hill Dr. B15: Edg 4A 116
Oakhill Dr. DY5: Brie H 4F 109
Oak Ho. WS6: Gt Wyr 4G 7
Oak House Mus. 5H 79
Oakhurst Rd. B27: A Grn 4H 135
B72: W Grn 5H 69
Oak Ind. Pk. DY6: K'wfrd 6C 74
Oakington Ho. B35: Cas V 4E 87
Oakland Cl. B91: Sol 3A 152
Oakland Dr. DY3: Gorn 5F 75
Oakland Rd. B13: Mose 2A 134
B21: Hand 1A 100
(not continuous)
WS3: Blox 2C 32
Oaklands B31: N'fld 3D 144
B62: Quin 1G 129
B76: Curd 1D 88
Oaklands, The
B37: Mars G 4C 122
WV3: Wolv 3F 43
Oaklands Av. B17: Harb 6F 115
Oaklands Cft. B76: Walm 6F 71
Oaklands Dr. B20: Hand 5B 82
B74: S'tly 2H 51
Oaklands Grn. WV14: Bils 3F 45
Oaklands Rd. B74: Four O 3H 53
WV3: Wolv 3F 43
Oaklands Sports & Social Cen. 1H 99
Oaklands Way B31: Longb 6H 143
WS3: Pels 4F 21
Oak La. B70: W Brom 4H 79
B92: Bars 6B 154
DY6: K'wfrd 6C 74

A-Z Birmingham Deluxe 209

Oaklea Dr.—Overend Rd.

Oaklea Dr. B64: Old H . . . 1H 111
Oakleaf Cl. B32: Bart G. . . . 3B 130
Oak Leaf Dr. B13: Mose . . . 2A 134
Oak Leasow B32: Quin . . . 1H 129
Oakleigh B31: N'fld. . . . 5G 145
Oakleigh Dr. DY3: Sed . . . 6G 59
WV8: Bilb . . . 4G 13
Oakleigh Rd. DY8: Stourb. . . . 3E 125
Oakleighs DY8: Word . . . 2A 108
Oakleigh Wlk. DY6: K'wfrd . . . 1C 92
Oakley Av. DY4: Tip . . . 1A 78
WS9: A'rdge . . . 4C 34
Oakley Cl. WV4: Penn. . . . 6B 42
Oakley Ct. B15: Edg . . . 6A 116
Oakley Gro. WV4: Penn . . . 6B 42
Oakley Rd. B10: Small H . . . 4C 118
(not continuous)
B30: Stir . . . 2D 146
WV4: Penn . . . 6B 42
Oak Leys WV3: Wolv. . . . 2A 42
Oakley Wood Dr. B91: Sol . . . 3A 152
Oakmeadow Av. B24: Erd . . . 4B 86
Oakmeadow Cl. B26: Yard . . . 6B 120
B33: Kitts G . . . 1H 121
Oakmeadow Way B24: Erd . . . 4B 86
Oakmount Cl. WS3: Pels . . . 4D 20
Oak Mt. Rd. B74: S'tly . . . 4A 52
Oak Pk. Ct. *B74: Four O . . . 6E 37*
(off Walsall Rd.)
Oak Pk. Leisure Cen. . . . 3B 22
Oak Pk. Rd. DY8: Word . . . 2D 108
Oakridge Cl. WV12: W'hall . . . 5C 30
Oakridge Dr. WS6: C Hay . . . 3F 7
WV12: W'hall . . . 5C 30
Oakridge Rd. B31: N'fld . . . 5H 145
Oak Ri. B46: Col . . . 4H 107
Oak Rd. B68: O'bry . . . 4H 113
B70: W Brom . . . 5H 79
DY1: Dud . . . 4E 77
DY4: Tip . . . 6G 61
WS3: Pels . . . 2D 20
WS4: S'fld . . . 6G 21
WS9: Wals W . . . 4C 22
WV13: W'hall . . . 1G 45
Oaks, The B17: Harb . . . 3F 115
B34: S End . . . 2F 105
B38: K Nor . . . 2B 160
B67: Smeth . . . 4D 98
B72: W Grn . . . 6H 69
B76: Walm . . . 2E 71
WS3: Blox . . . 6G 19
WS3: Wolv . . . 1E 43
Oaks Cres. WV3: Wolv . . . 2E 43
Oaks Dr. WV3: Wolv . . . 1E 43
WV5: Wom . . . 2G 73
Oakslade Dr. B92: Sol. . . . 5A 138
Oak St. B64: Crad H . . . 2F 111
DY2: Neth . . . 5G 95
DY5: Quar B . . . 2B 110
DY6: K'wfrd . . . 4A 92
WV3: Wolv . . . 2E 43
WV14: Cose . . . 6D 60
Oak St. Ind. Est. *B64: Crad H . . . 2F 111*
(off Oak St.)
Oak St. Trad. Est. DY5: Quar B. . . . 2B 110
Oakthorpe Dr. B37: K'hrst. . . . 4B 106
Oakthorpe Gdns. B69: Tiv. . . . 5A 78
Oak Tree Cl. B93: Ben H . . . 5A 166
Oak Tree Ct. B28: Hall G . . . 2G 149
B70: W Brom . . . 4H 79
Oaktree Cres. B62: Quin . . . 5F 113
Oak Tree Dr. B8: Salt . . . 3D 102
Oak Tree Gdns. B28: Hall G . . . 4E 149
DY8: Word . . . 2E 109
Oak Tree La. B29: S Oak. . . . 4A 132
B47: H'wd . . . 3B 162
Oaktree Ri. WV8: Cod . . . 3E 13
Oaktree Rd. WS10: W'bry . . . 2H 63
Oak Trees B47: H'wd . . . 3H 161
Oak Vw. WS2: Wals. . . . 6E 31
Oak Wlk., The B31: Longb . . . 6E 145
Oak Way B76: Walm . . . 3D 70
Oakwood Cl. WS9: Wals W. . . . 3A 22
WV11: Ess . . . 4B 18
Oakwood Cres. DY2: Dud . . . 3B 94
Oakwood Cft. B91: Sol . . . 6G 151
Oakwood Dr. B14: K Hth . . . 3F 147
B74: S'tly . . . 3G 51
Oakwood Rd. B11: S'hll . . . 2C 134
B47: H'wd . . . 3A 162
B67: Smeth. . . . 5D 98
B73: Bold . . . 3E 69
WS3: Blox. . . . 2C 32
Oakwood St. B70: W Brom. . . . 2H 79
Oast Ho. B8: W End . . . 5A 104
Oasthouse Cl. DY6: W Hth. . . . 2G 91
Oaston Rd. B36: Cas B . . . 1H 105
Oatfield Cl. WS7: Chase. . . . 1C 10
Oatlands Wlk. B14: K Hth. . . . 5E 147
Oatlands Way WV6: Pert . . . 6D 24
Oat Mill Cl. WS10: W'bry . . . 6E 47
Oban Rd. B92: Olton. . . . 4D 136
Oberon Cl. B45: Fran . . . 5G 143
Oberon Dr. B90: Shir . . . 6G 149
Occupation Rd. WS8: Wals W . . . 3C 22
Occupation St. DY1: Dud . . . 5C 76
Ocean Dr. WS10: W'bry . . . 4D 62
Ockam Cft. B31: N'fld. . . . 5G 145
OCKER HILL . . . 5C 62
Ocker Hill Rd. DY4: Tip . . . 4B 62
O'Connor Dr. DY4: Tip . . . 4C 62
Oddingley Ct. B23: Erd . . . 4C 84
Oddingley Rd. B31: N'fld . . . 5G 145
Odell Cres. WS3: Blox . . . 2A 32
Odell Pl. B5: Edg. . . . 6E 117
Odell Rd. WS3: Blox. . . . 2H 31
Odell Way WS3: Blox . . . 2H 31
Odensil Grn. B92: Sol . . . 3F 137
Odeon Cinema . . . 1G 117 (5E 5)
Offa's Dr. WV6: Pert . . . 4E 25
Offenham Covert B38: K Nor . . . 1A 160
Offini Cl. B70: W Brom. . . . 5D 80
Offmoor Rd. B32: Bart G. . . . 5H 129
Ogbury Cl. B14: K Hth. . . . 5E 147
Oglay Hay Rd. WS7: Chase . . . 3C 10
Ogley Cres. WS8: Bwnhls. . . . 6C 10
Ogley Dr. B75: S Cold. . . . 6D 54
Ogley Hay Rd. WS8: Bwnhls . . . 3C 10
Ogley Rd. WS8: Bwnhls . . . 6C 10
O'Hare Ho. WS4: Wals . . . 6D 32
O'Keeffe Cl. B11: S'brk. . . . 5B 118
Okehampton Dr. B71: W Brom . . . 1A 80
Okement Dr. WV11: Wed . . . 4D 28
Old Abbey Gdns. B17: Harb . . . 1H 131
Oldacre Cl. B76: Walm . . . 1B 86
Old Acre Dr. B21: Hand. . . . 2A 100
Oldacre Rd. B68: O'bry . . . 4G 113
Old Bank Pl. B72: S Cold . . . 6A 54
Old Bank Top B31: N'fld . . . 5F 145
Old Barn Rd. B30: B'vlle. . . . 1H 145
DY8: Word . . . 2E 109
Old Beeches B23: Erd. . . . 5C 68
Old Bell Rd. B23: Erd . . . 1H 85
Oldberrow Cl. B90: M'path . . . 3E 165
Old Birchills WS2: Wals . . . 6A 32
Old Birmingham Rd. B45: Lick. . . . 6F 157
Old Bri. St. B19: Hock. . . . 3E 101
Old Bri. Wlk. B65: Row R. . . . 4H 95
Old Bromford La. B8: W End . . . 2H 103
Old Brookside B33: Stech. . . . 1C 120
OLDBURY . . . 1G 97
Oldbury Bus. Cen. B68: O'bry . . . 1G 113
Oldbury Grn. Retail Pk. B69: O'bry . . . 1F 97
Oldbury Leisure Cen. . . . 3D 96
Oldbury Ringway B69: O'bry. . . . 1F 97
Oldbury Rd. B65: Row R . . . 1D 112
B66: Smeth. . . . 2A 98
B70: W Brom . . . 4E 79
Oldbury Rd. Ind. Est. B66: Smeth . . . 2B 98
B70: W Brom . . . 5F 79
Oldbury St. WS10: W'bry . . . 2H 63
Old Bush St. DY5: Brie H . . . 6A 94
Old Camp Hill B11: S'brk . . . 3A 118
Old Canal Wlk. DY4: Tip. . . . 2B 78
Old Castle Gro. WS8: Bwnhls. . . . 3B 10
Old Chapel, The B3: Birm . . . 6F 101 (2C 4)
Old Chapel Rd. B67: Smeth . . . 6D 98
Old Chapel Wlk. B68: O'bry . . . 5G 97
Old Chu. Av. B17: Harb. . . . 6G 115
Old Chu. Grn. B33: Stech . . . 1C 120
Old Chu. Rd. B17: Harb. . . . 6F 115
B46: Wat O . . . 4D 88
Old Ct. Cft. B9: Bord G . . . 2C 118
Old Cft. La. B34: S End . . . 1F 105
B36: Cas B . . . 1F 105
Old Cross B4: Birm . . . 2G 5
Old Cross St. DY4: Tip . . . 2G 77
Old Crown Cl. B32: Bart G . . . 4H 129
Old Damson La. B92: Sol. . . . 3B 138
Old Dickens Heath Rd. B90: Dic H. . . . 4G 163
Old Edwardians Sports Club . . . 1A 150
Olde Hall La. WS6: Gt Wyr. . . . 1F 7
Olde Hall Rd. WV10: F'stne . . . 1E 17
Old End La. WV14: Cose. . . . 6E 61
Old Fails Cl. WS6: C Hay . . . 2D 6
OLD FALLINGS . . . 1B 28
Old Fallings Cres. WV10: Bush . . . 2A 28
Old Fallings La. WV10: Bush . . . 6B 16
Old Farm Dr. WV8: Bilb . . . 3G 13
Old Farm Gro. B14: Yard W . . . 2D 148
Old Farm Mdw. WV3: Wolv . . . 3A 42
Old Farm Rd. B33: Stech . . . 5C 104
Oldfield Dr. DY8: Stourb. . . . 2E 125
Oldfield Rd. B12: Bal H. . . . 5A 118
WV14: Cose . . . 5C 60
Oldfields B64: Crad H . . . 3F 111
Oldfield Trad. Est. B64: Crad H. . . . 3F 111
Old Fire Sta., The B17: Harb . . . 5H 115
Old Flour Mills B70: W Brom. . . . 5A 80
Old Fordrove B76: Walm. . . . 2B 70
Old Forest Way B34: S End. . . . 3F 105
Old Forge Cl. WS1: Wals . . . 3D 48
Old Forge Trad. Est. DY9: Lye . . . 5A 110
Old Grange Rd. B11: S'hll. . . . 1C 134
Old Grn. La. B93: Know . . . 6B 168
Old Gro. Gdns. DY9: W'cte. . . . 2H 125
Old Hall Cl. DY8: Amb . . . 3E 109
Old Hall Ind. Est. WS3: Blox . . . 1A 32
Old Hall La. WS9: A'rdge . . . 6D 50
Old Hall St. WV1: Wolv . . . 2H 43 (4C 170)
Old Ham La. DY9: Pedm . . . 3G 125
Old Hampton La. WV10: Bush . . . 5D 16
Old Hawne La. B63: Hale . . . 6A 112
Old Heath Cres. WV1: Wolv . . . 2C 44
Old Heath Rd. WV1: Wolv . . . 2C 44
Old High St. DY5: Quar B . . . 2B 110
OLD HILL . . . 3B 112
Old Hill WV6: Tett. . . . 4B 26
Old Hill By-Pass B64: Old H. . . . 1H 111
Old Hill Station (Rail) . . . 3A 112
Old Hobicus La. B68: O'bry . . . 4H 97
Old Horns Cres. B43: Gt Barr . . . 3E 67
Oldhouse Farm Cl. B28: Hall G. . . . 1F 149
Old Ho. La. B62: Roms. . . . 6B 142
Oldington Gro. B91: Sol . . . 1F 165
Old Kingsbury Rd. B76: Min. . . . 2G 87
Oldknow Rd. B10: Small H . . . 5E 119
Old Landywood La. WV11: Ess . . . 1C 18
Old La. WS3: Blox. . . . 2A 32
WV6: Tett. . . . 1F 41
Old Langley Hall B75: S Cold . . . 1F 71
Old Level Way DY2: Neth. . . . 5F 95
Old Lime Gdns. B38: K Nor . . . 1A 160
Old Lindens Cl. B74: S'tly . . . 4G 51
Old Lode La. B92: Sol. . . . 1F 137
Old Mnr., The WV6: Tett. . . . 4B 26
Old Masters Cl. WS1: Wals . . . 2E 49
Old Mdw. Rd. B31: Longb . . . 2G 159
Old Meeting Rd. WV14: Cose . . . 5E 61
Old Meeting St. B70: W Brom . . . 2H 79
(not continuous)
Old Mill Cl. B90: Shir . . . 5D 148
Old Mill Ct. B46: Col. . . . 2H 107
Old Mill Gdns. B33: Stech . . . 1C 120
WS4: S'fld . . . 5G 21
Old Mill Gro. B20: Hand . . . 5E 83
Old Mill House Cl. WS4: S'fld. . . . 6F 21
Old Mill Rd. B46: Col . . . 2H 107
Old Moat Dr. B31: N'fld . . . 4F 145
Old Moat Way B8: W End. . . . 3H 103
OLD MOXLEY . . . 1A 62
Oldnall Cl. DY9: W'cte . . . 1B 126
Oldnall Rd. B63: Crad. . . . 1B 126
DY9: W'cte . . . 1B 126
Old Oak Cl. WS9: A'rdge. . . . 1D 34
Old Oak Rd. B38: K Nor . . . 5C 146
OLD OSCOTT . . . 4G 67
Old Oscott Hill B44: Gt Barr . . . 4G 67
Old Oscott La. B44: Gt Barr . . . 5G 67
Old Pk. B31: N'fld . . . 2E 145
Old Pk. Cl. B6: Aston . . . 2G 101
Old Pk. La. B69: O'bry . . . 4G 97
Old Pk. Rd. DY1: Dud . . . 3B 76
WS10: Darl, W'bry . . . 5E 47
Old Pk. Trad. Est. WS10: W'bry . . . 1E 63
Old Pk. Wlk. B6: Aston. . . . 2G 101
Old Penns La. B46: Col . . . 2H 107
Old Pl. WS3: Blox . . . 1A 32
Old Pleck Rd. WS2: Wals. . . . 3H 47
Old Port Cl. DY4: Tip . . . 5B 78
Old Portway B38: K Nor . . . 2A 160
Old Postway B19: Loz . . . 2F 101
Old Quarry Cl. B45: Rubery . . . 1F 157
Old Quarry Dr. DY3: Up Gor. . . . 2H 75
Old Rectory Gdns. WS9: A'rdge . . . 3E 35
Old Repertory Theatre, The . . . 1F 117 (5D 4)
Old School Cl. WV13: W'hall . . . 1A 46
Old School Dr. B65: Row R . . . 6B 96
Old Scott Cl. B33: Kitts G. . . . 1G 121
Old Snow Hill B4: Birm . . . 5F 101 (1D 4)
Old Sq. B4: Birm . . . 6G 101 (3F 5)
Old Sq. Shop. Pct. WS1: Wals . . . 2C 48
Old Stables Wlk. B7: Nech . . . 2C 102
Old Sta. Rd. B33: Stech . . . 5B 104
B92: H Ard . . . 3H 139
Old Stone Cl. B45: Fran. . . . 6F 143
Old Stow Heath La. WV1: Wolv . . . 2E 45
OLD SWINFORD . . . 3E 125
Old Tokengate B17: Harb . . . 5H 115
Old Town Cl. B38: K Nor. . . . 5B 146
Old Town La. WS3: Pels . . . 4D 20
Old Union Mill B16: Birm. . . . 1D 116
Old Vicarage Cl. WS3: Pels . . . 5E 21
WV5: Wom . . . 6H 57
Old Walsall Rd. B42: P Barr. . . . 1B 82
Old Warstone La. WV11: Ess . . . 5B 6
Old Warwick Ct. B92: Olton . . . 4C 136
Old Warwick Rd. B92: Olton. . . . 4C 136
Oldway Dr. B91: Sol . . . 5A 152
Old Well Cl. WS4: Rus . . . 2F 33
Old Wharf Rd. DY8: Amb . . . 5D 108
Olga Dr. DY4: Tip . . . 4B 62
Olinthus Av. WV11: Wed . . . 2G 29
Olive Av. WV4: E'shll. . . . 6A 44
Olive Dr. B62: B'hth . . . 3C 112
Olive Hill Rd. B62: B'hth . . . 3D 112
Olive La. B62: B'hth . . . 3C 112
Olive Mt. B69: O'bry. . . . 1D 96
Olive Pl. B14: K Hth. . . . 6H 133
Oliver Cl. DY2: Dud . . . 1G 95
Oliver Ct. B65: Row R. . . . 1B 112
Oliver Cres. WV14: Bils . . . 3G 61
Oliver Rd. B16: Birm. . . . 1B 116
B23: Erd . . . 1F 85
B66: Smeth. . . . 6G 99
Oliver St. B7: Birm . . . 4A 102
Ollerton Rd. B26: Yard . . . 4D 120
Ollison Dr. B74: S'tly . . . 1H 51
Olliver Cl. B62: Quin. . . . 2G 129
Olorenshaw Rd. B26: Sheld . . . 6H 121
OLTON . . . 4C 136
Olton Blvd. E. B27: A Grn. . . . 3G 135
Olton Blvd. W. B11: Tys . . . 2F 135
Olton Cft. B27: A Grn . . . 2H 135
Olton Mere B92: Olton. . . . 4C 136
Olton Rd. B90: Shir. . . . 3H 149
Olton Station (Rail) . . . 4C 136
Olton Wharf B92: Olton. . . . 3C 136
Olympus Dr. DY4: Tip. . . . 1D 78
Ombersley Cl. B69: O'bry. . . . 4D 96
Ombersley Rd. B12: Bal H . . . 5A 118
B63: Hale . . . 3H 127
Omersley Way B31: N'fld. . . . 5H 145
One Stop Shop. Cen. B42: P Barr. . . . 4F 83
Onibury Rd. B21: Hand. . . . 6F 81
Onslow Cres. B92: Olton. . . . 4E 137
Onslow Rd. B11: Tys . . . 1G 135
Ontario Cl. B38: K Nor . . . 1C 160
Oozells Sq. B1: Birm . . . 1E 117 (5A 4)
Oozells St. B1: Birm. . . . 1E 117 (5A 4)
Oozells St. Nth. B1: Birm . . . 1D 116 (5A 4)
Open Fld. Cl. B31: N'fld . . . 5F 145
Openfield Cft. B46: Wat O. . . . 5E 89
Oracle Bldg. B90: Bly P . . . 6E 165
Oratory, The . . . 2B 116
Orchard, The B37: Mars G . . . 3B 122
B68: O'bry. . . . 5A 98
WS3: Blox. . . . 5B 20
WV6: Tett . . . 3C 26
WV14: Bils . . . 6G 45
Orchard Av. B91: Sol . . . 2H 151
Orchard Blythe B46: Col. . . . 3H 107
Orchard Cl. B21: Hand . . . 5B 82
B46: Col . . . 2H 107
B63: Crad . . . 5E 111
B65: Row R . . . 6A 96
B73: Bold . . . 5G 69
B76: Curd. . . . 1D 88
WS4: Rus. . . . 4G 33
WS6: C Hay. . . . 2E 7
WV3: Wolv . . . 4H 41
WV13: W'hall . . . 2B 46
Orchard Ct. B23: Erd. . . . 3B 84
(Marsh Hill)
B23: Erd . . . 2G 85
(Sutton Rd.)
B65: Row R . . . 6B 96
DY6: K'wfrd . . . 3B 92
Orchard Cres. WV3: Wolv. . . . 4H 41
Orchard Dr. B31: Longb . . . 2D 158
Orchard Gro. B74: Four O. . . . 6F 37
DY3: Lwr G . . . 4F 75
WS9: A'rdge . . . 5D 34
WV4: Penn . . . 1E 59
Orchard Ho. B24: Erd . . . 3F 85
Orchard La. WV8: Bilb . . . 4H 13
Orchard Mdw. Wlk. B35: Cas V . . . 4F 87
Orchard Ri. B26: Yard. . . . 4D 120
Orchard Rd. B12: Bal H . . . 5H 117
B24: Erd . . . 2G 85
DY2: Neth . . . 1E 111
WS5: Wals. . . . 2F 65
WV11: Wed. . . . 2E 29
WV13: W'hall . . . 2B 46
Orchards, The B47: H'wd . . . 2A 162
B74: Four O . . . 3G 53
B90: Ches G . . . 5B 164
Orchard St. DY4: Tip. . . . 5H 77
DY5: Brie H. . . . 5G 93
Orchards Way B12: Bal H . . . 5G 117
Orchard Way B27: A Grn . . . 1H 135
B43: Gt Barr . . . 4B 66
B47: H'wd . . . 1A 162
B64: Old H . . . 2H 111
Orcheston Wlk. B14: K Hth. . . . 6F 147
Orchid Cl. B66: Smeth . . . 2B 98
Oregon Cl. DY6: K'wfrd . . . 3D 92
Oregon Dr. WV12: W'hall . . . 2E 31
Orford Gro. B21: Hand . . . 1G 99
Oriel Cl. DY1: Dud . . . 5A 76
Oriel Dr. WV10: F'hses . . . 4H 15
Oriel Ho. B37: F'bri. . . . 6C 106
Oriel Vs. *B11: S'hll . . . 6C 118*
(off Warwick Rd.)
Orion Cl. B8: W End . . . 5H 103
WS6: Gt Wyr. . . . 4F 7
Orkney Av. B34: Hodg H . . . 3D 104
Orkney Cft. B36: Cas B . . . 2D 106
Orlando Cl. WS1: Wals . . . 3C 48
Orlando Ho. *WS1: Wals . . . 3D 48*
(off Barleyfield Row)
Orme Cl. DY5: Brie H . . . 3E 109
Ormes La. WV6: Tett. . . . 6A 26
Ormonde Cl. B63: Crad. . . . 4D 110
Ormond Pl. WV14: Bils. . . . 5H 45
Ormond Rd. B45: Fran . . . 6E 143
Ormsby Ct. B15: Edg. . . . 4A 116
Ormsby Gro. B27: A Grn. . . . 6H 135
Ormscliffe Rd. B45: Redn. . . . 3H 157
Orphanage Rd. B24: Erd. . . . 2G 85
B72: W Grn. . . . 1A 86
Orpington Rd. B44: Gt Barr . . . 2G 67
Orpwood Rd. B33: Yard. . . . 1E 121
Orslow Wlk. WV10: Wolv . . . 4C 28
ORTON . . . 2F 57
Orton Av. B76: Walm . . . 1D 86
Orton Cl. B46: Wat O . . . 4C 88
Orton Gro. WV4: Penn . . . 1B 58
Orton La. WV4: Lwr P. . . . 2F 57
WV5: Wom . . . 2F 57
Orton Way B35: Cas V. . . . 6E 87
Orwell Cl. DY8: Stourb . . . 1A 124
WV11: Wed. . . . 4H 29
Orwell Dr. B38: K Nor . . . 1F 159
B71: W Brom . . . 1B 80
Orwell Pas. B5: Birm. . . . 1G 117 (5F 5)
Orwell Rd. WS1: Wals. . . . 3F 49
Osberton Dr. DY1: Dud. . . . 5B 76
Osborn Ct. B73: W Grn. . . . 4H 69
Osborne Dr. WS10: Darl . . . 3D 46
Osborne Gro. B19: Loz . . . 2E 101
Osborne Rd. B21: Hand . . . 1B 100
B23: Erd . . . 2F 85
B70: W Brom . . . 4A 80
WV4: Penn . . . 6D 42
Osborne Rd. Sth. B23: Erd . . . 3F 85
Osborne Twr. B6: Aston . . . 1A 102
Osborn Rd. B11: S'brk . . . 5C 118
Osbourne Cl. B6: Aston . . . 2A 102
DY5: Quar B . . . 3B 110
Osbourne Cft. B90: Ches G. . . . 4B 164
Oscott Ct. B23: Erd . . . 5E 69
Oscott Gdns. B42: P Barr . . . 4G 83
Oscott Rd. B6: Witt. . . . 4G 83
B42: P Barr. . . . 4G 83
Oscott School La.
B44: Gt Barr . . . 3G 67
Osier Gro. B23: Erd. . . . 1B 84
Osier Pl. WV1: Wolv. . . . 1B 44
Osier St. WV1: Wolv. . . . 1B 44
Osler St. B16: Birm. . . . 1B 116
Osmaston Rd. B17: Harb . . . 2E 131
DY8: Stourb . . . 3C 124
Osmington Gro.
B63: Crad . . . 5F 111
Osprey Dr. DY1: Dud. . . . 6B 76
Osprey Rd. B23: Erd . . . 1C 84
B27: A Grn . . . 3B 136
Ostler Cl. DY6: W Hth. . . . 2G 91
Oswestry Ct. B11: S'brk . . . 5B 118
Oswin Pl. WS3: Wals . . . 4D 32
Oswin Rd. WS3: Wals. . . . 4D 32
Other Rd. B45: Coft H . . . 4A 158
Otley Gro. B9: Bord G. . . . 6A 104
Ottawa Twr. B5: Bal H . . . 4F 117
Otter Cft. B34: S End . . . 4H 105
Otterstone Cl. DY3: Sed . . . 3G 59
Oughton Rd. B12: Birm. . . . 4A 118
Oundle Rd. B44: K'sdng . . . 6H 67
OUNSDALE . . . 1E 73
Ounsdale Cres. WV5: Wom . . . 6G 57
Ounsdale Dr. DY2: Neth . . . 6E 95
Ounsdale Rd. WV5: Wom. . . . 6E 57
Ounty John La. DY8: Stourb . . . 5E 125
Outfields B14: K Hth. . . . 1G 147
Outmore Rd. B33: Sheld . . . 2F 121
Out Wood Dr. B31: Longb. . . . 6B 144
Oval, The B67: Smeth. . . . 6B 98
DY1: Dud . . . 1A 94
WS10: W'bry. . . . 1F 63
Oval Rd. B24: Erd . . . 6E 85
DY4: Tip . . . 6H 61
Overbrook Cl. DY3: Gorn . . . 5G 75
Over Brunton Cl. B31: N'fld. . . . 5F 145
Overbury Cl. B31: N'fld. . . . 4G 145
B63: Hale . . . 3B 128
Overbury Rd. B31: N'fld . . . 3G 145
Overdale Av. B76: Walm. . . . 2D 86
Overdale Cl. WS2: Wals . . . 6C 30
Overdale Ct. B13: Mose . . . 1H 133
Overdale Dr. WV13: W'hall. . . . 6C 30
Overdale Rd. B32: Quin . . . 1C 130
Overend Rd. B63: Crad . . . 4F 111
B64: Crad H. . . . 4F 111

210 A-Z Birmingham Deluxe

Overend St.—Passfield Rd.

Overend St. B70: W Brom . . . 4B 80
Overfield Dr. WV14: Cose. . . . 2C 60
Overfield Rd. B32: Bart G. . . . 4C 130
DY1: Dud . . . 1A 94
Over Grn. Dr. B37: K'hrst . . . 3B 106
Overhill Rd. WS7: Burn . . . 1C 10
Overlea Av. B27: A Grn. . . . 2H 135
Over Mill Dr. B29: S Oak . . . 3D 132
Over Moor Cl. B19: Loz. . . . 2E 101
Over Pool Rd. B8: W End . . . 3G 103
Overseal Rd. WV11: Wed. . . . 1G 29
Overslade Rd. B91: Sol . . . 6D 150
Oversley Rd. B76: Walm. . . . 1E 87
Overstrand WV9: Pend . . . 4D 14
Overton Cl. B28: Hall G. . . . 1G 149
Overton Dr. B46: Wat O. . . . 4E 89
Overton Gro. B27: A Grn. . . . 5A 136
Overton La. WS7: Hamm . . . 1E 11
Overton Pl. B7: Birm. . . . 6A 102
B71: W Brom . . . 1B 80
Overton Rd. B27: A Grn . . . 5H 135
Overton Wlk. WV4: Penn . . . 5A 42
Over Wood Cft. B8: Salt . . . 6D 102
Owen Pl. WV14: Bils. . . . 5F 45
Owen Rd. WV3: Wolv . . . 2E 43
WV13: W'hall . . . 2C 46
WV14: Bils . . . 4F 45
Owen Rd. Ind. Est. WV13: W'hall. . . . 2C 46
Owens Cft. B38: K Nor . . . 6C 146
Owen St. DY2: Dud. . . . 1G 95
DY4: Tip . . . 2G 77
WS10: Darl. . . . 4D 46
Owens Way B64: Old H. . . . 2A 112
Ownall Rd. B34: S End. . . . 3G 105
Oxbarn Av. WV3: Wolv . . . 5C 42
Oxenton Cft. B63: Hale . . . 3F 127
Oxford Cl. B8: W End . . . 4H 103
WS6: Gt Wyr. . . . 2F 7
Oxford Ct. B29: W Cas . . . 6G 131
Oxford Dr. B27: A Grn. . . . 1B 136
DY8: Stourb . . . 1D 124
Oxford Ho. B31: Longb. . . . 1D 158
Oxford Pas. DY1: Dud. . . . 6D 76
Oxford Rd. B13: Mose . . . 3H 133
B23: Erd . . . 3F 85
B27: A Grn . . . 2A 136
B66: Smeth. . . . 1E 99
(not continuous)
B70: W Brom . . . 4H 79
Oxford St. B5: Birm. . . . 2H 117 (6G 5)
B30: Stir. . . . 6C 132
DY1: Dud . . . 6D 76
WS2: Wals . . . 4A 48
WS10: W'bry . . . 2H 63
WV1: Wolv . . . 2A 44
WV14: Bils . . . 6G 45
Oxford St. Ind. Est.
WV14: Bils . . . 6H 45
Oxford Ter. WS10: W'bry . . . 3H 63
Oxford Way DY4: Tip. . . . 3F 77
Oxhayes Cl. CV7: Bal C. . . . 6H 169
Oxhill Rd. B21: Hand . . . 5G 81
B90: Shir. . . . 5C 148
Ox Leasow B32: Bart G. . . . 3A 130
OXLEY . . . 1F 27
Oxley Av. WV10: Oxl. . . . 3G 27
Oxley Cl. DY2: Neth . . . 1D 110
WS6: Gt Wyr. . . . 4F 7
Oxley Ct. Cvn. Pk.
WV10: Oxl. . . . 1E 27
Oxley Gro. B29: W Cas . . . 5E 131
Oxley La. WV1: Wolv . . . 6G 27
Oxley Links Rd.
WV10: Oxl . . . 1F 27
Oxley Moor Rd. WV9: Pend . . . 1E 27
WV10: Oxl. . . . 1E 27
Ox Leys Rd. B75: S Cold. . . . 1F 71
B76: Walm, Wis . . . 1F 71
Oxley St. WV1: Wolv . . . 5G 27
Oxlip Cl. WS5: Wals . . . 2E 65
Oxpiece Dr. B36: Hodg H . . . 1B 104
Oxstall Cl. B76: Min . . . 2H 87
Ox St. DY3: Up Gor. . . . 2H 75
Oxted Cl. WV11: Wed. . . . 4H 29
Oxted Cft. B23: Erd . . . 4E 85
Oxwood La. B32: Fran . . . 3D 142
B62: Hunn . . . 3D 142

P

Pace Cres. WV14: Bils . . . 3A 62
Pacific Av. WS10: W'bry. . . . 4D 62
Packhorse La. B38: Head H . . . 3F 161
B47: H'wd. . . . 3F 161
Packington Av. B34: S End. . . . 4G 105
Packington Ct. B74: Four O. . . . 5E 37
Packmores B90: Dic H . . . 4G 163
Packwood Cl. B20: Hand . . . 5C 82
B93: Ben H . . . 5A 166
WV13: W'hall . . . 3H 45
Packwood Cotts. B93: Dorr . . . 6G 167
Packwood Ct. B29: W Cas . . . 4D 130
B91: Sol . . . 2G 151
Packwood Dr. B43: Gt Barr. . . . 4H 65
PACKWOOD GULLET . . . 6F 167
Packwood Rd. B26: Sheld . . . 3F 121
B69: Tiv . . . 6A 78
Padarn Cl. DY3: Sed. . . . 4G 59
Padbury WV9: Pend . . . 4F 15
Paddington Rd. B21: Hand. . . . 6G 81
Paddington Wlk. WS2: Wals . . . 5F 31
Paddock, The B31: N'fld. . . . 3G 145
DY3: Up Gor. . . . 2A 76
DY9: Pedm . . . 4F 125
WV4: Penn . . . 5F 43
WV5: Wom . . . 1E 73
WV6: Pert. . . . 5D 24
WV8: Cod . . . 5F 13
WV14: Cose . . . 4F 61
Paddock Dr. B26: Sheld . . . 4E 121
B93: Dorr . . . 6H 167
Paddock La. WS1: Wals . . . 2D 48
(not continuous)
WS6: Gt Wyr . . . 2G 7
WS9: A'rdge . . . 4C 34
Paddocks, The B15: Edg. . . . 3D 116
B76: Walm . . . 1E 71
Paddocks Dr. B47: H'wd. . . . 3H 161
Paddocks Grn. B18: Hock. . . . 4C 100
Paddock Vw. WV6: Wolv. . . . 3F 27
Paddys Wide Water Ind. Est.
DY5: Brie H. . . . 4G 93
Padgate Cl. B35: Cas V. . . . 4F 87
Padstow Rd. B24: Erd. . . . 3B 86
Paganal Dr. B70: W Brom . . . 6C 80
Paganel Dr. DY1: Dud. . . . 4E 77
Paganel Rd. B29: W Cas. . . . 3E 131
Pagan Pl. *B9: Birm. . . . 6H 5*
(off Gibb St.)
Pageant Ct. B12: Bal H. . . . 6G 117
Pages Cl. B75: S Cold. . . . 6A 54
Pages Ct. B43: Gt Barr . . . 4A 66
Pages La. B43: Gt Barr. . . . 4A 66
Paget Cl. WV14: Cose . . . 5D 60
Paget Ho. DY4: Tip . . . 4B 78
Paget M. B76: Walm. . . . 3D 70
Paget Rd. B24: Erd . . . 3B 86
WV6: Wolv . . . 1D 42
Paget St. WV1: Wolv. . . . 6F 27
Pagham Cl. WV9: Pend . . . 5D 14
Pagnell Gro. B13: Mose . . . 1C 148
Paignton Rd. B16: Edg. . . . 6H 99
Pailton Gro. B29: W Cas . . . 4F 131
Pailton Rd. B90: Shir. . . . 2H 149
Painswick Cl. WS5: Wals . . . 2F 65
Painswick Rd. B28: Hall G . . . 6E 135
Paintcup Row DY2: Neth. . . . 1E 111
Painters Cnr. *B66: Smeth. . . . 4G 99*
(off Grove La.)
Painters Cft. WV14: Cose. . . . 4G 61
Pakefield Rd. B30: K Nor . . . 4E 147
Pakenham Cl. B76: Walm. . . . 5D 70
Pakenham Dr. B76: Walm . . . 5D 70
Pakenham Ho. B76: Walm . . . 5D 70
Pakenham Rd. B15: Edg. . . . 4E 117
Pakenham Village *B15: Edg. . . . 4E 117*
(off Gilldown Pl.)
Pakfield Wlk. B6: Aston . . . 1H 101
Palace Cl. B65: Row R. . . . 5D 96
Palace Dr. B66: Smeth . . . 1B 98
Palace Rd. B9: Small H. . . . 1E 119
Palefield Rd. B90: M'path . . . 3D 164
Pale La. B17: Harb . . . 3D 114
Pale St. DY3: Up Gor . . . 2A 76
Palethorpe Rd. DY4: Tip. . . . 5A 62
PALFREY . . . 4A 48
Palfrey Rd. DY8: Stourb . . . 6B 108
Pallasades Shop. Cen., The
B2: Birm. . . . 1F 117 (5D 4)
Palmcourt Av. B28: Hall G. . . . 6E 135
Palm Cft. DY5: Brie H. . . . 3G 109
Palmer Cl. WV11: Wed. . . . 6H 17
Palmers Cl. WV8: Bilb . . . 6A 14
B90: Shir . . . 2H 149
PALMER'S CROSS . . . 1B 26
Palmers Gro. B36: Hodg H. . . . 1C 104
Palmerston Dr. B69: Tiv. . . . 5D 78
Palmerston Rd. B11: S'brk. . . . 5B 118
Palmer St. B9: Birm . . . 1A 118
Palmer's Way WV8: Bilb. . . . 6A 14
Palm Ho. B20: Hand. . . . 4B 82
Palmvale Cft. B26: Sheld . . . 5E 121
Palomino Pl. B16: Birm . . . 1B 116
Pamela Rd. B31: N'fld . . . 5E 145
Pan Cft. B36: Hodg H . . . 2A 104
Panjab Gdns. B67: Smeth . . . 3D 98
Pannel Cft. B19: Hock. . . . 3F 101
Panther Cft. B34: S End . . . 4H 105
Paper Mill End B44: Gt Barr . . . 1F 83
Paper Mill End Ind. Est. B44: Gt Barr. . . . 1F 83
Papyrus Way B36: Hodg H . . . 6D 86
Parade B1: Birm. . . . 6E 101 (3A 4)
B72: S Cold . . . 1H 69
(Holland St.)
B72: S Cold. . . . 6A 54
(Newhall Wlk.)
Parade, The B37: K'hrst . . . 3C 106
B64: Crad H . . . 3G 111
DY1: Dud . . . 5D 76
DY6: W Hth . . . 2H 91
WS8: Bwnhls . . . 4A 10
Parade Vw. WS8: Bwnhls. . . . 5A 10
PARADISE . . . 1F 95
Paradise DY2: Dud . . . 1F 95
Paradise Cir. Queensway
B1: Birm. . . . 1E 117 (3B 4)
Paradise Ct. B28: Hall G. . . . 1D 148
Paradise Gro. WS3: Pels . . . 4D 20
Paradise La. B28: Hall G. . . . 1E 149
WS3: Pels. . . . 4D 20
Paradise Pl. B3: Birm . . . 1E 117 (4C 4)
Paradise St. B1: Birm . . . 1F 117 (4C 4)
Pardington Cl. B92: Sol . . . 5A 138
Pargeter Ct. WS2: Wals . . . 1A 48
Pargeter Rd. B67: Smeth . . . 1D 114
Pargeter St. DY8: Stourb . . . 1D 124
WS2: Wals . . . 1A 48
Par Grn. B38: K Nor . . . 6H 145
Parish Gdns. DY9: Pedm. . . . 4F 125
Park & Ride
Bescot Cres. . . . 6B 48
Corser St. . . . 2B 44
Elmdon La. . . . 4B 122
Monkspath . . . 4F 151
Plascom . . . 2C 44
Priestfield . . . 4C 44
Science Park . . . 3G 27
Park App. B23: Erd . . . 5C 84
Park Av. B12: Bal H. . . . 6H 117
B18: Hock. . . . 2C 100
B30: K Nor . . . 2C 146
B46: Col . . . 3H 107
B65: Row R . . . 6C 96
B67: Smeth. . . . 5D 98
B68: O'bry . . . 6H 97
B91: Sol . . . 4H 151
DY4: Tip . . . 2G 77
WV1: Wolv. . . . 6F 27 (1A 170)
WV4: Penn . . . 6G 43
WV5: Wom . . . 2F 73
WV13: W'hall . . . 1H 45
Park Bldgs. *DY3: Lwr G . . . 3G 75*
(off Park Rd.)
Park Cir. B6: Aston . . . 2H 101
(not continuous)
Park Cl. B24: Erd . . . 2B 86
B69: Tiv . . . 2C 96
B92: Sol . . . 3H 137
DY1: Dud . . . 6D 60
WS6: C Hay. . . . 2E 7
WS8: Bwnhls . . . 5B 10
Park Ct. B65: Row R. . . . 6C 96
B73: Bold . . . 4F 69
Park Cres. B71: W Brom. . . . 3B 80
WV1: Wolv . . . 1F 43
Park Cft. B47: H'wd. . . . 4A 162
PARK DALE . . . 6E 27
Park Dale WS5: Wals . . . 5G 49
Parkdale DY3: Sed . . . 5H 59
Parkdale Av. WS10: W'bry . . . 1G 63
Parkdale Cl. B24: Erd . . . 5F 85
Park Dale Ct. WV1: Wolv . . . 6E 27
Parkdale Dr. B31: Longb. . . . 2E 159
Park Dale E. WV1: Wolv. . . . 6E 27
Parkdale Rd. B26: Sheld . . . 6G 121
Park Dale W. WV1: Wolv . . . 6E 27
Park Dr. B74: Four O. . . . 1G 53
B74: Lit A . . . 5C 36
WV4: Penn . . . 6G 43
Park Edge B17: Harb. . . . 4G 115
Park End B32: Bart G . . . 4B 130
Parker Ho. B14: K Hth . . . 4H 147
Parker Paul Ind. Est. WV2: Wolv. . . . 4G 43
Parker Rd. WV11: Wed. . . . 6H 17
Parker St. B16: Edg . . . 2B 116
WS3: Blox. . . . 6G 19
Parkes Av. WV8: Cod . . . 5H 13
Parkes' Hall Rd. DY1: Dud. . . . 1C 76
Parkes Ho. B69: O'bry . . . 2G 97
Parkes La. DY3: Sed. . . . 6C 60
DY4: Tip . . . 5H 61
Parkes St. B67: Smeth . . . 5D 98
DY5: Brie H. . . . 6H 93
WV13: W'hall . . . 2B 46
Parkeston Cres. B44: K'sdng . . . 4C 68
Park Farm Rd. B43: Gt Barr . . . 1D 66
PARKFIELD . . . 6B 44
Parkfield B32: Bart G. . . . 3F 129
Parkfield Chalet Land (Cvn. Pk.)
WV2: Wolv . . . 5H 43
Parkfield Cl. B15: Edg. . . . 4E 117
B62: Quin . . . 6G 113
Parkfield Colliery WV4: E'shll. . . . 6B 44
Parkfield Ct. B46: Col. . . . 2H 107
(Park Rd.)
B46: Col . . . 3H 107
(Sumner Rd.)
Parkfield Cres. WV2: E'shll. . . . 5A 44
Parkfield Dr. B36: Cas B. . . . 6G 87
Parkfield Gro. WV2: E'shll . . . 5A 44
Parkfield Ho. B23: Erd . . . 6E 85
Parkfield Pl. DY8: Stourb . . . 6F 109
Parkfield Rd. B8: Salt . . . 6E 103
B46: Col . . . 2H 107
B68: O'bry . . . 6G 97
DY2: Dud. . . . 3F 95
DY8: Stourb . . . 6E 109
WV4: E'shll . . . 5H 43
Park Gdns. DY9: W'cte . . . 2B 126
Park Gro. B10: Small H. . . . 3D 118
B46: Wat O . . . 4E 89
Park Hall Cl. WS5: Wals. . . . 5G 49
Park Hall Cres. B36: Cas B . . . 1F 105
Parkhall Cft. B34: S End . . . 2G 105
Park Hall Rd. WS5: Wals . . . 4G 49
WV4: Penn . . . 1H 59
Parkhead Cres. DY2: Dud. . . . 1D 94
Parkhead Rd. DY2: Dud . . . 1D 94
Park Hill B13: Mose . . . 1G 133
B65: B'hth. . . . 2B 112
WS10: W'bry . . . 1H 63
Park Hill Dr. B20: Hand . . . 3B 82
Park Hill Rd. B17: Harb . . . 5G 115
B67: Smeth. . . . 4D 98
Parkhill Rd. B76: Walm . . . 1D 86
Parkhill St. DY2: Dud. . . . 1G 95
Park Ho. B66: Smeth . . . 4G 99
WV11: Ess . . . 4A 18
Parkhouse Av. WV11: Wed. . . . 3D 28
Parkhouse Dr. B23: Erd . . . 2A 84
Parkhouse Gdns.
DY3: Lwr G. . . . 3G 75
Parklands B45: Redn . . . 1G 157
B91: Sol . . . 4E 151
Parklands, The B23: Erd. . . . 1D 84
DY9: Pedm . . . 2G 125
WV3: Wolv . . . 2B 42
Parklands Ct. B45: Redn . . . 1G 157
WS3: Blox. . . . 6H 19
Parklands Dr. B74: Four O . . . 3F 53
Parklands Gdns.
WS1: Wals . . . 3E 49
Parklands Rd. WS10: Darl . . . 6E 47
WV1: Wolv . . . 2C 44
WV14: Cose . . . 3F 61
Park La. B6: Aston . . . 2G 101
B20: Hand . . . 2F 81
B21: Hand. . . . 2F 81
B35: Cas V . . . 3F 87
B63: Crad . . . 5C 110
B69: O'bry . . . 3G 97
B76: Min. . . . 3G 87
CV7: Bal C . . . 5G 155
DY6: K'wfrd . . . 2C 92
WS6: Gt Wyr. . . . 2F 7
WS10: Darl . . . 4F 47
WV10: Bush, Wolv . . . 3A 28
Park La. E. DY4: Tip. . . . 3A 78
Park La. Est., The B69: O'bry. . . . 2G 97
Park La. Ind. Est. B71: W Brom . . . 6F 81
Park La. Trad. Est.
WV10: Wolv . . . 4A 28
Park La. W. DY4: Tip . . . 2G 77
Park Lime Dr. WS4: Wals . . . 5F 33
Park Mall WS1: Wals . . . 1C 48
Park Mdw. Av. WV14: Bils . . . 3E 45
Park M. B29: S Oak. . . . 4F 131
Park Mill Wlk. B7: Nech . . . 2C 102
Park Pl. B7: Nech . . . 2C 102
Park Retreat B66: Smeth. . . . 5F 99
Park Ridge B74: S Cold . . . 4G 53
Park Ridge Dr. B63: Crad . . . 5D 110
Park Ri. WV3: Wolv . . . 1C 42
Park Rd. B6: Aston . . . 2A 102
B11: S'hll . . . 2C 134
B13: Mose . . . 1H 133
B18: Hock. . . . 3B 100
B23: Erd . . . 5C 84
B46: Col . . . 3H 107
B63: Crad . . . 6C 110
B67: Smeth. . . . 1D 114
B69: Tiv . . . 1C 96
B73: S Cold . . . 6H 53
B91: Sol . . . 4G 151
DY1: Dud . . . 1D 76
DY2: Neth . . . 3E 95
DY3: Lwr G. . . . 3G 75
DY5: Quar B . . . 3B 110
DY8: Woll . . . 6B 108
WS3: Blox. . . . 6H 19
(not continuous)
WS4: Rus . . . 4G 33
WS5: Wals . . . 6H 49
WV13: W'hall . . . 6H 29
WV14: Bils . . . 6E 45
Park Rd. E. WV1: Wolv. . . . 6F 27
Park Rd. Nth. B6: Aston . . . 2A 102
Park Rd. Sth. B18: Hock. . . . 4D 100
Park Rd. W. DY8: Woll . . . 6A 108
WV1: Wolv . . . 6E 27
Parkrose Ind. Est. B66: Smeth . . . 1F 99
Parks Cres. WV11: Ess. . . . 4A 18
Parkside B32: Bart G. . . . 3A 130
B37: Mars G . . . 4F 123
Parkside Av. WV13: W'hall . . . 1G 45
Parkside Cl. WS10: W'bry . . . 2H 63
Parkside Ind. Est. WV1: Wolv . . . 2B 44
Parkside Rd. B20: Hand . . . 2A 82
B63: Crad . . . 6F 111
Parkside Way B31: Longb . . . 6A 144
B74: S'tly . . . 2A 52
Park Sq. B37: Mars G . . . 3F 123
Parkstone Cl. WS4: S'fld . . . 1G 33
Park St. B5: Birm. . . . 1G 117 (5F 5)
B6: Aston . . . 2A 102
(not continuous)
B64: Crad H . . . 1G 111
B65: B'hth. . . . 2D 112
B69: O'bry. . . . 3F 97
B70: W Brom . . . 4B 80
DY1: Dud . . . 3B 94
DY4: Tip . . . 2A 78
DY6: K'wfrd . . . 3B 92
DY8: Amb. . . . 3D 108
DY8: Stourb . . . 6E 109
DY9: Lye. . . . 6B 110
WS1: Wals . . . 1C 48
WS6: C Hay. . . . 2E 7
WS10: Darl . . . 6C 46
WS10: W'bry. . . . 2F 63
Park St. Arc. *WS1: Wals. . . . 1C 48*
(off Park St.)
Park St. Sth. WV2: Wolv . . . 5G 43
Park Ter. B21: Hand . . . 1A 100
WS10: Darl . . . 5B 46
Park Trad. Est. B18: Hock. . . . 3C 100
Pk. Tree Wlk. B24: Erd . . . 3B 86
Park Vw. B10: Small H . . . 4D 118
B18: Win G . . . 5A 100
B73: S Cold . . . 5G 53
B91: Sol . . . 5F 151
WS10: Darl. . . . 5C 46
Park View Community Leisure Cen. . . . 4F 103
Parkview Ct. DY6: W Hth . . . 1H 91
Parkview Cres. WS2: Wals. . . . 5G 31
Parkview Dr. B8: W End . . . 3G 103
WS8: Bwnhls . . . 3B 10
Park Vw. Rd. B31: N'fld . . . 4C 144
B74: Four O . . . 6D 36
DY9: W'cte . . . 1B 126
WV14: Bils . . . 3E 45
Park Vw. Trad. Est. B30: K Nor . . . 4B 146
PARK VILLAGE . . . 4B 28
Park Village Youth Media Activity Cen. . . . 4B 28
Parkville Av. B17: Harb. . . . 1F 131
Park Wlk. DY5: Quar B . . . 3B 110
Park Way B45: Redn. . . . 6H 143
WV11: Wed. . . . 6A 18
Parkway B8: W End . . . 4G 103
Parkway, The DY4: Tip. . . . 4D 62
WS4: S'fld . . . 1G 33
WV6: Pert. . . . 3D 24
Parkway Ind. Cen. B7: Birm . . . 5A 102 (1H 5)
Parkway Ind. Est., The WS10: W'bry. . . . 4E 63
Parkway Rd. DY1: Dud. . . . 5C 76
Parkway Rdbt. WS10: W'bry . . . 4E 63
Parkwood Cl. WS8: Wals W . . . 2C 22
Park Wood Ct. B74: Four O. . . . 1F 53
Parkwood Cft. B43: Gt Barr . . . 4D 66
Parkwood Dr. B73: New O . . . 3C 68
Parkyn St. WV2: Wolv. . . . 3A 44
Parliament St. B6: Aston . . . 3G 101
B10: Small H. . . . 3C 118
B70: W Brom . . . 6B 80
Parry Rd. WV11: Wed. . . . 1A 30
Parsonage Dr. B45: Coft H . . . 5B 158
B63: Crad . . . 4C 110
Parsonage St. B69: O'bry. . . . 2H 97
B71: W Brom . . . 1B 80
Parsons Hill B30: K Nor . . . 5C 146
B68: O'bry . . . 2H 113
Parson's St. DY1: Dud . . . 6E 77
Parsons Way WS2: Wals. . . . 3F 31
Partons Rd. B14: K Hth . . . 1F 147
Partridge Av. WS10: Darl . . . 5B 46
Partridge Cl. B37: Chel W. . . . 6E 107
Partridge Ct. B4: Birm. . . . 1E 5
WS10: W'bry . . . 2F 63
Partridge Mill WS3: Pels . . . 4C 20
Partridge Rd. B26: Yard . . . 2E 121
DY8: Stourb . . . 1A 124
Passey Rd. B13: Mose . . . 3D 134
Passfield Rd. B33: Yard . . . 6E 105

Pineways—Priory Av.

Pineways B74: Four O ... 6C 36
DY8: Word ... 1A 108
Pineways, The B69: O'bry ... 4C 96
Pineways Dr. WV6: Wolv ... 5C 26
Pinewood Cl. B44: Gt Barr ... 6G 67
B45: Rubery ... 1D 156
WS5: Wals ... 6E 49
WS8: Bwnhls ... 3A 10
WV3: Wolv ... 3G 41
WV5: Wom ... 1G 73
WV12: W'hall ... 3D 30
Pinewood Dr. B32: Bart G ... 4G 129
Pinewood Gro. B91: Sol ... 5D 150
Pinewoods B31: N'fld ... 5D 130
B32: Bart G ... 3G 129
B62: Quin ... 4G 113
Pinewood Wlk. DY6: K'wfrd ... 1C 92
Pinfold, The WS3: Blox ... 1A 32
Pinfold Ct. WS10: Darl ... 6C 46
Pinfold Cres. WV4: Penn ... 5B 42
Pinfold Gdns. WV11: Wed ... 4F 29
Pinfold Gro. WV4: Penn ... 5B 42
Pinfold Ind. Est. WS3: Blox ... 1A 32
Pinfold La. WS9: A'rdge ... 6C 50
WS11: Nort C ... 1C 8
WV4: Penn ... 5B 42
Pinfold Rd. B91: Sol ... 2A 152
Pinfold St. B2: Birm ... 1F 117 (4C 4)
B69: O'bry ... 1G 97
WS10: Darl ... 6C 46
(not continuous)
WV14: Bils ... 6F 45
Pinfold St. Extension WS10: Darl ... 6C 46
Pinford La. WS6: C Hay ... 3C 6
Pingle Cl. B71: W Brom ... 4D 64
Pingle La. WS7: Hamm ... 1F 11
Pinkney Pl. B68: O'bry ... 6A 98
Pink Pas. B66: Smeth ... 5F 99
Pinley Gro. B43: Gt Barr ... 2E 67
Pinley Way B91: Sol ... 1E 165
Pinner Ct. B17: Harb ... 5G 115
Pinner Gro. B32: Quin ... 1C 130
Pinson Gdns. WV13: W'hall ... 1H 45
Pinson Rd. WV13: W'hall ... 1H 45
Pintail Dr. B23: Erd ... 5C 84
Pinto Cl. B16: Birm ... 1B 116
Pinza Cft. B36: Hodg H ... 1B 104
Pioli Pl. WS2: Wals ... 4B 32
Pioneer Way B35: Cas V ... 5F 87
Piper Cl. WV6: Pert ... 5F 25
Piper Pl. DY8: Amb ... 3D 108
Piper Rd. WV3: Wolv ... 3A 42
Pipers Grn. B28: Hall G ... 2F 149
Piper's Row WV1: Wolv ... 1H 43 (3D 170)
Pipes Mdw. WV14: Bils ... 6G 45
Pippin Av. B63: Crad ... 4D 110
Pirbright Cl. WV14: Bils ... 2G 61
Pirrey Cl. WV14: Cose ... 4G 61
Pitcairn Cl. B30: Stir ... 1D 146
Pitcairn Dr. B62: Hale ... 6B 112
Pitcairn Rd. B67: Smeth ... 2B 114
Pitclose Rd. B31: N'fld ... 6F 145
Pitfield Rd. B33: Kitts G ... 2A 122
Pitfield Row DY1: Dud ... 6D 76
Pitfields Cl. B68: O'bry ... 3G 113
Pitfields Rd. B68: O'bry ... 3G 113
Pitfield St. DY1: Dud ... 6E 77
Pithall Rd. B34: S End ... 4H 105
Pit Leasow Cl. B30: Stir ... 5D 132
Pitman Rd. B32: Quin ... 6A 114
Pitmaston Ct. B13: Mose ... 2F 133
Pitmaston Rd. B28: Hall G ... 1G 149
Pitmeadow Ho. *B14: K Hth ... 5G 147*
(off Pound Rd.)
Pitsford St. B18: Hock ... 4C 100
Pitt La. B92: Bick ... 3F 139
Pitts Farm Rd. B24: Erd ... 2A 86
Pitt St. B4: Birm ... 6A 102
WV3: Wolv ... 2G 43 (4A 170)
Pixall Dr. B15: Edg ... 4D 116
Pixhall Wlk. B35: Cas V ... 4F 87
(not continuous)
Plainview Cl. WS9: A'rdge ... 1G 51
Plaistow Av. B36: Hodg H ... 2A 104
Plane Gro. B37: Chel W ... 2D 122
Planetary Ind. Est. WV13: W'hall ... 6E 29
Planetary Rd. WV13: W'hall ... 5D 28
Plane Tree Rd. B74: S'tly ... 3F 51
WS5: Wals ... 1F 65
Planet Rd. DY5: Brie H ... 5H 93
Plank La. B46: Wat O ... 5C 88
Planks La. WV5: Wom ... 1F 73
Plantation, The DY5: P'ntt ... 2F 93
Plantation Dr. B75: S Cold ... 5D 54
Plantation La. DY3: Himl ... 3H 73
Plantation Rd. WS5: Wals ... 1E 65
Plant Ct. *DY5: Brie H ... 1H 109*
(off Hill St.)
Plantsbrook Community Nature Reserve
... 3B 70
Plants Brook Nature Reserve ... 2E 87
Plants Brook Rd. B76: Walm ... 1D 86
Plants Cl. B73: New O ... 4D 68
WS6: Gt Wyr ... 5G 7
Plants Gro. B24: Erd ... 2B 86
Plants Hollow DY5: Brie H ... 2A 110
Plant St. B64: Old H ... 2F 111
DY8: Word ... 1C 108
Plant Way WS3: Pels ... 3D 20
Plascom Rd. WV1: Wolv ... 2C 44
Platts Cres. DY8: Amb ... 3C 108
Platts Dr. DY8: Amb ... 3C 108
Platts Rd. DY8: Amb ... 3C 108
Platt St. WS10: Darl ... 6D 46
Playdon Gro. B14: K Hth ... 4A 148
Pleasant Cl. DY6: K'wfrd ... 5A 92
Pleasant St. B70: W Brom ... 5A 80
(Farm St.)
B70: W Brom ... 5G 63
(Lee St.)
Pleasant Vw. DY3: Gorn ... 5H 75
PLECK ... 3H 47
Pleck Bus. Pk. WS2: Wals ... 2A 48
Pleck Ho. *B14: K Hth ... 6E 147*
(off Winterbourne Cft.)
Pleck Ind. Est. WS2: Wals ... 3A 48
Pleck Rd. WS2: Wals ... 3A 48
Pleck Wlk. B38: K Nor ... 6C 146
Plestowes Cl. B90: Shir ... 2H 149
Plimsoll Gro. B32: Quin ... 6A 114
Plough & Harrow Rd. B16: Edg ... 2B 116
Plough Av. B32: Bart G ... 3A 130
Ploughmans Pl. B75: R'ley ... 5B 38
Ploughmans Wlk. DY6: W Hth ... 2G 91
WV8: Pend ... 6C 14
Plover Cl. WV10: F'stne ... 1D 16
Plover Ct. B33: Stech ... 6C 104
Ploverdale Cres. DY6: K'wfrd ... 2E 93
Plowden Rd. B33: Stech ... 5D 104
Plume St. B6: Aston ... 1C 102
Plummers Ho. B6: Aston ... 2G 101
Plumstead Rd. B44: K'sdng ... 5A 68
Plym Cl. WV11: Wed ... 4E 29
Plymouth Cl. B31: Longb ... 2E 159
Plymouth Rd. B30: Stir ... 6D 132
Plympton M. B71: W Brom ... 1A 80
Pocklington Pl. B31: N'fld ... 1G 145
Poets Cnr. B10: Small H ... 4D 118
Point 3 B3: Birm ... 6E 101 (2B 4)
Pointon Cl. WV14: Cose ... 3C 60
Polars, The DY5: P'ntt ... 2F 93
Polden Cl. B63: Hale ... 4E 127
Polesworth Gro. B34: S End ... 3F 105
Pollard Rd. B27: A Grn ... 4A 136
Pollards, The B23: Erd ... 5E 69
Polly Brooks Yd. DY9: Lye ... 6A 110
Polo Flds. DY9: Pedm ... 4F 125
Pomeroy Rd. B32: Bart G ... 4A 130
B43: Gt Barr ... 1F 67
Pommel Cl. WS5: Wals ... 1D 64
Pond La. WV2: Wolv ... 3H 43
Pool Cotts. WS7: Chase ... 1A 10
Poole Cres. B17: Harb ... 2G 131
WS8: Bwnhls ... 3G 9
WV14: Cose ... 3F 61
Poole Ho. Rd. B43: Gt Barr ... 2A 66
Pool End Cl. B93: Know ... 3B 166
Pooles La. WV12: W'hall ... 1E 31
Poole St. DY8: Stourb ... 1C 124
Pool Farm Rd. B27: A Grn ... 4H 135
Pool Fld. Av. B31: N'fld ... 6C 130
Poolfield Dr. B91: Sol ... 4D 150
POOL GREEN ... 4B 34
Pool Grn. WS9: A'rdge ... 4C 34
Pool Grn. Ter. WS9: A'rdge ... 4C 34
Pool Hall Cres. WV3: Wolv ... 3F 41
Pool Hall Rd. WV3: Wolv ... 3F 41
Pool Hayes La.
WV12: W'hall ... 4A 30
Pool Ho. Rd. WV5: Wom ... 2D 72
Pool La. B69: O'bry ... 5F 97
Pool Mdw. WS6: C Hay ... 4D 6
Poolmeadow B76: Walm ... 5E 71
Pool Mdw. Cl. B13: Mose ... 4C 134
B91: Sol ... 6B 152
Pool Rd. B63: Hale ... 2B 128
B66: Smeth ... 4F 99
WS7: Chase ... 1A 10
(not continuous)
WS8: Bwnhls ... 3A 10
WV11: Wed ... 3A 30
Pool St. DY1: Dud ... 1C 76
WS1: Wals ... 2D 48
WV2: Wolv ... 3G 43 (6A 170)
(not continuous)
Pooltail Wlk. B31: Longb ... 6B 144
Pool Vw. WS4: Rus ... 2H 33
WS6: Gt Wyr ... 1G 7
Pool Way B33: Yard ... 2E 121
Pope Rd. WV10: Bush ... 1C 28
Popes La. B69: O'bry ... 3H 97
B30: K Nor ... 3H 145
B38: K Nor ... 3H 145
WV6: Tett ... 3G 25
Pope St. B1: Birm ... 6D 100
B66: Smeth ... 2F 99
Poplar Arc. *B91: Sol ... 3G 151*
(off Gardeners Wlk.)
Poplar Av. B11: S'brk ... 5B 118
B12: Bal H ... 1A 134
B14: K Hth ... 5H 133
B17: Edg ... 2E 115
B19: Loz ... 1E 101
B23: Erd ... 3F 85
B37: Chel W ... 3E 123
B69: O'bry ... 5G 97
B69: Tiv ... 1B 96
B70: W Brom ... 5C 80
B75: S Cold ... 4D 54
DY4: Tip ... 2F 77
WS2: Wals ... 6D 30
WS5: Wals ... 1E 65
WS8: Bwnhls ... 5C 10
WV11: Wed ... 2D 28
Poplar Cl. B69: Tiv ... 6C 78
WS2: Wals ... 5E 31
WV5: Wom ... 1H 73
Poplar Cres. DY1: Dud ... 4D 76
DY8: Stourb ... 2C 124
Poplar Dr. B6: Witt ... 2H 83
B8: Salt ... 3D 102
Poplar Grn. DY1: Dud ... 1C 76
Poplar Gro. B19: Loz ... 1E 101
B66: Smeth ... 6F 99
B70: W Brom ... 6C 80
Poplar La. B62: Roms ... 3A 142
Poplar Ri. B42: Gt Barr ... 6D 66
B69: Tiv ... 1C 96
B74: Lit A ... 4D 36
Poplar Rd. B11: S'hll ... 6B 118
B14: K Hth ... 5G 133
B66: Smeth ... 2E 115
B69: O'bry ... 1G 97
B91: Sol ... 3G 151
B93: Dorr ... 5B 166
DY6: K'wfrd ... 4C 92
DY8: Stourb ... 2C 124
WS6: Gt Wyr ... 4F 7
WS8: Bwnhls ... 5B 10
WS10: W'bry ... 5G 47
WV3: Wolv ... 5E 43
WV14: Bils ... 4H 45
Poplars, The B11: S'brk ... 5C 118
B16: Birm ... 5B 100
DY8: Word ... 1D 108
Poplars Dr. B36: Cas B ... 1F 105
WV8: Cod ... 5F 13
Poplars Ind. Est., The B6: Witt ... 2H 83
Poplar St. B66: Smeth ... 4G 99
WV2: Wolv ... 5H 43
Poplar Trees *B47: H'wd ... 3A 162*
(off May Farm Cl.)
Poplar Way Shop. Cen. B91: Sol ... 3G 151
Poplarwoods B32: Bart G ... 3H 129
Poppy Dr. WS5: Wals ... 2D 64
Poppy Gro. B8: Salt ... 5F 103
Poppy La. B24: Erd ... 2A 86
Poppymead B23: Erd ... 5B 68
Porchester Cl. WS9: Wals W ... 4C 22
Porchester Dr. B19: Hock ... 3F 101
Porchester St. B19: Hock ... 3F 101
Porlock Cres. B31: N'fld ... 4B 144
Porlock Rd. DY8: Amb ... 5E 109
Portal Rd. WS2: Wals ... 1F 47
Portchester Dr. WV11: Wed ... 4F 29
Porter Cl. B72: W Grn ... 6H 69
Porters Cft. B17: Harb ... 3E 115
Porter's Fld. DY2: Dud ... 6F 77
Portersfield Ind. Est. B64: Crad H ... 4F 111
Portersfield Rd. B64: Crad H ... 3E 111
Portershill Dr. B90: Shir ... 6A 150
Porter St. DY2: Dud ... 6F 77
Porter St. Sth. DY2: Dud ... 6F 77
Porters Way B9: Bord G ... 1E 119
Portfield Dr. DY4: Tip ... 4A 78
Portfield Gro. B23: Erd ... 1G 85
Porth Kerry Gro. DY3: Sed ... 6F 59
Port Hope Rd. B11: S'brk ... 4A 118
Porthouse Gro. WV14: Cose ... 2D 60
Portia Av. B90: Shir ... 5H 149
Portland Av. WS9: A'rdge ... 4D 34
Portland Ct. WS9: A'rdge ... 4D 34
Portland Cres. DY9: Pedm ... 4F 125
Portland Dr. B69: Tiv ... 5D 78
DY9: Pedm ... 4F 125
Portland Pl. WV14: Cose ... 6D 60
Portland Rd. B16: Edg ... 1G 115
B17: Edg ... 6F 99
WS9: A'rdge ... 3D 34
Portland St. B6: Aston ... 2A 102
WS2: Wals ... 6C 32
Port La. WV9: Coven ... 1H 13
Portman Rd. B13: Mose ... 6H 133
PORTOBELLO ... 3G 45
Portobello Cl. WV13: W'hall ... 2F 45
Portobello Rd. B70: W Brom ... 5G 63
Portrush Av. B38: K Nor ... 6G 145
Portrush Rd. WV6: Pert ... 5D 24
Portsdown Cl. WV10: Bush ... 2B 28
Portsdown Rd. B63: Hale ... 4E 127
Portsea St. WS3: Blox ... 3A 32
Port St. WS1: Wals ... 4B 48
Portswood Cl. WV9: Pend ... 6D 14
PORTWAY ... 4C 96
Portway, The DY6: K'wfrd ... 4C 92
Portway Cl. B91: Sol ... 6C 150
DY6: K'wfrd ... 4C 92
Portway Hill B65: Row R ... 3B 96
Portway Rd. B65: Row R ... 5B 96
B69: O'bry ... 2E 97
WS10: W'bry ... 2E 63
WV14: Bils ... 4G 45
Portway Rd. Ind. Est. B69: O'bry ... 2E 97
Portway Wlk. B65: Row R ... 3C 96
Posey Cl. B21: Hand ... 4H 81
Post Office Rd. WV5: Seis ... 2A 56
Poston Cft. B14: K Hth ... 3F 147
Potland Ter. *B18: Hock ... 4C 100*
(off Crabtree Rd.)
Potter Cl. B23: Erd ... 5D 68
Potter Ct. *DY5: Brie H ... 1H 109*
(off Promenade, The)
Potters Brook DY4: Tip ... 2B 78
Potters La. WS10: W'bry ... 3E 63
B6: Aston ... 3G 101
Potterton Way B66: Smeth ... 1D 98
Pottery Rd. B66: Smeth ... 2E 99
B68: O'bry ... 2A 114
Pouk Hill Cl. WS2: Wals ... 6G 31
Pouk La. WS14: Hilt ... 5G 11
Poultney St. B70: W Brom ... 6F 63
Poulton Cl. B13: Mose ... 3A 134
Pound Cl. B68: O'bry ... 6F 97
Pound Grn. B8: Salt ... 3F 103
Pound La. B32: Fran ... 4F 143
B46: Col ... 5H 107
Poundley Cl. B36: Cas B ... 1G 105
Pound Rd. B14: K Hth ... 6G 147
B68: O'bry ... 6F 97
(not continuous)
WS10: W'bry ... 2G 63
Pountney St. WV2: Wolv ... 3G 43 (6A 170)
Powell Av. B32: Quin ... 5G 113
Powell Pl. DY4: Tip ... 2C 78
WV14: Bils ... 2G 61
Powells Ho. B73: New O ... 3C 68
Powell St. B1: Birm ... 6D 100
B63: Hale ... 2B 128
WV10: Wolv ... 5B 28
Powerleague Soccer Cen. ... 6C 84
Power Way DY4: Tip ... 5D 62
Powick Pl. B19: Loz ... 2E 101
Powick Rd. B23: Erd ... 6D 84
Powis Av. DY4: Tip ... 1A 78
Powke La. B64: Old H ... 6H 95
B65: Row R ... 1A 112
Powke La. Ind. Est. B65: Row R ... 1A 112
Powlers Cl. DY9: W'cte ... 3A 126
Powlett St. WV2: Wolv ... 2H 43 (5D 170)
Poxon Rd. WS9: Wals W ... 3C 22
Poynings, The WV6: Tett ... 4A 26
Precinct, The WV12: W'hall ... 4B 30
Premier Bus. Pk. WS2: Wals ... 2B 48
Premier Ct. B30: K Nor ... 4E 147
Premier Pk. B73: New O ... 3D 68
Premier Partnership Ind. Est.
DY6: K'wfrd ... 6F 93
Premier St. B7: Nech ... 1D 102
Premier Trad. Est. B7: Birm ... 4H 101
Prescot Rd. DY9: Lye ... 1G 125
Prescott St. B18: Hock ... 5D 100
Prestbury Rd. B6: Aston ... 1G 101
Presthope Rd. B29: W Cas ... 6F 131
Preston Av. B76: Walm ... 2C 70
Preston Ho. *WS1: Wals ... 2D 48*
(off Paddock La.)
Preston Rd. B18: Win G ... 3A 100
B26: Yard ... 5B 120
Prestons Row WV14: Cose ... 2C 60
Prestwick Cl. B75: S Cold ... 3A 54
Prestwick Rd. B35: Cas V ... 3F 87
DY6: K'wfrd ... 3A 92
Prestwood Av. WV11: Wed ... 2F 29
Prestwood Rd. B29: W Cas ... 5F 131
WV11: Wed ... 4C 28
Prestwood Rd. W. WV11: Wed ... 3C 28
Pretoria Rd. B9: Bord G ... 6E 103
Priam Gro. WS3: Pels ... 1F 21
Price Cres. WV14: Bils ... 4F 45
Price Rd. WS10: W'bry ... 2A 64
Prices Rd. DY3: Gorn ... 4G 75
Price St. B4: Birm ... 5G 101 (1E 5)
B66: Smeth ... 4F 99
B70: W Brom ... 4A 80
DY2: Dud ... 1G 95
WV14: Bils ... 6H 45
PRIESTFIELD ... 5D 44
Priestfield WV2: E'shll ... 4C 44
Priestfield Cl. B44: Gt Barr ... 3E 67
Priestfield St. WV14: Bils ... 5D 44
Priestland Rd. B34: S End ... 2F 105
Priestley Cl. B20: Hand ... 6C 82
B63: Crad ... 5D 110
Priestley Rd. B11: S'brk ... 4A 118
WS2: Wals ... 4G 31
Priestly Wharf B7: Birm ... 5H 101 (1H 5)
Priest St. B64: Old H ... 2H 111
Primley Av. B36: Hodg H ... 2B 104
WS2: Wals ... 2H 47
Primley Cl. WS2: Wals ... 1H 47
Primrose Av. B11: S'hll ... 5C 118
DY4: Tip ... 5C 62
WV10: F'hses, Bush ... 4H 15
Primrose Bank B68: O'bry ... 5H 97
Primrose Cl. B64: Crad H ... 3D 110
WS3: Pels ... 2E 21
Primrose Cres. DY1: Dud ... 3E 77
Primrose Cft. B23: Erd ... 6C 68
B28: Hall G ... 2F 149
Primrose Gdns. B38: K Nor ... 1B 160
WV8: Cod ... 4G 13
PRIMROSE HILL ... 5F 95
Primrose Hill B38: K Nor ... 6B 146
(not continuous)
B67: Smeth ... 5B 98
DY8: Word ... 2C 108
Primrose Hill Trad. Est. DY2: Neth ... 5F 95
Primrose La. B28: Hall G ... 2F 149
B90: Dic H ... 4G 163
WV10: Bush ... 3A 16
(Cromwell Rd.)
WV10: Bush ... 1B 28
(Old Fallings La.)
Primrose Pk. DY5: P'ntt ... 2G 93
Primrose Rd. DY2: Neth ... 5E 95
Primroses, The WS5: Wals ... 1F 65
Primrose Woods B32: Bart G ... 3H 129
Primsland Cl. B90: M'path ... 2G 165
Prince Albert St. B9: Small H ... 2D 118
(not continuous)
Prince Andrew Cres. B45: Fran ... 5E 143
Prince Charles Cl. B45: Fran ... 5E 143
Prince Charles Rd. WV14: Bils ... 2H 61
Prince Edward Dr. B45: Fran ... 5E 143
Prince George Rd. WS10: W'bry ... 6G 47
Prince of Wales La.
B14: K Hth, Yard W ... 5C 148
Prince of Wales Way B66: Smeth ... 4G 99
Princep Cl. B43: Gt Barr ... 1F 67
Prince Philip Cl. B45: Fran ... 5E 143
Prince Rd. B30: K Nor ... 4B 146
Princes Av. WS1: Wals ... 3E 49
Princes Dr. WV8: Cod ... 4G 13
PRINCES END ... 5H 61
Princes End Ind. Est. DY4: Tip ... 4G 61
Princes Gdns. WV8: Cod ... 4F 13
Princes Ga. B91: Sol ... 3F 151
Princes Rd. B69: Tiv ... 5A 78
DY8: Stourb ... 3B 124
Princess Alice Dr. B73: New O ... 3D 68
Princess All. WV1: Wolv ... 1H 43 (3C 170)
Princess Anne Dr. B45: Fran ... 5E 143
Princess Anne Rd. WS2: Wals ... 6F 31
WV14: Bils ... 2H 61
Princess Ct. WV10: Wolv ... 3C 28
Princess Cres. B63: Hale ... 5G 111
Princess Diana Way B45: Fran ... 5E 143
Princess Gro. B71: W Brom ... 5B 64
Princess Pde. B70: W Brom ... 4B 80
Princes Sq. WV1: Wolv ... 1H 43 (2C 170)
Princess Rd. B5: Bal H ... 5G 117
B68: O'bry ... 1B 114
Princess Sq. WV14: Bils ... 2H 61
Princess St. WV1: Wolv ... 1H 43 (3C 170)
Princess Way WS10: Darl ... 3C 46
Prince St. B64: Crad H ... 3F 111
DY2: Neth ... 3E 95
WS2: Wals ... 3A 48
WS9: Wals W ... 5B 22
Prince's Way B91: Sol ... 3F 151
Princethorpe Cl. B34: S End ... 2H 105
B90: Shir ... 5G 149
Princethorpe Rd. B29: W Cas ... 4E 131
Princeton Gdns. WV9: Pend ... 5D 14
Prince William Cl. B23: Erd ... 5D 84
Principal Ct. B67: Smeth ... 4E 99
Princip St. B4: Birm ... 5G 101 (1E 5)
Printing Ho. St. B4: Birm ... 6G 101 (2E 5)
Priors Cl. CV7: Bal C ... 3H 169
Priors Mill DY3: Up Gor ... 2A 76
Priors Way B23: Erd ... 5C 68
Priory, The ... 4E 77
Priory, The DY3: Sed ... 5H 59
Priory Av. B29: S Oak ... 3D 132

Priory Chambers—Rectory Av.

Priory Chambers DY1: Dud. 6E 77
(off Priory St.)
Priory Cl. B46: Col 4H 107
B66: Smeth. 5G 99
B70: W Brom 5D 80
DY1: Dud 5D 76
DY8: Stourb 2F 125
Priory Ct. B90: M'path. 2F 165
DY1: Dud 6E 77
DY8: Stourb 2F 125
WS9: Wals W 3C 22
WV1: Wolv. 6G 27 (1A 170)
Priory Dr. B68: O'bry 4A 98
Priory Fld. Cl. WV14: Cose 4B 60
Priory Fields Nature Reserve 5D 148
Priory Gdns. B28: Hall G 3D 148
Priory Ga. Way B9: Bord G. 1E 119
Priory Ho. B63: Hale. 6H 111
Priory Ho. Ind. Est. B18: Hock 4C 100
Priory La. DY3: Sed 6H 59
Priory New Way Ind. Est. B6: Aston 4G 101
Priory Queensway, The
B4: Birm 6G 101 (3E 5)
Priory Rd. B5: Edg 5D 116
B6: Aston 1B 102
B14: K Hth 6E 133
B15: Edg. 5D 116
B28: Hall G 2D 148
B62: Hale 1E 129
DY1: Dud 2E 77
DY8: Stourb 2F 125
Priory Sq. Shop. Cen. B4: Birm 3F 5
Priory St. DY1: Dud 6E 77
Priory Wlk. B4: Birm 6G 101 (3F 5)
B72: W Grn. 6A 70
Priory Woods Nature Reserve. 3E 81
Pritchard Av. WV11: Wed 3G 29
Pritchard Cl. B66: Smeth 4F 99
Pritchard St. DY5: Brie H 6F 93
WS10: W'bry 2G 63
Pritchatts Rd. B15: Edg 6A 116
Pritchett Av. WV4: E'shll 2B 60
Pritchett Rd. B31: Longb. 2F 159
Pritchett St. B6: Birm 4G 101
Pritchett Twr. B10: Small H. 2C 118
Private Way B45: Coft H. 5A 158
Privet Cl. B44: Gt Barr 2G 67
Probert Rd. WV10: Oxl 1E 27
Proctor St. B7: Birm 4A 102
Proffitt Cl. WS2: Wals. 5C 32
WS8: Bwnhls 2C 22
Proffitt St. WS2: Wals. 5C 32
Prole St. WV10: Wolv 5A 28
Promenade, The DY5: Brie H. 1H 109
Prospect Gdns. DY8: Stourb. 1E 125
Prospect Hill DY8: Stourb. 1E 125
Prospect La. B91: Sol 2B 150
Prospect Pl. B12: Bal H 6H 117
Prospect Rd. B13: Mose. 4H 133
B62: Hale 6C 112
DY3: Gorn. 5F 75
Prospect Row DY2: Dud 2F 95
DY8: Stourb 2E 125
Prospect St. DY4: Tip 4C 62
WV14: Bils 5G 45
Prospect Trad. Est. B1: Birm 3A 4
Prosper Mdw. DY6: K'wfrd. 2C 92
Prospero Cl. B45: Fran 5G 143
Prosser St. WV10: Wolv 4A 28
WV14: Bils 6F 45
Prossers Wlk. B46: Col. 2H 107
Prouds La. WV14: Bils 3F 45
Provence Cl. WV10: Wolv. 5B 28
Providence Cl. WS3: Blox. 2A 32
(not continuous)
Providence Dr. DY9: Lye. 5A 110
Providence Ind. Est. DY9: Lye 5A 110
Providence La. WS3: Blox 3A 32
Providence Row WV14: Cose. 5D 60
Providence St. B64: Crad H 2F 111
DY4: Tip 2C 78
DY9: Lye. 5A 110
Pruden Av. WV4: E'shll 2B 60
Pryor Rd. B68: O'bry. 6A 98
Pudsey Dr. B75: Four O 6A 38
Pugh Cres. WS2: Wals 1E 47
Pugh Rd. B6: Aston. 2A 102
WV14: Bils 2G 61
WV14: Cose 3B 60
Pugin Cl. WV6: Pert 6D 24
Pugin Gdns. B23: Erd 5D 68
Pumphouse Way B69: O'bry. 5F 97
Pump St. WV2: E'shll 4C 44
Puppy Grn. DY4: Tip. 2A 78
Purbeck Cl. B63: Hale 4F 127
Purbeck Cft. B32: Harb. 6D 114
Purbrook Rd. WV1: Wolv 3B 44
Purcel Rd. WV10: Bush 1H 27
Purdy Rd. WV14: Bils. 3G 61
Purefoy Rd. B13: Mose. 2C 148
Purley Gro. B23: Erd. 2A 84
Purnells Way B93: Know 4C 166
Purslet Rd. WV1: Wolv. 2C 44
Purslow Gro. B31: N'fld 5E 145
Putney Av. B20: Hand 6E 83
Putney La. B62: Roms 5A 142
Putney Rd. B20: Hand 6D 82
Putney Wlk. B37: F'bri 6D 106
Pype Hayes Cl. B24: Erd. 3B 86
Pype Hayes Rd. B24: Erd 3B 86
Pype Marshbrook Rd. B24: Erd 3B 86
Pytchley Ho. B20: Hand 4B 82
Pytman Dr. B76: Walm 6E 71

Q

Quadrangle, The B30: B'vlle. 1B 146
B90: Shir. 1C 164
Quadrant, The DY3: Sed. 4H 59
Quadrille Lawns WV9: Pend. 5D 14
Quail Grn. WV6: Tett 1F 41
Qualcast Rd. WV1: Wolv 1B 44
Quantock Cl. B45: Fran. 5H 143
B63: Hale. 3F 127
WS8: Wals W 3C 22
Quantock Rd. DY8: Amb 5F 109
Quantry La. DY9: Belb 1A 156
Quarrington Gro. B14: K Hth 4A 148
QUARRY BANK 2C 110
Quarry Brow DY3: Up Gor. 2A 76
Quarry Cl. WS6: C Hay 2E 7
Quarry Hill B63: Hale 3H 127
Quarry Ho. B45: Rubery 1F 157
Quarry Ho. Cl. B45: Fran. 6F 143
Quarry La. B31: N'fld 4D 144
B63: Hale 3H 127
Quarry Pk. Rd. DY8: Stourb 5E 125
Quarry Ri. B69: Tiv 1B 96
Quarry Rd. B29: W Cas 4D 130
DY2: Neth 1D 110
Quarry Wlk. B45: Redn. 2G 157
Quasar Cen. WS1: Wals 1C 48
Quatford Gdns. WV10: Wolv. 4A 28
Quayle Gro. DY8: Word 6B 92
Quayside B18: Win G 4C 100
Quayside Cl. B69: O'bry 1E 97
Quayside Dr. WS2: Wals. 3A 48
Qube 3A 4
Queen Eleanors Dr. B93: Know 1D 166
Queen Elizabeth Av. WS2: Wals 6F 31
Queen Elizabeth Ct. B19: Hock 3D 100
Queen Elizabeth Rd. B45: Fran. 5E 143
Queen Mary St. WS1: Wals 5B 48
Queen Mother Ct. B30: B'vlle. 5H 131
Queen Mother Gdns.
B17: Harb 5E 115
Queen's Arc. WV1: Wolv 1G 43 (3B 170)
Queens Av. B14: K Hth 5G 133
B90: Shir 6H 149
B18: Hock 3B 100
B69: Tiv 6B 78
Queensbridge Rd. B13: Mose. 3F 133
Queens Cl. B24: Erd 5F 85
B67: Smeth. 4E 99
Queens Ct. B1: Birm 2E 117 (6B 4)
B3: Birm. 5F 101 (1C 4)
B91: Sol 3H 151
WV10: Wolv 3C 28
Queens Ct. Trad. Est.
B70: W Brom 4F 79
Queens Cres. DY8: Amb 4E 109
WV14: Cose 4C 60
Queen's Cross DY1: Dud 1D 94
Queens Dr. B65: Row R 5D 96
B5: Birm. 1F 117 (5D 4)
B30: K Nor 3C 146
WS7: Chase 1B 10
Queens Dr., The B62: Hale 6C 112
Queens Gdns. B23: Erd. 6B 68
DY2: Neth 5E 95
WS10: W'bry. 2E 63
WV8: Cod 4F 13
WV14: Bils 4F 45
Queen's Head Rd. B21: Hand. 2A 100
Queens Hospital Cl.
B15: Birm 2E 117
Queens Lea WV12: W'hall 4C 30
Queens Pde. WS3: Blox 6H 19
Queen's Pk. Rd. B32: Harb. 5D 114
Queen Sq. WV1: Wolv 1G 43 (3B 170)
Queen's Ride B5: Edg 1E 133
Queens Rd. B23: Erd 4C 84
B67: Smeth. 5B 98
DY8: Stourb 5D 108
WS5: Wals. 5F 49
B6: Aston 1A 102
B26: Yard 2D 120
DY3: Sed. 5A 60
DY4: Tip 2H 77
WS4: Rus 2G 33
Queens Sq. B70: W Brom. 4B 80
Queen St. B12: Bal H 6B 118
B63: Hale 1A 128
B64: Crad H. 2F 111
B69: O'bry 4G 97
B70: W Brom 4B 80
B72: S Cold. 1A 70
DY4: Tip 5H 61
DY5: P'ntt. 3G 93
(not continuous)
DY5: Quar B 3C 110
(not continuous)
DY6: K'wfrd 2B 92
DY8: Stourb 6D 108
DY8: Word 6B 92
WS2: Wals 2B 48
WS6: C Hay 2D 6
WS7: Chase 1B 10
WS9: Wals W 5A 22
WS10: Darl 3D 46
WS10: W'bry. 2E 63
WV1: Wolv. 1H 43 (3C 170)
(not continuous)
WV14: Bils 6G 45
(Bridge St.)
WV14: Bils 1B 62
(Tudor Rd.)
Queen St. Ind. Est. WS7: Chase. 1B 10
Queen St. Pas. DY5: Quar B. 3C 110
Queensway B1: Birm. 1E 117
B6: Witt 4H 83
B63: Hale 2A 128
B68: O'bry 2H 113
B74: S'tly 3A 52
DY9: W'cte 3A 126
Queensway Cl. B68: O'bry 2H 113
Queensway Mall B63: Hale. 2B 128
(off Hagley Mall)
Queensway Trad. Est. B5: Birm 3G 5
Queenswood Rd. B13: Mose 1A 134
B75: Four O 2H 53
Quenby Dr. DY1: Dud 4C 76
Quendale WV5: Wom 1E 73
Quentin Dr. DY1: Dud 1B 94
Queslade Cl. B43: Gt Barr 4C 66
QUESLETT 3F 67
Queslett Pk. Golf Cen. 5E 67
(off Booth's La.)
Queslett Rd. B43: Gt Barr. 4B 66
(not continuous)
Queslett Rd. E. B74: S'tly. 6G 51
Quicksand La. WS9: A'rdge 5B 34
Quillets Rd. DY8: Word 6A 92
Quilter Cl. WS2: Wals 6F 31
WV14: Cose 5C 60
Quilter Rd. B24: Erd 5H 85
Quincey Dr. B24: Erd 4A 86
Quincy Ri. DY5: Brie H 4G 109
QUINTON 5A 114
Quinton Av. WS6: Gt Wyr 2F 7
Quinton Bus. Pk. B32: Quin 6G 113
Quinton Cl. B92: Sol. 2H 137
Quintondale B90: Shir. 1A 164
Quinton Expressway
B32: Quin 1H 129
Quinton La. B32: Quin 5A 114
Quinton Pl. WS11: Nort C 1E 9
Quinton Rd. B17: Harb 2E 131
Quinton Rd. W. B32: Quin 6H 113
Quinsnam Ct. B13: Mose 3B 134
Quorn Cres. DY8: Word 6A 92
Quorn Gro. B24: Erd. 5H 85
Quorn Ho. B20: Hand 4B 82

R

Rabone La. B66: Smeth 3F 99
Raby Cl. B69: Tiv 1H 95
Raby St. WV2: Wolv 3H 43 (6D 170)
Racecourse La. DY8: Stourb 3C 124
Racecourse Rd. WV6: Wolv 4E 27
Racecourse Rd. Ind. Est. WV6: Wolv. 4E 27
Racemeadow Cres. DY2: Neth 2E 111
Raceway, The 6D 80
Rachael Gdns. WS10: W'bry 1H 63
Rachel Cl. DY4: Tip 4C 62
Rachel Gdns. B29: S Oak 3H 131
Radbourn Dr. B74: S Cold. 4A 54
Radbourne Dr. B63: Crad 4C 110
Radbourne Rd. B90: Shir 4B 150
Radcliffe Dr. B62: Quin. 5E 113
Radcliffe Twr. B12: Birm 3H 117
Raddens Rd. B62: Hale 2F 129
Raddington Dr. B92: Olton 5B 136
Raddlebarn Farm Dr. B29: S Oak. 4B 132
Raddlebarn Rd. B29: S Oak 4A 132
Radford Cl. WS5: Wals 2E 65
Radford Dr. WS4: S'fld 5G 21
Radford La. WV3: Wolv. 5F 41
WV4: Lwr P. 5F 41
Radford Ri. B91: Sol. 2A 152
Radford Rd. B29: W Cas. 1E 145
Radley Ct. B26: Sheld. 4G 121
Radley Gro. B29: W Cas 3E 131
Radley Rd. DY9: W'cte 1B 126
WS4: Rus 2G 33
Radleys, The B33: Kitts G, Sheld 4G 121
Radley's Wlk. B33: Sheld. 4G 121
Radlow Cres. B37: Mars G. 3D 122
Radnell Ho. B69: O'bry 3D 96
Radnor Cl. B45: Fran 5H 143
Radnor Ct. WS9: Wals W 3B 22
Radnor Cft. WS5: Wals. 2G 65
Radnor Grn. B71: W Brom 6A 64
Radnor Rd. B20: Hand 1D 100
B68: O'bry 4H 113
DY3: Sed 5G 59
Radnor St. B18: Hock 3C 100
Radstock Av. B36: Hodg H 2A 104
Radstock Rd. WV12: W'hall 6C 18
Radway Rd. B90: Shir. 2C 164
Raeburn Rd. B43: Gt Barr. 1E 67
Raford Rd. B23: Erd 1D 84
Ragees Rd. DY6: K'wfrd. 5D 92
Raglan Av. B66: Smeth. 5G 99
WV6: Pert 6F 25
Raglan Cl. DY3: Sed 6F 59
WS9: A'rdge 6H 35
Raglan Rd. B5: Edg. 5F 117
B21: Hand. 1G 99
B66: Smeth. 5G 99
Raglan St. DY5: Brie H. 5G 93
WV3: Wolv. 1F 43 (3A 170)
Raglan Way B37: Chel W 1F 123
Ragley Cl. B93: Know. 2D 166
WS3: Blox. 6G 19
Ragley Dr. B26: Sheld 5G 121
B43: Gt Barr 3H 65
WV13: W'hall 3H 45
Ragley Wlk. B65: Row R 6C 96
Ragnall Av. B33: Sheld. 4H 121
Rail Bri. Est. B70: W Brom 6G 79
Railswood Dr. WS3: Pels 4E 21
Railway Dr. WV1: Wolv. 1H 43 (2D 170)
WV14: Bils 6G 45
Railway La. WV13: W'hall 2A 46
Railway Rd. B20: Hand 5H 83
B73: S Cold 6H 53
Railwayside Cl. B66: Smeth. 2C 98
(off Forest Cl.)
Railway St. B70: W Brom. 3H 79
DY4: Tip 2C 78
WV1: Wolv 1H 43 (2D 170)
WV13: W'hall 2A 46
WV14: Bils 6G 45
Railway Ter. B7: Nech 3B 102
B42: Gt Barr 1B 82
WS10: W'bry 3F 63
Railway Vw. B10: Small H 4C 118
Railway Wlk. WS11: Nort C 1E 9
Railwharf Sidings DY2: Neth 5F 95
Rainbow St. WV2: Wolv 3G 43
WV14: Cose 2F 61
Rainford Way B38: K Nor. 1G 159
(off Nearhill Rd.)
Rainham Cl. DY4: Tip 2F 77
Rainsbrook Dr. B90: M'path 3D 164
Rake Way B15: Birm 2D 116 (6A 4)
Raleigh Cl. B21: Hand. 6F 81
Raleigh Cft. B43: Gt Barr 2A 66
Raleigh Ind. Est. B21: Hand 6F 81
Raleigh Rd. B9: Bord G 6D 102
WV14: Bils 2H 61
Raleigh St. B71: W Brom 3A 80
WS2: Wals 1A 48
Ralph Barlow Gdns. B44: K'sdng 5B 68
Ralph Gdns. B44: K'sdng 5B 68
Ralph Rd. B8: Salt 5D 102
B90: Shir 3H 149
Ralphs Mdw. B32: Bart G. 3B 130
Ralston Cl. WS3: Blox 3G 19
Ramblers Way B75: R'ley. 6C 38
Ramillies Cres. WS6: Gt Wyr 4F 7
Ramp Rd. B26: Birm A 6E 123
Ramsay Rd. B68: O'bry 2A 114
Ramsden Cl. B29: W Cas 6F 131
Ramsey Cl. B45: Fran. 6E 143
B71: W Brom 5D 64
Ramsey Ho. WS2: Wals 4A 48
Ramsey Rd. B7: Nech. 2C 102
DY4: Tip 6G 61
WS2: Wals 4G 31
Randall Cl. DY6: K'wfrd 5D 92
Randall Lines Ho. WV1: Wolv 6G 27
Randle Dr. B75: R'ley 6A 38
Randle Rd. DY9: Lye 1G 125
Randwick Gro. B44: Gt Barr 4F 67
Ranelagh Ho. WV2: Wolv. 4H 43
(off Blakenhall Gdns.)
Ranelagh Rd. WV2: Wolv. 5G 43
Rangeview Cl. B74: S'tly 5H 51
Rangeways Rd. DY6: K'wfrd 5D 92
Rangoon Rd. B92: Sol 1A 138
Ranleigh Av. DY6: K'wfrd. 5D 92
Rannoch Cl. DY5: Brie H. 3F 109
Ranscombe Dr. DY3: Gorn. 5H 75
Ransom Rd. B23: Erd 3C 84
Ranworth Ri. WV4: Penn 1H 59
Ratcliffe Cl. DY3: Sed. 6B 60
Ratcliffe Rd. B91: Sol. 6G 137
WV11: Wed. 3A 30
Ratcliff Wlk. B69: O'bry 2G 97
Ratcliff Way DY4: Tip 1D 78
Rathbone Cl. B5: Bal H. 4G 117
WV14: Bils 6F 45
Rathbone Rd. B67: Smeth 1D 114
Rathlin Cl. WV9: Pend 4E 15
Rathlin Cft. B36: Cas B. 3D 106
Rathmore Cl. DY8: Stourb 3B 124
Rathwell Cl. WV9: Pend 5E 15
Rattle Cft. B33: Stech. 6C 104
Ravenall Cl. B34: S End 2F 105
Raven Cl. WS6: C Hay 3D 6
Raven Ct. DY5: Brie H 1H 109
(off Lit. Potter St.)
Raven Cres. WV11: Wed 1H 29
Ravenfield Cl. B8: W End 4F 103
Ravenhayes La. B32: Fran 6G 129
Raven Hays Rd. B31: Longb. 5A 144
Ravenhill Dr. WV8: Cod 4G 13
Ravenhurst Dr. B43: Gt Barr. 2A 66
Ravenhurst M. B23: Erd 4E 85
Ravenhurst Rd. B17: Harb 4G 115
Raven Rd. WS5: Wals. 5F 49
Ravensbourne Gro. WV13: W'hall 1C 46
Ravens Ct. WS8: Bwnhls 6B 10
Ravenscroft DY8: Woll 5A 108
Ravenscroft Rd. B92: Olton 5E 137
WV12: W'hall 4B 30
Ravensdale Cl. WS5: Wals 4F 49
Ravensdale Gdns. WS5: Wals 5F 49
Ravensdale Rd. B10: Small H. 4F 119
Ravenshaw B91: Sol. 5D 152
Ravenshaw La. B91: Sol. 3C 152
(not continuous)
Ravenshaw Rd. B16: Edg. 1G 115
Ravenshaw Way B91: Sol. 5C 152
Ravenshill Rd. B14: Yard W. 3C 148
Ravensholme WV6: Tett 1F 41
Ravenside Retail Pk. B24: Erd. 4C 86
Ravensitch Wlk. DY5: Brie H 2A 110
Ravenswood B15: Edg 3A 116
Ravenswood Cl. B74: Four O 3H 53
Ravenswood Dr. B91: Sol. 6D 150
Ravenswood Dr. Sth. B91: Sol 6C 150
Ravenswood Hill B46: Col 2H 107
Raven Wlk. B15: Edg 4E 117
Rawdon Gro. B44: K'sdng. 5B 68
Rawlings Rd. B67: Smeth 1D 114
Rawlins Cft. B35: Cas V. 4G 87
Rawlins St. B16: Birm 2C 116
Raybon Cft. B45: Redn. 3G 157
Raybould's Bri. Rd. WS2: Wals. 5A 32
Raybould's Fold DY2: Neth. 4E 95
Rayford Dr. B71: W Brom. 3D 64
Ray Hall La. B43: Gt Barr. 4E 65
Rayleigh Ho. B27: A Grn 2B 136
Rayleigh Rd. WV3: Wolv 3E 43
Raymond Av. B42: Gt Barr 1D 82
Raymond Cl. WS2: Wals. 4B 32
Raymond Gdns. WV11: Wed 4G 29
Raymond Rd. B8: Salt. 5E 103
Raymont Gro. B43: Gt Barr. 1D 66
Rayners Cft. B26: Yard 2D 120
Raynor Rd. WV10: Wolv. 3B 28
RBSA Gallery 6E 101 (2B 4)
Rea Av. B45: Rubery. 1E 157
Reabrook Rd. B31: Longb 1D 158
Rea Bus. Pk. B7: Birm 5C 102
Rea Cl. B31: Longb. 2E 159
Readers Wlk. B43: Gt Barr. 4B 66
Rea Fordway B45: Fran. 6F 143
Reansway Sq. WV6: Wolv 5E 27
Reapers Cl. WV12: W'hall 4D 30
Reapers Wlk. WV8: Pend. 6D 14
Rea Rd. B31: N'fld 6D 144
Reaside Cres. B14: K Hth. 2D 146
Reaside Cft. B12: Bal H 5G 117
Reaside Dr. B45: Redn 1H 157
Rea St. B5: Birm 2H 117 (6G 5)
Rea St. Sth. B5: Birm. 3G 117
Rea Ter. B5: Birm 1H 117 (5H 5)
Rea Twr. B19: Birm. 4E 101
(off Mosborough Cres.)
Rea Valley Dr. B31: N'fld 5F 145
Reaview Dr. B29: S Oak 3D 132
Reaymer Cl. WS2: Wals. 3H 31
Reay Nadin Dr. B73: S'tly. 1B 68
Rebecca Dr. B29: S Oak 3A 132
Rebecca Gdns. WV4: Penn. 1D 58
Recreation St. DY2: Neth 4F 95
Rectory Av. WS10: Darl 5D 46

Rectory Cl.—Rochford Cl.

Rectory Cl. DY8: Stourb 2F **125**
Rectory Flds. DY8: Word 1C **108**
Rectory Gdns. B36: Cas B 1E **105**
B68: O'bry 4H **97**
B91: Sol 4G **151**
DY8: Stourb 2F **125**
Rectory Gro. B18: Win G 3A **100**
Rectory La. B36: Cas B 1E **105**
Rectory Pk. Av. B75: S Cold 1C **70**
Rectory Pk. Cl. B75: S Cold 1C **70**
Rectory Pk. Ct. B75: S Cold 5D **54**
Rectory Pk. Rd. B26: Sheld 6F **121**
Rectory Rd. B31: N'fld 4F **145**
B75: S Cold 6A **54**
B91: Sol 4G **151**
DY8: Stourb 2F **125**
Rectory St. DY8: Word 6B **92**
Redacre Rd. B73: Bold 3F **69**
Redacres WV6: Tett 3C **26**
Redbank Av. B23: Erd 4C **84**
Redbourn Rd. WS3: Blox 3G **19**
Red Brick Cl. B64: Crad H 4F **111**
Redbrook Covert B38: K Nor 1A **160**
Red Brook Rd. WS2: Wals 4G **31**
Redbrooks Cl. B91: Sol 6E **151**
Redburn Dr. B14: K Hth 5F **147**
Redcar Cft. B36: Hodg H 1A **104**
Redcar Rd. WV10: F'hses 3H **15**
Redcliffe Dr. WV5: Wom 1H **73**
Redcott's Cl. WV10: Bush 1C **28**
Redcroft Dr. B24: Erd 2A **86**
Redcroft Rd. DY2: Dud 3G **95**
Red Cross Wlk. WV1: Wolv 6G **27**
Reddal Hill Rd. B64: Old H 2G **111**
REDDICAP HEATH 1C **70**
Reddicap Heath Rd. B75: S Cold 1C **70**
Reddicap Hill B75: S Cold 1C **70**
Reddicap Trad. Est. B75: S Cold 6B **54**
Reddicroft B73: S Cold 6A **54**
Reddings, The B47: H'wd 4A **162**
Reddings La. B11: Tys 3E **135**
Reddings Rd. B13: Mose 3F **133**
Redditch Ho. B33: Kitts G 1A **122**
Redditch Rd. B31: Longb 3G **159**
B48: Hopw 6G **159**
Redfern Cl. B92: Olton 4F **137**
Redfern Dr. WS7: Burn 1D **10**
Redfern Pk. Way B11: Tys 6G **119**
Redfern Rd. B11: Tys 6F **119**
Redfly La. DY5: P'ntt 3G **93**
Redford Cl. B13: Mose 3B **134**
Redgate Cl. B38: K Nor 5H **145**
Redhall Rd. B32: Harb 4C **114**
DY3: Gorn 5G **75**
Red Hill DY8: Stourb 1F **125**
Redhill DY2: Dud 1F **95**
Redhill Av. WV5: Wom 1G **73**
Red Hill Cl. DY8: Stourb 1F **125**
Redhill Ct. DY8: Stourb 2F **125**
Red Hill Gro. B38: K Nor 2B **160**
Redhill La. B45: Rubery 4C **156**
B61: C'wich 4C **156**
Redhill Pl. B62: Hunn 6A **128**
Redhill Rd. B25: Yard 5G **119**
B31: Longb 1F **159**
B38: K Nor, Head H 1F **159**
Red Hill St. WV1: Wolv 6G **27**
Redholme Ct. DY8: Stourb 1E **125**
Red Ho. Av. WS10: W'bry 2H **63**
Redhouse Cl. B93: Ben H 4A **166**
Redhouse Cone & Mus. 2C **108**
Redhouse Ind. Est. WS9: A'rdge 3H **33**
Redhouse La. WS9: A'rdge 4A **34**
Red Ho. Pk. Rd. B43: Gt Barr 3A **66**
Redhouse Rd. B33: Stech 6C **104**
WV6: Tett 4G **25**
Redhouse St. WS1: Wals 4C **48**
Redhurst Dr. WV10: F'hses 4F **15**
Redlake Dr. DY9: Pedm 4F **125**
Redlake Rd. DY9: Pedm 4F **125**
Redlands Cl. B91: Sol 2H **151**
Redlands Rd. B91: Sol 2G **151**
Redlands Way B74: S'tly 2A **52**
Red La. DY3: Sed 5F **59**
WV11: Ess 6C **18**
Red Leasowes Rd. B63: Hale 2H **127**
Redliff Av. B36: Cas B 6H **87**
Red Lion Av. WS11: Nort C 1E **9**
Red Lion Cl. B69: Tiv 1A **96**
Red Lion Cres. WS11: Nort C 1E **9**
Red Lion La. WS11: Nort C 1E **9**
Red Lion St. WS2: Wals 6C **32**
WV1: Wolv 1G **43** (2A **170**)
Redmead Cl. B30: K Nor 3G **145**
Redmoor Gdns. WV4: Penn 6E **43**
Redmoor Way B76: Min 1H **87**
REDNAL 3H **157**
Rednal Hill La. B45: Rubery 3F **157**
Rednall Dr. B75: R'ley 6A **38**
Rednal Mill Dr. B45: Redn 2B **158**
Rednal Rd. B38: K Nor 1G **159**
Redoak Ho. WV10: Wolv 6B **28**
Redpine Crest WV12: W'hall 5D **30**
Red River Rd. WS2: Wals 4G **31**
Red Rock Dr. WV8: Cod 5F **13**
Red Rooster Ind. Est. WS9: A'rdge 3A **34**
Redruth Cl. DY6: K'wfrd 1B **92**
WS5: Wals 4H **49**
Redruth Rd. WS5: Wals 4H **49**
Redstone Dr. WV11: Wed 4H **29**
Redstone Farm Rd. B28: Hall G 1H **149**
Redstone Way DY3: Lwr G 3H **75**
Redthorn Gro. B33: Stech 6B **104**
Redvers Rd. B9: Small H 2E **119**
Redway Ct. B75: S Cold 1C **70**
Redwing Cl. WS7: Hamm 1F **11**
Redwing Gro. B23: Erd 6B **68**
Red Wing Wlk. B36: Cas B 1C **106**
Redwood Av. DY1: Dud 2B **76**
Redwood Bus. Pk. B66: Smeth 2A **98**
Redwood Cl. B30: K Nor 3A **146**
B74: S'tly 1H **51**
Redwood Cft. B14: K Hth 6G **133**
Redwood Dr. B69: Tiv 5B **78**
Redwood Gdns. B27: A Grn 6H **119**
Redwood Ho. B37: K'hrst 4C **106**
Redwood Rd. B30: K Nor 3A **146**
WS5: Wals 1F **65**
WV14: Cose 3F **61**
Redwood Way WV12: W'hall 1B **30**
Redworth Ho. *B45: Rubery* *1F 157*
(off Deelands Rd.)
Reedham Gdns. WV4: Penn 6B **42**
Reedly Rd. WV12: W'hall 6C **18**
Reedmace Cl. B38: K Nor 1B **160**
Reedswood Cl. WS2: Wals 6A **32**
Reedswood Gdns. WS2: Wals 6A **32**
Reedswood La. WS2: Wals 6A **32**
Reedswood Retail Pk. WS2: Wals 5H **31**
Reedswood Way WS2: Wals 5G **31**
Rees Dr. WV5: Wom 6H **57**
Reeves Gdns. WV8: Cod 3G **13**
Reeves Rd. B14: K Hth 1E **147**
Reeves St. WS3: Blox 1H **31**
Reflex Ind. Pk. WV13: W'hall 6H **29**
Reform St. B70: W Brom 4B **80**
Regal Cft. B36: Hodg H 1H **103**
Regal Dr. WS2: Wals 3A **48**
Regan Av. B90: Shir 6G **149**
Regan Ct. B75: S Cold 6G **55**
Regan Cres. B23: Erd 1E **85**
Regan Dr. B69: O'bry 1D **96**
Regency Cl. B9: Small H 2D **118**
Regency Ct. WV1: Wolv 6G **27** (1A **170**)
Regency Dr. B38: K Nor 5B **146**
Regency Gdns. B14: Yard W 4C **148**
Regency Wlk. B74: Four O 4D **36**
Regent Av. B69: Tiv 6A **78**
Regent Cl. B5: Edg 5F **117**
B63: Hale 1A **128**
B69: Tiv 1A **96**
DY6: K'wfrd 3B **92**
Regent Ct. *B62: Quin* *4G 113*
(off Binswood Rd.)
B66: Smeth 4E **99**
Regent Dr. B69: Tiv 6A **78**
Regent Ho. *WS2: Wals* *6B 32*
(off Green La.)
WV1: Wolv 6F **27** (2A **170**)
Regent Pde. B1: Birm 5E **101** (1A **4**)
Regent Pk. Rd. B10: Small H 3C **118**
Regent Pl. B1: Birm 5E **101** (1A **4**)
B69: Tiv 5B **78**
Regent Rd. B17: Harb 5H **115**
B21: Hand 1H **99**
B69: Tiv 1A **96**
WV4: Penn 6C **42**
Regent Row B18: Birm 5E **101** (1A **4**)
Regents, The B15: Edg 3H **115**
Regent St. B1: Birm 5E **101** (1A **4**)
B30: Stir 6C **132**
B64: Old H 1H **111**
B66: Smeth 3E **99**
DY1: Dud 1E **77**
DY4: Tip 5G **61**
WV13: W'hall 6A **30**
WV14: Bils 5F **45**
Regents Way B75: S Cold 5D **54**
Regent Wlk. B8: W End 2H **103**
Regina Av. B44: Gt Barr 5F **67**
Regina Cl. B45: Fran 5E **143**
Regina Cres. WV6: Tett 5H **25**
Regina Dr. B42: P Barr 4E **83**
WS4: Wals 5F **33**
Reginald Rd. B8: Salt 5D **102**
B67: Smeth 1D **114**
Regis Beeches WV6: Tett 4A **26**
Regis Gdns. B65: Row R 1C **112**
Regis Heath Rd. B65: Row R 1D **112**
Regis Rd. B65: Row R 2C **112**
WV6: Tett 4H **25**
Regus Bldg. B90: Bly P 6D **164**
Reid Av. WV12: W'hall 3D **30**
Reid Rd. B68: O'bry 2A **114**
Reigate Av. B8: W End 5H **103**
Reliance Trad. Est. WV14: Bils 6D **44**
Relko Dr. B36: Hodg H 2A **104**
Remembrance Rd. WS10: W'bry 2A **64**
Remington Pl. WS2: Wals 4A **32**
Remington Rd. WS2: Wals 3H **31**
Renaissance Ct. B12: Birm 2A **118**
Renfrew Cl. DY8: Word 6A **92**
Renfrew Sq. B35: Cas V 3F **87**
Rennie Gro. B32: Quin 6B **114**
Rennison Dr. WV5: Wom 1G **73**
Renown Cl. DY5: P'ntt 1F **93**
Renton Gro. WV10: Oxl 6E **15**
Renton Rd. WV10: Oxl 6E **15**
Repington Way B75: S Cold 5F **55**
Repton Av. WV6: Pert 6E **25**
Repton Gro. B9: Bord G 6H **103**
Repton Ho. B23: Erd 1F **85**
Repton Rd. B9: Bord G 6H **103**
Reservoir Cl. WS2: Wals 3H **47**
Reservoir Pas. WS10: W'bry 2F **63**
Reservoir Pl. WS2: Wals 3H **47**
Reservoir Retreat B16: Edg 2B **116**
Reservoir Rd. B16: Edg 1B **116**
B23: Erd 3D **84**
B29: S Oak 2F **131**
B45: Coft H 6A **158**
B65: Row R 6C **96**
B68: O'bry 5A **98**
B92: Olton 5D **136**
Reservoir St. WS2: Wals 3H **47**
Retallack Cl. B66: Smeth 1F **99**
Retford Dr. B76: Walm 1C **70**
Retford Gro. B25: Yard 5A **120**
Retreat, The B64: Crad H 4G **111**
Retreat Gdns. DY3: Sed 6A **60**
Retreat St. WV3: Wolv 3F **43** (6A **170**)
Revesby Wlk. B7: Birm 5A **102**
Rex Cl. WS3: Blox 6H **19**
Reynards Cl. DY3: Sed 6C **60**
Reynolds Cl. DY3: Swind 5E **73**
Reynolds Ct. B68: O'bry 4H **113**
Reynolds Gro. WV6: Pert 4F **25**
Reynolds Ho. *B19: Loz* *2G 101*
(off Newbury Rd.)
Reynolds Rd. B21: Hand 2A **100**
Reynoldstown Rd. B36: Hodg H 1A **104**
Reynolds Wlk. WV11: Wed 1B **30**
Rhayader Rd. B31: N'fld 2C **144**
Rhodes Cl. DY3: Lwr G 3E **75**
Rhone Cl. B11: S'hll 2C **134**
Rhoose Cft. B35: Cas V 4F **87**
Rhys Thomas Cl. WV12: W'hall 5D **30**
Rian Ct. B64: Crad H 3F **111**
Ribbesford Av. WV10: Oxl 1F **27**
Ribbesford Cl. B63: Crad 6F **111**
Ribbesford Cres. WV14: Cose 4F **61**
Ribble Ct. B73: S Cold 6H **53**
Ribblesdale Rd. B30: Stir 6C **132**
Ribble Wlk. B36: Cas B 1B **106**
Richard Lighton Ho. B1: Birm 3A **4**
Richard Pl. WS5: Wals 3G **49**
Richard Rd. WS5: Wals 3G **49**
Richards Cl. B31: Longb 3D **158**
B65: Row R 5E **97**
Richards Ho. B69: O'bry 5D **96**
WS2: Wals *6B 32*
(off Burrowes St.)
Richardson Dr. DY8: Amb 3C **108**
Richards Rd. DY4: Tip 4H **61**
Richards St. WS10: Darl 3D **46**
Richard St. B6: Aston 4H **101**
B7: Birm 4H **101**
B70: W Brom 4H **79**
Richard St. Sth. B70: W Brom 5A **80**
Richard St. W. B70: W Brom 5H **79**
Richard Williams Rd. WS10: W'bry 3H **63**
Richborough Dr. DY1: Dud 4A **76**
Riches St. WV6: Wolv 6D **26**
Richford Gro. B33: Kitts G 1H **121**
Richmere Ct. WV6: Tett 6H **25**
Richmond Ashton Dr. DY4: Tip 2A **78**
Richmond Av. B12: Bal H 6H **117**
WV3: Wolv 2D **42**
Richmond Cl. B20: Hand 4C **82**
B47: H'wd 2B **162**
Richmond Ct. *B15: Edg* *3D 116*
(off Enfield Rd.)
B29: W Cas 6G **131**
B63: Hale 2G **127**
B68: O'bry 4A **98**
B72: W Grn 6H **69**
DY9: Pedm *4F 125*
(off Redlake Rd.)
Richmond Cft. B42: Gt Barr 1B **82**
Richmond Dr. WV3: Wolv 2C **42**
WV6: Pert 5F **25**
Richmond Gdns. DY8: Amb 4D **108**
WV5: Wom 2G **73**
Richmond Gro. DY8: Woll 3C **108**
Richmond Hill B68: O'bry 4A **98**
Richmond Hill Gdns. B15: Edg 4A **116**
Richmond Hill Rd. B15: Edg 5A **116**
Richmond Ho. B37: Chel W 2E **123**
Richmond Pk. DY6: W Hth 1A **92**
Richmond Pl. B14: K Hth 5H **133**
Richmond Rd. B18: Hock 3D **100**
B33: Stech 1B **120**
B45: Rubery 2E **157**
B66: Smeth 1E **115**
B73: S Cold 5H **53**
B92: Olton 4C **136**
DY2: Dud 1E **95**
DY3: Sed 6A **60**
WV3: Wolv 1C **42**
Richmond St. B63: Hale 1A **128**
B70: W Brom 1F **79**
WS1: Wals 2D **48**
Richmond St. Sth.
B70: W Brom 2E **79**
Richmond Way B37: Chel W 6E **107**
Rickard Cl. B93: Know 4A **166**
Rickman Dr. B15: Birm 3F **117**
Rickyard Cl. B25: Yard 2B **120**
B29: W Cas 1E **145**
Rickyard Piece B32: Quin 1C **130**
Riddfield Rd. B36: Hodg H 1C **104**
Ridding La. WS10: W'bry 3F **63**
Riddings, The B33: Stech 5C **104**
B76: Walm 5F **71**
DY9: W'cte 3H **125**
WV10: Bush 2C **28**
Riddings Cres. WS3: Pels 3D **20**
Riddings Hill CV7: Bal C 5H **169**
RIDGACRE 5B **114**
Ridgacre Ent. Pk. B71: W Brom 1H **79**
Ridgacre La. B32: Quin 5H **113**
Ridgacre Rd. B32: Quin 5H **113**
(not continuous)
B71: W Brom 1H **79**
Ridgacre Rd. W. B32: Quin 5G **113**
Ridge Cl. B13: Mose 1C **148**
WS2: Wals 6D **30**
Ridgefield Rd. B62: B'hth 3C **112**
Ridge Gro. DY9: Lye 6G **109**
Ridge Hill DY8: Word 6D **92**
Ridge La. WV11: Wed 2F **29**
Ridgemount Dr. B38: K Nor 2H **159**
Ridge Rd. DY6: K'wfrd 4H **91**
Ridge St. DY8: Woll 5A **108**
Ridgewater Cl. B45: Redn 3H **157**
Ridge Way B32: Quin 1G **129**
Ridgeway B17: Edg 1F **115**
WS9: A'rdge 5D **34**
Ridgeway, The B23: Erd 1A **84**
DY3: Sed 1H **75**
WS7: Burn 1C **10**
Ridgeway Av. B62: Quin 5G **113**
Ridgeway Ct. WS2: Wals 2F **47**
Ridgeway Dr. WV4: Penn 2D **58**
Ridgeway Rd. DY4: Tip 5A **62**
DY8: Word 1D **108**
Ridgewood B34: S End 3F **105**
Ridgewood Av. DY8: Woll 4A **108**
Ridgewood Cl. WS1: Wals 3D **48**
Ridgewood Dr. B75: Four O 2H **53**
Ridgewood Gdns. B44: Gt Barr 6G **67**
Ridgmont Cft. B32: Quin 6C **114**
Riding Cl. B71: W Brom 5D **64**
Riding Way WV12: W'hall 4C **30**
Ridley St. B1: Birm 2E **117** (6B **4**)
Ridpool Rd. B33: Kitts G 6F **105**
Rifle St. WV14: Cose 5C **60**
Rigby St. WS10: W'bry 4F **63**
Riland Av. B75: S Cold 6B **54**
Riland Ct. B72: W Grn 6A **70**
Riland Gro. B75: S Cold 6A **54**
Riland Ind. Est. B75: S Cold 6B **54**
Riland Rd. B75: S Cold 6B **54**
Riley Cres. WV3: Wolv 5D **42**
Riley Dr. B36: Cas B 6C **88**
Riley Rd. B14: Yard W 4D **148**
Riley St. WV13: W'hall 1B **46**
Rilstone Rd. B32: Harb 6D **114**
Rindleford Av. WV4: Penn 5A **42**
Ring, The B25: Yard 3A **120**
Ringhills Rd. WV8: Bilb 5H **13**
Ringinglow Rd. B44: Gt Barr 3E **67**
Ringmere Av. B36: Cas B 1F **105**
Ring Rd. Nth. B15: Edg 1B **132**
Ring Rd. St Andrews
WV1: Wolv 1F **43** (3A **170**)
Ring Rd. St Davids
WV1: Wolv 1H **43** (3D **170**)
Ring Rd. St Georges
WV2: Wolv 2H **43** (5C **170**)
Ring Rd. St Johns
WV2: Wolv 2G **43** (5A **170**)
Ring Rd. St Marks
WV3: Wolv 2F **43** (4A **170**)
Ring Rd. St Patricks
WV1: Wolv 6H **27** (1C **170**)
Ring Rd. St Peters
WV1: Wolv 1G **43** (2A **170**)
Ring Rd. Sth. B15: Edg 1B **132**
Ringswood Rd. B92: Olton 1C **136**
Ringway Bus. Pk. B7: Birm 4A **102**
Ringwood Av. WS9: A'rdge 4D **34**
Ringwood Dr. B45: Fran 6G **143**
Ringwood Rd. WV10: Bush 6H **15**
Ripley Cl. B69: Tiv 1H **95**
Ripley Gro. B23: Erd 2B **84**
Ripon Dr. B71: W Brom 4B **64**
Ripon Rd. B14: Yard W 3C **148**
WS2: Wals 1H **47**
WV10: Oxl 2G **27**
Rippingille Rd. B43: Gt Barr 1E **67**
Ripple Rd. B30: Stir 6D **132**
Risborough Ho. B31: Longb 1D **158**
Rischale Way WS4: Rus 1H **33**
Rise, The B37: Mars G 4C **122**
B42: Gt Barr 5C **66**
B48: Hopw 5F **159**
DY6: K'wfrd 4C **92**
Rise Av. B45: Redn 2G **157**
Riseley Cres. B5: Bal H 5F **117**
Rising Brook WV6: Tett 5H **25**
Rissington Av. B29: S Oak 5C **132**
Ritchie Cl. B13: Mose 4A **134**
Rivendell Ct. B28: Hall G 4E **135**
Rivendell Gdns. WV6: Tett 4H **25**
Riverbank Rd. WV13: W'hall 1D **46**
River Brook Dr. B30: Stir 5D **132**
River Lee Rd. B11: Tys 6E **119**
Rivermead Pk. B34: S End 4E **105**
Riversdale Rd. B14: Yard W 4D **148**
Riverside Ct. B38: K Nor 4H **145**
B46: Col *2H 107*
(off Prossers Wlk.)
Riverside Cres. B28: Hall G 3D **148**
Riverside Dr. B29: S Oak 2E **133**
B33: Stech 5B **104**
B91: Sol 5A **152**
Riverside Gdns. WV8: Bilb 3H **13**
Riversleigh Dr. DY8: Word 3C **108**
River St. B5: Birm 1A **118** (5H **5**)
Riverway WS10: W'bry 3H **63**
Rivington Cl. DY8: Stourb 1C **124**
Rivington Cres. B44: K'sdng 4C **68**
Roach Cl. B37: Chel W 6E **107**
DY5: Brie H 4H **93**
Roach Cres. WV11: Wed 1H **29**
Roach Pool Cft. B16: Edg 1G **115**
Robert Av. B23: Erd 1E **85**
Robert Ct. B13: Mose 3B **134**
Robert Rd. B20: Hand 6D **82**
DY4: Tip 1H **77**
Roberts Cl. WS9: Wals W 5B **22**
WS10: Mox 1B **62**
Roberts Ct. B24: Erd 1A **86**
Roberts Grn. Rd. DY3: Up Gor 3A **76**
Roberts La. DY9: Pedm 5F **125**
Robertson Knoll B36: Hodg H 2D **104**
Robertsons Gdns. B7: Nech 2C **102**
Roberts Rd. B27: A Grn 2A **136**
WS3: Wals 4D **32**
WS10: W'bry 2C **64**
Robert St. DY3: Lwr G 3H **75**
Robert Wynd WV14: Cose 4B **60**
Robeson Cl. DY4: Tip 2F **77**
Robin Cl. B36: Cas B 1C **106**
DY6: K'wfrd 3E **93**
Robin Gro. WV11: Wed 2E **29**
Robin Hood Crematorium B90: Shir 2H **149**
Robin Hood Cres. B28: Hall G 6E **135**
Robin Hood Cft. B28: Hall G 1F **149**
Robin Hood Island *B28: Hall G* *2G 149*
(off Stratford Rd.)
Robin Hood La. B28: Hall G 6D **134**
Robin Hood Rd. DY5: Quar B 1B **110**
Robin Rd. B23: Erd 3E **85**
Robins Bus. Pk. DY4: W Brom 6E **63**
Robins Cl. DY8: Stourb 2E **125**
WS6: C Hay 4D **6**
Robins Ct. B14: K Hth 4H **133**
Robinsfield Dr. B31: Longb 2E **159**
Robinsons Way B76: Min 2H **87**
Robin Wlk. WS2: Wals 6F **31**
Robottom Cl. WS2: Wals 3H **31**
Robson Cl. WS8: Bwnhls 2C **22**
Rocester Av. WV11: Wed 2G **29**
Rochdale Wlk. B10: Small H 4C **118**
Roche Rd. WS3: Blox 6F **19**
Rochester Cft. WS2: Wals 5G **31**
Rochester Rd. B31: N'fld 3E **145**
Roche Way WS3: Blox 6F **19**
Rochford Cl. B45: Rubery 2E **157**
B63: Hale 3H **127**
B76: Walm 5E **71**
WS2: Wals 4A **48**

Rochford Ct.—Rutland Ter.

Rochford Ct. B90: M'path 3E 165
Rochford Gro. WV4: Penn. 6B 42
Rock, The WV6: Tett 4B 26
Rock Av. B45: Redn 2A 158
Rocket Pool Dr. WV14: Bils 3H 61
Rockface, The 6H 101 (2H 5)
Rockford Rd. B42: Gt Barr 6C 66
Rock Gro. B92: Olton 2C 136
Rockingham Cl. B93: Dorr 6H 165
DY3: Gorn 4F 75
WS3: Blox 6H 19
Rockingham Dr. WV6: Pert 6E 25
Rockingham Gdns. B74: S Cold 5H 53
Rockingham Hall Gdns.
DY9: Hag 6H 125
Rockingham Rd. B25: Yard 3B 120
Rockland Dr. B33: Stech 5C 104
Rockland Gdns. WV13: W'hall 3H 45
Rocklands Dr. B75: S Cold 3H 53
Rockley Gro. B45: Redn 2H 157
Rockley Rd. B65: Row R 3A 96
Rockmead Av. B44: Gt Barr 3H 67
Rockmoor Cl. B37: K'hrst 6A 106
Rock Rd. B92: Olton 2C 136
WV14: Cose 5B 60
Rocks Hill DY5: Brie H 2H 109
Rock St. DY3: Up Gor 2A 76
Rockville Rd. B8: Salt 5G 103
Rocky La. B6: Aston 3A 102
B7: Nech 3A 102
B42: Gt Barr 1C 82
Rodborough Rd. B26: Sheld 5F 121
B93: Dorr 6F 167
Rodbourne Rd. B17: Harb 2G 131
Roddis Cl. B23: Erd 5D 68
Roderick Dr. WV11: Wed 2F 29
Roderick Rd. B11: S'brk 6C 118
Rodlington Av. B44: Gt Barr 4H 67
Rodman Cl. B15: Edg 3H 115
Rodney Cl. B16: Birm 1C 116
B92: Olton 4F 137
Rodney Rd. B92: Olton 4F 137
Rodway Cl. B19: Loz 2G 101
DY5: Quar B 4H 109
WV4: E'shll 2H 59
Rodwell Gro. B44: K'sdng 5A 68
Roebuck Cl. B34: S End 4A 106
Roebuck Glade WV12: W'hall 5E 31
Roebuck La. B66: Smeth 2C 98
B70: W Brom 6C 80
Roebuck Pl. WS3: Blox 3C 32
Roebuck Rd. WS3: Blox 3C 32
Roebuck St. B70: W Brom 6D 80
Roedean Cl. B44: K'sdng 6B 68
Roford Ct. DY3: Up Gor 1A 76
Rogerfield Rd. B23: Erd 1G 85
Rogers Cl. WV11: Wed 6A 18
Rogers Rd. B8: W End 4H 103
Rokeby Cl. B76: Walm 1C 70
Rokeby Rd. B43: Gt Barr 3B 66
Rokeby Wlk. B34: Hodg H 3D 104
Rokewood Cl. DY6: K'wfrd 6B 74
Roland Gdns. B19: Loz 1E 101
Roland Gro. B19: Loz 1E 101
Rolan Dr. B90: Maj G 1E 163
Roland Rd. B19: Loz 1E 101
Roland Vernon Way
DY4: Tip 6C 62
Rolfe St. B66: Smeth 3E 99
Rollason Rd. B24: Erd 4G 85
DY2: Dud 1F 95
Rollesby Dr. WV13: W'hall 3H 45
Rollingmill Bus. Pk.
WS2: Wals 2A 48
Rolling Mill Cl. B5: Bal H 4G 117
Rollingmill St. WS2: Wals 2A 48
Rollswood Dr. B91: Sol 3D 150
Roman Cl. WS8: Bwnhls 3A 10
Roman Ct. B38: K Nor 1C 160
Roman La. B74: Lit A 5B 36
Roman Pk. B46: Col 6H 89
B74: Lit A 5B 36
Roman Pl. B74: Lit A 1B 52
Roman Rd. B74: Lit A 4C 36
DY7: Stourb 3A 124
DY8: Stourb 1A 124
(not continuous)
Roman Vw. WS11: Cann 1F 7
Roman Way B15: Edg 2H 131
B46: Col 5G 89
B65: Row R 5C 96
Romany Rd. B45: Fran 6D 142
Romany Way DY8: Stourb 2A 124
Roma Rd. B11: Tys 6E 119
Romford Cl. B26: Sheld 5F 121
Romilly Av. B20: Hand 5D 82
Romilly Cl. B76: Walm 1E 71
DY8: Woll 5C 108
Romney Cl. B28: Hall G 6F 135
Romney Ho. Ind. Est. *WS10: Darl* 4B 46
(off Wolverhampton St.)
Romney Way B43: Gt Barr 1F 67
Romsey Gro. WV10: F'hses 4G 15
Romsey Rd. WV10: F'hses 4G 15
Romsey Way WS3: Blox 4F 19
ROMSLEY 3A 142
Romsley Cl. B45: Rubery 1E 157
B63: Hale 3B 128
WS4: S'fld 5G 21
ROMSLEY HILL 5A 142
Romsley Rd. B32: Bart G 5H 129
B68: O'bry 1H 113
DY9: Lye 6G 109
Romulus Cl. B20: Hand 4D 82
Ronald Gro. B36: Cas B 6H 87
Ronald Pl. B9: Bord G 1E 119
Ronald Rd. B9: Bord G 1D 118
Ron Davis Cl. B66: Smeth 4F 99
ROOD END 3A 98
Rood End Rd. B68: O'bry 3A 98
B69: O'bry 2A 98
Rooker Av. WV2: E'shll 4A 44
Rooker Cres. WV2: E'shll 5B 44
Rookery, The B62: Quin 3G 129
Rookery Av. DY5: Brie H 1E 109
WV4: E'shll 2C 60
Rookery La. WS9: A'rdge 3D 34
WV3: Wolv 5E 43
Rookery Pde. WS9: A'rdge 3D 34
Rookery Pk. DY5: P'ntt 4F 93
Rookery Ri. WV5: Wom 1H 73
Rookery Rd. B21: Hand 1A 100
B29: S Oak 3B 132
WV4: E'shll 2C 60
WV5: Wom 1H 73
Rookery St. WV11: Wed 4E 29
Rookwood Dr. WV6: Tett 1F 41
Rookwood Rd. B27: A Grn 1H 135
Rooth St. WS10: W'bry 1H 63
Roper Wlk. DY3: Sed 1B 76
Roper Way DY3: Sed 1B 76
Rope Wlk. WS1: Wals 2E 49
Rosafield Av. B62: Quin 5F 113
Rosalind Av. DY1: Dud 6D 60
Rosalind Gro. WV11: Wed 4A 30
Rosamond St. WS1: Wals 4B 48
Rosary Rd. B23: Erd 4D 84
Rosary Vs. B11: S'hll 6B 118
Rose Av. B68: O'bry 4B 114
DY6: K'wfrd 4D 92
Rose Bank B74: Lit A 4D 36
Rose Bank Dr. WS3: Wals 5C 32
Rosebay Av. B38: K Nor 1B 160
Rosebay Gro. WV5: Wom 1E 73
Rosebery Rd. B66: Smeth 5G 99
Rosebery St. B18: Hock 5C 100
Rosebriars B90: Maj G 2E 163
Rose Cl. B66: Smeth 4G 99
Rose Cott. Dr. *DY8: Word* 6B 92
(off Barnett La.)
Rose Cotts. B29: S Oak 3B 132
B30: Stir 1C 146
Rose Ct. CV7: Bal C 1H 169
Rosecroft Rd. B26: Sheld 5G 121
Rosedale Av. B23: Erd 4E 85
B66: Smeth 4G 99
Rosedale Gro. B25: Yard 3A 120
Rosedale Pl. WV13: W'hall 3A 46
Rosedale Rd. B25: Yard 3A 120
Rosedale Wlk. DY6: K'wfrd 1C 92
Rosedene Dr. B20: Hand 5B 82
Rose Dr. WS8: Clay 1A 22
Rosefield Ct. B67: Smeth 5E 99
Rosefield Cft. B6: Aston 2H 101
Rosefield Rd. B67: Smeth 5E 99
Rosefields B31: N'fld 2F 145
Rose Gdns., The B63: Hale 3G 127
Rosehall Cl. B91: Sol 6D 150
Rose Hill B45: Coft H, Lick 6G 157
DY5: Quar B 2C 110
WV13: W'hall 3A 46
Rose Hill Cl. B36: Cas B 1F 105
Rosehill Ct. *DY1: Dud* 6E 77
(off Wolverhampton St.)
Rose Hill Gdns. WV13: W'hall 2A 46
Rose Hill Rd. B21: Hand 2C 100
Rosehip Cl. WS5: Wals 2E 65
Roseland Av. DY2: Dud 6H 77
Roseland Way B15: Birm 2D 116
Rose La. B69: Tiv 5C 78
Roseleigh Rd. B45: Redn 3H 157
Rosemary Av. WS6: C Hay 2D 6
WV4: Penn 5G 43
WV14: Bils 5H 45
Rosemary Cl. WS8: Clay 1H 21
Rosemary Ct. WV11: Wed 2H 29
Rosemary Cres. DY1: Dud 1B 76
WV4: Penn 6G 43
Rosemary Cres. W. WV4: Penn 6F 43
Rosemary Dr. B74: Lit A 6C 36
Rosemary Hill Rd. B74: Four O 6C 36
Rosemary La. DY8: Stourb 2B 124
Rosemary Nook B74: Lit A 4D 36
Rosemary Rd. B33: Stech 1D 120
B63: Hale 3F 127
DY4: Tip 1A 78
WS6: C Hay 1D 6
(not continuous)
Rosemoor Dr. DY5: Brie H 4F 109
Rosemount B32: Quin 1C 130
Rose Pl. B18: Birm 5E 101 (1A 4)
Rose Rd. B17: Harb 5H 115
B46: Col 1H 107
Rose St. WV14: Bils 3H 61
ROSEVILLE 6D 60
Roseville Ct. *WV14: Cose* 5E 61
(off Castle St.)
Roseville Gdns. WV8: Cod 3G 13
Roseville Pct. *WV14: Cose* 5E 61
(off Castle St.)
Rosewood Cl. B74: Lit A 4D 36
Rosewood Dr. B23: Erd 5D 84
WV12: W'hall 1B 30
Rosewood Gdns. WV11: Ess 4B 18
Rosewood Pk. WS6: C Hay 3D 6
Rosewood Rd. DY1: Dud 2D 76
Roshven Rd. B12: Bal H 1A 134
Roslin Gro. B19: Hock 3E 101
Roslyn Cl. B66: Smeth 3E 99
Ross B65: Row R 1B 112
Ross Cl. WV3: Wolv 1C 42
Ross Dr. DY6: K'wfrd 2A 92
Rosse Ct. B92: Sol 5B 138
Rossendale Cl. B63: Crad 5F 111
Ross Hgts. B65: Row R 6B 96
Rosslyn Rd. B76: Walm 1D 86
Ross Rd. WS3: Wals 3D 32
Rostrevor Rd. B10: Small H 2F 119
Rotary Ho. DY1: Dud 6B 76
Rotherby Gro. B37: Mars G 4D 122
Rotherfield Rd. B26: Sheld 3F 121
Rothesay Cft. B32: Bart G 6H 129
Rothesay Dr. DY8: Word 6A 92
Rothesay Way WV12: W'hall 3B 30
Rothley Wlk. B38: K Nor 1G 159
Rothwell Dr. B91: Shir 2B 150
Rotton Pk. Rd. B16: Edg 5H 99
(not continuous)
Rotton Pk. St. B16: Birm 6B 100
ROTTON ROW 5E 167
Rough Coppice Wlk. B35: Cas V 5E 87
ROUGH HAY 4C 46
Rough Hay Pl. WS10: Darl 4C 46
Rough Hay Rd. WS10: Darl 4C 46
Rough Hill Dr. B65: Row R 3H 95
Rough Hills Cl. WV2: E'shll 5B 44
Rough Hills Rd. WV2: E'shll 5B 44
Roughlea Av. B36: Hodg H 2D 104
ROUGHLEY 6A 38
Roughley Dr. B75: R'ley 1A 54
Roughley Farm Rd. B75: R'ley 6C 38
Rough Rd. B44: K'sdng 2A 68
Rough Wood Country Pk. 3E 31
Rouncil Cl. B92: Sol 6H 137
Roundabout, The B31: Longb 6B 144
Round Cft. WV13: W'hall 1A 46
Round Hill DY3: Sed 3H 59
Round Hill Av. DY9: Pedm 4G 125
Roundhill Cl. B76: Walm 2C 70
Roundhill Ho. DY6: K'wfrd 6B 74
Roundhills Rd. B62: B'hth 3F 113
Roundhill Ter. B62: B'hth 2E 113
Roundhill Way WS8: Bwnhls 3B 10
Roundhouse Rd. DY3: Up Gor 3A 76
Roundlea Cl. WV12: W'hall 1B 30
Roundlea Rd. B31: N'fld 5C 130
Round Moor Wlk. B35: Cas V 4E 87
ROUND OAK 5H 93
Round Rd. B24: Erd 5H 85
Roundsaw Cft. B45: Rubery 1F 157
ROUND'S GREEN 2E 97
Round's Grn. Rd. B69: O'bry 2E 97
Rounds Hill Rd. WV14: Cose 5F 61
Rounds Rd. WV14: Cose 2F 61
Round St. DY2: Neth 3E 95
Roundway Down WV6: Pert 6E 25
Rounton Cl. B74: Four O 5D 36
Rousay Cl. B45: Fran 6F 143
Rousdon Gro. B43: Gt Barr 5H 65
Rover Dr. B27: A Grn 1B 136
B36: Cas B 6B 88
Rovex Bus. Pk. B11: Tys 6F 119
Rowallan Rd. B75: R'ley 2B 54
Rowan Cl. B47: H'wd 4B 162
B76: Walm 3D 70
Rowan Ct. B30: K Nor 5C 146
B66: Smeth 1B 98
Rowan Cres. WV3: Wolv 4C 42
WV14: Cose 4D 60
Rowan Dr. B28: Hall G 2G 149
WV11: Ess 4B 18
Rowan Grange B74: Lit A 4C 36
Rowan Ri. DY6: K'wfrd 3C 92
Rowan Rd. B72: S Cold 3A 70
DY3: Sed 4B 60
WS5: Wals 1D 64
Rowantrees B45: Redn 4H 157
Rowan Way B31: Longb 6D 144
B37: Chel W 2E 123
Roway La. B69: O'bry 6E 79
Rowbrook Cl. B90: Maj G 1E 163
Rowchester Ct. B4: Birm 2E 5
Rowcroft Covert B14: K Hth 4E 147
Rowdale Rd. B42: Gt Barr 6E 67
Rowden Dr. B23: Erd 1G 85
B91: Sol 5C 150
Rowena Gdns. DY3: Sed 3G 59
Rowheath Ho. B30: B'vlle 1A 146
Rowheath Rd. B30: K Nor 3B 146
Rowington Av. B65: Row R 6D 96
Rowington Rd. B34: S End 3A 106
Rowland Gdns. WS2: Wals 6A 32
Rowland Hill Dr. DY4: Tip 2C 78
Rowlands Av. WS2: Wals 6E 31
WV1: Wolv 1D 44
Rowlands Cl. WS2: Wals 5E 31
Rowlands Cres. B91: Sol 5F 137
Rowlands Rd. B26: Yard 4C 120
Rowland St. WS2: Wals 6A 32
Rowley Gro. B33: Kitts G 6H 105
Rowley Hall Av. B65: Row R 5C 96
Rowley Hill Vw. B64: Crad H 3H 111
Rowley Pl. WS4: Rus 2F 33
ROWLEY REGIS 6C 96
Rowley Regis Crematorium
B65: Row R 1A 112
Rowley Regis Station (Rail) 1E 113
Rowley St. WS1: Wals 1D 48
Rowley Vw. B70: W Brom 4H 79
WS10: Darl 1C 62
WV14: Bils 2A 62
Rowley Village B65: Row R 6C 96
Rowney Cft. B28: Hall G 2E 149
Rowood Dr. B91: Sol 6G 137
B92: Sol 6H 137
Rowthorn Cl. B74: S'tly 4A 52
Rowthorn Dr. B90: M'path 3E 165
Rowton Av. WV6: Pert 6E 25
Rowton Dr. B74: S'tly 6H 51
Roxburgh Gro. B43: Gt Barr 1E 67
Roxburgh Rd. B73: S Cold 2G 69
Roxby Gdns. WV6: Wolv 4E 27
Royal Arch Apartments
B1: Birm 2E 117 (6B 4)
Royal Cl. B65: Row R 4C 96
DY5: Brie H 3G 109
Royal Ct. B72: W Grn 3H 69
Royal Doulton Crystal 4D 108
Royal Gro. B23: Erd 6B 68
Royal Oak Rd. B62: Quin 1F 129
B65: Row R 4H 95
Royal Rd. B72: S Cold 6A 54
Royal Scot Gro. WS1: Wals 6C 48
Royal Star Cl. B33: Kitts G 1G 121
Royal Stop, The (MM) 2A 44
Royal Way DY4: Tip 5A 78
Roydon Rd. B27: A Grn 5A 136
Roylesden Cres. B73: New O 3C 68
Royston Chase B74: Lit A 6B 36
Royston Ct. *B13: Mose* 3B 134
(off Wake Grn. Pk.)
Royston Cft. B12: Bal H 5H 117
Royston Way DY3: Sed 5G 59
RSPB Sandwell Valley Nature Reserve
1G 81
Rubens Cl. DY3: Up Gor 2H 75
RUBERY 2F 157
Rubery By-Pass B45: Rubery 2E 157
Rubery Ct. WS10: Darl 4C 46
Rubery Farm Gro. B45: Rubery 1F 157
Rubery Fld. Cl. B45: Redn 6G 143
Rubery La. B45: Fran 6F 143
Rubery La. Sth. B45: Rubery 1F 157
Rubery St. WS10: Darl 3D 46
Ruckley Av. B19: Loz 2E 101
Ruckley Rd. B29: W Cas 5E 131
Rudd Gdns. WV10: Wolv 5D 28
Ruddington Way B19: Hock 4G 101
Rudge Av. WV1: Wolv 6D 28
Rudge Cl. WV12: W'hall 5C 30
Rudge Cft. B33: Kitts G 5E 105
Rudge St. WV14: Cose 3G 61
Rudge Wlk. B18: Hock 6C 100
Rudgewick Cft. B6: Aston 3H 101
Rudyard Cl. WV10: Bush 3A 16
Rudyard Gro. B33: Kitts G 6F 105
Rudyngfield Dr. B33: Stech 6D 104
Rufford Cl. B23: Erd 5D 68
Rufford Rd. DY9: Lye 1G 125
Rufford St. DY9: Lye 5H 109
Rufford Way WS9: A'rdge 2A 34
Rugby Rd. DY8: Woll 4B 108
Rugby St. WV1: Wolv 6F 27
Rugeley Av. WV12: W'hall 1D 30
Rugeley Cl DY4: Tip 2G 77
Ruislip Cl. B35: Cas V 3E 87
RUITON 3H 75
Ruiton St. DY3: Lwr G 3H 75
Rumbow B63: Hale 1B 128
RUMBUSH 6E 163
Rumbush La. B90: Dic H 3G 163
(Dickens Heath Rd.)
B90: Dic H, Tid G 6E 163
(Norton La.)
B94: Earls 6E 163
Runcorn Cl. B37: F'bri 5E 107
Runcorn Rd. B12: Bal H 6H 117
Runnymede Dr. CV7: Bal C 6H 169
Runnymede Rd. B11: S'hll 2E 135
Rupert St. B7: Birm 5A 102
WV3: Wolv 1E 43
RUSHALL 2F 33
Rushall Cl. DY8: Word 3C 108
WS4: Wals 5F 33
Rushall Ct. *B43: Gt Barr* 6A 66
(off West Rd.)
Rushall Mnr. Cl. WS4: Wals 5F 33
Rushall Mnr. Rd. WS4: Wals 5F 33
Rushall Rd. WV10: Bush 5A 16
Rushbrook Cl. B92: Olton 3C 136
WS8: Clay 1A 22
Rushbrooke Cl. B13: Mose 1H 133
Rushbrooke Dr. B73: New O 2C 68
Rushbrook Gro. B14: K Hth 4E 147
Rushbury Cl. B90: Shir 3B 150
WV14: Bils 6D 44
Rushden Cft. B44: K'sdng 4H 67
Rushes Mill WS3: Pels 4C 20
Rushey La. B11: Tys 6G 119
Rushford Av. WV5: Wom 1G 73
Rushford Cl. B90: M'path 2E 165
Rush Grn. B32: Bart G 3C 130
Rushlake Grn. B34: S End 4F 105
Rushleigh Rd. B90: Maj G 1E 163
Rushmead Gro. B45: Redn 2G 157
Rushmere Rd. DY4: Tip 5A 62
Rushmoor Cl. B74: S Cold 5H 53
Rushmore Ho. B45: Rubery 1F 157
Rushton Cl. CV7: Bal C 5H 169
Rushwater Cl. WV5: Wom 1E 73
Rushwick Cft. B34: S End 3H 105
Rushwick Gro. B90: M'path 3E 165
Rushwood Cl. WS4: Wals 6E 33
Rushy Piece B32: Bart G 2B 130
Ruskin Av. B65: Row R 1D 112
DY3: Lwr G 2E 75
WV4: E'shll 3B 60
Ruskin Cl. B6: Aston 2H 101
Ruskin Ct. B66: Smeth 2B 98
B68: O'bry 3H 113
Ruskin Gro. B27: A Grn 3H 135
Ruskin Hall Gro. B6: Aston 2H 101
Ruskin Rd. WV10: Bush 1B 28
Ruskin St. B71: W Brom 2A 80
Russell Bank Rd. B74: Four O 5E 37
Russell Cl. B69: Tiv 5D 78
DY4: Tip 4C 62
WV11: Wed 6H 17
Russell Ct. B74: Four O 6D 36
WV3: Wolv 2F 43
Russell Ho. WS10: W'bry 3F 63
WV8: Cod 3E 13
Russell Rd. B13: Mose 2F 133
B28: Hall G 3E 135
WV14: Bils 4H 45
Russells, The B13: Mose 2F 133
RUSSELL'S HALL 6B 76
Russells Hall Rd. DY1: Dud 6A 76
Russell St. DY1: Dud 6D 76
WS10: W'bry 3F 63
WV3: Wolv 2F 43
WV13: W'hall 1B 46
Russett Cl. WS5: Wals 3A 50
Russett Way DY5: P'ntt 2F 93
Russet Wlk. WV8: Pend 6C 14
Russet Way B31: N'fld 1C 144
Ruston St. B16: Birm 2D 116
Ruthall Cl. B29: W Cas 6G 131
Ruth Cl. DY4: Tip 3C 62
Rutherford Rd. B23: Erd 6E 69
WS2: Wals 3G 31
Rutland Av. WV4: Penn 1B 58
Rutland Cl. B29: W Cas 6G 131
Rutland Cres. WS9: A'rdge 6D 22
WV14: Bils 4F 45
Rutland Dr. B26: Yard 4C 120
Rutland Pas. DY1: Dud 6E 77
Rutland Pl. DY8: Woll 3B 108
Rutland Rd. B66: Smeth 2E 115
B71: W Brom 6A 64
WS10: W'bry 1A 64
Rutland St. WS3: Wals 4C 32
Rutland Ter. *B18: Hock* 4C 100
(off Crabtree Rd.)

Rutley Gro.—Sampson Rd. Nth.

Rutley Gro. B32: Quin. 1D 130
Rutters Mdw. B32: Quin 1H 129
Rutter St. WS1: Wals 4B 48
Ryan Av. WV11: Wed 1A 30
Ryan Pl. DY2: Neth 3E 95
(not continuous)
Rycroft Gro. B33: Kitts G 1G 121
Rydal Cl. B74: S'tly. 1H 51
WV11: Wed. 2E 29
Rydal Dr. WV6: Pert 5F 25
Rydal Ho. B69: O'bry 4D 96
Rydal Way B28: Hall G 6F 135
Rydding La. B71: W Brom 5H 63
Rydding Sq. B71: W Brom 5H 63
Ryde Gro. B27: A Grn. 4G 135
Ryde Pk. Rd. B45: Redn. 3A 158
Ryder Ho. B70: W Brom 4E 79
Ryders Grn. Rd.
B70: W Brom 3E 79
Ryders Hayes La. WS3: Pels 3E 21
Ryder St. B4: Birm. 6G 101 (2F 5)
B70: W Brom 2F 79
DY8: Word 1B 108
Ryebank Cl. B30: B'vlle 2G 145
Ryeclose Cft. B37: Chel W 6F 107
RYECROFT. 5B 32
Rye Cft. B27: A Grn. 6A 120
B47: H'wd. 4A 162
DY9: W'cte 2A 126
Ryecroft Av. WV4: Penn 6F 43
Ryecroft Cl. DY3: Sed. 5G 59
Ryecroft Pk. WS2: Wals 6C 32
Ryecroft Pl. WS3: Wals 3D 32
Ryecroft St. WS2: Wals 6C 32
Ryefield WV8: Pend 5C 14
Ryefield Cl. B91: Sol 2C 150
Ryefield Way DY6: K'wfrd 3A 92
Rye Grass Wlk. B35: Cas V. 4F 87
Rye Gro. B11: Tys 1F 135
Ryemarket DY8: Stourb 6E 109
Ryhope Wlk. WV9: Pend. 4E 15
(not continuous)
Ryknild Cl. B74: Four O. 3F 37
Ryland Cl. B63: Hale. 3G 127
DY4: Tip 2B 78
Ryland Ho. *B19: Birm* *4F 101*
(off Gt. Hampton Row)
Ryland Rd. B11: S'hll 1D 134
B15: Edg. 4E 117
B24: Erd 6F 85
Rylands Dr. WV4: Penn 1D 58
Ryland St. B16: Birm 2D 116
Ryle St. WS3: Blox 5B 20
Rymond Rd. B34: Hodg H. 3C 104
Ryton Cl. B73: S Cold. 6H 53
WV10: Wolv 4C 28
Ryton End La. B92: Bars. 6C 154
Ryton Gro. B34: S End 2H 105

S

Sabell Rd. B67: Smeth. 3D 98
Sabrina Rd. WV6: Tett 2E 41
Saddlers Cen. WS1: Wals. 2C 48
Saddlers Cl. B63: Crad. 6D 110
Saddlers Ct. WS2: Wals 4H 47
Saddlers Ct. Ind. Est. WS2: Wals 2G 31
Saddlers M. B91: Sol 6G 151
Saddleworth Rd. WS3: Blox. 3G 19
Sadler Cres. *B11: S'hll*. *1D 134*
(off Lea Rd.)
Sadler Ho. *B19: Hock* *3E 101*
(off Guest Gro.)
Sadler Rd. B75: S Cold. 4D 54
WS8: Bwnhls 6C 10
Sadlers Mill WS8: Bwnhls 6C 10
Sadlers Wlk. B16: Edg 2C 116
Saffron Gdns. WV4: Penn 1E 59
Saffron Ho. B38: K Nor. 1A 160
Sage Cft. B31: N'fld 2D 144
St Agatha's Rd. B8: W End. 4H 103
St Agnes Cl. B13: Mose 3B 134
St Agnes Rd. B13: Mose. 3B 134
St Aidans Wlk. B10: Small H 3C 118
St Albans Cl. B67: Smeth. 3C 98
WV11: Wed. 1A 30
St Albans Ho. B32: Harb. 6D 114
St Albans Rd. B67: Smeth 3C 98
B13: Mose 2A 134
St Alphege Cl. B91: Sol 4G 151
St Andrew's Av. WS3: Pels 2E 21
St Andrews Cl. WV6: Wolv 5E 27
B32: Bart G 2E 131
DY3: Lwr G 4E 75
DY8: Stourb 3D 124
St Andrews Dr. B69: Tiv 2B 96
WV6: Pert. 4D 24
St Andrews Ind. Est.
B9: Bord G 1C 118
St Andrews Rd. B9: Birm 1B 118
B75: S Cold. 4A 54
St Andrews Stadium 2C 118
St Andrews St. DY2: Neth. 4E 95
B9: Birm 1B 118
St Annes Cl. WS7: Chase 1A 10
B20: Hand. 3B 82
St Annes Ct. WV13: W'hall. 2B 46
B13: Mose 1G 133
B44: K'sdng 6A 68
B64: Crad H 2E 111
St Annes Gro. B93: Know. 3C 166
St Annes Ind. Est.
WV13: W'hall 6B 30
St Annes Rd. B64: Crad H. 2E 111
WV10: Oxl 5G 15
WV13: W'hall 6B 30
St Anne's Way B44: K'sdng. 1A 84
St Ann's Ter. WV13: W'hall. 6B 30
St Anthony's Dr. WS3: Pels 2F 21
St Athan Cft. B35: Cas V 4F 87
St Audries Ct. B91: Sol. 5D 150
St Augustine's Rd. B16: Edg 2H 115
St Augustus Cl. B70: W Brom 5D 80
St Austell Rd. WS5: Wals. 4A 50
St Bartholomew's Ter. WS10: W'bry. 2F 63
St Benedict's Cl. B70: W Brom 5D 80
St Benedicts Rd. B10: Small H 4F 119
WV5: Wom. 1G 73
St Bernards Rd. B92: Olton 2B 150
B72: W Grn. 3A 70
St Blaise Av. B46: Wat O 5D 88
St Blaise Rd. B75: R'ley 6B 38
St Brades Cl. B69: Tiv. 2C 96
St Brides Cl. DY3: Sed 5G 59
WV5: Wom 1F 73
Saintbury Dr. B91: Sol 2G 165
St Caroline Cl. B70: W Brom 5D 80
St Catharines Cl. WS1: Wals 4E 49
St Catherines Cl. DY2: Dud 6A 78
B75: S Cold 4D 54
St Catherine's Ct. B91: Sol. 3F 151
St Catherine's Cres. WV4: Penn. 1D 58
St Chads WV14: Cose. 6D 60
St Chads Cir. Queensway
B4: Birm. 5F 101 (1D 4)
St Chad's Cl. DY3: Lwr G 4F 75
St Chads Ind. Est. B19: Birm 4F 101
St Chad's Queensway
B4: Birm 5G 101 (2D 4)
St Chads RC Cathedral. 5G 101 (1D 4)
St Chads Rd. B45: Rubery 2F 157
B75: S Cold. 6C 54
WV10: Bush 1B 28
WV14: Bils 4H 45
St Christopher Cl. B70: W Brom 5D 80
St Christophers B20: Hand 3B 82
St Clements Av. WS3: Blox. 2B 32
St Clements Ct. B63: Hale 2A 128
St Clements La. B71: W Brom 3B 80
St Clements Rd. B7: Nech 3C 102
St Columbas Dr. B45: Redn 2A 158
St Cuthbert's Cl. B70: W Brom. 5D 80
St David's Cl. B70: W Brom 5D 80
WS3: Pels 2F 21
St Davids Ct. B69: O'bry. 2G 97
St Davids Dr. B32: Quin 6H 113
St Davids Gro. B20: Hand. 3B 82
St Davids Pl. WS3: Blox. 5B 20
St Denis Rd. B29: W Cas 1E 145
St Dennis Ho. *B16: Edg* *2H 115*
(off Melville Rd.)
St Dominic's Rd. B24: Erd 6E 85
(not continuous)
St Edburgh's Rd. B25: Yard 2C 120
St Edmund's Cl. B70: W Brom 5D 80
WV6: Wolv 6D 26
St Edwards Rd. B29: S Oak 3B 132
St Eleanors Cl. B70: W Brom. 5D 80
St Francis Av. B91: Sol. 1C 150
St Francis' Cl. WS3: Pels 2F 21
St Francis Factory Est.
B70: W Brom 5B 80
St George Dr. B66: Smeth. 2E 99
ST GEORGES. 2H 43 (4C 170)
St Georges Av. B23: Erd. 2G 85
St Georges Cl. B75: S Cold 5D 54
WS10: Darl. 4D 46
B15: Edg. 4C 116
St Georges Ct. *WS10: Darl*. *4D 46*
(off St George's St.)
B30: B'vlle. 6A 132
B74: Four O. 4E 37
WS1: Wals *1D 48*
(off Persehouse St.)
St George's Pde. WV2: Wolv. 2H 43 (4C 170)
St Georges Pl. B70: W Brom 4A 80
WS1: Wals 1D 48
St Georges Rd. DY2: Dud 3F 95
DY8: Stourb 3B 124
B90: Shir. 1B 164
St George's St. B19: Birm. 5F 101
WS10: Darl. 4D 46
St Gerards Ct. B91: Sol. 5C 150
St Gerards Rd. B91: Sol 5C 150
St Giles Av. B65: Row R 5B 96
St Giles Cl. B65: Row R 5C 96
St Giles Ct. B65: Row R 6D 96
WV13: W'hall 2B 46
St Giles Cres. WV1: Wolv. 1C 44
St Giles Rd. B33: Kitts G 1H 121
WV1: Wolv 1C 44
WV13: W'hall 2B 46
St Giles Row *DY8: Stourb*. *5E 109*
(off Lwr. High St.)
St Giles St. DY2: Neth. 4E 95
St Helens Av. DY4: Tip 2C 78
St Helens Pas. B1: Birm 5E 101 (1A 4)
St Helens Rd. B91: Sol. 1E 151
St Heliers Rd. B31: N'fld 3C 144
St Ives Rd. WS5: Wals 4H 49
St James Av. B65: Row R. 5B 96
St James Cl. B70: W Brom. 5D 80
WS3: Pels 2F 21
St James Gdns. WS8: Bwnhls 6B 10
St James Pl. B7: Birm 6A 102
B15: Edg. 3D 116
B90: Shir 5H 149
St James Rd. B69: O'bry 1D 96
B75: Four O 1A 54
B21: Hand. 1H 99
St James's Rd. DY1: Dud. 5D 76
St James's Ter. DY1: Dud. 5C 76
St James St. WS10: W'bry 3E 63
WV1: Wolv 2A 44
DY3: Lwr G. 4H 75
St James Wlk. *WS8: Bwnhls* *6B 10*
(off Short St.)
St John Bosco Cl. B71: W Brom. 6H 63
St John Cl. B75: R'ley 5B 38
St John's Arc. WV1: Wolv 1G 43 (3B 170)
St Johns Av. B65: Row R 5B 96
St John's Cl. B70: W Brom. 5D 80
B93: Know 3D 166
DY3: Swind. 5D 72
WS9: Wals W 4B 22
St Johns Ct. B31: N'fld 6F 145
B17: Harb 5F 115
DY5: Brie H. *1H 109*
(off Hill St.)
WS3: Blox. 6H 19
WS10: W'bry. 3F 63
St Johns Gro. B37: K'hrst 6B 106
St John's Ho. B70: W Brom 5A 80
St Johns Retail Pk. WV2: Wolv . . . 2G 43 (6B 170)
St Johns Rd. B11: S'hll. 6C 118
B17: Harb 5H 115
B63: Hale 1G 127
B68: O'bry. 4A 98
DY2: Dud 1G 95
DY8: Stourb 5E 109
WS2: Wals 3H 47
WS3: Pels 2F 21
DY4: Tip 6H 61
WS8: Bwnhls 2C 22
WS10: Darl 6C 46
WV11: Ess 4A 18
St John's Sq. WV2: Wolv. 2G 43 (5B 170)
St John's St. DY2: Neth. 4E 95
WV1: Wolv 3B 170
St Johns Wlk. B42: P Barr. 3F 83
St John's Way B93: Know. 3E 167
St Johns Wood B45: Redn 4H 157
St Joseph's Av. B31: N'fld. 2F 145
St Josephs Cl. WS3: Pels 3E 21
St Joseph's Ct. WV4: Penn. 5A 42
St Joseph's Rd. B8: W End 4A 104
St Joseph St. DY2: Dud. 6F 77
St Judes Cl. B14: K Hth 5H 147
B75: S Cold 5D 54
St Jude's Ct. WV6: Wolv. 6D 26
St Judes Pas. B5: Birm 2F 117 (6D 4)
St Jude's Rd. WV6: Wolv 6D 26
St Jude's Rd. W. WV6: Wolv 6D 26
St Katherines Rd. B68: O'bry. 1H 113
St Kenelms Av. B63: Hale. 4G 127
St Kenelm's Cl. B70: W Brom 5D 80
St Kenelm's Rd. B62: Roms. 3A 142
St Kilda's Rd. B8: Salt. 5E 103
St Laurence M. B31: N'fld. 4E 145
St Laurence Rd. B31: N'fld 2F 145
St Lawrence Cl. B93: Know 4D 166
St Lawrence Ho. *B16: Edg* *2H 115*
(off Melville Rd.)
St Lawrence Way WS10: Darl 4D 46
St Leonard's Cl. B37: Mars G. 4C 122
St Loye's Cl. B62: B'hth 3D 112
St Lukes Cl. B65: Row R 5B 96
St Luke's Rd. B5: Birm 3F 117
(not continuous)
WS10: W'bry 2G 63
St Lukes St. B64: Crad H. 2F 111
St Luke's Ter. DY1: Dud 1C 94
St Margaret's B74: Four O 6C 36
St Margarets Av. B8: W End. 3H 103
St Margaret's Ct. B92: Olton. 4C 136
St Margarets Dr. B63: Hale. 3H 127
St Margarets Rd. B8: W End 3G 103
B43: Gt Barr 3B 66
B92: Olton. 4C 136
WS3: Pels 3E 21
St Marks Cl. WS6: Gt Wyr. 1F 7
St Marks Cres. B1: Birm 6C 100
St Mark's Factory Cen. DY9: Lye 6H 109
St Marks Rd. DY2: Dud 5H 77
DY4: Tip 5H 61
WS3: Pels 3E 21
WV3: Wolv 2E 43
(not continuous)
B67: Smeth. 6B 98
DY9: Lye. 6H 109
WS8: Bwnhls 2C 22
St Marks St. WV3: Wolv. 2F 43 (4A 170)
B1: Birm 6D 100
St Martins Cl. B70: W Brom. 5D 80
WV2: E'shll 5A 44
St Martins Dr. DY4: Tip. 2A 78
St Martins Ind. Est. B69: O'bry 3H 97
(Engine St.)
B69: O'bry 2H 97
(Parsonage St.)
St Martin's Queensway
B2: Birm 1G 117 (5E 5)
St Martin's Rd. B75: S Cold 6D 54
St Martin's St. B15: Birm. 2D 116
St Martin's Ter. WV14: Bils 1G 61
St Marys Cl. B24: Erd. 3B 86
B27: A Grn 2H 135
DY3: Sed. 5B 60
St Marys Ct. *WV13: W'hall*. *1A 46*
(off Wolverhampton St.)
DY5: Brie H. 1H 109
St Mary's Hall WV2: Wolv. 2H 43 (5C 170)
St Mary's La. DY8: Stourb 2F 125
St Mary's Mobile Home Pk. B47: Wyt 6G 161
St Mary's Rd. B17: Harb. 6G 115
B67: Smeth. 2D 114
WS10: W'bry. 2F 63
St Marys Row B4: Birm. 6G 101 (2E 5)
B13: Mose 2H 133
St Mary's St. WV1: Wolv. 1H 43 (2C 170)
St Mary's Vw. B23: Erd. 5D 68
St Marys Way WS9: A'rdge. 4C 34
St Matthews Cl. WS3: Pels 2F 21
WS1: Wals 2D 48
St Matthews Rd. B66: Smeth 4G 99
B68: O'bry 1G 113
(not continuous)
St Matthews St. WV1: Wolv 2B 44
St Mawes Rd. WV6: Pert. 6F 25
St Mawgan Cl. B35: Cas V 3G 87
St Michaels Cl. WS3: Pels 5E 21
St Michaels Ct. B70: W Brom. 4A 80
WV6: Tett 4C 26
St Michaels Cres. B69: O'bry 5F 97
St Michael's Gro. DY2: Dud 6A 78
St Michael's Hill B18: Hock 2C 100
St Michael's M. B69: Tiv 5A 78
St Michael's Rd. B18: Hock 2C 100
B73: Bold 5F 69
DY3: Lwr G. 2D 74
St Michael St. B70: W Brom 4A 80
WS1: Wals 3C 48
St Michaels Way DY4: Tip 4A 78
St Nicholas Cl. WS3: Pels. 3E 21
St Nicholas Gdns. B38: K Nor 5B 146
St Nicholas Wlk. B76: Curd 1D 88
St Oswald's Cl. B10: Small H 3E 119
St Oswald's Rd. B10: Small H. 3E 119
St Patricks Cl. B14: K Hth 2G 147
St Paul's Av. B12: Bal H 6A 118
St Paul's Cl. WS1: Wals 1C 48
St Pauls Ct. B46: Wat O 4D 88
B65: B'hth. 2D 112
St Paul's Cres. B46: Col. 2H 107
B70: W Brom 6E 63
WS3: Pels 3F 21
St Pauls Dr. B62: B'hth. 2D 112
DY4: Tip 3B 78
St Paul's Rd. B12: Bal H. 5H 117
B66: Smeth. 2B 98
DY2: Neth 4F 95
WS10: W'bry 6H 47
St Paul's Sq. B3: Birm. 6E 101 (2B 4)
St Pauls Stop (MM) 5F 101 (1C 4)
St Paul's St. WS1: Wals 1C 48
St Pauls Ter. B3: Birm. 5E 101 (1B 4)
St Peters Cl. B72: W Grn 2H 69
DY4: Tip. 3D 78
WS9: Ston 3G 23
B28: Hall G 1D 148
B46: Wat O. 5D 88
WV1: Wolv. 1G 43 (2B 170)
St Peters Ct. WS3: Blox 6H 19
St Peter's Dr. WS3: Pels. 3E 21
St Peters La. B92: Bick. 4F 139
St Peters Rd. B17: Harb 6F 115
B20: Hand. 6E 83
DY2: Dud, Neth. 3F 95
DY9: Pedm. 4G 125
St Peter's Sq. WV1: Wolv 1G 43 (2B 170)
St Peters Ter. WS2: Wals 5C 32
St Philips Av. WV3: Wolv. 4D 42
St Philips Cathedral. 6F 101 (3D 4)
St Philips Gro. WV3: Wolv. 4D 42
St Philips Pl. B3: Birm. 6G 101 (3E 5)
St Phillips Ct. B46: Col. 2H 107
St Quentin St. WS2: Wals. 3A 48
St Saviours Cl. WV2: E'shll. 5B 44
St Saviour's Rd. B8: Salt 5D 102
St Silas' Sq. B19: Loz. 2D 100
St Simons Cl. B75: S Cold 5D 54
St Stephens Av. WV13: W'hall 1H 45
St Stephen's Cen. B21: Hand 3A 100
St Stephen's Ct. WV13: W'hall. 2H 45
St Stephens Gdns. WV13: W'hall 1A 46
St Stephens Rd. B29: S Oak. 5D 132
B71: W Brom 6F 81
St Stephen's St. B6: Aston. 3G 101
St Thomas Cl. B75: S Cold. 6D 54
WS3: Wals 3C 32
WS9: A'rdge 6D 22
St Thomas' Rd. B23: Erd 4D 84
St Thomas St. DY2: Neth 4E 95
DY8: Stourb 6D 108
St Valentines Cl. B70: W Brom 5D 80
St Vincent Cres. B70: W Brom. 1F 79
St Vincent St. B16: Birm. 1D 116
St Vincent St. W. B16: Birm. 1C 116
Saladin Av. B69: O'bry 4E 97
Salcombe Av. B26: Sheld 6G 121
Salcombe Dr. DY5: Brie H 4G 109
Salcombe Gro. WV14: Cose 4F 61
Salcombe Rd. B66: Smeth 4F 99
Saldavian Ct. WS2: Wals 5H 47
Salem St. DY4: Tip. 2D 78
Salford Circ. B6: Aston. 6D 84
Salford St. B6: Aston 1C 102
Salford Trad. Est. B6: Aston. 1C 102
Salisbury Cl. B13: Mose. 1G 133
DY1: Dud 4B 76
Salisbury Ct. B91: Sol 3G 151
Salisbury Dr. B46: Wat O 4E 89
Salisbury Gro. B72: W Grn. 6A 70
Salisbury Rd. B8: Salt. 4E 103
B13: Mose 1G 133
B19: Loz 1F 101
B66: Smeth 5F 99
B70: W Brom 6C 80
Salisbury St. WS10: Darl 4E 47
Salisbury Twr. B18: Hock 6C 100
Sallow Gro. WS8: Bwnhls. 4B 10
Sally Ward Dr. WS9: Wals W 3C 22
Salop Cl. B71: W Brom 1H 79
Salop Dr. B68: O'bry. 1A 114
Salop Rd. B68: O'bry 6A 98
Salop St. B12: Birm 3H 117
B69: O'bry. 6E 79
DY1: Dud 5D 76
WV3: Wolv. 2G 43 (4A 170)
WV14: Bils 1G 61
Salstar Cl. B6: Aston 3G 101
Saltash Gro. B25: Yard 2A 120
Saltbrook Rd. B63: Crad. 4C 110
DY9: Lye. 4B 110
Saltbrook Trad. Est. B63: Crad. 4C 110
Salter Rd. DY4: Tip. 6H 61
Salter's La. B71: W Brom. 3C 80
Salter's Rd. WS9: Wals W 3C 22
SALTER STREET 6A 164
Salter St. B94: Earls, H'ley H 6A 164
Salters Va. B70: W Brom 6C 80
SALTLEY 5D 102
Saltley Bus. Pk. B8: Salt 3D 102
Saltley Cotts. B24: Erd 1F 103
Saltley Ind. Cen. B8: Salt. 6C 102
Saltley Leisure Cen. 6G 103
Saltley Rd. B7: Birm. 4B 102
Saltley Trad. Est. B8: Salt 3D 102
Saltley Viaduct B7: Birm. 4C 102
B8: Salt. 4C 102
Saltney Cl. B24: Erd 2B 86
Saltwells La. DY2: Neth 1C 110
DY5: Brie H, Quar B 1B 110
Saltwells Nature Reserve 6C 94
Saltwells Rd. DY2: Neth. 1D 110
Salwarpe Gro. B29: W Cas. 3D 130
Sambourn Cl. B91: Sol 1A 152
Sambourne Dr. B34: S End. 2H 105
Sambrook Rd. WV10: Wolv 3C 28
Sampson Cl. B21: Hand 6G 81
B69: Tiv 2C 96
Sampson Rd. B11: S'brk. 4B 118
Sampson Rd. Nth. B11: S'brk. 3B 118

Sampson St.—Shaver's End

Sampson St. WS10: W'bry 2H 63
Sams La. B70: W Brom 5A 80
Samuels Rd. B32: Quin 6G 113
Samuel St. WS3: Blox 6H 19
Sanda Cft. B36: Cas B 3D 106
Sandalls Cl. B31: Longb 6B 144
Sandal Ri. B91: Sol 4A 152
Sandals Ri. B62: Hale 2D 128
Sandalwood Cl. WV12: W'hall 1B 30
Sandbank WS3: Blox 6G 19
Sandbarn Cl. B90: M'path 3D 164
Sandbeds Rd. WV12: W'hall 5C 30
Sandbourne Rd. B8: W End 5G 103
Sanderling Ri. DY6: K'wfrd 3E 93
Sanders Cl. DY2: Dud 2G 95
Sanders St. DY4: Tip 2B 78
Sandfield B66: Smeth 2C 98
Sandfield Bri. DY5: P'ntt 6F 75
Sandfield Cl. B90: Shir 1G 163
Sandfield Farm Home Pk. WS8: Bwnhls 4D 10
Sandfield Gro. DY3: Gorn 5F 75
Sandfield Rd. B71: W Brom 4C 64
DY8: Word 1D 108
Sandfields Av. B10: Small H 3B 118
Sandfields Rd. B68: O'bry 1A 114
Sandford Av. B65: Row R 6C 96
Sandford Ri. WV6: Tett 3C 26
Sandford Rd. B13: Mose 1A 134
DY1: Dud 6A 76
Sandford Wlk. B12: Bal H 6H 117
Sandgate Rd. B28: Hall G 3F 149
DY4: Tip 5A 62
Sandhill Farm Cl. B19: Loz 2F 101
Sandhills Cres. B91: Sol 1F 165
Sandhill St. WS3: Blox 6G 19
Sandhurst Av. B36: Hodg H 3B 104
DY9: W'cte 3H 125
Sandhurst Dr. WV4: Penn 1E 59
Sandhurst Gro. DY8: Word 6C 92
Sandhurst Ho. B38: K Nor 6C 146
Sandhurst Rd. B13: Mose 3G 133
B74: Four O 4F 37
DY6: K'wfrd 5E 93
Sandland Cl. WV14: Bils 5H 45
Sandland Rd. WV12: W'hall 1D 30
Sandmartin Cl. DY2: Neth 1E 111
Sandmeadow Pl. DY6: K'wfrd 4A 92
Sandmere Gro. B14: Yard W 4D 148
Sandmere Ri. WV10: Bush 6A 16
Sandmere Rd. B14: Yard W 4D 148
Sandon Gro. B24: Erd 3H 85
Sandon Rd. B17: Edg 2E 115
B66: Smeth 1E 115
DY9: W'cte 1B 126
WV10: F'hses 5F 15
Sandown Av. WS6: C Hay 2E 7
Sandown Ct. B29: W Cas 6G 131
Sandown Dr. WV6: Pert 5F 25
Sandown Rd. B36: Hodg H 1B 104
Sandown Twr. B31: N'fld 6E 145
Sandpiper Cl. DY9: W'cte 6B 110
Sandpiper Gdns. B38: K Nor 2B 160
Sandpiper Way B23: Erd 1C 84
Sandpit Cl. WS10: W'bry 3C 64
Sand Pits B1: Birm 6D 100 (3A 4)
Sandpits, The B30: B'vlle 5A 132
Sandpits Cl. B76: Curd 1D 88
Sandpits Ind. Est. B1: Birm 6D 100
Sandra Cl. WS9: A'rdge 4D 34
Sandringham Av. WV12: W'hall 2B 30
Sandringham Ct. B43: Gt Barr 4B 66
Sandringham Dr. B65: Row R 5C 96
WS9: A'rdge 6D 22
Sandringham Pl. DY8: Word 2B 108
Sandringham Rd. B42: P Barr 1D 82
B62: Hale 4B 112
DY8: Word 2A 108
WV4: Penn 1E 59
WV5: Wom 1F 73
Sandringham Way DY5: Brie H 3G 109
Sandstone Av. B45: Rubery 1G 157
Sandstone Cl. DY3: Lwr G 3H 75
Sand St. B70: W Brom 3E 79
Sandway Gdns. B8: Salt 3D 102
Sandway Gro. B13: Mose 6C 134
SANDWELL 1E 99
Sandwell & Dudley Station (Rail) 6G 79
Sandwell Av. WS10: Darl 6B 46
Sandwell Bus. Development Cen.
B66: Smeth 2A 98
Sandwell Bus. Pk. B66: Smeth 1A 98
Sandwell Cen. B70: W Brom 4B 80
Sandwell Ct. B21: Hand 1H 99
Sandwell Ind. Est. B66: Smeth 1A 98
Sandwell Pk. Farm 4D 80
Sandwell Pl. B66: Smeth 1E 99
WV12: W'hall 2D 30
Sandwell Rd. B21: Hand 6H 81
B70: W Brom 3A 80
WV10: Oxl 6F 15
Sandwell Rd. Nth. B71: W Brom 3B 80
Sandwell Rd. Pas. B70: W Brom 3A 80
Sandwell St. WS1: Wals 3D 48
Sandwell Valley Country Pk.
Forge La. 1E 81
Salter's La. 3D 80
Tanhouse Av. 1G 81
Sandwell Wlk. WS1: Wals 3D 48
Sandwood Dr. B44: Gt Barr 5H 67
Sandy Acre Way DY8: Stourb 6F 109
Sandy Cres. WV11: Wed 1A 30
Sandy Cft. B13: Mose 6C 134
Sandycroft B72: W Grn 2A 70
Sandyfields Rd. DY3: Lwr G, Sed 2D 74
Sandy Gro. WS8: Bwnhls 4B 10
Sandy Hill Ri. B90: Shir 3G 149
Sandy Hill Rd. B90: Shir 3G 149
Sandy Hollow WV6: Tett 1A 42
Sandy La. B6: Aston 2B 102
B42: Gt Barr 5E 67
B61: L Ash, Wild 4A 156
DY8: Stourb 1B 124
WS10: W'bry 2D 64
WV6: Tett 3C 26
WV8: Cod 3F 13
WV10: Bush 6A 16
Sandy Mt. WV5: Wom 6H 57
Sandymount Rd. WS1: Wals 3D 48
Sandy Rd. DY8: Stourb 4B 124
Sandys Gro. DY4: Tip 2G 77
Sandy Way B15: Birm 2D 116 (6A 4)
Sangwin Rd. WV14: Cose 6E 61
Sansome Ri. B90: Shir 5F 149
Sansome Rd. B90: Shir 5F 149
Sanstone Cl. WS3: Blox 4A 20
Sanstone Rd. WS3: Blox 4H 19
Santolina Dr. WS5: Wals 2E 65
Sant Rd. B31: Longb 2F 159
Sapcote Bus. Pk. B10: Small H 5E 119
Sapcote Trad. Cen. B64: Old H 6H 95
Saplings, The B76: Walm 5E 71
Sapphire Ct. B3: Birm 5E 101 (1B 4)
B92: Olton 4D 136
Sapphire Hgts. B1: Birm 6D 100
Sapphire Ho. E. B91: Sol 3E 151
Sapphire Ho. W. B91: Sol 3E 151
Sapphire Twr. *B6: Aston* *3H 101*
(off Park La.)
Saracen Dr. B75: S Cold 5D 54
CV7: Bal C 3E 169
Sara Cl. B74: Four O 6G 37
Sarah Cl. WV14: Bils 4G 61
Sarah Ct. B73: New O 4D 68
Sarah Gdns. WS5: Wals 1D 64
Sarah St. B9: Birm 1B 118
Saredon Cl. WS3: Pels 6E 21
Saredon Rd. WS6: C Hay 1B 6
WV10: Share 1A 6
(not continuous)
Sarehole Mill Mus. 5D 134
Sarehole Rd. B28: Hall G 6D 134
Sargent Cl. B43: Gt Barr 1F 67
Sargent Ho. B16: Birm 1D 116
Sargent's Hill WS5: Wals 5G 49
Sargent Turner Trad. Est.
DY9: Lye 5B 110
Sark Dr. B36: Cas B 3D 106
Satellite Ind. Pk.
WV13: W'hall 5F 29
Saturday Bri. B1: Birm 6B 4
Saunton Rd. WS3: Blox 4G 19
Saunton Way B29: S Oak 4G 131
Saveker Dr. B76: Walm 1C 70
Savernake Cl. B45: Fran 5G 143
Saville Cl. B45: Redn 2H 157
Savoy Cl. B32: Harb 6D 114
Saw Mill Cl. WS4: Wals 6C 32
Saxelby Cl. B14: K Hth 5G 147
(not continuous)
Saxelby Ho. B14: K Hth 5G 147
Saxon Cl. WS6: Gt Wyr 3G 7
Saxon Ct. WV6: Tett 4A 26
Saxondale Av. B26: Sheld 5D 120
Saxon Dr. B65: Row R 5C 96
Saxonfields WV6: Tett 4A 26
Saxons Way B14: K Hth 5A 148
Saxon Way B37: K'hrst 6B 106
Saxon Wood Cl. B31: N'fld 3E 145
Saxon Wood Rd.
B90: Ches G 4B 164
Saxton Dr. B74: Four O 3F 37
Scafell Dr. B23: Erd 2D 84
WV14: Bils 4H 45
Scafell Rd. DY8: Amb 5F 109
Scampton Cl. WV6: Pert 4E 25
Scarborough Cl. WS2: Wals 3H 47
Scarborough Rd. WS2: Wals 3H 47
Scarecrow La. B75: R'ley 5C 38
Scarsdale Rd. B42: Gt Barr 5F 67
Schofield Av. B71: W Brom 5H 63
Schofield Rd. B37: K'hrst 4C 106
Scholars Ga. B33: Kitts G 1F 121
Scholars Wlk. WS4: Rus 2F 33
Scholefield Twr. *B19: Birm* *4F 101*
(off Uxbridge St.)
Schoolacre Ri. B74: S'tly 2G 51
Schoolacre Rd. B34: S End 3F 105
School Av. WS3: Blox 1A 32
WS8: Bwnhls 5B 10
School Cl. B35: Cas V 4F 87
B37: K'hrst 3C 106
B69: Tiv 2C 96
WV3: Wolv 4H 41
WV5: Try 5C 56
WV8: Cod 3G 13
School Dr. B47: Wyt 6A 162
B73: S Cold 1H 69
DY8: Amb 3D 108
WV14: Bils 3A 62
School Dr., The DY2: Dud 2F 95
Schoolgate Cl. B8: W End 3G 103
WS4: S'fld 6H 21
School Grn. WV14: Bils 3E 45
Schoolhouse Cl. B38: K Nor 5D 146
School La. B33: Yard 2D 120
B34: S End 3F 105
B63: Hale 3H 127
B91: Sol 2H 151
DY5: Brie H 5F 93
DY9: Hag 6H 125
WS3: Lit W 3C 8
WS3: Pels 3D 20
WV3: Wolv 2G 43 (4A 170)
WV10: Bush 5H 15
School Pas. DY5: Quar B 2C 110
School Rd. B13: Mose 4H 133
B14: Yard W 3B 148
B28: Hall G 5F 135
B45: Rubery 3E 157
B90: Shir 5H 149
DY3: Himl 4H 73
DY5: Quar B 1C 110
WS10: W'bry 3B 64
WV5: Try 5C 56
WV5: Wom 6H 57
WV6: Tett 5G 25
WV11: Wed 3D 28
School St. B64: Crad H 2F 111
DY1: Dud 6D 76
(not continuous)
DY3: Sed 5A 60
DY5: P'ntt 2H 93
School St. DY8: Stourb 5D 108
WS4: S'fld 6H 21
WS10: Darl 5C 46
(Alma St.)
WS10: Darl 6E 47
(Nowell St., not continuous)
WV3: Wolv 2G 43 (4A 170)
WV13: W'hall 1H 45
WV14: Cose 5E 61
School St. W. WV14: Cose 5E 61
School Ter. B29: S Oak 3B 132
School Wlk. WV14: Bils 3E 45
Scorers Cl. B90: Shir 1H 149
Scotchings, The B36: Hodg H 1C 104
Scotland La. B32: Bart G 5H 129
Scotland Pas. B70: W Brom 4B 80
SCOTLANDS 1C 28
Scotland St. B1: Birm 6E 101 (3A 4)
Scott Arms Shop. Cen. B42: Gt Barr 4B 66
Scott Av. WS10: W'bry 3H 63
WV4: Penn 1C 58
Scott Cl. B71: W Brom 2B 80
Scott Gro. B92: Olton 2C 136
Scott Ho. B43: Gt Barr 6B 66
Scott Rd. B43: Gt Barr 3B 66
B92: Olton 2C 136
WS5: Wals 5H 49
SCOTT'S GREEN 1C 94
Scotts Grn. Cl. DY1: Dud 1B 94
Scotts Grn. Island DY1: Dud 2B 94
Scott's Rd. DY8: Stourb 5D 108
Scott St. DY4: Tip 2C 78
Scotwell Cl. B65: Row R 6B 96
Scout Cl. B33: Kitts G 1G 121
Scribbans Cl. B66: Smeth 5F 99
Scriber's La. B28: Hall G 3D 148
Scribers Mdw. B28: Hall G 3E 149
Scrimshaw Ho. *WS2: Wals* *4A 48*
(off Pleck Rd.)
Seacroft Av. B25: Yard 2C 120
Seafield Cl. DY6: K'wfrd 5C 92
Seaforth Gro. WV12: W'hall 6B 18
Seagar St. B71: W Brom 3C 80
Seagers La. DY5: Brie H 1H 109
Seagull Bay Dr. WV14: Cose 4F 61
Seal Cl. B76: Walm 1C 70
Seals Grn. B38: K Nor 2H 159
Seamless Dr. WV11: Wed 5F 29
Sear Hills Cl. CV7: Bal C 3H 169
Sear Retail Pk. B90: Shir 6B 150
Seaton Cl. WV11: Wed 4H 29
Seaton Gro. B13: Mose 4F 133
Seaton Pl. DY8: Word 1A 108
Seaton Rd. B66: Smeth 4F 99
Second Av. B6: Witt 4H 83
B9: Bord G 2E 119
B29: S Oak 2D 132
DY6: P'ntt 2D 92
WS8: Bwnhls 4C 10
WV10: Bush 2A 28
Second Exhibition Av. B40: Nat E C 1F 139
Security Ho. WV1: Wolv 2G 43 (4B 170)
Sedge Av. B38: K Nor 4B 146
Sedgeberrow Covert B38: K Nor 1A 160
Sedgeberrow Rd. B63: Hale 3A 128
Sedgebourne Way B31: Longb 6A 144
Sedgefield Cl. DY1: Dud 4A 76
Sedgefield Gro. WV6: Pert 5F 25
Sedgefield Way WS11: Nort C 1E 9
Sedgeford Cl. DY5: Brie H 3H 109
Sedgehill Av. B17: Harb 1F 131
Sedgemere Gro. CV7: Bal C 6H 169
WS4: S'fld 1G 33
Sedgemere Rd. B26: Yard 2D 120
SEDGLEY 5H 59
Sedgley Gro. B20: Hand 3A 82
Sedgley Hall Av. DY3: Sed 5G 59
Sedgley Hall Est. DY3: Sed 4G 59
Sedgley Rd. DY1: Dud 1D 76
WV4: Penn 2C 58
Sedgley Rd. E. DY4: Tip 3A 78
Sedgley Rd. W. DY4: Tip 1F 77
Seedhouse Ct. B64: Old H 3A 112
Seeds La. WS8: Bwnhls 5B 10
Seeleys Rd. B11: Tys 6D 118
Sefton Dr. B65: Row R 3H 95
Sefton Gro. DY4: Tip 3C 62
Sefton Rd. B16: Edg 1B 116
Segbourne Rd. B45: Rubery 1E 157
Segundo Cl. WS5: Wals 1D 64
Segundo Rd. WS5: Wals 1D 64
SEISDON 3A 56
Seisdon Hollaway WV5: Seis 2A 56
Seisdon Rd. WV5: Seis, Try 3A 56
Selborne Cl. WS1: Wals 2E 49
Selborne Gro. B13: Mose 2C 148
Selborne Rd. B20: Hand 5C 82
DY2: Dud 2F 95
Selborne St. WS1: Wals 2E 49
Selbourne Cres. WV1: Wolv 2D 44
Selby Cl. B26: Yard 2D 120
Selby Gro. B13: Mose 2B 148
Selby Ho. B69: O'bry 3D 96
Selby Way WS3: Blox 5E 19
Selcombe Way B38: K Nor 2B 160
Selco Way B76: Min 2E 87
Selcroft Av. B32: Harb 6D 114
Selecta Av. B44: Gt Barr 3F 67
Selkirk Cl. B71: W Brom 1A 80
Selly Av. B29: S Oak 3C 132
Selly Cl. B29: S Oak 3D 132
Selly Hall Cft. B30: B'vlle 1C 146
Selly Hill Rd. B29: S Oak 3B 132
SELLY OAK 4A 132
Selly Oak Ind. Est. B29: S Oak 4A 132
Selly Oak Rd. B30: B'vlle 6A 132
Selly Oak Station (Rail) 3A 132
SELLY PARK 3D 132
Selly Pk. Rd. B29: S Oak 2C 132
Selly Wharf B29: S Oak 3A 132
Selly Wick Dr. B29: S Oak 3D 132
Selly Wick Rd. B29: S Oak 3C 132
Sellywood Rd. B30: B'vlle 6H 131
Selma Gro. B14: Yard W 2D 148
Selman's Hill WS3: Blox 4A 20
Selman's Pde. WS3: Blox 5A 20
Selsdon Cl. B47: Wyt 4C 162
Selsdon Rd. WS3: Blox 4F 19
Selsey Av. B17: Edg 6F 99
Selsey Rd. B17: Edg 6F 99
Selston Rd. B6: Aston 2G 101
Selvey Av. B43: Gt Barr 2D 66
Selworthy Rd. B36: Cas B 2B 106
Selwyn Cl. WV2: Wolv 4G 43
Selwyn Ho. B37: Chel W 6F 107
Selwyn Rd. B16: Edg 6H 99
WV14: Bils 5H 45
Selwyn Wlk. B74: Lit A 5C 36
Senior Cl. WV11: Ess 4A 18
Senneley's Pk. Rd.
B31: N'fld 5C 130
Sennen Cl. WV13: W'hall 2H 45
Sensall Rd. DY9: W'cte 2B 126
Sentry Way B75: S Cold 5D 54
Serpentine Rd. B6: Aston 6A 84
B17: Harb 5G 115
B29: S Oak 2C 132
Servite Ct. B14: K Hth 5A 148
Servite Ho. B44: Gt Barr 3H 67
B92: Olton 6B 136
Seth Somers Track 3C 128
Settle Av. B34: Hodg H 3E 105
Settle Cft. B37: F'bri 2B 122
Setton Dr. DY3: Sed 6A 60
Seven Acres WS9: A'rdge 4D 34
Seven Acres Rd. B31: N'fld 6G 145
B62: Quin 6G 113
Sevendwellings Vw.
DY5: Brie H 2G 109
Seven Star Rd. B91: Sol 2E 151
Seven Stars Rd. B69: O'bry 2G 97
Severn Cl. B36: Cas B 2B 106
DY4: Tip 2H 77
WV12: W'hall 2A 30
Severn Ct. B23: Erd 4B 84
B73: S Cold 6H 53
Severn Dr. DY5: P'ntt 2F 93
WV6: Pert 5E 25
Severne Gro. B27: A Grn 4A 136
Severne Rd. B27: A Grn 5A 136
Severn Gro. B11: S'brk 5C 118
B19: Loz 2E 101
(not continuous)
Severn Rd. B63: Crad 6D 110
DY8: Stourb 2D 124
WS3: Blox 6C 20
WS8: Bwnhls 3G 9
Severn St. B1: Birm 2F 117 (6C 4)
Severn St. Pl. B1: Birm 6C 4
Severn Twr. B7: Nech 4B 102
Severn Way B47: Wyt 6G 161
Sevington Cl. B91: Sol 1G 165
Seymour Cl. B29: S Oak 3C 132
WS6: C Hay 4D 6
Seymour Gdns. B74: Four O 6E 37
Seymour Rd. B69: O'bry 2A 98
DY4: Tip 4C 62
DY9: W'cte 6B 110
Shackleton Dr. WV6: Pert 4E 25
Shackleton Hall B15: Edg 5C 116
Shackleton Rd. WS3: Blox 5B 20
Shadowbrook La.
B92: H Ard 5F 139
Shadwell Dr. DY3: Lwr G 4H 75
Shadwell St. B4: Birm 5F 101 (1D 4)
Shady La. B44: Gt Barr 3F 67
Shadymoor Dr. DY5: Brie H 3G 109
Shaftesbury Av. B63: Crad 4D 110
DY9: Pedm 2G 125
Shaftesbury Rd. WS10: W'bry 3H 63
Shaftesbury Sq. B71: W Brom 2A 80
Shaftesbury St. B70: W Brom 3A 80
B71: W Brom 3A 80
Shaftmoor Ind. Est.
B28: Hall G 3F 135
Shaftmoor La. B27: A Grn 3G 135
B28: Hall G 3E 135
Shaftsbury Cl. WV14: Bils 4H 45
Shaftsbury Rd. B26: Sheld 6G 121
Shahjalal Rd. B8: Salt 4D 102
Shakespeare Cl. WV14: Cose 3F 61
Shakespeare Cres. WS3: Blox 1C 32
(not continuous)
Shakespeare Dr. B90: Shir 6G 149
Shakespeare Ho. B31: Longb 1E 159
Shakespeare Pl. WS3: Blox 2C 32
Shakespeare Rd. B23: Erd 4B 84
B67: Smeth 5C 98
B90: Shir 6B 150
DY3: Lwr G 3E 75
DY4: Tip 5A 62
Shakespeare St. B11: S'hll 6C 118
WV1: Wolv 2A 44
Shaldon Wlk. B66: Smeth 4F 99
Shales, The WV5: Wom 2E 73
Shale St. WV14: Bils 6E 45
Shalford Rd. B92: Olton 1C 136
Shallcross La. DY3: Lwr G 4H 75
Shalnecote Gro. B14: K Hth 2E 147
Shambles, The WS10: W'bry 3F 63
Shandon Cl. B32: Bart G 2D 130
Shanklyn Cl. WS6: Gt Wyr 2F 7
Shannon Dr. WS8: Bwnhls 3G 9
Shannon Rd. B38: K Nor 2H 159
Shannon Wlk. WS8: Bwnhls 3G 9
Shanti Niketan WV2: Wolv 4H 43
Shapinsay Dr. B45: Fran 6F 143
SHARD END 2G 105
Shard End Cres. B34: S End 3G 105
Shardlow Rd. WV11: Wed 1G 29
Shardway, The B34: S End 4G 105
(not continuous)
Sharesacre St. WV13: W'hall 6B 30
Sharington Cl. DY2: Dud 1G 95
Sharman Rd. WV10: Bush 3A 28
SHARMANS CROSS 3C 150
Sharmans Cross Rd. B91: Sol 3C 150
Sharon Cl. WV4: E'shll 6A 44
Sharps Cl. B45: Redn 2G 157
Sharrat Fld. B75: R'ley 1B 54
Sharrocks St. WV2: Wolv 2A 44
SHAVER'S END 4D 76

Shawberry Av. B35: Cas V 4E 87
Shawberry Rd. B37: K'hrst 4B 106
SHAWBROOK 5H 161
Shawbrook Gro. B14: K Hth 4A 148
Shawbury Gro. B12: Birm 3H 117
WV6: Pert 4E 25
Shawbury Rd. WV10: Wolv 4B 28
Shaw Dr. B33: Yard 1C 120
Shawfield B47: H'wd 4A 162
Shaw Hall La. WV10: Cov H 1F 15
Shawhellier Av. DY5: Brie H 1A 110
Shaw Hill Gro. B8: W End 5G 103
Shaw Hill Rd. B8: W End 5G 103
Shawhurst Cft. B47: H'wd 2A 162
Shawhurst Gdns. B47: H'wd 2B 162
Shawhurst La. B47: H'wd 4A 162
Shaw La. WV6: Tett 6H 25
Shawley Cft. B27: A Grn 1C 136
Shaw Pk. Bus. Village
WV10: Bush 3H 27
Shaw Rd. DY2: Dud 2D 94
(not continuous)
DY4: Tip 3C 78
WV2: Wolv 5G 43
WV10: Bush 3G 27
(not continuous)
WV14: Cose 4D 60
Shawsdale Rd. B36: Hodg H 2D 104
Shaws La. WS6: Gt Wyr 3G 7
Shaw's Pas. B5: Birm 1H 117 (5G 5)
Shaw St. B70: W Brom 5E 63
WS2: Wals 1B 48
Sheaf La. B26: Sheld 6F 121
Sheapecote Ho. B71: W Brom 3D 64
Shearers Pl. B75: R'ley 6C 38
Shearwater Cl. B45: Rubery 3F 157
Shearwater Dr. DY5: Brie H 4G 109
Shearwater Wlk. B23: Erd 6B 68
Sheaves Cl. WV14: Cose 2D 60
Shedden St. DY2: Dud 1F 95
Sheddington Rd. B23: Erd 6D 68
Sheen Rd. B44: Gt Barr 1G 67
Sheepclose Dr. B37: F'bri 6C 106
Sheepcote St. B16: Birm 1D 116 (6A 4)
Sheepfold Cl. B65: Row R 5A 96
Sheepmoor Cl. B17: Harb 3D 114
Sheepwash La. DY4: Tip 2D 78
Sheepwash Nature Reserve 3D 78
Sheffield Rd. B73: Bold 6G 69
Sheffield St. DY5: Quar B 2C 110
Shefford Rd. B6: Aston 4H 101
Sheila Av. WV11: Wed 2G 29
Shelah Rd. B63: Hale 5H 111
Shelbourne Cl. B69: Tiv 5D 78
SHELDON 6H 121
Sheldon Av. WS10: W'bry 1G 63
Sheldon Cl. WV14: Bils 2F 61
Sheldon Country Pk. 5G 121
Sheldon Dr. B31: Longb 5B 144
Sheldonfield Rd. B26: Sheld 6H 121
Sheldon Gro. B26: Sheld 6F 121
Sheldon Hall Av. B33: Kitts G 6H 105
(not continuous)
Sheldon Health Leisure Cen. 3G 121
Sheldon Heath Rd. B26: Yard, Sheld 2E 121
Sheldon Rd. B71: W Brom 5C 64
WV10: Oxl 6E 15
Sheldon Wlk. B33: Sheld 2G 121
SHELFIELD 6G 21
Shelfield Rd. B14: K Hth 4E 147
Shelley Av. DY4: Tip 5A 62
Shelley Cl. DY3: Lwr G 2E 75
DY8: Amb 3E 109
Shelley Dr. B23: Erd 4B 84
B74: Four O 3F 37
Shelley Rd. WV10: F'hses 5H 15
WV12: W'hall 2E 31
Shelley Twr. B31: N'fld 4G 145
Shelly Cl. B37: F'bri 1B 122
Shelly Cres. B90: M'path 2F 165
Shelly Cft. B33: Kitts G 6E 105
Shelly Ho. B68: O'bry 5H 97
Shelly La. B90: M'path 3F 165
Shelly Manor Mus. 5B 132
Shelly Shop. Cen. B90: M'path 2F 165
Shelsley Av. B69: O'bry 4D 96
Shelsley Dr. B13: Mose 4B 134
Shelsley Way B91: Sol 6F 151
Shelton Cl. WS10: W'bry 1C 64
Shelton La. B63: Crad 6G 111
Shelwick Gro. B93: Dorr 5A 166
Shenley Av. DY1: Dud 1D 76
Shenley Court Leisure Cen. 6C 130
SHENLEY FIELDS 1C 144
Shenley Flds. Dr. B31: N'fld 5C 130
Shenley Flds. Rd. B29: W Cas 6D 130
Shenley Gdns. B29: W Cas 6E 131
Shenley Grn. B29: W Cas 1E 145
Shenley Hill B31: N'fld 1C 144
Shenley La. B29: W Cas 4D 130
Shenley Lane Community & Sports Cen.
1E 145
Shenstone Av. B62: Hale 6E 113
DY8: Stourb 2B 124
Shenstone Cl. B74: Four O 3E 37
Shenstone Ct. B90: Shir 5D 148
WV3: Wolv 5E 43
Shenstone Dr. CV7: Bal C 3G 169
WS9: A'rdge 1C 34
Shenstone Flats B62: Quin 6F 113
Shenstone Rd. B14: K Hth 6A 148
B16: Edg 6G 99
B43: Gt Barr 5A 66
Shenstone Trad. Est. B63: Hale 1C 128
Shenstone Valley Rd. B62: Quin 5E 113
Shenstone Wlk. B62: Hale 6D 112
SHENSTONE WOODEND 1G 37
Shenton Wlk. B37: K'hrst 4C 106
Shepheard Rd. B26: Sheld 6H 121
Shepherd Dr. WV12: W'hall 4C 30
Shepherds Brook Rd. DY9: Lye 6H 109
Shepherds Fold B65: Row R 1B 112
Shepherds Gdns. B15: Birm 2D 116
Shepherds Grn. Rd. B24: Erd 5F 85
Shepherds La. CV7: Mer 2G 141
Shepherds Pool Rd. B75: R'ley 1C 54
Shepherds Standing
B34: S End 3F 105
Shepherds Wlk. WV8: Pend 5D 14
Shepherds Way B23: Erd 5C 68
Shepley Rd. B45: Redn 3H 157
Sheppey Dr. B36: Cas B 4D 106
SHEPWELL GREEN 1C 46
Shepwell Grn. WV13: W'hall 2C 46
Sherard Cft. B36: Cas B 3D 106
Sheraton Cl. WS9: A'rdge 3D 34
Sheraton Grange DY8: Stourb 3D 124
Sherborne Cl. B46: Col 5H 107
WS3: Blox 2A 32
Sherborne Gdns. WV8: Cod 4G 13
Sherborne Gro. B1: Birm 6C 100
Sherborne Lofts B16: Birm 1D 116
Sherborne Rd. WV10: Bush 6H 15
Sherborne St. B16: Birm 1D 116
Sherborne Wharf B16: Birm 1D 116
Sherbourne Ct. B27: A Grn 1A 136
Sherbourne Dr. B27: A Grn 1A 136
Sherbourne Rd. B12: Bal H 5H 117
(Arter St.)
B12: Bal H 4G 117
(Longmore St.)
B27: A Grn 1A 136
B64: Old H 3A 112
DY8: Stourb 1F 125
Sherdmore Cft. B90: M'path 3E 165
Sheridan Cl. WS2: Wals 4H 47
Sheridan Gdns. DY3: Lwr G 2D 74
Sheridan St. B71: W Brom 3B 80
WS2: Wals 4H 47
Sheridan Wlk. B35: Cas V 4E 87
Sheriff Dr. DY5: Quar B 1B 110
Sherifoot La. B75: Four O 5H 37
Sheringham B15: Edg 3A 116
Sheringham Rd. B30: K Nor 4D 146
Sherington Dr. WV4: Penn 6H 43
Sherlock Cl. WV12: W'hall 4D 30
Sherlock St. B5: Birm 4G 117
Sherrans Dell WV4: E'shll 2A 60
Sherratt Cl. B76: Walm 5D 70
Sherringham Dr. WV11: Ess 6C 18
Sherron Gdns. B12: Bal H 6H 117
Sherston Covert B30: K Nor 5E 147
Shervale Cl. WV4: Penn 5E 43
Sherwin Av. WV14: Cose 3C 60
Sherwood Av. DY4: Tip 3H 77
Sherwood Cl. B28: Hall G 2F 149
B92: Olton 6D 136
Sherwood Dr. DY5: Quar B 2B 110
Sherwood M. B28: Hall G 1E 149
Sherwood Rd. B28: Hall G 6E 135
B67: Smeth 2E 115
DY8: Woll 4C 108
Sherwood St. WV1: Wolv 6G 27
Sherwood Wlk. B45: Fran 4H 143
WS9: A'rdge 2A 34
Shetland Cl. B16: Birm 1B 116
WV6: Wolv 4F 27
Shetland Dr. B66: Smeth 2B 98
Shetland Wlk. B36: Cas B 3D 106
Shidas La. B69: O'bry 2E 97
Shifnal Rd. WV7: Alb 6A 12
Shifnal Wlk. B31: Longb 1D 158
Shifrall Way B75: S Cold 4D 54
Shillcock Gro.
B19: Birm 4G 101
Shilton Cl. B90: M'path 3D 164
Shilton Gro. B29: W Cas 5D 130
Shilwell Cres. B69: Tiv 5D 78
Shipbourne Cl. B32: Harb 6D 114
Shipley Flds. B24: Erd 4G 85
Shipley Gro. B29: W Cas 5E 131
Shipston Rd. B31: N'fld 6F 145
Shipton Cl. DY1: Dud 4A 76
Shipton Rd. B72: S Cold 2A 70
Shipway Rd. B25: Yard 4G 119
Shirebrook Cl. B6: Aston 1G 101
Shire Brook Ct. B19: Loz 1F 101
Shire Cl. B16: Birm 1B 116
B68: O'bry 1H 113
Shireland Brook Gdns.
B18: Win G 5H 99
Shireland Cl. B20: Hand 4A 82
Shireland Rd. B66: Smeth 5F 99
Shire Lea WS8: Bwnhls 1D 22
SHIRE OAK 2B 22
Shire Oak Pk. (Nature Reserve) 3D 22
Shire Ridge WS9: Wals W 3C 22
Shirestone Rd. B33: Kitts G 1H 121
Shireview Gdns.
WS3: Pels 3F 21
Shireview Rd. WS3: Pels 3E 21
Shirland Rd. B37: Mars G 2C 122
SHIRLEY 4H 149
Shirleydale B90: Shir 6A 150
Shirley Dr. B72: S Cold 1A 70
SHIRLEY HEATH 1H 163
Shirley Pk. Rd. B90: Shir 5H 149
Shirley Rd. B27: A Grn 4H 135
B28: Hall G 1G 149
B30: K Nor 2C 146
B68: O'bry 3A 98
DY2: Dud 1G 95
Shirley Station (Rail) 6F 149
SHIRLEY STREET 5H 149
Shirley Trad. Est. B90: Shir 1D 164
Shirrall Dr. B78: Dray B 5G 39
Shirrall Gro. B37: K'hrst 4B 106
Sholing Cl. WV8: Pend 6D 14
Shooters Cl. B5: Bal H 5F 117
Shooters Hill B72: S Cold 3B 70
Shop La. WV6: Tres 4B 40
WV8: Oaken 6C 12
Shopton Rd. B34: S End 2E 105
Shoreham Cl. WV13: W'hall 2F 45
Short Acre St. WS2: Wals 6B 32
SHORT CROSS 1H 127
Shorters Av. B14: K Hth 3B 148
Shortfield Cl. CV7: Bal C 2H 169
SHORT HEATH
Erdington 1D 84
Willenhall 4D 30
Short Heath Ct. B23: Erd 2F 85
Short Heath Rd. B23: Erd 1D 84
Shortland Cl. B93: Know 2C 166
Shortlands Cl. B30: K Nor 5C 146
Shortlands La. WS3: Pels 3D 20
Short La. WS6: C Hay 2E 7
Short Rd. B67: Smeth 6B 98
WV10: Bush 6A 16
Short St. B63: Hale 1H 127
B65: B'hth, Row R 1C 112
(not continuous)
B90: Dic H 4G 163
DY1: Dud 5C 76
DY4: Tip 5G 61
DY8: Stourb 6D 108
WS2: Wals 2B 48
WS8: Bwnhls 5B 10
WS10: Darl 4F 47
WS10: W'bry 2E 63
WV1: Wolv 1H 43 (2C 170)
WV12: W'hall 4C 30
WV14: Bils 5F 45
Shorwell Pl. DY5: Brie H 3G 109
Shottery Cl. B76: Walm 4D 70
Shottery Gro. B76: Walm 4D 70
Shottery Rd. B90: Shir 6H 149
Shotteswell Rd. B90: Shir 2H 163
Showcase Cinema
Dudley 5G 77
Tyburn 5B 86
Walsall 2G 47
Showell Cir. WV10: Bush 2A 28
SHOWELL GREEN 1B 134
Showell Grn. La. B11: S'hll 2B 134
Showell Ho. B69: O'bry 2G 97
Showell La. WV4: Lwr P 2G 57
Showell Rd. WV10: Bush 2H 27
Showell Rd. Ind. Est. WV10: Wolv 3H 27
Showells Gdns. B7: Nech 2C 102
Shrawley Cl. B45: Rubery 2F 157
B63: Hale 3A 128
Shrawley Rd. B31: N'fld 5G 145
Shrewley Cres. B33: Kitts G 2A 122
Shrewsbury Cl. WS3: Blox 6F 19
Shrewton Av. B14: K Hth 6F 147
Shrubbery, The B16: Birm 6B 100
DY1: Dud 5D 76
DY4: Tip 1C 78
Shrubbery Av. DY4: Tip 2F 77
Shrubbery Cl. B76: Walm 1B 86
Shrublands Av. B68: O'bry 4H 113
Shrub La. B24: Erd 3H 85
Shugborough Cl. WS3: Blox 6H 19
Shugborough Dr. DY1: Dud 5A 76
Shustoke La. WS5: Wals 1F 65
Shustoke Rd. B34: S End 3G 105
B91: Sol 2H 151
SHUT END 6E 75
Shutlock La. B13: Mose 4F 133
Shyltons Cft. B16: Birm 1C 116
Sibdon Gro. B31: Longb 1E 159
Sidaway Cl. B65: Row R 3C 96
Sidaway St. B64: Old H 2G 111
Sidbury Gro. B93: Dorr 6A 166
Sidcup Cl. WV14: Cose 2D 60
Sidcup Rd. B44: K'sdng 4A 68
Siddeley Wlk. B36: Cas B 6B 88
Siddons Factory Est. B70: W Brom 5F 63
Siddons Rd. WV14: Cose 3F 61
Siddons Way B70: W Brom 6G 63
Sidenhill Cl. B90: Shir 1H 163
Sidford Gdns. B24: Erd 4A 86
Sidford Gro. B23: Erd 6E 69
Sidings, The B20: Hand 1E 101
B70: W Brom 5A 80
Sidlaw Cl. B63: Hale 3F 127
WV10: Oxl 3G 27
Sidney St. WV2: Wolv 3G 43 (6A 170)
Sidwick Cres. WV2: E'shll 5D 44
Sigmund Cl. WV1: Wolv 6D 28
Signal Gro. WS3: Blox 6G 19
Signal Hayes Rd. B76: Walm 3D 70
(not continuous)
Silesbourne Cl. B36: Cas B 1G 105
Silhill Hall Rd. B91: Sol 1E 151
Silva Av. DY6: K'wfrd 5D 92
Silver Birch Cl. B8: Salt 3D 102
Silver Birch Coppice B74: Four O 4D 36
Silverbirch Ct. B24: Erd 1H 85
Silver Birch Dr. B47: H'wd 3B 162
Silver Birch Rd. B24: Erd 1H 85
B37: K'hrst 3B 106
B74: S'tly 2H 51
WS11: Nort C 1F 9
WV2: Wolv 4H 43
Silverbirch Rd. B91: Sol 4A 152
Silver Ct. WS8: Bwnhls 6B 10
Silver Ct. Gdns. WS8: Bwnhls 6B 10
Silvercroft Av. B20: Hand 4G 81
Silverdale Dr. WV10: Wolv 5A 28
Silverdale Gdns. DY8: Word 6A 92
Silverdale Rd. B24: Erd 2B 86
SILVER END 2F 109
Silver End Bus. Est. DY5: Brie H 2G 109
Silver End Ind. Est. DY5: Brie H 2F 109
Silverfield Cl. B14: K Hth 5G 133
Silver Innage B63: Crad 4E 111
Silverlands Av. B68: O'bry 6H 97
Silverlands Cl. B28: Hall G 4F 135
Silvermead Ct. B47: Wyt 4H 161
Silvermead Rd. B73: W Grn 4G 69
Silvermere Rd. B26: Sheld 5H 121
Silvers Cl. WS3: Pels 2D 20
Silverstone Cl. WS2: Wals 6E 31
Silverstone Dr. B74: S'tly 5H 51
SILVER STREET 4G 161
Silver St. B14: K Hth 5G 133
B38: Head H 4F 161
B47: Wyt 4G 161
DY5: Brie H 2G 109
WS8: Bwnhls 6A 10
Silverthorne Av. DY4: Tip 2F 77
Silverthorne La. B64: Crad H 2D 110
Silverton Cres. B13: Mose 4D 134
Silverton Hgts. B67: Smeth 3D 98
Silverton Rd. B67: Smeth 3C 98
Silverton Way WV11: Wed 4H 29
Silvertrees Rd. DY4: Tip 2G 77
Silvester Ct. B70: W Brom 4B 80
Silvester Rd. WV14: Bils 5G 45
Silvester Way DY5: Brie H 3F 109
Silvington Cl. B29: W Cas 6G 131
Simcox Gdns. B32: Bart G 3B 130
Simcox Rd. WS10: W'bry 6F 47
Simeon Bissell Cl. DY4: Tip 2A 78
Simeon's Wlk. DY5: Quar B 4B 110
Simmonds Cl. WS3: Blox 4B 20
Simmonds Pl. WS3: Blox 4B 20
WS10: Darl 4E 47
Simmonds Rd. WS3: Blox 4B 20
Simmonds Way WS8: Bwnhls 2C 22
Simmons Dr. B32: Quin 6A 114
Simmons Leasow
B32: Bart G 3B 130
Simmons Rd. WV11: Wed 6B 18
Simms La. B47: H'wd 4A 162
(not continuous)
DY2: Neth 4E 95
Simon Cl. B71: W Brom 4C 64
Simon Rd. B47: H'wd 2A 162
Simpkins Cl. WS9: Wals W 4C 22
Simpson Gro. WV10: Bush 3A 28
Simpson Rd. B72: W Grn 4A 70
WS2: Wals 4H 31
WV10: Bush 3A 28
Simpson St. B69: O'bry 2G 97
Sinclair Ct. B13: Mose 1G 133
Singer Cft. B36: Cas B 6B 88
Singh Cl. B21: Hand 4A 82
Sion Cl. DY5: Brie H 6H 93
Sir Alfred's Way B76: Walm 2C 70
Sir Harrys Rd. B15: Edg 5D 116
Sir Hilton's Rd. B31: Longb 2F 159
Sir Johns Rd. B29: S Oak 2E 133
Sir Richards Dr. B17: Harb 4D 114
Sisefield Rd. B38: K Nor 6C 146
Siskin Cl. WS7: Hamm 1F 11
Siskin Dr. B12: Bal H 5G 117
Siskin Rd. DY9: W'cte 2H 125
Sister Dora Bldgs. *WS1: Wals 2C 48*
(off Bridge, The)
Sister Dora Gdns. WS1: Wals 2C 48
Siviters Cl. B65: Row R 6C 96
Siviters La. B65: Row R 6B 96
Six Acres B32: Quin 1A 130
Sixes Sports Cen. 6C 74
Six Foot Rd. DY2: Neth 4E 95
Six Towers Rd. WS2: Wals 5A 32
Six Ways B23: Erd 3F 85
Skelcher Rd. B90: Shir 3G 149
Skemp Cl. WV14: Bils 2F 61
Sketchley Cl. B66: Smeth 4E 99
Skidmore Av. WV3: Wolv 3D 42
Skidmore Dr. B70: W Brom 4G 79
Skidmore Rd. WV14: Cose 3F 61
Skinner La. B5: Birm 2G 117
Skinner St. WV1: Wolv 1G 43 (3A 170)
Skip La. WS5: Wals 6H 49
Skipton Grn. WV6: Wolv 4E 27
Skipton Rd. B16: Edg 2C 116
Skomer Cl. B45: Fran 6E 143
Skye Cl. B36: Cas B 3D 106
Skye Wlk. B64: Old H 2G 111
Sky Lark Cl. DY5: P'ntt 6G 75
Skylark Cl. B23: Erd 6C 68
Skywalk B40: Nat E C 1F 139
Slack La. B20: Hand 5A 82
Slacky La. WS3: Blox 6C 20
Slade Cl. B71: W Brom 3D 64
Sladefield Rd. B8: W End 4G 103
Slade Gdns. WV8: Cod 3G 13
Slade Gro. B93: Know 3B 166
Slade Hill WV6: Wolv 6D 26
Slade La. B28: Hall G 4E 149
B75: R'ley 6E 39
Slade Lanker B34: Stech 4E 105
Sladepool Farm Rd. B14: K Hth 4H 147
Slade Rd. B23: Erd 3D 84
B63: Crad 5E 111
B75: R'ley, Can 6C 38
WV10: F'hses 4G 15
Slaithwaite Rd. B71: W Brom 3C 80
Slaney Ct. WS2: Wals 4A 48
Slaney Rd. WS2: Wals 5H 47
Slater Rd. B67: Smeth 1C 114
Slate La. WV8: Cod 2D 12
Slateley Cres. B90: M'path 3E 165
Slater Cl. B64: Old H 2H 111
Slate Row WS3: Pels 4E 21
Slater Rd. B93: Ben H 5A 166
Slater's La. WS2: Wals 4H 47
Slater's Pl. WS2: Wals 4H 47
Slater St. DY4: Tip 3A 78
(Crompton Rd.)
DY4: Tip 2D 78
(Sheepwash La.)
WS10: Darl 4D 46
WV13: W'hall 6C 30
WV14: Bils 1G 61
Sleaford Gro. B28: Hall G 6G 135
Sleaford Rd. B28: Hall G 6H 135
Sledmore Rd. DY2: Dud 2F 95
Slieve, The B20: Hand 4C 82
Slim Av. WV14: Bils 2G 61
Slimbridge Cl. B90: M'path 3E 165
Slim Rd. WS2: Wals 1E 47
Sloanes Ga. B63: Hale 1A 128
Sling, The DY2: Neth 3E 95
Slingfield Rd. B31: N'fld 5G 145
Slitting Mill Cl. B21: Hand 1G 99
Sloane Ho. B1: Birm 2A 4
Sloane St. B1: Birm 6E 101 (3A 4)
Slough La. B38: Head H 1G 161
B47: H'wd 1G 161
Smallbrook La. WV5: Wom 6H 57
Smallbrook Queensway
B5: Birm 2F 117 (6D 4)
Small Cl. B67: Smeth 4B 98
Smalldale Rd. B42: Gt Barr 6F 67
SMALL HEATH 3D 118
Small Heath Bri. B10: Small H 3B 118
B11: S'brk 4B 118

Small Heath Bus. Pk.—Stackhouse Dr.

Small Heath Bus. Pk. B10: Small H 4F 119
Small Heath Highway B10: Small H 3B 118
Small Heath Leisure Cen. 3D 118
Small Heath Station (Rail) 4D 118
Small Heath Trad. Est. B11: Small H 5D 118
Smallshire Cl. WV11: Wed 4H 29
Smallshire Way DY8: Word 3B 108
Small St. B71: W Brom 1H 79
WS1: Wals 3C 48
Smallwood Cl. B24: Erd 4B 86
B76: Walm 2C 70
Smallwood Rd. WV8: Pend 5C 14
Smarts Av. WS14: Shen W 2G 37
Smeaton Gdns. B18: Win G 5A 100
Smeed Gro. B24: Erd 4H 85
SMESTOW 3C 72
Smestow Ga. DY3: Swind 2B 72
Smestow La. DY3: Swind 3C 72
Smestow St. WV10: Wolv 5H 27
Smestow Valley Local Nature Reserve
. . . . 3D 26
Smestow Wildlife Cen. 3D 72
SMETHWICK 4E 99
Smethwick Galton Bridge Station (Rail)
. . . . 2C 98
Smethwick New Ent. Cen.
B66: Smeth 3E 99
Smethwick Rolfe Street Station (Rail)
. . . . 3E 99
Smethwick Swimming Cen. 1D 114
Smirrells Rd. B28: Hall G 2E 149
Smith Av. WS10: Darl 1D 62
Smith Cl. B67: Smeth 6B 98
WV14: Cose 4C 60
Smithfield Rd. WS3: Blox 6B 20
Smithfields DY8: Stourb 6E 109
Smithfield St. B5: Birm 2G 117 (6G 5)
Smith Ho. WS3: Blox 4A 20
Smithmoor Cres. B71: W Brom 5D 64
Smith Pl. DY4: Tip 3B 78
Smith Rd. WS2: Wals 5A 48
WS10: W'bry 4E 63
Smiths Cl. B32: Bart G 3H 129
Smiths La. B93: Know 3A 166
Smith St. B19: Birm 4E 101
DY2: Dud 2F 95
WV14: Bils 6F 45
Smiths Way B46: Wat O 4C 88
SMITH'S WOOD 2C 106
Smithy, The B26: Sheld 5G 121
Smithy Dr. WS3: Pels 3E 21
Smithy La. DY5: P'ntt 6F 75
Smout Cres. WV14: Cose 3B 60
Snapdragon Dr. WS5: Wals 2D 64
Snape Rd. WV11: Wed 6A 18
Snapes Lodge WV12: W'hall 3C 30
Sneyd Hall Cl. WS3: Blox 1G 31
Sneyd Hall Rd. WS3: Blox 6G 19
Sneyd La. WS3: Blox 6F 19
WV11: Ess 5B 18
Snowberry Dr. DY5: P'ntt 6G 75
Snowberry Gdns.
B27: A Grn 6A 120
Snowdon Gro. B63: Hale 4F 127
Snowdon Ri. DY3: Sed 1H 75
Snowdon Rd. DY8: Amb 5F 109
Snowdon Way WV10: Oxl 3F 27
WV12: W'hall 6B 18
Snowdrop Cl. WS8: Clay 1H 21
Snowford Cl. B90: Shir 6F 149
Snow Hill WV2: Wolv 2H 43 (4C 170)
Snow Hill Junc.
WV2: Wolv 2H 43 (5C 170)
Snow Hill Queensway
B4: Birm 6G 101 (2D 4)
Snow Hill Station (Rail & MM) . . . 6F 101 (2D 4)
Snowshill Dr. B90: Ches G 4B 164
Snowshill Gdns. DY1: Dud 3B 76
Soberton Cl. WV11: Wed 2H 29
SOHO 2G 99
Soho Av. B18: Hock 2C 100
Soho Benson Road Stop (MM) 3B 100
Soho Cl. B66: Smeth 4G 99
Soho Hill B19: Hock 2C 100
Soho Ho. B66: Smeth 4G 99
Soho Pool Way B18: Hock 3C 100
Soho Rd. B21: Hand 1A 100
Soho St. B66: Smeth 3G 99
Soho Way B66: Smeth 3F 99
Solari Cl. DY4: Tip 5C 62
Solent Cl. WV9: Pend 5D 14
Solent Ct. B73: S Cold 6H 53
SOLIHULL 4G 151
Solihull By-Pass B91: Sol 2G 151
Solihull Ice Rink 2F 137
Solihull La. B28: Hall G 1G 149
SOLIHULL LODGE 5C 148
Solihull Parkway B37: Mars G 4F 123
Solihull Retail Pk. B90: Shir 6B 150
Solihull Rd. B11: S'hll 2D 134
B90: Shir 4A 150
B92: H Ard 1E 153
Solihull Station (Rail) 3E 151
Soliway Cl. WS10: W'bry 1A 64
Solly Gro. DY4: Tip 6D 62
Solva Cl. WV1: Wolv 2D 44
Somerby Dr. B91: Sol 1E 165
Somercotes Rd. B42: Gt Barr 5F 67
Somerdale Rd. B31: N'fld 3G 145
Somerfield Cl. WS4: S'fld 6G 21
Somerfield Rd. WS3: Blox 1H 31
Somerford Cl. WS6: Gt Wyr 4E 7
Somerford Gdns. WV10: Bush 5A 16
Somerford Pl. WV13: W'hall 2H 45
Somerford Rd. B29: W Cas 5D 130
Somerford Way WV14: Cose 5D 60
Somerland Rd. B26: Yard 2E 121
Somerset Cres. WS10: W'bry 1B 64
Somerset Dr. B31: Longb 2D 158
DY8: Woll 4B 108
Somerset Rd. B15: Edg 5A 116
B20: Hand 5B 82
B23: Erd 1F 85
B71: W Brom 1B 80
WS4: Wals 5E 33
WV13: W'hall 1D 46
Somers Rd. B62: Hale 6C 112
CV7: Mer 4F 141
WS2: Wals 4G 47
Somers Wood Cvn. & Camping Pk.
CV7: Mer 4F 141
Somerton Dr. B23: Erd 1G 85
B37: Mars G 4C 122
Somerville Ct. B73: S Cold 3G 69
Somerville Dr. B73: S Cold 1G 69
Somerville Ho. B37: Chel W 6F 107
Somerville Rd. B10: Small H 3D 118
B73: S Cold 1G 69
Somery Rd. B29: W Cas 3E 131
DY1: Dud 4E 77
Sommerfield Rd. B32: Bart G 3A 130
Sonning Dr. WV9: Pend 5D 14
Sopwith Cft. B35: Cas V 5E 87
Sorrel Cl. B69: Tiv 5B 78
Sorrel Dr. WS5: Wals 2E 65
Sorrel Gro. B24: Erd 4B 86
Sorrel Ho. B24: Erd 4B 86
Sorrell Dr. B27: A Grn 3H 135
Sorrel Wlk. DY5: Brie H 5F 109
Sorrento Ct. B13: Mose 2A 134
Sot's Hole Nature Reserve 2C 80
Souters Ho. B32: Bart G 5B 130
Southacre Av. B5: Birm 3G 117
(not continuous)
Southall Cres. WV14: Cose 4E 61
Southall Rd. WV11: Wed 1A 30
Southalls La. DY1: Dud 6D 76
Southam Cl. B28: Hall G 5E 135
Southam Dr. B73: W Grn 4H 69
Southam Ho. B13: Mose 6A 134
Southampton St.
WV1: Wolv 6H 27 (1D 170)
Southam Rd. B28: Hall G 5E 135
South Av. DY8: Stourb 1D 124
WV11: Wed 4E 29
Southbank Rd. B64: Old H 2G 111
Southbank Vw. DY6: K'wfrd 5C 92
Southbourne Av. B34: Hodg H 3B 104
WS2: Wals 2H 47
Southbourne Cl. B29: S Oak 3C 132
Southbourne Rd. WV10: F'hses 4G 15
Sth. Car Pk. Rd. B40: Nat E C 2G 139
Southcote Gro. B38: K Nor 6H 145
Southcott Av. DY5: Brie H 3H 109
South Cres. WV10: F'stne 1D 16
South Dene B67: Smeth 4D 98
Southdown Av. B18: Hock 3C 100
South Dr. B5: Edg 1E 133
B46: Col 2F 107
B75: S Cold 5A 54
Southern Cl. DY6: K'wfrd 6D 92
Southerndown Rd. DY3: Sed 6F 59
Southern Rd. B8: W End 4A 104
Southern Way WS10: Mox 2C 62
WS10: W'bry 2C 62
Southey Cl. B91: Sol 1F 165
WV12: W'hall 1E 31
Southfield Av. B16: Edg 6H 99
B36: Cas B 1E 105
Southfield Cl. WS9: A'rdge 3C 34
Southfield Dr. B28: Hall G 2G 149
Southfield Gro. WV3: Wolv 4A 42
Southfield Rd. B16: Edg 6H 99
WV11: Wed 4H 29
Southfields Cl. B46: Col 5H 107
Southfields Rd. B91: Sol 6D 150
Southfield Way WS6: Gt Wyr 3F 7
Southgate B64: Crad H 3F 111
WV1: Wolv 1F 43
Southgate Rd. B44: Gt Barr 3G 67
South Grn. WV4: Penn 6B 42
South Gro. B6: Aston 1F 101
B19: Hand 1D 100
B23: Erd 2F 85
South Holme B9: Bord G 1C 118
Southlands Rd. B13: Mose 4A 134
Southminster Dr. B14: K Hth 1G 147
South Oval DY3: Up Gor 2A 76
South Pde. B72: S Cold 6A 54
South Pk. M. DY5: Brie H 1G 109
South Range B11: Bal H 5B 118
South Rd. B11: S'brk 4B 118
B14: K Hth 5G 133
B18: Hock 2C 100
B23: Erd 3F 85
B31: N'fld 5D 144
B67: Smeth 4D 98
DY4: Tip 5B 62
DY8: Stourb 1B 124
South Rd. Av. B18: Hock 3C 100
South Roundhay B33: Kitts G 6E 105
Southside Bus. Cen. *B12: Bal H* *6A 118*
(off Ladypool Rd.)
Sth. Staffordshire Bus. Pk.
WS11: Cann 1C 6
South Staffordshire Golf Course 3B 26
South St. B17: Harb 6H 115
DY5: Brie H 1G 109
WS1: Wals 3B 48
WV10: Oxl 3G 27
WV13: W'hall 2H 45
South St. Gdns. WS1: Wals 3B 48
South Vw. B43: Gt Barr 6A 66
South Vw. Cl. WV8: Bilb 5H 13
WV10: F'stne 1D 16
Southview Ridge DY5: Brie H 4H 109
South Vw. Rd. DY3: Sed 5G 59
Southville Bungalows B14: K Hth 3B 148
South Wlk. B31: N'fld 6G 145
South Way B40: Nat E C 2H 139
Southway Ct. DY6: K'wfrd 5D 92
Southwick Pl. WV14: Bils 4F 45
Southwick Rd. B62: B'hth 3D 112
Southwold Av. B30: K Nor 4E 147
Southwood Av. B34: S End 2F 105
Southwood Cl. DY6: K'wfrd 4C 92
Southwood Covert B14: K Hth 5F 147
SOUTH YARDLEY 5B 120
Sovereign Ct. B1: Birm 6E 101 (2A 4)
Sovereign Dr. DY1: Dud 5A 76
Sovereign Hgts. B31: Longb 6A 144
Sovereign Rd. B30: K Nor 3B 146
Sovereign Wlk. WS1: Wals 1E 49
Sovereign Way B13: Mose 1H 133
Sowerby March B24: Erd 3B 86
Sowers Cl. WV12: W'hall 4D 30
Sowers Ct. B75: R'ley 5B 38
Sowers Gdns. WV12: W'hall 4D 30
Spa Gro. B30: Stir 5E 133
SPARKBROOK 4B 118
SPARKHILL 1C 134
Sparkhill Pool & Fitness Cen. 1C 134
Spark St. B11: S'brk 4A 118
Sparrey Dr. B30: Stir 5C 132
Sparrow Cl. WS10: W'bry 6H 47
Spartan Ind. Cen. B70: W Brom 1E 79
Speakers Cl. B69: Tiv 2B 96
Speed Rd. DY4: Tip 1G 77
Speedwell Cl. B25: Yard 5G 119
WS9: A'rdge 4B 34
WV11: Wed 4G 29
Speedwell Dr. CV7: Bal C 3G 169
Speedwell Gdns. DY5: Brie H 5F 109
Speedwell Ho. B38: K Nor 6C 146
Speedwell Rd. B5: Bal H 5F 117
B25: Yard 5G 119
Speedwell Trad. Est. B11: Tys 5G 119
Spelter Works WS3: Blox 2G 31
Spencer Av. WV14: Cose 5E 61
Spencer Cl. B24: Erd 3B 86
B69: Tiv 1B 96
B71: W Brom 5D 64
DY3: Lwr G 3E 75
Spencer St. B18: Birm 4E 101 (1A 4)
(not continuous)
Spenser Av. WV6: Pert 5F 25
Spernall Gro. B29: W Cas 4E 131
Spey Cl. B5: Edg 5F 117
Spiceland Rd. B31: N'fld 1D 144
Spiers Cl. B93: Know 3C 166
Spies Cl. B62: Quin 5F 113
Spies La. B62: Quin 6F 113
Spills Mdw. DY3: Up Gor 2A 76
Spilsbury Cft. B91: Sol 1E 165
Spindle La. B90: Dic H 3G 163
(not continuous)
Spinners End Dr. B64: Crad H 2F 111
Spinners End Ind. Est. B64: Crad H 3F 111
Spinney, The B15: Edg 6A 116
B20: Hand 3A 82
B38: K Nor 6B 146
B47: Wyt 5B 162
B74: Lit A 4B 36
B91: Sol 1G 165
DY3: Gorn 5G 75
WV3: Wolv 2B 42
Spinney Cl. B31: N'fld 4E 145
DY8: Word 6A 92
WS3: Pels 5E 21
Spinney Dr. B90: Ches G 5B 164
Spinney Wlk. B76: Walm 6D 70
Spiral Cl. B62: B'hth 3E 113
Spiral Ct. B24: Erd 5E 85
B76: Walm 2D 70
DY3: Lwr G *4H 75*
(off Yorkdale Cl.)
DY8: Stourb 1E 125
WV11: Wed 2F 29
Spiral Grn. B24: Erd 3A 86
Spitfire Pk. B24: Erd 5B 86
Spitfire Rd. B24: Erd 5A 86
Spitfire Way B35: Cas V 5E 87
Spondon Gro. B34: S End 4G 105
Spondon Rd. WV11: Wed 1G 29
Spon La. B70: W Brom 6B 80
Spon La. Ind. Est. B66: Smeth 1B 98
Spon La. Sth. B66: Smeth 1B 98
B70: Smeth, W Brom 1B 98
Spon La. Trad. Est. B70: W Brom 5B 80
Spoon Dr. B38: K Nor 5H 145
Spooner Cft. B5: Birm 3G 117
Spooners Cl. B92: Sol 6B 138
Spot La. WS8: Clay 1B 22
Spouthouse La. B43: Gt Barr 6A 66
Spout La. WS1: Wals 4C 48
(not continuous)
Spreadbury Cl. B17: Harb 3D 114
Sprig Cft. B36: Hodg H 1A 104
Spring Av. B65: Row R 1C 112
Spring Avon Cft. B17: Harb 5F 115
SPRING BANK 6B 30
Springbank B9: Bord G 6F 103
Spring Bank Ho. WV13: W'hall 6A 30
Springbank Rd. B15: Edg 4E 117
Springbrook Cl. B36: Cas B 6H 87
Spring Cl. B91: Sol 4D 150
WS4: S'fld 5G 21
Spring Coppice Dr. B93: Dorr 6C 166
Spring Ct. B66: Smeth 4G 99
B70: W Brom 5B 80
WS1: Wals 4E 49
Spring Cres. B64: Crad H 4H 111
Springcroft Rd. B11: Tys 3F 135
Spring Dr. WS6: Gt Wyr 3G 7
Spring Dr. Ind. Est. WV4: E'shll 1C 60
SPRINGFIELD
Moseley 4D 134
Rowley Regis 3H 95
Wolverhampton 6A 28
Springfield B23: Erd 4D 84
Springfield Av. B12: Bal H 5A 118
B68: O'bry 5A 98
DY3: Sed 4A 60
DY9: W'cte 1A 126
Springfield Cl. B65: Row R 4A 96
Springfield Ct. B28: Hall G 5F 135
B75: S Cold 6G 55
Springfield Cres. B70: W Brom 6C 80
B76: Walm 1E 71
B92: Sol 2G 137
DY2: Dud 1H 95
Springfield Dr. B14: K Hth 4G 133
B62: B'hth 4D 112
Springfield Grn. DY3: Sed 4A 60
Springfield Gro. DY3: Sed 4H 59
Springfield Ind. Est. B69: O'bry 2H 97
Springfield La. B65: Row R 4H 95
WV10: F'hses 3H 15
Springfield Rd. B13: Mose 4D 134
B14: K Hth 5H 133
B36: Cas B 1H 105
B62: B'hth 4D 112
B68: O'bry 5A 98
B76: Walm 3D 70
DY5: Brie H 1F 109
WV10: Wolv 5A 28
WV14: Bils 4G 45
Springfields B46: Col 4H 107
WS4: Rus 2F 33
Springfield Ter. B65: Row R 4H 95
Spring Gdns. B21: Hand 2A 100
B66: Smeth 6F 99
DY2: Dud 1F 95
DY3: Gorn 5G 75
Spring Gro. B19: Hock 3D 100
Spring Gro. Gdns. B18: Hock 3B 100
Spring Head WS10: W'bry 3F 63
SPRING HILL 1A 58
SPRINGHILL
Essington 2D 18
Lynn 6G 11
Spring Hill B1: Birm 6D 100
B18: Hock 5C 100
B24: Erd 4F 85
Springhill Av. WV4: Penn 2A 58
Springhill Cl. WS4: S'fld 6H 21
WV12: W'hall 2D 30
Springhill Ct. WS1: Wals 3E 49
Springhill Gro. WV4: Penn 1A 58
Spring Hill Ind. Est.
B18: Hock 6C 100
Springhill La. WV4: Lwr P 6F 41
WV4: Penn 2A 58
Springhill Pk. WV4: Penn 2H 57
Springhill Rd. WS1: Wals 2D 48
WS8: Bwnhls 6C 10
WV11: Wed 1G 29
Spring Hill Ter. WV4: Penn 5E 43
Spring Ho. B37: K'hrst 4D 106
Spring La. B24: Erd 4G 85
WS4: S'fld 5G 21
WV12: W'hall 5B 30
Spring Mdw. B63: Hale 3H 127
B64: Old H 2H 111
DY4: Tip 1C 78
WS6: C Hay 4D 6
Springmeadow Gro. B19: Hock 3F 101
Springmeadow Rd. DY2: Neth 1E 111
Spring Mdws. Cl. WV8: Bilb 3H 13
Spring Parklands DY1: Dud 1C 94
Spring Rd. B11: Tys 2F 135
B15: Edg 4F 117
B66: Smeth 1B 98
DY2: Neth 3F 95
WS4: S'fld 6H 21
WV4: E'shll 6C 44
Spring Rd. Ind. Est. WV4: E'shll 1C 60
Spring Road Station (Rail) 3G 135
Springs, The B64: Old H 2A 112
Springslade B32: Harb 6D 114
Springslade Dr. B24: Erd 4B 86
SPRINGS MIRE 1A 94
Spring St. B15: Birm 3F 117
B63: Crad 5E 111
DY4: Tip 2A 78
(Alexandra Rd.)
DY4: Tip 5C 62
(Oaker Hill Rd.)
DY9: Lye 1A 126
Springthorpe Grn. B24: Erd 3A 86
Springthorpe Rd. B24: Erd 4B 86
(Pype Hayes Rd.)
B24: Erd 3B 86
(Woodcote Rd.)
SPRING VALE 1D 60
Springvale Av. WS5: Wals 4G 49
WV14: Bils 1D 60
Springvale Bus. Cen. WV14: Bils 1D 60
Spring Va. Cl. WV14: Cose 4C 60
Spring Va. Ind. Pk. WV14: Bils 6E 45
Spring Va. Rd. B65: Row R 4A 96
Springvale St. WV13: W'hall 6B 30
Springvale Way WV14: Bils 1E 61
Spring Vs. B63: Hale 2A 128
Spring Wlk. B63: Hale 4F 127
B69: O'bry 4G 97
WS2: Wals 6H 31
Sproat Av. WS10: Darl 6C 46
Spruce Gro. B24: Erd 5H 85
Spruce Rd. WS5: Wals 2B 64
Spruce Way WV3: Wolv 2B 42
Spur Tree Av. WV3: Wolv 2G 41
Squadron Cl. B35: Cas V 3G 87
Square, The B15: Birm 2D 116
B17: Harb *6G 115*
(off High St.)
B17: Harb 5F 115
(Carless Av.)
B91: Sol 4G 151
DY2: Dud 3B 94
DY4: Tip 6D 62
WS9: A'rdge 3D 34
WV2: Wolv 3H 43 (6D 170)
WV8: Cod 3F 13
WV12: W'hall 1D 30
Square Cl. B32: Bart G 2A 130
Squires Ct. DY5: Brie H 3G 109
Squires Cft. B76: Walm 4E 71
Squires Ga. Wlk. B35: Cas V 4E 87
Squires Wlk. WS10: W'bry 2F 63
Squirrel Hollow B76: Walm 3E 71
Squirrels Hollow B68: O'bry 4B 114
Squirrel Wlk. B74: Lit A 4C 36
WV4: Penn 1E 59
Stable Cl. DY3: Sed 1A 76
Stable Cft. B71: W Brom 6D 64
Stableford Cl. B32: Bart G 2D 130
Stables, The B29: S Oak 3C 132
Stablewood Gro. WS1: Wals 4E 49
Stacey Cl. B64: Old H 2G 111
Stacey Dr. B13: Mose 2A 148
Stacey Grange Gdns. B45: Redn 3G 157
Stackhouse Cl. WS9: Wals W 3C 22
Stackhouse Dr. WS3: Pels 3E 21

Tower Vw. Rd.—Up. Trinity St.

Tower Vw. Rd. WS6: Gt Wyr 5F 7
Tower Works Ind. Est. WV3: Wolv 2E 43
Town End Sq. WS1: Wals 1C 48
(off Park St.)
Townend St. WS2: Wals 1C 48
Town Fold WS3: Pels 3E 21
Town Ga. Retail Pk.
DY1: Dud 5H 77
Town Hall Stop (MM) 4A 80
Townley Gdns. B6: Aston 6G 83
Townsend Av. DY3: Sed 5H 59
Townsend Dr. B76: Walm 6D 70
Townsend Pl. DY6: K'wfrd 3B 92
Townsend Way B1: Birm 6D 100 (3A 4)
Townshend Gro. B37: K'hrst 5B 106
Townson Rd. WV11: Wed 1A 30
Townwell Fold WV1: Wolv 1G 43 (3A 170)
Town Wharf Bus. Pk.
WS2: Wals 2B 48
Town Yd. WV13: W'hall 2A 46
Towpath Cl. B9: Birm 1B 118
Towyn Rd. B13: Mose 3D 134
Toy's La. B63: Crad 6E 111
Tozer St. DY4: Tip 6H 61
Traceys Mdw. B45: Redn 2G 157
Tractor Spares Ind. Est.
WV13: W'hall 1F 45
Trafalgar Ct. B69: Tiv 6B 78
Trafalgar Gro. B25: Yard 5G 119
Trafalgar Rd. B13: Mose 2H 133
B21: Hand 1A 100
B24: Erd 4F 85
B66: Smeth 5F 99
B69: Tiv 6B 78
Trafalgar Ter. B66: Smeth 5F 99
Trajan Hill B46: Col 6H 89
Tram Way B66: Smeth 2A 98
Tramway Cl. WS10: Darl 4E 47
WV14: Bils 4H 45
Tranter Rd. B8: W End 4G 103
Tranwell Cl. WV9: Pend 5D 14
Traquain Dr. DY1: Dud 4C 76
Travellers Way B37: Chel W 6F 107
Treaford La. B8: W End 5H 103
Treddles La. B70: W Brom 4B 80
Tredington Cl. B29: W Cas 6E 131
Tree Acre Gro. B63: Crad 1E 127
Treeford Cl. B91: Sol 6D 150
Trees Rd. WS1: Wals 5D 48
Treeton Cft. B33: Yard 1E 121
Tree Tops WV5: Wom 5E 57
Treetops Dr. WV12: W'hall 4E 31
Trefoil Cl. B29: W Cas 6E 131
(not continuous)
Tregarron Rd. B63: Crad 6E 111
Tregea Ri. B43: Gt Barr 6G 65
Trehern Cl. B93: Know 4C 166
Trehernes Dr. DY9: Pedm 4F 125
Trehurst Av. B42: Gt Barr 5E 67
Trejon Rd. B64: Crad H 3G 111
Tremaine Gdns. WV10: Wolv 5H 27
Trenchard Cl. B75: S Cold 6D 54
Trent Cl. DY8: Stourb 1E 125
WV6: Pert 5E 25
Trent Ct. B73: S Cold 6H 53
Trent Cres. B47: Wyt 6G 161
Trent Dr. B36: Cas B 1B 106
Trentham Av. WV12: W'hall 4A 30
Trentham Gro. B26: Yard 6C 120
Trentham Ri. WV2: E'shll 4B 44
Trent Pl. WS3: Blox 1B 32
Trent Rd. WS3: Pels 6E 21
Trent St. B5: Birm 1H 117 (5H 5)
Trent Twr. B7: Birm 5A 102
Trenville Av. B11: S'hll 6B 118
B12: Bal H 6B 118
Tresco Cl. B45: Fran 6E 143
TRESCOTT 4B 40
Trescott Rd. B31: N'fld 4B 144
Tresham Rd. B44: Gt Barr 4G 67
DY6: K'wfrd 1B 92
Trevanie Av. B32: Quin 5A 114
Trevelyan Ho. B37: Chel W 2E 123
Trevor Av. WS6: Gt Wyr 2G 7
Trevorne Cl. B12: Bal H 5H 117
Trevor Rd. WS3: Pels 3D 20
Trevor St. B7: Nech 3C 102
Trevor St. W. B7: Nech 3C 102
Trevose Cl. WS3: Blox 4F 19
Trevose Retreat B12: Bal H 6H 117
Trewman Cl. B76: Walm 5D 70
Treyamon Rd. WS5: Wals 4H 49
Treynham Cl. WV1: Wolv 2E 45
TRIANGLE 1D 10
Triangle, The B18: Hock 3A 100
Trickley Dr. B75: S Cold 5D 54
Tricorn Ho. B16: Edg 2C 116
Trident Blvd. B35: Cas V 5F 87
Trident Cen. DY1: Dud 6E 77
Trident Cl. B23: Erd 6G 69
B76: Walm 6D 70
Trident Ct. B20: Hand 4C 82
B37: Mars G 3G 123
Trident Dr. B68: O'bry 4H 97
WS10: W'bry 2D 62
Trident Ho. B15: Birm 2E 117 (6A 4)
Trident Retail Pk. B9: Birm 1A 118
Trident Rd. B26: Birm A 1E 139
Trigen Ho. B90: Bly P 6D 164
Trigo Cft. B36: Hodg H 1C 104
Trimpley Cl. B93: Dorr 6A 166
Trimpley Gdns. WV4: Penn 2C 58
Trimpley Rd. B32: Bart G 5H 129
Trinder Rd. B67: Smeth 1B 114
Trindle Cl. DY2: Dud 6F 77
Trindle Rd. DY2: Dud 6F 77
Tring Ct. WV6: Wolv 5D 26
Trinity Cen. B64: Old H 1G 111
Trinity Cl. B92: Olton 4F 137
DY8: Word 1B 108
Trinity Ct. B6: Aston 6F 83
B64: Old H 2G 111
WV3: Wolv 1E 43
WV13: W'hall 2G 45
Trinity Gro. WS10: W'bry 2G 63
Trinity Hill B72: S Cold 6A 54
Trinity Pk. B37: Mars G 2F 139
Trinity Pl. B72: S Cold 6A 54
Trinity Rd. B6: Aston 6F 83
B75: Four O 2H 53
DY1: Dud 6E 77
DY8: Amb 3E 109
WV12: W'hall 3D 30
WV14: Bils 6H 45
(not continuous)
Trinity Rd. Nth. B70: W Brom 6B 80
(not continuous)
Trinity Rd. Sth. B70: W Brom 6B 80
Trinity St. B64: Old H 2G 111
B67: Smeth 3E 99
B69: O'bry 4G 97
B70: W Brom 5B 80
DY5: Brie H 6H 93
Trinity Ter. B11: S'brk 3A 118
Trinity Way B70: W Brom 6B 80
Trinity Way Stop (MM) 6B 80
Trippleton Av. B32: Bart G 5H 129
Tristram Av. B31: N'fld 6F 145
Triton Cl. WS6: Gt Wyr 4F 7
Trittiford Rd. B13: Mose 1B 148
Triumph Wlk. B36: Cas B 6C 88
Tromans Cl. B64: Crad H 4G 111
Tromans Ind. Est. DY2: Neth 6F 95
Troon Cl. B75: S Cold 3B 54
WS3: Blox 4G 19
Troon Ct. WV6: Pert 4D 24
Troon Pl. DY8: Word 6A 92
Trotter's La. B71: W Brom 6G 63
Trouse La. WS10: W'bry 2E 63
Troutbeck Dr. DY5: Brie H 3F 109
Troy Gro. B14: K Hth 3F 147
Truck Stop Bus. Pk. B11: Tys 6H 119
Truda St. WS1: Wals 4B 48
TRUEMAN'S HEATH 2C 162
Trueman's Heath La.
B47: H'wd 2B 162
B90: Maj G 2B 162
Truro Cl. B65: Row R 5E 97
Truro Rd. WS5: Wals 4H 49
Truro Twr. B16: Birm 1C 116
Truro Wlk. B37: Chel W 1C 122
Trustin Cres. B92: Sol 5A 138
Tryon Pl. WV14: Bils 5G 45
TRYSULL 4C 56
Trysull Av. B26: Sheld 1G 137
Trysull Gdns. WV3: Wolv 4B 42
Trysull Holloway WV5: Try 1C 56
Trysull Rd. WV3: Wolv 4B 42
WV5: Wom 5E 57
Trysull Way DY2: Neth 6E 95
Tudbury Rd. B31: N'fld 3B 144
Tudman Cl. B76: Walm 6E 71
Tudor Cl. B13: Mose 1H 147
B14: K Hth 6A 148
B73: New O 3D 68
CV7: Bal C 3G 169
WS6: C Hay 2E 7
Tudor Ct. B1: Birm 3A 4
B72: S Cold 6A 54
B74: Four O 1G 53
DY4: Tip 3A 78
WV11: Ess 4H 17
Tudor Cres. WV2: Wolv 5F 43
Tudor Cft. B37: F'bri 2B 122
Tudor Gdns. B23: Erd 4E 85
DY8: Stourb 6C 108
Tudor Grange Pk. 4E 151
Tudor Grange Sports Cen. 4F 151
Tudor Gro. B74: S'tly 3A 52
TUDOR HILL 5H 53
Tudor Hill B73: S Cold 5G 53
Tudor Ind. Est. B11: Tys 6H 119
Tudor Pk. Ct. B74: Four O 6F 37
Tudor Pl. DY3: Up Gor 1A 76
Tudor Rd. B13: Mose 3H 133
B65: Row R 4C 96
B68: O'bry 5A 98
B73: S Cold 6H 53
DY3: Up Gor 1A 76
WV10: Wolv 5C 28
WV14: Bils 1B 62
Tudors Cl. B10: Small H 3C 118
Tudor St. B18: Win G 5H 99
DY4: Tip 3A 78
Tudor Ter. B17: Harb 5G 115
DY2: Dud 6G 77
Tudor Va. DY3: Up Gor 1A 76
Tudor Way B72: W Grn 3H 69
WS6: C Hay 4D 6
Tufnell Gro. B8: W End 2G 103
Tugford Rd. B29: W Cas 6G 131
Tulips Gdns. B29: W Cas 6D 130
Tulip Wlk. B37: Chel W 3E 123
Tulsi Cen. B19: Birm 5E 101
Tulyar Cl. B36: Hodg H 1A 104
Tunnel La. B30: K Nor, K Hth 3D 146
Tunnel Rd. B70: W Brom 5G 63
Tunnel St. WV14: Cose 5E 61
Tunstall Rd. DY6: K'wfrd 4E 93
Turchill Dr. B76: Walm 5E 71
Turf Cl. WS11: Nort C 1E 9
Turfpits La. B23: Erd 1D 84
Turf Pitts La. B75: Can 6D 38
(not continuous)
Turks Head Way
B70: W Brom 5A 80
Turley St. DY1: Dud 1C 76
Turls Hill Rd. DY3: Sed 5A 60
WV14: Cose 5C 60
Turls St. DY3: Sed 5A 60
Turnberry Cl. WV6: Pert 4D 24
Turnberry Rd. B42: Gt Barr 5D 66
WS3: Blox 4F 19
Turner Av. WV14: Cose 3B 60
Turner Dr. DY5: Quar B 4H 109
Turner Gro. WV6: Pert 5G 25
Turners Cft. B71: W Brom 5E 65
Turners Gro. DY3: Lwr G 3G 75
TURNER'S HILL 3B 96
Turner's Hill B65: Row R 3B 96
Turners Hill Rd. DY3: Lwr G 3G 75
Turner's La. DY5: Brie H 3G 109
Turner St. B11: S'brk 5A 118
B70: W Brom 3G 79
DY1: Dud 1D 94
DY3: Lwr G 4H 75
DY4: Tip 6H 61
Turney Rd. DY8: Stourb 5D 108
Turnham Grn. WV6: Pert 6E 25
Turnhouse Rd. B35: Cas V 3F 87
Turnley Rd. B34: S End 3G 105
Turnpike Cl. B11: S'brk 5A 118
CV7: Bal C 2H 169
Turnpike Dr. B46: Wat O 4E 89
Turnstone Dr. WV10: F'stne 1D 16
Turton Cl. WS3: Blox 3G 19
Turton Rd. B70: W Brom 5H 79
DY4: Tip 4H 61
Turtons Cft. WV14: Cose 2D 60
TURVES GREEN 6E 145
Turves Grn. B31: Longb, N'fld 2D 158
Turves Green Leisure & Adult Education Cen.
6E 145
Turville Rd. B20: Hand 6E 83
Tustin Gro. B27: A Grn 5A 136
Tutbury Av. WV6: Pert 6F 25
Tuxford Cl. WV10: Wolv 5A 28
Twatling Rd. B45: B Grn, Lick 6G 157
Tweeds Well B32: Bart G 6H 129
Tweed Twr. B20: Hand 5F 83
Twickenham Ct. DY8: Woll 4A 108
Twickenham Rd. B44: K'sdng 4B 68
Two Gates B63: Crad 6D 110
Two Gates La. B63: Crad 6E 111
Two Locks DY5: Brie H 5C 94
Two Woods La. DY5: Brie H 2A 110
Twycross Gro. B36: Hodg H 2B 104
Twydale Av. B69: Tiv 5C 78
Twyford Cl. WS9: A'rdge 4D 34
Twyford Gro. WV11: Wed 2H 29
Twyford Rd. B8: W End 4A 104
Twyning Rd. B16: Edg 5H 99
B30: Stir 6D 132
Tyber Dr. B20: Hand 4D 82
Tyberry Cl. B90: Shir 6G 149
TYBURN 4E 87
Tyburn Gro. B24: Erd 4B 86
Tyburn Rd. B24: Erd 6D 84
WV1: Wolv 2E 45
Tyburn Sq. B24: Erd 4B 86
Tyburn Trad. Est. B35: Cas V 5B 86
Tyebeams B34: S End 4G 105
Tye Gdns. DY9: Pedm 4F 125
Tyler Ct. B24: Erd 4F 85
Tyler Gdns. WV13: W'hall 2B 46
Tyler Gro. B43: Gt Barr 4C 66
Tyler Rd. WV13: W'hall 3A 46
Tylers Grn. B38: K Nor 5D 146
Tylers Gro. B90: M'path 3D 164
Tylney Cl. B5: Bal H 4F 117
Tyndale Cres. B43: Gt Barr 2E 67
Tyndall Wlk. B32: Bart G 3G 129
Tyne Cl. B37: F'bri 5D 106
WS8: Bwnhls 3G 9
Tyne Ct. B73: S Cold 6H 53
Tynedale Cres. WV4: E'shll 2A 60
Tynedale Rd. B11: Tys 2F 135
Tyne Gro. B25: Yard 3B 120
Tyne Pl. DY5: Quar B 1B 110
Tyning Cl. WV9: Pend 5E 15
Tyninghame Av. WV6: Tett 3B 26
Tynings La. WS9: A'rdge 4C 34
Tyrley Cl. WV6: Tett 1H 41
Tyrol Cl. DY8: Woll 6B 108
TYSELEY 6G 119
Tyseley Hill Rd. B11: Tys 1G 135
Tyseley Ind. Est. B11: Tys 6E 119
Tyseley La. B11: Tys 1G 135
Tyseley Station (Rail) 6G 119
Tysoe Dr. B76: Walm 1D 70
Tysoe Rd. B44: K'sdng 6H 67
Tythebarn Dr. DY6: W Hth 2G 91
Tythe Barn La. B90: Dic H 3E 163
(not continuous)
Tyzack Cl. DY5: Brie H 1G 109

U

UCI Cinema
Brierley Hill 1A 110
Shirley 2C 164
Udall Rd. WV14: Cose 2F 61
Uffculme Rd. B30: Stir 5F 133
Uffmoor Est. B63: Hale 3G 127
Uffmoor La. B62: Roms, Hale 6F 127
B63: Hale 4G 127
Uffmoor Wood Nature Reserve 6G 127
Ufton Cl. B90: Shir 4C 150
Ufton Cres. B90: Shir 4B 150
UGC Cinema
Birmingham 2G 117 (6E 5)
Bishopsgate St. 2D 116
Rednal 1G 157
Ullenhall Rd. B76: Walm 4D 70
B93: Know 3C 166
Ullenwood B21: Hand 2H 99
Ulleries Rd. B92: Olton 3D 136
Ullrick Grn. B24: Erd 5F 85
Ullswater Cl. B32: Bart G 3D 130
Ullswater Gdns. DY6: K'wfrd 3B 92
Ullswater Ho. B69: O'bry 4D 96
Ullswater Ri. DY5: Brie H 4H 93
Ullswater Rd. WV12: W'hall 6B 18
Ulster Dr. DY6: K'wfrd 5C 92
Ulverley Ct. B92: Olton 5D 136
Ulverley Cres. B92: Olton 5D 136
ULVERLEY GREEN 5D 136
Ulverley Grn. Rd. B92: Olton 4C 136
Ulwine Dr. B31: N'fld 3D 144
Umberslade Rd. B29: S Oak 4B 132
Uncle Ben's Cl. B69: O'bry 5F 97
Underhill La. WV10: Bush 4B 16
Underhill Rd. B8: Salt 6F 103
DY4: Tip 1C 78
Underhill St. B69: O'bry 4G 97
Underhill Wlk. B69: O'bry 4G 97
Underley Cl. DY6: W Hth 2H 91
Underpass, The B40: Nat E C 1F 139
Underwood Cl. B15: Edg 1H 131
B23: Erd 3C 84
Underwood Rd. B20: Hand 2A 82
Unett Ct. B66: Smeth 4G 99
Unett St. B19: Hock 4E 101
(not continuous)
B66: Smeth 5G 99
Unett Wlk. B19: Birm 4E 101
Union Cen. WS10: W'bry 3F 63
Union Dr. B73: Bold 3F 69
Union La. WV5: Try 4D 56
Union Mill St. WV1: Wolv 1A 44
Union Pas. B2: Birm 1G 117 (4E 5)
Union Pl. B29: S Oak 3D 132
Union Rd. B6: Aston 1B 102
B69: O'bry 6E 79
B70: W Brom 5F 79
B90: Shir 5A 150
B91: Sol 3G 151
Union Row B21: Hand 1B 100
Union St. B2: Birm 1G 117 (4E 5)
B65: B'hth 2C 112
B70: W Brom 1B 98
DY2: Dud 6E 77
DY4: Tip 5H 61
(Attwell Rd.)
DY4: Tip 2H 77
(Unity Wlk.)
DY8: Stourb 6E 109
DY9: Lye 6A 110
WS1: Wals 1D 48
WS10: W'bry 3F 63
WV1: Wolv 1H 43 (3D 170)
WV13: W'hall 1A 46
WV14: Bils 6E 45
Unisant Trad. Est. B64: Old H 1H 111
Unitt Dr. B64: Old H 3G 111
Unity Cl. WS10: Darl 1C 62
Unity Pl. B29: S Oak 3B 132
B69: O'bry 1G 97
Unity Wlk. DY4: Tip 2G 77
University of Aston
Chemical Engineering Building
6H 101
Gem Sports Hall 6H 101
University of Birmingham
Edgbaston Pk. Rd. 6B 116
Selly Oak Campus 5H 131
University Rd. E. 1B 132
University of Central England
Bournville Campus 6A 132
Department of Art 6F 101 (3C 4)
Gosta Green Campus 5H 101 (1G 5)
Hamstead Campus 4A 82
Perry Barr Campus 4F 83
School of Jewellery 5E 101 (1A 4)
Sycamore Rd. 6B 132
Westbourne Campus 3C 116
University of Wolverhampton
Molineux Rd. 6G 27 (1B 170)
St Peter's Sq. 1G 43 (2B 170)
Walsall Campus 4E 49
University Rd. E. B15: Edg 1B 132
University Rd. W. B15: Edg 1A 132
University Station (Rail) 1A 132
Unketts Rd. B67: Smeth 6C 98
Unwin Cres. DY8: Stourb 6C 108
Upavon Cl. B35: Cas V 3E 87
Upland Rd. B29: S Oak 3C 132
Uplands B63: Hale 3F 127
Uplands, The B67: Smeth 4D 98
Uplands Av. B65: Row R 6D 96
WV3: Wolv 3B 42
WV13: W'hall 2F 45
Uplands Cl. DY2: Dud 2H 95
Uplands Dr. DY3: Sed 5H 59
WV3: Wolv 3C 42
WV5: Wom 1G 73
Uplands Gro. WV13: W'hall 2E 45
Uplands Rd. B21: Hand 5H 81
DY2: Dud 2G 95
WV13: W'hall 2E 45
Up. Ashley St. B62: B'hth 2C 112
Up. Balsall Heath Rd.
B12: Bal H 5H 117
Up. Brook St. WS2: Wals 2B 48
Up. Castle St. WS10: Darl 3D 46
Up. Chapel St. B69: Tiv 5B 78
Up. Church La. DY4: Tip 5H 61
Up. Clifton Rd. B73: S Cold 6H 53
Upper Cl. B32: Bart G 2B 130
Up. Conybere St. B12: Birm 4H 117
Up. Dean St. B5: Birm 2G 117 (6E 5)
Up. Ettingshall Rd.
WV14: Cose 5C 60
Up. Forster St. WS4: Wals 6D 32
UPPER GORNAL 2A 76
Up. Gough St. B1: Birm 2F 117 (6C 4)
Upper Grn. WV6: Tett 4B 26
Up. Grosvenor Rd. B20: Hand 5D 82
Up. Hall La. WS1: Wals 2C 48
Up. Highgate St. B12: Birm 4H 117
Up. High St. B64: Crad H 2F 111
WS10: W'bry 2F 63
Up. Holland Rd. B72: S Cold 1A 70
UPPER LANDYWOOD 5E 7
Up. Landywood La. WS6: C Hay 4D 6
Up. Lichfield St. WV13: W'hall 1A 46
Up. Mall E. B5: Birm 1G 117 (5F 5)
Up. Mall W. B5: Birm 1G 117 (5E 5)
Up. Marshall St. B1: Birm 2F 117 (6C 4)
Up. Meadow Rd. B32: Quin 6A 114
Up. Navigation St. WS2: Wals 1B 48
Up. Portland St. B6: Aston 2A 102
Up. Rushall St. WS1: Wals 2D 48
Up. Russell St. WS10: W'bry 3F 63
Up. St Mary's Rd. B67: Smeth 2D 114
Up. Short St. WS2: Wals 2B 48
Up. Sneyd Rd. WV11: Ess 5B 18
Up. Stone Cl. B76: Walm 1C 70
Upper St. WV6: Tett 4B 26
Up. Sutton St. B6: Aston 2H 101
Up. Thomas St. B6: Aston 2H 101
(not continuous)
Up. Trinity St. B9: Birm 2A 118

224 A-Z Birmingham Deluxe

Up. Vauxhall—Walsall Enterprise Pk.

Up. Vauxhall WV1: Wolv. 1E 43
Up. Villiers St. WV2: Wolv. 5G 43
Up. William St. B1: Birm. 2E 117 (6A 4)
Up. Zoar St. WV3: Wolv 3F 43
Upton Ct. *B23: Erd* *4B 84*
(off Alwynn Wlk.)
Upton Gdns. WV14: Bils 6E 45
Upton Gro. B33: Stech 2A 120
Upton Rd. B33: Stech 1A 120
Upton St. DY2: Neth 4E 95
Upwey Av. B91: Sol 3E 151
USAM Trad. Est.
WV10: F'hses 5H 15
Usk Way B36: Cas B 1B 106
Uttoxeter Cl. WV6: Wolv 3F 27
Uxbridge Cl. DY3: Lwr G 4H 75
Uxbridge Ct. WS7: Chase 1A 10
Uxbridge St. B19: Birm 4F 101

V

Valbourne Rd. B14: K Hth 3E 147
Vale, The B11: S'hll 3C 134
B15: Edg 5C 116
Vale Av. DY3: Up Gor 1H 75
WS9: A'rdge 6F 35
Vale Cl. B32: Bart G 2D 130
Vale Head Dr. WV6: Tett 1G 41
Valencia Cft. B35: Cas V 3F 87
Valentine Cl. B74: S'tly 5H 51
Valentine Ct. B14: K Hth 4H 133
Valentine Rd. B14: K Hth 4G 133
B68: O'bry 1A 114
Valepits Rd. B33: Sheld 2G 121
Valerian B74: Four O 5F 37
Valerie Gro. B43: Gt Barr 5G 65
Vale Rd. DY2: Neth 5G 95
Vale Row DY3: Up Gor 2H 75
Vales Cl. B76: Walm 6C 70
Vale St. B71: W Brom 1C 80
DY3: Up Gor 2H 75
DY8: Amb 3E 109
WV2: E'shll 5C 44
Vale Vw. WS9: A'rdge 5D 34
Valiant Ho. B35: Cas V 2F 87
Valiant Way B92: Sol 5G 137
Vallan Cft. B36: Hodg H 2D 104
Valley Farm Rd. B45: Rubery 3F 157
Valley Grn. WS6: C Hay 3E 7
Valley Rd. B43: Gt Barr 6G 65
B62: B'hth 3F 113
B64: Crad H 4G 111
B67: Smeth 6D 98
B74: S'tly 4H 51
B92: Sol 2G 137
DY3: Up Gor 1A 76
DY9: Lye 6B 110
Valley Rd. WS3: Blox 1A 32
WV10: Wolv 4B 28
Valleyside WS3: Pels 5D 20
Valley Vw. WS8: Bwnhls 6C 10
Vanborough Wlk. DY1: Dud 5C 76
Vanbrugh Ct. WV6: Pert 6E 25
Van Diemans Rd. WV5: Wom 2E 73
Vanguard Cl. B36: Hodg H 1C 104
Vanguard Rd. B26: Birm A 1E 139
Vann Cl. B10: Small H 3C 118
(not continuous)
Vantage Point *B70: W Brom* *5A 80*
(off Blacksmith Way)
Varden Cft. B5: Bal H 4F 117
Vardon Way B38: K Nor 6H 145
Varley Rd. B24: Erd 3B 86
Varley Va. B24: Erd 3B 86
Varlins Way B38: K Nor 2H 159
Varney Av. B70: W Brom 5B 80
Vaughan Cl. B74: Four O 3F 37
Vaughan Gdns. WV8: Cod 3F 13
Vaughan Rd. WV13: W'hall 2F 45
Vaughan Trad. Est. DY4: Tip 3B 78
Vaughton Dr. B75: S Cold 5C 54
Vaughton St. B12: Birm 3H 117
Vaughton St. Sth. B5: Birm 3G 117
B12: Birm 3G 117
VAUXHALL 4B 102
Vauxhall Av. WV1: Wolv 1E 43
Vauxhall Bus. Pk. B7: Birm 4C 102
Vauxhall Cres. B36: Cas B 6B 88
Vauxhall Gdns. DY2: Dud 2G 95
Vauxhall Gro. B7: Birm 6B 102
Vauxhall Ho. *WV1: Wolv* *1E 43*
(off Upper Vauxhall)
Vauxhall Pl. B7: Birm 6A 102
Vauxhall Rd. B7: Birm 6A 102
DY8: Stourb 6E 109
Vauxhall St. DY1: Dud 1D 94
Vauxhall Ter. B7: Birm 5B 102
Vauxhall Trad. Est. B7: Birm 5B 102
Vector Ind. Pk. B71: W Brom 1A 80
Velsheda Rd. B90: Shir 5G 149
Venetia Rd. B9: Bord G 1C 118
Venice Ct. B13: Mose 3B 134
Venning Gro. B43: Gt Barr 6H 65
Ventnor Av. B19: Hock 2E 101
B36: Hodg H 2B 104
Ventnor Cl. B68: O'bry 4A 114
Ventnor Rd. B92: Sol 2G 137
Venture Ct. WV10: F'hses 2H 15
Venture Way B7: Birm 5H 101 (1H 5)
Vera Rd. B26: Yard 4C 120
Verbena Gdns. B7: Birm 4A 102
Verbena Rd. B31: N'fld 1D 144
Vercourt B74: Lit A 6B 36
Verdun Cres. DY2: Dud 5H 77
Vere St. B5: Birm 3F 117
Verity Wlk. DY8: Word 2C 108
Verney Av. B33: Sheld 4H 121
Vernier Av. DY6: K'wfrd 4E 93
Vernon Av. B20: Hand 3B 82
DY4: Tip 3G 77
WS8: Bwnhls 5C 10
Vernon Cl. B62: B'hth 3C 112
B74: Four O 4E 37
WV11: Ess 3H 17
WV13: W'hall 2G 45
Vernon Ct. B16: Edg 2A 116
B68: O'bry 4H 113
Vernon Rd. B16: Edg 2H 115
B62: B'hth 3C 112
B68: O'bry 3A 98
WV14: Bils 5H 45
Vernon St. B70: W Brom 4E 79
WV14: Cose 3G 61
Vernon Trad. Est. B62: B'hth 3C 112
Vernon Way WS3: Blox 6D 18
Veronica Av. WV4: E'shll 6A 44
Veronica Cl. B29: W Cas 1D 144
Veronica Rd. DY6: K'wfrd 3E 93
Verstone Cft. B31: N'fld 5E 145
Verstone Rd. B90: Shir 3A 150
Verwood Cl. WV13: W'hall 2F 45
Vesey Cl. B46: Wat O 5D 88
B74: Four O 1F 53
Vesey Rd. B73: W Grn 4H 69
Vesey St. B4: Birm 5G 101 (1E 5)
Vestry Cl. B64: Old H 2H 111
Vestry Ct. DY8: Woll 5C 108
Viaduct Dr. WV6: Wolv 3F 27
Viaduct St. B7: Birm 6A 102
Vibart Rd. B26: Yard 3D 120
Vicarage Cl. B30: Stir 6E 133
B42: Gt Barr 6F 67
DY4: Tip 2G 77
DY5: Brie H 3G 109
WS8: Bwnhls 5C 10
(not continuous)
Vicarage Gdns. B65: B'hth 2C 112
B76: Walm 6D 70
Vicarage La. B46: Wat O 5D 88
DY5: P'ntt 1H 93
Vicarage Pl. WS1: Wals 2C 48
Vicarage Prospect DY1: Dud 6D 76
Vicarage Rd. B6: Aston 2A 102
(not continuous)
B14: K Hth 1E 147
B15: Edg 3B 116
B17: Harb 6F 115
B18: Hock 2C 100
B33: Yard 2C 120
B62: B'hth 2C 112
B67: Smeth 4D 98
B68: O'bry 5H 97
B71: W Brom 1B 80
B94: Earls 6A 164
DY3: Up Gor 2B 76
DY5: Brie H 4G 109
DY8: Amb 4E 109
DY8: Woll 4A 108
DY9: Lye 6B 110
WS3: Pels 5E 21
WS8: Bwnhls 6B 10
WS10: W'bry 2F 63
WV2: Wolv 3H 43
WV4: Penn 2B 58
WV11: Wed 3D 28
WV14: Cose 6E 61
Vicarage Rd. Sth. DY9: Lye 6A 110
Vicarage Rd. W. DY1: Dud 1D 76
Vicarage St. B68: O'bry 4H 97
Vicarage Ter. WS2: Wals 3A 48
Vicarage Wlk. WS1: Wals 2C 48
Vicar St. DY2: Dud 6E 77
DY3: Sed 5H 59
WS10: W'bry 2G 63
Vicars Wlk. DY9: W'cte 3A 126
Viceroy Cl. B5: Edg 5E 117
DY6: K'wfrd 4E 93
Victor Cl. WV2: E'shll 5D 44
Victoria Arc. WV1: Wolv 1G 43 (3B 170)
Victoria Av. B10: Small H 3D 118
B21: Hand 1B 100
B62: Quin 5F 113
B66: Smeth 4E 99
WS3: Blox 6H 19
Victoria Bldgs. *B16: Birm* *6A 100*
(off Barford Rd.)
Victoria Ct. B13: Mose 1H 133
B62: Quin *4G 113*
(off Binswood Rd.)
B66: Smeth 3F 99
DY5: Brie H 6H 93
WS11: Nort C 1F 9
Victoria Fold WV1: Wolv 2G 43 (4A 170)
Victoria Gdns. B64: Old H 1H 111
Victoria Gro. B18: Win G 5A 100
WV5: Wom 5G 57
Victoria Ho. *B16: Birm* *1D 116*
(off Bellcroft)
WS3: Blox 1B 32
WS10: Darl *5C 46*
(off Factory St.)
Victoria M. B69: O'bry 6F 97
WS4: Wals 6E 33
Victoria New Works WS10: Darl 3D 46
Victoria Pk. Rd. B66: Smeth 4F 99
Victoria Pas. DY8: Stourb 6E 109
WV1: Wolv 1G 43 (3B 170)
Victoria Rd. B6: Aston 2G 101
(not continuous)
B17: Harb 6F 115
B21: Hand 2A 100
B23: Erd 4D 84
B27: A Grn 3A 136
(not continuous)
B30: Stir 6C 132
B33: Stech 6B 104
B62: B'hth 2D 112
B64: Old H 1H 111
B68: O'bry 3A 98
B72: S Cold 6A 54
DY3: Sed 5A 60
DY4: Tip 2H 77
DY5: Quar B 2C 110
WS3: Pels 4E 21
WS10: Darl 5D 46
WV3: Wolv 4C 42
WV6: Tett 4C 26
WV10: Wolv 4B 28
WV11: Wed 3D 28
Victoria Sq. B2: Birm 1F 117 (4C 4)
WV1: Wolv 1H 43 (3C 170)
Victoria St. B9: Small H 2D 118
B63: Hale 1A 128
B70: W Brom 2F 79
(Phoenix St.)
B70: W Brom 4A 80
(Price St.)
DY5: Brie H 6H 93
DY5: P'ntt 2G 93
DY6: W Hth 6H 73
DY8: Stourb 6E 109
WS10: W'bry 3E 63
WV1: Wolv 2G 43 (4B 170)
WV13: W'hall 6A 30
Victoria Ter. WS4: Wals 6E 33
Victor Rd. B18: Win G 3A 100
B92: Sol 2H 137
Victor St. WS1: Wals 4C 48
WS3: Pels 6E 21
Victor Twr. B7: Nech 3B 102
Victory Av. B65: Row R 1B 112
WS10: Darl 1C 62
Victory Ho. B13: Mose 1H 133
Victory La. WS2: Wals 5G 31
Victory Ri. B71: W Brom 2A 80
View Dr. DY2: Dud 1G 95
Viewfield Cres. DY3: Sed 6H 59
Viewlands Dr. WV6: Tett 1G 41
View Point B69: Tiv 1B 96
VIGO 4B 22
Vigo Cl. WS9: Wals W 5B 22
Vigo Pl. WS9: A'rdge 1B 34
Vigo Rd. WS9: Wals W 5B 22
Vigo Ter. WS9: Wals W 5B 22
Viking Ri. B65: Row R 5C 96
VILLAGE, THE 2C 92
Village, The DY6: K'wfrd 2C 92
Village M., The WV6: Tett 4A 26
Village Rd. B6: Aston 6A 84
Village Sq. B31: Longb 5A 144
Village Wlk. WS10: W'bry 2H 63
Village Way B76: Walm 5D 70
WV14: Bils 6E 45
Villa Park 6H 83
Villa Rd. B19: Hock 2C 100
Villa St. B19: Loz 2D 100
(not continuous)
DY8: Amb 3E 109
Villa Wlk. B19: Hock 3E 101
Villette Gro. B14: Yard W 3C 148
Villiers Av. WV14: Bils 4F 45
Villiers Ho. *WV2: Wolv* *4G 43*
(off Blakenhall Gdns.)
Villiers Pl. WV14: Bils 4F 45
Villiers Sq. WV14: Bils 4F 45
Villiers St. WS1: Wals 4C 48
WV13: W'hall 1A 46
Villiers Trad. Est. WV2: Wolv 4F 43
Vimy Rd. B13: Mose 6B 134
WS10: W'bry 1G 63
Vimy Ter. WS10: W'bry 1G 63
Vincent Cl. B12: Bal H 5H 117
Vincent Dr. B15: Edg 2H 131
Vincent Pde. B12: Bal H 5H 117
Vincent Rd. B75: S Cold 4C 54
Vincent St. B12: Bal H 6H 117
(not continuous)
WS1: Wals 4D 48
Vince St. B66: Smeth 6E 99
Vinculum Way WV13: W'hall 3B 46
Vine Av. B12: Bal H 6A 118
Vine Cres. B71: W Brom 1B 80
Vine Gdns. B64: Old H 1H 111
Vine La. B63: Hale 2B 128
Vineries, The B27: A Grn 1B 136
Vine St. B6: Aston 2B 102
DY5: Brie H 4A 94
DY8: Word 2C 108
Vine Ter. B17: Harb 6G 115
Vineyard Cl. B18: Hock 2B 100
Vineyard Rd. B31: N'fld 2D 144
Vinnall Gro. B32: Bart G 5H 129
Vintage Cl. B34: Stech 4E 105
Violet Cft. DY4: Tip 4C 62
Virgin Active 6D 164
Virginia Dr. WV4: Penn 1D 58
Viscount Cl. B35: Cas V 5E 87
Viscount Dr. B35: Cas V 5F 87
Viscount Ho. B26: Birm A 1E 139
Vista, The DY3: Sed 4H 59
Vista Grn. B38: K Nor 6C 146
(not continuous)
Vittoria St. B1: Birm 5E 101 (1A 4)
B66: Smeth 3H 99
Vivian Cl. B17: Harb 6G 115
Vivian Rd. B17: Harb 6G 115
Vixen Cl. B76: Walm 6B 70
Vue Cinema *1D 102*
(in Star City)
Vulcan Ind. Est. WS2: Wals 3A 32
Vulcan Rd. B91: Sol 1G 151
WV14: Bils 6H 45
Vulcan Rd. Ind. Est. B91: Sol 1G 151
Vyrnwy Gro. B38: K Nor 1A 160
Vyse St. B6: Aston 1B 102
B18: Birm 4E 101 (1A 4)

W

Wadbarn B90: Dic H 4G 163
Waddell Cl. WV14: Cose 3B 60
Waddens Brook La. WV11: Wed 4G 29
Waddington Av. B43: Gt Barr 4A 66
Wades Cl. DY4: Tip 2G 77
Wadesmill Lawns WV10: Bush 3A 16
Wadham Cl. B65: Row R 3C 96
Wadham Ho. B37: Chel W 6E 107
Wadhurst Rd. B17: Edg 1F 115
Wadley's Rd. B91: Sol 1D 150
Waen Cl. DY4: Tip 5B 62
Waggoners La. B78: Hints 2H 39
Waggon St. B64: Old H 1H 111
Waggon Wlk. B38: K Nor 1G 159
(not continuous)
Wagoners Cl. B8: Salt 3F 103
Wagon La. B92: Olton 1D 136
Wagstaff Cl. WV14: Cose 5F 61
Waine Ho. WS8: Bwnhls 1C 22
Wainwright Cl. DY6: W Hth 2G 91
Wainwright St. B6: Aston 2A 102
Waite Rd. WV13: W'hall 3G 45
Wakefield Cl. B73: Bold 3G 69
Wakefield Ct. B13: Mose 3B 134
B29: W Cas *6G 131*
(off Abdon Av.)
Wakefield Gro. B46: Wat O 4D 88
Wakeford Rd. B31: N'fld 6G 145
WAKE GREEN 3A 134
Wake Grn. Pk. B13: Mose 3B 134
Wake Grn. Rd. B13: Mose 2H 133
DY4: Tip 4A 62
Wakelam Gdns. B43: Gt Barr 4H 65
Wakelams Fold DY3: Gorn 4G 75
Wakeley Hill WV4: Penn 1D 58
Wakelin Rd. B90: Shir 2H 163
Wakeman Ct. WV11: Ess 4H 17
Wakeman Dr. B69: Tiv 1B 96
Wakeman Gro. B33: Sheld 4H 121
Wakes Cl. WV13: W'hall 2B 46
Wakes Rd. WS10: W'bry 3G 63
Walcot Cl. B75: Four O 6H 37
Walcot Dr. B43: Gt Barr 1B 82
Walcot Gdns. WV14: Bils 1D 60
Walcot Grn. B93: Dorr 6H 167
Waldale Cl. WV11: Ess 6C 18
Walden Gdns. WV4: Penn 5C 42
Walden Rd. B11: Tys 2G 135
Waldeve Gro. B92: Sol 5B 138
Waldley Gro. B24: Erd 4A 86
Waldon Wlk. B36: Cas B 1B 106
Waldron Av. DY5: Brie H 1F 109
Waldron Cl. WS10: W'bry 5F 47
Waldrons Moor B14: K Hth 2E 147
Walford Av. WV3: Wolv 3D 42
Walford Dr. B92: Sol 2H 137
Walford Grn. B32: Bart G 6H 129
Walford Rd. B11: S'brk 5B 118
Walford St. B69: Tiv 5A 78
Walhouse Cl. WS1: Wals 1D 48
Walhouse Rd. WS1: Wals 1D 48
(not continuous)
Walk, The DY3: Sed 4H 59
Walker Av. B69: Tiv 2C 96
DY5: Quar B 4H 109
DY9: W'cte 2H 125
WV10: Bush 1A 28
Walker Dr. B24: Nech 1E 103
Walker Grange DY4: Tip 6H 61
Walker Pl. WS3: Blox 1C 32
Walker Rd. WS3: Blox 1B 32
Walkers Fold WV12: W'hall 3D 30
WALKER'S HEATH 5C 146
Walkers Heath Rd. B38: K Nor 6D 146
Walker St. DY2: Neth 5E 95
DY4: Tip 6B 62
Walk La. WV5: Wom 6G 57
Walkmill La. WS11: Cann 1D 6
Wallace Cl. B69: O'bry 3D 96
WS11: Nort C 1D 8
Wallace Ct. WS6: C Hay 4D 6
Wallace Ho. B69: O'bry 4D 96
Wallace Ri. B64: Crad H 4G 111
Wallace Rd. B29: S Oak 3D 132
B69: O'bry 3D 96
WS8: Bwnhls 5A 10
WV14: Bils 2A 62
Wall Av. B46: Col 4H 107
Wallbank Rd. B8: W End 3G 103
WALLBROOK 5F 61
Wallbrook St. WV14: Cose 5F 61
Wall Cft. WS9: A'rdge 2D 34
Wall Dr. B74: Four O 5F 37
Wall End Cl. WS2: Wals 2G 31
Wallface B71: W Brom 6G 63
WALL HEATH 1H 91
Wallheath Cres. WS9: Ston 2G 23
Wall Heath La. WS9: Ston 2H 23
Walling Cft. WV14: Cose 2D 60
Wallington Cl. WS3: Blox 5H 19
WALLINGTON HEATH 5G 19
Wallington Heath WS3: Blox 5H 19
Wallis Ct. B13: Mose 3B 134
Wallows Ind. Est., The
DY5: Brie H 4H 93
Wallows La. WS1: Wals 5A 48
WS2: Wals 5A 48
Wallows Pl. DY5: Brie H 4G 93
Wallows Rd. DY5: Brie H 5G 93
Wallows Wood DY3: Lwr G 3E 75
Wall St. WV1: Wolv 1D 44
Wall Well B63: Hale 2H 127
Wall Well La. B63: Hale 2H 127
Walmead Cft. B17: Harb 4D 114
Walmer Gro. B23: Erd 2B 84
Walmer Mdw. WS9: A'rdge 2D 34
Walmers, The WS9: A'rdge 2D 34
Walmers Wlk., The B31: Longb 6B 144
Walmer Way B37: Chel W 6E 107
Walmesley Way B31: N'fld 4C 144
WALMLEY 5D 70
WALMLEY ASH 2D 86
Walmley Ash La. B76: Walm 1F 87
Walmley Ash Rd. B76: Walm, Min 6D 70
Walmley Cl. B63: Crad 4D 110
B76: Walm 5D 70
Walmley Rd. B76: Walm 1C 70
Walnut Av. WV8: Bilb 4G 13
Walnut Cl. B37: Chel W 2D 122
DY9: Pedm 4F 125
Walnut Dr. B66: Smeth 4F 99
WV3: Wolv 2B 42
Walnut Ho. B20: Hand 4B 82
Walnut La. WS10: W'bry 3G 63
Walnut Rd. WS5: Wals 1E 65
Walnut Way B31: Longb 1D 158
Walpole St. WV6: Wolv 6E 27
Walpole Wlk. B70: W Brom 6B 80
WALSAL END 4A 154
Walsal End La. B92: H Ard 4H 153
WALSALL 2D 48
Walsall Bus. Pk. WS9: A'rdge 6A 34
Walsall Enterprise Pk. WS2: Wals 3A 48

Wheldrake Av.—Windyridge Rd.

Wheldrake Av. B34: S End 4G 105
Whernside Dr. WV6: Wolv 4E 27
Wherretts Well La. B91: Sol 2A 152
Whetstone Cl. B15: Edg 6B 116
Whetstone Grn. WV10: Bush 6H 15
Whetstone Gro. WV10: Bush 1H 27
Whetstone La. WS9: A'rdge 5D 34
Whetstone Rd. WV10: Bush 1H 27
Whetty Bri. Rd. B45: Rubery 3E 157
Whetty La. B45: Rubery 2E 157
Whichbury Ct. B65: Row R 5D 96
Whichford Cl. B76: Walm 1B 86
Whichford Gro. B9: Bord G 1H 119
While Rd. B72: S Cold 1H 69
Whilmot Cl. WV10: F'stne 1D 16
Whinberry Ri. DY5: P'ntt 6G 75
Whisley Brook La. B28: Hall G 3F 135
Whistler Gro. WV10: Bush 1C 28
Whiston Av. WV11: Wed 2A 30
Whiston Gro. B29: W Cas 5F 131
Whiston Ho. WS1: Wals 2D 48
Whitacre La. WS14: Lynn 6G 11
Whitacre Rd. B9: Bord G 6E 103
B93: Know 2D 166
Whitbourne Cl. B12: Bal H 6B 118
Whitburn Av. B42: P Barr 2C 82
Whitburn Cl. WV9: Pend 5E 15
Whitby Cl. WS3: Blox 4F 19
Whitby Rd. B12: Bal H 1A 134
Whitchurch La. B90: Dic H 3G 163
Whitcot Gro. B31: Longb 1D 158
Whitebeam Cl. DY3: Lwr G 3G 75
WS8: Clay 1A 22
Whitebeam Cft. B38: K Nor 6A 146
Whitebeam Rd. B37: Chel W 3E 123
White City Rd. DY5: Quar B 2C 110
White Cl. DY9: Pedm 3G 125
Whitecrest B43: Gt Barr 3B 66
Whitecroft Rd. B26: Sheld 6G 121
White Falcon Ct. B91: Sol 5D 150
White Farm Rd. B74: Four O 4E 37
Whitefield Av. B17: Harb 5E 115
Whitefield Cl. WV8: Bilb 5H 13
Whitefields Cres. B91: Sol 5F 151
Whitefields Ga. B91: Sol 6E 151
Whitefields Rd. B91: Sol 6E 151
(not continuous)
Whitefriars Dr. B63: Hale 1A 128
Whitegates Rd. WV14: Cose 2F 61
Whitehall Dr. B63: Hale 1B 128
DY1: Dud 5C 76
Whitehall Ind. Pk. DY4: Tip 2E 79
Whitehall Rd. B9: Small H 1D 118
B21: Hand 2C 100
B63: Hale 1B 128
B64: Crad H 3E 111
B70: W Brom 2E 79
DY4: Tip 2D 78
DY6: K'wfrd 3A 92
DY8: Stourb 3F 125
WS1: Wals 4C 48
WV4: Penn 1F 59
White Hart, The *WS1: Wals* 3C 48
(off Caldmore Grn.)
Whitehead Dr. B76: Min 1H 87
Whitehead Gro. CV7: Bal C 2H 169
Whitehead Rd. B6: Aston 2G 101
Whiteheath Ct. *B69: O'bry* 5E 97
(off Birchfield La.)
White Hill B31: N'fld 2F 145
Whitehill La. B29: W Cas 2E 145
White Hollies WS3: Pels 3D 20
White Horse Rd. WS8: Bwnhls 3A 10
Whitehouse Av. WS10: Darl 4B 46
WS10: W'bry 2F 63
WV3: Wolv 3B 42
WV11: Wed 2H 29
White Ho. Cl. B91: Sol 4D 150
WHITEHOUSE COMMON 4D 54
Whitehouse Comn. Rd. B75: S Cold 3C 54
Whitehouse Ct. B75: S Cold 6D 54
Whitehouse Cres. B75: S Cold 3C 54
WV11: Wed 6H 17
Whitehouse Dr. B66: Smeth 2E 99
WHITEHOUSE GATE 5E 97
White Ho. Grn. B91: Sol 4D 150
Whitehouse La. DY3: Swind 6A 72
DY7: Env 6A 72
WV8: Cod, Cod W 1B 12
White Ho. Pl. B45: Rubery 3F 157
White Ho's. La. WV10: F'stne 1C 16
(not continuous)
Whitehouse St. B6: Aston 3H 101
DY4: Tip 5A 78
WS2: Wals 6B 32
WV14: Cose 5E 61
White Ho. Way B91: Sol 4E 151
Whitehouse Way WS9: A'rdge 5B 34
Whitemoor Dr. B90: M'path 2E 165
White Oak Dr. DY6: K'wfrd 3A 92
WV3: Wolv 3A 42
Whitepoplars Cl. DY5: Brie H 5G 93
White Rd. B11: S'brk 4C 118
B32: Quin 5B 114
B67: Smeth 3C 98
White Row WV5: Try 4C 56
Whites Dr. DY3: Sed 5A 60
Whiteslade Cl. B93: Know 2C 166
Whitesmiths Cl. DY3: Sed 5H 59
Whitesmiths Cft. B14: K Hth 5G 133
Whites Rd. B71: W Brom 1A 80
WHITE STITCH 1H 141
Whitestitch La. CV7: Mer 2H 141
Whitestone Rd. B63: Hale 5A 112
White St. B12: Bal H 6A 118
WS1: Wals 3C 48
Whites Wood WV5: Wom 2G 73
Whitethorn Cres. B74: S'tly 2F 51
Whitethorn Rd. DY8: Word 2E 109
Whitewood Glade WV12: W'hall 5E 31
Whitford Dr. B90: M'path 2F 165
Whitgreave Av. WV10: Bush 1A 28
WV10: F'stne 1D 16
Whitgreave Ct. WV10: F'stne 1D 16
Whitgreave St. B70: W Brom 4E 79
Whitland Cl. B45: Redn 3H 157
Whitland Dr. B14: K Hth 4H 147
Whitley Cl. WV6: Tett 1H 41
Whitley Ct. B20: Hand 4A 82
Whitley Ct. Rd. B32: Quin 5A 114
Whitley Dr. B74: S'tly 3A 52
Whitley St. WS10: W'bry 2E 63
Whitlock Gro. B14: K Hth 4A 148
WHITLOCKS END 4E 163
Whitlock's End Station (Rail) 2E 163
Whitminster Av. B24: Erd 4H 85
Whitminster Cl.
WV12: W'hall 5C 30
Whitmore Hill WV1: Wolv 1G 43 (2A 170)
Whitmore Ho. WV6: Wolv 5E 27
WHITMORE REANS 5E 27
Whitmore Rd. B10: Small H 3C 118
DY8: Stourb 6B 108
Whitmore St. B18: Hock 4D 100
WS1: Wals 4B 48
WV1: Wolv 1H 43 (2C 170)
Whitnash Cl. CV7: Bal C 3G 169
Whitney Av. DY8: Woll 5B 108
Whittaker St. WV2: E'shll 5A 44
Whittall St. B4: Birm 6G 101 (2E 5)
Whittimere St. WS1: Wals 1D 48
Whittingham Gro. WV11: Wed 3H 29
Whittingham Rd. B63: Hale 6A 112
Whittington Cl. B14: K Hth 2G 147
B71: W Brom 5D 64
Whittington Gro. B33: Yard 1D 120
Whittington Hall La.
DY7: Kinv 1A 124
Whittington Oval B33: Yard 1E 121
Whittington Rd. DY8: Stourb 2B 124
Whittle Cft. B35: Cas V 4D 86
Whittleford Gro. B36: Cas B 6G 87
Whitton St. WS10: Darl 5E 47
Whitwell Cl. B90: M'path 4E 165
Whitworth Cl. WS10: Darl 4E 47
Whitworth Dr. B71: W Brom 4C 64
Whitworth Ind. Pk. B9: Bord G 1C 118
Whyle St. B63: Hale 1B 128
Whyley St. B70: W Brom 3G 79
Whyley Wlk. B69: O'bry 4G 97
Whynot St. B63: Crad 6D 110
Wibert Cl. B29: S Oak 4C 132
Wichnor Rd. B92: Olton 6D 120
Wicketts Twr. B5: Edg 6E 117
Wickham Gdns. WV11: Wed 3D 28
Wickham Sq. B70: W Brom 5H 79
Wicklow Cl. B63: Hale 4F 127
Wideacre Dr. B44: Gt Barr 6G 67
Wide Acres B45: Fran 6F 143
Widney Av. B29: S Oak 3G 131
WS9: A'rdge 6D 22
Widney Cl. B93: Ben H 4B 166
Widney La. B91: Sol 6C 150
Widney Mnr. Rd. B91: Sol 5G 151
Widney Manor Station (Rail) 1G 165
Widney Rd. B93: Ben H, Know 4A 166
Wiggin Cotts. B17: Harb 6G 115
Wiggin Ho. WS3: Blox 4A 20
Wiggins Cft. B76: Walm 2D 70
Wiggins Hill Rd. B76: Min, Wis 1B 88
Wigginsmill Rd. WS10: W'bry 4D 62
Wiggin St. B16: Birm 6B 100
Wight Cft. B36: Cas B 3D 106
Wightwick Bank WV6: Tett 2G 41
Wightwick Cl. WS3: Blox 6H 19
Wightwick Ct. WV6: Tett 1G 41
Wightwick Gro. WV6: Tett 1G 41
Wightwick Hall Rd. WV6: Tett 2E 41
Wightwick Leys WV6: Tett 1F 41
Wightwick Manor 2F 41
Wigland Way B38: K Nor 6C 146
Wigmore Gro. B44: K'sdng 5B 68
Wigmore La. B71: W Brom 5E 65
(not continuous)
Wigorn La. DY9: Pedm 5F 125
Wigorn Rd. B67: Smeth 2D 114
Wilberforce Way B92: Sol 6B 138
Wilbraham Rd. WS2: Wals 2A 48
Wilcote Gro. B27: A Grn 5A 136
Wildacres DY8: Woll 5A 108
Wilday Cl. DY4: Tip 2A 78
Wilde Cl. B14: K Hth 3F 147
Wilden Cl. B31: N'fld 4A 144
Wilderness La. B43: Gt Barr 3H 65
Wildfell Rd. B27: A Grn 3B 136
WILDMOOR 5A 156
Wildmoor La. B61: Cats, Wild 6A 156
Wildmoor Rd. B90: Shir 2H 149
Wildside Activity Cen. 4D 26
Wildtree Av. WV10: Bush 5C 16
Wiley Av. WS10: Darl 5C 46
Wiley Av. Sth. WS10: Darl 6C 46
Wilford Gro. B76: Walm 1F 87
B91: Sol 5F 151
Wilford Rd. B71: W Brom 1B 80
Wilkes Av. WS2: Wals 1F 47
Wilkes Cl. WS3: Pels 4C 20
Wilkes Cft. DY3: Sed 6H 59
Wilkes Rd. WV8: Cod 3F 13
Wilkes St. B71: W Brom 6C 64
WV13: W'hall 2A 46
Wilkin, The WS8: Bwnhls 3G 9
Wilkin Rd. WS8: Bwnhls 3G 9
Wilkins Ho. *WS3: Blox* 6G 19
(off Sandbank)
Wilkinson Av. WV14: Bils 2G 61
Wilkinson Cl. B73: W Grn 3H 69
Wilkinson Cft. B8: W End 3A 104
Wilkinson Rd. WS10: Mox 6A 46
Wilkins Rd. WV14: Bils 4F 45
Wilks Grn. B21: Hand 4H 81
Willard Rd. B25: Yard 5A 120
Willaston Rd. B33: Sheld 4H 121
Willclare Rd. B26: Sheld 5E 121
Willcock Rd. WV2: Wolv 4A 44
WILLENHALL 1B 46
Willenhall Ind. Est. WV13: W'hall 6C 30
Willenhall La. WS2: Wals 2F 31
WS3: Blox 2F 31
Willenhall La. Ind. Est. WS3: Blox 1G 31
Willenhall Leisure Cen. 2B 46
Willenhall Library & Mus. 2B 46
Willenhall Rd. WS10: Darl 2D 46
WV1: Wolv 2C 44
WV13: W'hall 2C 44
WV14: Bils 5H 45
Willenhall St. WS10: Darl 3C 46
Willenhall Trad. Est. WV13: W'hall 2A 46
Willerby Fold WV10: Bush 3B 16
Willersey Rd. B13: Mose 5D 134
Willes Ct. *B62: Quin* 4G 113
(off Binswood Rd.)
Willes Rd. B18: Win G 3A 100
Willett Av. WS7: Chase 1A 10
Willett Rd. B71: W Brom 5C 64
Willetts Dr. B63: Crad 1D 126
Willetts Rd. B31: N'fld 6E 145
Willetts Way B64: Old H 1H 111
Willey Gro. B24: Erd 5H 85
William Bentley Ct. WV11: Wed 4E 29
William Booth La. B4: Birm 5F 101 (1D 4)
William Cook Rd. B8: W End 4H 103
William Ct. B13: Mose 1H 133
B16: Edg 2A 116
William Edward St. B12: Birm 3H 117
William Grn. Rd. WS10: W'bry 2A 64
William Harper Rd.
WV13: W'hall 2B 46
William Kerr Rd. DY4: Tip 2C 78
William Rd. B31: N'fld 6D 144
B67: Smeth 6B 98
William's Cl. WV12: W'hall 4C 30
Williamson St. WV3: Wolv 3F 43 (6A 170)
William St. B15: Birm 2E 117 (6A 4)
B70: W Brom 2F 79
DY5: Brie H 6G 93
WS4: Wals 6D 32
William St. Nth. B19: Birm 5F 101
William St. W. B66: Smeth 2F 99
William Wiggin Av. WS3: Blox 5H 19
Willingsworth Rd.
WS10: W'bry 4C 62
Willingworth Cl. WV14: Cose 2C 60
Willis Pearson Av. WV14: Bils 3H 61
Willmore Gro. B38: K Nor 1B 160
Willmore Rd. B20: Hand 5F 83
Willmott Cl. B75: R'ley 6B 38
Willmott Rd. B75: R'ley 6B 38
Willoughby Dr. B91: Sol 6F 151
Willoughby Gro. B29: W Cas 4E 131
Willow Av. B17: Edg 1E 115
WS10: W'bry 1F 63
WV11: Wed 1C 28
Willow Bank WV3: Wolv 2A 42
Willowbank Rd. B93: Know 3B 166
Willow Cl. B21: Hand 1H 99
B64: Old H 2G 111
Willow Coppice B32: Bart G 4A 130
Willow Ct. B13: Mose 2A 134
B66: Smeth 1B 98
Willowdale Grange WV6: Tett 4C 26
Willow Dr. B21: Hand 6G 81
B69: Tiv 2C 96
B90: Ches G 5B 164
WV8: Bilb 4H 13
Willow End DY9: W'cte 2H 125
Willow Gdns. B16: Birm 5B 100
Willow Gro. WV11: Ess 4B 18
Willow Hgts. B64: Crad H 3A 112
Willowherb Cl. WS5: Wals 2E 65
Willowherb Way B90: Dic H 4G 163
Willow Ho. *B7: Birm* 5A 102
(off Vauxhall Rd.)
Willow M. B29: S Oak 4F 131
Willow Pk. Dr. DY8: Stourb 3E 125
Willow Ri. DY5: Brie H 2G 109
Willow Rd. B30: B'vlle 5B 132
B43: Gt Barr 4B 66
B91: Sol 5C 150
DY1: Dud 3C 76
WV3: Wolv 3B 42
Willows, The B27: A Grn 3H 135
B47: H'wd 3A 162
B74: Four O 1F 53
B76: Walm 3D 70
DY2: Neth 4G 95
WV5: Wom 2F 73
Willowsbrook Rd. B62: B'hth 3F 113
Willows Cres. B12: Bal H 6F 117
Willowside WS4: S'fld 1G 33
Willows Rd. B12: Bal H 6G 117
WS1: Wals 2E 49
WS4: S'fld 1G 33
Willow Wlk. B76: Walm 6D 70
Willow Way B37: Chel W 1D 122
Wills Av. B71: W Brom 5H 63
Willsbridge Covert
B14: K Hth 5F 147
Wills Ho. B70: W Brom 5A 80
Willson Cft. B28: Hall G 4D 148
Wills St. B19: Loz 2D 100
Wills Way B66: Smeth 5G 99
Wilmcote Cl. B12: Bal H 5G 117
Wilmcote Dr. B75: Four O 6H 37
Wilmcote Rd. B91: Sol 1D 150
Wilmcote Twr. B12: Birm 4H 117
Wilmington Rd. B32: Quin 5H 113
Wilmore La. B47: Wyt 5H 161
Wilmot Av. B46: Col 3H 107
Wilmot Cl. CV7: Bal C 1H 169
Wilmot Dr. B23: Erd 1G 85
DY4: Tip 1G 77
Wilmot Gdns. DY1: Dud 5C 76
Wilnecote Gro. B42: P Barr 3F 83
Wilner's Vw. WS3: Pels 2D 20
Wilsford Cl. B14: K Hth 6F 147
WS4: S'fld 1G 33
Wilson Dr. B75: S Cold 6E 55
(not continuous)
Wilson Rd. B19: Loz 1F 101
B66: Smeth 6F 99
B68: O'bry 3B 114
DY5: Brie H 5G 93
WV14: Cose 6E 61
Wilsons Rd. B93: Know 3E 167
Wilson St. DY4: Tip 2A 78
WV1: Wolv 6H 27
Wilton Cl. DY3: Sed 6A 60
Wilton Rd. B11: S'hll 6B 118
B20: Hand 6D 82
B23: Erd 2G 85
CV7: Bal C 3H 169
Wilton St. B19: Loz 1F 101
Wiltshire Cl. WS2: Wals 5B 32
Wiltshire Ct. *B29: W Cas* 6G 131
(off Tugford Rd.)
Wiltshire Dr. B63: Crad 4D 110
Wiltshire Way B71: W Brom 6A 64
Wimbledon Dr. DY8: Stourb 3F 125
Wimborne Rd. WV10: Wolv 3C 28
Wimbourne Rd. B16: Edg 6H 99
B76: Walm 1E 71
Wimhurst Mdw. WV10: Bush 3B 16
Wimperis Way B43: Gt Barr 1E 67
Wimpole Gro. B44: K'sdng 6B 68
Wincanton Cft. B36: Hodg H 1A 104
Winceby Rd. WV6: Pert 6F 25
Winchcombe Cl. B92: Olton 3F 137
DY1: Dud 4A 76
Winchcombe Rd. B92: Olton 3F 137
Winchester Cl. B65: Row R 5E 97
DY9: Hag 6E 125
Winchester Ct. *B74: Four O* 1F 53
(off Vesey Cl.)
Winchester Dr. B37: Chel W 1C 122
DY8: Stourb 2E 125
Winchester Gdns. B31: N'fld 4E 145
Winchester Gro. B21: Hand 1G 99
Winchester M. WS9: A'rdge 5D 34
Winchester Ri. DY1: Dud 5C 76
Winchester Rd. B20: Hand 6F 83
B71: W Brom 5H 63
WV10: F'hses 4G 15
Winchfield Dr. B17: Harb 3D 114
Wincote Dr. WV6: Tett 5A 26
Wincrest Way B34: S End 4G 105
Windermere Dr. B74: S'tly 6H 35
DY6: K'wfrd 3B 92
Windermere Ho. *B15: Edg* 2H 131
(off Vincent Rd.)
B69: O'bry 4D 96
Windermere Rd. B13: Mose 4B 134
B21: Hand 5A 82
WV6: Tett 1B 26
Windfall Ct. B24: Erd 3B 86
Winding Mill Nth. DY5: Quar B 4A 110
Winding Mill Sth. DY5: Quar B 4A 110
Windlass Cft. B31: N'fld 2D 144
Windleaves Rd. B36: Cas B 1A 106
Windley Cl. B19: Birm 4E 101
Windley Ho. B73: New O 3C 68
Windmill Av. B45: Rubery 1E 157
B46: Col 2H 107
Windmill Bank WV5: Wom 6G 57
Windmill Cl. B31: N'fld 2G 145
Windmill Cres. B66: Smeth 4G 99
WV3: Wolv 2G 41
Windmill End DY2: Neth 4G 95
Windmill Gro. DY6: W Hth 1H 91
Windmill Hill B31: N'fld 2F 145
B63: Crad 5E 111
Windmill La. B66: Smeth 5F 99
WV3: Wolv 2G 41
Windmill Pct. B66: Smeth 4F 99
Windmill Rd. B90: Shir 5E 149
Windmill St. B1: Birm 2F 117 (6D 4)
DY1: Dud 5C 76
DY3: Up Gor 2H 75
WS1: Wals 3C 48
WS10: W'bry 2G 63
Windmill Ter. WS10: W'bry 2G 63
Windmill Vw. DY1: Dud 6D 60
Windridge Cres. B92: Sol 5B 138
Windrow, The WV6: Pert 5D 24
Windrush Cl. B92: Olton 3E 137
Windrush Gro. B29: S Oak 5C 132
Windrush Rd. B47: H'wd 2B 162
Windsor Arc. B4: Birm 6G 101 (3E 5)
Windsor Av. B68: O'bry 6G 97
WV4: Penn 5C 42
Windsor Cl. B31: Longb 3E 159
B45: Fran 5G 143
B63: Hale 2H 127
B65: Row R 5C 96
DY3: Gorn 6F 75
Windsor Ct. B38: K Nor 6B 146
Windsor Cres. DY2: Dud 3F 95
Windsor Dr. B24: Erd 2A 86
B92: Sol 2F 137
Windsor Gdns. WV3: Wolv 4G 41
WV8: Cod 4F 13
Windsor Ga. WV12: W'hall 5C 30
Windsor Gro. DY8: Word 2C 108
WS4: S'fld 5G 21
Windsor Ho. B23: Erd 1F 85
Windsor Ind. Est. B7: Birm 4A 102
Windsor Lodge B92: Olton 5B 136
Windsor Pl. B7: Birm 6A 102
B23: Erd 4E 85
Windsor Rd. B30: Stir 2D 146
B36: Cas B 2B 106
B63: Hale 1H 127
B65: Row R 5C 96
B68: O'bry 6G 97
B71: W Brom 5H 63
B73: New O 4D 68
DY4: Tip 5A 62
DY8: Stourb 2B 124
WS6: C Hay 1E 7
WV4: E'shll 6B 44
WV5: Wom 1F 73
Windsor St. B7: Birm 4H 101
WS1: Wals 4C 48
WV14: Bils 5E 45
Windsor St. Sth. B7: Birm 5A 102
Windsor Ter. B16: Edg 2B 116
Windsor Vw. B32: Bart G 6H 129
Windsor Wlk. WS10: Darl 3D 46
Windsor Way WS4: Rus 2H 33
Winds Point DY9: Hag 6E 125
Windward Way B36: Cas B 1B 106
Windward Way Ind. Est. B36: Cas B 1B 106
Windy Mnr. Rd. B93: Know 5G 151
Windyridge Rd. B76: Walm 1D 86

Winford Av.—Wood St.

Winford Av. DY6: K'wfrd 5C 92
Wingate Cl. B30: K Nor 3B 146
Wingate Ct. B74: Four O 5E 37
Wingate Rd. WS2: Wals 1E 47
Wing Cl. WS2: Wals 5F 31
Wingfield Cl. B37: F'bri 6B 106
Wingfield Ho. B37: K'hrst 4B 106
Wingfield Rd. B42: Gt Barr 6E 67
B46: Col 4H 107
Wingfoot Av. WV10: Bush 1A 28
Wingfoot Way B24: Erd 6A 86
Wing Yip Cen. B7: Nech 3B 102
Winifride Ct. B17: Harb 6F 115
Winkle St. B70: W Brom 3H 79
Winleigh Rd. B20: Hand 5B 82
Winnall Cl. WV14: Cose 3F 61
Winn Ho. *WS2: Wals* *6B 32*
(off Burrowes St.)
Winnie Rd. B29: S Oak 4A 132
Winnington Rd. B8: W End 2G 103
Winnipeg Rd. B38: K Nor 1C 160
Winrush Cl. DY3: Gorn 4H 75
Winscar Cft. DY3: Lwr G 4A 76
Winsford Cl. B63: Hale 5A 112
B76: Walm 2C 70
CV7: Bal C 3G 169
Winsham Gro. B21: Hand 1A 100
Winslow Av. B8: W End 5H 103
Winslow Dr. WV6: Wolv 5D 26
Winslow Ho. B29: S Oak 4F 131
WINSON GREEN 4A 100
Winson Green/ Outer Circle Stop (MM) 2A 100
Winson Grn. Rd. B18: Win G 4A 100
Winson St. B18: Win G 5H 99
Winspear Cl. CV7: Mer 4H 141
Winstanley Rd. B33: Stech 1B 120
Winster Av. B93: Dorr 5A 166
Winster Gro. B44: Gt Barr 3F 67
Winster Gro. Ind. Est. B44: Gt Barr 3F 67
Winster Rd. B43: Gt Barr 5H 65
WV1: Wolv 2D 44
Winston Churchill Ct. WV14: Bils 3E 45
Winston Dr. B20: Hand 6D 82
B62: Roms 3A 142
Winston Rd. DY3: Swind 5E 73
Winterbourne Cft. B14: K Hth 6E 147
Winterbourne Rd. B91: Sol 3D 150
Winterdene CV7: Bal C 2H 169
Winterley Gdns. DY3: Sed 1A 76
Winterley La. WS4: Rus 2G 33
Winterton Rd. B44: K'sdng 2A 68
Winthorpe Dr. B91: Sol 1G 165
Wintney Cl. B17: Harb 4E 115
Winton Gro. B76: Walm 1E 87
Winwood Rd. B65: Row R 6E 97
Winwoods Gro. B32: Bart G 5G 129
Wiremill Cl. B44: Gt Barr 1G 83
Wirral Rd. B31: N'fld 1D 144
Wiseacre Cft. B90: Shir 5E 149
Wiseman Gro. B23: Erd 4D 68
Wisemore WS1: Wals 1C 48
(not continuous)
Wishaw Cl. B90: Shir 5E 149
Wishaw Gro. B37: K'hrst 4B 106
Wishaw La. B76: Curd 1D 88
B76: Min, Wis 1H 87
Wisley Way B32: Harb 6D 114
Wistaria Cl. B31: N'fld 1E 145
Wisteria Dr. WS5: Wals 1D 64
WS8: Bwnhls 3G 9
Wisteria Gro. B44: Gt Barr 3G 67
Wistmans Cl. DY1: Dud 5A 76
Wistwood Hayes WV10: Bush 3B 16
Witham Cl. B76: Walm 4E 71
Witham Ct. B91: Sol 6G 151
Withdean Cl. B11: S'brk 6D 118
Witherford Cl. B29: S Oak 5G 131
Witherford Cft. B91: Sol 5B 150
Witherford Way B29: S Oak 5G 131
Withern Way DY3: Gorn 4G 75
Withers Rd. WV8: Bilb 4H 13
Withers Way B71: W Brom 3B 80
Withington Covert B14: K Hth 5F 147
Withington Gro. B93: Ben H, Dorr 5A 166
Withybrook Rd. B90: Shir 1H 163
Withy Gro. B37: K'hrst 4B 106
Withy Hill Rd. B75: S Cold 4D 54
Withymere La. WV5: Wom 5A 58
Withymoor Rd. DY2: Neth 5G 95
DY8: Amb 4E 109
WITHYMOOR VILLAGE 2H 109
Withy Rd. WV14: Bils 2E 61
Withy Rd. Ind. Est. WV14: Bils 2E 61
Withywood Cl. WV12: W'hall 6C 18
Witley Av. B63: Hale 1G 127
B91: Sol 5G 151
Witley Cres. B69: O'bry 4E 97
Witley Farm Cl. B91: Sol 5G 151
Witley Rd. B31: N'fld 5H 145
Witney Dr. B37: F'bri 1B 122
Witney Gro. WV10: F'hses 4F 15
Wittersham Ct. *WV13: W'hall* *1B 46*
(off Birmingham St.)
WITTON 4H 83
Witton Bank B62: Quin 4F 113
Witton La. B6: Aston 6H 83
B71: W Brom 5G 63
Witton Lodge Rd. B23: Erd 6B 68
Witton Rd. B6: Aston 1G 101
WV4: Penn 5E 43
Witton Station (Rail) 6H 83
Witton St. B9: Birm 1B 118
DY8: Stourb 1C 124
Wixford Cft. B34: S End 2E 105
Wixford Gro. B90: Shir 5B 150
Wobaston Rd. WV9: Pend 4B 14
WV10: F'hses 3E 15
Woburn Av. WV12: W'hall 3B 30
Woburn Cres. B43: Gt Barr 4H 65
Woburn Dr. B62: Hale 4B 112
DY5: Brie H 4F 109
Woburn Gro. B27: A Grn 4A 136
Woburn Ho. *B15: Edg* *4E 117*
(off Woodview Dr.)
Wodehouse Cl. WV5: Wom 2E 73
Wodehouse La. DY3: Sed 5A 58
WV5: Wom 5A 58
Woden Av. WV11: Wed 3E 29
Woden Cl. WV5: Wom 6F 57
Woden Cres. WV11: Wed 3E 29
Woden Pas. WS10: W'bry 3F 63
Woden Rd. WV10: Wolv 5A 28
Woden Rd. E. WS10: W'bry 1H 63
Woden Rd. Nth. WS10: W'bry 6E 47
Woden Rd. Sth. WS10: W'bry 4F 63
Woden Rd. W. WS10: Darl 1D 62
WS10: W'bry 1D 62
Wodensfield Twr. WV11: Wed 4E 29
Woden Way WV11: Wed 3E 29
Wolcot Gro. B6: Witt 2H 83
Wold Wlk. B13: Mose 1B 148
Wolfsbane Dr. WS5: Wals 2E 65
Wolfson Dr. B15: Edg 1H 131
WOLLASTON 5B 108
Wollaston Ct. DY8: Woll 5A 108
WS1: Wals *1D 48*
(off Lwr. Rushall St.)
Wollaston Cres. WV11: Wed 3F 29
Wollaston Rd. DY7: Stourt 4A 108
DY8: Amb 4C 108
Wollerton Gro. B75: S Cold 5D 54
WOLLESCOTE 6B 110
Wollescote Bus. Pk. DY9: Lye 6B 110
Wollescote Dr. B91: Sol 6F 151
Wollescote Rd. DY9: W'cte 2G 125
(not continuous)
Wolmer Rd. WV11: Wed 5H 17
Wolseley Av. B27: A Grn 1B 136
Wolseley Bank WV10: Bush 2B 28
Wolseley Cl. B36: Cas B 6C 88
WV10: Bush 2B 28
Wolseley Dr. B8: W End 2G 103
Wolseley Ga. WV10: Bush 2B 28
Wolseley Rd. B70: W Brom 6E 63
WV14: Bils 4D 44
Wolseley St. B9: Birm 1B 118
(not continuous)
Wolston Cl. B90: Shir 2H 149
WOLVERHAMPTON 1A 44 (4D 170)
Wolverhampton Art Gallery & Mus. *2C 170*
(off Lichfield St.)
Wolverhampton Race Course 3E 27
Wolverhampton Rd. B68: O'bry 6G 97
B69: O'bry 2D 96
DY3: Sed 4H 59
DY6: W Hth 6A 74
WS2: Wals 1G 47
(not continuous)
WS3: Blox 6H 19
WS3: Pels 4C 20
WS6: C Hay 4B 6
WS11: Cann 1B 6
WV6: Nur 6A 24
WV8: Cod 3F 13
(not continuous)
WV10: Share 3A 6
(Saredon Rd., not continuous)
WV10: Share 4B 6
(Warstone Rd.)
WV10: Wolv 6B 28
WV11: Ess 4H 17
Wolverhampton Rd. E. WV4: Penn 6H 43
Wolverhampton Rd. Sth. B32: Quin 4C 114
Wolverhampton Rd. W. WS2: Wals 1C 46
WV13: W'hall 1C 46
Wolverhampton Science Pk.
WV10: Wolv 3G 27
Wolverhampton Sports Arena 4E 27
Wolverhampton Station (Rail) 1H 43 (2D 170)
Wolverhampton St. DY1: Dud 5D 76
WS2: Wals 1B 48
WS10: Darl 4B 46
WV13: W'hall 2H 45
WV14: Bils 5E 45
Wolverhampton Wanderers FC 6G 27 (1A 170)
Wolverley Av. DY8: Woll 5A 108
WV4: Penn 6B 42
Wolverley Cres. B69: O'bry 4D 96
Wolverley Rd. B32: Bart G 5H 129
B63: Hale 3H 127
B92: Sol 3H 137
Wolverson Cl. WV12: W'hall 5C 30
Wolverson Rd. WS9: Wals W 3C 22
Wolverton Rd. B37: Mars G 4D 122
B45: Redn 3A 158
DY2: Dud 6G 77
WOMBOURNE 2F 73
Wombourne Cl. DY3: Sed 5G 59
Wombourne Ent. Pk. WV5: Wom 2D 72
Wombourne Leisure Cen. 6F 57
Wombourne Pk. WV5: Wom 2F 73
Wombourne Rd. DY3: Swind 5E 73
Wombrook Bus. Cen.
WV5: Wom 1E 73
Wombrook Dale WV5: Wom 1D 72
Woodacre Rd. B24: Erd 3A 86
Woodall Rd. B6: Aston 6H 83
Woodall St. B64: Crad H 2E 111
WS3: Blox 6A 20
(not continuous)
Woodard Rd. DY4: Tip 6C 62
Wood Av. DY3: Lwr G 3G 75
WV11: Wed 3F 29
Wood Bank B26: Yard 4C 120
Wood Bank Rd. WV3: Wolv 3G 41
Woodbank Rd. DY3: Sed 6G 59
Woodberry Dr. B76: Walm 3E 71
Woodberry Wlk. B27: A Grn 2B 136
Woodbine Av. B10: Small H 3D 118
Woodbine Cft. B26: Sheld 5E 121
Woodbine Wlk. B37: Chel W 1F 123
Woodbourne B15: Edg 3H 115
(not continuous)
Woodbourne Rd. B15: Edg 3G 115
B17: Harb 3F 115
B67: Smeth 1C 114
Woodbridge Cl. WS3: Blox 4G 19
WS4: S'fld 6H 21
Woodbridge Rd. B13: Mose 2H 133
Woodbrooke Gro. B31: N'fld 1G 145
Woodbrooke Rd. B30: B'vlle 6H 131
Woodbrook Ho. B37: Chel W 1D 122
Woodburn Rd. B66: Smeth 2H 99
Woodbury Cl. B62: B'hth 3F 113
DY5: Brie H 1A 110
Woodbury Gro. B91: Sol 6F 151
Woodbury Rd. B62: B'hth 3F 113
B62: Quin 4F 113
Woodchester Rd. B93: Dorr 6F 167
Woodchurch Grange B73: Bold 5F 69
Wood Cl. B46: Col 2H 107
Woodclose Rd. B37: F'bri 6B 106
Woodcock Cl. B31: Longb 6A 144
WOODCOCK HILL 6C 130
Woodcock La. B27: A Grn 2B 136
(not continuous)
B31: N'fld 6C 130
Woodcock La. Nth. B27: A Grn 1B 136
Woodcock Sports Cen. *5H 101*
(off Woodcock St.)
Woodcock St. B7: Birm 5H 101 (1G 5)
Woodcombe Cl. DY5: Brie H 4F 109
Wood Comn. Grange WS3: Pels 3D 20
Woodcote Dr. B8: Salt 4F 103
B93: Dorr 6H 167
Woodcote Pl. B19: Loz 2E 101
Woodcote Rd. B24: Erd 2B 86
WV6: Tett 5A 26
Woodcote Way B18: Hock 4C 100
B74: S'tly 5H 51
Wood Ct. B20: Hand 5C 82
Woodcroft B47: H'wd 3B 162
Woodcroft Av. B20: Hand 4A 82
DY4: Tip 2E 77
Woodcroft Cl. B64: Old H 3H 111
WOODCROSS 3B 60
Woodcross La. WV14: Cose 3C 60
Woodcross St. WV14: Cose 3B 60
WOOD END 2E 29
Woodend B20: Hand 1A 82
Wood End La. B24: Erd 4F 85
Woodend Pl. WV6: Tett 5H 25
Wood End Rd. B24: Erd 4F 85
WS5: Wals 3H 49
WV11: Wed 2F 29
Woodend Way WS9: A'rdge 6D 22
Woodfall Av. B30: K Nor 2B 146
Woodfield Av. B64: Crad H 3F 111
B69: O'bry 5G 97
DY5: P'ntt 2F 93
DY9: W'cte 3B 126
WV4: Penn 5D 42
Woodfield Cl. B74: Four O 3H 53
WS5: Wals 6A 50
Woodfield Cres. B12: Bal H 5A 118
Woodfield Hgts. WV6: Tett 5B 26
Woodfield Rd. B12: Bal H 5A 118
B13: K Hth 5H 133
B91: Sol 1F 151
DY3: Lwr G 3G 75
Woodfield Social & Sports Club 5E 43
Woodfold Cft. WS9: A'rdge 2D 34
Woodford Av. B36: Cas B 1F 105
Woodford Cl. WV9: Pend 5D 14
Woodford Grn. Rd. B28: Hall G 5G 135
Woodford La. WV5: Try, Wom 5C 56
Woodford Way WV5: Wom 1D 72
Woodfort Rd. B43: Gt Barr 6A 66
WOODGATE 5H 129
Woodgate Bus. Pk. B32: Bart G 3H 129
Woodgate Dr. B32: Bart G 4G 129
Woodgate Gdns. B32: Bart G 3G 129
Woodgate La. B32: Bart G 3G 129
Woodgate Valley Country Pk. 3H 129
Woodgate Valley Country Pk. Vis. Cen. 3H 129
Woodgate Valley Urban Farm
B32: Bart G 3G 129
Woodglade Cft. B38: K Nor 5A 146
WOOD GREEN 6H 47
Wood Grn. WS6: C Hay 1E 7
Woodgreen Cft. B68: O'bry 4A 114
Wood Grn. Rd. B18: Win G 5H 99
WS10: W'bry 1G 63
Woodgreen Rd. B68: O'bry 4A 114
Woodhall Cl. DY4: Tip 5A 62
Woodhall Cft. B92: Olton 2D 136
Woodhall Ho. *WS3: Blox* *1A 32*
(off Woodhall St.)
Woodhall Rd. WV4: Penn 1C 58
Woodham Cl. B45: Fran 6E 143
Woodhaven WS4: S'fld 6H 21
WOOD HAYES 6E 17
Wood Hayes Cft. WV10: Bush 5E 17
Wood Hayes Rd. WV10: Bush 5D 16
WV11: Wed 6E 17
Woodhill Cl. WV5: Wom 1F 73
Wood Hill Dr. WV5: Wom 2F 73
Wood Ho. WS1: Wals 4D 48
Woodhouse Ct. DY5: Quar B 2C 110
Woodhouse Fold WV11: Wed 4F 29
Woodhouse Rd. B32: Quin 5C 114
WV6: Tett 5H 25
Woodhouse Rd. Nth. WV6: Tett 5H 25
Woodhouse Way B64: Crad H 2E 111
Woodhurst Rd. B13: Mose 1A 134
Wooding Cres. DY4: Tip 4B 62
Woodington Rd. B75: S Cold 6E 55
Woodland Av. DY1: Dud 4E 77
DY5: Quar B 2C 110
WV6: Tett 6H 25
Woodland Cl. DY9: Pedm 4H 125
WV12: W'hall 3D 30
Woodland Ct. WS14: Shen W 2G 37
Woodland Cres. WV3: Wolv 4B 42
Woodland Dr. B66: Smeth 2C 98
WS6: C Hay 1E 7
Woodland Gro. B43: Gt Barr 2A 66
DY3: Gorn 4F 75
Woodland Ri. B64: Crad H 3H 111
B73: S Cold 1H 69
Woodland Rd. B21: Hand 1G 99
B31: N'fld 4F 145
B62: B'hth 3D 112
WV3: Wolv 4B 42
Wood Lands, The B75: S Cold 5E 55
Woodlands, The B64: Crad H 4A 112
DY8: Stourb 3E 125
WV8: Cod 5G 13
Woodlands Av. B46: Wat O 5D 88
WS5: Wals 6A 50
Woodlands Cen., The WV12: W'hall 2E 31
Woodlands Cotts. WV4: Penn 1C 58
Woodlands Crematorium B46: Col 4E 107
Woodlands Cres. WS3: Pels 2D 20
Woodlands Farm Rd. B24: Erd 3D 86
Woodlands La. B90: Shir 1H 163
Woodlands Paddock WV4: Penn 1C 58
Woodlands Pk. Rd. B30: B'vlle 1G 145
Woodlands Rd. B8: Salt 5F 103
B11: S'hll 2B 134
B45: Rubery 2D 156
WV5: Wom 2G 73
Woodlands St. B66: Smeth 4G 99
Woodlands Wlk. WV4: Penn 6C 42
Woodlands Way B37: Chel W 6F 107
Wood La. B17: Harb 5E 115
B20: Hand 5C 82
B24: Erd 6G 85
B32: Bart G 4G 129
(not continuous)
B37: Mars G 3C 122
B70: W Brom 4G 79
B74: S'tly 2G 51
B92: Bars 5G 153
WS3: Pels 2D 20
WS9: A'rdge 6H 23
WS14: Foot 6H 23
WV10: F'hses 6H 15
WV12: W'hall 2E 31
Wood La. Cl. WV12: W'hall 2E 31
Woodlawn B91: Sol 3A 152
Woodlawn Gro. DY6: K'wfrd 4B 92
Woodlea Dr. B24: Erd 5F 85
B91: Sol 2C 150
Wood Leasow B32: Bart G 3B 130
Wood Leaves B47: H'wd 1H 161
Woodleigh Av. B17: Harb 1H 131
Woodleigh Cl. B63: Hale 5A 112
Woodleigh Ct. B38: K Nor 6B 146
Woodleigh Rd. B72: W Grn 4A 70
Woodleys, The B14: K Hth 3B 148
Woodloes Rd. B90: Shir 1H 163
Woodman Cl. B63: Hale 2C 128
WS10: W'bry 1H 63
Woodman Gro. B75: R'ley 6C 38
Woodman La. WS6: C Hay 1E 7
Woodman Rd. B14: K Hth 6A 148
B63: Hale 2C 128
Woodman Wlk. B23: Erd 2A 84
Woodmeadow Rd. B30: K Nor 4D 146
Woodnorton Dr. B13: Mose 3G 133
Woodnorton Rd. B65: Row R 1F 113
Woodpecker Gro. B36: Cas B 2C 106
Woodperry Av. B91: Sol 6G 151
Woodridge B6: Aston 6G 83
Woodridge Av. B32: Quin 1H 129
Woodridge Rd. B63: Hale 6A 112
Wood Rd. DY3: Lwr G 4G 75
WV5: Wom 5H 57
WV6: Tett 6H 25
WV8: Cod 2D 12
Woodrough Dr. B13: Mose 3H 133
Woodrow Cres. B93: Know 4C 166
Woodrow La. B61: Cats 6B 156
Woodruff Way WS5: Wals 1D 64
Woodrush Dr. B47: H'wd 4A 162
WOODS, THE 1A 64
Woods, The B14: K Hth 4H 133
WOODS BANK 5D 46
Woods Bank Est., The WS10: Darl 1D 62
Woods Bank Ter. WS10: Darl 6C 46
Woods Cres. DY5: Quar B 2C 110
WOODSETTON 1B 76
Woodsetton Cl. DY1: Dud 1D 76
Woodshires Rd. B92: Olton 6C 136
WOODSIDE 3B 94
Wood Side WV11: Wed 1A 30
Woodside B37: K'hrst 4A 106
B74: Four O 1E 53
Woodside Cl. WS5: Wals 5H 49
Woodside Cres. B93: Know 5D 166
Woodside Dr. B74: Lit A 4C 36
Woodside Gro. WV8: Bilb 4H 13
Woodside Ho. B34: S End 4A 106
Woodside Ind. Est. DY5: Brie H 4B 94
Woodside Rd. B29: S Oak 4C 132
(not continuous)
DY2: Dud 3B 94
WS5: Wals 5H 49
Woodside Way B32: Bart G 5G 129
B91: Sol 2C 150
WS9: A'rdge 4D 34
WV12: W'hall 2E 31
Woods La. B64: Crad H 3E 111
DY5: Brie H 4H 109
Woodsome Gro. B23: Erd 6C 68
Woodsorrel Rd. DY1: Dud 3B 76
Woodstile Cl. B75: R'ley 6B 38
Woodstile Way B34: S End 3F 105
Woodstock Cl. DY1: Dud 1C 94
DY8: Word 2A 108
WS5: Wals 2E 65
Woodstock Cres. B93: Dorr 6B 166
Woodstock Dr. B74: Four O 5D 36
DY8: Word 2A 108
Woodstock Ho. B13: Mose 6A 134
Woodstock Rd. B13: Mose 1A 134
B21: Hand 1B 100
WV1: Wolv 2D 44
Woodston Gro. B91: Sol 1G 165
Wood St. B16: Birm 1C 116
DY2: Dud 3B 94
DY4: Tip 1G 77
DY8: Woll 4B 108
DY9: Lye 6B 110
WS10: Darl 5F 47
WV4: E'shll 2C 60
WV10: Wolv 4B 28
WV13: W'hall 1A 46
WV14: Bils 6F 45

A-Z Birmingham Deluxe 229

HOSPITALS and HOSPICES

covered by this atlas with their map square reference

N.B. Where Hospitals and Hospices are not named on the map,
the reference given is for the road in which they are situated.

ACORNS CHILDREN'S HOSPICE 5A **132**
103 Oak Tree Lane
BIRMINGHAM
B29 6HZ
Tel: 0121 2484850

ACORNS CHILDREN'S HOSPICE (WALSALL) 6D **48**
Walstead Road
WALSALL
WS5 4NL
Tel: 01922 422500

BIRMINGHAM CHILDREN'S HOSPITAL
(DIANA PRINCESS OF WALES HOSPITAL) 6G **101** (2F **5**)
Steelhouse Lane
BIRMINGHAM
B4 6NH
Tel: 0121 3339999

BIRMINGHAM DENTAL HOSPITAL 6G **101** (2E **5**)
St Chad's Queensway
BIRMINGHAM
B4 6NN
Tel: 0121 2368611

BIRMINGHAM HEARTLANDS HOSPITAL 1H **119**
Bordesley Green East
BIRMINGHAM
B9 5ST
Tel: 0121 4242000

BIRMINGHAM NUFFIELD HOSPITAL, THE 6B **116**
22 Somerset Road
BIRMINGHAM
B15 2QQ
Tel: 0121 4562000

BIRMINGHAM WOMENS HOSPITAL 1H **131**
Metchley Park Road
BIRMINGHAM
B15 2TG
Tel: 0121 4721377

BLOXWICH HOSPITAL 1H **31**
Reeves Sreet
WALSALL
WS3 2JJ
Tel: 01922 858600

BRADBURY HOSPICE 1H **113**
494 Wolverhampton Road
OLDBURY
B68 8DG
Tel: 0121 5442712

BUSHEY FIELDS HOSPITAL 2A **94**
Bushey Fields Rd.
DUDLEY
DY1 2LZ
Tel: 01384 457373

CITY HOSPITAL (BIRMINGHAM) 5B **100**
Dudley Road
BIRMINGHAM
B18 7QH
Tel: 0121 5543801

COMPTON HOSPICE 1A **42**
Compton Road West
WOLVERHAMPTON
WV3 9DH
Tel: 01902 774500

CORBETT HOSPITAL 4E **109**
Vicarage Rd.
STOURBRIDGE
DY8 4JB
Tel: 01384 456111

DOROTHY PATTISON HOSPITAL 2H **47**
Alumwell Close
WALSALL
WS2 9XH
Tel: 01922 858000

EDWARD STREET HOSPITAL 4A **80**
Edward Street
WEST BROMWICH
B70 8NL
Tel: 0121 5537676

GOOD HOPE HOSPITAL 5B **54**
Rectory Road
SUTTON COLDFIELD
B75 7RR
Tel: 0121 3782211

GOSCOTE HOSPITAL 1D **32**
Goscote Lane
WALSALL
WS3 1SJ
Tel: 01922 710710

GUEST HOSPITAL 4G **77**
Tipton Rd.
DUDLEY
DY1 4SE
Tel: 01384 456111

HAMMERWICH HOSPITAL 1D **10**
Hospital Rd.
BURNTWOOD
WS7 0EH
Tel: 01543 675754

HEATH LANE HOSPITAL 6B **64**
Heath Lane
WEST BROMWICH
B71 2BG
Tel: 0121 5531831

HIGHCROFT HOSPITAL 4D **84**
Fentham Road
BIRMINGHAM
B23 6AL
Tel: 0121 6235500

JOHN TAYLOR HOSPICE 2A **86**
76 Grange Road
BIRMINGHAM
B24 0DF
Tel: 0121 2552400

LITTLE ASTON BUPA HOSPITAL 4B **36**
Little Aston Hall Dri.
SUTTON COLDFIELD
B74 3UP
Tel: 0121 3532444

LITTLE BLOXWICH DAY HOSPICE 4B **20**
Stoney Lane
WALSALL
WS3 3DW
Tel: 01922 858735

MANOR HOSPITAL (WALSALL) 2A **48**
Moat Road
WALSALL
WS2 9PS
Tel: 01922 721172

MARY STEVENS HOSPICE 3F **125**
221 Hagley Rd.
STOURBRIDGE
DY8 2JR
Tel: 01384 443010

MOSELEY HALL HOSPITAL 2G **133**
Alcester Road
BIRMINGHAM
B13 8JL
Tel: 0121 4424321

MOSSLEY DAY UNIT 6G **19**
Sneyd Lane
WALSALL
WS3 2LW
Tel: 01922 858680

NEW CROSS HOSPITAL (WOLVERHAMPTON) 4D **28**
Wolverhampton Road
WOLVERHAMPTON
WV10 0QP
Tel: 01902 307999

NORTHCROFT HOSPITAL 3D **84**
Reservoir Road
BIRMINGHAM
B23 6DW
Tel: 0121 3782211

PARKWAY BUPA HOSPITAL 2A **152**
1 Damson Parkway
SOLIHULL
B91 2PP
Tel: 0121 7041451

PENN HOSPITAL 1C **58**
Penn Road
WOLVERHAMPTON
WV4 5HN
Tel: 01902 444141

PRIORY HOSPITAL, THE 6D **116**
Priory Road
BIRMINGHAM
B5 7UG
Tel: 0121 4402323

QUEEN ELIZABETH HOSPITAL 1A **132**
Edgbaston
BIRMINGHAM
B15 2TH
Tel: 0121 6271627

QUEEN ELIZABETH PSYCHIATRIC HOSPITAL 1A **132**
Mindelsohn Way
BIRMINGHAM
B15 2QZ
Tel: 0121 678000

RIDGE HILL HOSPITAL 6C **92**
Brierly Hill Rd.
STOURBRIDGE
DY8 5ST
Tel: 01384 456111

ROWLEY REGIS COMMUNITY HOSPITAL 1B **112**
Moor Lane
ROWLEY REGIS
B65 8DA
Tel: 0121 6073465

ROYAL ORTHOPAEDIC HOSPITAL 2F **145**
Bristol Road South
BIRMINGHAM
B31 2AP
Tel: 0121 685 4000

RUSSELLS HALL HOSPITAL 2H **93**
Pensnett Rd.
DUDLEY
DY1 2HQ
Tel: 01384 456111

ST DAVID'S HOUSE (DAY HOSPITAL) 6G **57**
Planks La.
WOLVERHAMPTON
WV5 8DU
Tel: 01902 326001

ST MARY'S HOSPICE 4C **132**
176 Raddlebarn Road
BIRMINGHAM
B29 7DA
Tel: 0121 4721191

SANDWELL DISTRICT GENERAL HOSPITAL 2B **80**
Lyndon
WEST BROMWICH
B71 4HJ
Tel: 0121 5531831

SELLY OAK HOSPITAL 4B **132**
Raddlebarn Road
BIRMINGHAM
B29 6JD
Tel: 0121 6271627

SOLIHULL HOSPITAL 3G **151**
Lode Lane
SOLIHULL
B91 2JL
Tel: 0121 4242000

SUTTON COLDFIELD COTTAGE HOSPITAL 1H **69**
Birmingham Road
SUTTON COLDFIELD
B72 1QH
Tel: 0121 255 4000

WARREN PEARL MARIE CURIE HOSPICE 3H **151**
911-913 Warwick Road
SOLIHULL
B91 3ER
Tel: 0121 2547800

WEST HEATH HOSPITAL 1G **159**
Rednal Road
BIRMINGHAM
B38 8HR
Tel: 0121 6271627

WEST MIDLANDS HOSPITAL 6F **111**
Colman Hill
HALESOWEN
B63 2AH
Tel: 01384 560123

WEST PARK REHABILITATION HOSPITAL 1E **43**
Park Road West
WOLVERHAMPTON
WV1 4PW
Tel: 01902 444000

WOLVERHAMPTON EYE INFIRMARY 1E **43**
Compton Road
WOLVERHAMPTON
WV3 9QR
Tel: 01902 307999

WOLVERHAMPTON NUFFIELD HOSPITAL 5A **26**
Wood Road
WOLVERHAMPTON
WV6 8LE
Tel: 01902 754177

WOODBOURNE PRIORY HOSPITAL 3G **115**
23 Woodbourne Road
BIRMINGHAM
B17 8BY
Tel: 0121 4344343

A-Z Digital Mapping

With the same familiar look as our paper maps and atlases, high quality digital mapping is available for a desktop PC, Pocket PC or mobile phone. For detailed system requirements and information please refer to our website, www.a-zmaps.co.uk

Memory-Map CD-ROM

Each title in this series covers a large urban conurbation. These CD-ROM's can be used on a desktop PC and downloaded to a Pocket PC or Windows® powered smartphone*.

Key features include:
- Pan and Zoom through four levels of street and road mapping.
- Create routes to calculate travel time, distances and direction.
- Add overlays such as text and icons.
- Fully searchable index to streets, places, stations, hospitals, etc., also Postcodes in 2006 editions onwards.
- GPS connection upgrade allows you to see your current position.
- Print maps for personal use.
  Pan and Zoom functionality only on Windows® powered smartphone.

In addition, the software allows you to copy either a section of mapping that you wish to navigate, or the whole atlas, to your Pocket PC or smartphone whilst retaining the same key features as above*.

Titles available:
- **Birmingham and West Midlands**.
- Bristol and Bath.
- Leeds, Bradford and West Yorkshire.
- Liverpool and Merseyside.
- Greater London.
- Greater Manchester.
- Nottingham and Derby.
- Sheffield and South Yorkshire.
- Southampton and Portsmouth.
- Great Britain Road Atlas

Mapping for Pocket PC

A-Z GB road and A-Z street mapping covering many British towns and cities is available for Pocket PC.

This is a downloadable product direct from our website and works on all Microsoft based Pocket PC's. Simply purchase the Viewer software from our website, www.a-zmaps.co.uk, and any map(s), and download instantly.

Depending on the amount of free memory, the Pocket A-Z Viewer will allow multiple maps to be saved on either storage cards or internal memory. This gives you the ability to build up a library of A-Z maps covering many towns and cities in Great Britain.

Key features include:
- Tap the screen and drag to move around the map.
- Navigation tools indicate direction of travel and distance.
- Save favourite places on the map.
- Zoom in and out of the map.
- Fully searchable index for easy street location.
- Connect a GPS to pinpoint your location, direction and speed of travel.

Mapping for Mobile Phones

The famous **A-Z Birmingham,** A-Z London, and Great Britain road mapping is now available for Symbian™ based mobile phones.

All mapping is installed onto a memory card by downloading the product direct from our website. For a list of compatible smartphones please see our website www.a-zmaps.co.uk.

Key features include:
- Simply use the navigation button on your phone to move the map.
- Fully searchable index to streets, districts, stations and selected places of interest.
- Zoom out to an overview showing your selected location by means of a pointer.